I0063141

# Exploring Windows 11

## 2025 Edition

**Kevin Wilson**

**elluminet Press**

www.elluminetpress.com

# Exploring Windows 11: 2025 Edition

Copyright © 2025 Elluminet Press

This work is subject to copyright. All rights are reserved by the Publisher, whether the whole or part of the material is concerned, specifically the rights of translation, reprinting, reuse of illustrations, recitation, broadcasting, reproduction on microfilms or in any other physical way, and transmission or information storage and retrieval, electronic adaptation, computer software, or by similar or dissimilar methodology now known or hereafter developed. Exempted from this legal reservation are brief excerpts in connection with reviews or scholarly analysis or material supplied specifically for the purpose of being entered and executed on a computer system, for exclusive use by the purchaser of the work. Duplication of this publication or parts thereof is permitted only under the provisions of the Copyright Law of the Publisher's location, in its current version, and permission for use must always be obtained from the Publisher. Permissions for use may be obtained through Rights Link at the Copyright Clearance Centre. Violations are liable to prosecution under the respective Copyright Law.

Trademarked names, logos, and images may appear in this book. Rather than use a trademark symbol with every occurrence of a trademarked name, logo, or image we use the names, logos, and images only in an editorial fashion and to the benefit of the trademark owner, with no intention of infringement of the trademark.

The use in this publication of trade names, trademarks, service marks, and similar terms, even if they are not identified as such, is not to be taken as an expression of opinion as to whether or not they are subject to proprietary rights.

While the advice and information in this book are believed to be true and accurate at the date of publication, neither the authors nor the editors nor the publisher can accept any legal responsibility for any errors or omissions that may be made. The publisher makes no warranty, express or implied, with respect to the material contained herein.

iStock.com/golibo, BONDART, PeopleImages, ymgerman. Photo 130859010 © Kaspars Grinvalds - Dreamstime.com. Photo 103557713 © Konstantin Kolosov - Dreamstime.com. Yuri Arcurs via Getty Images

Publisher: Elluminet Press
Director: Kevin Wilson
Lead Editor: Steven Ashmore
Technical Reviewer: Mike Taylor, Robert Ashcroft
Copy Editors: Joanne Taylor, James Marsh
Proof Reader: Mike Taylor
Indexer: James Marsh
Cover Designer: Kevin Wilson

eBook versions and licenses are also available for most titles. Any source code or other supplementary materials referenced by the author in this text is available to readers at www.elluminetpress.com/resources

For detailed information about how to locate your book's resources, go to www.elluminetpress.com/resources

# Table of Contents

# About the Author

With over 20 years' experience in the computer industry, Kevin Wilson has made a career out of technology and showing others how to use it. After earning a master's degree in computer science, software engineering, and multimedia systems, Kevin has held various positions in the IT industry including graphic & web design, programming, building & managing corporate networks, and IT support.

He serves as senior writer and director at Elluminet Press Ltd, he periodically teaches computer science at college, and works as an IT trainer in England while researching for his PhD. His books have become a valuable resource among the students in England, South Africa, Canada, and in the United States.

Kevin's motto is clear: "If you can't explain something simply, then you haven't understood it well enough." To that end, he has created the Exploring Tech Computing series, in which he breaks down complex technological subjects into smaller, easy-to-follow steps that students and ordinary computer users can put into practice.

# Acknowledgements

Thanks to all the staff at Luminescent Media & Elluminet Press for their passion, dedication and hard work in the preparation and production of this book.

To all my friends and family for their continued support and encouragement in all my writing projects.

To all my colleagues, students and testers who took the time to test procedures and offer feedback on the book

Finally thanks to you the reader for choosing this book. I hope it helps you to use your computer with greater understanding.

Have fun!

# 1 New Features & Updates

Windows 11 is the successor to Windows 10 and the most recent major release of Microsoft's desktop operating system. It was officially released on October 5, 2021, and made available as a free upgrade for eligible Windows 10 systems. However, it introduced stricter hardware requirements—including support for UEFI with Secure Boot, TPM 2.0, and modern 64-bit processors—which rendered many older machines ineligible for official support.

Windows 11 is developed under Microsoft's continuous update model, with periodic feature releases and monthly quality updates. Major updates are identified by version numbers (e.g. 21H2, 22H2, 23H2, 24H2), each introducing new functionality, interface refinements, and security improvements.

To help you better understand this section, take a look at the video resources. Scan the QR code, or open your web browser and type the following directly into the address bar at the top (don't use a search engine):

 elluminetpress.com/win-11

# What's New?

Windows 11 continues to evolve with each major update. Version 24H2, released in the second half of 2024, introduces a wide range of features—including artificial intelligence enhancements, user interface improvements, system performance optimizations, expanded security measures, and support for emerging hardware standards.

First is the Copilot+ PC (pronounced Copilot Plus), which is a new type of Windows PC introduced alongside version 24H2. These PCs are equipped with a dedicated Neural Processing Unit (NPU) capable of performing over 40 trillion operations per second (TOPS), enabling advanced AI workloads to run locally rather than in the cloud. This architecture supports faster, more private, and more energy-efficient execution of AI-powered features such as those listed below.

Recall is a timeline-based feature that periodically captures snapshots of desktop activity—including open applications, documents, and websites—and organizes them into a searchable index. All data is processed and stored locally, secured using on-device encryption and Windows Hello authentication. While Recall is designed to enhance productivity by making past content easy to retrieve, it has raised privacy concerns due to its continuous background capture model.

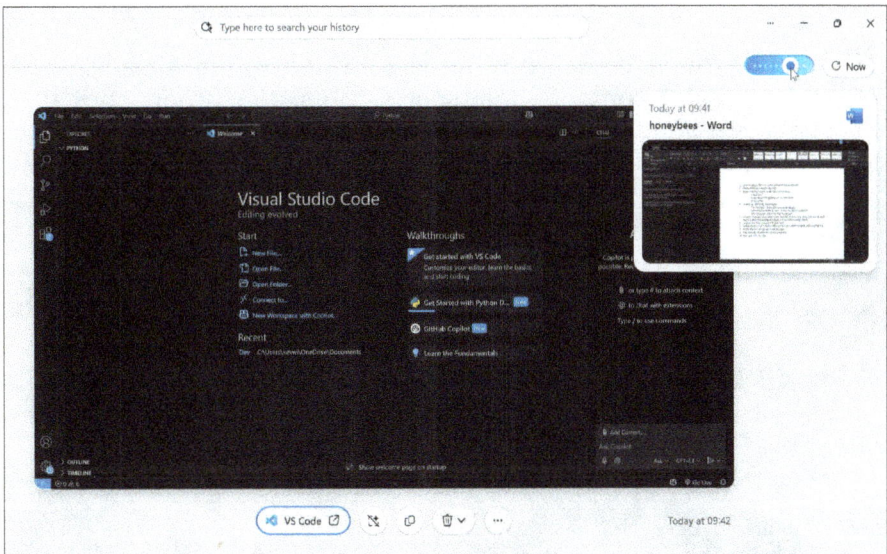

AI Super Resolution applies deep learning models to enhance the visual quality of supported games and video applications by upscaling lower-resolution content in real time.

# Chapter 1: New Features & Updates

Cocreator in Paint introduces generative AI capabilities to the classic drawing application. It allows users to create images from text prompts and integrates with Paint's new support for layers and transparency, making it useful for creative exploration, prototyping, and digital illustration. Also available in the Photos App.

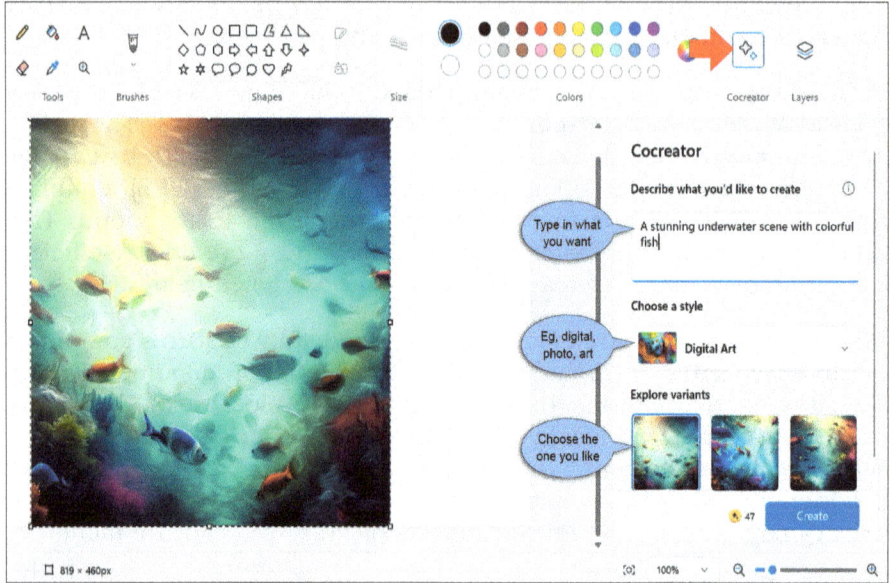

Live Captions with Translation delivers on-device, real-time subtitles for spoken audio content. It supports translation from more than 40 languages into English, improving accessibility for international communication and media consumption.

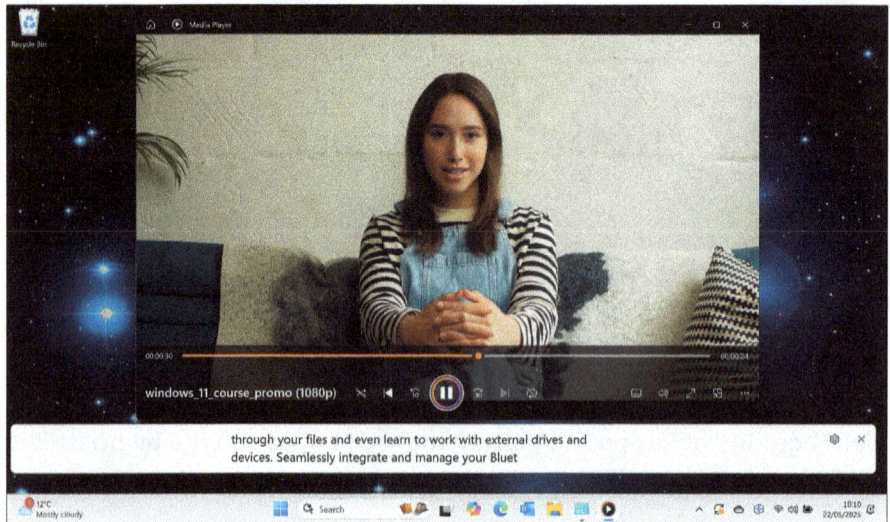

Click to Do offers intelligent, contextual actions—such as summarizing text, annotating documents, or creating calendar events—based on the content currently displayed or selected on screen.

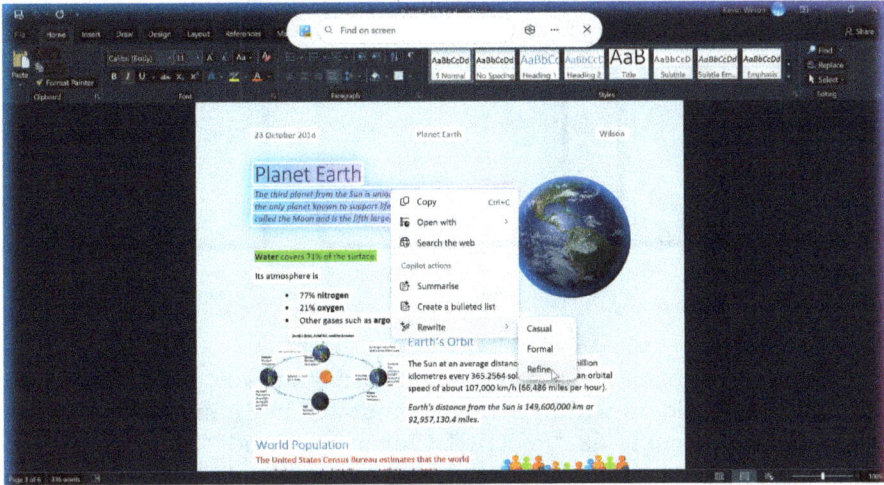

Windows Studio Effects uses hardware acceleration to enhance video conferencing with features such as background blur, automatic framing, voice isolation, and eye contact correction.

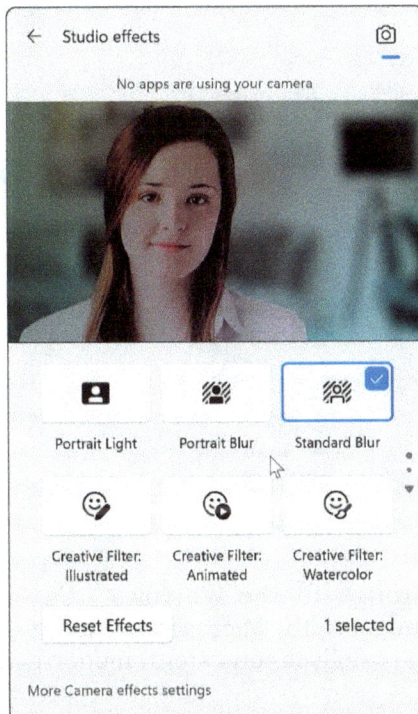

# Chapter 1: New Features & Updates

The Start menu in version 24H2 introduces a more flexible layout with expanded support for pinned apps, allowing you to customize the grid with more apps per row. This enhancement streamlines access to frequently used apps and reduces reliance on search, especially on high-resolution displays.

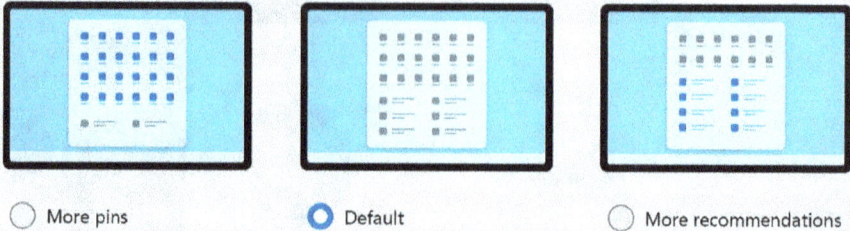

○ More pins          ● Default          ○ More recommendations

File Explorer now features a refined tabbed interface, allowing you to open multiple folders within a single window. The Home view includes organized tabs such as "Recent," "Favorites," and "Shared," which automatically categorize files based on usage and collaboration status.

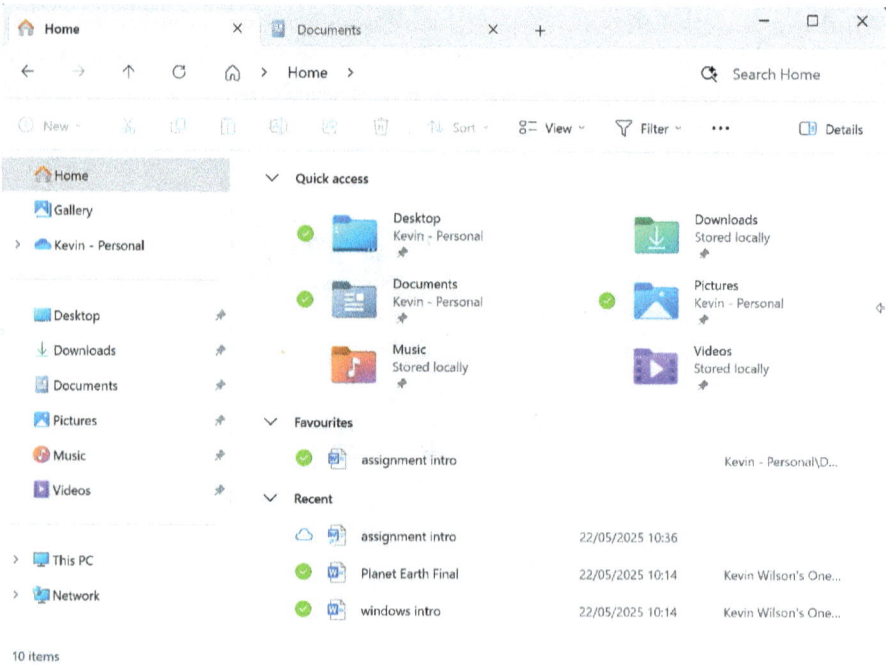

Visual elements throughout the Windows 11's interface have been refined to better align with Microsoft's Fluent Design System—a framework intended to deliver consistent, modern, and accessible user experiences.

These updates include changes to typography, layout spacing, and color schemes within File Explorer, the Settings app, and common system dialog boxes. While system icons have not been comprehensively redesigned, minor adjustments contribute to a more cohesive overall appearance.

The Quick Settings panel has been improved in version 24H2. You can now scroll vertically through the available controls. Additionally, you can drag and drop the controls to reorder them directly within the panel, allowing you to personalize the layout by adding, removing, or rearranging system toggles such as Wi-Fi, Bluetooth, brightness, and Focus Assist.

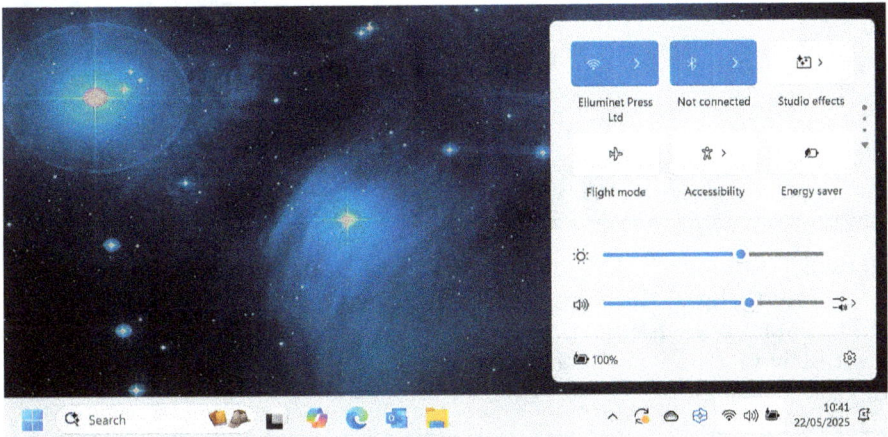

Additionally, a redesigned volume flyout includes a built-in Volume Mixer that provides per-app sound control, offering more granular audio management without launching the full Settings app.

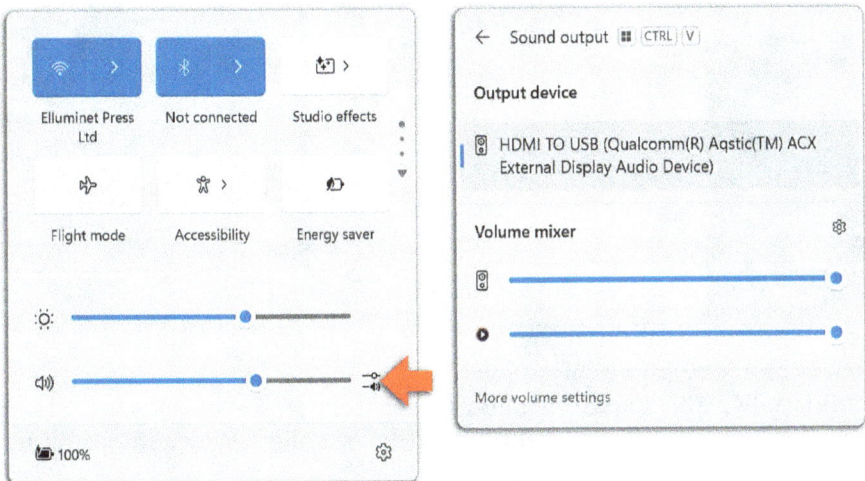

# Chapter 1: New Features & Updates

Snap Layouts, first introduced in earlier versions of Windows 11, have been enhanced in version 24H2 to be more responsive and context-aware. Hovering over the maximize button now reveals a refined layout menu that adapts to your screen size and orientation, offering more relevant snapping options.

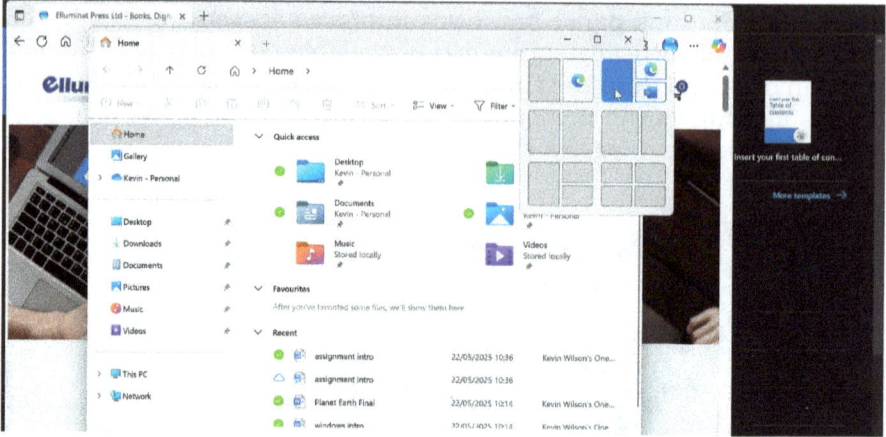

Version Windows 11 version 24H2 introduces deeper integration with Phone Link. The Start menu now includes a dedicated panel that displays real-time phone information—such as battery status, connectivity state, and recent messages or calls—when a compatible device is paired.

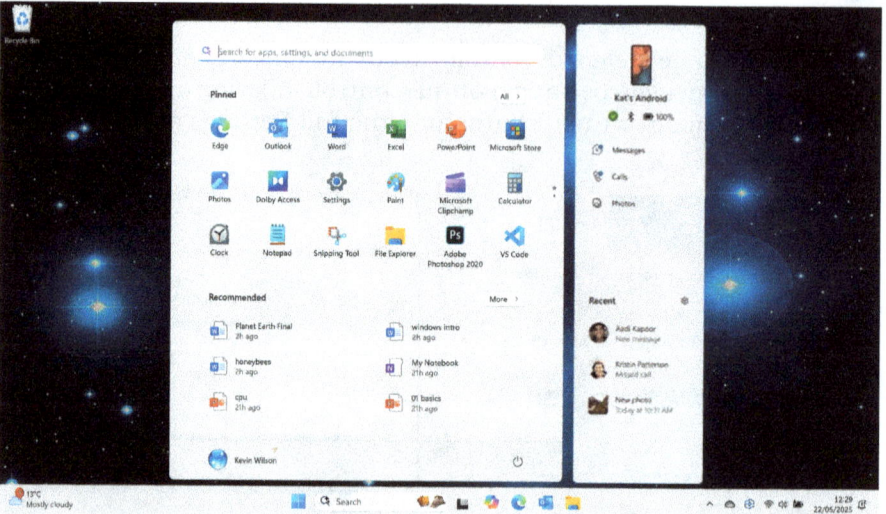

Additionally, File Explorer gains a new section for quickly accessing files transferred from a linked android mobile device, streamlining wireless file sharing.

Windows 11 now includes built-in support for extracting and compressing .7z, .tar, and Zip—without needing third-party tools. This is part of Microsoft's broader initiative to enhance File Explorer's functionality.

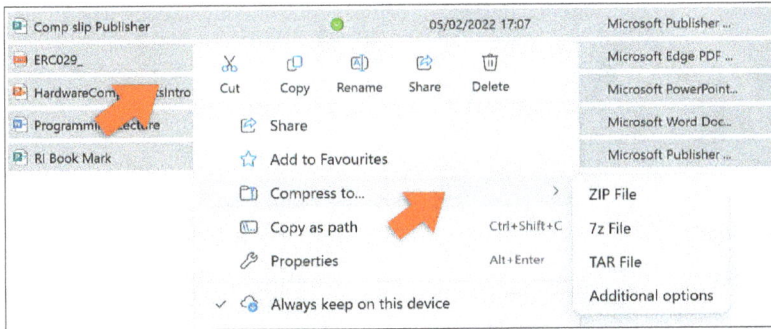

Subtle animation enhancements improve the responsiveness and fluidity of user interactions across the Windows 11 interface. Window transitions, menu expansions, and context shifts now feature smoother motion with more consistent timing, reducing visual stutter and enhancing perceived performance. These refinements contribute to a more polished and cohesive user experience, in line with Microsoft's Fluent Design principles.

The Settings app continues its gradual replacement of legacy Control Panel functionality.

With the release of Windows 11—and particularly with updates such as version 23H2 and 24H2—Microsoft has continued to phase out legacy components and streamline the system.

WordPad was removed in 24H2; Microsoft recommends using Word instead.

Maps app is deprecated and will be removed from the Microsoft Store by July 2025. Google and Bing Maps are good alternatives.

Movies & TV was removed from default installs, but is still available from the Microsoft Store.

Groove Music has been replaced by the new Media Player, which supports both music and video playback.

Cortana has been deprecated and has been replaced by the AI-powered Windows Copilot.

The Mail, Calendar, and People apps are being phased out in favor of the new Outlook for Windows app.

# 2

# Installing Windows 11

Most new laptops, tablets, and desktop PCs come with Windows 11 preinstalled—typically the Home edition for consumer devices, though higher-end business models may include Windows 11 Pro.

If you have an older machine purchased in 2018 or later, you may be able to upgrade to Windows 11. It is unlikely older machines will be able to run Windows 11.

In this chapter we'll take a look at:

- Upgrading to Windows 11
- System Requirements
- TPM & Secure Boot
- Supported CPUs
- Checking your PC
- Upgrading from Windows 10
- Installation Assistant
- Media Creation Tool
- Running Windows 11 for the First Time

To help you better understand this section, take a look at the video resources. Scan the QR code, or open your web browser and type the following directly into the address bar at the top (don't use a search engine):

elluminetpress.com/using-win-11

# Upgrading to Windows 11

If you have a fully licensed version of Windows 10 installed, then if your PC is compatible, you will receive the Windows 11 update for free on Windows update.

## Requirements

If you're upgrading, make sure your PC meets the following specification.

| | |
|---|---|
| **Processor:** | 1 gigahertz (GHz) or faster with 2 or more cores on a compatible 64-bit processor or System on a Chip (SoC) |
| **RAM:** | 4 gigabyte (GB) |
| **Hard Disk:** | 64 GB or larger storage device |
| **System firmware:** | UEFI, Secure Boot capable |
| **TPM:** | Trusted Platform Module (TPM) version 2.0 |
| **Graphics card:** | Compatible with DirectX 12 or later with WDDM 2.0 driver |
| **Display:** | High definition (720p) display that is greater than 9" diagonally, 8 bits per colour channel |

A few things to take note of. First, your device must include a Trusted Platform Module version 2.0 (TPM 2.0). TPM is a security chip—either discrete or firmware-based—that provides hardware-level protection by securely storing cryptographic keys, digital certificates, and passwords. It helps ensure that sensitive data is protected from unauthorized access and tampering by malware or other threats. TPM 2.0 is a mandatory requirement for official support in Windows 11. Most systems manufactured from 2016 onward include TPM 2.0 or firmware-based equivalents (such as Intel PTT or AMD fTPM), although it may need to be enabled in the UEFI settings. You can check this in device manager. Right click on the start button, select 'device manager' from the menu.

Scroll down the list and double-click 'Security devices'. You should see 'Trusted Platform Module 2.0' listed. If you don't see it, or if it shows 'Trusted Platform Module 1.2', then your device does not meet the TPM 2.0 requirement for Windows 11.

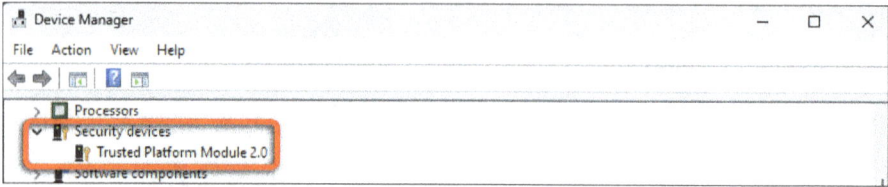

For a more detailed view, press Windows + R on your keyboard, type `tpm.msc` then press Enter. This opens the TPM Management Console, where you can confirm if TPM 2.0 is present and ready for use.

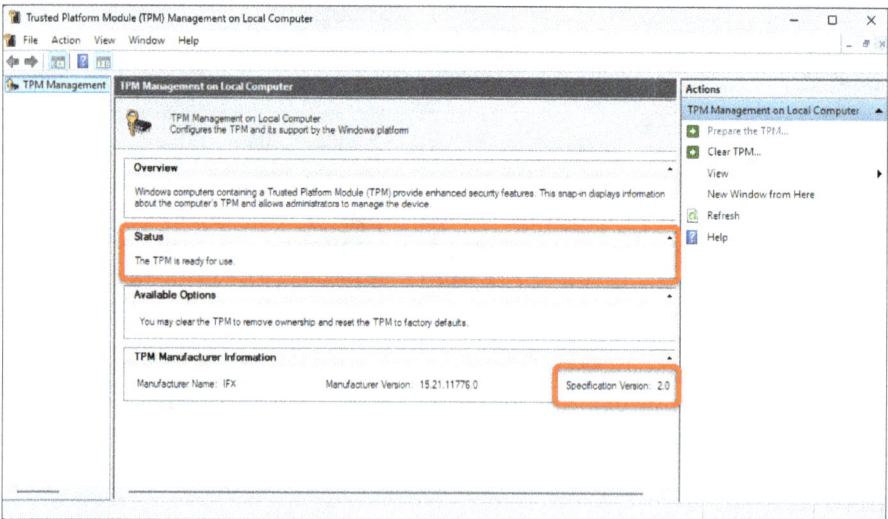

Secondly, your device will also need secure boot enabled. Most modern devices include this feature. Secure Boot is a security feature that only allows approved operating systems to boot up, thereby preventing malware from taking control of your device at boot time.

Windows 11 also requires a 64-bit CPU that appears on Microsoft's official compatibility list. For Intel-based systems, supported CPUs begin with 8th-generation Core CPUs (Coffee Lake), such as the Core i5-8250U, Core i7-8565U, and Core i9-9900K. Support extends to later generations as well, including select 10th-generation CPUs like the Core i5-10210U and i7-10510U (Comet Lake), 11th-generation CPUs such as the i5-1135G7 and i7-1165G7 (Tiger Lake), and newer 12th- and 13th-generation mobile CPUs like the i5-1240P, i7-1260P (Alder Lake), i5-1335U, and i7-1365U (Raptor Lake).

For AMD systems, Windows 11 requires second-generation Ryzen CPUs (Zen+ architecture) or newer. Supported CPUs include the Ryzen 5 2600 and Ryzen 7 2700X (Zen+), Ryzen 5 3600 (Zen 2), Ryzen 7 5800X (Zen 3), and Ryzen 7 7700X (Zen 4). On mobile systems, compatible models range from the Ryzen 5 3500U and 3700U (Zen+), to Ryzen 5 4500U and 4700U (Zen 2), and up to Ryzen 5 5600U, 5800U (Zen 3), 7730U, and Ryzen 9 7940HS (Zen 3+/4).

For ARM-based devices, Windows 11 is officially supported only on Qualcomm Snapdragon chips, starting with the Snapdragon 850, and continuing through the Snapdragon 7c, 8c, 8cx (Gen 1–3), and the high-performance Snapdragon X Elite platform.

As of version 24H2, Microsoft enforces several mandatory CPU instruction sets—such as SSE4.2 and POPCNT—which are used to accelerate low-level operations like string handling, checksums, and bitwise population counts.

While most PCs manufactured after 2018 include supported hardware, users should confirm compatibility by checking Microsoft's official CPU lists.

## Check your PC

To check if your PC is compatible, use the PC Health Check tool. To do this go to

`www.microsoft.com/en-us/software-download/windows11`

Click 'PC Health Check' at the top of the web page.

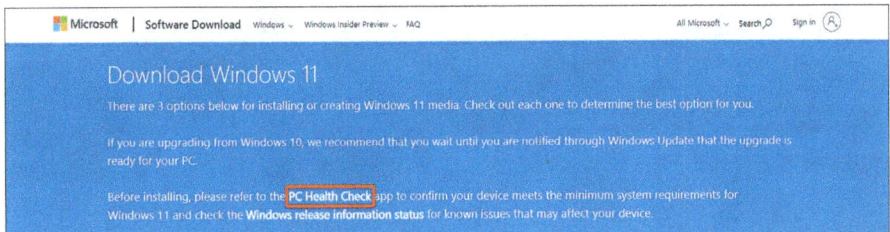

Click 'download pc health check app'

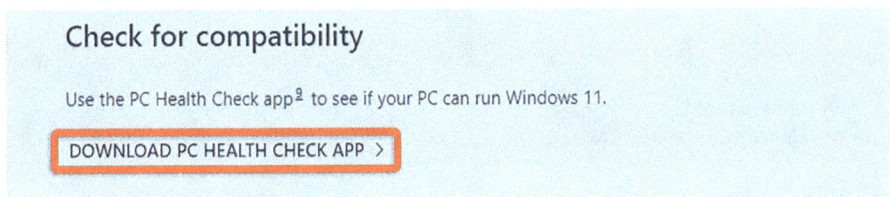

## Chapter 2: Installing up Windows 11

Click 'open' when prompted by your browser. Run through the installation wizard. Once the installation is complete, click 'check now' at the top of the screen.

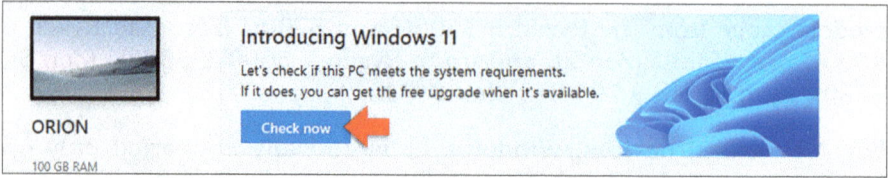

If you see the message on the left, you're all set, otherwise you can't install Windows 11.

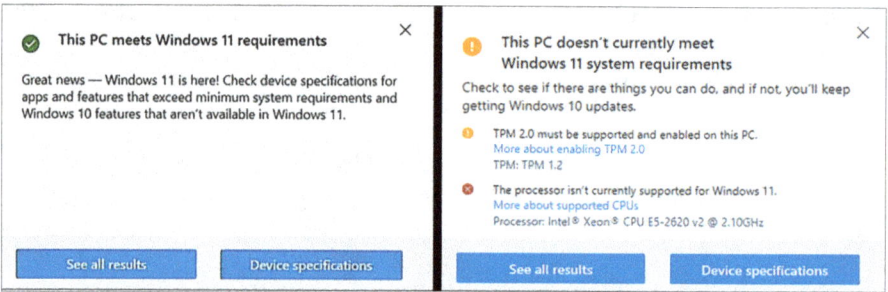

# Upgrade using Windows Update on Windows 10

If you are running Windows 10 and your device meets the requirements, then you should automatically receive a notification in Windows Update. In Windows 10, open the Start Menu. Click the settings icon.

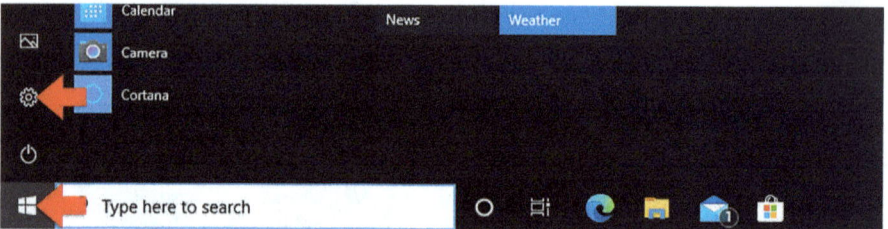

Click 'update & security'.

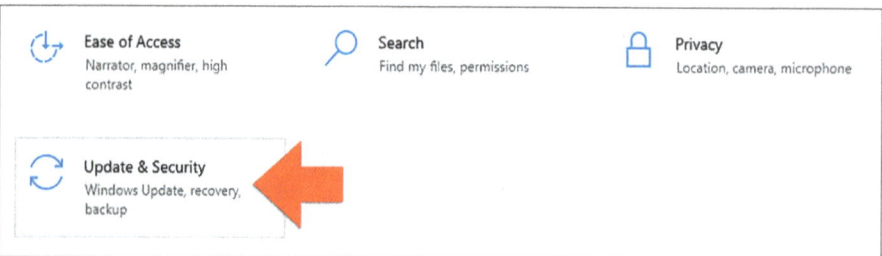

Then select 'Windows Update' from the list on the list. Then click 'check for updates'.

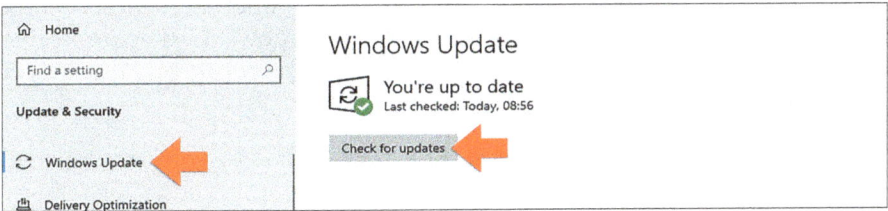

Windows 10 will check for any available updates. When Windows 11 is available, you'll see a 'feature update' notification in windows update. Click 'download and install now'.

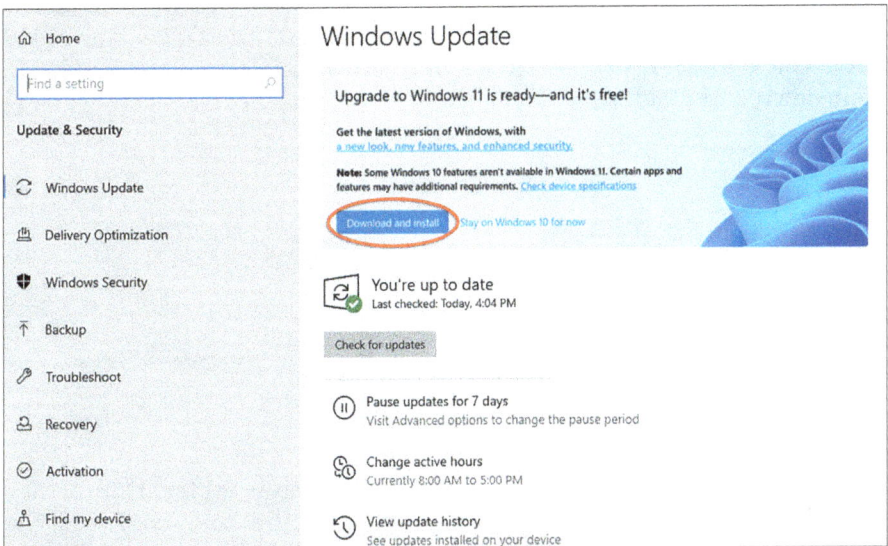

To complete the update, you'll need to restart your machine when it's finished. Go to Start > Power Icon > 'Update & Restart'.

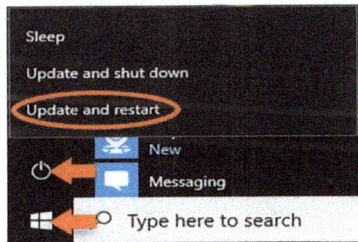

If you only see 'restart' on the menu, then the update hasn't finished downloading yet. Once the installation is complete see "Running Windows 11 the First Time" on page 35.

# Windows 11 Installation Assistant

The Windows 11 Installation Assistant is a Microsoft utility that downloads and installs the latest version of Windows 11 on compatible devices. It's useful if your PC meets the requirements but hasn't yet received the upgrade through Windows Update.

First, download the health check tool, then run it to confirm your PC is compatible. See page 27.

Next, you'll need to download installation assistant. To do this, open your web browser and navigate to the following website.

```
www.microsoft.com/en-us/software-download/windows11
```

Scroll down to 'Windows 11 installation assistant', then click 'download now'. Click 'save' if prompted by your browser. You'll find the file in your downloads folder.

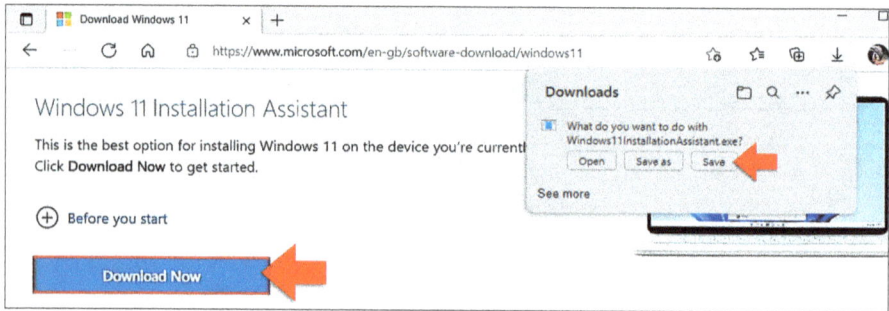

Open file explore, then navigate to your downloads folder. Double lick on windows11installationassistant.exe Once the tool confirms the device hardware is compatible. You'll land on the 'install windows 11' screen. Click 'accept and install'

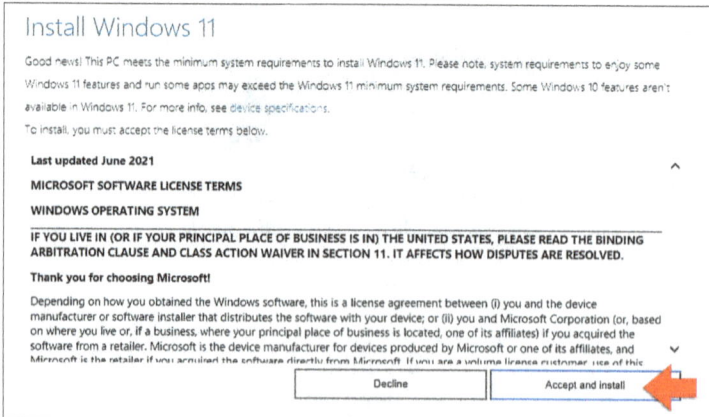

The tool will download the Windows 11 installation files, which may take some time depending on your internet speed and system performance. Once the download is complete, you'll be prompted to restart your PC.

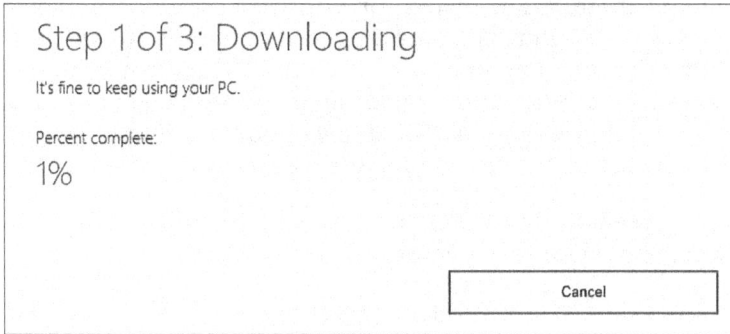

---

## Step 1 of 3: Downloading

It's fine to keep using your PC.

Percent complete:

1%

| | Cancel |
|---|---|

---

Click "Restart now" to begin installation.

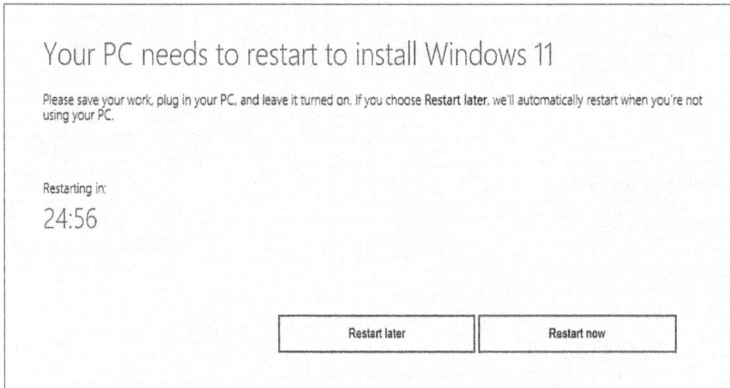

---

## Your PC needs to restart to install Windows 11

Please save your work, plug in your PC, and leave it turned on. If you choose Restart later, we'll automatically restart when you're not using your PC.

Restarting in:

24:56

| Restart later | Restart now |
|---|---|

---

Your PC will reboot and proceed with installing Windows 11. This part of the process may take a while and may involve multiple restarts. Do not turn off your computer during this time.

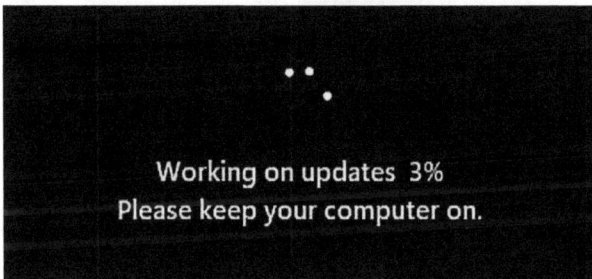

Working on updates 3%
Please keep your computer on.

Once installation is complete, you'll need to go through the first-time setup procedure. "Running Windows 11 the First Time" on page 35.

# Media Creation Tool

The Media Creation Tool is an official Microsoft utility that allows you to create installation media for Windows 11. This is particularly useful if your computer isn't working correctly, fails to start, or needs a clean installation. For instance, if your PC has been infected with malware, shows persistent errors, or if you've replaced your hard drive or SSD, the Media Creation Tool allows you to reinstall Windows 11 from scratch without relying on recovery partitions or factory software.

First, you'll need to download the utility. To do this, open your web browser and navigate to the following website.

`www.microsoft.com/software-download/windows11`

Scroll down to 'create windows 11 installation media', then click 'download now'.

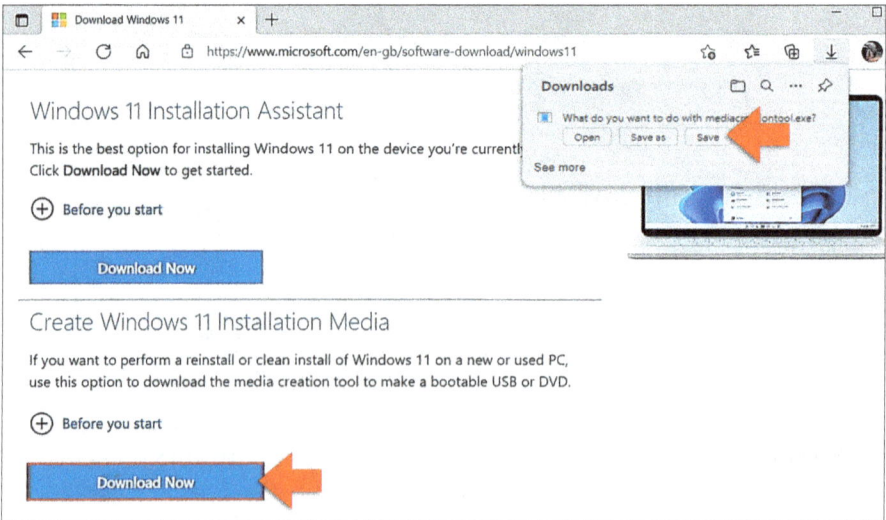

Click on the file in the downloads prompt, or click 'save' if prompted by your browser. You'll find the file in your downloads folder.

## Creating a Windows 11 Installation Disk

Once the file has finished downloading, open File Explorer, then navigate to your downloads folder. Double-click on `MediaCreationTool.exe`

When the Media Creation Tool opens, you'll be asked to accept Microsoft's license terms. Click Accept to continue.

To create the installation media, you'll need a USB flash drive with at least 8GB of storage. Plug the USB flash drive into your PC.

Choose your language, edition of Windows 11 (Home or Pro), and system architecture (typically 64-bit). In most cases, the Media Creation Tool will automatically detect and select the appropriate settings based on your current system.

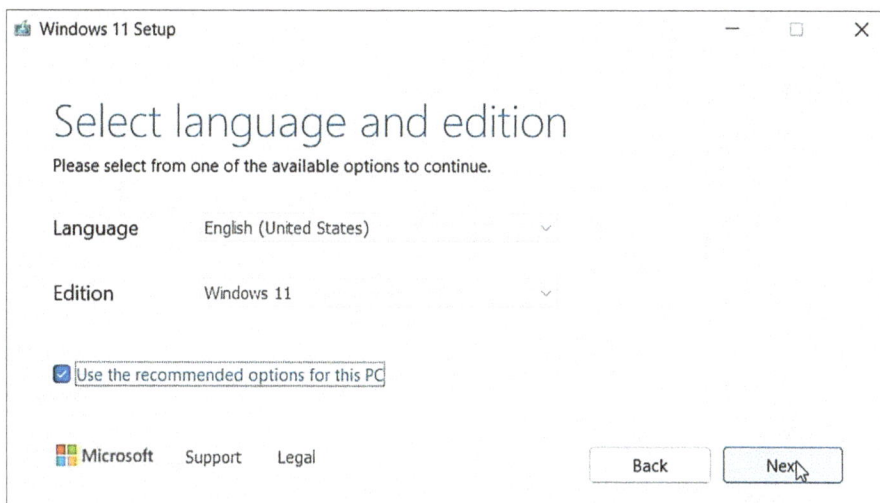

If you need to make changes—such as creating installation media for a different PC with a different language, edition, or architecture— untick "Use the recommended options for this PC", then select the language, edition, and architecture manually. For most users, the correct architecture is x64, which is standard for modern Intel and AMD processors; select ARM64 only if you're installing Windows 11 on a device with an ARM-based processor. Click Next to continue.

Select your installation media. Select USB flash drive. *If you want an ISO image you can burn to a DVD select ISO file.* Click next.

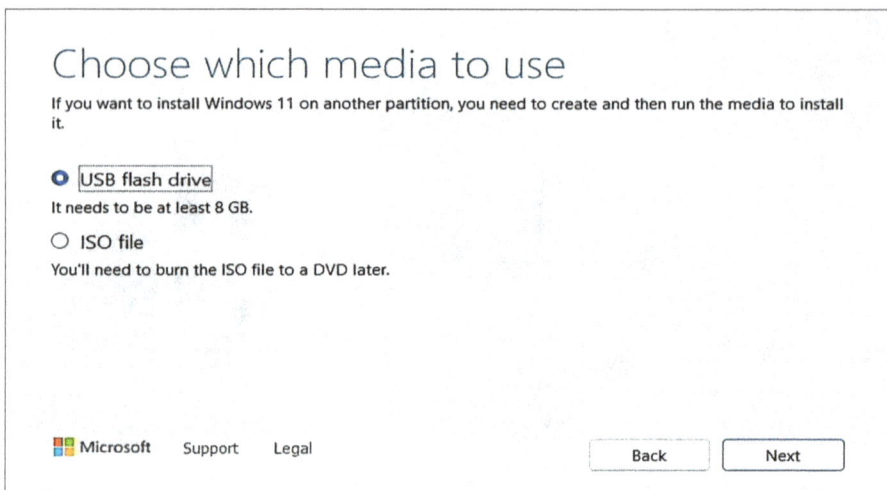

## Choose which media to use

If you want to install Windows 11 on another partition, you need to create and then run the media to install it.

○ USB flash drive
It needs to be at least 8 GB.

○ ISO file
You'll need to burn the ISO file to a DVD later.

▓ Microsoft     Support     Legal                    Back        Next

The Media Creation Tool will scan for available USB drives. Select your USB flash drive from the list under Removable drives, then click 'next' to start.

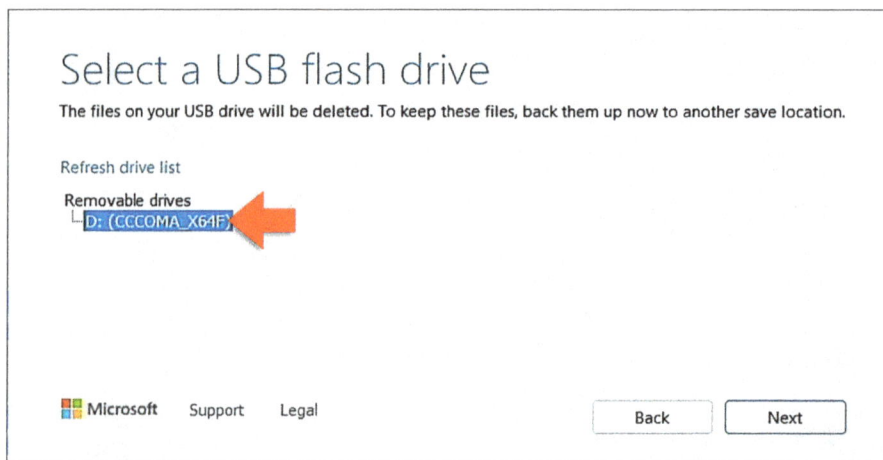

## Select a USB flash drive

The files on your USB drive will be deleted. To keep these files, back them up now to another save location.

Refresh drive list

Removable drives
  └ D: (CCCOMA_X64F)

▓ Microsoft     Support     Legal                    Back        Next

The Media Creation Tool will begin downloading the latest installer and write it to your USB drive. This process may take some time depending on your internet connection and system performance. Once the media has been created, you'll see a confirmation message. Click 'finish', then safely remove the USB drive.

If you run into problems with your PC, you can always start it up using the flash drive you just created.

# Running Windows 11 the First Time

If you've just bought a new computer with Windows 11, or installed a fresh copy, you'll need to run through the initial set up procedure. This will allow you to connect your computer to your WiFi/Internet, enter your Microsoft Account email address and password, and set a login method such as a PIN, fingerprint, or Windows Hello Face (face ID).

Select your country or region from the list and click 'yes'.

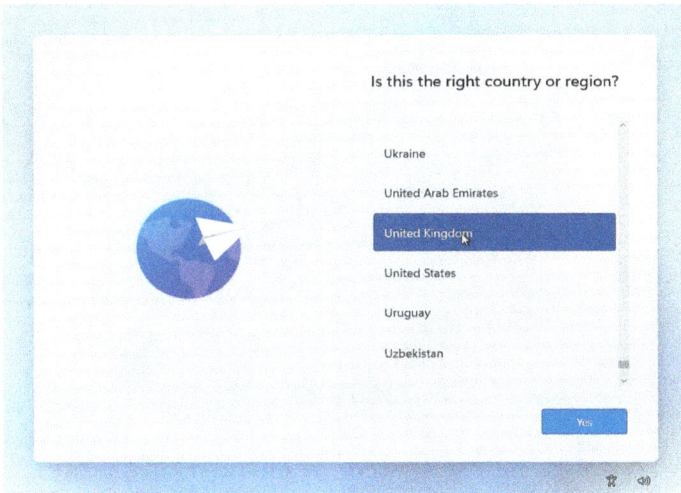

Select keyboard layout for your country, then click 'yes'.

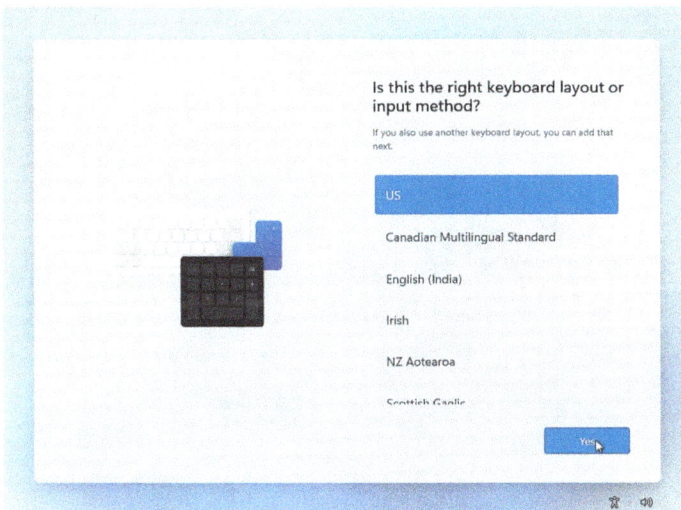

Skip secondary keyboard if you don't have one.

Click 'sign in'.

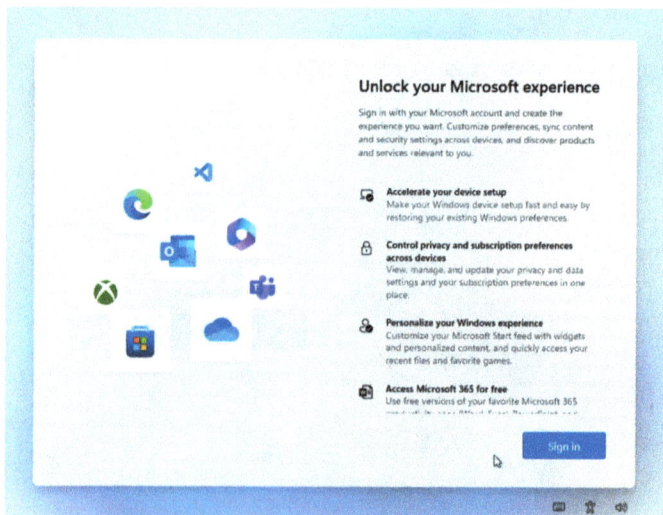

Sign in with your Microsoft Account email address and password. Click 'next'. This allows you to make use of OneDrive, email, purchase apps from the App Store, buy music and films.

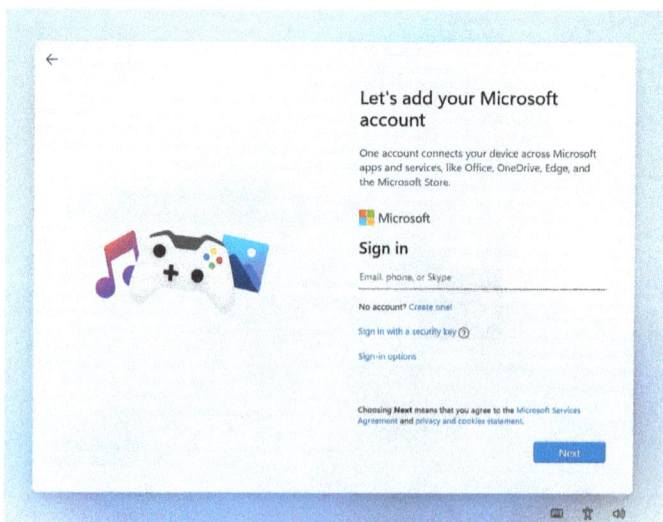

If you're setting up a new PC or if you have to reinstall Windows, you will see the last backup available from the previous PC you've used with your Microsoft Account (if any). If you want to restore specific folders, click 'folders' then select the folders you want to include. Similarly with apps, settings and credentials.

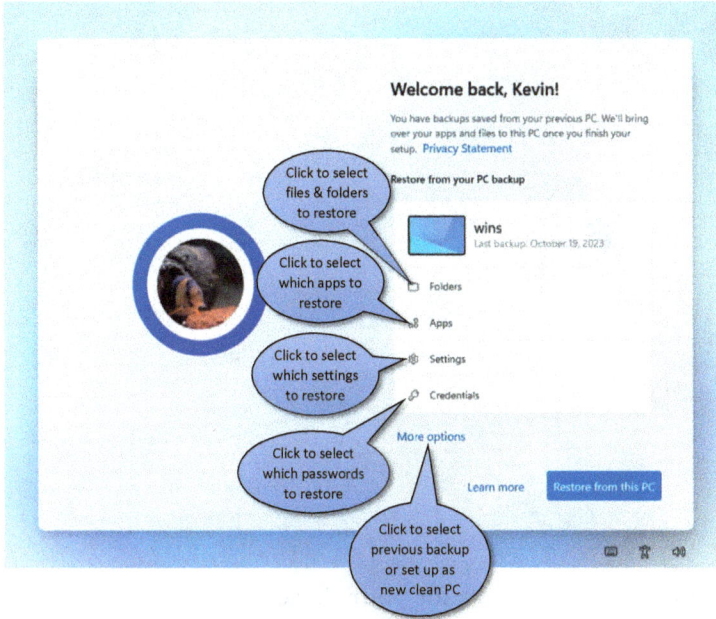

If you want to restore a previous backup, or if you want to set your device up as a new PC without restoring a backup, click 'more options'. Either select the backup you want to restore from the list, or click 'setup as new pc'. Note that 'setting up as a new pc' will execute a clean install meaning no previous settings, apps or documents will be restored.

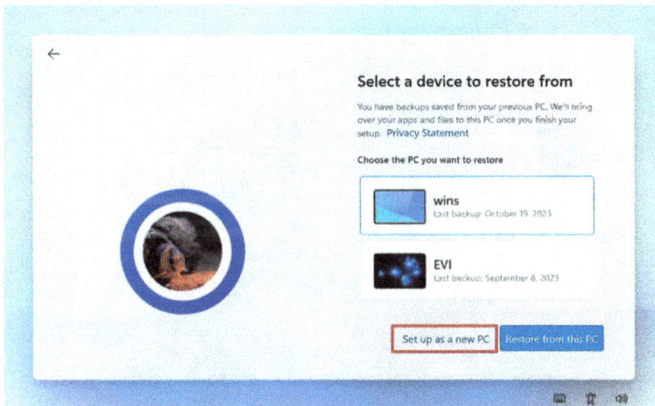

Set up your sign in method. You'll have certain options available depending on your device. If you have a finger print scanner on your device select that option. If no other options are available, select PIN. Click 'create pin', then enter a 4 digit pin code. This is the code you'll use to sign into Windows on your device, so don't forget it.

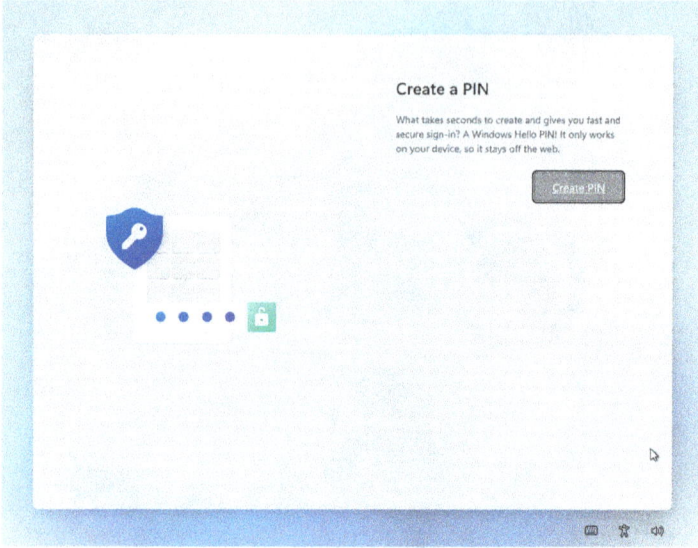

Choose the privacy settings for your device. 'Location' allows windows to determine your physical location. This enables you to use location based apps such as weather, local interest, news as well as maps, and getting directions.

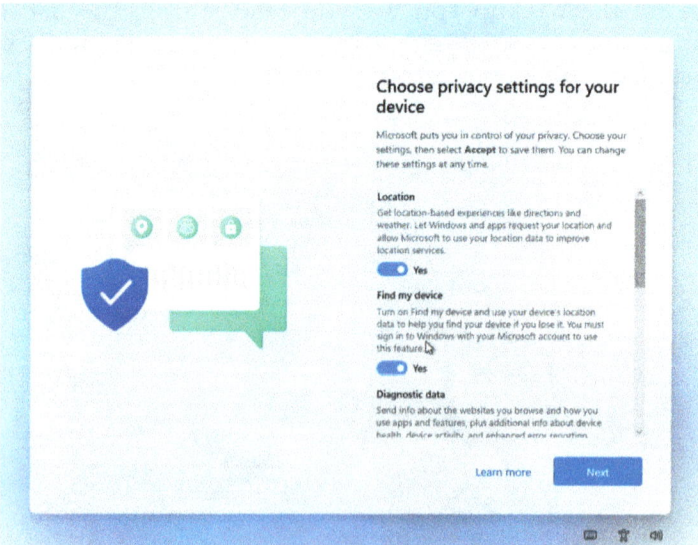

'Find my device' is useful if you're setting up a tablet and allows windows to periodically report its location. This can help if you lose your device or it is stolen. You'll be able to see its location in your Microsoft Account settings.

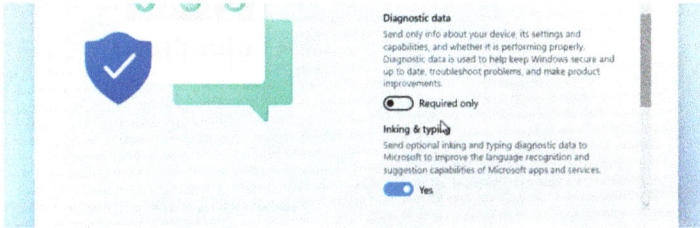

'Diagnostic data' is what Microsoft uses to troubleshoot problems and make improvements to its services. I'd suggest you select 'required only', so the only data that is sent to Microsoft is your device settings and its current state of operation,

'Inking & Typing' data is collected when you use Windows Ink and allows Microsoft to use the data to improve its product.

'Advertising ID' means any ads that appear will be tailored to your personal computing habits.

Next, you can further customise Windows 11. If you're a gamer, click the 'gaming' box. If you're a creative, click 'creativity', and follow the steps. You can skip this section for now and customise Windows later. Click 'skip'.

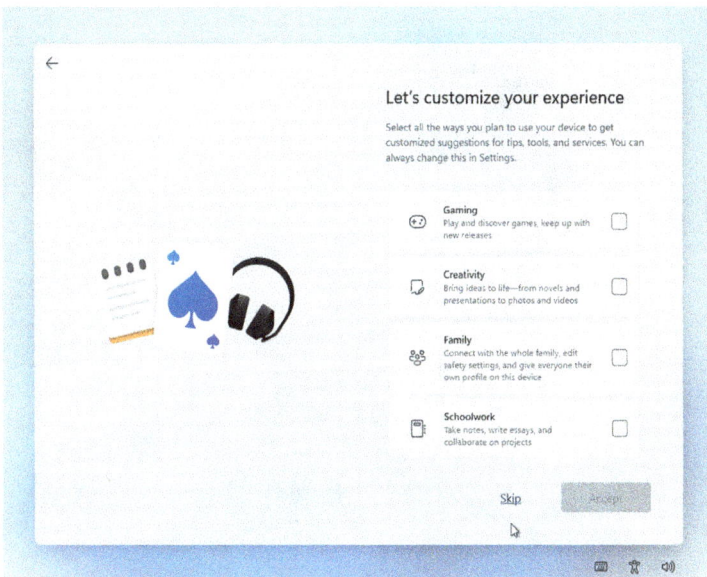

Next, you can link your Android phone to your PC. If you want to do this, use your phone to scan the code and follow the instructions. If not, click 'skip'.

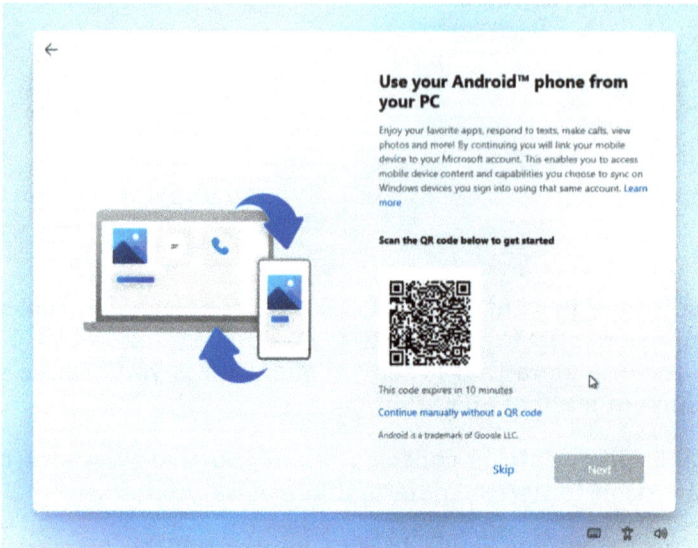

**Allow have your recent browsing data** allows you to synchronize your browsing data across devices where you use Microsoft Edge. This means if you log into Microsoft Edge on a different device with the same Microsoft account, you'll find your browsing information waiting for you.

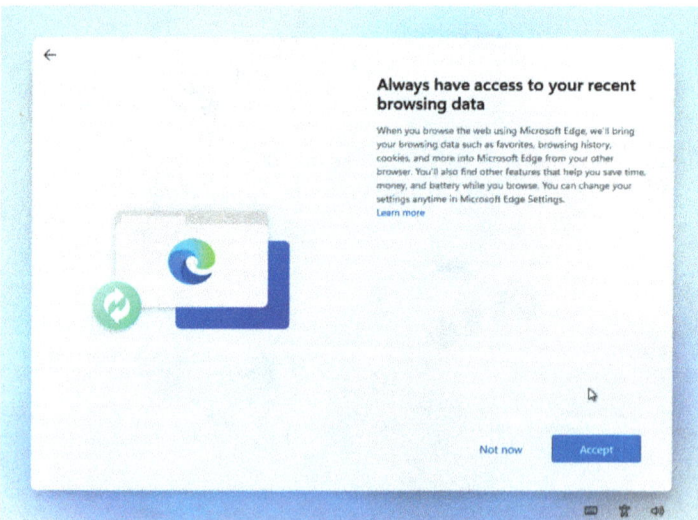

Click 'accept.

On the next screen, you can sign up for a free trial of Microsoft 365 to get access to Microsoft Word, Excel, PowerPoint, etc. Note that there is a charge for this service. If you already have Microsoft 365 or don't want to use it, click 'decline'. If you want to sign up and pay the subscription fee, then click 'continue'.

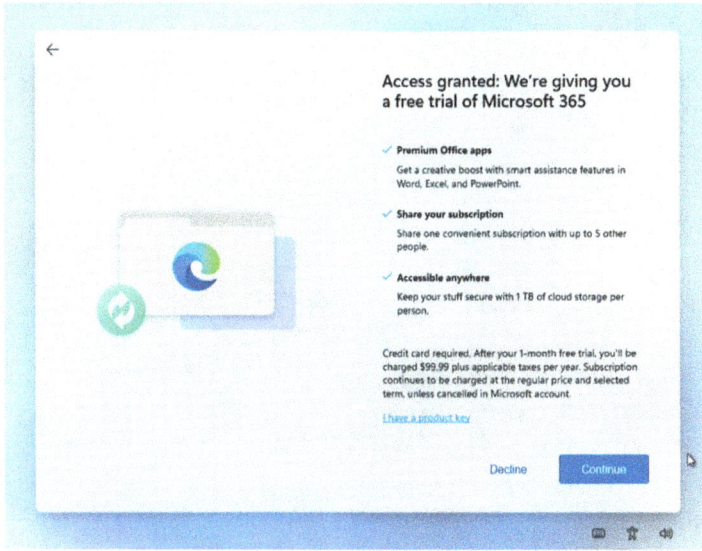

The next screen is about purchasing more storage space on OneDrive. With a Microsoft Account you get 5GB of free space on OneDrive.

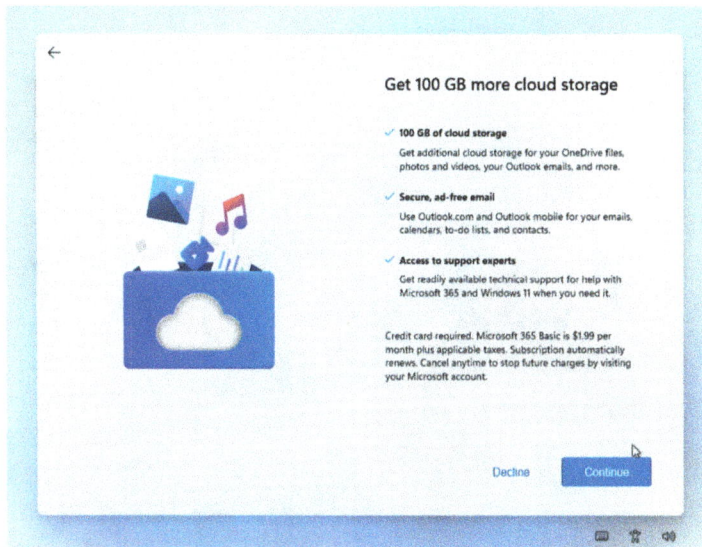

Click 'decline'. You can always purchase more space later on.

Next, you can sign up for a Game Pass if you intend to play games. Click 'skip for now'. You can always sign up for these later.

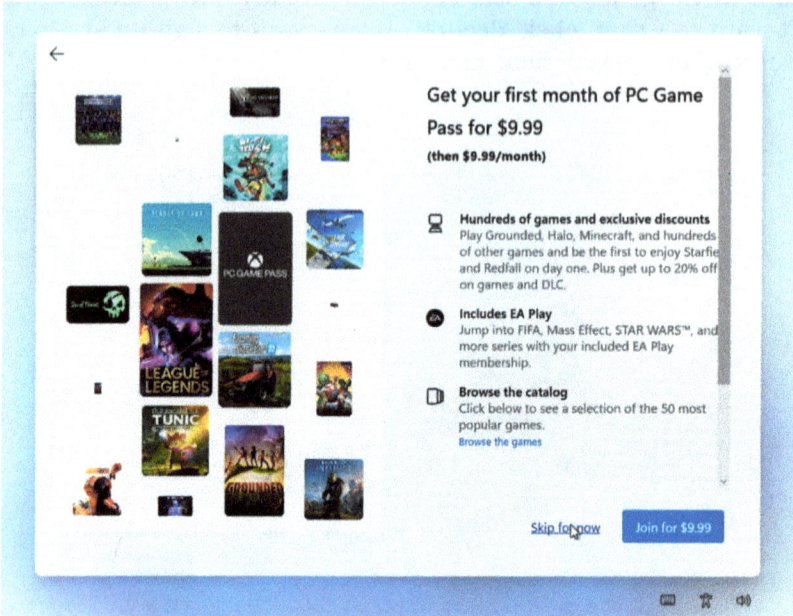

Allow Windows 11 to finish checking for updates. This might take a while, and your PC may restart a few times if required.

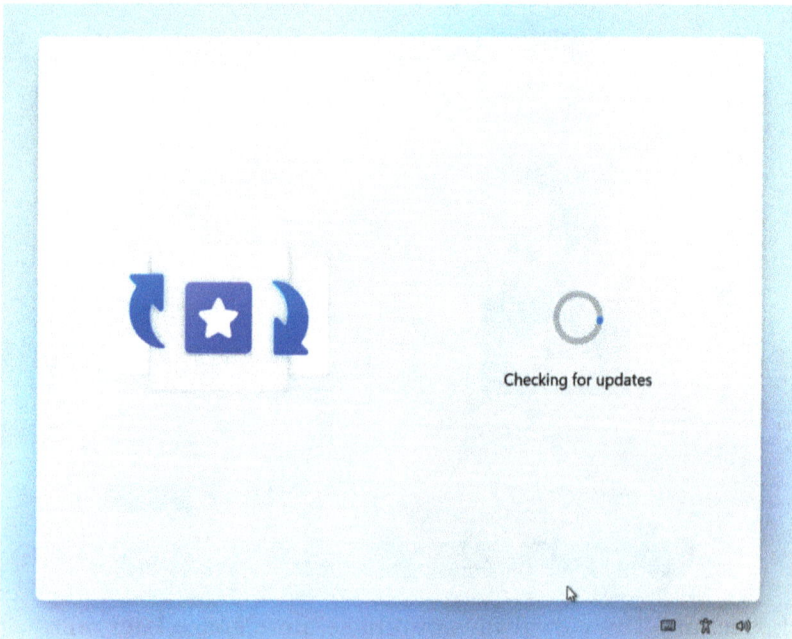

Allow your PC to configure itself.

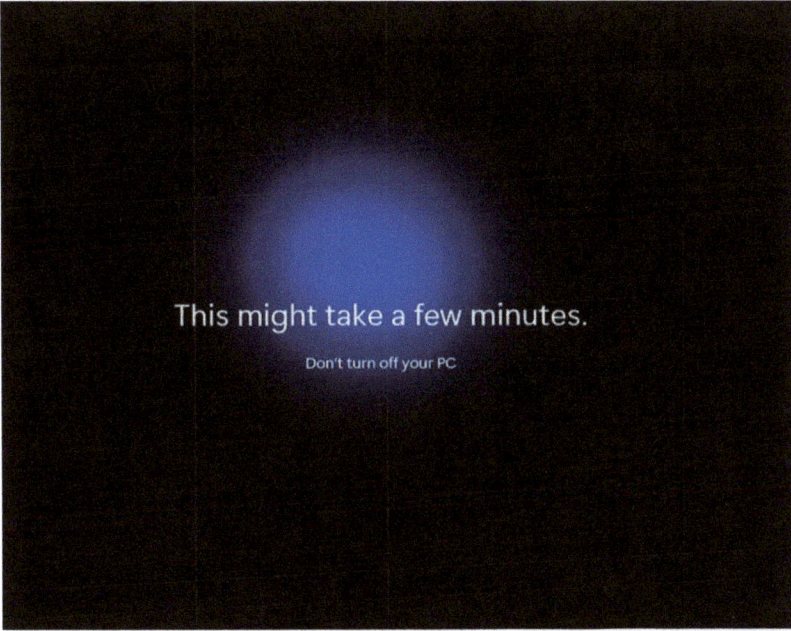

When the configuration is complete, you'll land on your desktop.

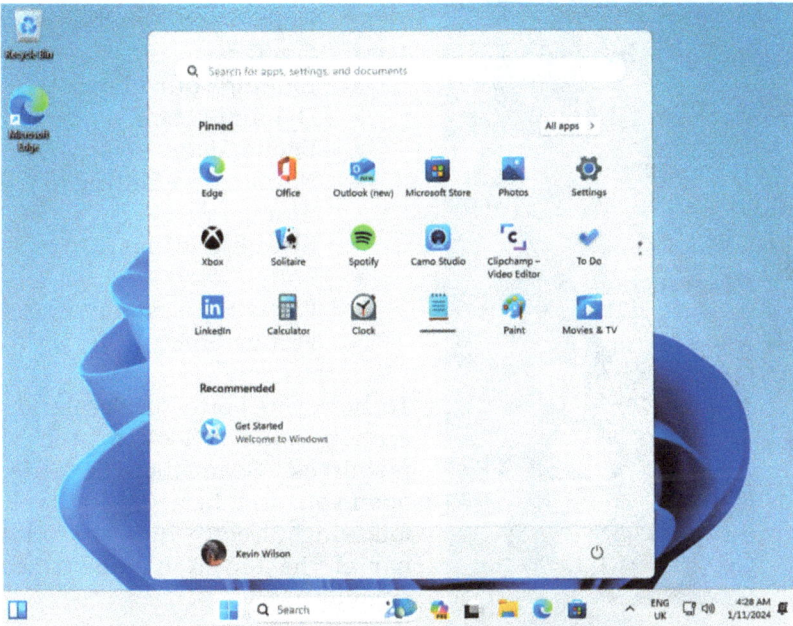

You can now use your PC.

# 3

# Settings and Personalise

You can personalise Windows according to your personal taste and how you intend to use your PC.

In this chapter, we'll take a look

- Adjusting System Settings
- General Settings
- Keyboard & Mouse
- Internet & Networks
- Printers & Bluetooth Devices
- Audio & Display Settings
- User Accounts & Windows Hello
- OneDrive
- Linking your Phone
- Dynamic Lock
- Focus Mode
- Notification Settings
- Storage Sense
- Search Settings
- Fonts
- Linux Subsystem
- Family Safety

To help you better understand this section, take a look at the video resources. Scan the QR code, or open your web browser and type the following directly into the address bar at the top (don't use a search engine):

elluminetpress.com/using-win-11

# Adjusting System Settings

To adjust system settings, you'll need to use the settings app.

## Settings App

To open the settings app, click the start button, then select the settings app icon. If you don't see it, select 'all apps' on the top right, scroll down to 'settings'.

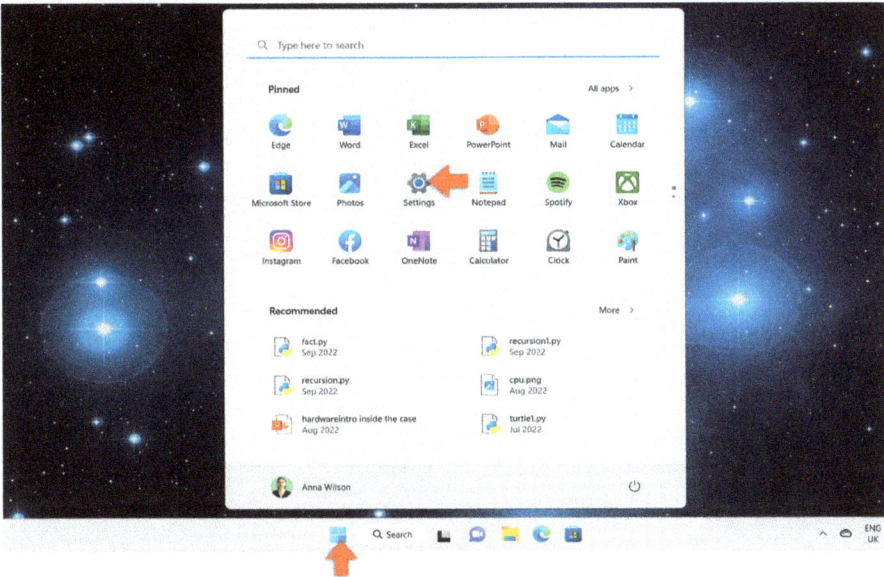

You'll land on the home page.

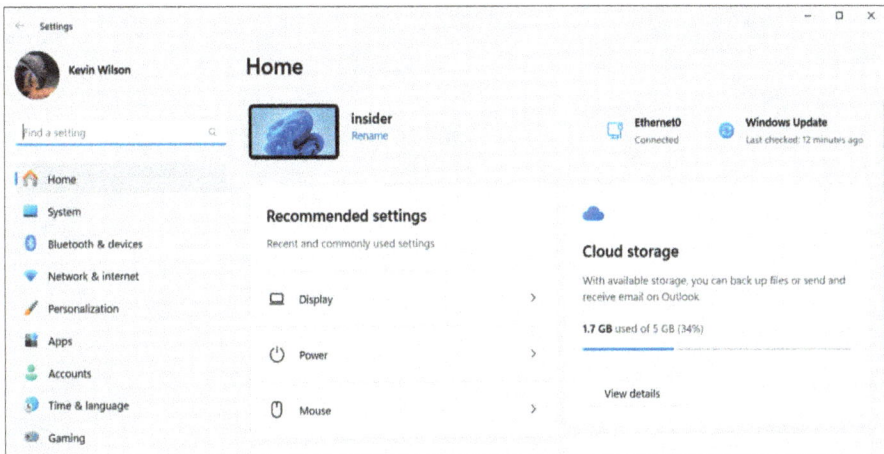

# Chapter 3: Settings and Personalisation

The home page features interactive cards that represent various device and account-related settings. These cards are designed to adjust and provide the most relevant and useful information based on how you use your device

Recommended Settings Card offers options that help save time by suggesting settings based on your usage patterns.

Cloud Storage Card displays your cloud storage usage and alerts you when you are nearing your storage capacity.

Account Recovery Card assists in adding more recovery information to your account to prevent being locked out.

Personalization Card allows you to quickly change your background theme or color mode with just one click.

Microsoft 365 Card provides a quick overview of your Microsoft 365 subscription status and benefits, along with key actions.

Xbox Card shows your Xbox subscription status and provides options to manage the subscription.

Bluetooth Devices Card enables quick access and connection to your favorite Bluetooth devices.

Down the left hand side you'll see a list of categories. Settings for different features and options are grouped into these categories.

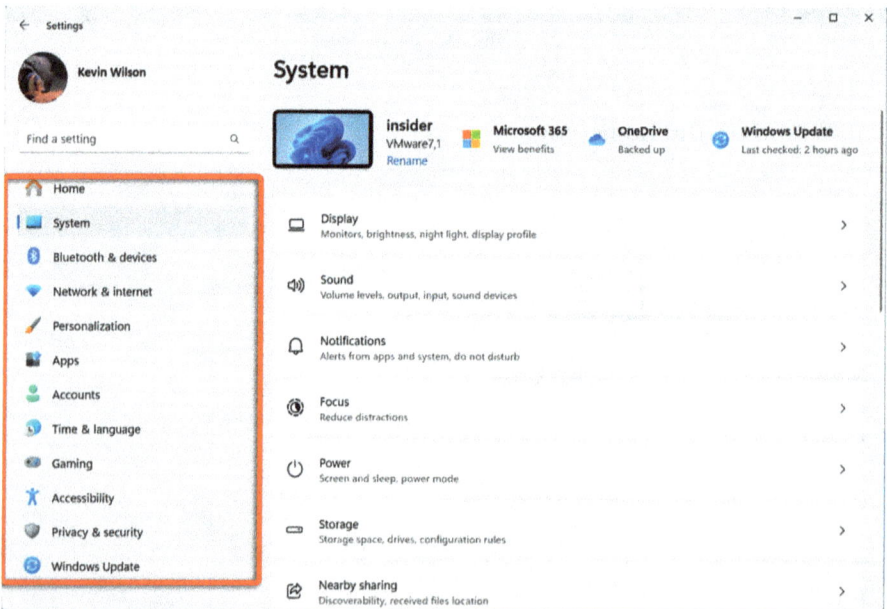

For example, all settings to do with devices such as printers, mice and keyboards can be found in the 'bluetooth & devices' category.

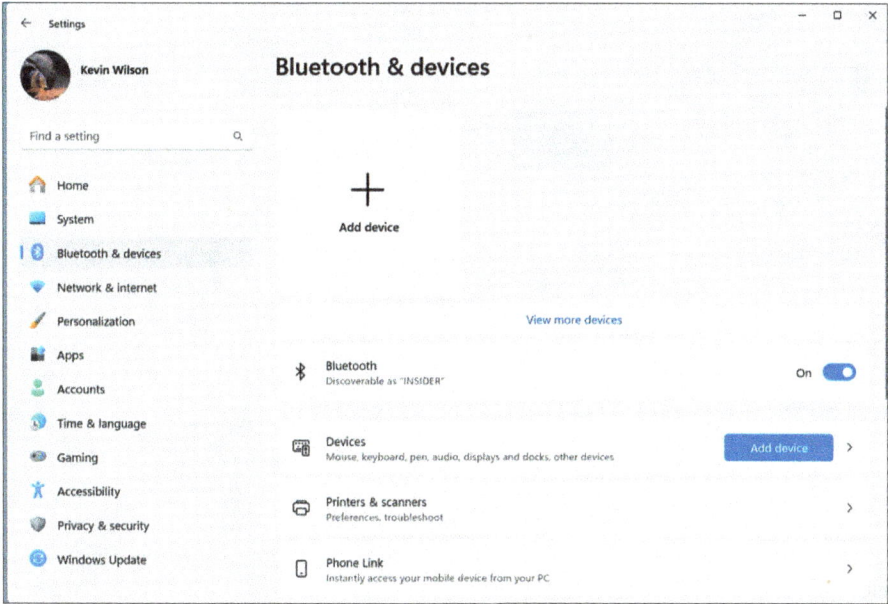

# Searching for Settings

The quickest way to change a setting is to search for it using the search field on the settings app.

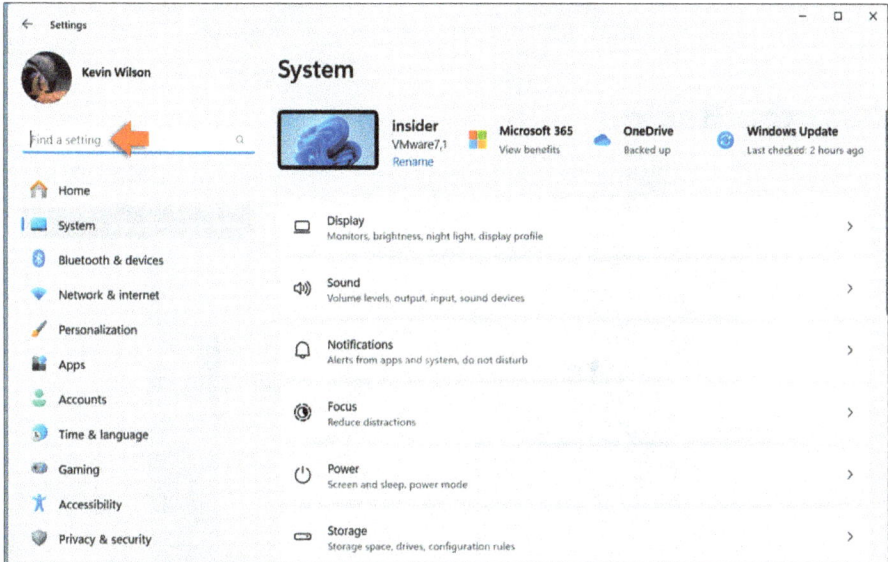

For example, if I wanted to change the printer settings, I'd just type 'printer' into the search field.

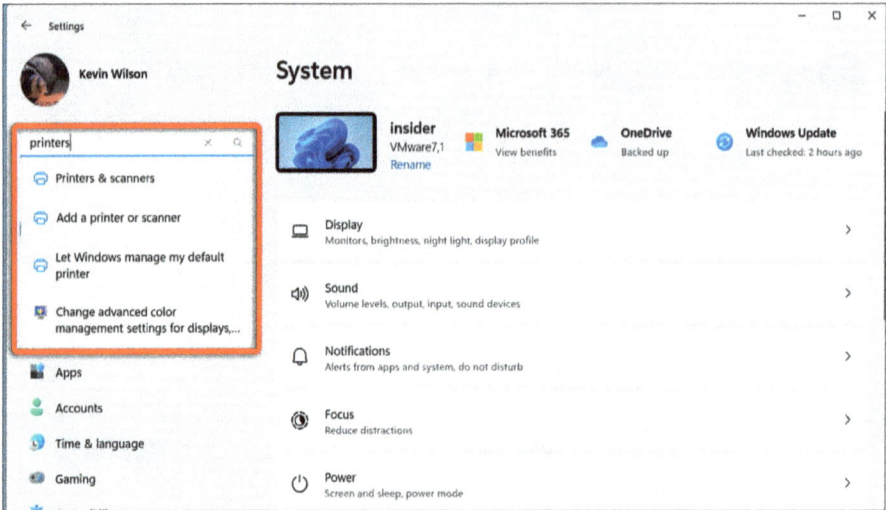

Click on 'Printers & Scanners' in the list of suggestions in the drop down box.

You can do this for any setting you need to change.

# General Settings

General configuration settings worth noting are date and time, power saving options, regional settings and keyboard layouts.

## Desktop Background

To change the wallpaper or background on your desktop, right click on your desktop, then from the popup menu, select 'personalise'.

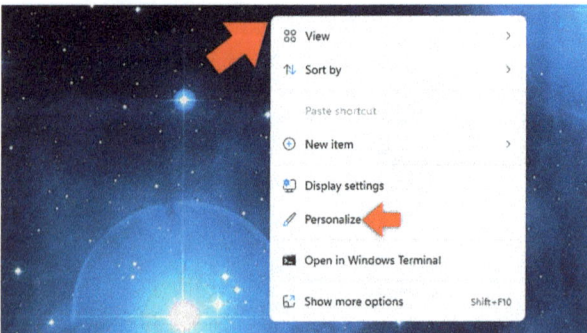

Scroll down the page, then click on 'background'.

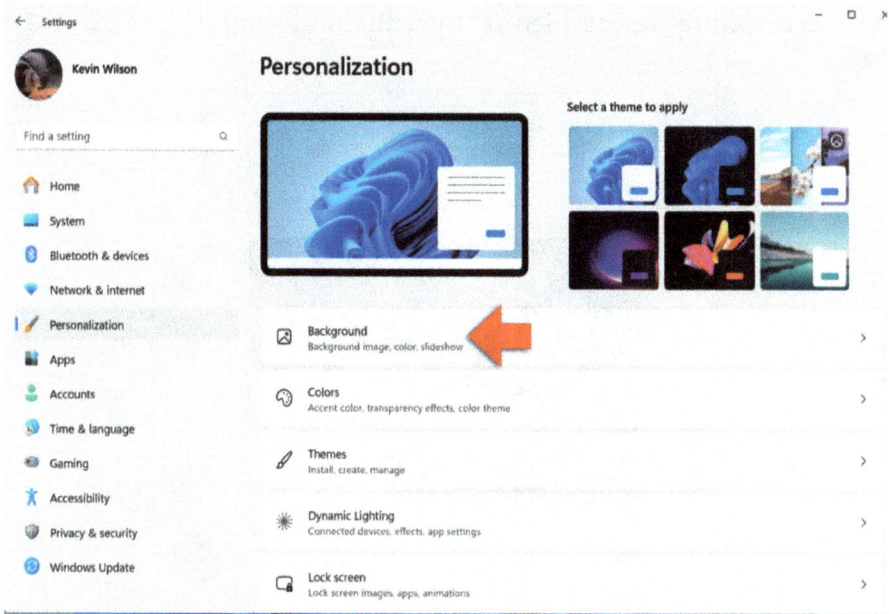

Scroll down to the 'personalise your background' section. You can put a picture in the background, a color, create a slideshow or use windows spotlight. Spotlight images are sourced from Bing and change daily or periodically.

## Color

To set the background to a color, change the dropdown box at the top from 'picture' to 'solid color'.

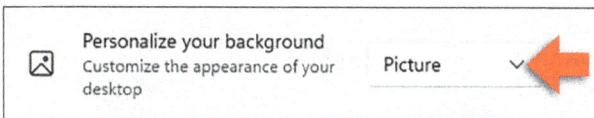

Select a color from the palette.

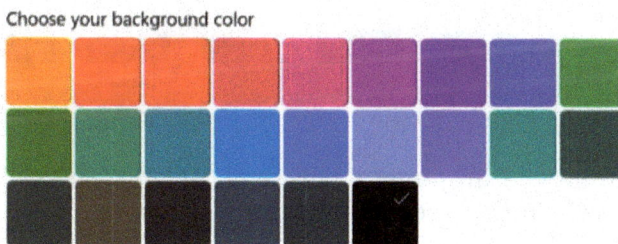

**49**

## Picture

To use a picture, select 'picture' from the first drop down box at the top.

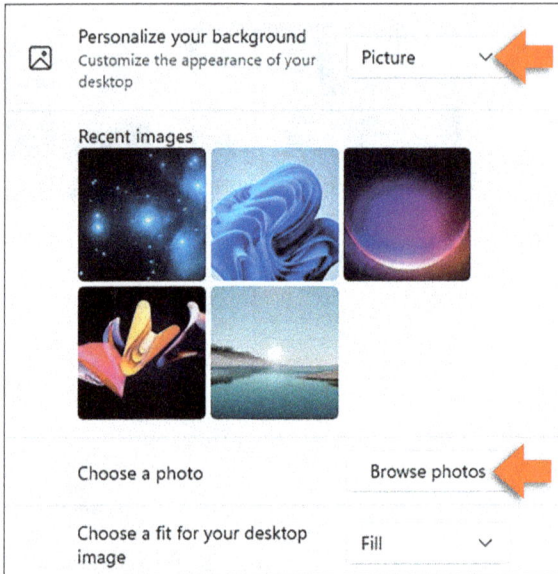

Select a picture from the recent images. If you want to add your own, click 'browse photos.

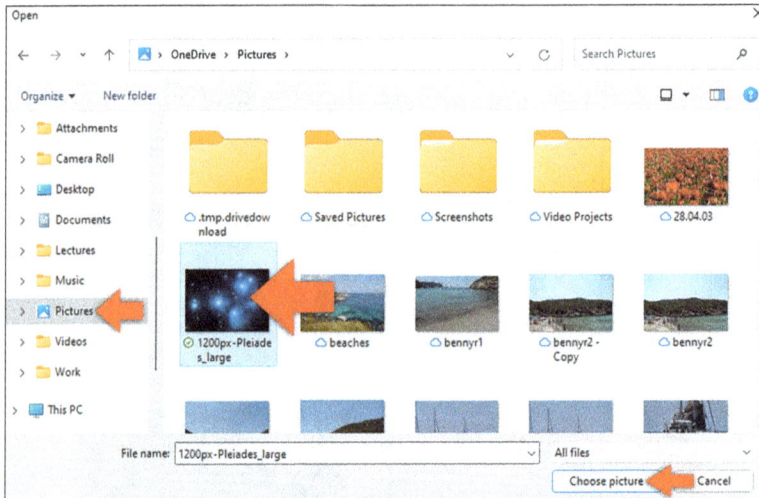

Select 'fill' from the drop down box that says 'choose a fit for your desktop image'. This will resize and crop your photo to fit your screen size.

## Slideshow

To create a slideshow, select 'slideshow' from the drop down box at the top.

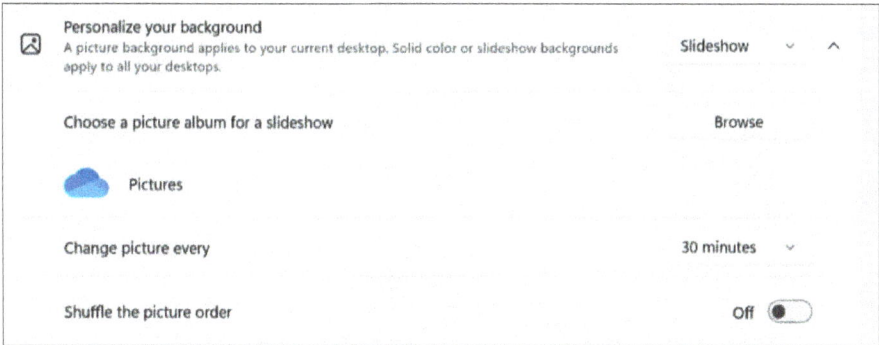

Click 'browse' to choose your photos. Navigate to your pictures folder, then click 'chose this folder'.

Set the amount of time to show each picture - eg 30 mins, or 1 hour...

Click the switch at the bottom to turn on 'shuffle the picture order'. This will select random photos from the pictures folder you selected above.

# Spotlight

Windows Spotlight is a feature that displays different background images on the lock screen and desktop. Based on user interactions and preferences, Windows Spotlight personalizes the content it displays, and fetches high-quality images from Bing. These images vary and can include landscapes, architectural wonders, and other photographic art.

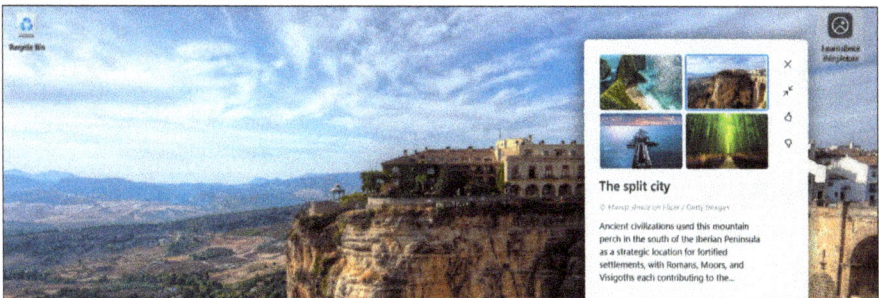

The feature often provides interesting facts or trivia about the image, making it an informative experience.

# Start Menu Personalization, Folders & Icons

You can add your documents, downloads, music and the settings icon to the bottom right of your start menu next to the power button. As well as change the layout to add more pinned apps, or more recommended apps/recent files.

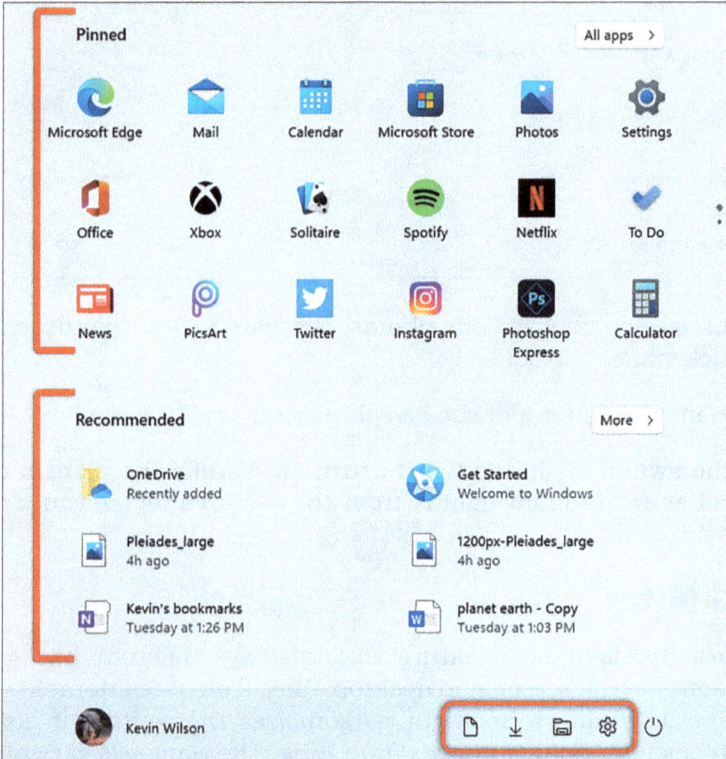

To do this, open your settings app, select 'personalisation' from the list on the left hand side. Scroll down the list on the right, select 'start'.

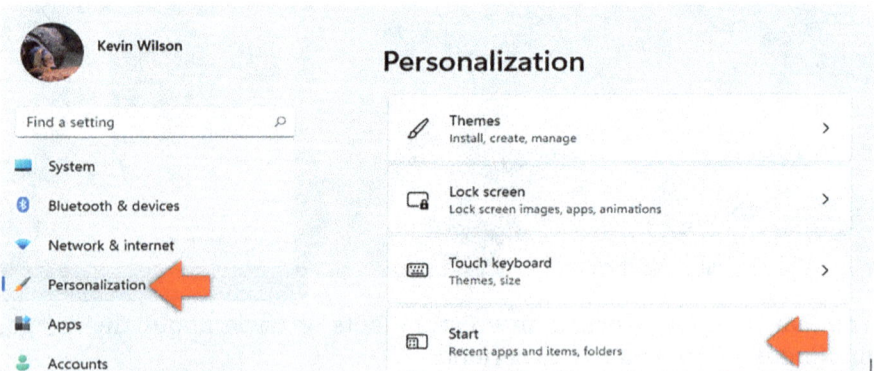

Here you can personalise your start menu. Along the top, you can select a layout for your start menu. You can show more pinned apps, or you can show more recent documents/apps that are listed in the 'recommended' section at the bottom of the start menu.

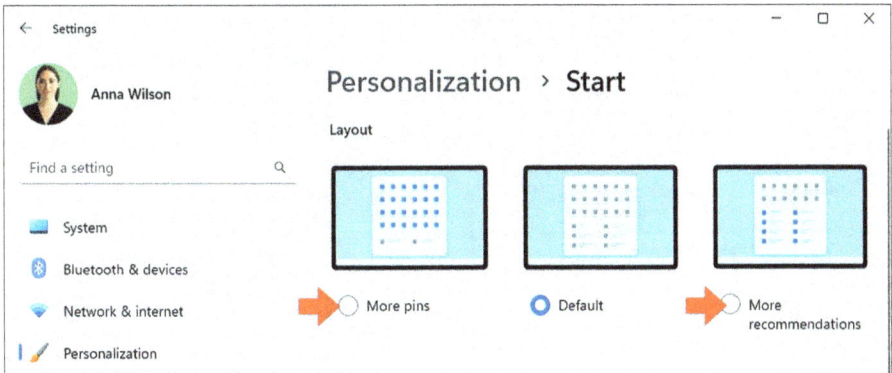

Just select 'more pins' to show more pinned apps, or 'more recommendations' to show more recent documents/apps.

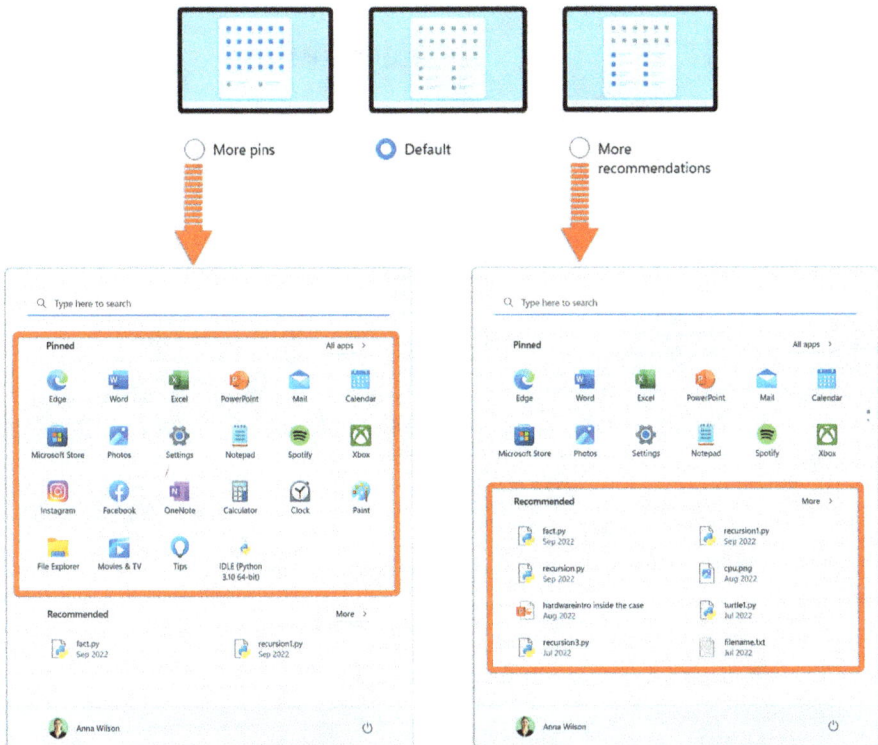

Scroll down the page.

# Chapter 3: Settings and Personalisation

Here, you can show recently added apps, most used apps, as well as jump lists and recently opened documents in file explorer.

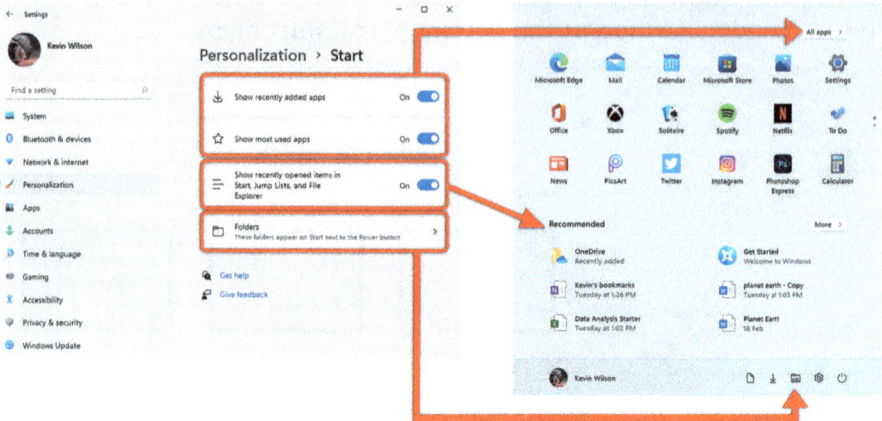

Underneath that, you can add your folder icons to the bottom right of the start menu. Click on 'folders'.

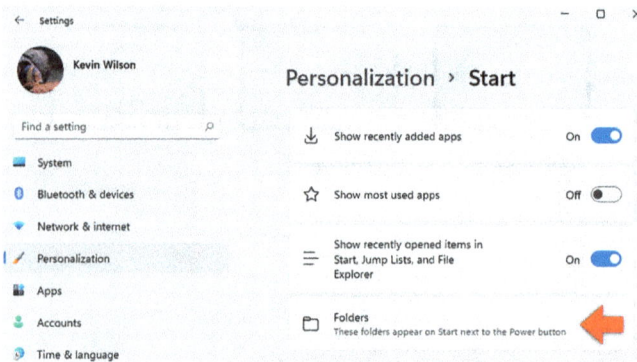

Choose the folders you want to appear on the bottom right of your start menu. It is useful to add your most used folders such as documents, downloads, or pictures, as well as the settings icon.

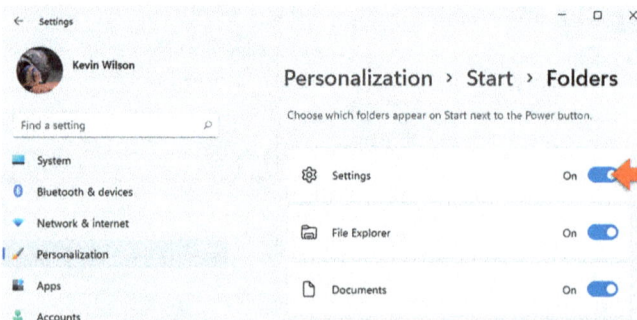

# Taskbar Personalisation and Alignment

You can personalise the taskbar in Windows 11. To do this, right click on the taskbar, then select 'taskbar settings' from the popup menu.

Click on the small arrows on the right to open up the sections. In the 'taskbar items' section you can add or remove the buttons that appear next to the start button. Here, you can change the search field to an icon, enable/disable the taskbar icon for copilot, taskview or the widgets icon.

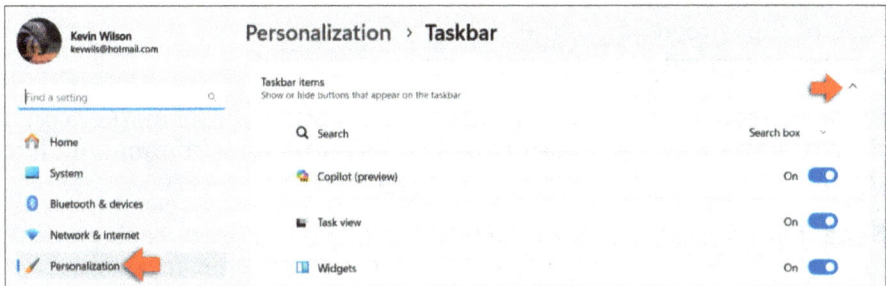

In the 'system tray icons' select which icons you want to appear in the corner. Turn the switch 'on' to show the icon in the overflow, turn the switch 'off' to hide it in the overflow.

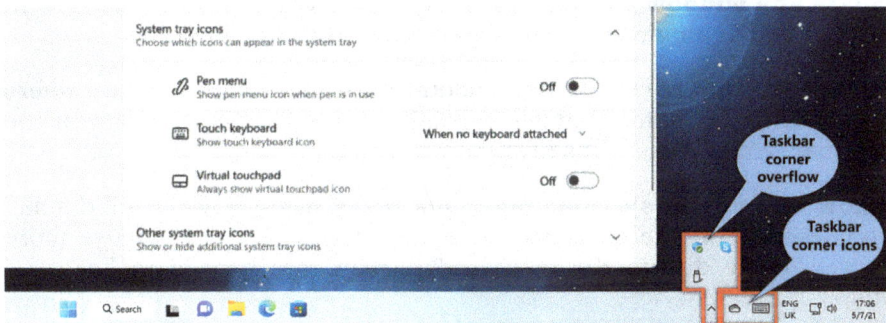

Pen menu, touch keyboard and virtual will show their respective icons in the system on tablets and touch-screen laptops.

The 'other system tray icons' section allows you to enable/disable additional icons in the system tray such as OneDrive, Windows Security, Bluetooth and so on.

# Chapter 3: Settings and Personalisation

In the 'taskbar behaviours' section, the Windows 11 taskbar is by default aligned to the center. You can change this if you prefer the traditional left aligned taskbar as seen in previous versions of Windows. Select 'left' from the 'taskbar alignment' drop down box.

**Automatically hide the taskbar** will hide the taskbar when not in use and will reappear when the you move the pointer to the bottom edge of the screen where the taskbar is located.

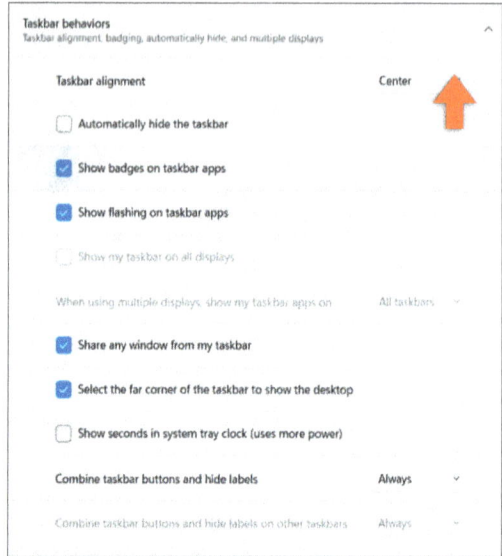

Taskbar behaviors
Taskbar alignment, badging, automatically hide, and multiple displays

| | |
|---|---|
| Taskbar alignment | Center |
| Automatically hide the taskbar | |
| Show badges on taskbar apps | |
| Show flashing on taskbar apps | |
| Show my taskbar on all displays | |
| When using multiple displays, show my taskbar apps on | All taskbars |
| Share any window from my taskbar | |
| Select the far corner of the taskbar to show the desktop | |
| Show seconds in system tray clock (uses more power) | |
| Combine taskbar buttons and hide labels | Always |
| Combine taskbar buttons and hide labels on other taskbars | Always |

**Show badges on taskbar apps:** Badges are small status markers on a taskbar app's icon that provide notifications or status information, like the number of unread emails or messages.

**Show flashing on taskbar apps:** Allows taskbar apps to flash or blink to alert the user of an action required, like a new chat message in an instant messaging application.

**Show my taskbar on all displays:** When using multiple monitors, this option ensures that the taskbar appears on each one.

**Share any window from my taskbar** allows you to share a window in a Microsoft Teams meeting using a menu on the taskbar icon.

**Select the far corner of the taskbar to show the desktop** refers to the 'Show Desktop' button, typically located at the far right of the taskbar, which minimizes all windows when clicked.

**Show seconds in system tray clock (uses more power)** will display the seconds on the clock in the system tray, which could use more power, likely due to the increased refresh rate needed to keep the display updated.

**Combine taskbar buttons and hide labels** determines whether open windows from the same app are grouped together as a single icon on the taskbar, and whether their window titles are hidden.

**Combine taskbar buttons and hide labels on other taskbars** applies this same grouping behavior to taskbars on other displays in a multi-monitor setup.

# Colors & Effects

You can change on screen colors and effects in Windows 11. To do this, right click on your desktop then select 'personalise' from the popup menu.

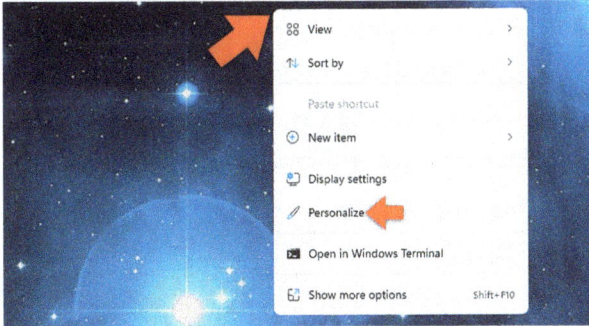

Scroll down the list on the right, select 'colors'.

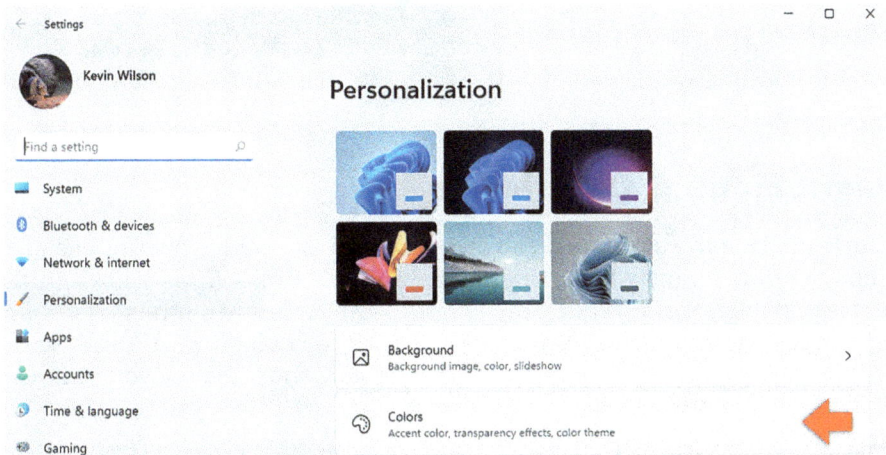

Scroll down to 'transparency effects' and 'accent colors'.

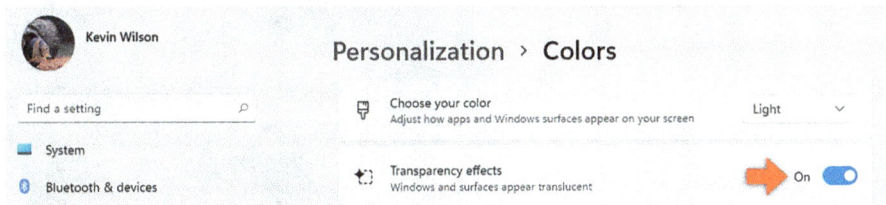

Transparency effects create panels that look like frosted sheets of glass such as the widgets panel, or the semi translucent start menus and windows. Use the switch to turn the effect on or off.

Accent colors are the colors of switches, scrollbars, progress bars, sliders, highlighted text, hyperlinks, and buttons.

Using the drop down box next to 'accent color', set this to 'automatic' to allow Windows to select a color based on your desktop background, or set it to 'manual' and select a color from the pallet below.

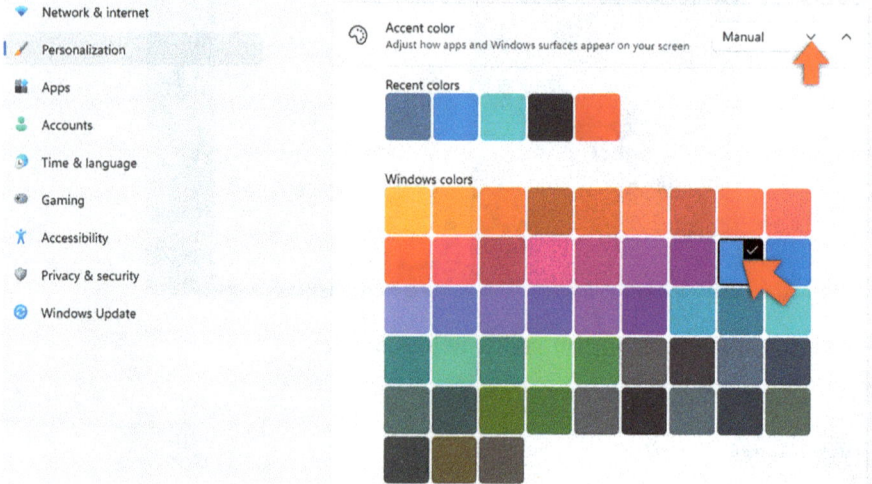

# Light Mode & Dark Mode

Dark mode makes looking at your screen a bit easier on the eyes. It replaces the bright white backgrounds in Windows Apps with a dark acrylic background. This only works with Windows Apps such as explorer, photos, news, media player, mail, or calendar, and not with applications such as Word, Chrome, or Photoshop. Below you can see light mode vs dark mode.

Right click on your desktop then select 'personalise' from the popup menu.

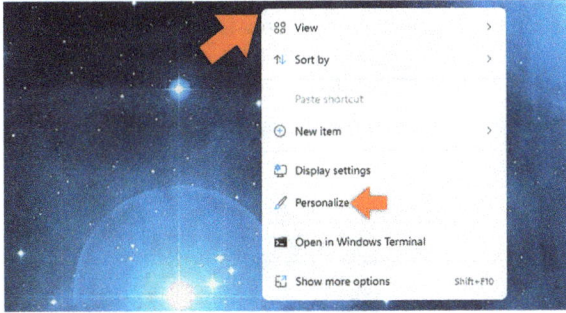

Scroll down the list on the right, select 'colors'.

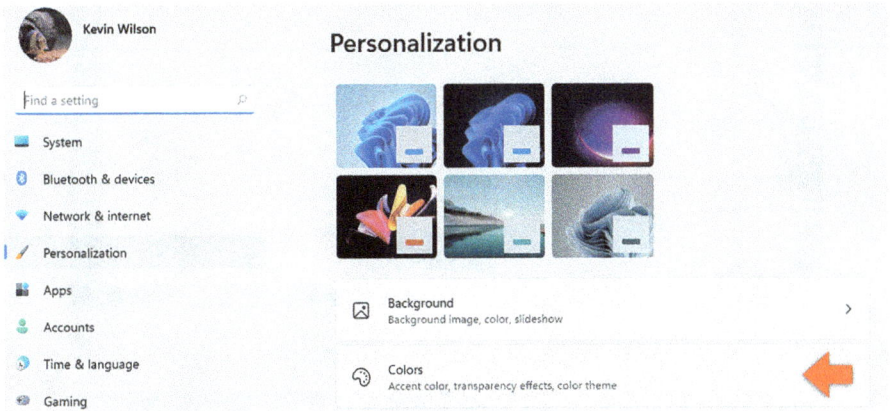

Scroll down until you see 'choose your color'. Select 'light' for light mode, and 'dark' for dark mode.

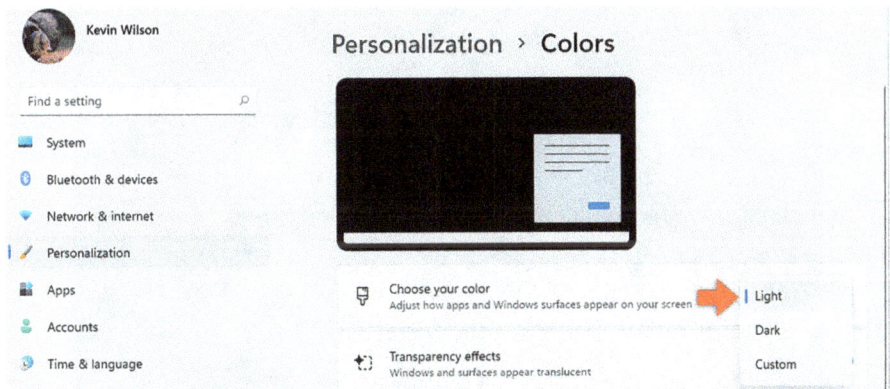

You can also customise the color. To do this select 'custom' from the drop down.

# Chapter 3: Settings and Personalisation

Now you can choose between dark and light mode. 'Windows Mode' sets the color mode for the start menu, taskbar, search, and system tray. 'App Mode' sets the color mode for all windows apps including, mail, calendar, file explorer, news, weather, app store, and so on.

Here, you can see windows is dark, and the app (eg settings) is light.

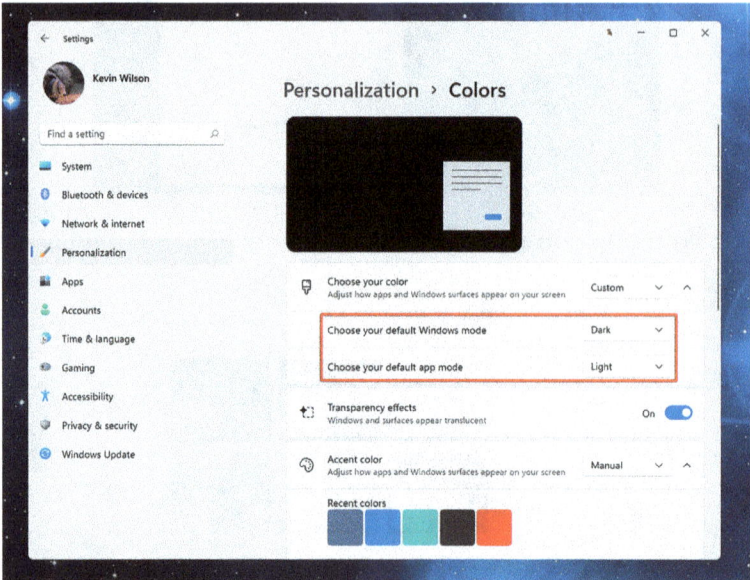

If I wanted the apps dark, and windows light...

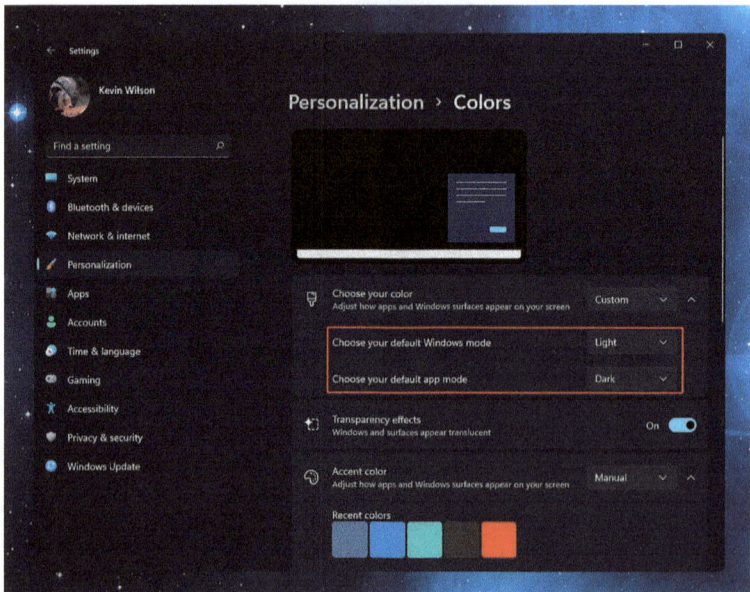

# Power Options

The power options allow you to set a time interval for windows to turn off your display or put your computer to sleep after a period of inactivity. If you need to change the power options, open your settings app, then select 'system' from the list on the left.

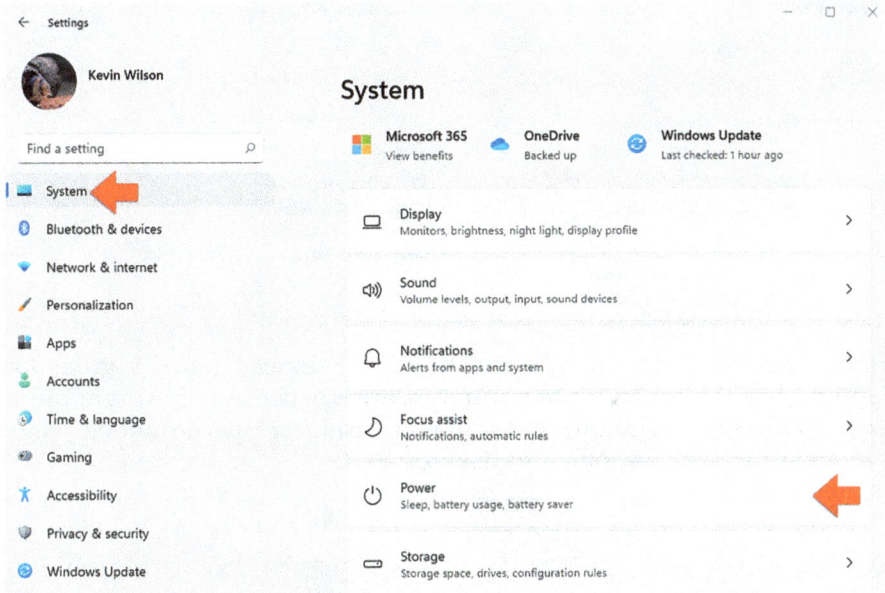

Here, you can set the amount of time before your computer turns off the screen and the amount of time before your computer goes into sleep mode. These times mean the length of time your computer is left unattended. Click the drop down box and select a time.

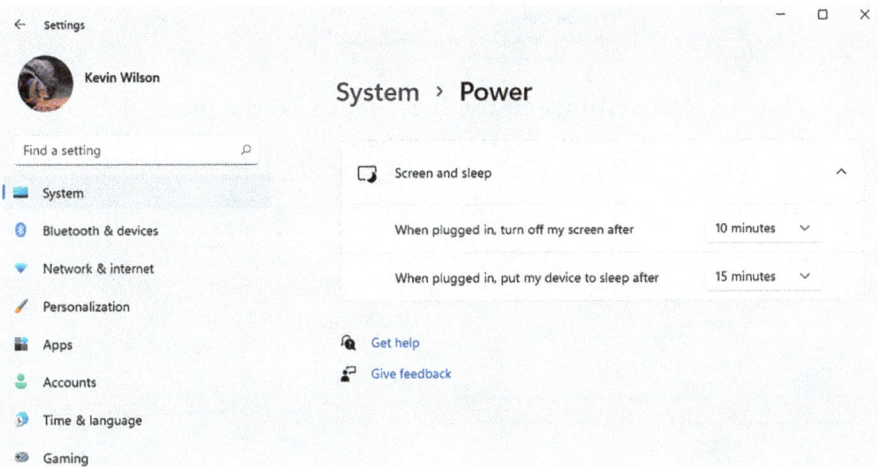

# Additional Power Options

To change your power schemes, click 'additional power settings', click on the search icon on the taskbar, type in `control panel`.

Select 'system & security'. Then click 'power options'.

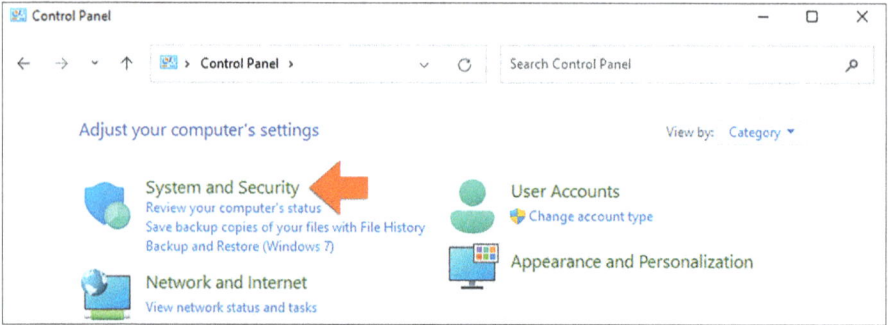

Here, you can select a power plan. The balanced plan is great for laptops and tablets as it gives you a balance between performance and power efficiency. Ultimate performance, and high performance plans are great for workstations and desktop PCs.

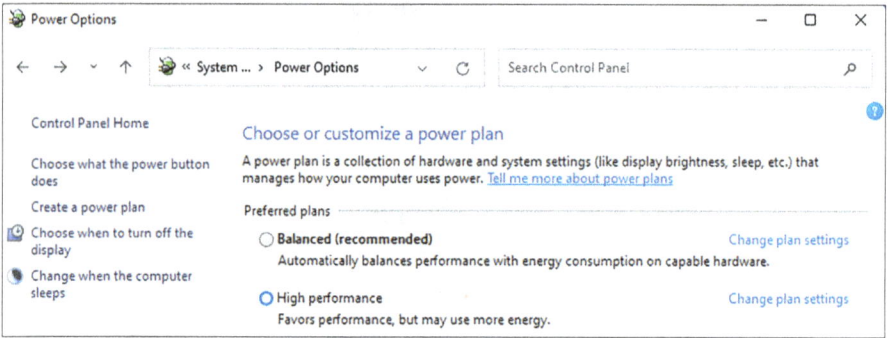

Click 'change plan settings' to further customise the plan.

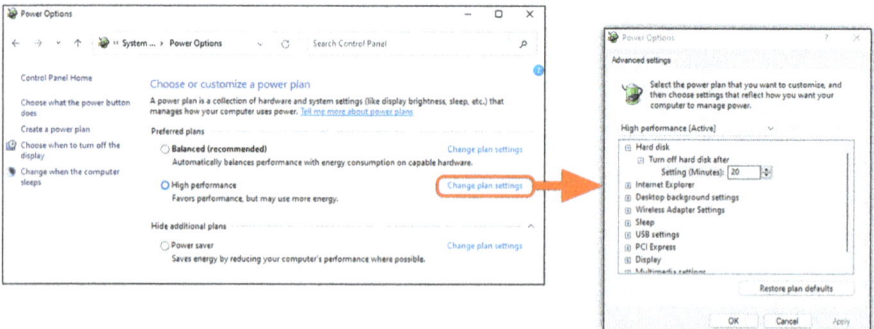

# Date and Time

To change the date and time, right click on the clock on the bottom right of the taskbar. Select 'adjust date and time' from the popup menu.

Here, you can select your time zone. Windows will automatically set the time when it connects to the internet.

**Set time zone automatically** requires location services to be enabled and will set the time zone based on your physical location. This is useful when traveling, as it adjusts the time zone to match your current region without manual intervention.

**Time zone** dropdown allows you to manually select your time zone from a list of available options.

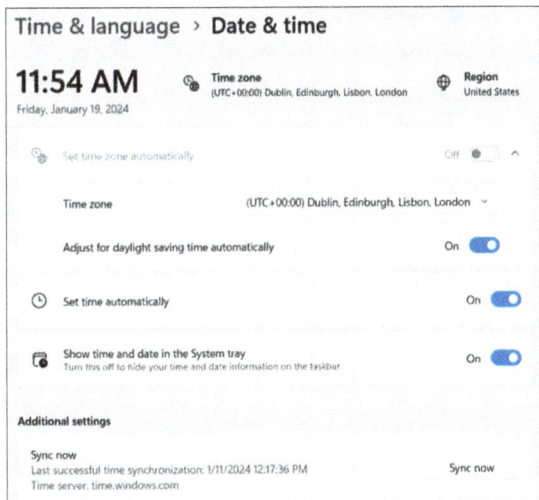

Time & language  >  **Date & time**

**11:54 AM**
Friday, January 19, 2024

Time zone
(UTC+00:00) Dublin, Edinburgh, Lisbon, London

Region
United States

Set time zone automatically — Off

Time zone — (UTC+00:00) Dublin, Edinburgh, Lisbon, London

Adjust for daylight saving time automatically — On

Set time automatically — On

Show time and date in the System tray
Turn this off to hide your time and date information on the taskbar — On

Additional settings

Sync now
Last successful time synchronization: 1/11/2024 12:17:36 PM
Time server: time.windows.com — Sync now

**Adjust for daylight saving time** automatically will automatically update the clock for daylight saving changes if your time zone observes this.

**Set time automatically** synchronize the computer's clock with an internet time server, ensuring that the time displayed is accurate.

**Show time and date in the System tray** displays the current time and date in the system tray, usually at the bottom right corner of the screen on the taskbar.

**Sync now** allows you to manually initiate a synchronization of your computer's clock with the selected internet time server.

**Time server** is server that your computer uses to synchronize its clock. In the screenshot above, it's set to time.windows.com, which is a default server provided by Microsoft.

# Regional Settings

If you need to change your language or the date/time format for your particular country, you can do that here. Open the settings app, then select 'time & language' from the list on the left. Select 'language & region' from the list on the right.

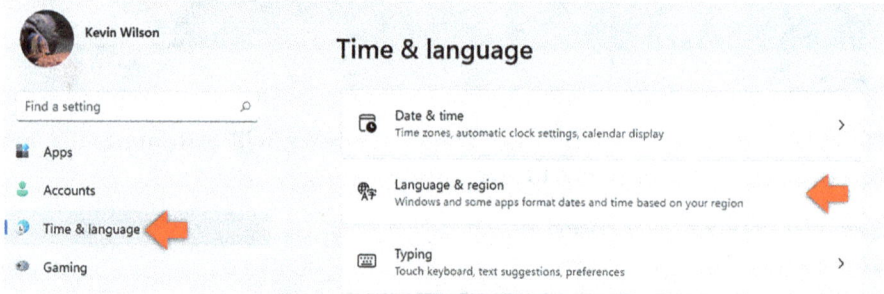

Here, you can select your country or region and regional format.

**Windows display language** allows you to choose the language in which Windows features like Settings and File Explorer will appear. Changing the display language can affect menus, dialog boxes, and other user interface items.

**Preferred languages** allow you to add multiple languages that you prefer to use with Windows and your applications.

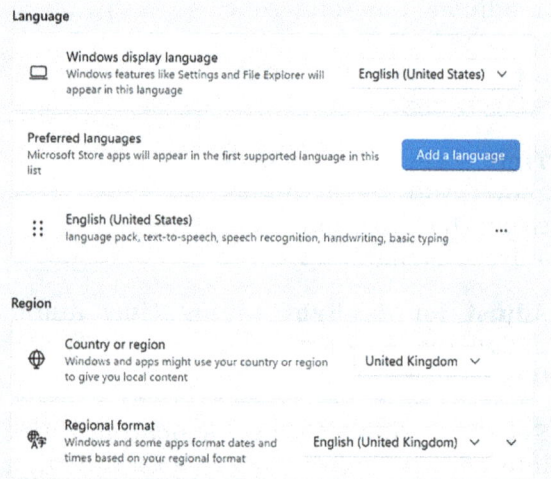

To add a language, click '**add a language**'. This allows you to add additional languages to your list of preferred languages. Useful for multilingual users or those learning a new language.

**Country or region** allows you choose your country or region so that Windows and apps can provide local content that is relevant to your location, such as news, weather, and local features. **Regional format** allows you to set the format Windows and some apps use for displaying dates, times, currency, and measurements.

# Keyboards

Most countries use a standard keyboard, however there are some regional differences with layouts and language.

## Layout & Language

Open your settings app, then select 'time & language' from the list on the left. Select 'language & region' from the list on the right.

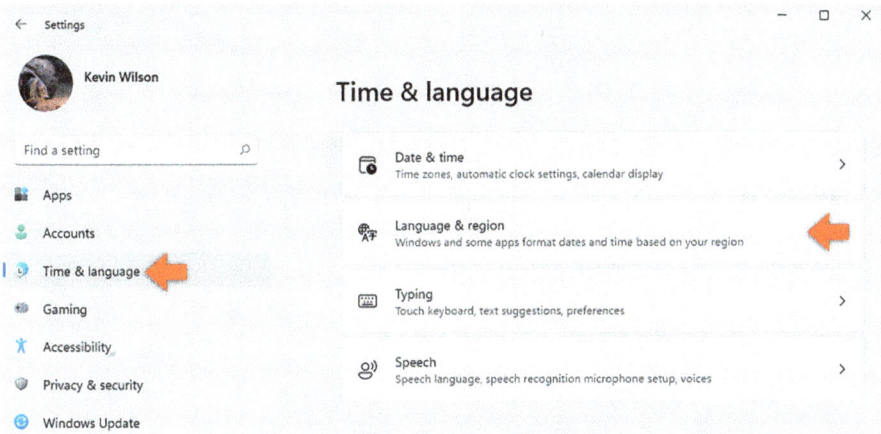

Click on the three dots icon on the right of your language, then select 'language options' from the drop down menu.

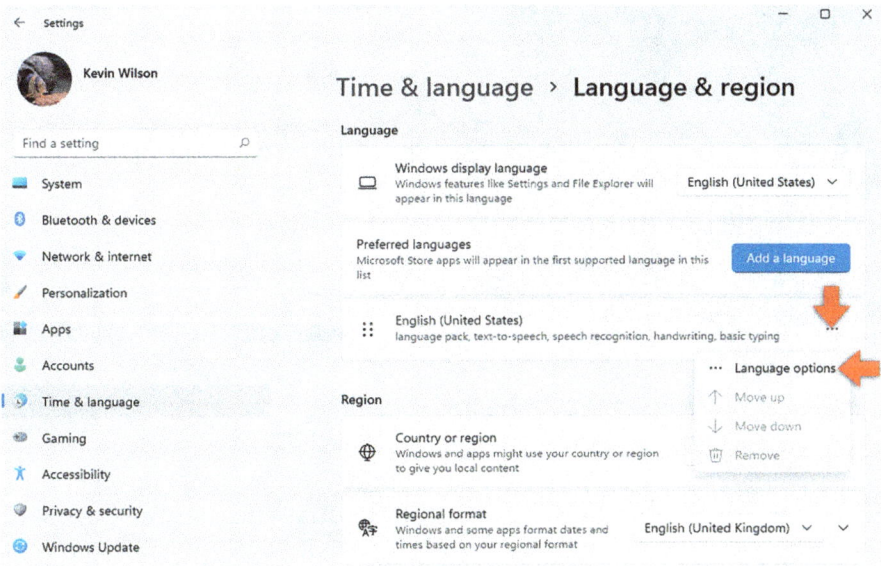

# Chapter 3: Settings and Personalisation

Scroll down to 'Keyboards' and then select 'Add a keyboard'. In the pop-up menu, select the keyboard language you want to add.

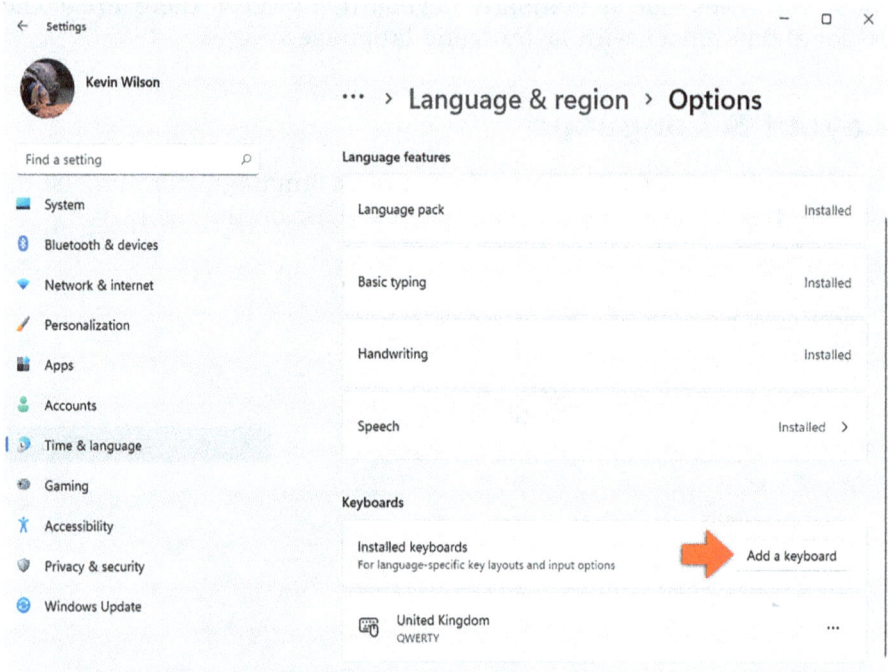

A language control popup box will appear above the taskbar on the bottom-right corner of the screen.

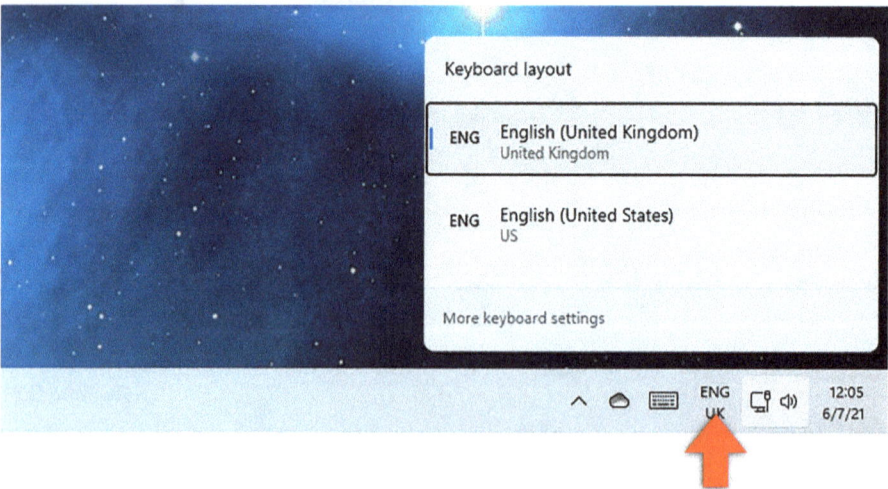

Here, you can switch between keyboards. Just click on the keyboard you just added.

# Touch Keyboard

On a touchscreen device such as a tablet, the touch keyboard appears along the bottom of the screen when you tap a text field, or need to start typing.

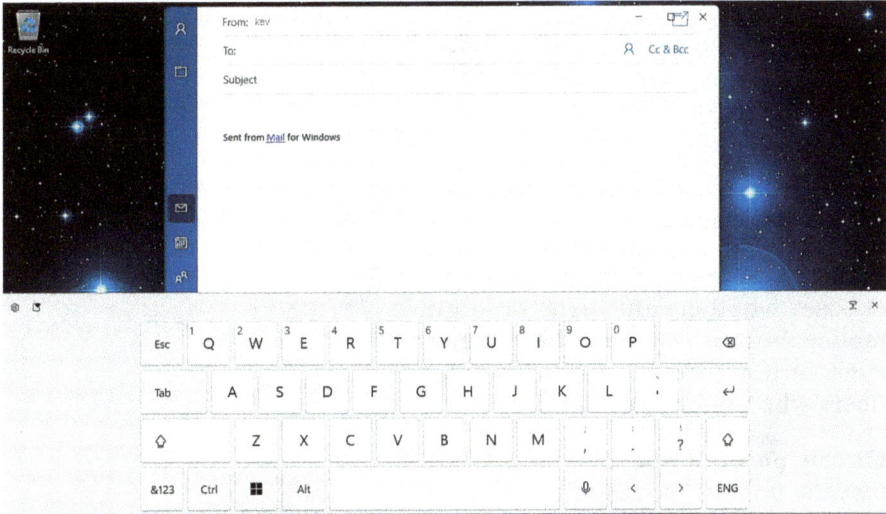

Open the settings app, select 'personalisation' from the list on the left, then click 'touch keyboard'.

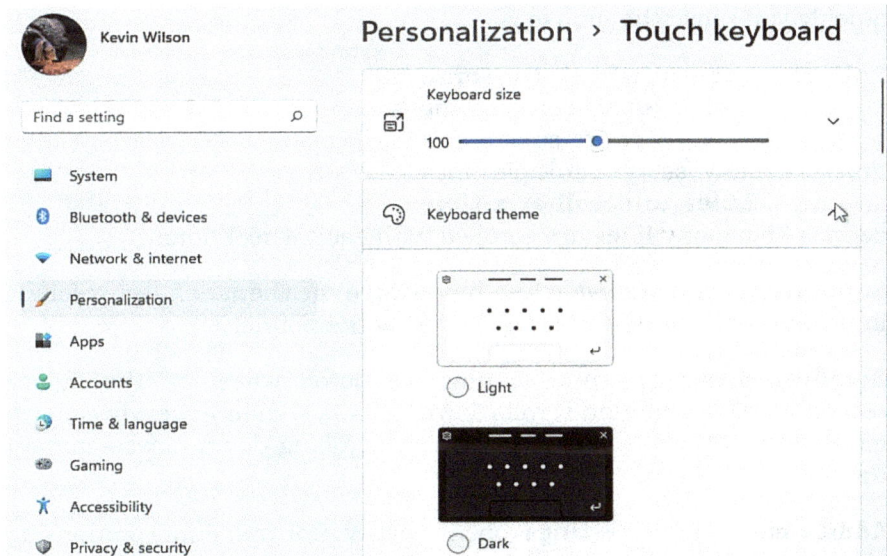

Here, you can change the keyboard size, and select a theme, or look, of your keyboard.

# Mouse

To adjust mouse pointer speed and scrolling, open your settings app, then select 'bluetooth & devices' from the list on the left. Scroll down the list on the right, then select 'mouse'.

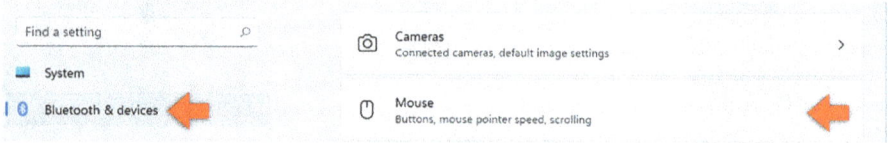

Here you can configure your mouse speed, pointer and scroll settings to suite your needs.

**Primary mouse button** lets you choose whether the left or right mouse button acts as the primary click button—useful for left-handed users who prefer to switch.

**Mouse pointer speed** controls how fast the pointer moves in response to physical movement of the mouse.

**Enhance pointer precision** adjusts the pointer's speed based on how quickly you move the mouse.

**Roll the mouse wheel to scroll** allows you to choose between scrolling several lines or an entire screen at a time - usually set to multiple lines at a time. **Lines to scroll at a time** defines how many lines are scrolled with each wheel notch.

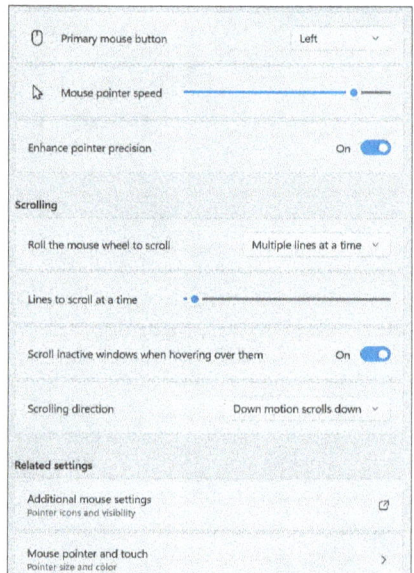

**Scroll inactive windows when hovering over them** enables scrolling in background windows just by hovering the pointer.

**Scrolling direction** controls how the scroll wheel on the mouse responds. "Down motion scrolls down" means scrolling the wheel down moves content down. If you reverse it, scrolling down moves content up.

**Additional mouse settings** opens legacy Control Panel options to change double-click speed, pointer trails, and hide pointer while typing.

**Mouse pointer and touch** opens the settings to customize the pointer's size and color for visibility and accessibility.

**68**

# Internet & Networks

You can connect to networks and the internet in a variety of ways. The most common is WiFi, but you can also connect using an Ethernet cable.

## WiFi

To locate nearby WiFi networks, click the Network/WiFi icon on the bottom right of the screen then tap 'available'.

Tap the name of the network you want to join, make sure 'connect automatically' is selected, then click 'connect'.

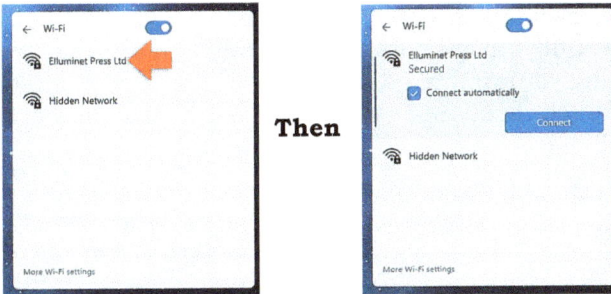

**Then**

Enter the WiFi password or network password, then click 'next'.

For your home WiFi, the network key or password is usually printed on the back of your router. Sometimes the network name is called an SSID.

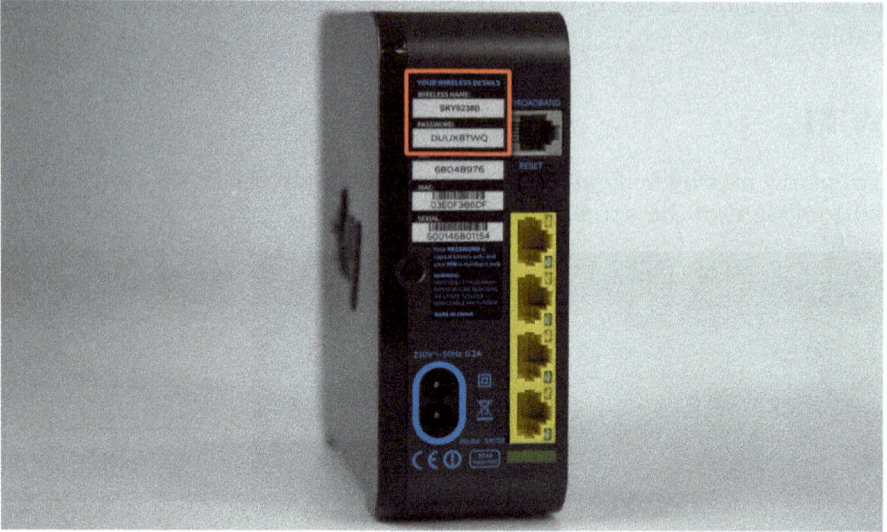

Use the same procedure if you are on a public hotspot such as in a cafe, library, hotel, airport and so on. You'll need to find the network key if they have one. Some are open networks and you can just connect.

When using public hotspots, keep in mind that most of them don't encrypt the data you send over the internet and aren't secure. So don't start checking your online banking account or shop online while using an unsecured connection, as anyone who is on the public WiFi hotspot potentially can gain access to anything you do.

## Ethernet

To connect via Ethernet, you'll need an Ethernet cable. Plug one end into your laptop or PC. Plug the other end of the cable into your router or switch.

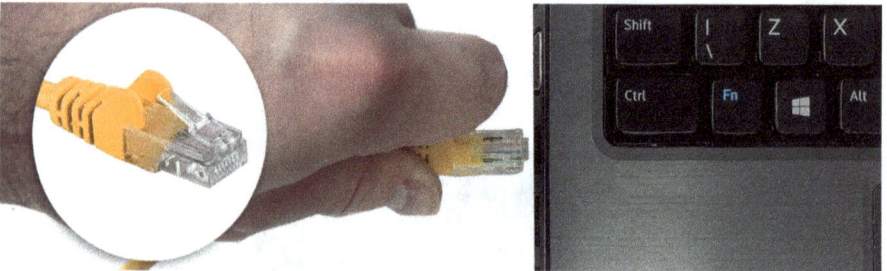

Most modern devices no longer include an Ethernet port. If this is the case and you need one, then you can buy a USB to Ethernet adapter.

## Mobile USB Modems

If you use your laptop on the go a lot or travel frequently, you should also consider using 3G/4G/5G LTE mobile data modem. You can get these from a phone provider such as AT&T, Verizon, $O_2$, T-Mobile, etc.

When you buy these from your phone provider, you can take out a contract or pay as you go in the same way you'd buy a cell/mobile phone.

## VPN

If you're concerned about security or often use public Wi-Fi—such as in cafés, airports, libraries or hotels—you should consider a VPN, or Virtual Private Network. A VPN encrypts your internet traffic and sends it through a secure tunnel to a remote VPN server, preventing your ISP or others on the local network from seeing your internet activity.

The diagram below illustrates how a VPN operates. While your PC connects to the internet via your ISP or a public Wi-Fi network, the VPN software establishes an encrypted tunnel between your PC and the VPN server. All data you transmit is securely routed through this tunnel to the VPN server, where it is decrypted and forwarded to its final destination on the internet. This protects your traffic from being monitored by anyone else connecting to the same Wi-Fi network or by your ISP. However, beyond the VPN server, your data is only encrypted if the destination website or service uses secure protocols such as HTTPS.

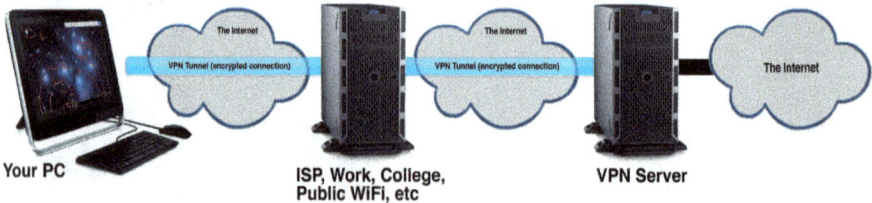

Your PC          ISP, Work, College,          VPN Server
                 Public WiFi, etc

There are a few good ones to choose from, some have a free option with a limited amount of data and others you pay a subscription.

Take a look at:

tunnelbear.com
windscribe.com
protonvpn.com
nordvpn.com
surfshark.com

With these VPN services, you can download an app that connects your computer to the secure servers for you. Here in the example below, we have Proton VPN running on windows. You can see the app provides a variety of different servers to connect to around the world, as well as the means to connect and disconnect the VPN.

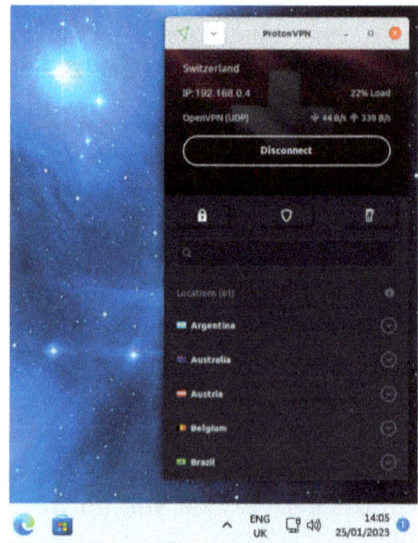

To set up a VPN manually, right click on the network/WiFi icon on the bottom right of the taskbar, select 'network and internet settings'. Select VPN from the list on the right.

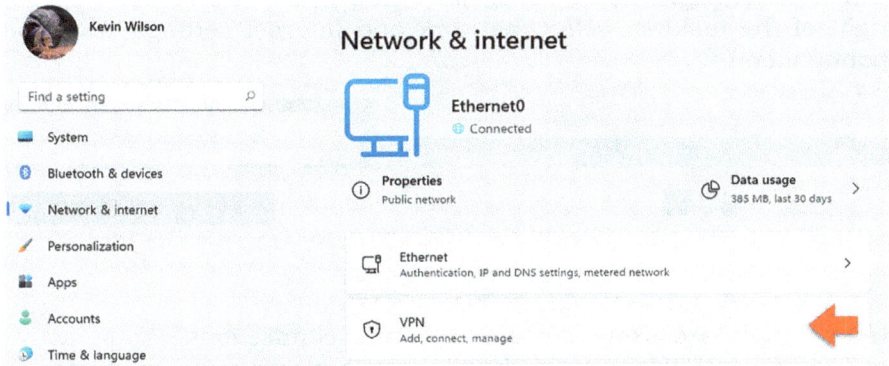

Click 'Add VPN'.

Enter the connection details. You'll need to get the connection information from your system administrator.

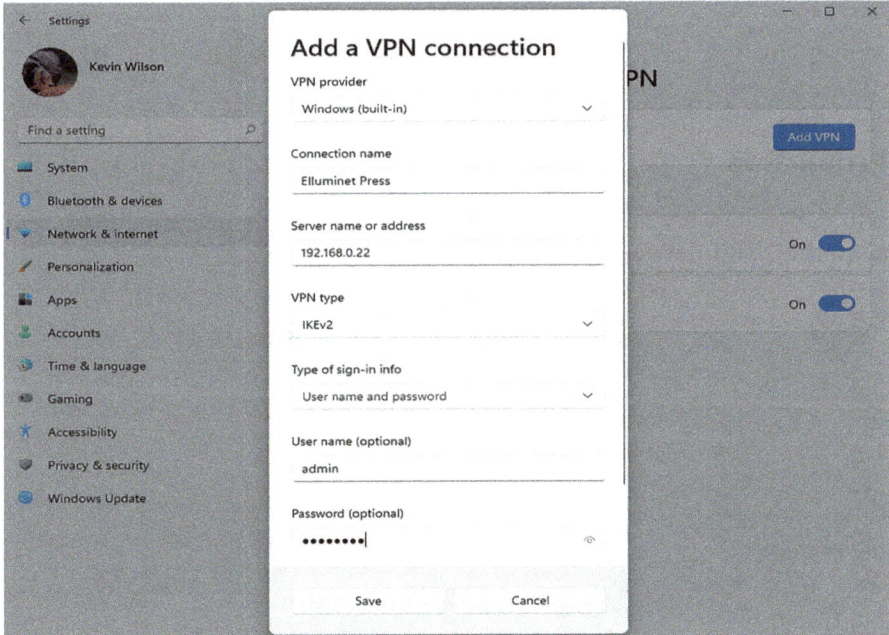

# Network Settings

Network settings is where you'll be able to configure your WiFi or Ethernet settings. Right click on the network/WiFi icon on the bottom right of the taskbar, select 'network and internet settings' from the popup menu.

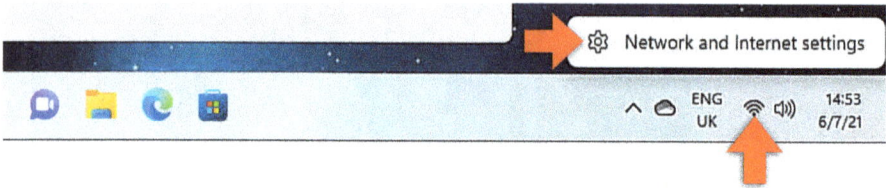

Here, you'll see your current network connections. Your active connection will be shown at the top - in this case we're connected to WiFi. Click on your connection to see settings

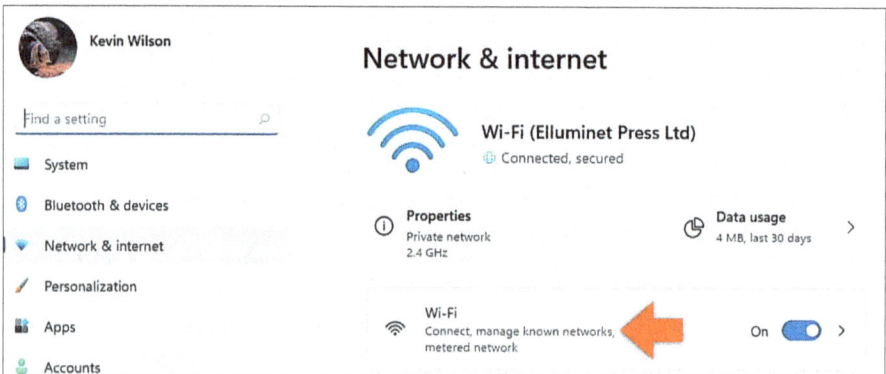

## Properties

You can view your connection properties such as IP address, DNS and available WiFi networks.

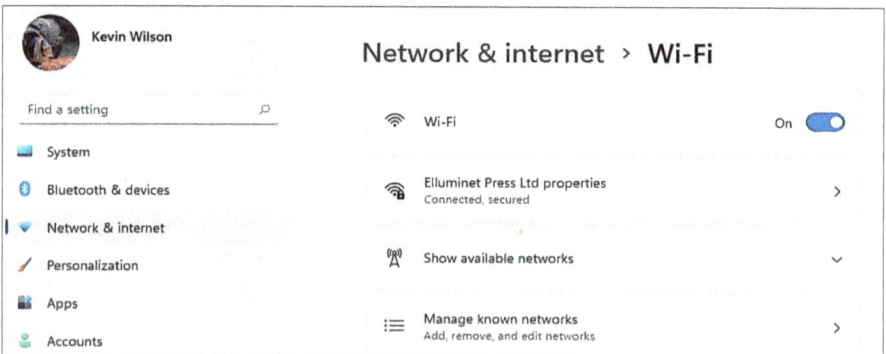

Available Networks will show you any WiFi networks that are in range. In 'manage known networks', you can add a network, or forget a network.

## DNS & IP Addresses

Open your network settings properties as in the previous section. Select your network connection, eg WiFi.

Select '...properties'.

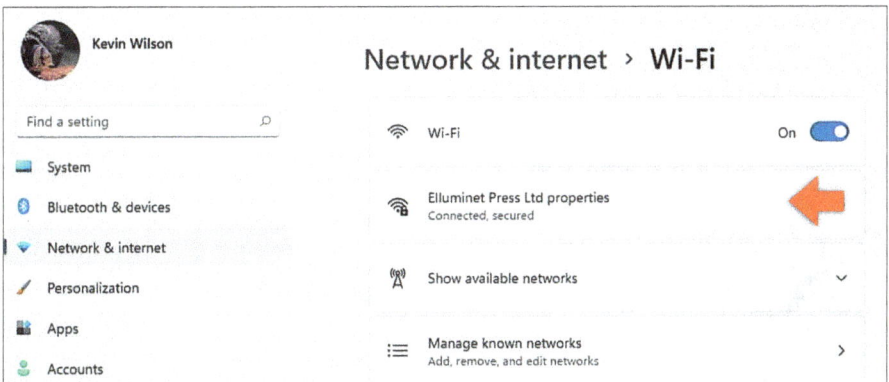

# Chapter 3: Settings and Personalisation

Scroll down the page, here you'll see assignments for your IP address and DNS server settings. Most of the time you can keep these on automatic (DHCP), but in certain circumstances you might need to change them.

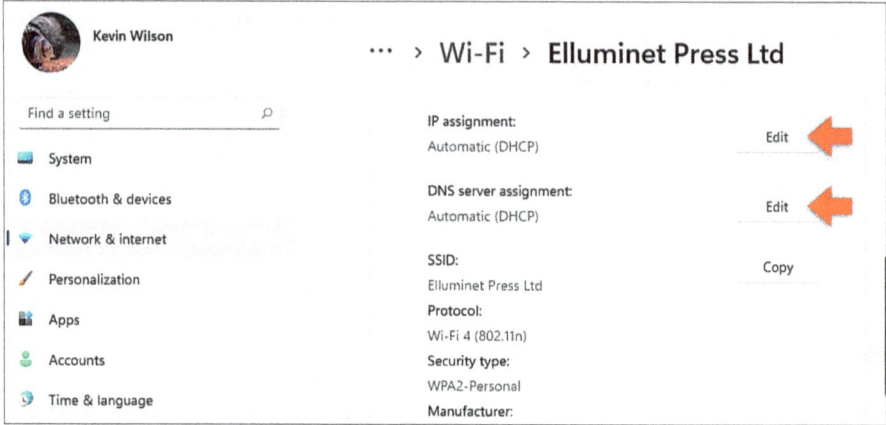

Your IP address is the unique address of your device that uniquely identifies it on the network. The DNS server converts website domain names into IP addresses.

To change the IP address, click 'edit' next to 'IP assignment'. Select 'manual', then enter the network details.

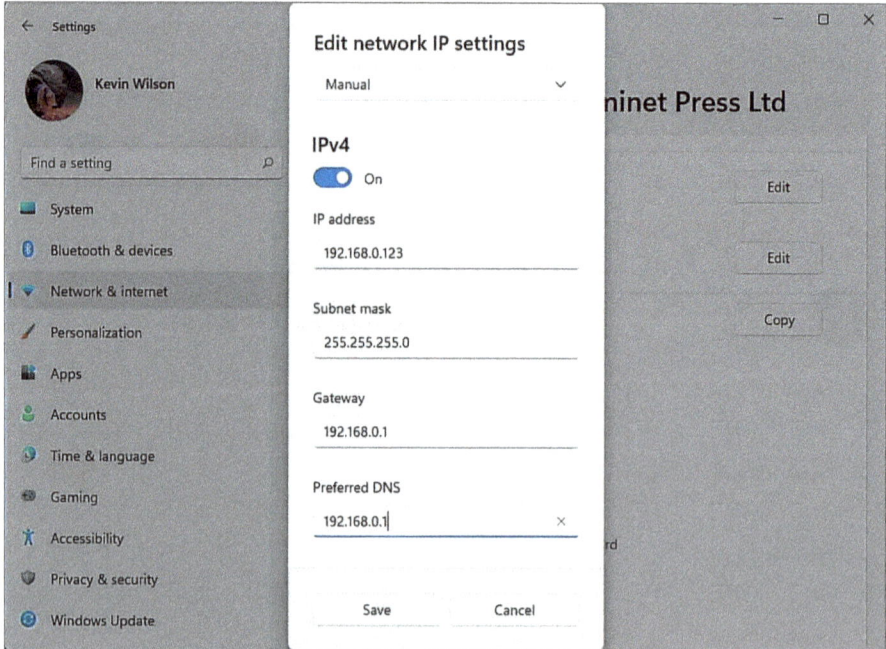

To change the DNS, click 'edit' next to 'DNS server assignment'. Select' 'manual', then enter the IP address of the DNS server. Try Cloudflare's DNS: 1.1.1.3 and 1.0.0.3

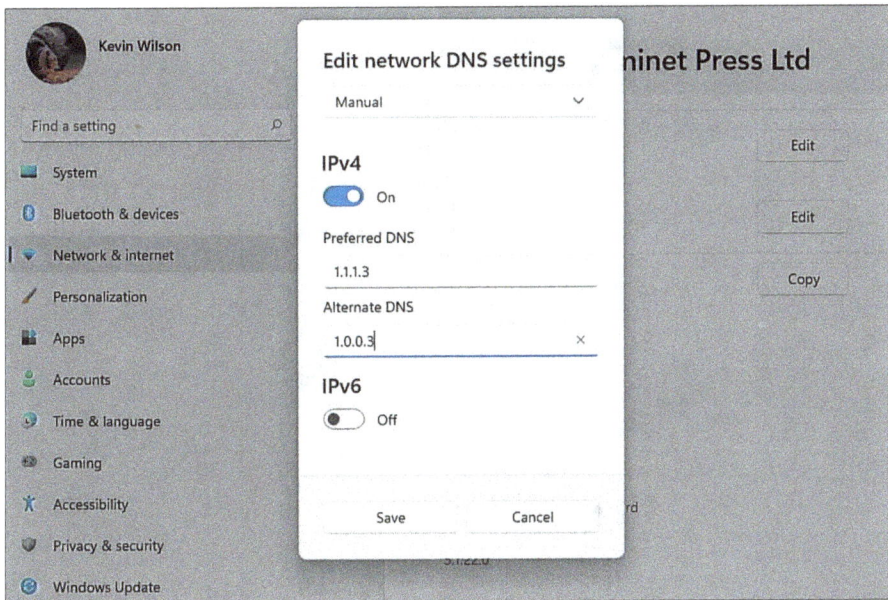

# Printers

You can connect a printer to your computer with a USB cable as well as using WiFi.

## WiFi

WiFi is definitely the way you'd want to connect to a printer if you are on a tablet or laptop. Unfortunately it is difficult to give specific instructions on printer setup as each model of printer and each manufacturer has their own method. However, I will provide some general guidelines you can use to get started.

## Chapter 3: Settings and Personalisation

If your printer is brand new, you'll need to connect it to your WiFi. Printers with LCD panels display step-by-step instructions for setting up the wireless connection when you first turn on the printer. So read the instructions for specifics on how to do this.

If your printer doesn't have an LCD panel, use the WPS method. You can use this method if you have a WPS button on your router - as shown in the photo below.

Refer to the printer's quick start guide to find the exact procedure for your printer model. Usually you have to press and hold the WiFi button on your printer for a few seconds, then go to your router and press the WPS button.

*If your router doesn't have a WPS button, you'll have to select your WiFi network (SSID) and enter your WiFi password on your printer.*

*You'll need to refer to the printer's instructions on exactly how to do that on your particular printer.*

Your printer will let you know when it's connected to your WiFi - the WiFi light usually stops flashing and lights up.

Once connected, on your computer open the settings app, then click 'bluetooth & devices' in the list on the left. Select 'printers & scanners' from the panel on the right hand side.

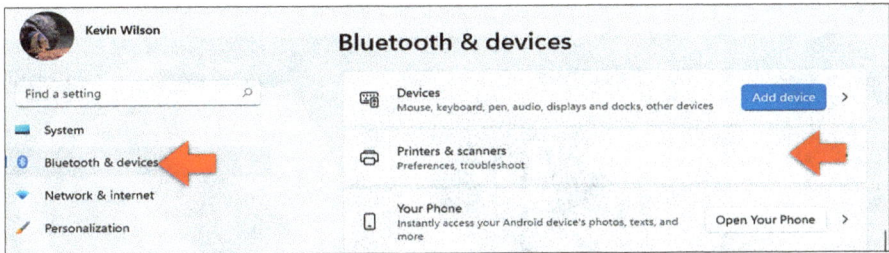

Click 'add device'.

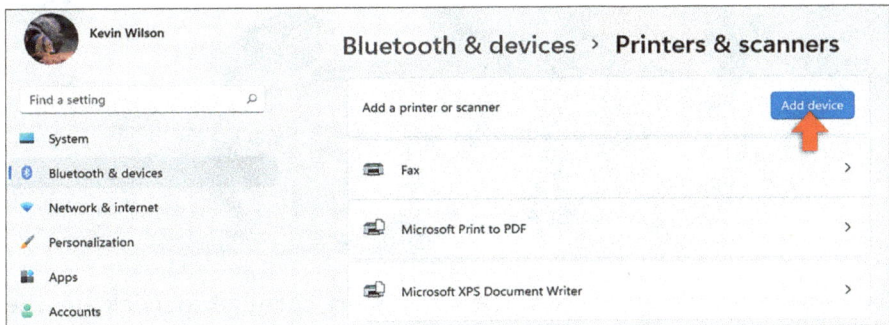

Windows will detect most modern printers, and display a list of any it finds. Click 'add device' next to your printer.

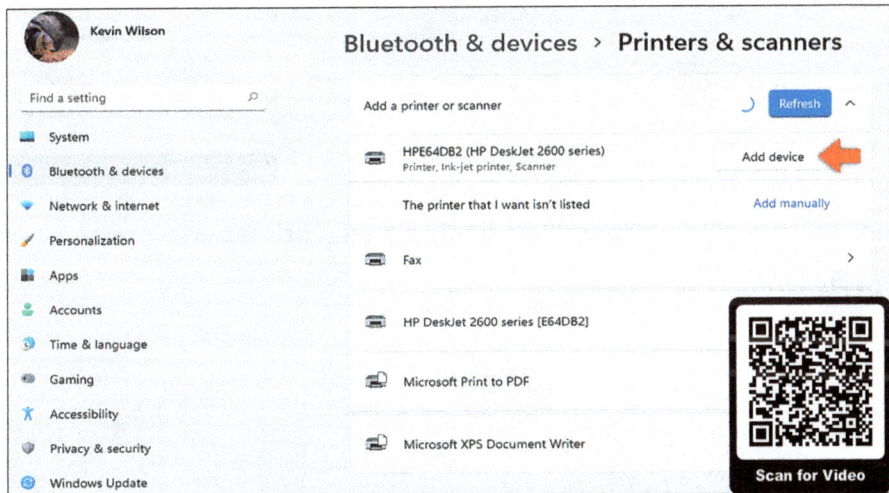

Windows will download and install the appropriate driver for your printer automatically.

**79**

# USB

Using a USB cable, plug the square end into the back of the printer, then plug the other end into a USB port on your computer.

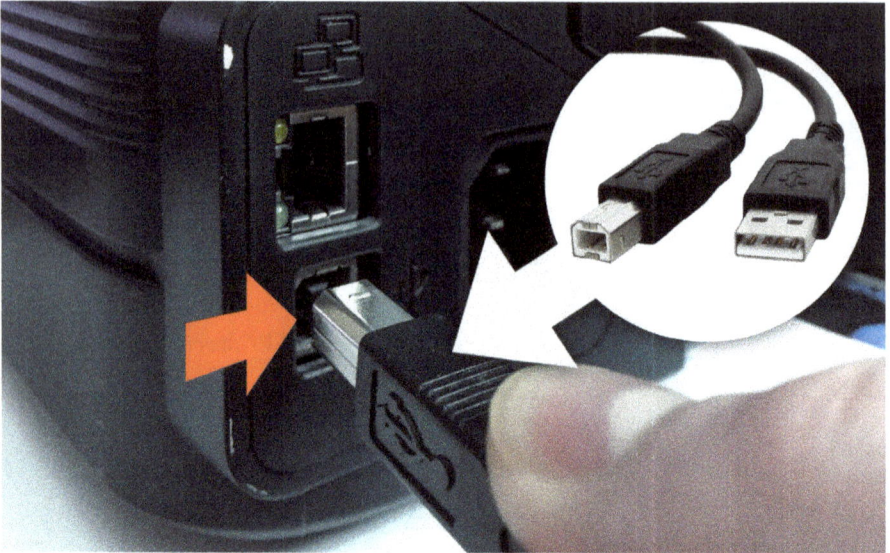

Turn on your printer, then open the start menu and click on the settings app icon. Select 'bluetooth & devices' from the list on the left.

Select 'printers & scanners', then click 'add a printer or scanner'.

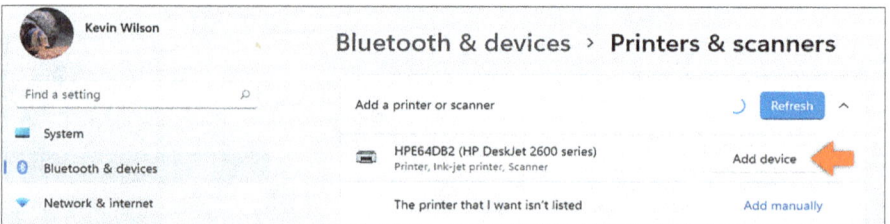

Windows will detect most modern printers. Select your printer from the list.

# Manufacturer's Printer Setup Programs

Many printer manufacturers include a setup program to install the printer on your computer.

## HP

HP have introduced a simplified setup method for their printers. To set up your printer, plug it in and turn it up. On your computer open your web browser and navigate to the following website

```
123.hp.com
```

Type your printer's model number into the search field.

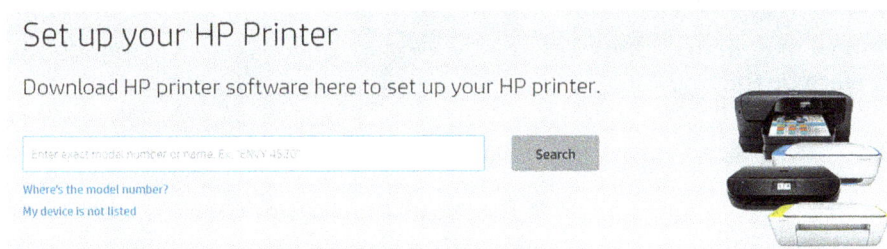

Click 'download' or 'get the app'. Follow the instructions on the screen to download and install the drivers or the app.

## Epson

To set up your printer, plug it in and turn it up. On your computer open your web browser and navigate to the following website

```
epson.sn
```

Type your printer's model number into the search field.

Click 'lets get started'. Scroll down the page.

Follow the instructions on the screen to download and install the drivers or the app.

## Chapter 3: Settings and Personalisation

### Canon

To set up your printer, plug it in and turn it up. On your computer open your web browser and navigate to the following website

    canon.com/ijsetup

Click 'setup', then type in your printer model number.

Follow the instructions on the screen to download and install the drivers or the app.

### Brother

To set up your printer, plug it in and turn it up. On your computer open your web browser and navigate to the following website

    support.brother.com

Select 'downloads'.

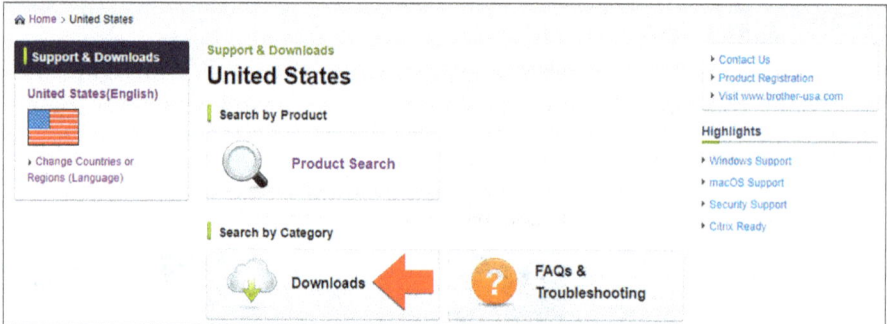

Type in your model number.

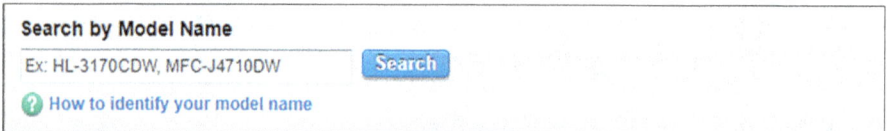

Select 'Windows 10' or 'Windows 11', then download the 'full driver & software package'. Follow the instructions on screen.

# Downloading Printer Drivers

If Windows 11 has trouble installing your printer, you'll need to download and install the printer software.

To do this, you'll need to go to the manufacturer's website and download the software.

For HP & Samsung printers go to

support.hp.com/drivers

For Canon printers go to

www.usa.canon.com/support

For Brother printers go to

support.brother.com

For Epson printers go to

support.epson.com

Somewhere on the manufacturer's website, there will be a product search field. Type in the model name of your printer. Click 'OK' or 'find'

In the example above, I'm installing an HP printer. In most cases you'll need to download the driver software from the manufacturer's website.

From the search results, select your Operating System if required, usually "Windows 10 (64bit)" or "Windows 11 (64bit)".

Click on the prompt at the bottom of your browser.

This will run the installation software. Click 'OK' or 'Yes' to the security prompt. If you don't see a prompt, go to your downloads folder in file explorer and double click on the EXE file you just downloaded. Follow the on screen instructions to connect to your printer.

# Managing Printers

You can get to the print queue from the Settings App on the start menu. From the Settings App, select 'bluetooth & devices' on the left. On the right hand side of the window, click 'printers & scanners'.

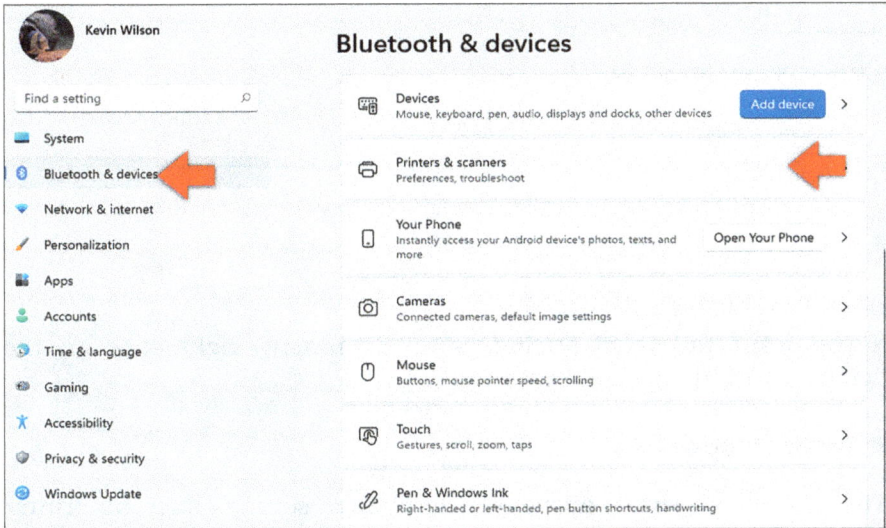

## Print Queue

Open 'printers & scanners as shown above, then select your printer.

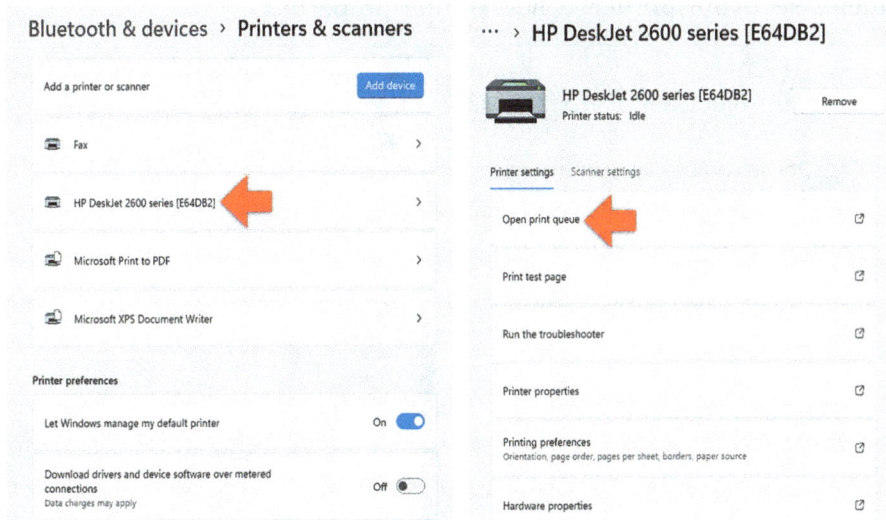

From the printer settings page, click 'open print queue'. This will open up the print queue for that printer.

**85**

# Chapter 3: Settings and Personalisation

Here you can see a list of documents that are queued for printing. If you click on three dots to the right of the print job in the list, you can cancel or pause all document.

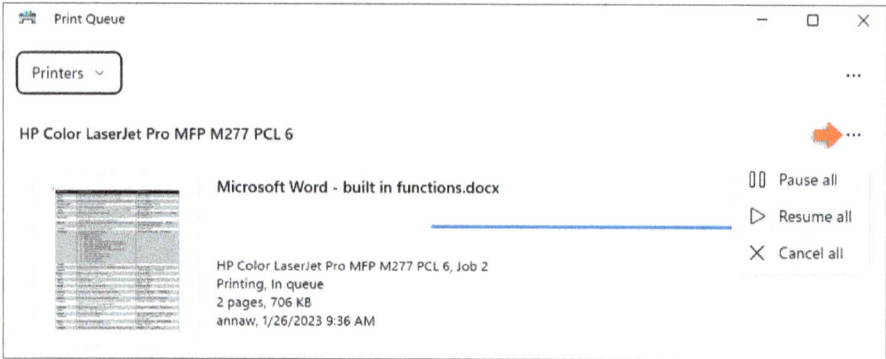

If you want to cancel an individual document, right click on the document in the list, select 'cancel'.

## Printer Properties

The printer properties allows you to change settings such as printer sharing - if you want to share your printer with another device on your network. You can also change the port the computer uses to print to the printer, as well as color management and various security settings.

Open 'printers & scanners as shown at the beginning of this section, then select your printer. Click 'printer properties'.

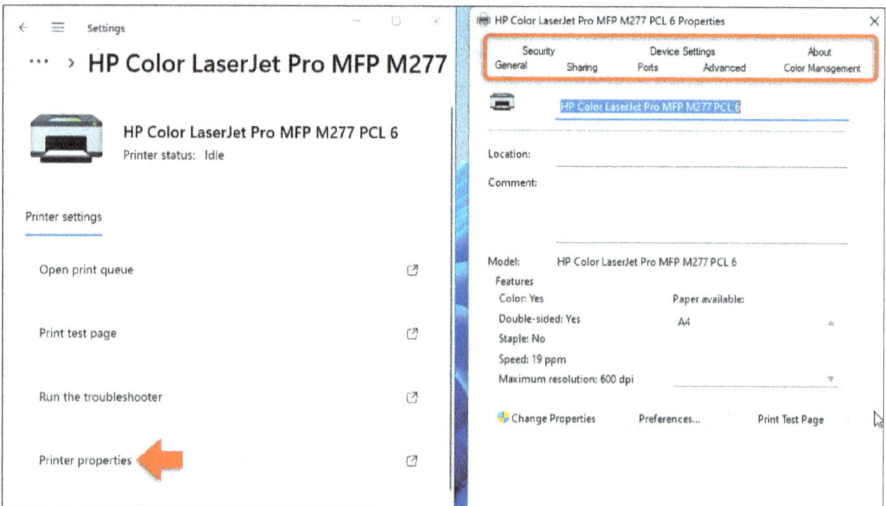

Use the tabs along the top of the properties window to change settings.

## Printer Preferences

The printer preferences allows you to change settings such as paper size, color/black and white printing, as well as various other settings.

Open 'printers & scanners as shown at the beginning of this section, then select your printer. Click 'printer preferences'.

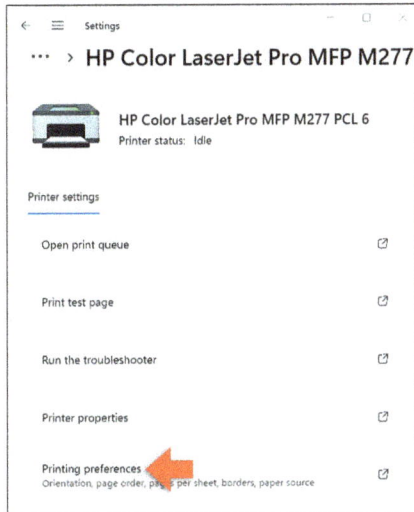

This window will look slightly different depending on your model of printer, but most of the functionality is similar. Here, you can change the paper sizes and type. For example, you can select A4 or letter size paper, you can choose if you want to print on to envelopes or card.

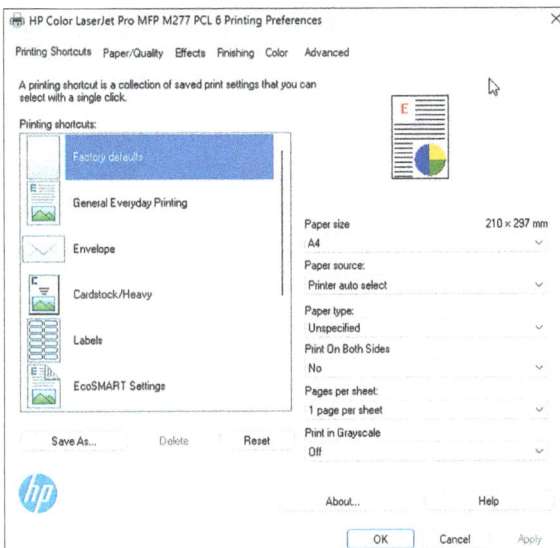

## Chapter 3: Settings and Personalisation

Using the tabs along the top of the window, you can change other settings. Here in the 'paper/quality' tab, we can change the paper size, type and so on.

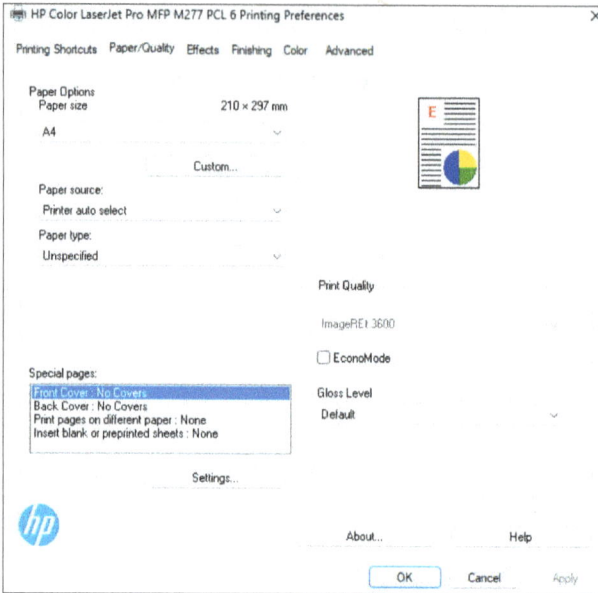

In the 'color' tab we can change color options and use grey scale printing.

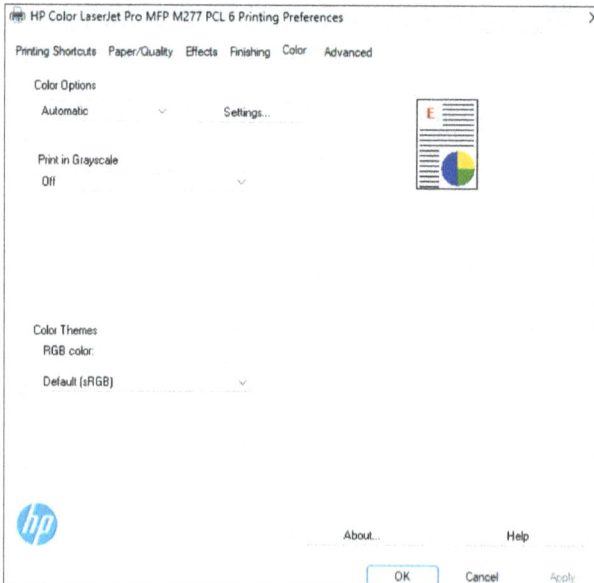

Click 'ok' when you're done

# Bluetooth Devices

You can pair any bluetooth device such as a mouse, keyboard, headphones, pens and so on. To do this go to the settings app on the start menu, select 'bluetooth & devices'.

## Pairing a Device

Shift the bluetooth slider to 'on'. Then click 'add device'.

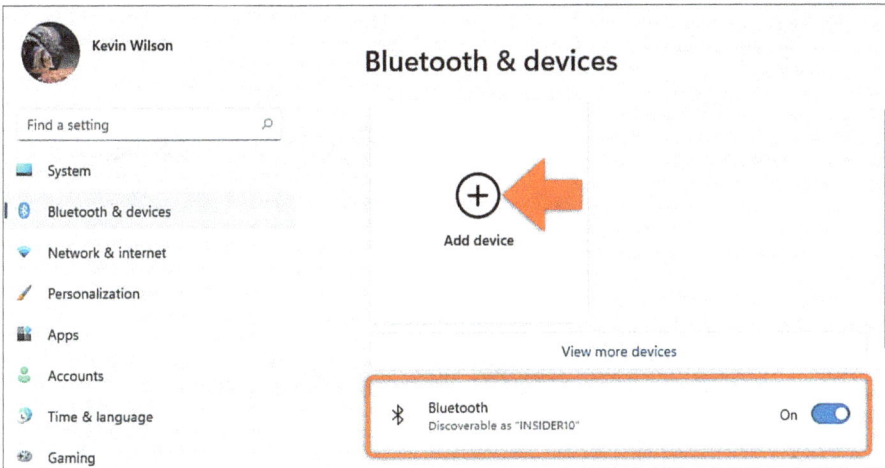

From the 'add a device' menu, select the type of device you're adding. In this example bluetooth.

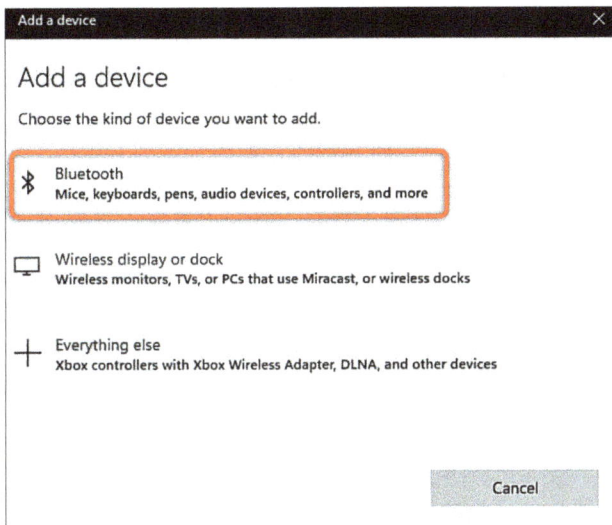

## Chapter 3: Settings and Personalisation

Put your device into discover mode. How you do this depends on the device, so you'll need to read the instructions that came with it to find out. In this example, I'm going to pair a bluetooth mouse. To put the mouse into pairing mode, press and hold the button on the bottom of the mouse until the light underneath starts flashing.

Press and hold the pairing button...

Your laptop or PC will start scanning for bluetooth devices, and list them in this window. Select your device from the list. Windows will add and setup the device automatically. Click 'done'.

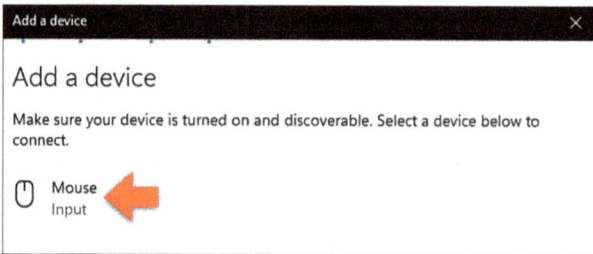

You'll see all your bluetooth devices appear along the top.

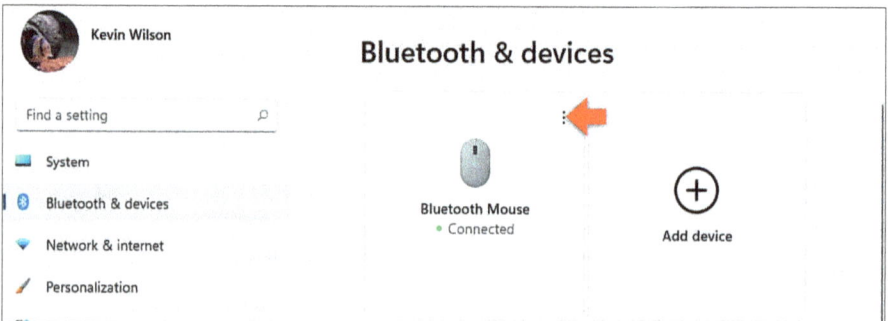

If you need to remove a device, click on the three dots icon on the top right of the device, then select 'remove device'.

**90**

# Audio Settings

You can adjust settings and configure your audio in Windows 11. Right-click the volume icon on the bottom right of your window, then select 'sounds' settings from the popup menu.

Here, you'll see the sound settings are split into sections. Let's take a look at the output section. Here you can manage the output played through speakers or headphones.

**Choose where to play sound** allows users to select the default audio output device, such as speakers or headphones.

**Pair a new output device** button will start the process to pair a new device.

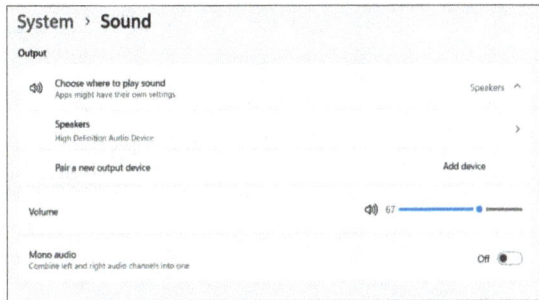

**Volume Slider** controls the master volume level for the output device.

**Mono audio** enables or disables mono audio. When turned on, it combines the left and right audio channels into one signal, which is useful for those with hearing impairments in one ear.

The input section, you can manage input devices such as microphones. **Choose a device for speaking or recording** allows users to select the default input device, like a microphone or a headset.

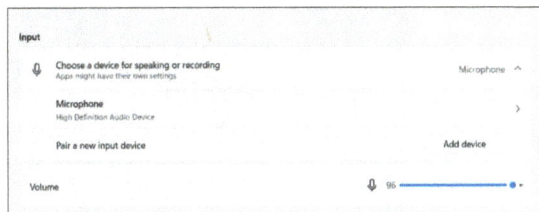

**Pair a new input device** starts the process to pair a new input device, such as a Bluetooth microphone.

**Volume Slider** controls the sensitivity of the input device or the microphone level.

## Chapter 3: Settings and Personalisation

## Configuring a Microphone

To configure your microphone, make sure it's plugged into the pink 3.5mm jack on the back of your computer, or in the microphone jack.

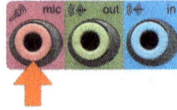

Scroll down to 'input', then select your microphone.

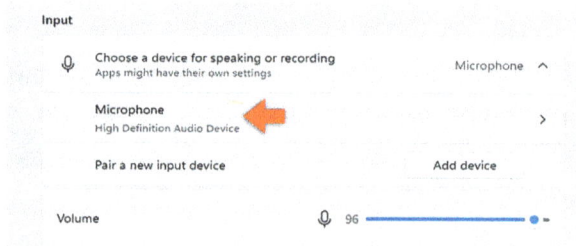

Here, you can adjust the input volume - this is how sensitive your microphone is. You can also change the format which also adjusts the quality: CD quality, DVD quality, or studio quality.

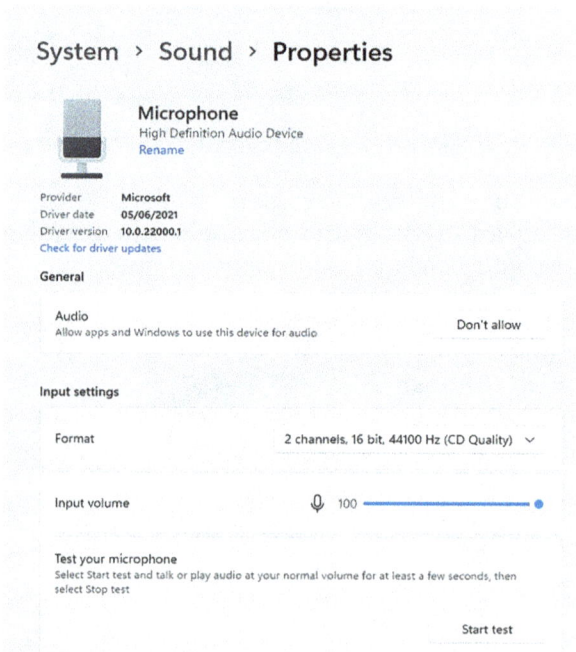

To test your microphone, click 'start test' at the bottom right of the screen.

Now, read the sentence displayed on your screen. Read the following paragraph into the microphone using your normal speaking voice.

*Peter dictates to his computer. He prefers it to typing, and particularly prefers it to pen and paper.*

You'll see the blue bar next to 'input volume' move as you speak. Windows 11 will adjust the input volume automatically depending on how loud you speak.

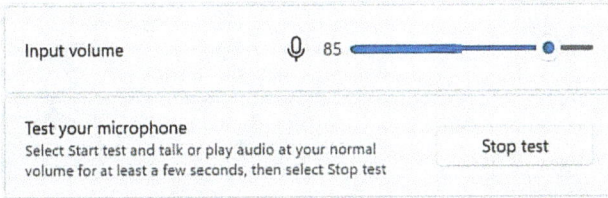

Once you're done, click 'stop test'.

## Adjust Microphone Recording Volume

Right-click the volume icon on the bottom right of your window, then select 'sound settings' from the popup menu.

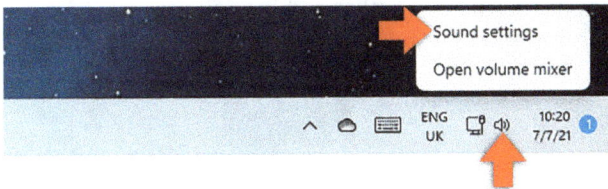

Scroll down to the bottom, then select 'more sound settings'.

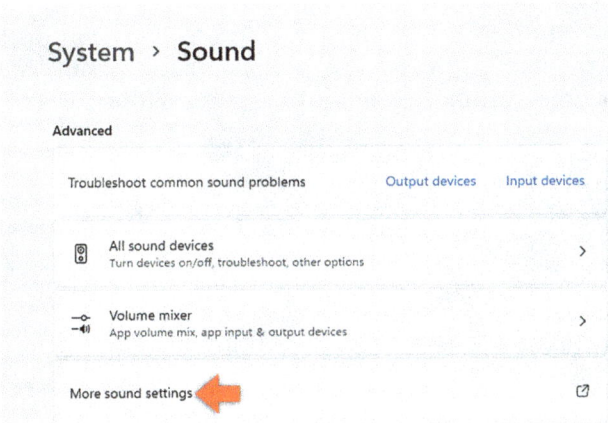

From the 'sounds' dialog box, select the 'recording' tab. Select your microphone, then click 'properties'.

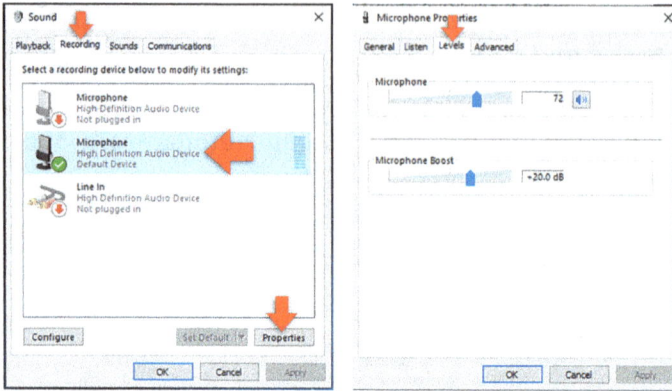

From the 'properties' window, select 'levels'. From here, set the microphone levels. Use the top slider to increase the recording levels of the microphone. Use the bottom slider to boost the microphone sensitivity - useful if your mic isn't picking up your voice clearly.

# Attaching Speakers

Make sure your speakers are plugged into the green 3.5mm jack on the back of your computer.

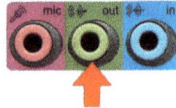

# Audio Levels

To adjust the audio volume, click on the speaker icon on the bottom right of the taskbar. Here, at the bottom of the popup box, you can adjust the overall volume. Click and drag the slider.

Click the 'side arrow' on the right of volume slider if you need to select a different device, such as speakers, headphones, etc.

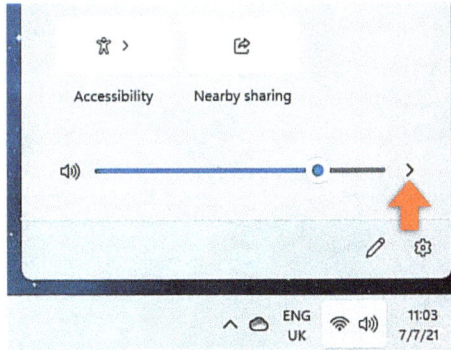

Select a device.

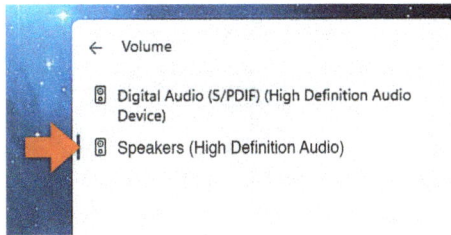

# Volume Mixer

Each application that generates sound such as iTunes, Web browser, Spotify and so on, will have its own volume control. This allows you to adjust the volume for individual apps. For example, you can turn down the system sounds, but keep your music playing louder, or you can turn down your music in the background if you're on a video call.

To open the mixer, right click on the speaker icon on the bottom right of the taskbar. Select 'open volume mixer'.

# Chapter 3: Settings and Personalisation

You'll see two sections: system and apps. Let's take a look at each section.

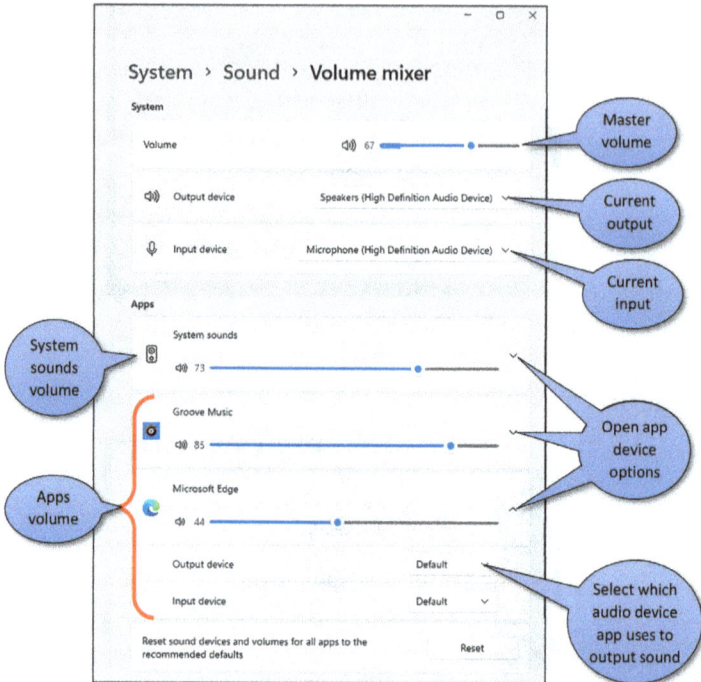

The **Volume** slider in the system section is the master volume control for the entire system. This affects the overall loudness of all sounds played by the computer.

**Output Device** shows the currently selected default audio output device (e.g., speakers or headphones) through which all sounds are played.

**Input Device** indicates the currently selected default audio input device (e.g., microphone) used for capturing sound.

In the Apps section, the **system sounds** slider controls the volume level of sounds generated by the windows itself.

The other sliders underneath control the volume of the other apps that are currently running - the apps that show up in this list depend on what you're running. Each app has its own volume control, allowing you to independently adjust how loud it is in relation to other apps and system sounds. In this example, I have Groove Music playing in the background and I have a video running in Edge. Here, I can turn down the volume of the music in Edge without turning down the volume on Groove Music. Just use the appropriate slider on the mixer.

# Display Settings

To adjust your display resolution, multiple monitor settings and so on, open your settings app.

## Screen Resolution & Scaling

The screen resolution is the number of horizontal pixels by the number of vertical pixels on a screen. For example a full HD screen is 1920x1080. Windows 11 does its best to automatically select the correct screen resolution for any screens it detects.

Open the settings app, then select 'system' from the left hand side. Select 'display' from the list on the right.

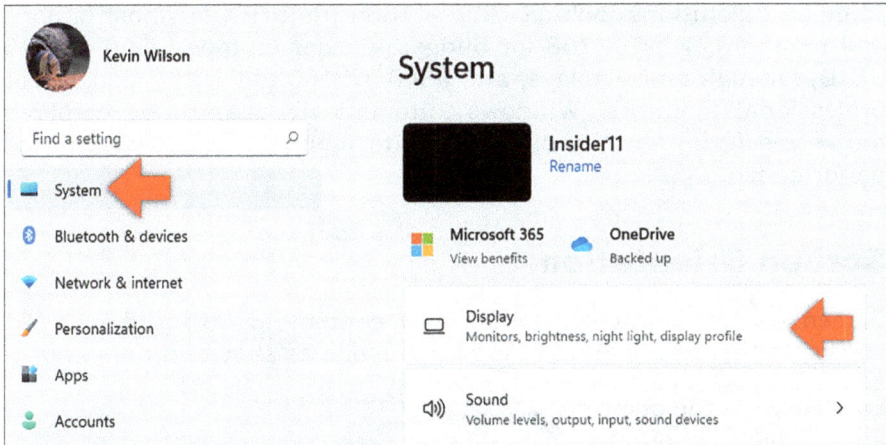

Select the screen whose resolution you want to change. If you only have one screen you wont get this option. I have selected screen 1.

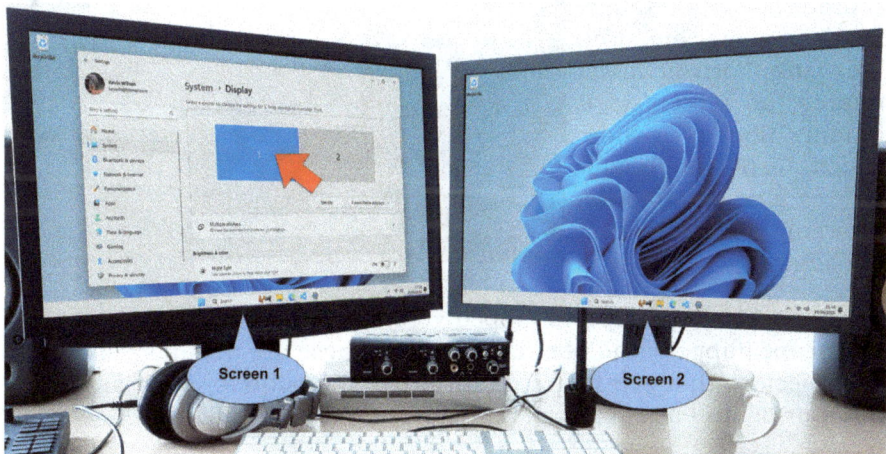

Scroll down to 'Scale & layout'. If you want make text and icons appear larger, use the Scale option at the top. 100% is the default size, while 125% and above increases the size of text, windows, and other interface elements.

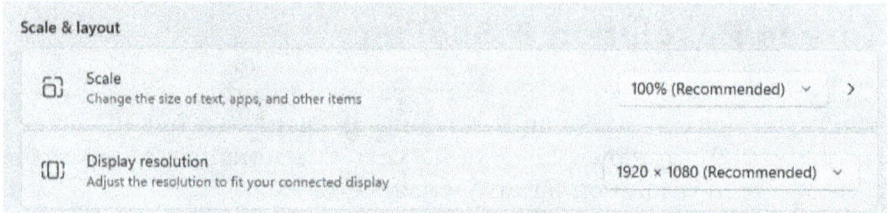

To change the resolution of the display, click the drop down box next to 'display resolution', then select a resolution from the list. The most common resolutions include 1920 × 1080 (Full HD) for most laptops and monitors, 1366 × 768 for budget or older laptops, 2560 × 1440 (QHD) for high-end displays, and 3840 × 2160 (4K UHD) for large or professional monitors. Windows automatically marks the display's native resolution as "Recommended" to ensure optimal clarity and performance.

# Screen Orientation

Screen orientation refers to the way content is arranged on your screen—either in portrait or landscape mode as shown in the photo.

Landscape is the default and most common orientation, where the screen is wider than it is tall, ideal for general computing tasks, media viewing, and web browsing. Portrait mode rotates the screen so it is taller than it is wide, which can be useful for reading documents, browsing long webpages, or coding.

Windows 11 also supports flipped versions of each of these settings - landscape (flipped) and portrait (flipped). These are useful for monitors or projectors that are mounted in unusual positions, such as upside down or behind a rear-projection surface.

# Multiple Screens

You can plug in more than one screen if your PC supports this.

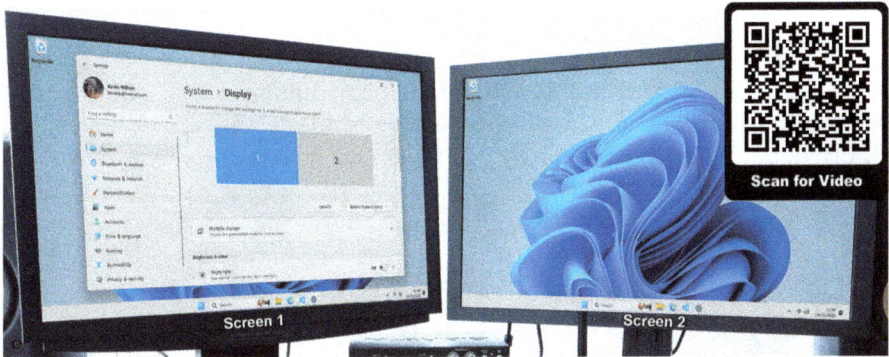

To set up your screens, open your settings app then select 'system' from the list on the left. Then select 'displays' from the list on the right.

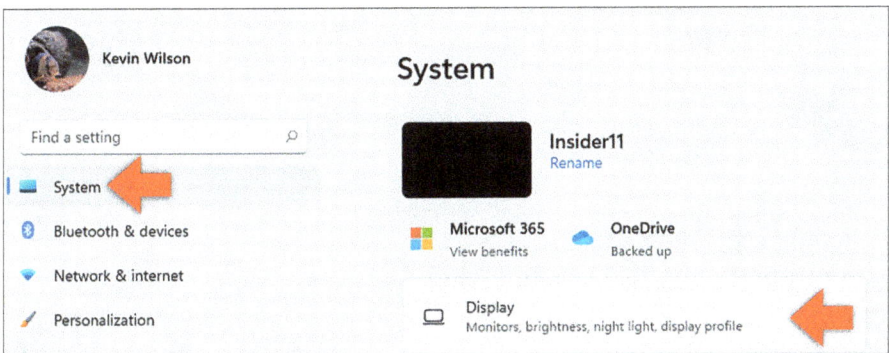

Here, you'll see a diagram with rectangles representing your screens. In this case, I have two screens, my main 24" display (screen 1) and second 24" display next to it on the right (screen 2).

You can drag these rectangles in any order. It is useful to have them in the same order as the physical arrangement on your desk - as shown in the photograph at the top of the page.

**99**

## Chapter 3: Settings and Personalisation

Click 'multiple displays' top expand the options.

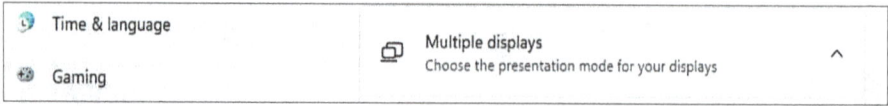

| | |
|---|---|
| ⊙ Time & language | ⊡ **Multiple displays** ∧ |
| | Choose the presentation mode for your displays |
| ⊕ Gaming | |

Here, you can force Windows to detect your displays. You can identify all your displays - this shows the display number on each screen: 1, 2, 3, etc depending on how many displays you have connected.

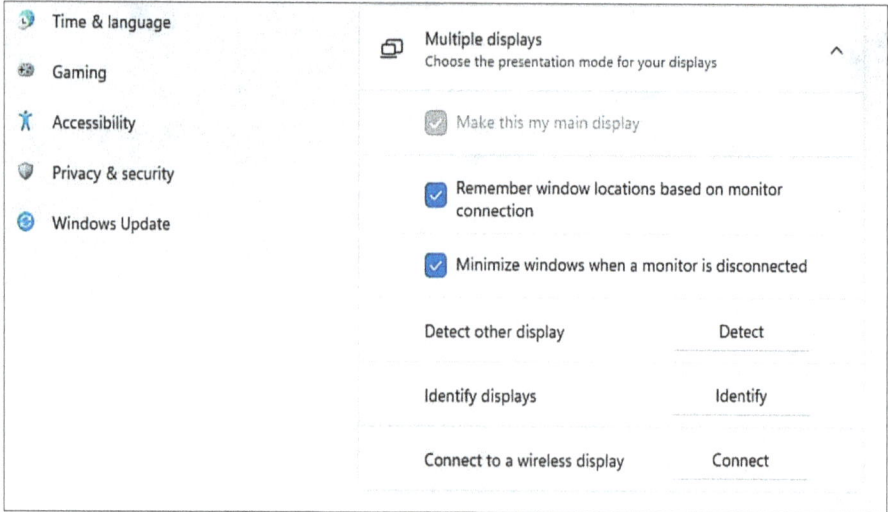

| | |
|---|---|
| ⊙ Time & language | ⊡ **Multiple displays** ∧ |
| | Choose the presentation mode for your displays |
| ⊕ Gaming | |
| 𝕏 Accessibility | ☑ Make this my main display |
| ⊙ Privacy & security | ☑ Remember window locations based on monitor connection |
| ⊙ Windows Update | ☑ Minimize windows when a monitor is disconnected |
| | Detect other display        Detect |
| | Identify displays        Identify |
| | Connect to a wireless display        Connect |

You can also connect to wireless displays using a feature called screen casting.

## Wireless Displays and Screen Casting

You can connect to wireless compatible displays such as Smart TVs. Your TV will need to support screen mirroring or Miracast for this to work. On your TV look for settings or apps such as 'Miracast', 'Screen Casting', or 'WiFi Casting'. Make sure you enable them. Also enable bluetooth if it isn't already. Check your TV's documentation for details on how to do this for your model.

If your TV doesn't support screen mirroring, you can buy a Micracast dongle such as the one below. Or a Microsoft Display Adapter.

To cast your screen, on your PC, press Windows K on your keyboard. Select your display or TV from the list of available displays.

Once connected, your laptop screen will show on the wireless display

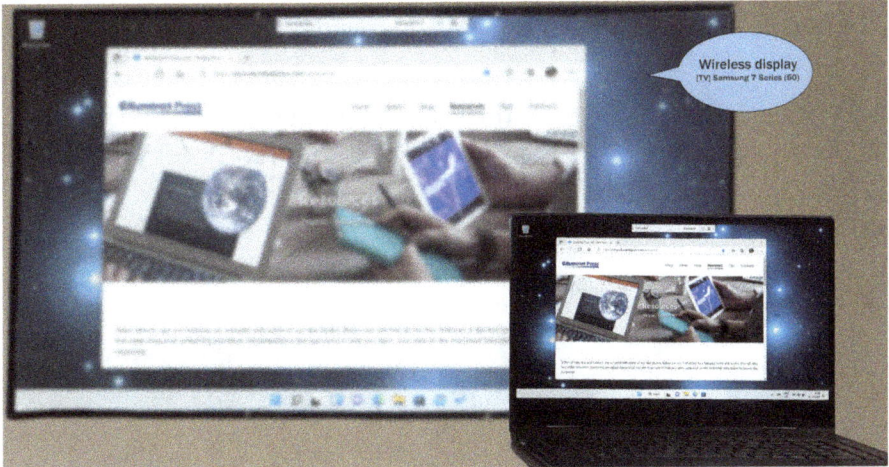

Note that at the time of writing, Miracast negotiates it's connection over WiFi using the 2.4GHz band. Some laptops and devices connect using the 5Ghz band, this may cause the connection to fail. To change this, on your laptop, right click on the start button, select 'device manager'. Click on network adapters to open it up, then right click on your WiFi adapter, select 'properties' from the popup menu.

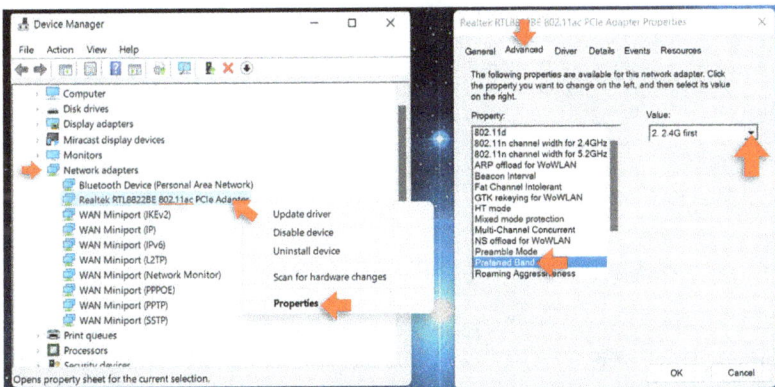

Select the 'advanced tab', scroll down to 'preferred band', change the value to '2. 2.4G first'.

# Screen Calibration

Screen calibration is the process of adjusting your display settings to ensure that colors, brightness, contrast, and gamma levels are rendered as accurately and consistently as possible. This is essential for professionals in photography, video editing, digital art, and design—accurate colors ensure that what you see is what others will see when the content is shared or printed.

To calibrate your screen, press Windows + S to open search, type "Calibrate display color", and select the result. This opens the Display Color Calibration wizard.

The wizard will guide you through adjusting gamma, brightness, contrast, and color balance. It provides reference images so you can make comparative judgments. Just follow the instructions on screen.

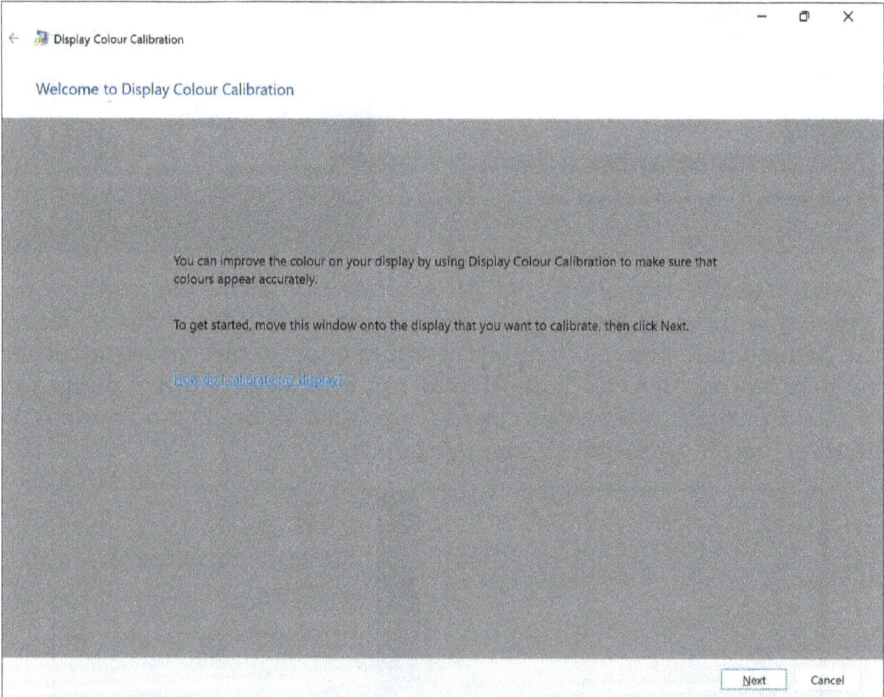

Repeat this on each screen if you have more than one.

For professional-level accuracy, hardware devices such as the X-Rite i1Display or Datacolor SpyderX can measure screen output and create highly accurate ICC profiles.

After calibration, Windows saves the new settings as a color profile.

# Color Profiles

A color profile defines the color characteristics of a device or image. It maps how colors should appear on your screen (a monitor profile), how they're interpreted by your printer (a printer profile), how a scanner captures them (a scanner profile), or how a camera records them (a camera profile). Each device has different color capabilities, and without proper color management, colors can appear inconsistent or incorrect across devices.

To address this, every display, camera, scanner, and printer uses a unique ICC profile (International Color Consortium profile) that acts as a translator between the device's native color space and a standardized color space—such as sRGB or Adobe RGB. By converting color data through a standard intermediary format, these profiles ensure that colors are accurately and consistently represented when transferred between devices, allowing for true-to-life reproduction across screens, printers, and applications.

To view and change color profiles in Windows 11, press Windows + R, type `colorcpl.exe` then press Enter to open the Color Management utility.

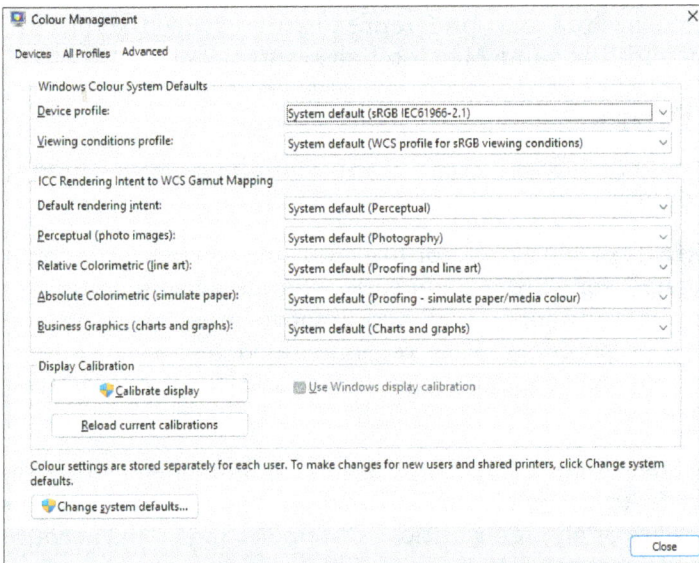

From here, you can view the current profiles associated with a device, as well as add, remove, or set a default profile. The Advanced tab allows you to configure system-wide color management settings, such as rendering intents and default profiles, which is especially useful in color-critical or professional workflows.

# User Accounts

You can set up multiple user accounts on your PC, allowing different people to sign in with their own credentials and access personalized settings, apps, OneDrive, email, and calendar data. Each user has a separate profile with isolated files, settings, and preferences.

## Account Types

Windows 11 supports two main types of accounts: A Local Account and a Microsoft Account.

A **local account** consists of a username and password used exclusively to sign in to a specific Windows device. It operates independently of Microsoft's cloud services and does not include features such as settings sync, OneDrive integration, or Microsoft Store access. It is ideal for users who prefer privacy or offline use. Online services can still be accessed separately by signing in to individual apps.

A **Microsoft Account** is an email-based login (e.g., outlook.com, hotmail.com, or a third-party email address registered with Microsoft). It provides access to cloud-based features including OneDrive, Microsoft 365, Outlook, Xbox Live, and the Microsoft Store. Settings, themes, passwords, and preferences can be synced across all devices signed in with the same Microsoft account.

## User Types

There are three different types of user: administrators, standard users and child users.

**Administrators** have full control over the system. They can install and uninstall software system wide, change system settings, manage security configurations, and add/remove other user accounts. For security best practices, it is recommended to use an administrator account only for configuration tasks and a standard account for everyday usage.

**Standard users** can launch applications, modify their own settings, and use most features in Windows. However, they cannot install system-wide software or changing critical system settings. This account type is well-suited for regular daily use and helps reduce the risk of accidental system changes or malware installation.

A **child account** is a type of Microsoft account that includes parental controls such as screen time limits, web filtering, content restrictions, activity reports, and purchase approvals. These settings can be managed via the Microsoft Family Safety dashboard.

It is considered best practice to have at least two accounts on your device: a local account set to an administrator type, and a Microsoft Account set to a standard user type. This allows you to use your standard Microsoft Account for every day activities, and the administrator account to change system settings and install software.

# Create a Microsoft Account

To set up a new Microsoft Account, open your web browser and navigate to the following address:

```
signup.live.com
```

Enter an email address you'd like to use for your Microsoft Account, click 'next'. Next, enter a password for the account. *Remember passwords must have at least 8 characters and contain at least one uppercase letter, lowercase letter, number, and a symbol (eg: \*, $, #, etc).* Click 'next'.

Enter your first and last names in the fields, click 'next'. Then enter the country you're living in and your date of birth.

Enter the captcha code in the field at the bottom

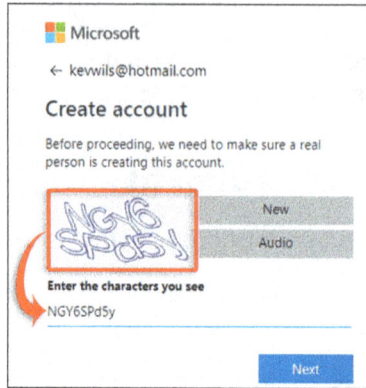

Click 'next'. Your account will be created. Close the browser window and you're good to go.

## Adding a New User with Microsoft Account

To add a new user, click the start menu, and select the settings app icon. Then select 'accounts' from the list on the left. Select 'other users'.

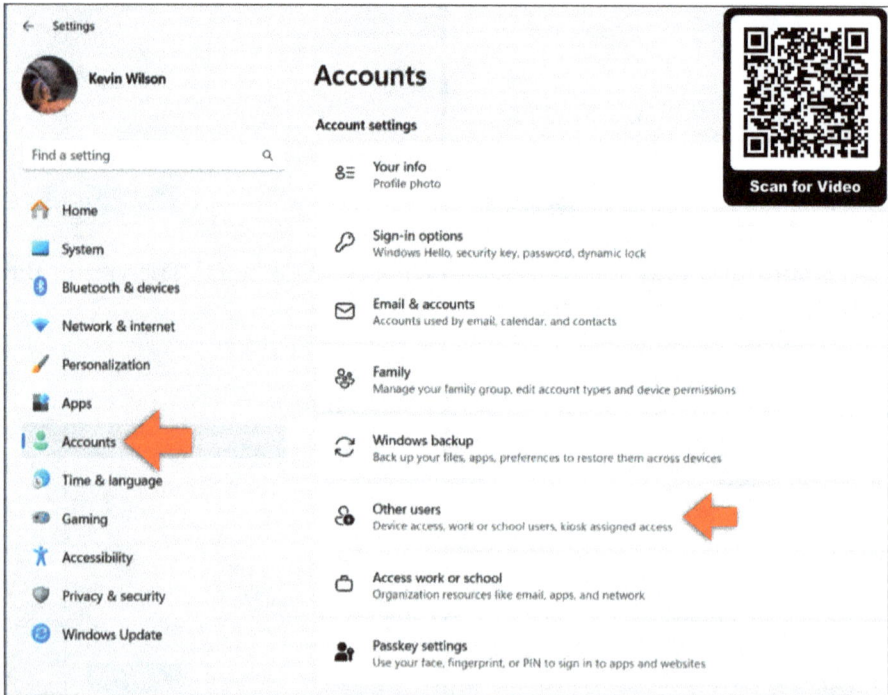

Scroll down to 'other users', then click 'add account'.

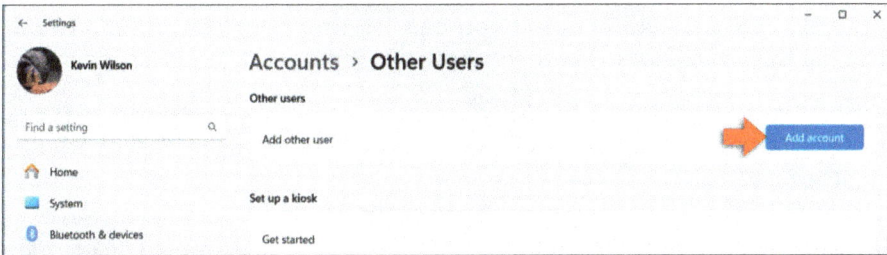

Enter the new user's Microsoft Account email address and password.

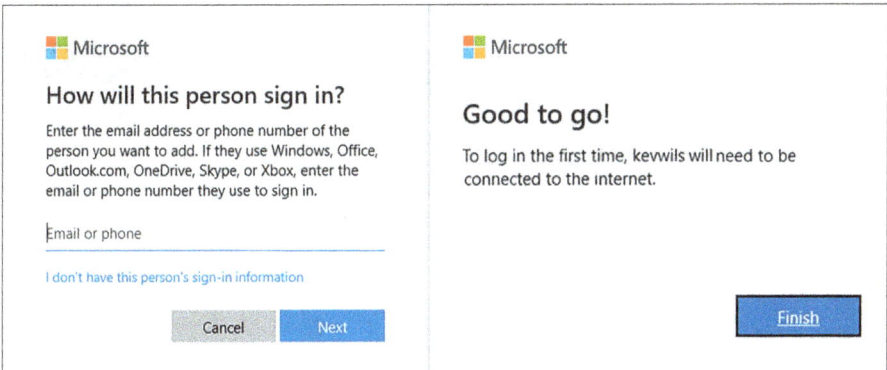

Select the account type for this user: administrator or standard. For other users, it is best to set their account type to standard.

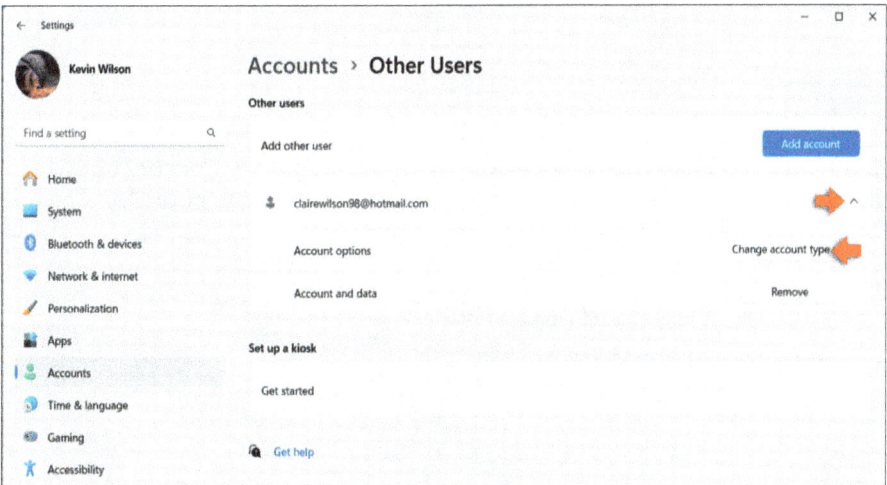

The new user will be able to log into Windows with their own account and can select it from the login screen.

# Adding a New User with Local Account

A local account is an account you can log into your computer without having to sign up for a Microsoft Account email address and password.

To add a local user, click on the start menu, then select the settings app. Click on 'accounts' on the settings app home page. Select 'Family & other users'.

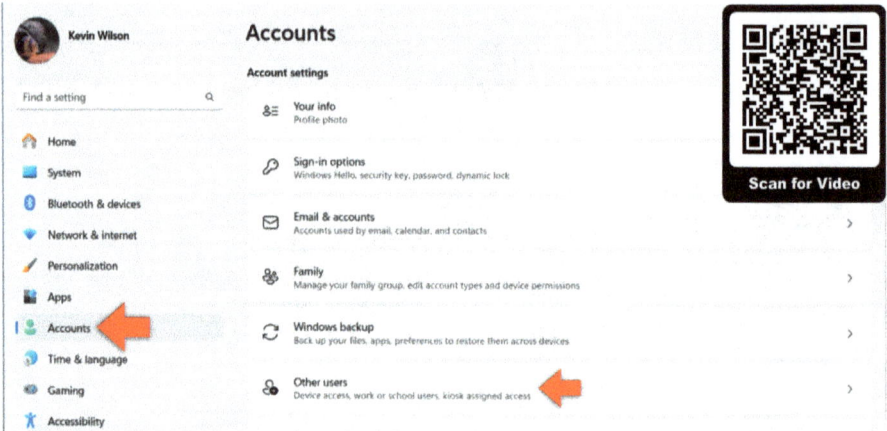

Scroll down the page, click 'Add account'.

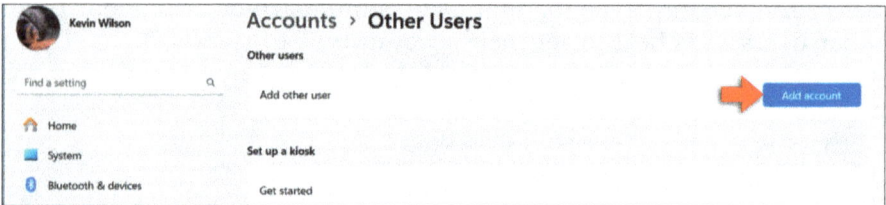

Click 'I don't have this person's sign-in information. On the 'create account' screen, select 'add user without Microsoft account'.

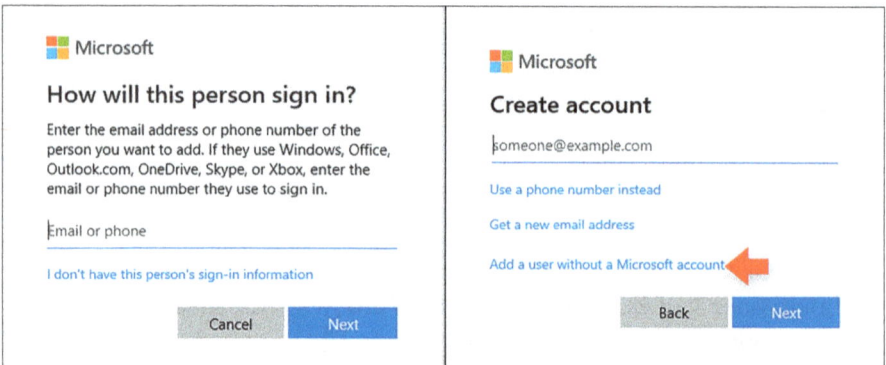

Enter the username and password for this user. Select three security questions - this is to verify your identity should you need to reset your password.

Click 'next'.

The new user will be able to log into Windows with their own account and can select it from the login screen.

## Change an Account Type

As we mentioned earlier, you can change an account to either a standard user or an administrator. Click on the start menu, then select the settings app icon. Click on 'accounts' on the settings app home page. Select 'Family & other users' from the list on the left.

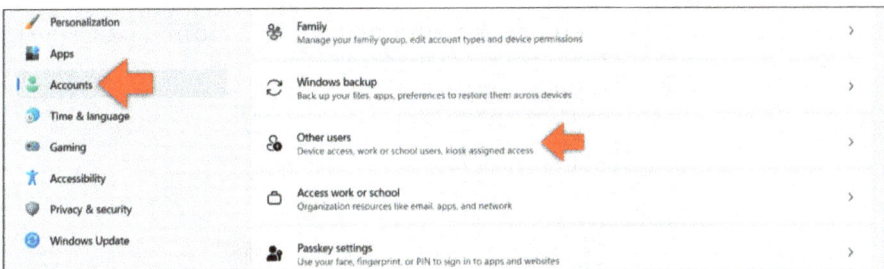

Scroll down to 'other users' select the user you want to change. From the options select 'change account type'.

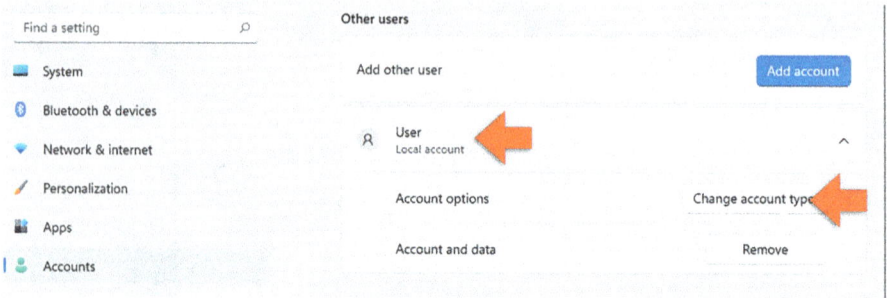

From the popup dialog box, select either 'administrator' or 'standard user', click 'ok'.

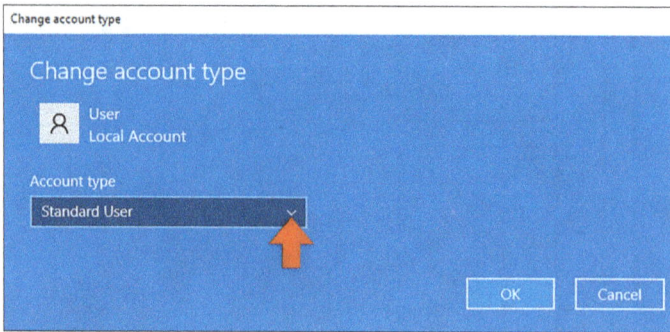

An administrator account allows complete control over the computer, which means an administrator can install apps and hardware, change system wide settings, or execute elevated tasks.

Standard user accounts can use apps, but they can't install new ones or change system settings without administrator approval. It is recommended that you have two accounts on your computer: an administrator account for changing settings or installing apps, and a standard account for everyday use.

This setup offers a more secure environment, any attempt to install new apps or change system settings while you are signed in with your standard account, will require the administrator account's password.

To remove the account, click 'remove'.

# Windows Hello & Sign In Options

Windows Hello is Microsoft's biometric authentication system integrated into Windows 11. It allows you to sign into your device and supported apps or services using facial recognition or a fingerprint, instead of a traditional password. To use Windows Hello, your device must include compatible hardware—either a fingerprint scanner or an infrared (IR) camera specifically certified for Windows Hello. Devices such as the Surface Pro, Surface Laptop, Dell XPS 13/15, HP Spectre x360, and Lenovo ThinkPad X1 Carbon are among the most common systems with built-in Windows Hello-compatible cameras. If your device doesn't have one built in, you can use an external camera like the Logitech BRIO 4K, which includes an IR sensor and is fully compatible with Windows Hello facial recognition.

To find the Windows Hello settings, open the settings app. Select 'accounts' from the list on the left, then click 'sign-in options'.

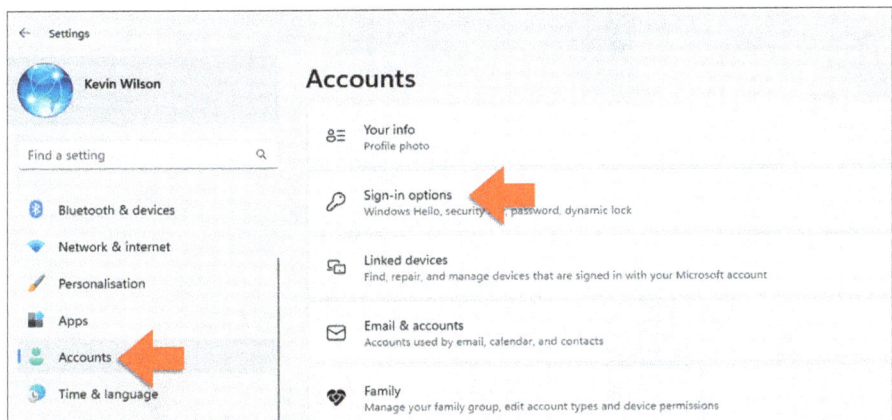

## Fingerprint

To setup the finger print scanner, select 'fingerprint recognition' from the sign in options. Then select 'set up' under the fingerprint section of the 'sign in' options under 'fingerprint'.

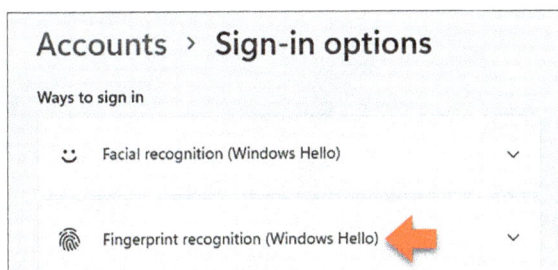

**111**

Scan your finger using the fingerprint reader. Most people use their index finger.

You may need to do this a few times. Keep going until Windows informs you the process is complete.

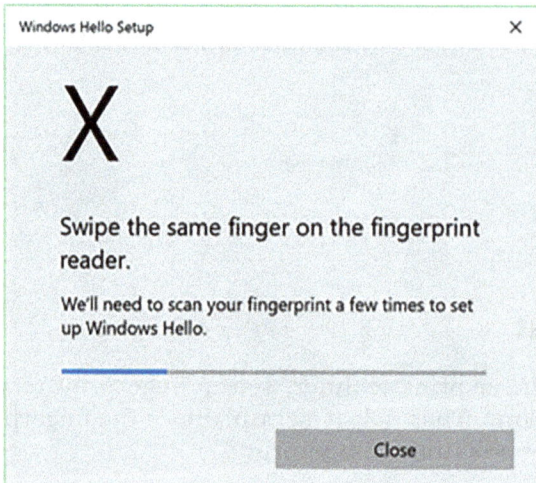

Select close on the bottom right.

You should now be able to sign in with your fingerprint from the lock screen. So instead of typing in a password, you can now just swipe or place your finger on the scanner to sign into your account.

# Facial Recognition

To use Windows Hello facial recognition, your device must have a camera that supports infrared (IR) depth sensing—standard webcams are not sufficient. A widely used external option is the Logitech BRIO 4K Ultra HD Webcam, which includes an IR sensor and is fully compatible with Windows Hello facial recognition. If you're using a Microsoft device such as the Surface Studio, Surface Pro tablet, or Surface Book laptop, a compatible IR camera is already built in, so no additional hardware is required.

To set it up, select 'facial recognition'.

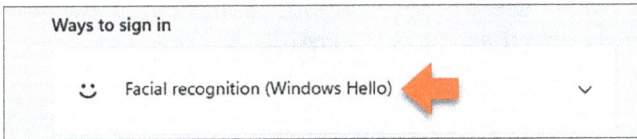

Under 'windows hello face' select 'set up'.

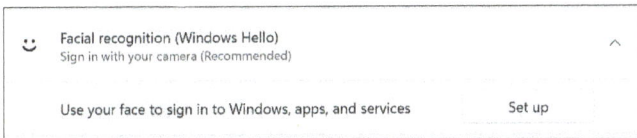

Enter your PIN if prompted.

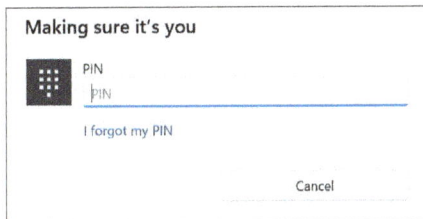

Click 'get started'.

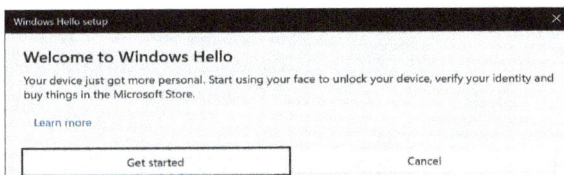

You'll see a live preview from your camera on the screen. Position yourself so that your entire face is clearly visible, centered, and well-lit. As the scan begins, a box will appear around your face to help you stay properly aligned. The box outline will gradually fill with blue, indicating that Windows is capturing and processing your facial data. Hold still and look directly at the screen until the process

Keep looking directly at your camera.

completes. You'll see a confirmation message indicating that facial recognition has been set up successfully. Click 'close'.

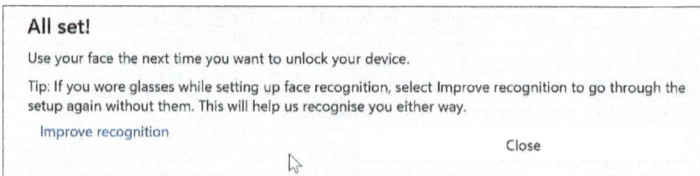

**All set!**

Use your face the next time you want to unlock your device.

Tip: If you wore glasses while setting up face recognition, select Improve recognition to go through the setup again without them. This will help us recognise you either way.

Improve recognition

Close

Once setup, you'll return to the Windows Hello settings screen where you can manage additional options.

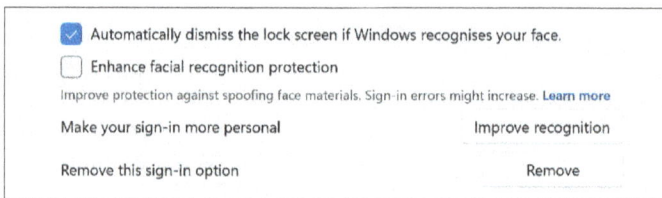

☑ Automatically dismiss the lock screen if Windows recognises your face.

☐ Enhance facial recognition protection

Improve protection against spoofing face materials. Sign-in errors might increase. **Learn more**

Make your sign-in more personal                 Improve recognition

Remove this sign-in option                       Remove

Here, you can enable the option to automatically dismiss the lock screen—this means that as soon as Windows recognises your face, you'll be signed in without needing to click or swipe. You also have the option to enhance facial recognition protection, which increases resistance to spoofing attempts (such as using photos or masks). If you want to improve recognition accuracy, particularly under different lighting conditions or with appearance changes (like wearing glasses), you can click "Improve recognition" to scan your face again. Finally, if you no longer wish to use facial recognition, you can click "Remove" to disable it and remove the stored biometric data.

# PIN

A PIN is usually 4 - 8 numbers you can use to sign into windows instead of using a password.

From the 'sign in options', select 'PIN' from the sign in options.

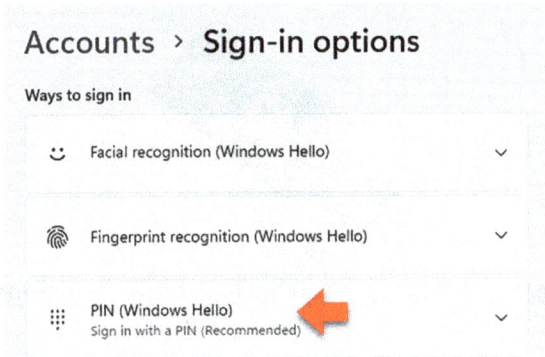

Tap 'add', then tap 'next'.

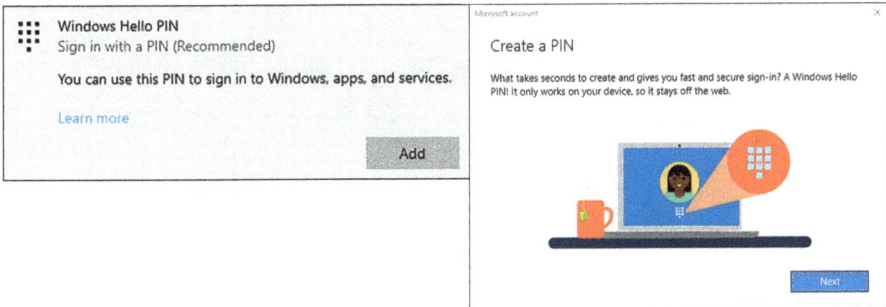

Enter your Microsoft account password if prompted. Enter your new PIN. Click 'ok'.

You can now sign in with a PIN instead of typing in your password.

# Security Key

A security key is a physical device that you can use to sign into your PC instead of a password or PIN. A security key can be a USB device that you can keep on your keyring, or an NFC device like a smartphone or access card.

You can buy a key such as YubiKey or Thetis from Amazon or some other retailer.

To it set up, insert your security key into a USB port on your PC.

Select 'Security Key" from the sign in options.

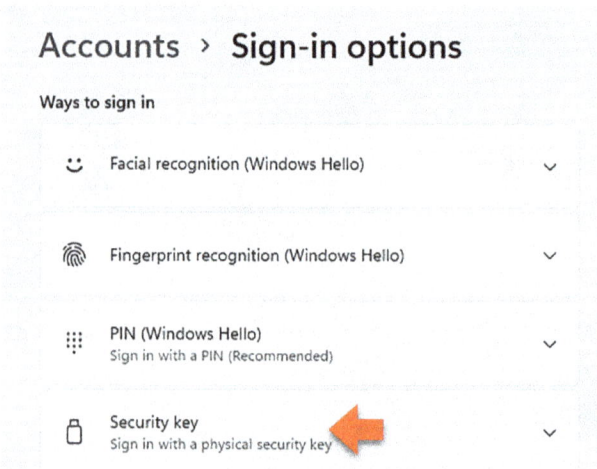

Click 'manage'.

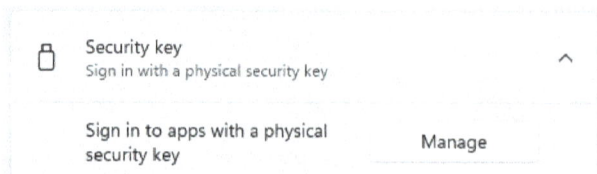

Under 'security key PIN', click 'add'. Type in and confirm a security key PIN, then select OK.

The security key will be updated with the new PIN for use with your work or school account.

# OneDrive

OneDrive comes with Windows 11 and is probably the safest place to store all your files as they are backed up in case your PC crashes.

The theory is, you work on the files on your local machine - you edit, update, create, save, and do the things you need to do. OneDrive automatically copies these updates onto your OneDrive Account in the Cloud. This is called synchronisation. This means you can access your files from any of your devices whether it is a tablet, phone, laptop, or on the web.

If you signed into Windows 11 with your Microsoft Account, then OneDrive is usually installed.

## Setup

If OneDrive isn't already set up, click the OneDrive icon on the bottom right hand side of the screen.

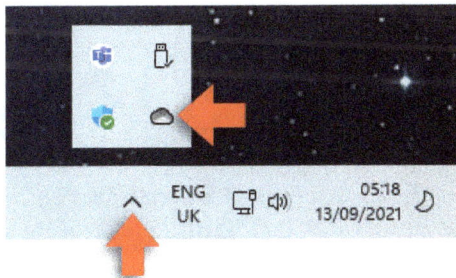

Enter your Microsoft Account email address and password then click 'sign in'.

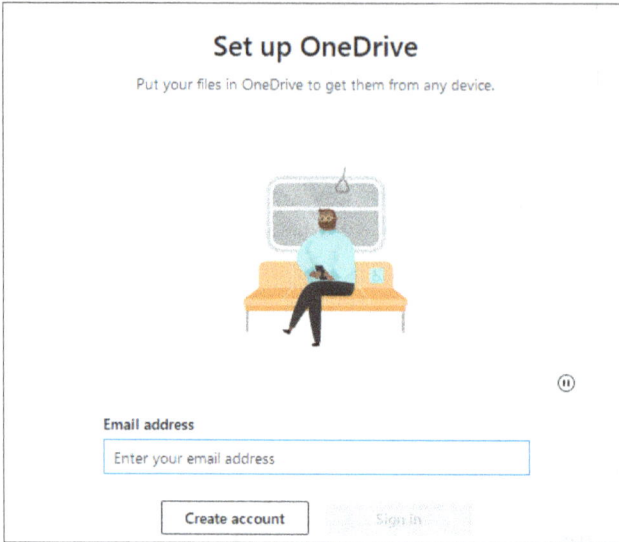

OneDrive will ask you where you want to store your OneDrive files on your computer while you work on them. Most of the time you can just leave it in it's default location.

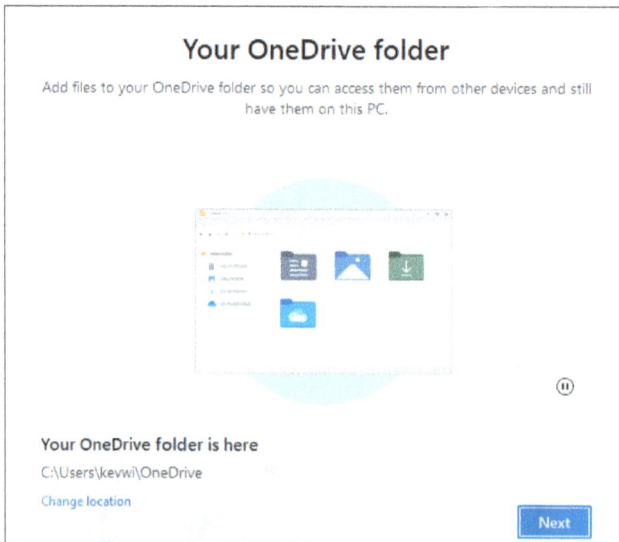

*If you want to specify a different location click 'change location', then browse to the drive and folder you want OneDrive to use. .*

Click 'next'

Click 'not now' to use OneDrive free. You get 5GB of storage for free. If you need more space, click 'go premium' and select a payment plan.

Run through the introduction... click 'next'.

On the 'get mobile app' screen, click 'later'.

You can download this app on your other devices such as iPad, tablet, or phone using the app store.

You'll find your OneDrive files in File Explorer. To open File Explorer, click the icon on your taskbar.

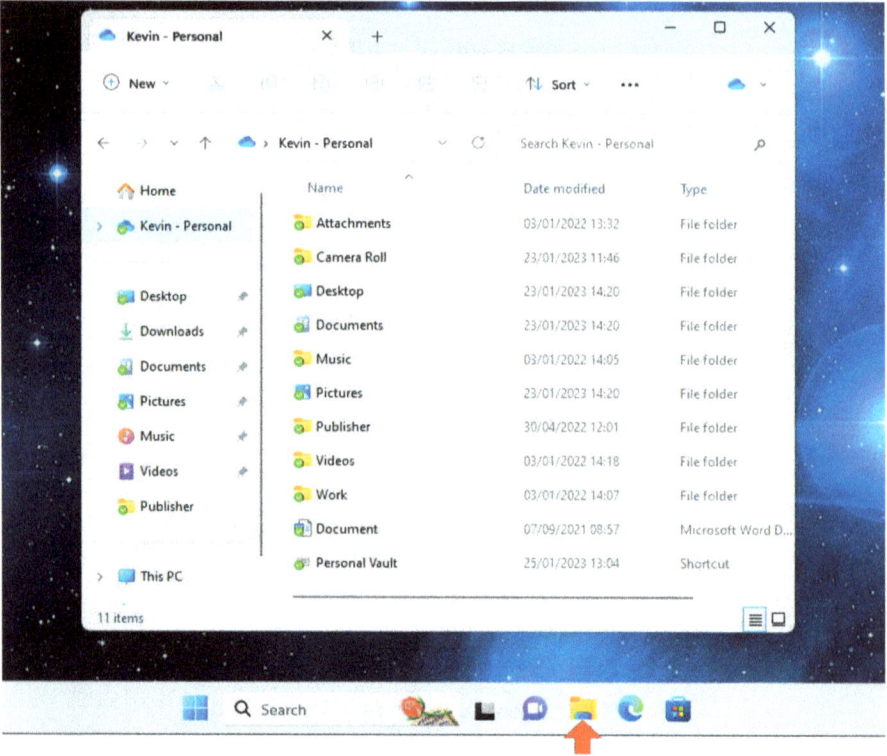

You'll find your OneDrive listed in the left hand pane. This is where you should save all your files you work on, in your apps.

## Changing Settings

To change OneDrive settings, click on the OneDrive icon on the bottom right of the screen. Click the settings icon, then select 'settings'.

## Sync & Backup Settings

On the 'sync & backup tab' you'll find some options, lets take a look.

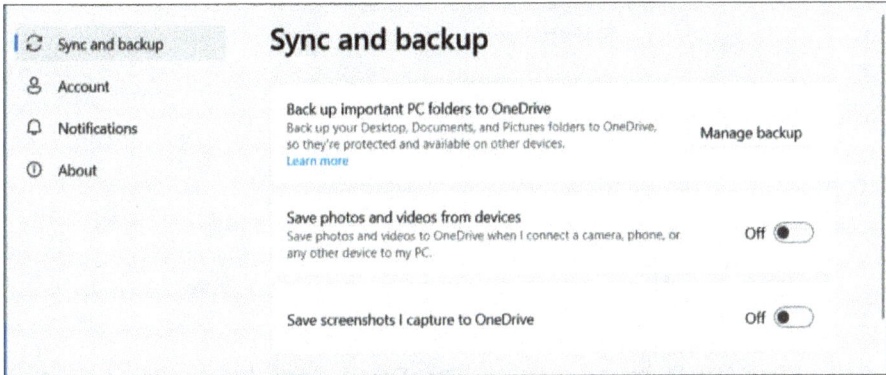

| | |
|---|---|
| ↻ Sync and backup | **Sync and backup** |
| ♒ Account | |
| ♪ Notifications | Back up important PC folders to OneDrive |
| ① About | Back up your Desktop, Documents, and Pictures folders to OneDrive, so they're protected and available on other devices. Learn more |

Back up important PC folders to OneDrive
Back up your Desktop, Documents, and Pictures folders to OneDrive, so they're protected and available on other devices.
Learn more                                                    Manage backup

Save photos and videos from devices
Save photos and videos to OneDrive when I connect a camera, phone, or     Off ⬤
any other device to my PC.

Save screenshots I capture to OneDrive                                    Off ⬤

**Back up important PC folders to OneDrive** allows you to automatically back up your Desktop, Documents, and Pictures folders to OneDrive, ensuring that your files are protected and accessible on other devices. There's a "Manage backup" button to configure this setting.

**Save photos and videos from devices** saves photos and videos you take with a camera, phone, or other devices directly to your PC via OneDrive.

**Save screenshots I capture to OneDrive** saves screenshots you take directly to your OneDrive pictures folder.

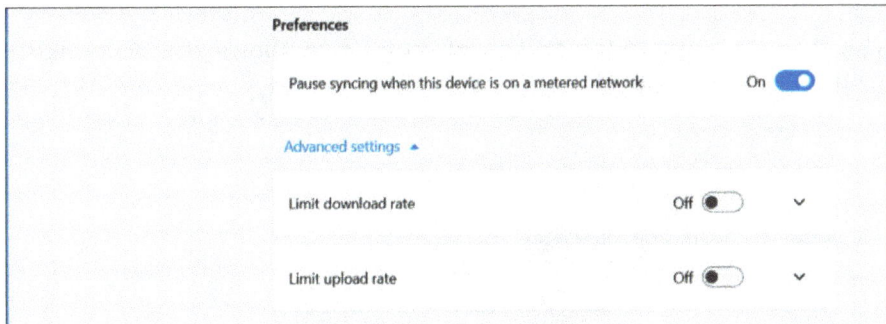

Preferences

Pause syncing when this device is on a metered network          On ⬤

Advanced settings ▲

Limit download rate                                             Off ⬤   ⌄

Limit upload rate                                               Off ⬤   ⌄

In the preferences section, **pause syncing when this device is on a metered network** will prevent OneDrive from syncing when your device is connected to a network that has data limitations, like a mobile hotspot, to avoid unnecessary data charges.

In the advanced settings, you can set a limit to how fast files upload and download from OneDrive to your PC, which can be useful to not saturate your internet connection.

**121**

**Excluded file extensions** section allows you specify certain file types that you do **not** want to be backed up to OneDrive. You can add file extensions that OneDrive will ignore during the sync process.

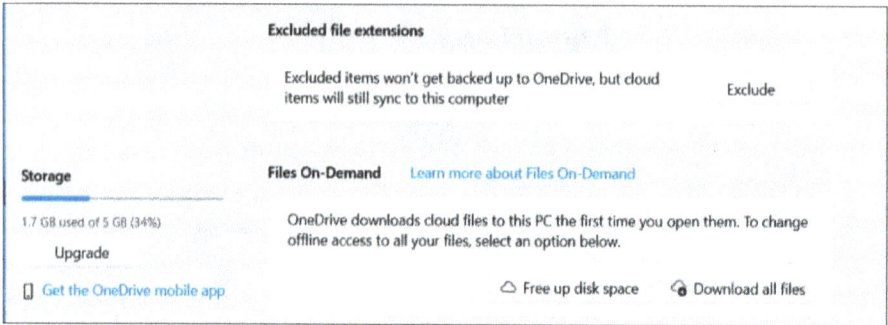

In the Files On-Demand section, **OneDrive downloads cloud files to this PC the first time you open them** allows you to access your files in OneDrive without having to download them all to your device first, saving space on your hard drive. When you open a file, it's downloaded at that moment. There are two options:

**Free up disk space** will make only online-only files visible on your PC, removing downloaded files and thus freeing up space.

**Download all files** will download all your OneDrive files to your PC for offline access.

## Account Settings

The account settings tab on the left hand side allows you to configure your OneDrive account.

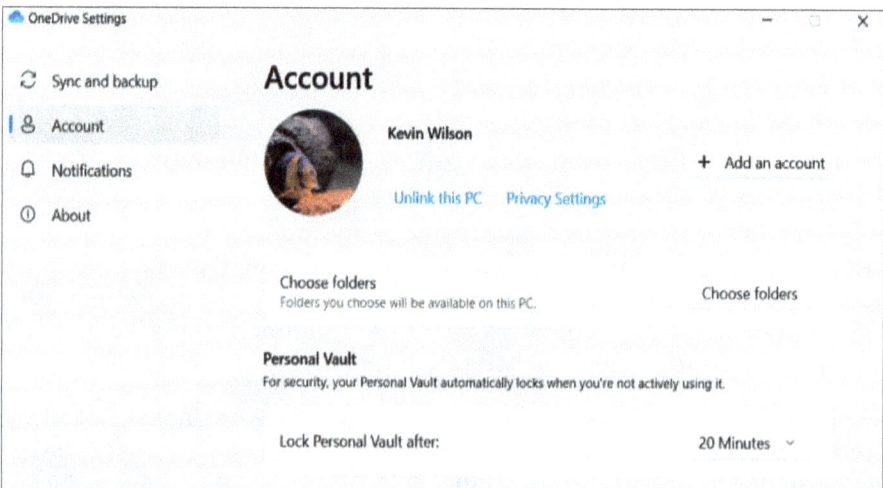

User Information appears along with a profile picture, indicating the name of the user who is currently logged into OneDrive.

**Unlink this PC** allows you to disconnect the current PC from the OneDrive account. After unlinking, OneDrive will no longer sync files to or from that particular computer.

**Privacy Settings** leads to options that allow you to manage your privacy settings, giving you control over how your usage data, diagnostic data and files are handled and shared.

**Add an account** allows you to add multiple account to OneDrive, which is useful if you want to switch between personal and work accounts or manage multiple OneDrive accounts from the same PC.

**Choose folders** allows you to select which folders from your OneDrive will be synced to your PC. This is useful for managing storage space on your device or for choosing specific documents you need for offline access.

The **Personal Vault** is a protected area within OneDrive that adds an extra layer of security with a more robust authentication method, like two-factor authentication, to access sensitive files. You can set it to lock automatically after a period of inactivity, in this example the Personal Vault will lock after 20 Minutes. This means if you are not actively using your Personal Vault, it will lock itself after 20 minutes to keep your files secure.

## Notification Settings

The notifications tab on the left allows you to enable/disable various notifications.

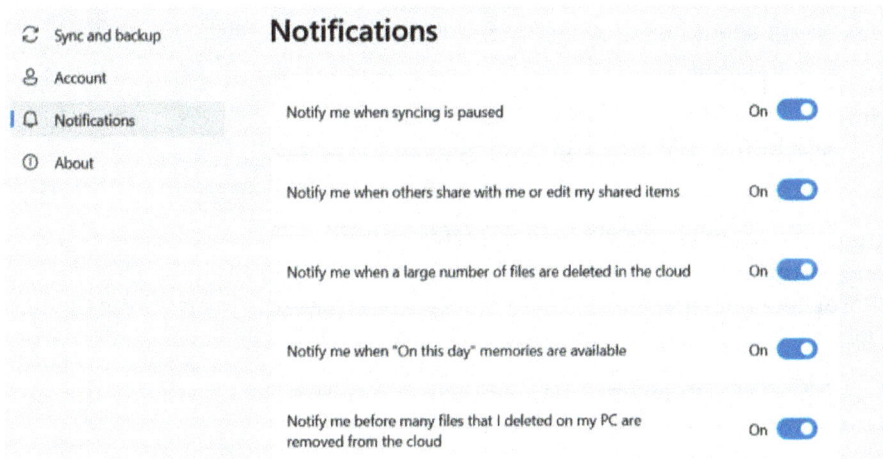

| | |
|---|---|
| ↻ Sync and backup | **Notifications** |
| ⚇ Account | |
| ⍰ Notifications | Notify me when syncing is paused |
| ① About | |

Notify me when others share with me or edit my shared items — On

Notify me when a large number of files are deleted in the cloud — On

Notify me when "On this day" memories are available — On

Notify me before many files that I deleted on my PC are removed from the cloud — On

**Notify me when syncing is paused** means you'll receive a notification if OneDrive stops syncing your files. This can happen for various reasons, such as when you're on a metered connection, and syncing is set to pause to save data, or if there's an error with syncing.

**Notify me when others share with me or edit my shared items** means you'll receive an alerts you when someone shares files or folders with you or when changes are made to files or folders you've shared with others.

**Notify me when a large number of files are deleted in the cloud** means you'll receive a notification notification when large numbers of files are deleted and serves as a safeguard against mass deletion of files from your OneDrive, which could be accidental or malicious.

**Notify me when "On this day" memories are available** will send you notifications about photos or documents you saved on the same day in past years, similar to a "memories" feature found in social media platforms.

**Notify me before many files that I deleted on my PC are removed from the cloud** will notify you if you delete a large number of files on your PC that are synced to OneDrive, this setting will ensure you're alerted before these changes affect the copies stored in the cloud.

**Notify me to load files from my other accounts to this PC** will notify you if you have multiple OneDrive accounts (like a personal and work account), this setting will notify you when you can load files from these other accounts onto your current PC.

## Storage Settings

On the bottom left of the settings dialog box you'll see some storage settings.

Storage Usage indicator shows how much storage space you've used and the maximum amount that you have on your account.

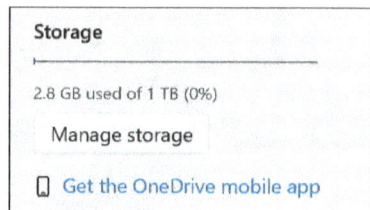

> **Storage**
>
> 2.8 GB used of 1 TB (0%)
>
> Manage storage
>
> ☐ Get the OneDrive mobile app

**Upgrade** button will guide you through the process of purchasing additional storage space. OneDrive offers various plans with different storage capacities, often tied to Microsoft 365 subscriptions, which provide more storage space than the free tier.

**Get the OneDrive mobile app** will allow you to download the app OneDrive App if you haven't already done so.

# Linking your Phone

You can link your smartphone—whether it's an Android device or an iPhone—to your Windows 11 PC using the Phone Link app. Once connected, you can view and respond to text messages, access recent photos, receive notifications, and even make calls. While iPhone support is available, it is currently limited to basic features like sending and receiving messages and calls via Bluetooth. For the full Phone Link experience, an Android phone running version 8.0 or later is recommended.

The first thing you'll need to do is open the 'phone link' app on your PC. Open the start menu, select 'all apps'. Scroll down to the bottom, then select 'phone link'.

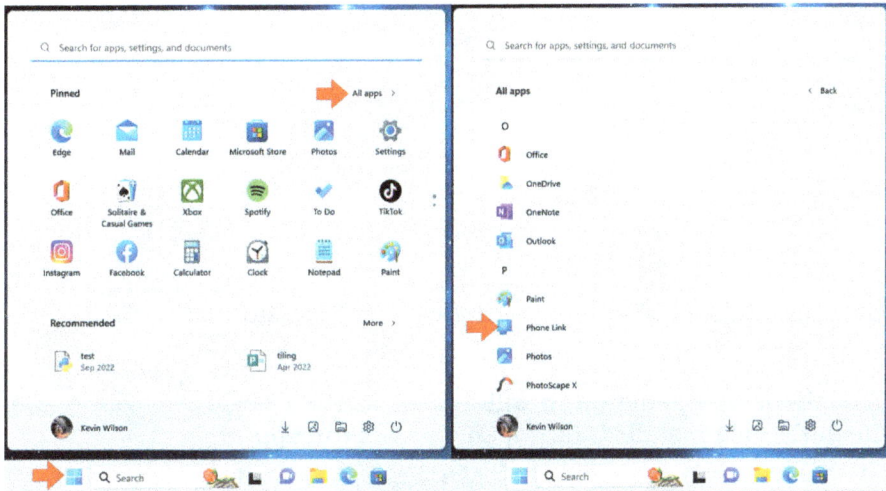

Select your type of phone: Android or iPhone. In this example, I'm using an Android phone.

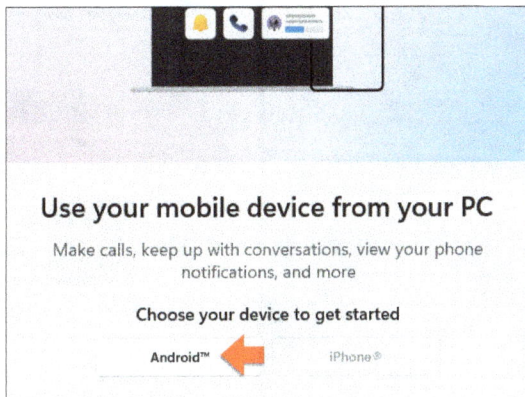

Sign in with your Microsoft Account if prompted. You'll see a QR code appear on your screen.

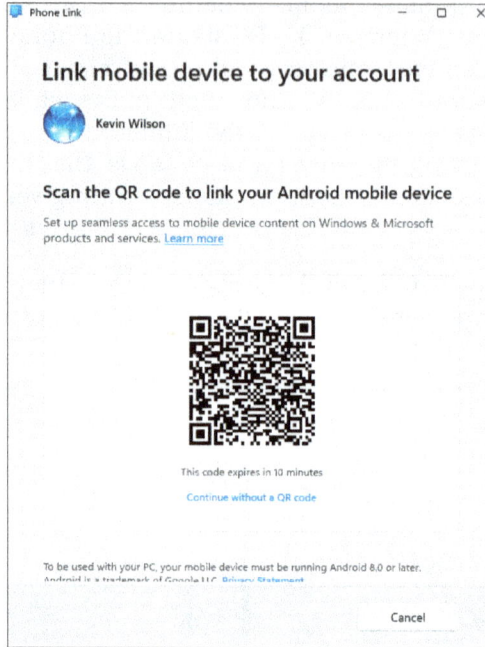

On your Android phone, go to the Google Play Store, search for `Link to Windows`, and install it.

The phone companion app will appear in the Google Play Store. Tap 'install'. Once installed, tap 'open' to start the app.

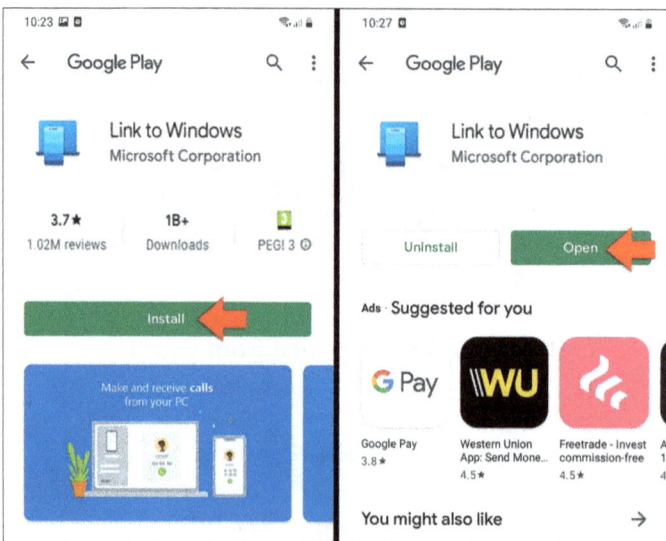

Once installed, open the app and sign in using the same Microsoft account as your PC. Tap Link your phone and PC.

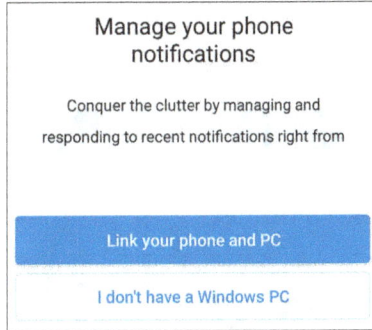

Scan the code on your PC's screen with your phone.

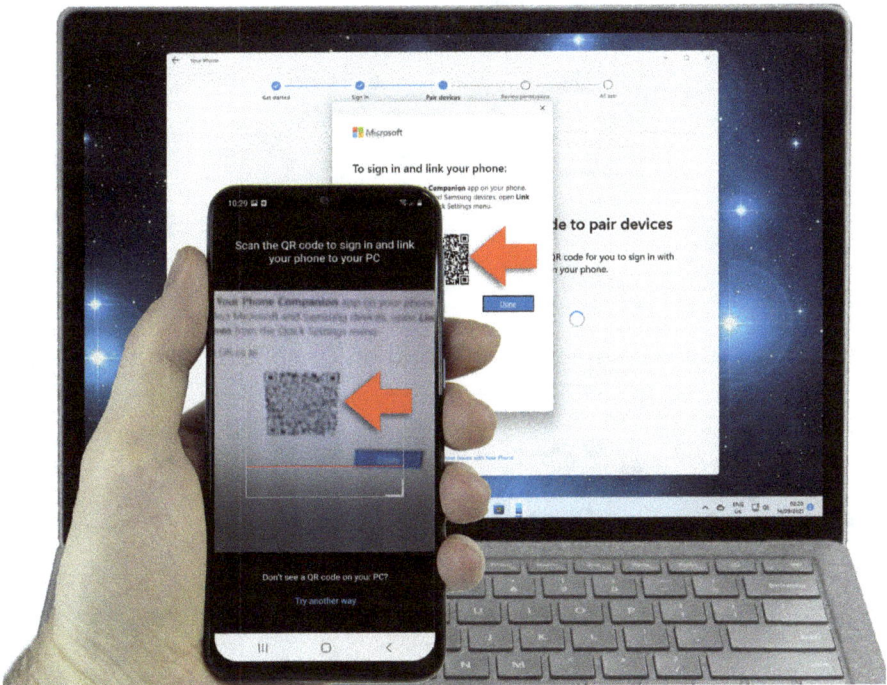

Tap Continue and Allow all permission requests (contacts, calls, SMS, photos, and notification access) to unlock all features.

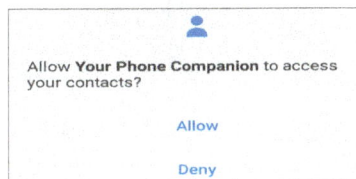

**127**

Tap 'done' to finish.

Now, on your PC, click 'continue';

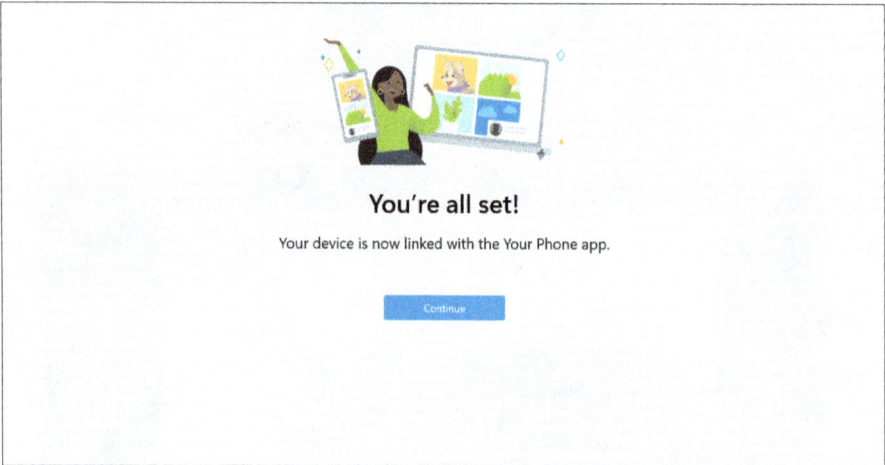

When the setup is complete, you'll land on the phone link home page.

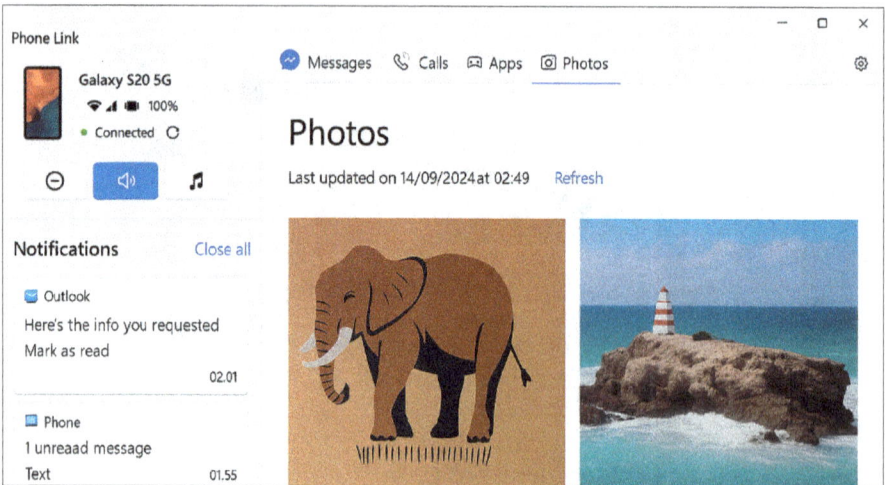

See "Phone Link" on page 364 for information on how to use Phone Link.

# Dynamic Lock

Dynamic lock allows you to automatically lock and unlock your PC using a paired bluetooth device - usually an Android phone. For this to work, you first need to pair your phone with your PC using bluetooth.

## Pair your Phone

Before activating the dynamic lock, you will first need to pair your device or phone with your PC or laptop via Bluetooth. To do this open your settings app and select 'bluetooth & devices'. Then in the right hand side, click 'add device'.

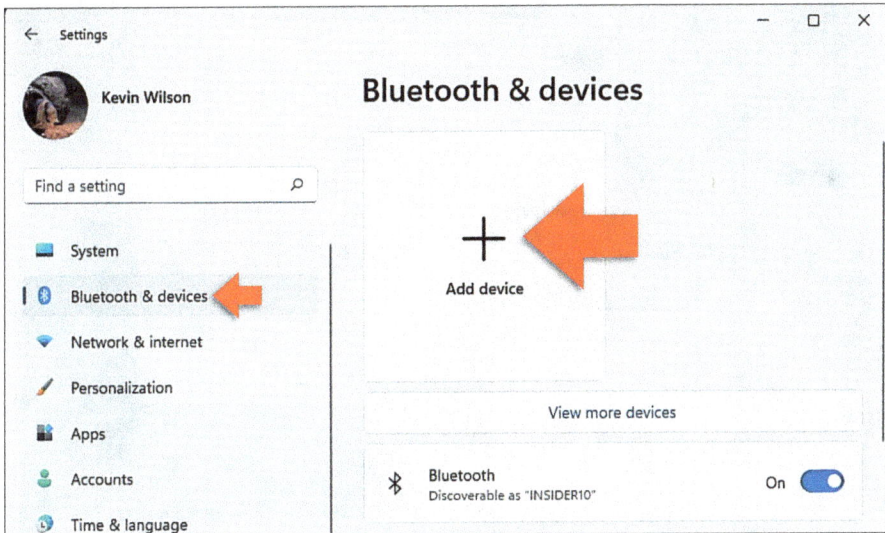

From the 'add a device' dialog box, select 'bluetooth'.

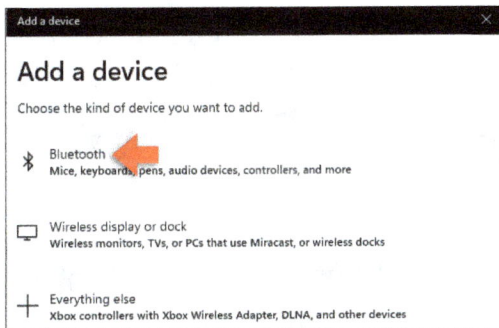

Windows will scan for your phone. Make sure your phone is turned on and unlocked. Open the bluetooth settings on your phone.

**129**

Give your PC a minute to detect your phone. Select the device from the list.

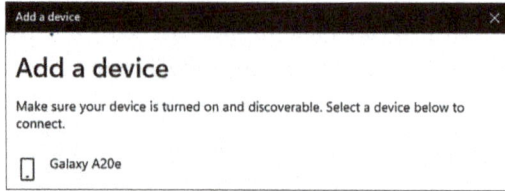

**Add a device**

Make sure your device is turned on and discoverable. Select a device below to connect.

Galaxy A20e

Windows will generate a code once your phone has been detected. Enter this code into your phone and tap 'pair'. .

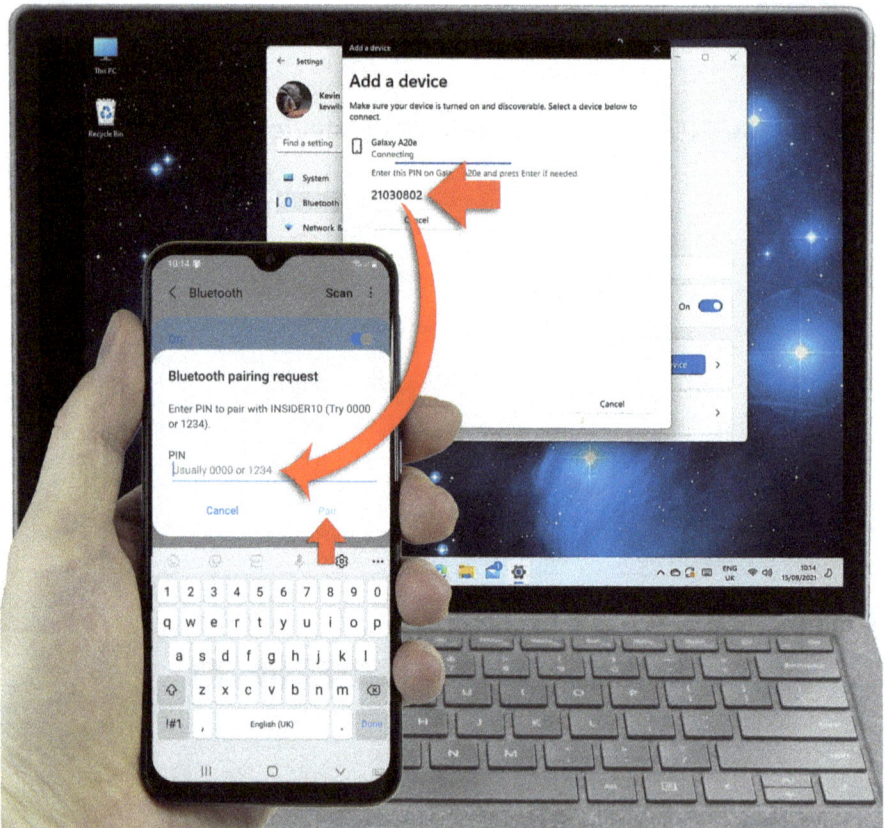

If you're having a bit of trouble connecting, try rebooting both devices.

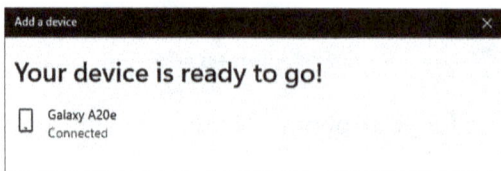

**Your device is ready to go!**

Galaxy A20e
Connected

# Enable Dynamic Lock

To enable dynamic lock, open the settings app, select 'accounts' from the list on the left, then click 'sign-in options'. Scroll down to 'dynamic lock'

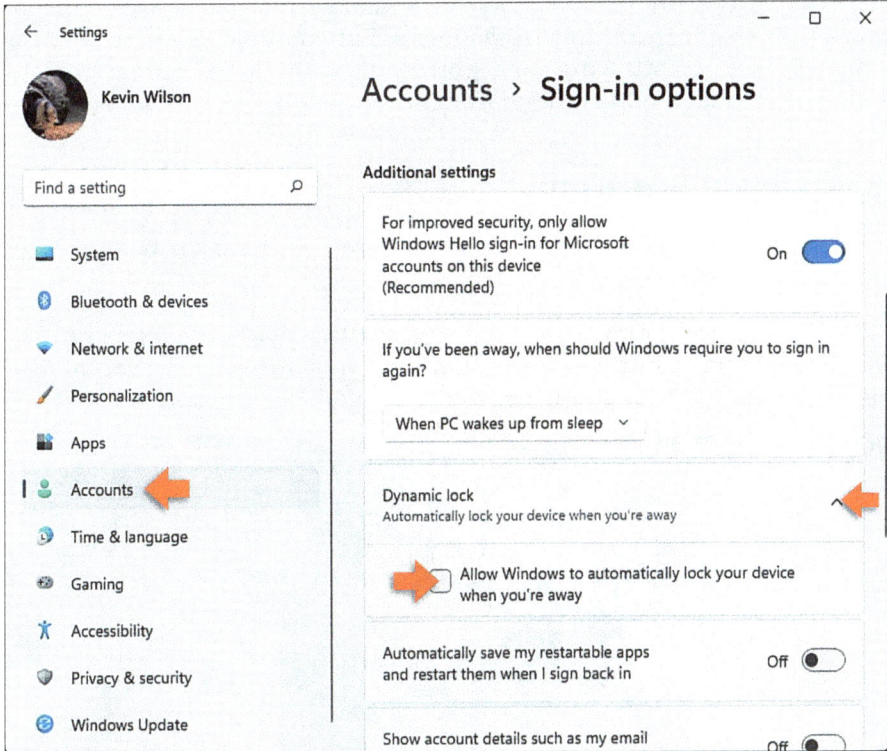

Tick the box next to 'Allow Windows to detect when you're away and automatically lock the device.'

When you move your phone away from your PC, it will automatically lock a minute or so after you're out of range.

**131**

# Focus Mode

Focus mode allows you to silence notifications during a period of time, so you can focus on your work without distraction. You can do this by setting a focus timer to create a focus session with a set amount of time, such as an hour. A focus session allows you to set aside time for work that requires uninterrupted focus. For example, if you're working on a project, or studying, and you don't want to be interrupted by email or message notifications from other people.

## Starting a Session

To start a focus session click on the date and time on bottom-right corner of the screen

Along the bottom of the panel, you'll see a timer and the focus button. Use the '+' and '-' buttons to set how long you want the session to last, for example, 60 minutes. Click 'focus' to start the session.

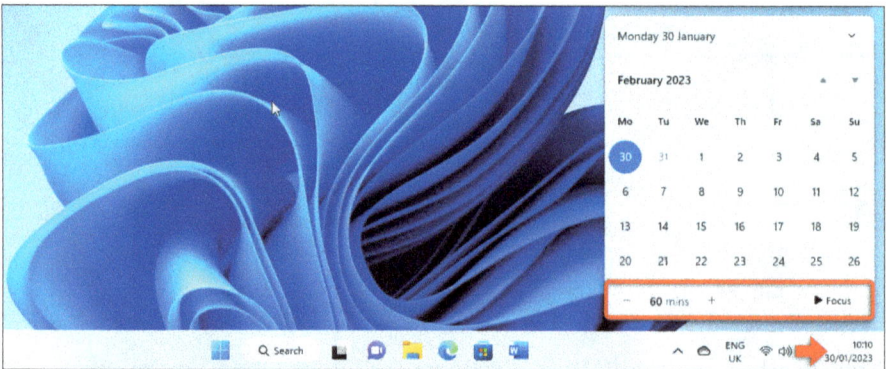

You'll see a focus panel appear, counting down the minutes of the session. Click the icon on the top left of to open the panel in the clock app.

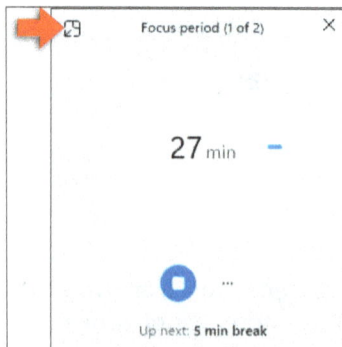

In the section on the top left, you'll see your focus period, this is a count down timer that will count down the remaining time. On the top right, you will see your progress and daily goals etc.

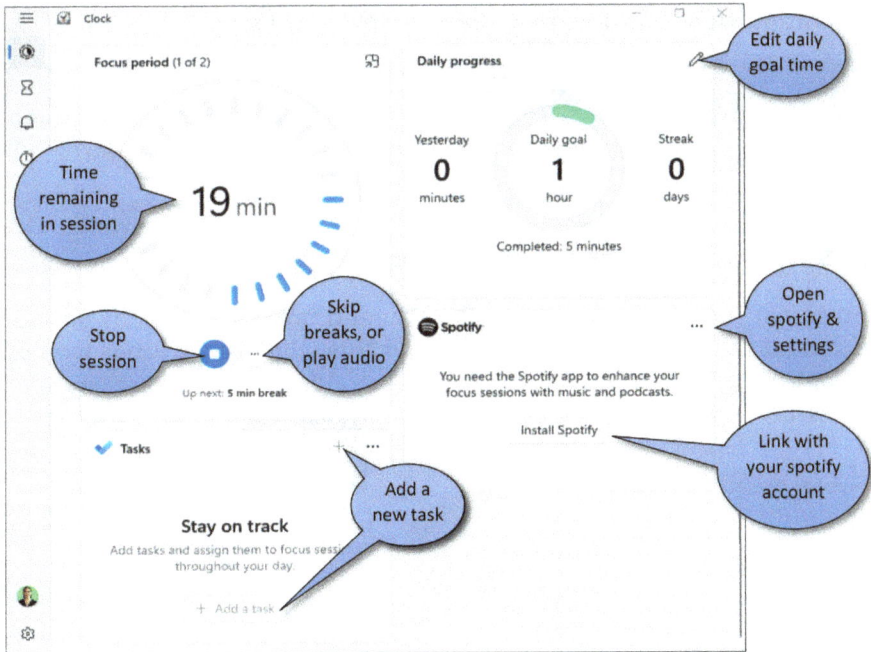

Along the bottom, you can use Microsoft To Do, to assign tasks to be completed during the focus session to help keep you on track. To do this, just click on 'add task' then enter the task name. To add additional tasks, click the '+' icon at the top of the 'tasks' section.

You can also play relaxing music while you work using spotify. To do this, click 'install spotify'. Follow the steps on screen to either sign in or open a new account. Once spotify is installed, you can select from certain relaxing tracks to play.

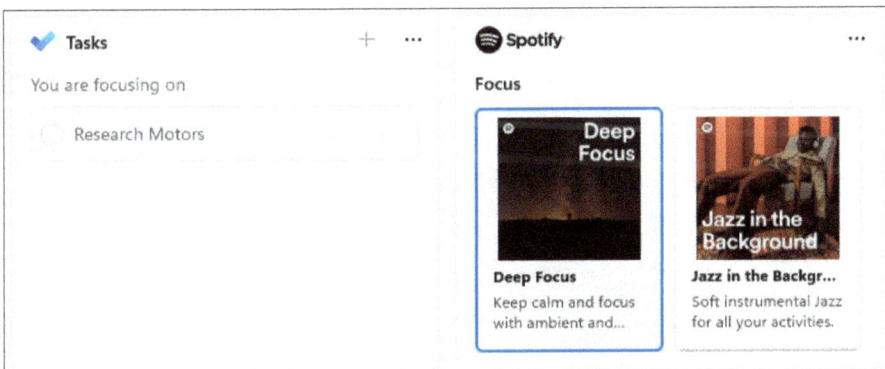

If you need to reopen the session, open the clock app from the start menu.

If you want to end a focus session early, click on the time and date on the bottom right hand corner, then click 'end session'.

# Customising Focus Sessions

You can adjust the focus session length, add breaks, or set any sounds effects for notifications or alarms. To do this, click the settings icon on the bottom left of the clock app.

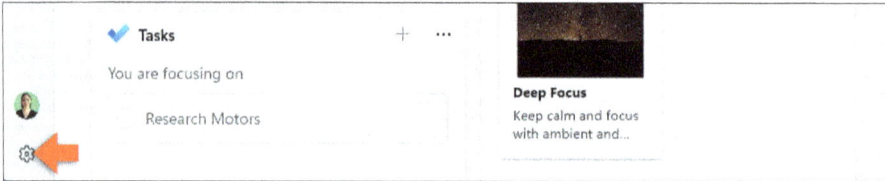

## Allowing & Customising Notifications

You can change the maximum focus period lengths for before a break. For example, you can set the focus period to 30 mins before a break, or 1 hour before a break. In the field below, you can select the length of time for each break, for example, 5 mins, 10 mins and so on.

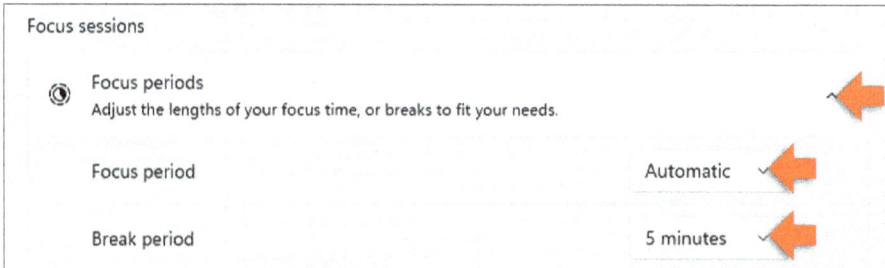

Next, you can set what sound effect to play when your session ends.

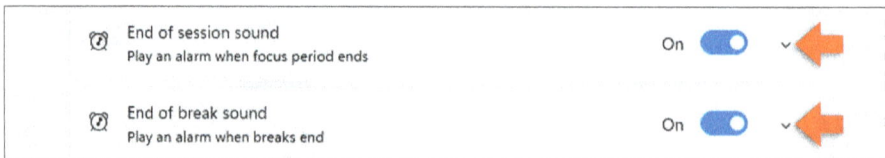

You can enable or disable the Spotify and To Do panels. Just click on the switch to enable/disable.

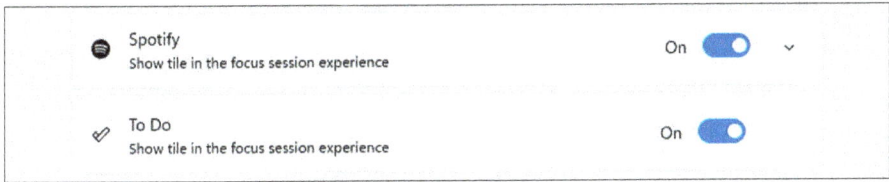

| | | | |
|---|---|---|---|
| ● | **Spotify** Show tile in the focus session experience | On ⬤ | ⌄ |
| ✐ | **To Do** Show tile in the focus session experience | On ⬤ | |

Click the small arrow to change your spotify settings

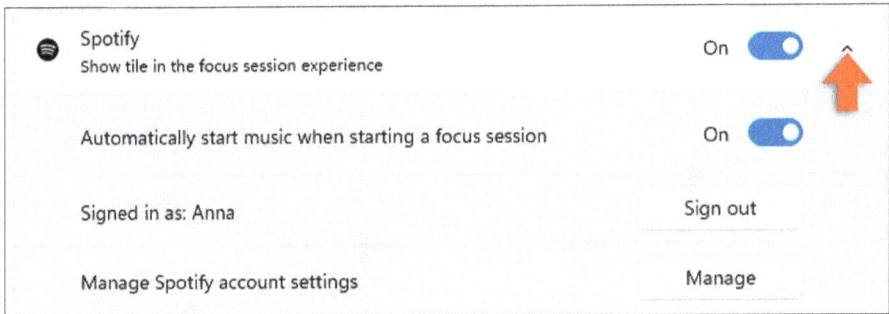

| | | |
|---|---|---|
| ● | **Spotify** Show tile in the focus session experience | On ⬤ ⌃ |
| | Automatically start music when starting a focus session | On ⬤ |
| | Signed in as: Anna | Sign out |
| | Manage Spotify account settings | Manage |

Scroll down and click 'change notification settings' to enable or disable specific notifications while you're in a focus session.

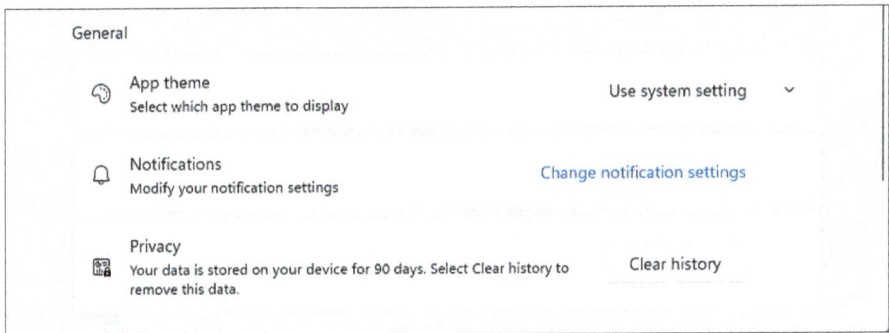

General

| | | |
|---|---|---|
| ☾ | **App theme** Select which app theme to display | Use system setting ⌄ |
| 🔔 | **Notifications** Modify your notification settings | Change notification settings |
| 🖼 | **Privacy** Your data is stored on your device for 90 days. Select Clear history to remove this data. | Clear history |

Click 'set priority notifications' to choose the notifications you can want to receive.

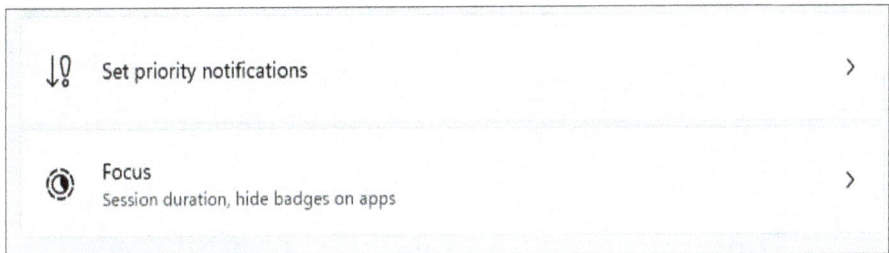

| | | |
|---|---|---|
| ↓♪ | **Set priority notifications** | ❯ |
| ◐ | **Focus** Session duration, hide badges on apps | ❯ |

**135**

# Chapter 3: Settings and Personalisation

Under 'calls and reminders' you can allow/disallow incoming calls or reminders that will interrupt your session. Untick the boxes to prevent incoming calls and reminders

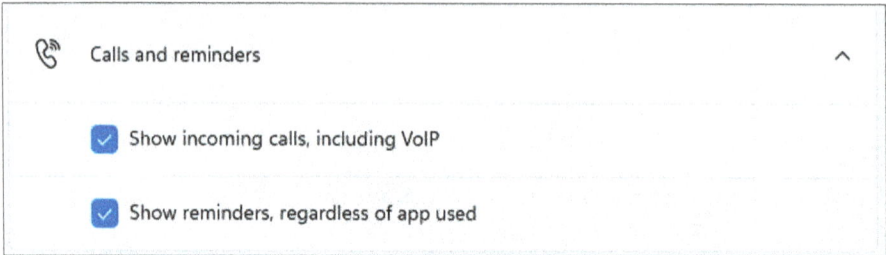

| | | |
|---|---|---|
| 📞 | Calls and reminders | ∧ |
| | ☑ Show incoming calls, including VoIP | |
| | ☑ Show reminders, regardless of app used | |

Any apps listed under the 'apps' section will also interrupt your session. To add apps, click on 'add apps', then select the app from the list.

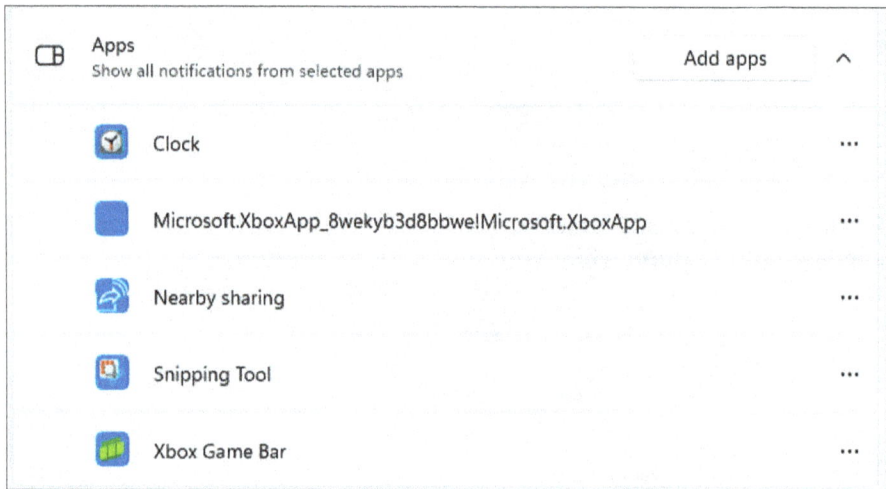

| | | | |
|---|---|---|---|
| ▢ | Apps<br>Show all notifications from selected apps | Add apps | ∧ |
| 🕐 | Clock | | ••• |
| 🟦 | Microsoft.XboxApp_8wekyb3d8bbwe!Microsoft.XboxApp | | ••• |
| 📶 | Nearby sharing | | ••• |
| 📷 | Snipping Tool | | ••• |
| 📊 | Xbox Game Bar | | ••• |

To remove apps from the list, click on the three dots icon to the right of the app in the list, then click 'remove'.

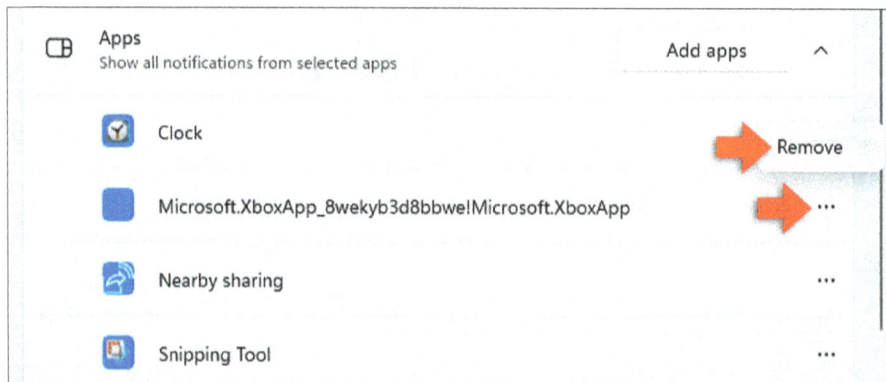

| | | | |
|---|---|---|---|
| ▢ | Apps<br>Show all notifications from selected apps | Add apps | ∧ |
| 🕐 | Clock | | Remove |
| 🟦 | Microsoft.XboxApp_8wekyb3d8bbwe!Microsoft.XboxApp | | ••• |
| 📶 | Nearby sharing | | ••• |
| 📷 | Snipping Tool | | ••• |

# Notification Settings

Open the settings app, then select 'system' from the list on the left hand side. Click on 'notifications'.

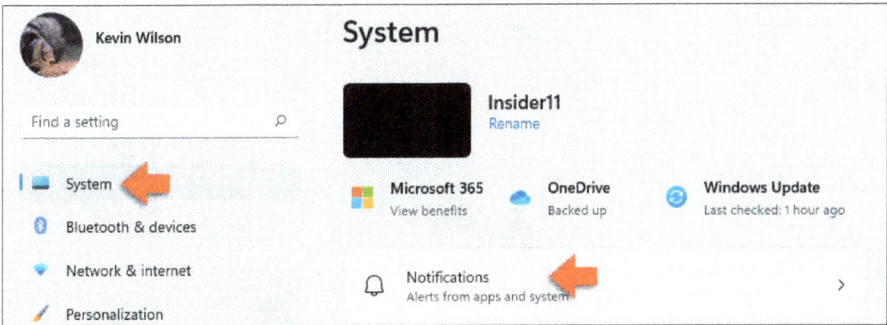

Here you can turn on/off notifications from apps.

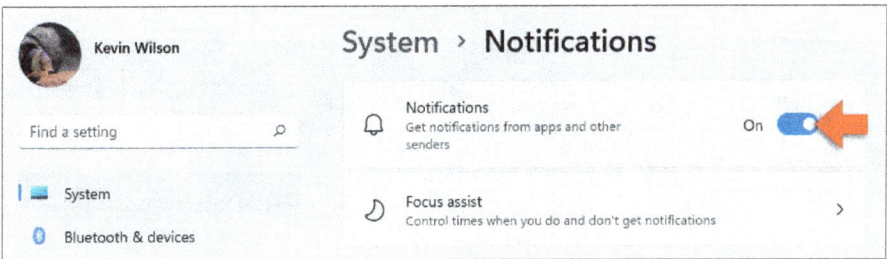

Scroll down to turn on/off individual apps. To do this, click the on/off switch.

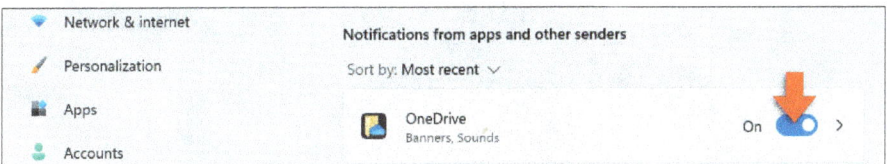

Click on the individual app to change the notification settings for that app. For example Mail.

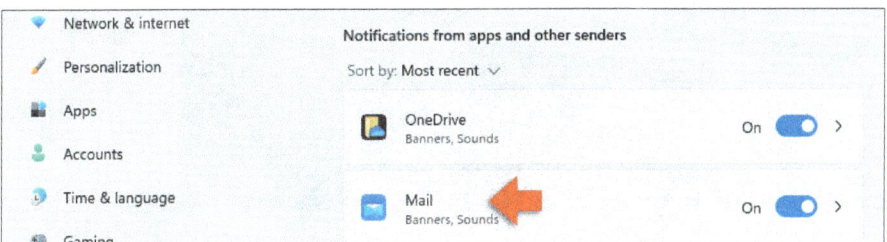

**137**

# Chapter 3: Settings and Personalisation

Here, you can turn on/off notifications for this app.

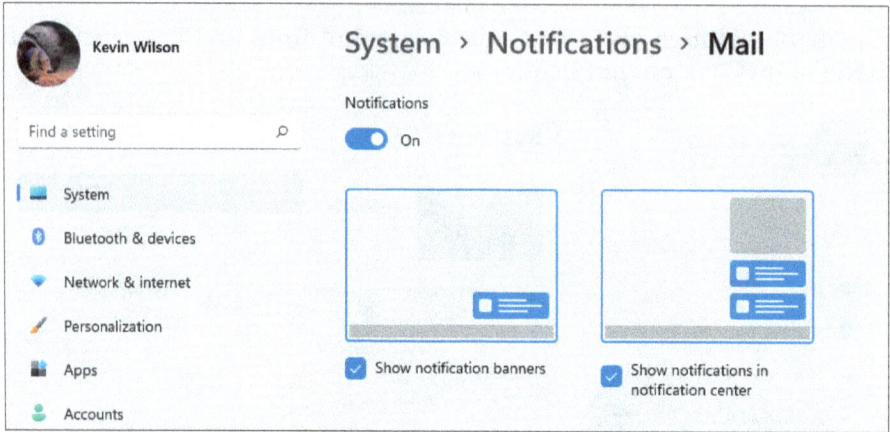

Underneath you can allow the app to show notifications on the bottom right of the desktop: "show notification banners".

Or on the notification center: "show notifications in notification center.

At the bottom, you can hide/show notifications from this app on the lock screen. Or play a sound when a notification arrives from this app. Just click on the switches to turn the features on or off.

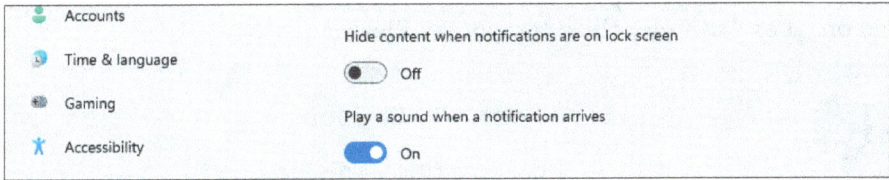

| | |
|---|---|
| Accounts | Hide content when notifications are on lock screen |
| Time & language | ⬤◯ Off |
| Gaming | Play a sound when a notification arrives |
| Accessibility | ⬤⬤ On |

Underneath, you can set the priority for this app. Top priority will always show notifications from this app at the top of the notifications, so they always appear first in the list. Useful for important apps such as reminders, email, or message.

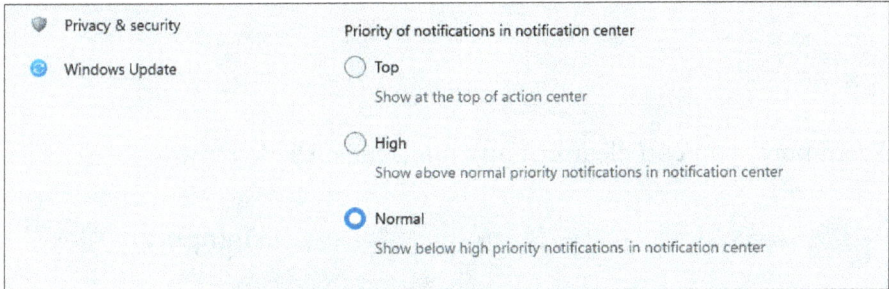

| | |
|---|---|
| Privacy & security | Priority of notifications in notification center |
| Windows Update | ◯ Top |
| | Show at the top of action center |
| | ◯ High |
| | Show above normal priority notifications in notification center |
| | ⦿ Normal |
| | Show below high priority notifications in notification center |

Apps set to 'normal' show at the bottom of the list in notification center. Apps set to 'high' show above any apps set to 'normal'.

# Storage Sense

Over time, temporary files, caches and files in the recycle bin start to accumulate. Storage sense monitors and deletes these files, keeping your system running smoothly. To find storage sense, open the settings app and select system on the left hand side. Click on 'storage'.

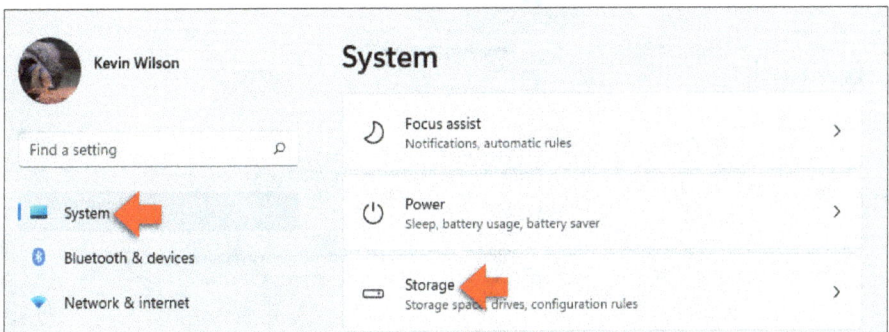

| Kevin Wilson | **System** | |
|---|---|---|
| Find a setting 🔍 | 🌙 Focus assist<br>Notifications, automatic rules | > |
| 🖥 System ⬅ | ⏻ Power<br>Sleep, battery usage, battery saver | > |
| 🔵 Bluetooth & devices | | |
| 📶 Network & internet | 🔲 Storage ⬅<br>Storage space, drives, configuration rules | > |

**139**

## Chapter 3: Settings and Personalisation

Scroll further down the page and you'll see your hard disk drive and various categories. This is a breakdown of how your storage is being used. You'll see space allocated to 'system & reserved' such as system files. You'll also see space allocated to 'apps & features', temp files and so on. For example, click 'temporary files'

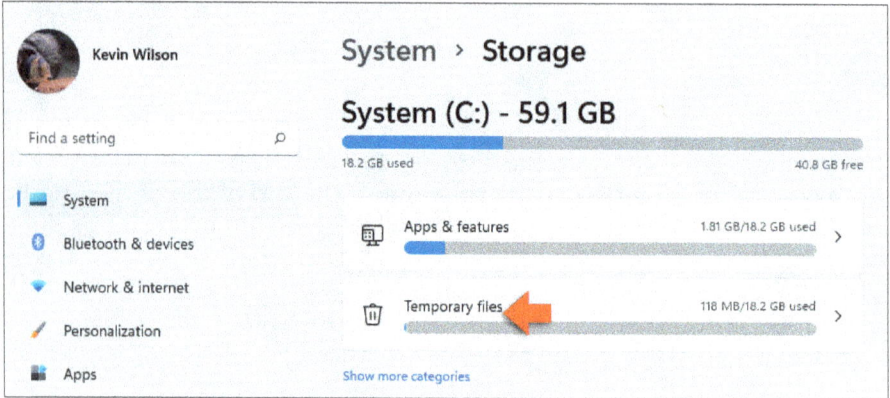

From here, you can clear out any temp files. Click 'remove files'.

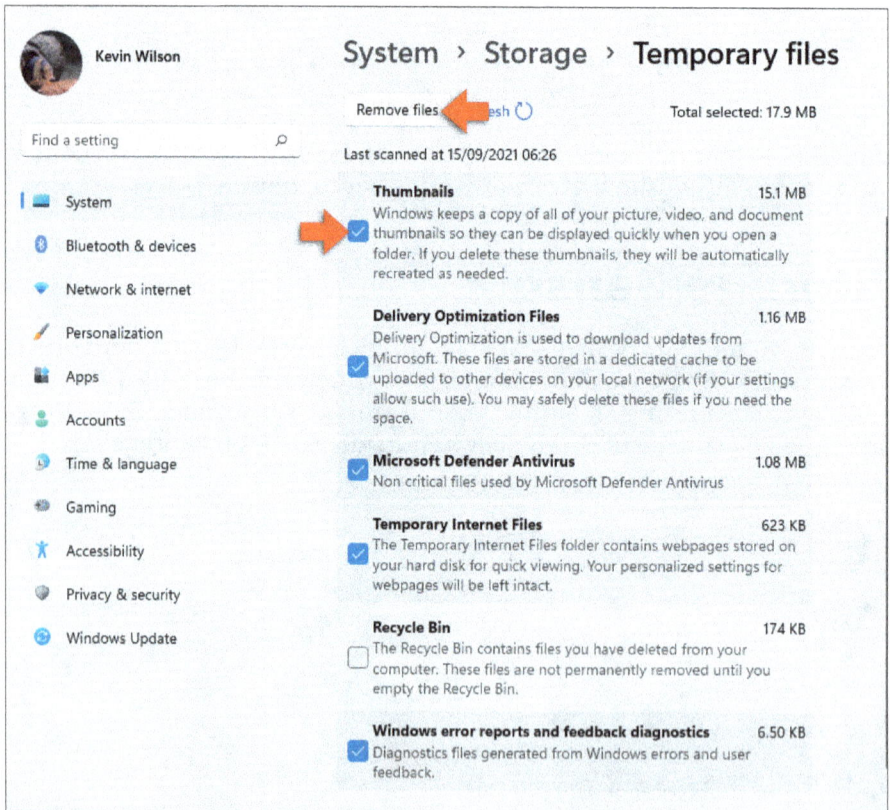

# Configure Storage Sense

Open the settings app and select system.

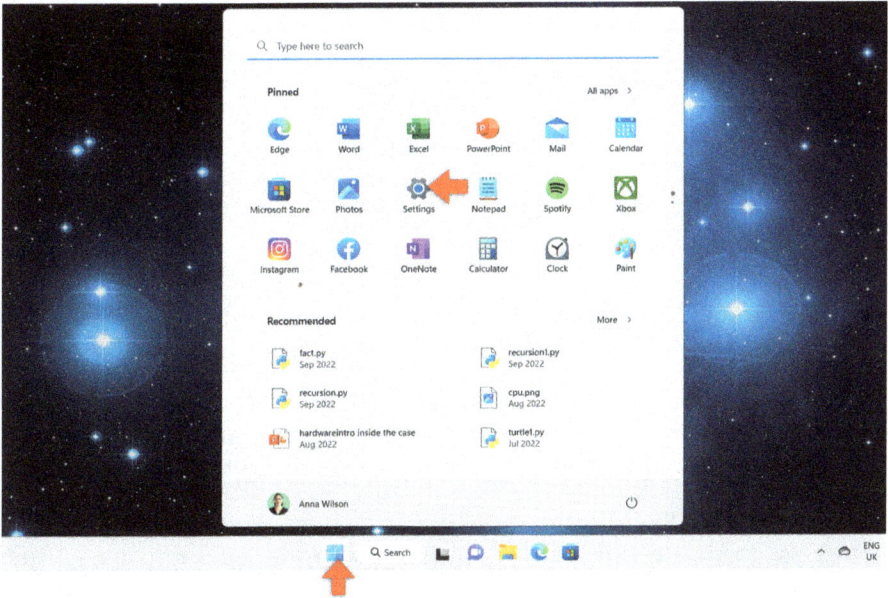

On the left hand panel select 'storage'. Click 'configure storage sense or run it now'.

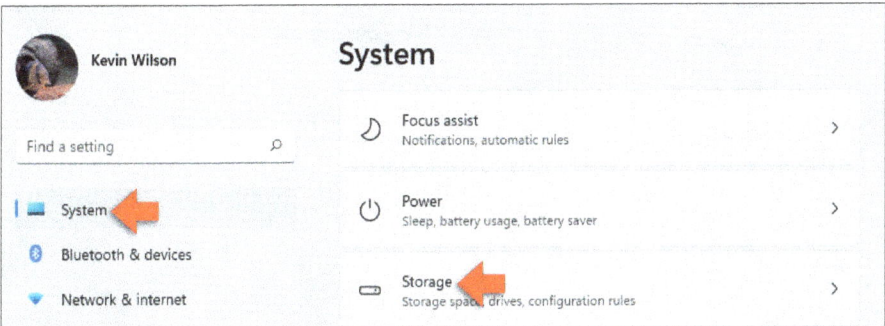

Click the switch to turn on 'storage sense', then click on 'storage sense'.

# Chapter 3: Settings and Personalisation

Under the 'temporary files' section, make sure there is a tick next to 'keep windows running smoothly'. This helps to automatically clean up system files

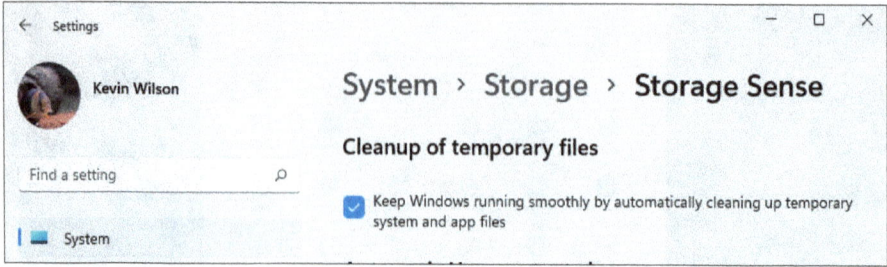

Under 'automatic user content cleanup', set 'run storage sense to 'once a month'. This will help to clear up temporary files.

Set 'delete files in my recycle bin' to '30 days'. This will ensure your recycle bin is cleared once a month. You can also set this to 'never' if you prefer not to clear the bin, or want to clear the bin yourself.

Set 'delete files in downloads folder' to 'never'. I don't usually allow Windows to delete files in my downloads folder, as sometimes I like to reuse or keep things I have downloaded from the web. However if you don't do this, then you can allow Windows to delete files in your downloads folder after a certain number of days - usually 30 days is a good setting.

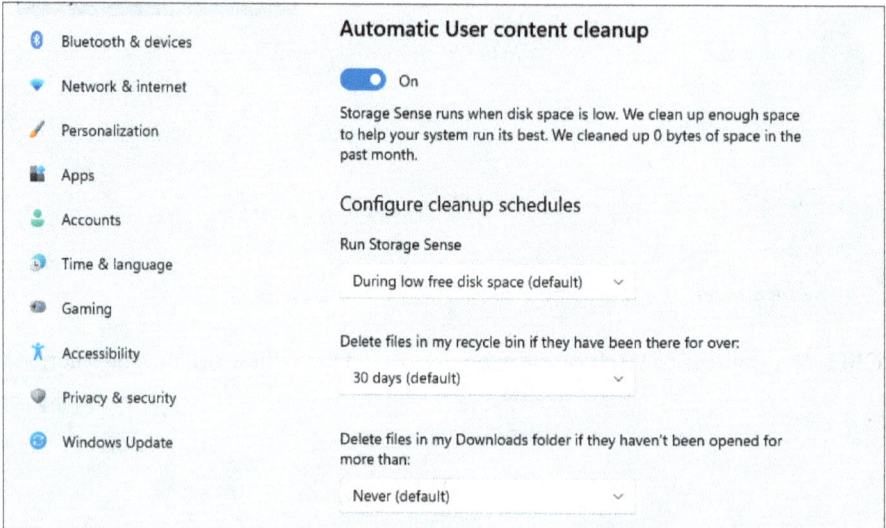

I have found this strategy works well for me. You can tweak the settings to find what works best for you.

Scroll down to the bottom of the page. Locally available cloud content is usually used when OneDrive's 'Files on Demand' feature is enabled. This allows storage sense to remove files from your device that have not been used in a while. These files are however still available on OneDrive - just not physically on your device. To be safe, set this feature to 'never'.

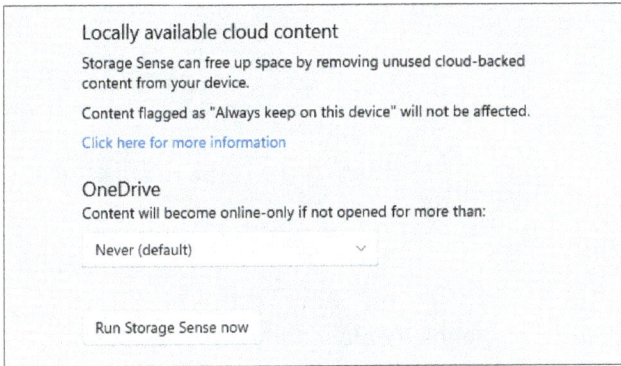

Locally available cloud content

Storage Sense can free up space by removing unused cloud-backed content from your device.

Content flagged as "Always keep on this device" will not be affected.

Click here for more information

OneDrive

Content will become online-only if not opened for more than:

Never (default)

Run Storage Sense now

Once you're done, click 'run storage sense now'. Windows will automatically clear temporary files.

# Cleanup Recommendations

Cleanup Recommendations is a feature designed to automate the process of identifying unused files, uninstalling unused apps, and clearing temporary files in order to free up hard drive space on your PC.

To view these recommendations under the 'storage management' section.

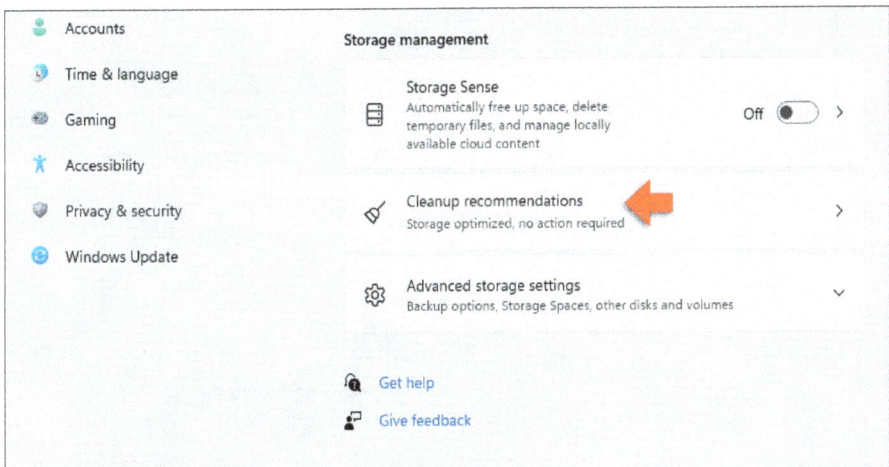

Accounts

Time & language

Gaming

Accessibility

Privacy & security

Windows Update

Storage management

Storage Sense
Automatically free up space, delete temporary files, and manage locally available cloud content                Off

Cleanup recommendations
Storage optimized, no action required

Advanced storage settings
Backup options, Storage Spaces, other disks and volumes

Get help

Give feedback

**143**

Here, you'll see a list of temporary files you can clean up. To see all the options click 'see advanced options'.

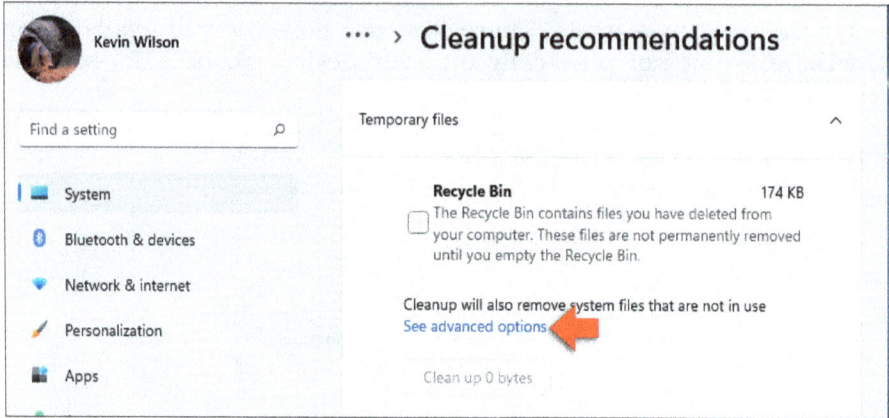

Select all the options, click 'remove files' to clear them.

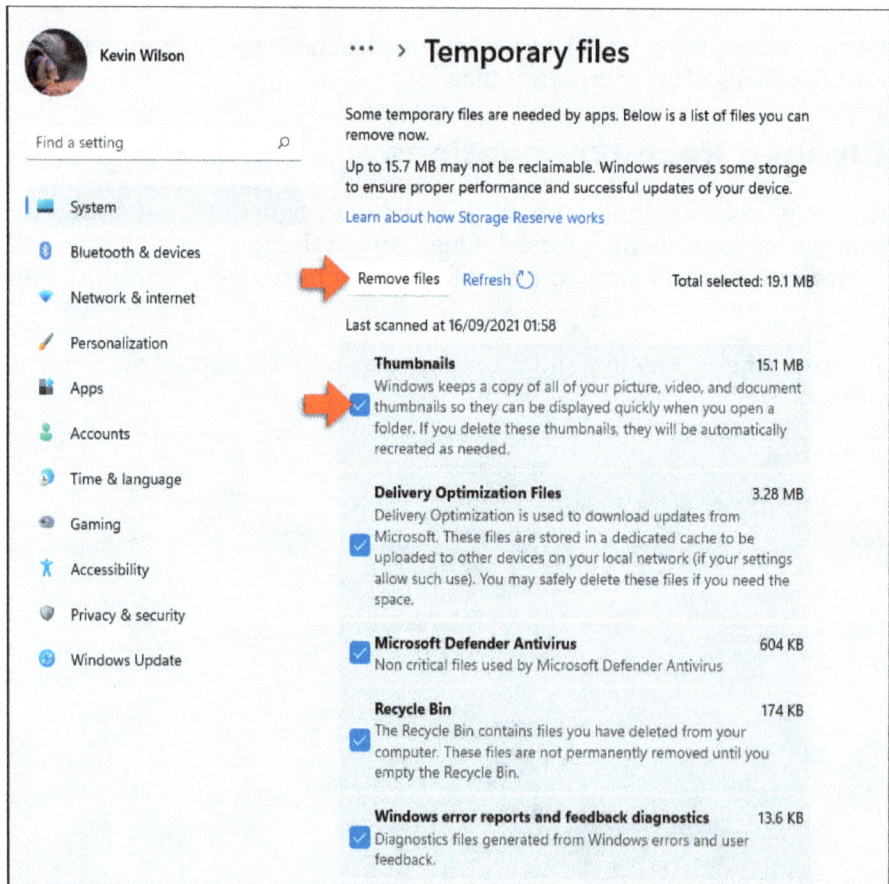

Click the back arrow on the top left of the screen to return to cleanup recommendations.

Further down the page, you'll see recommendations for removing large or unused files, synced files, and unused apps.

Click on 'large or unused files'. Look at the dates to see when you last used the file. Click the tickbox next to the filename. *Warning! This will delete these files, make sure you don't need them. If in doubt, leave the file un-ticked.* Click 'clean up' to remove selected files.

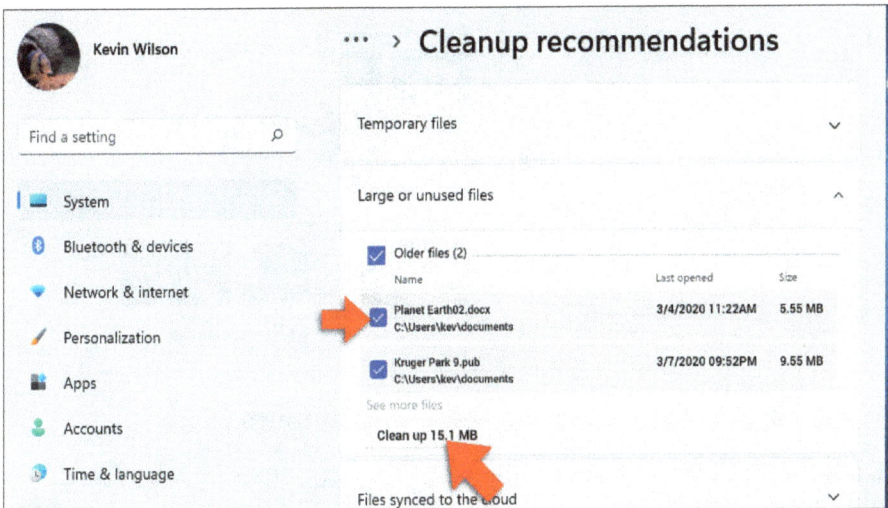

Click on 'unused apps'. Look at the date to see when you last used the app. Click the tickbox on the apps you don't use. Click 'clean up'.

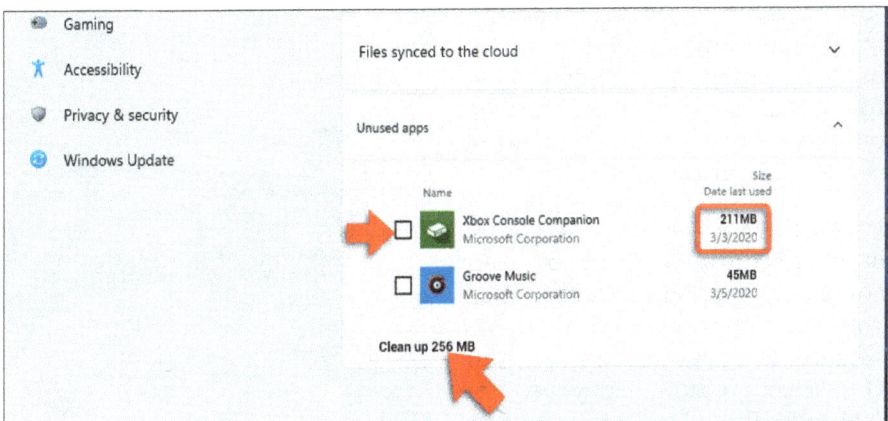

# Search Settings

You can customise the search settings. To do this, click the search field on the taskbar.

Click the three dots icon on the top right. Select 'search settings' from the drop down menu

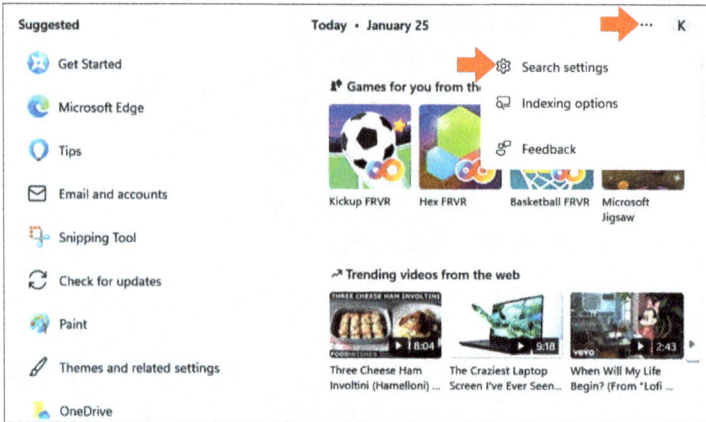

You'll land on the permissions and history settings page.

Under 'SafeSearch' you can filter out web search results. This means you can remove adult images and text from web sites that appear in windows search results. This is set to 'moderate' by default, and only filters out images, but you can also set it to 'strict' if you have children or don't want to see any adult content including text.

If you have a Microsoft Account, or an account supplied by your company, school/college, then you can control whether windows search can search files on your OneDrive, email, photos, or messages linked to your accounts.

**SafeSearch**

In Windows Search, web previews will not automatically load web results if they may contain adult content. If you choose to preview web results, we'll apply the following setting:

○ Strict — Filter out adult text, images, and videos from my web results

● Moderate — Filter adult images and videos but not text from my web results

○ Off — Don't filter adult content from my web results

**Cloud content search**

Windows Search can personalise your search results by including your content from OneDrive, SharePoint, Outlook, Bing, and other services.

Microsoft account

Allow Windows Search to provide results from the apps and services that you are signed in to with your Microsoft account.

🔵 On

Work or School account

Allow Windows Search to provide results from the apps and services that you are signed in to with your work or school account.

🔵 On

**146**

Further down the page, you'll see search history. You can turn this on or off using the switch. To clear the search history, click 'clear device search history'.

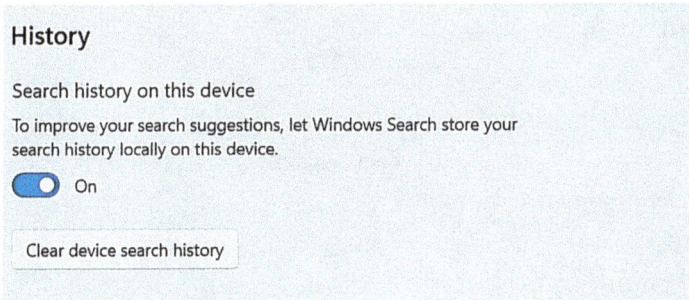

**History**

Search history on this device

To improve your search suggestions, let Windows Search store your search history locally on this device.

On

Clear device search history

The search history allows windows search to save previous searches. You'll see these on the search screen.

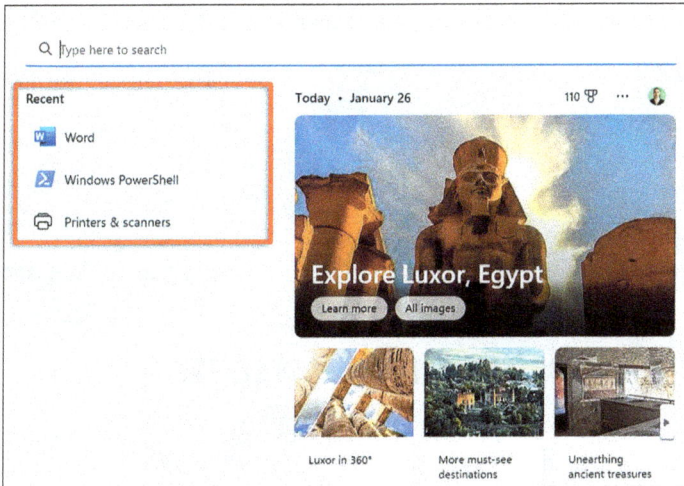

Q Type here to search

Recent

Word

Windows PowerShell

Printers & scanners

Today • January 26    110 ⚐ ··· 

Explore Luxor, Egypt

Learn more    All images

Luxor in 360°    More must-see destinations    Unearthing ancient treasures

Scroll down to the bottom of the search settings page, you'll see a section called 'more settings'. Show search highlights will show trending web searches and areas of interest on the right hand side of the search window

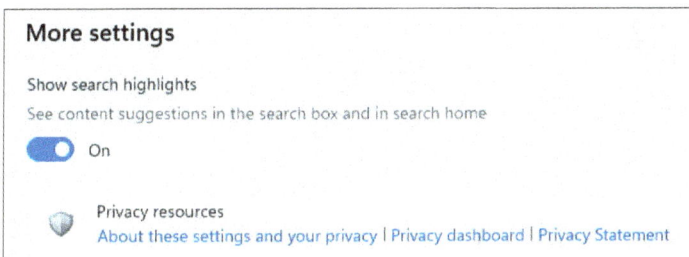

**More settings**

Show search highlights

See content suggestions in the search box and in search home

On

Privacy resources

About these settings and your privacy | Privacy dashboard | Privacy Statement

If you turn off 'show search highlights', this will remove the highlights. Instead on the right of the search window, you'll see common quick searches you can use to search for common settings you've used before. Underneath you'll find a list of 'top apps', this is a list of your most used apps.

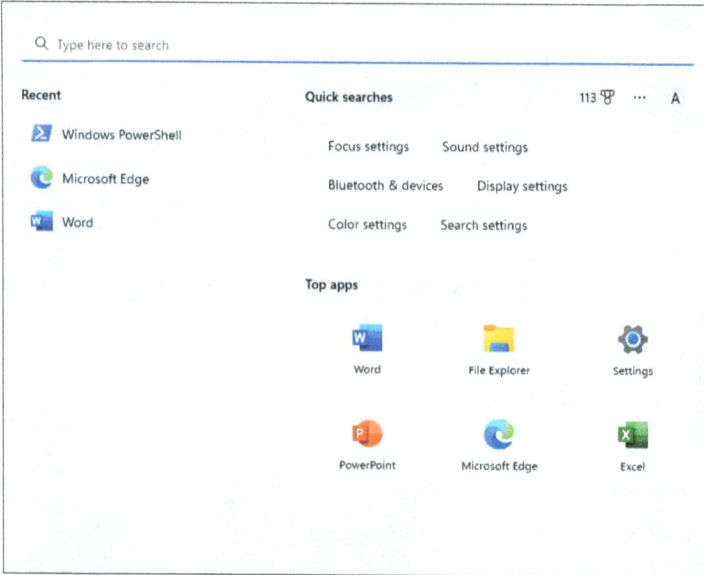

I find this setup a lot more useful than showing the highlights.

# Search Indexing Options

You can change how Windows indexes files on your machine. You can add network locations, other drives, folders and so on. To adjust the indexing options, click the three dots icon on the top right of the search screen.

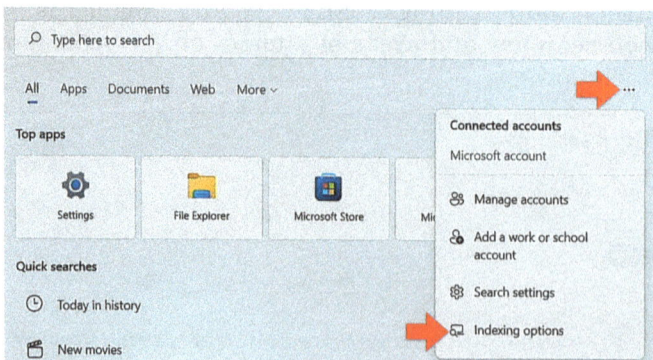

Under 'find my files' you'll see two modes. Classic mode is the default and will only index files in your own profile folders such as documents, desktop, as well as apps on your start menu. Enhanced mode turns on indexing for all files and apps on other drives and on other folders but doesn't search the content of the files. For most situations, classic mode is best.

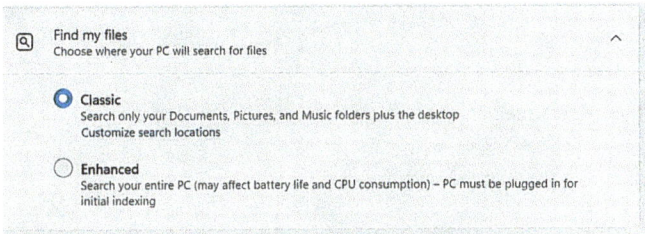

You can add locations to this search if you want to include other drives. To do this click 'customise search locations' under the 'classic' option.

Here, you'll see a list of folders windows search will index. Click 'modify' to add or remove folders.

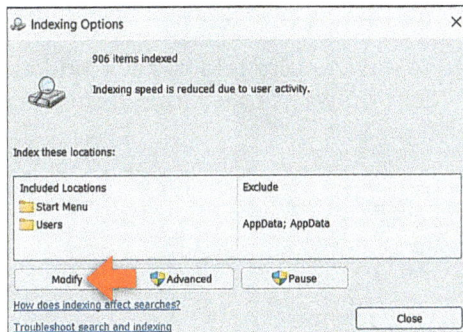

On the 'indexed locations' dialog box, select the folders to include. Click 'ok'.

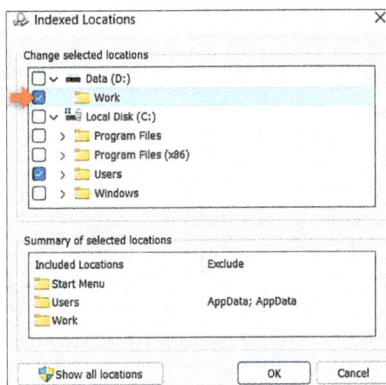

# Chapter 3: Settings and Personalisation

You can also choose which folders to exclude from the search. These are usually folders that contain temporary data, caches and other folders that don't contain any useful information. As you can see in the settings below, these folders are program data.

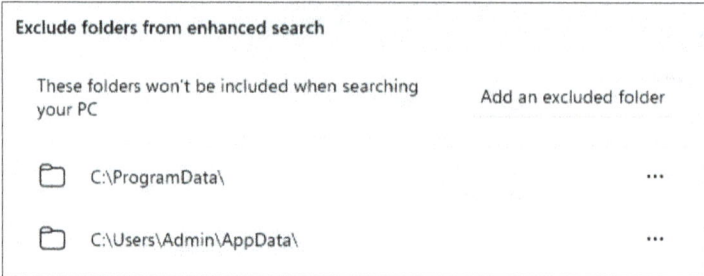

If you want to remove a folder, click the three dots icon next to the folder, then select 'remove'.

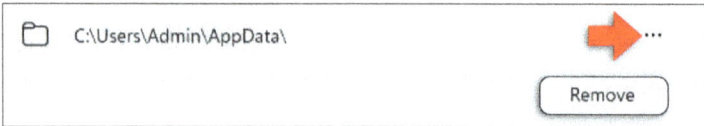

If you want to exclude a particular folder, click 'add an excluded folder', then choose the folder you want to exclude from the search.

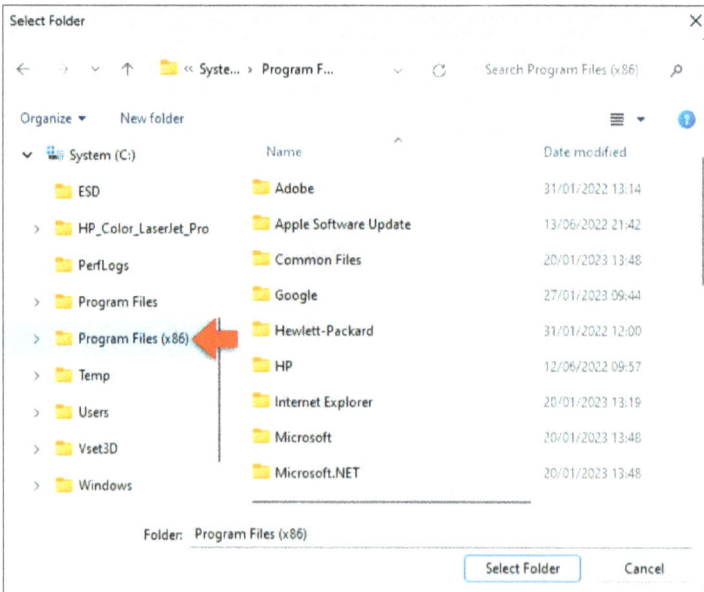

Click 'select folder'. This will add the folder to the exclusion list and windows won't search this folder.

# Fonts

You can download and install new fonts. This is useful if you are a designer or want a different font for a document you are working on.

You can download endless types of fonts from various websites on the internet. Many of these are free, but there are one or two you'd have to pay for. Here are a few useful sites offering fonts to download.

```
fonts.google.com
www.dafont.com
www.fontsquirrel.com
```

To install fonts you have downloaded, open File Explorer, then select your 'downloads' folder from the left hand side.

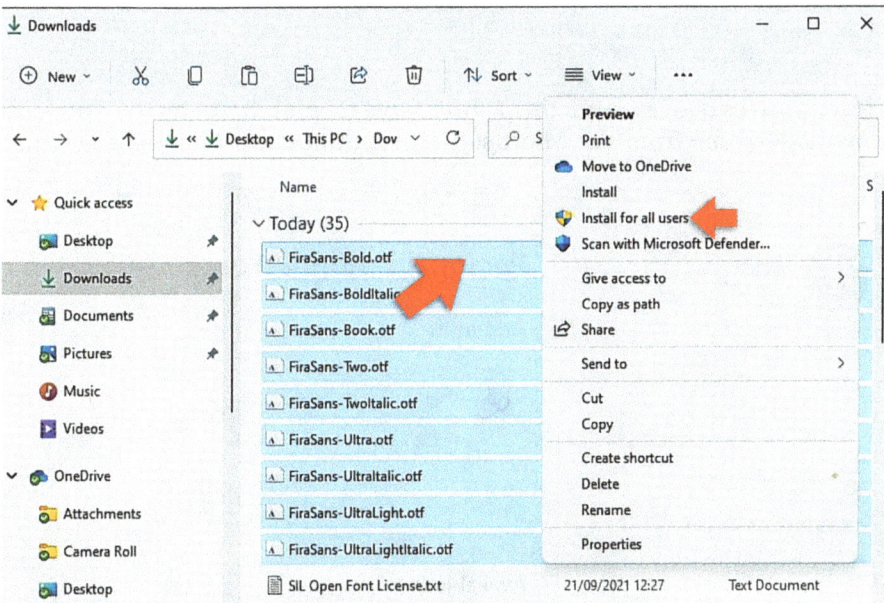

Select all the font files you have downloaded, right click on the selection, click 'show more options', then select 'install for all users'.

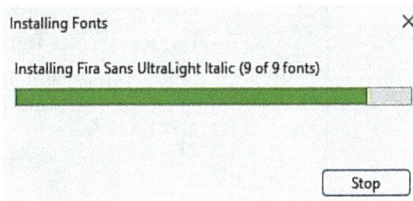

Allow the fonts to install.

# Chapter 3: Settings and Personalisation

You can see all your installed fonts using the settings app. Click the settings app icon on your start menu and select 'personalisation'. Select 'fonts' from the list.

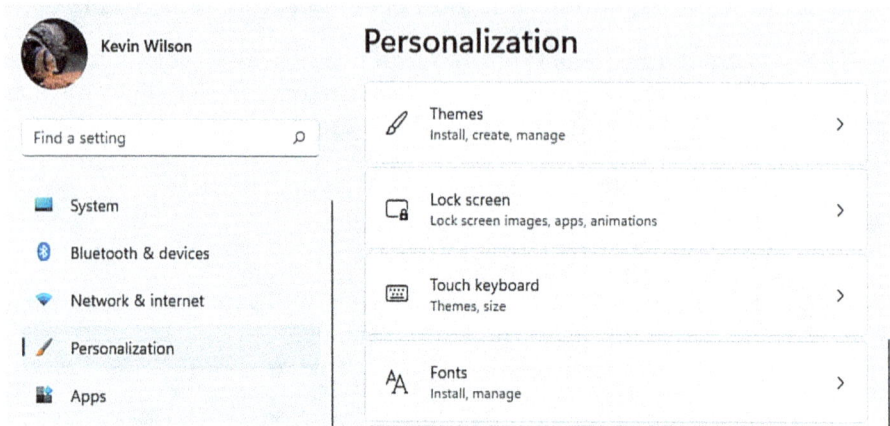

**Kevin Wilson**

## Personalization

Find a setting

- System
- Bluetooth & devices
- Network & internet
- Personalization
- Apps

| | Themes<br>Install, create, manage | > |
|---|---|---|
| | Lock screen<br>Lock screen images, apps, animations | > |
| | Touch keyboard<br>Themes, size | > |
| AA | Fonts<br>Install, manage | > |

Here, you can drag and drop font files to install them, or you can download some from the Microsoft store. Just click 'Microsoft store'

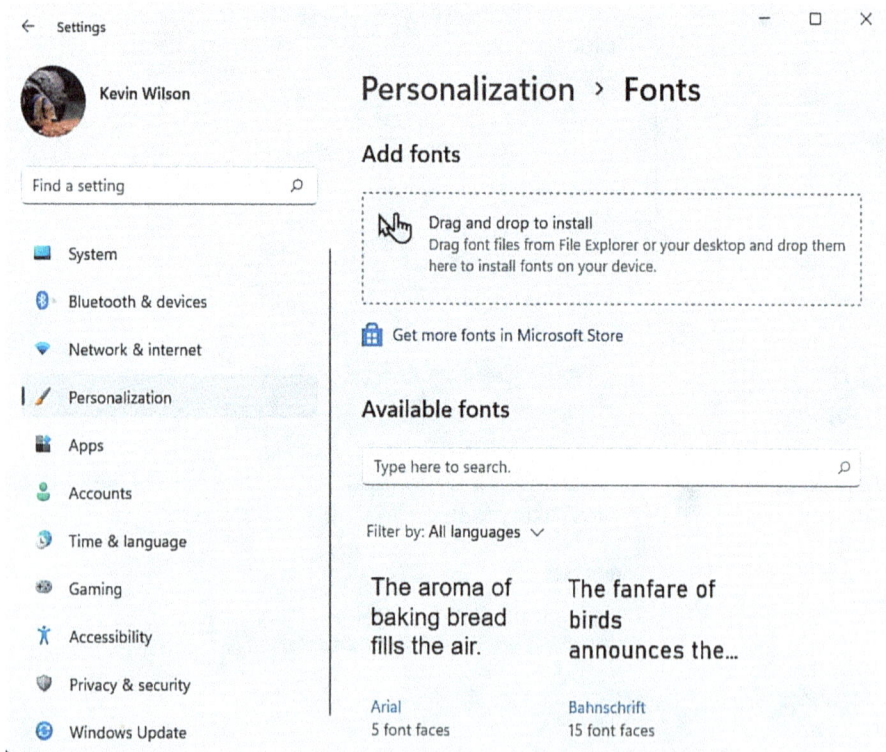

← Settings      — □ ✕

**Kevin Wilson**

Find a setting

- System
- Bluetooth & devices
- Network & internet
- Personalization
- Apps
- Accounts
- Time & language
- Gaming
- Accessibility
- Privacy & security
- Windows Update

## Personalization › Fonts

### Add fonts

Drag and drop to install
Drag font files from File Explorer or your desktop and drop them here to install fonts on your device.

Get more fonts in Microsoft Store

### Available fonts

Type here to search.

Filter by: All languages ⌄

| The aroma of baking bread fills the air. | The fanfare of birds announces the... |
|---|---|
| Arial<br>5 font faces | Bahnschrift<br>15 font faces |

Underneath, you'll see all the fonts installed on your PC.

**152**

# Windows Subsystem for Linux

Windows Subsystem for Linux (WSL) allows you to run native Linux command-line tools natively on Windows, alongside your Windows apps and is primarily aimed at developers.

## Enable WSL

To enable this feature, click the search icon on the taskbar then type 'turn windows features on or off'. Click 'turn windows features on or off'

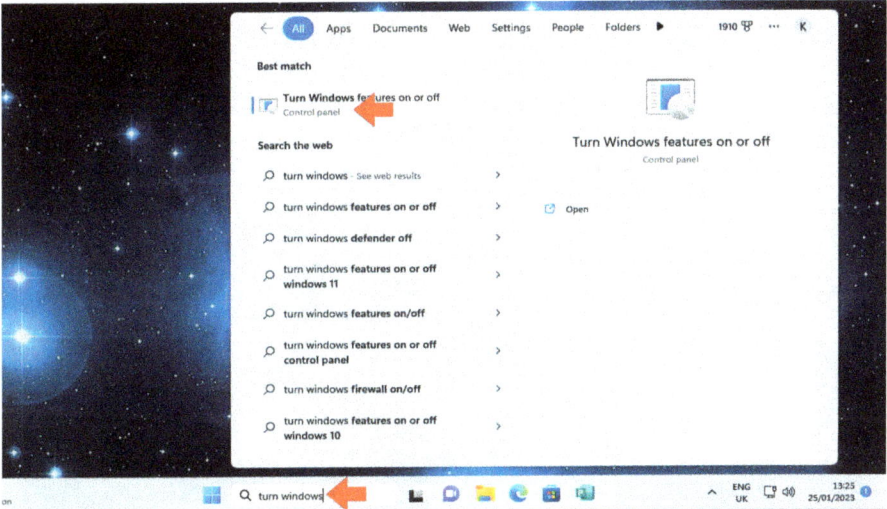

Scroll down the list, select 'windows subsystem for linux.

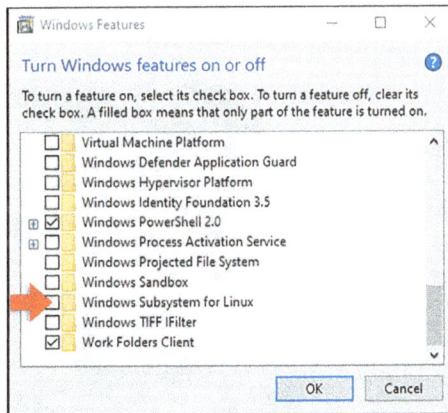

Click ok. Restart your machine when prompted.

## Installing a Linux Distribution

Now that you have the system enabled, you need to install a linux distribution. To do this, open up your Microsoft Store and search for linux. Eg 'ubuntu linux'.

Click the distribution in the search results

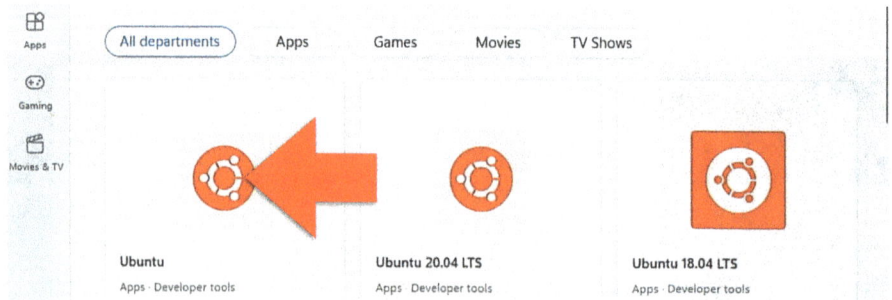

Click 'install', on the info page.

Now, find the distribution on your start menu, and run the app. It will take a few minutes to install. Run through the setup wizard, enter a username and a password. This will be used to log into linux.

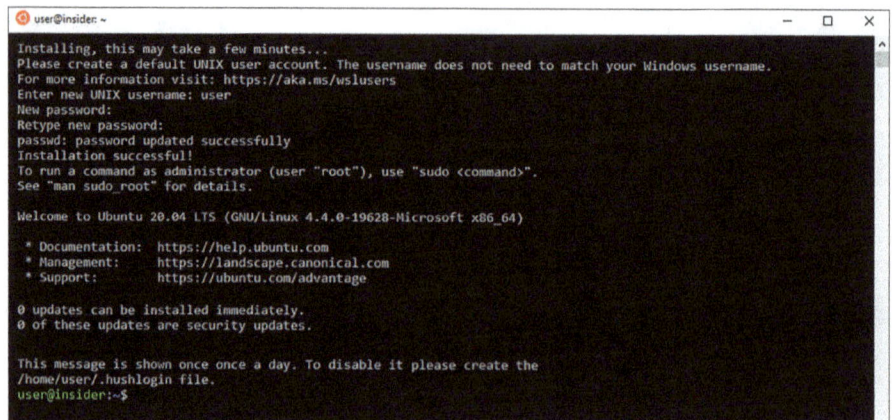

# Family Safety

You can create child accounts for your children either on your devices or their own devices. These are special, restricted accounts you can monitor and tailor to your child. It is not a good idea to allow a young child to use your account. Child accounts are used for children under 13.

## Child Accounts

On your child's computer or tablet, sign in as an administrator (your own account). Open the Settings App and click 'accounts'. Select 'family'.

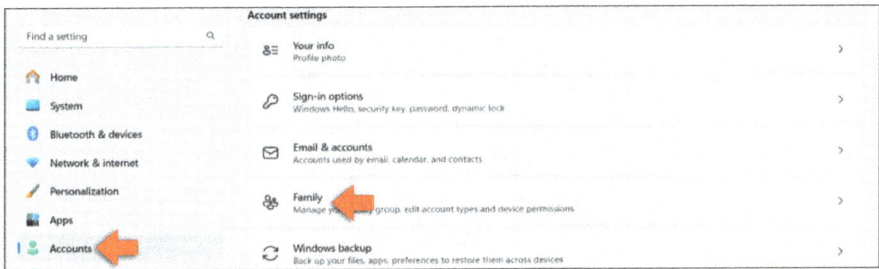

Under 'your family, click 'add someone'.

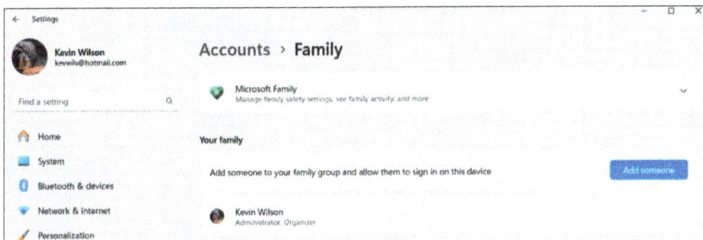

Click 'create one for a child'.

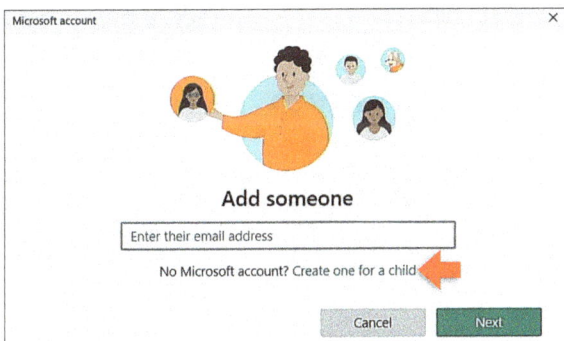

## Chapter 3: Settings and Personalisation

Enter an email address for them, click 'next'. Then enter a password, click 'next'.

Enter the child's name, click 'next'.

Enter your country and the child's date of birth

Click 'next'.

Sign in with the account you just created. If the child is under 13, you'll need to give parental consent. To do this, click 'I'm a parent or guardian', then click 'continue'.

Sign in with your Microsoft Account email address and password.

On the 'give consent' screen. Scroll to the bottom, click 'I agree'.

Do you want to allow your child to access all games and apps, or only those published by Microsoft?. Tick the box to allow all apps, click 'continue'.

**Can Sophie use non-Microsoft apps with this account?**

If you want, you can let your child use their new Microsoft account to sign in to games and apps that aren't published by Microsoft.
If you don't allow, they'll only have access to sign in to apps published by Microsoft.

☐ My child can sign in to non-Microsoft apps

...ecking this box, you agree to let your child use their Microsoft account to ...n in to games and apps that aren't published by Microsoft. These third-party apps may collect information from your child or allow your child to communicate with others. You can manage permissions for your child at any time from their Account Settings page.

Continue

Adjust the safety settings if you need to. You can age limit apps - just click the drop down box and select an age.

**Sophie is now in the family group**

How do these recommended safety settings look for them?

**Age limit on apps and games**
For stuff in Microsoft Store above their age limit, child will need your approval.

12 ˅

You can monitor their activity, filter their web search results, or use 'ask to buy' which alerts you when your child attempts to make a purchase.

**Activity reporting**
Keep an eye on screen time, plus get a weekly report sent to your inbox.

**Web and search filters**
Use Microsoft Edge to filter out mature content and websites.

**Ask to buy**
Child needs permission to buy apps from Microsoft Store.

Sign out    Family Safety

Leave them all on, then click 'sign out' to sign out of your account.

Now you can sign out of your account. On the lock screen allow your child to sign in using the account you just created. Select the child's account from the bottom left, click 'sign in'. Follow the on-screen prompts to finalise the account.

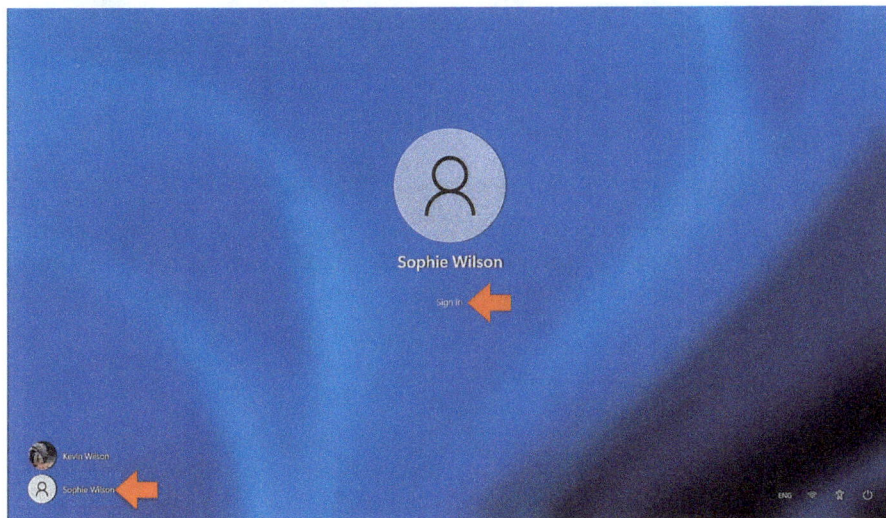

## Monitoring Activity

You can log on to your family safety website by opening your web browser and navigating to the following address. Click 'sign in' and enter your Microsoft Account email address and password.

```
account.microsoft.com/family
```

On the main family screen you'll see a list of child accounts.

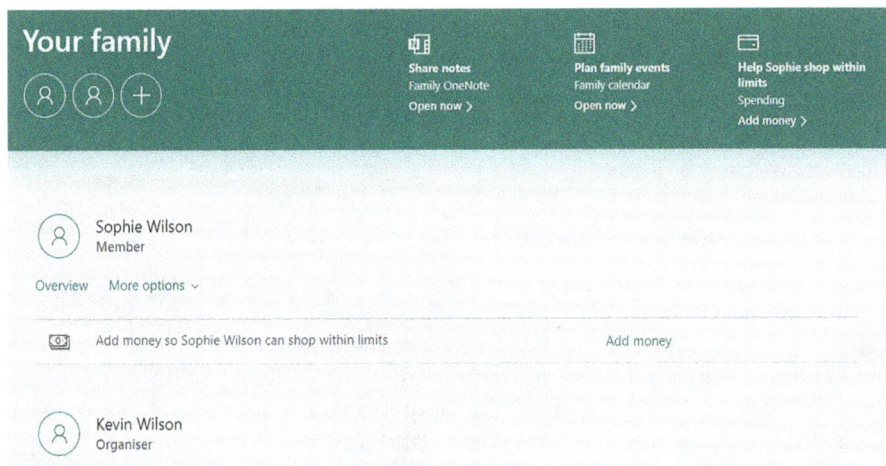

## Chapter 3: Settings and Personalisation

Under their name, click 'overview'.

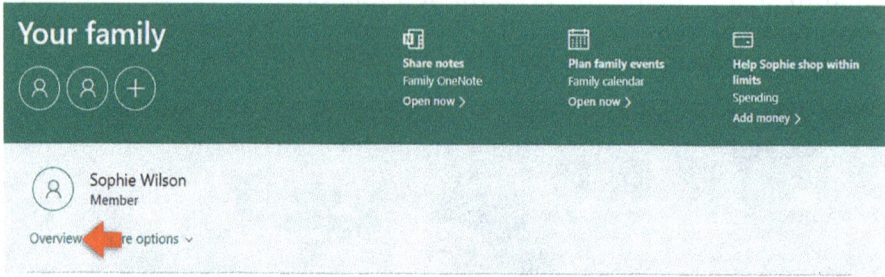

You'll see the overview page. Down the left hand side, you'll see a menu. Screen Time, allows you to set limits and curfews to control how long your child uses the computer and times they are allowed access.

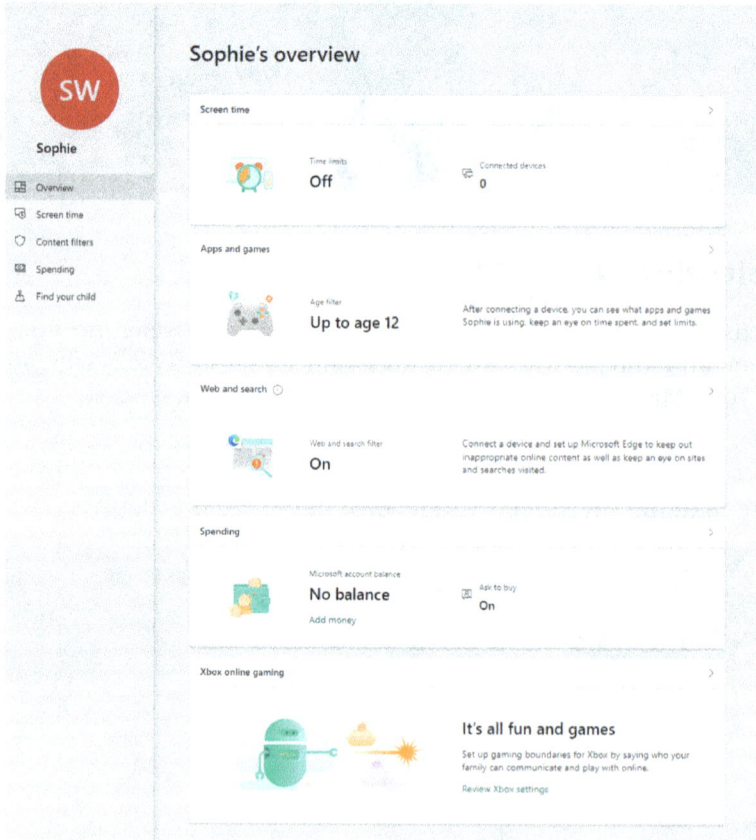

Content filters allow you to block types of apps, and restrict content according to age. You can also monitor your child's spending, as well as add some money for your child to spend in the Microsoft Store. Find your child allows you to track your child's physical location.

# Screen Time

You can set curfews and limits to the amount of time your children can use their devices. To do this select 'screen time' from the menu on the top left.

Select 'devices' from the top left.

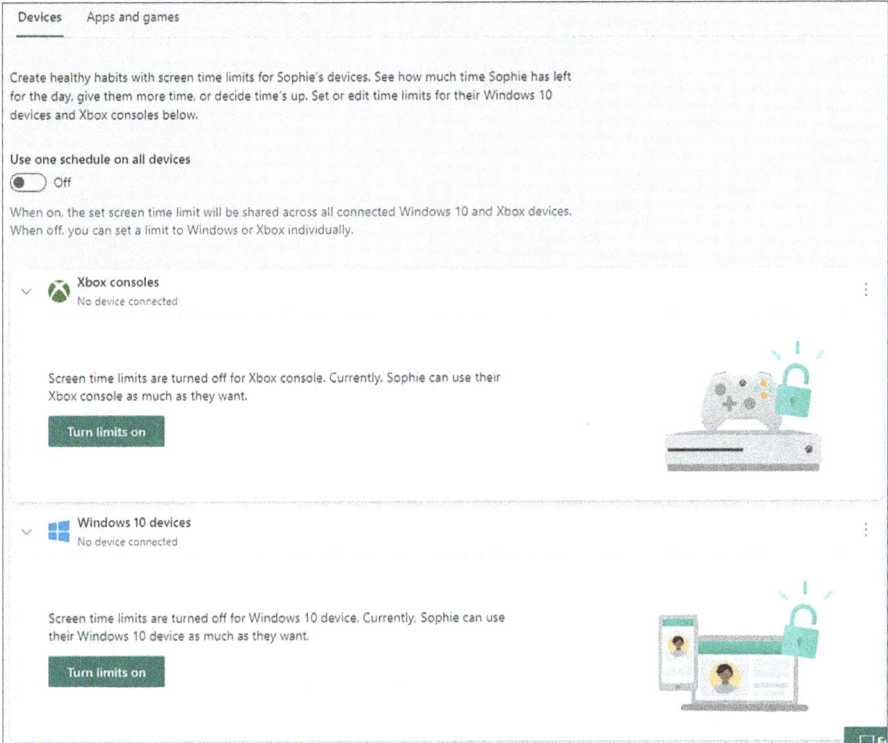

Under 'windows 10 devices' click 'turn on limits'.

Click the days you want to allow your child to use the computer.

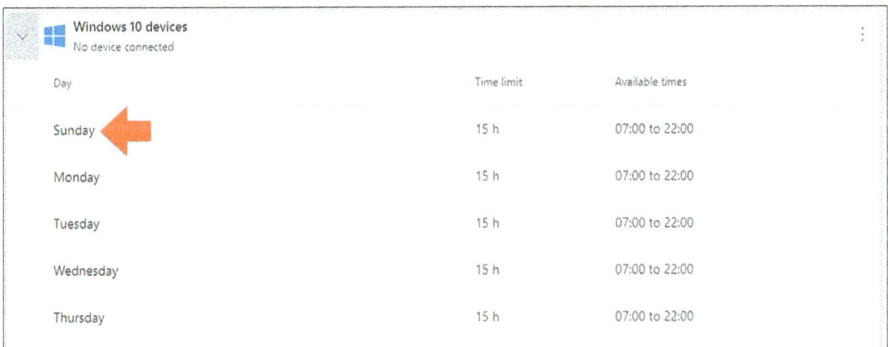

Change the day at the top to 'every day'. Drag the slider to select the amount of time. Then set the time window you want to allow your child to use the computer. *The example below shows the child can use the computer for two hours each day, between 4pm and 8pm.* Click 'finish.

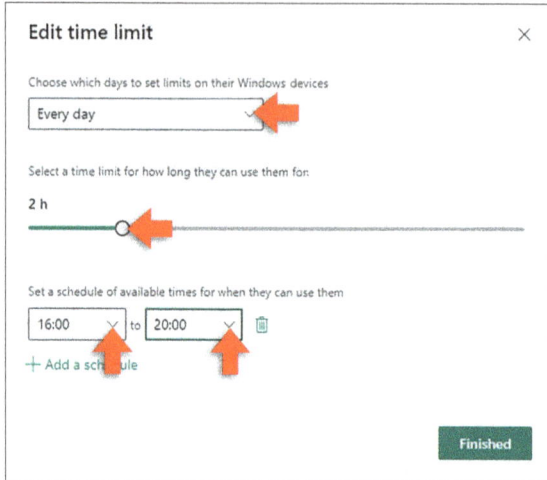

Click on a day to edit the times etc.

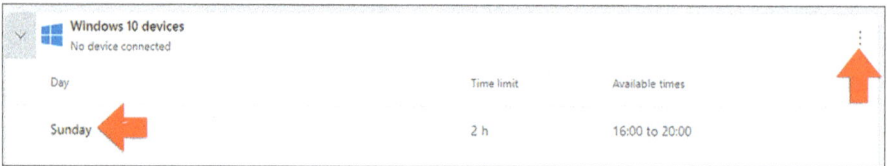

To remove the restriction, click the three dots icon on the top right, select 'turn limits off'.

## Content Filters

You can view your child's web activity and what apps they've been using. You can also filter out websites, or block certain apps.

To see this, select 'content filters' from the menu on the top left of the screen.

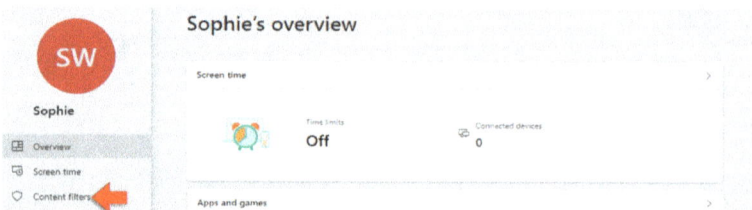

## Web Activity

Select 'web and search' from the two options along the top. Here, you'll see web activity.

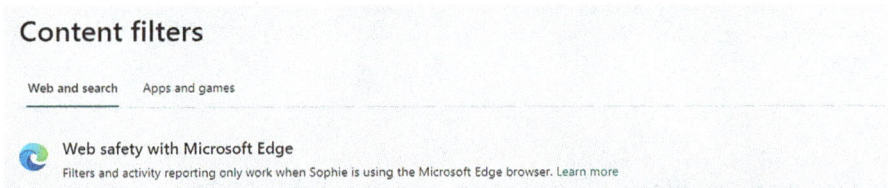

**Content filters**

Web and search    Apps and games

**Web safety with Microsoft Edge**
Filters and activity reporting only work when Sophie is using the Microsoft Edge browser. Learn more

Select the date on the top right, then scroll down to the 'activity' section where you'll see a list of websites and web searches. Click the small side arrow to the left of the site to view all pages visited. If you want to block the site click 'block'.

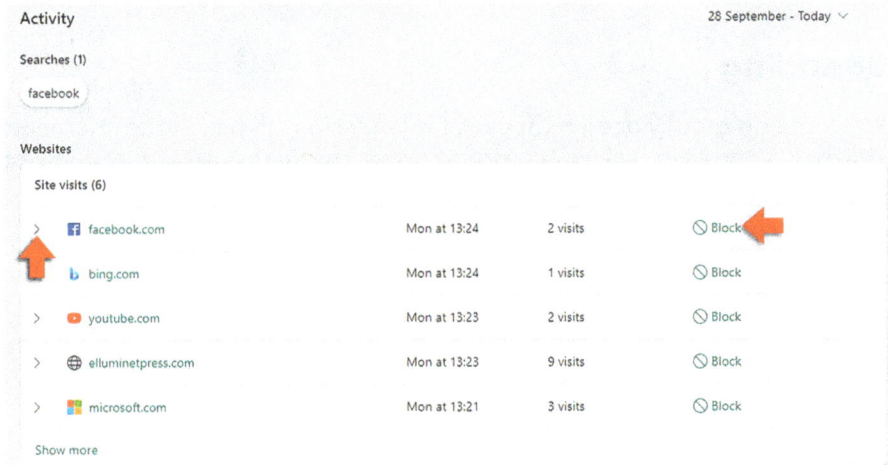

Activity             28 September - Today

Searches (1)

facebook

Websites

Site visits (6)

| > | facebook.com | Mon at 13:24 | 2 visits | Block |
|---|---|---|---|---|
| > | bing.com | Mon at 13:24 | 1 visits | Block |
| > | youtube.com | Mon at 13:23 | 2 visits | Block |
| > | elluminetpress.com | Mon at 13:23 | 9 visits | Block |
| > | microsoft.com | Mon at 13:21 | 3 visits | Block |

Show more

Scroll down to 'filter settings'. Block mature content using the 'filter inappropriate websites' switch.

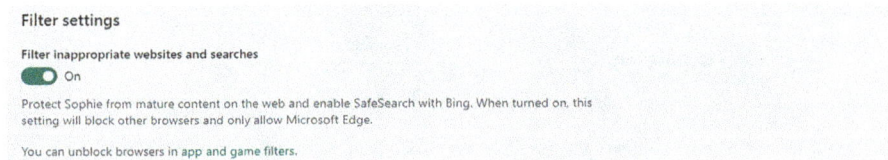

**Filter settings**

Filter inappropriate websites and searches
On

Protect Sophie from mature content on the web and enable SafeSearch with Bing. When turned on, this setting will block other browsers and only allow Microsoft Edge.

You can unblock browsers in app and game filters.

At the bottom you can allow only certain websites and block all others. To use this, turn on 'only use allowed websites'.

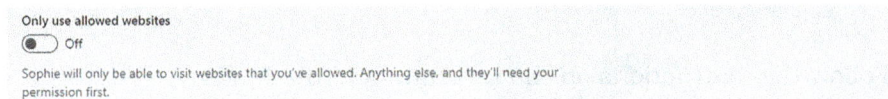

**Only use allowed websites**
Off

Sophie will only be able to visit websites that you've allowed. Anything else, and they'll need your permission first.

Under 'allowed websites', click 'add a website', then type the URL, eg facebook.com

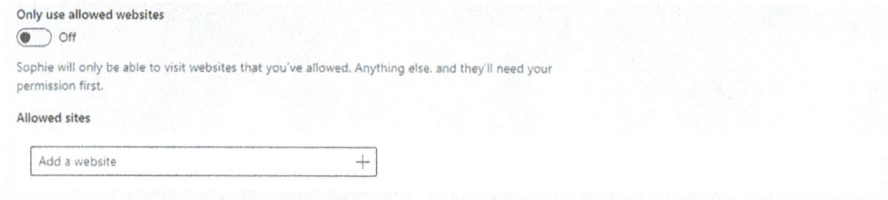

If you want to block a particular website, under 'blocked websites', type in the URL, eg youtube.com

# Spending

You can add money or a credit card for your child to use in the microsoft store. To see this, select 'spending' from the menu on the top left of the screen.

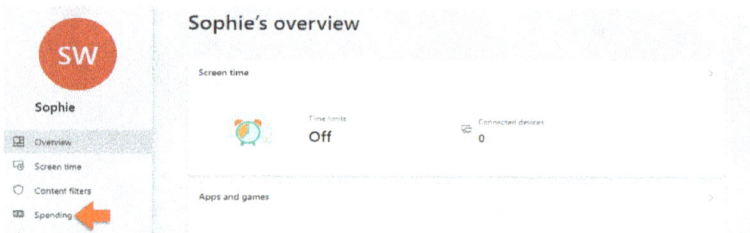

Select 'add money' in the 'microsoft account balance' section.

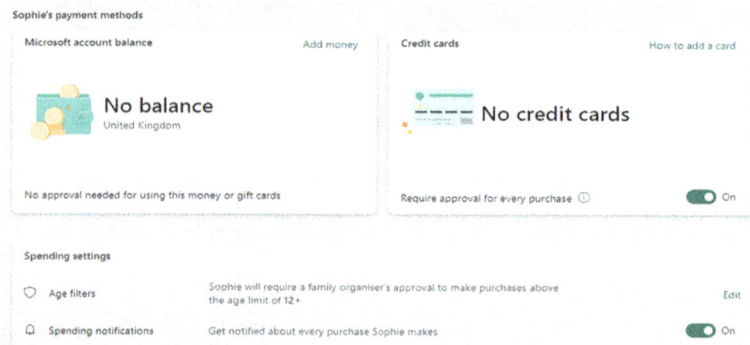

Follow the instructions on the screen to add the funds.

**164**

# Find your Child

You can track your child's physical location. To use this feature, you'll need to install the family safety app on the device the child uses. Currently this only works with iPhones/iPad or Android phones and tablets.

On your Phone/tablet, open the app store, search for Microsoft Family Safety, then download and install the app. Once installed, open the app, then sign in with your Microsoft Account.

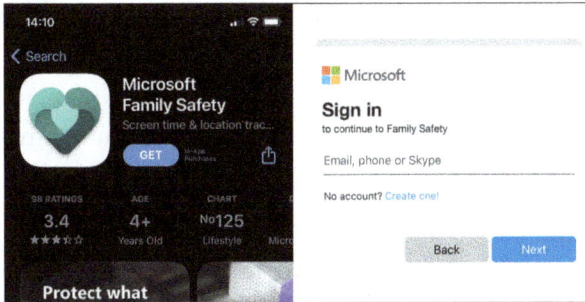

On your child's phone/tablet, open the app store then search for Microsoft Family Safety. Download and install the app.

Once the app is installed, open it, then sign in with your child's Microsoft Account.

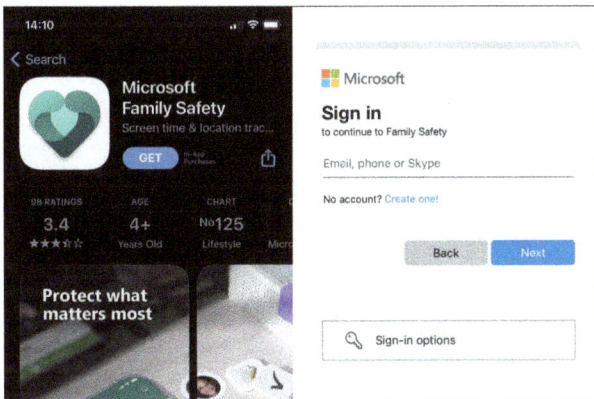

Click the profile icon on the top left to open the settings.

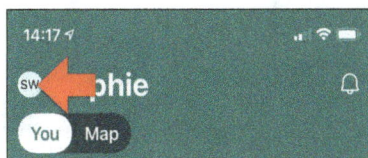

**165**

# Chapter 3: Settings and Personalisation

Select settings, then turn on 'share your location'.

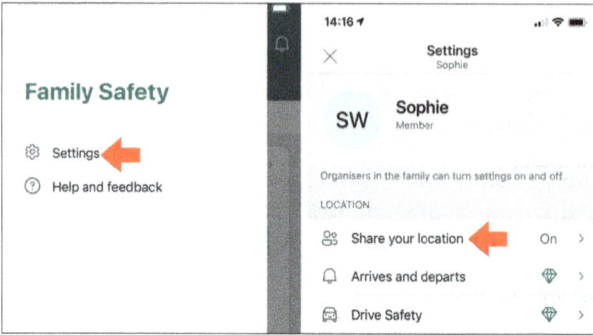

Now on your Phone, you'll be able to track your child's device. Tap 'map' on the top left. You'll see the members of your family appear on the map.

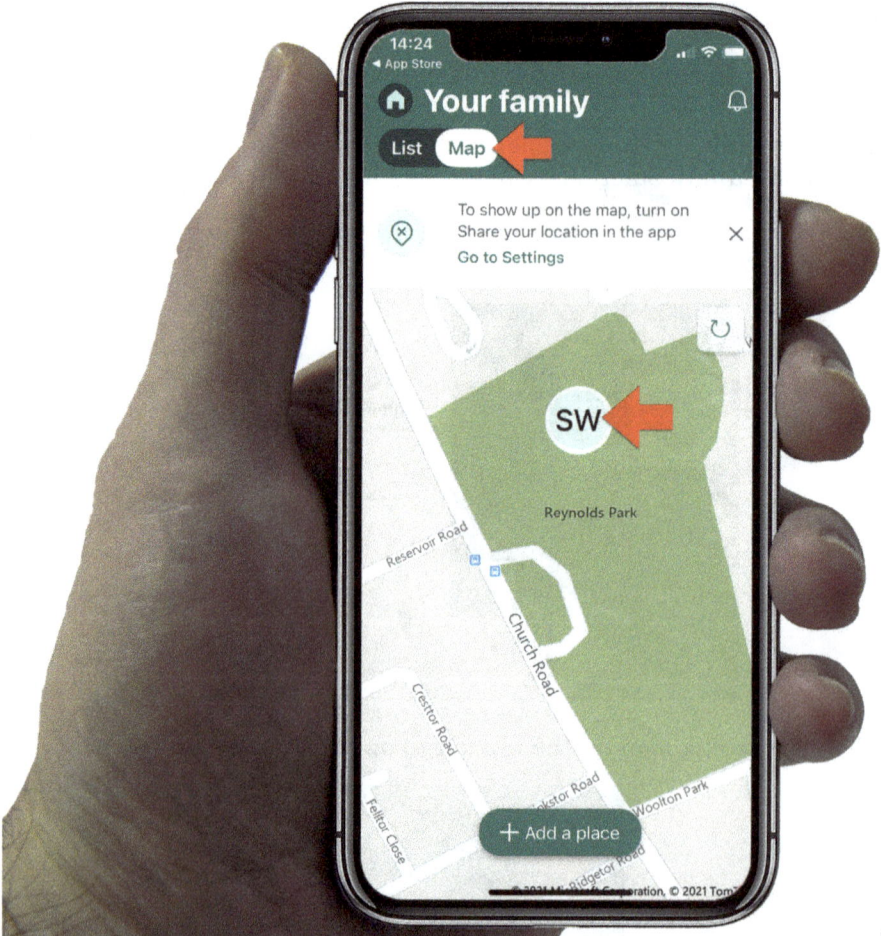

# Gaming Settings

Windows 11 offers a range of features designed to enhance the gaming experience.

## Game Mode

Game Mode is a feature in Windows 11 that optimizes your system's performance for gaming. When enabled, it prioritizes gaming processes and manages system resources to provide a smoother gaming experience. To enable/disable it open the Settings app, select 'gaming'. Click 'game mode' and toggle the switch to on/off.

## Xbox Game Bar

The Xbox Game Bar is a customizable overlay that provides quick access to gaming features, including screen capture, performance monitoring, and social interaction. To use the Xbox Game Bar, press Win G.

## Graphics Settings

Graphics settings in Windows 11 are crucial for optimizing visual performance, especially for gaming or graphic-intensive tasks.

Open settings, select 'system', 'display', 'graphics'. Click on the app, select 'options'. You can specify performance preferences for individual games.

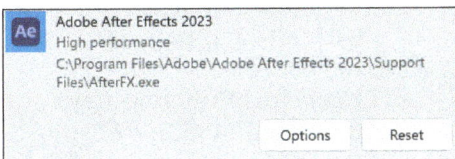

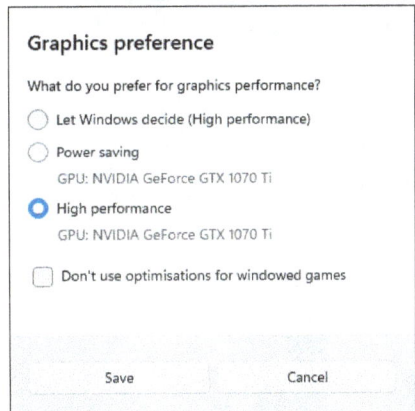

After selecting an app, choose whether you want it to have "High performance" (favoring GPU power) or "Power saving" (favoring battery life).

# 4

# Basic Navigation

With a PC and a laptop, you'll be using a keyboard and mouse or touchpad for navigating around Windows.

There are various different types of mice and keyboards available on the market.

Pens are also available for hybrid devices with touch screens such as the surface book and tablet.

In this chapter we'll take a look at

- Using the Mouse
- Left click, right click & scrolling with your mouse
- Using the Touch Pad
- Left click, right click & scroll with a touch pad
- Keyboards
- Keyboard Function Keys
- Keyboard Modifier Keys
- Pens

To help you better understand this section, take a look at the video resources. Scan the QR code, or open your web browser and type the following directly into the address bar at the top (don't use a search engine):

 elluminetpress.com/win-11-nav

# Mouse

Computer mice come in various different shapes, however most of them have two click buttons and a scroll wheel. Some have other buttons you can assign various functions to. You'll want to find a mouse that fits comfortably in your hand allowing you to use both buttons and the scroll wheel without straining your wrist. Mice can be wired or wireless. Wireless mice are nice to use as they don't have a wire hanging out the side which can get in the way. These mice either need batteries or recharged.

## Using the Mouse

When using your mouse, make sure it fits securely into the palm of your hand. This will allow you to use both mouse buttons comfortably and reduce wrist strain. When you move the mouse, try keep wrist movement to a minimum.

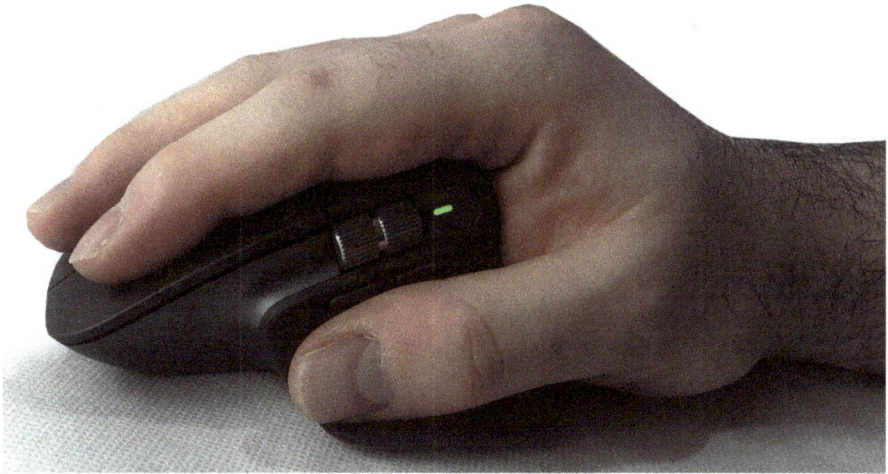

Move the mouse along your desk, while keeping an eye on the mouse pointer on the screen.

### Left Click

The most common function of your mouse is the left click. This is used to select something on the screen. You can select an icon, file, button, or text field.

Move your mouse pointer to the object on the screen, then click once with the left mouse button.

## Chapter 4: Basic Navigation

### Double Click

To start an app, application, or open a file, you need to double click. This means clicking the left mouse button twice in quick succession.

### Right Click

The right mouse button opens a context menu on an object such as a file or app. This provides in context functionality for that file or app.

Here, in the screen on the right, you'll see I've right clicked on a file in File Explorer. This brings up the context menu with additional functions you can perform on that file.

### Scroll Wheel

The scroll wheel allows you to scroll up and down pages in a document, a window such as File Explorer, or a web page in Chrome or Edge. Move your mouse pointer over the page you want to scroll, use your index finger to move the wheel up or down.

# Touch Pad

The touchpad is usually found on laptop devices and allows you to control the mouse pointer using your finger. Slide your finger left, right, up, or down on the touchpad to move the mouse pointer on screen.

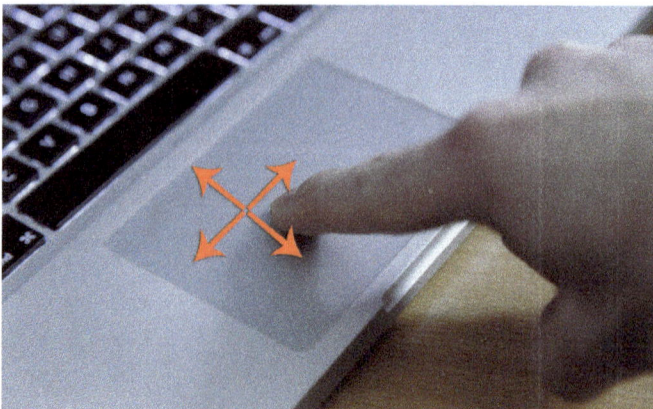

## Left Click on Something

Use one finger to tap on the touch pad. Tap on the touch pad to select something, double tap to open an app or file.

## Right Click on Something

To right click on something - to open a popup menu, move the mouse pointer to an icon, then tap with two fingers.

## Scroll

Use two fingers up and down the touch pad to scroll up and down web pages, documents or emails.

# Keyboards

Computer keyboards come with the standard QWERTY layout. There are other layouts for other regions and languages but we'll concentrate on the QWERTY design. Here is a common example

# Function Keys

Along the top of the keyboard you'll see some function keys. These are usually assigned a standard function within windows.

Lets take a look at what each key does.

| Key | Function |
|-----|----------|
| F1 | Used to access the help screen |
| F2 | Renames a selected icon, folder or file |
| F3 | Often opens a search |
| F4 | Open the address bar in file explorer |
| F5 | Refresh document, page or window |
| F6 | Jumps to address bar in browser |
| F7 | Spell/grammar check in Word |
| F8 | |
| F9 | Refreshes a document in  Word or sends and receives emails in Outlook |
| F10 | Activates the menu bar of an open application. |
| F11 | Full screen mode |
| F12 | Save as in most windows programs. Also opens developer tools in web browser |

# Modifier Keys

Modifier keys are used when executing a keyboard short cut, such as CTRL C to copy text. CTRL, or control is the modifier key. Here are some useful keyboard shortcuts.

| | |
|---|---|
| Windows + Tab | Opens thumbnail list of open applications |
| Windows + A | Open Windows 10 notification centre |
| Windows + D | Show Windows desktop |
| Windows + E | Open Windows Explorer |
| Windows + K | Connect to wireless displays and audio devices |
| Windows + P | Project a screen |
| Windows + R | Run a command |
| Windows + X | Open Start button context menu |
| Windows key + Arrow key | Snap app windows left, right, corners, maximize, or minimize |
| Windows key + Comma | Temporarily peek at the desktop |
| Windows Key | Show windows start menu |
| Alt + Tab | Switch to previous window |
| Alt + Space | Reveals drop down menu on current window: Restore, move, size, minimize, maximize or close. |
| Alt + F4 | Close current app |
| Ctrl + Shift + Esc | Open Task Manager |
| Ctrl + Z | Undo Command |
| Ctrl + X | Cut selected text |
| Ctrl + C | Copy selected text |
| Ctrl + V | Paste selected text at cursor position |
| Ctrl + P | Print |

Modifier keys live at the bottom of the keyboard next to the space bar.

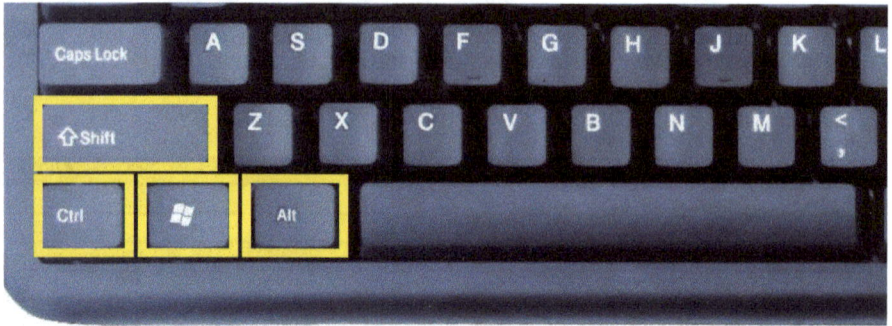

Some keyboard will have special keys on the right hand side such as insert or home, page up and page down. 'Home' moves the cursor to the beginning of the line, 'end' moves it to the end. You can use these when typing a document as they help when moving around the page.

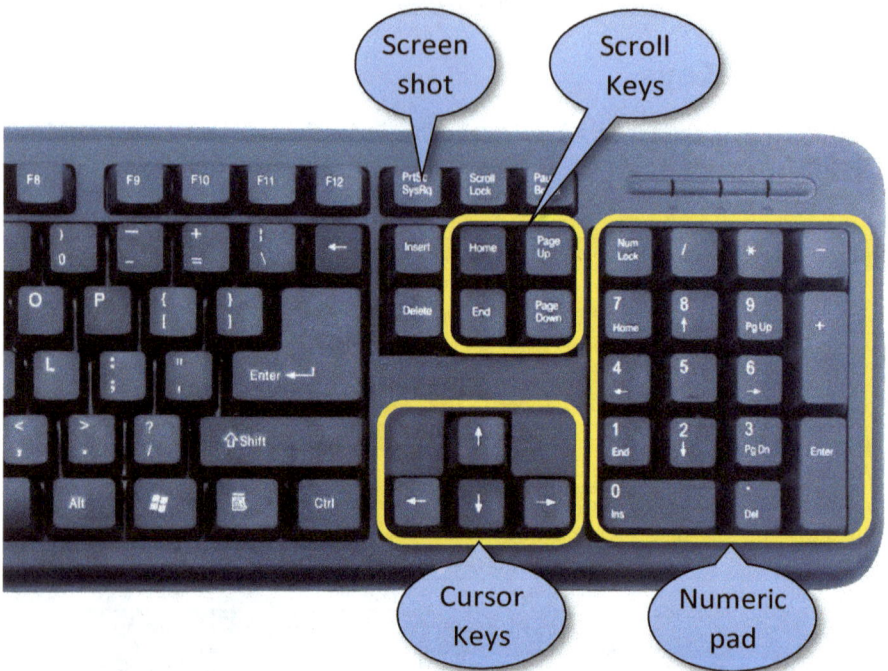

Below that, you'll see some cursor keys. These are useful when moving up and down a page, or moving your cursor around a word document.

On the far right you'll see a numeric pad. These keys are useful if you work with numbers as the keypad makes it easier and faster to enter numbers.

# Pens

You can use a pen or stylus to interact with any Windows 11 device that has a touchscreen—such as a tablet, touchscreen laptop, or Microsoft Surface. Pens are especially useful for handwriting notes in OneNote, drawing in art apps, or marking up documents.

If you have a Surface Pro, Surface Laptop Studio, or Surface Go, you can use the Surface Pen or Surface Slim Pen. These support pressure sensitivity, tilt for shading, palm rejection, and a shortcut button. Some models, like the Surface Slim Pen 2, charge wirelessly and attach magnetically to the device.

Other touchscreen laptops—like those from Dell, HP, Lenovo, or ASUS—don't always include a pen, but many support pens that use the Microsoft Pen Protocol (MPP). These are available in electronics stores and online.

You can use the pen to write, draw, or tap through apps, icons, and menus.

# 5

# Getting around Windows 11

In this chapter we will take a look at the different parts of Windows 11, as well as

- The Desktop
- Start Menu
- Task Bar
- Widgets Panel
- Windows Search
- Virtual Desktops
- Quick Settings (Action Center)
- Notifications
- Windows Ink
- Arranging Windows on the Desktop
- Multiple Screens
- Cloud Clipboard
- Character Map & Symbols
- Taking Screenshots
- Task Manager
- File Explorer
- Managing your Files
- External Drives

To help you better understand this section, take a look at the video resources. Scan the QR code, or open your web browser and type the following directly into the address bar at the top (don't use a search engine):

elluminetpress.com/using-win-11

# The Desktop

The desktop is the basic working area on your PC. It's the equivalent of your workbench or office desk, hence why it is called a desktop.

**Scan for Video**

## Desktop Anatomy

On the desktop itself you can save files such as documents or photos - these will appear as file icons. On some devices you may see other icons such as the trash can for deleted files or network connections.

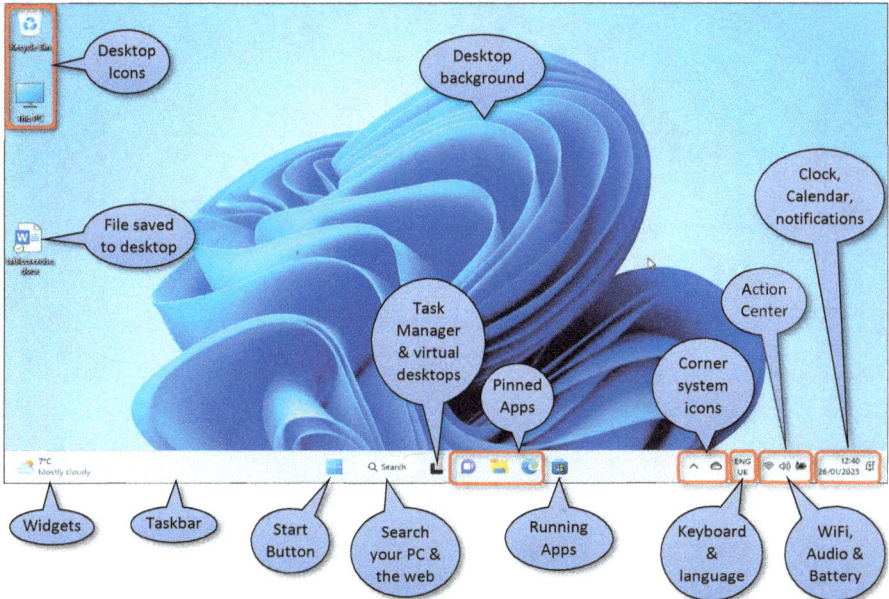

If you've come from using Windows 10, you'll notice some differences. First, the start button and the other icons on the taskbar are now centred. The Action Center has been split into two separate areas: Quick Settings and the Notification Center. Quick Settings appears when you click the network, sound, or battery icons in the bottom-right corner of the taskbar, and includes toggles for Wi-Fi, Bluetooth, Airplane Mode, volume, screen brightness (on laptops), battery status, and Focus mode. Clicking the clock on the far right of the taskbar opens the Notification Center, where you'll find recent alerts and a collapsible calendar view. The Search function appears on the taskbar as either a button, icon with label, or full search box. A Widgets button near the bottom-left corner of the taskbar opens a customizable panel with news, weather, calendar events, and other live information. You can view and create virtual desktops, or view all running tasks using the task manager icon on the taskbar.

# Start Menu

The start menu is the central launch point for apps, changing settings, as well as system shut down, reset, hibernate, and sleep.

## Opening

To open the Start menu, click the Start button located at the center or bottom-left of the taskbar. You can also press the Windows key on your keyboard.

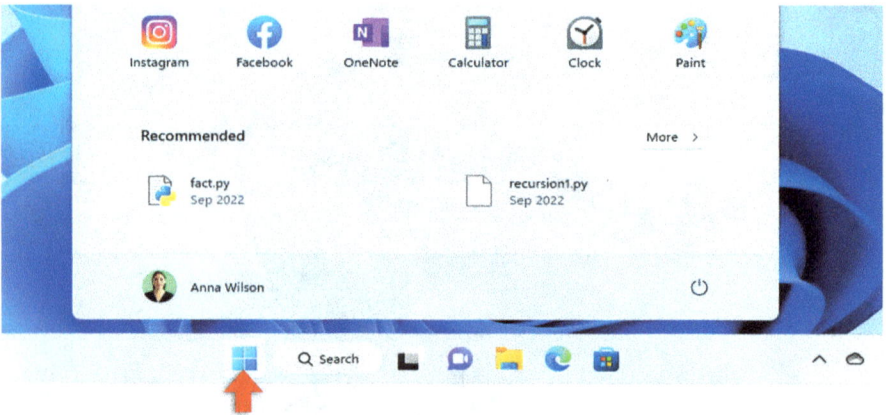

Lets take a closer look at the different parts of the menu.

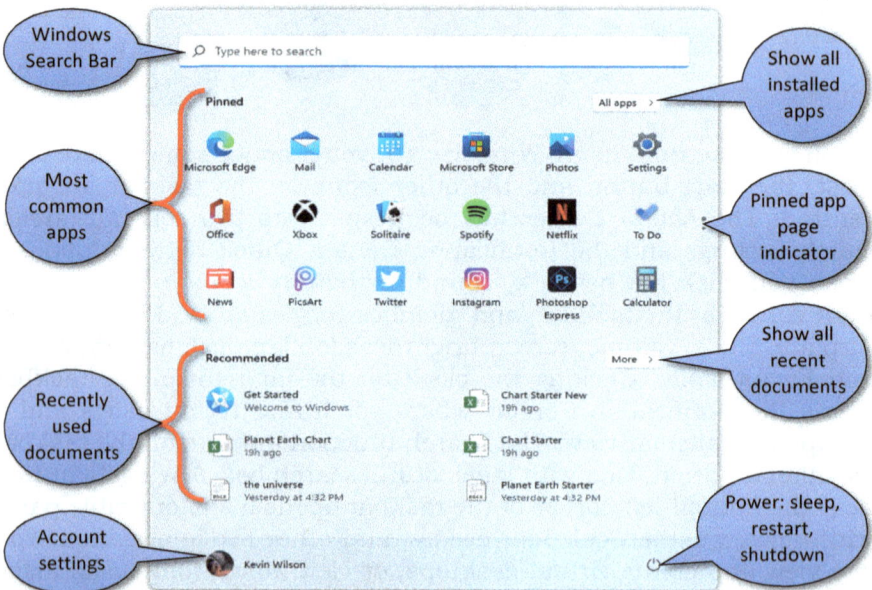

## Pinning Apps

At the top of the Start menu, you'll find the Pinned apps section. These are apps you've chosen to keep there for quick access. To pin an app, click on the 'all apps' icon on the top right.

Right click on the app you want to pin - eg 'groove music'. Select 'pin to start'.

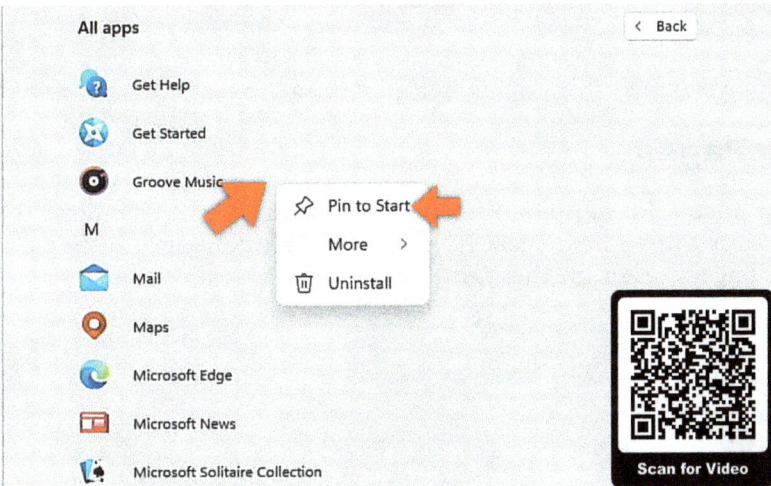

You'll see the app appear in the 'pinned apps' section.

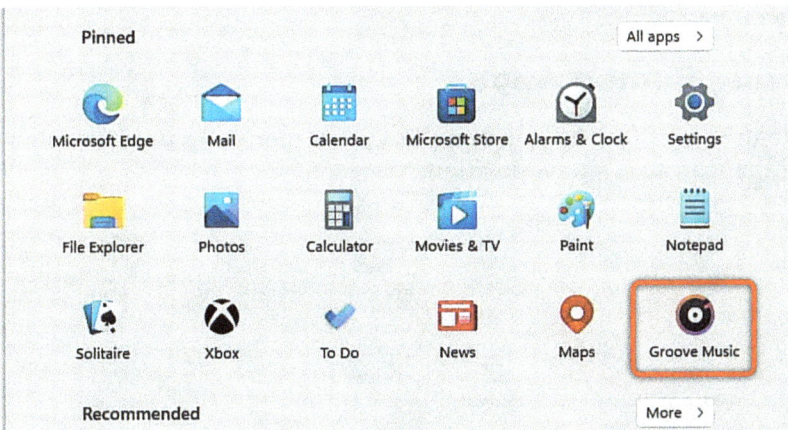

## App Folders

You can group similar apps together into app folders. To do this just click and drag one app on top of another.

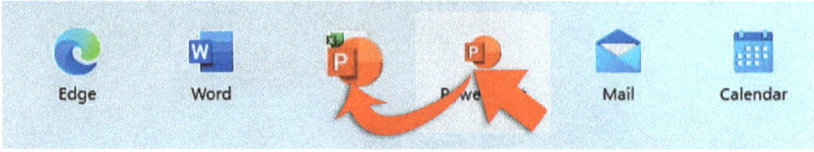

A new app folder will appear. Click on the folder to open it up.

To remove an app from the folder, just drag it back onto the start menu

## App Pages

If you have a lot of apps pinned to your start menu, Windows 11 will split your apps into pages. If you have multiple pages of apps, you'll see a page marker on the right hand side of the start menu.

Click on the small dot, or use the scroll wheel on your mouse to move between pages.

## Moving Pinned Apps

You can rearrange the apps on your start menu. To do this, click and drag the icon to it's new position.

**180**

The other icons will move out the way so you can drop the app icon where you want it.

## Remove App

Right click on the app you want to remove, select 'unpin from start'.

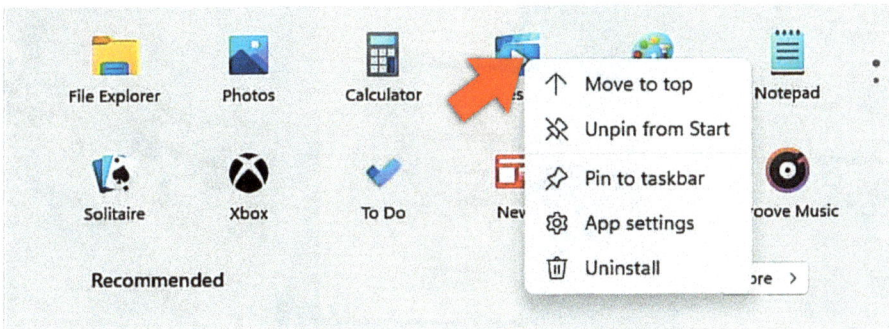

## Search Bar

At the top of the start menu, you'll see a shortcut to Windows search.

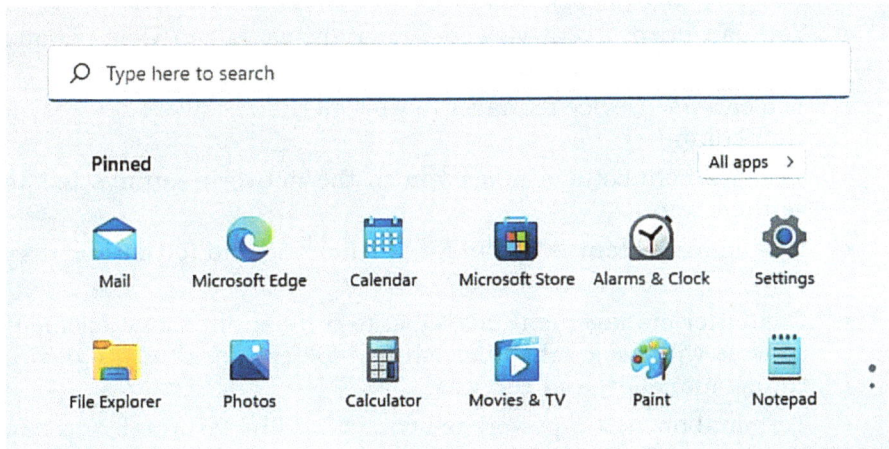

See windows search on page 189.

## Hidden Start Menu

To open the secondary start menu, right click on the start button on your taskbar.

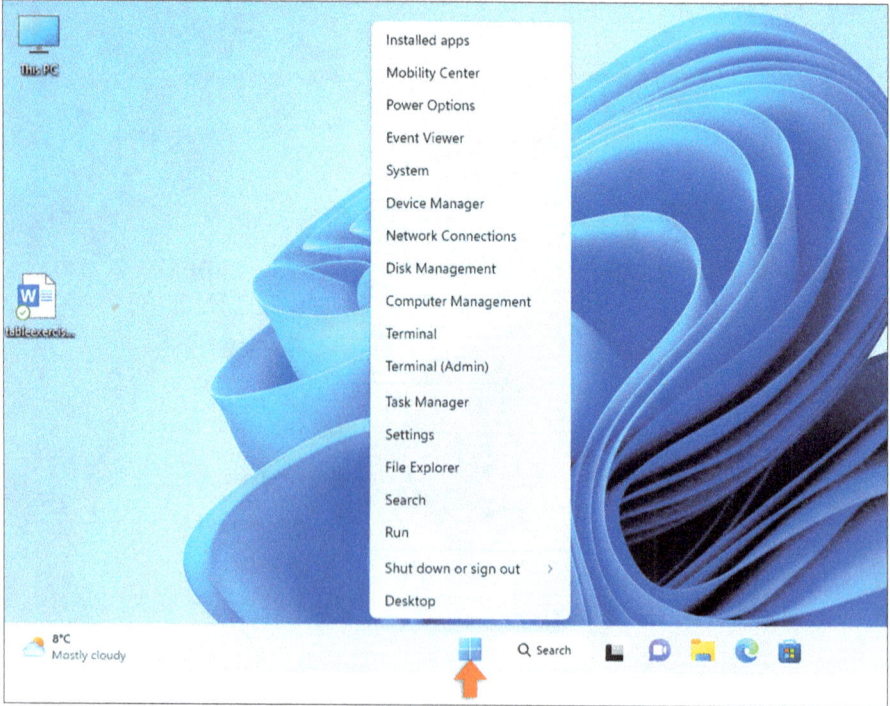

Here, you can quick access:

- 'Apps and features' and 'power options' in the settings app.
- You can open 'Event viewer' which allows you to view various event logs and is useful for troubleshooting.
- You can use Device manager to view all the hardware devices on your computer
- Network connections takes you to the network settings in the settings app.
- Disk management is useful for partitioning and formatting disk drives.
- Computer management takes you to the computer management console with task scheduler, shared folders, local users, device & disk manager, and services.
- Terminal opens up powershell command line terminal. You can also access Task manager, Settings App, File Explorer, Search, and Run.

# Task Bar

The taskbar is a core user interface element usually located at the bottom of the screen, and is designed to provide quick access to apps, settings, and notifications.

**Scan for Video**

## Anatomy

On the far left of the taskbar, you'll see the widgets icon (if enabled). This icon may show the weather and alerts from widgets such as your calendar or local news. Click the icon to reveal the widgets sidebar.

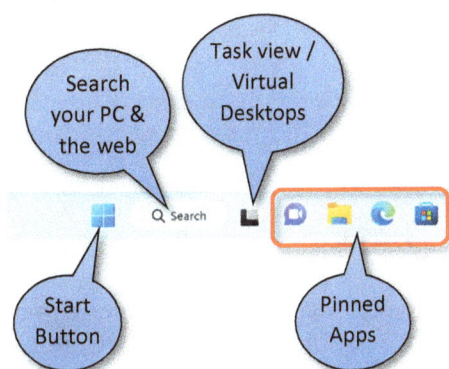

8°C
Mostly cloudy

Widget Sidebar

Task view / Virtual Desktops

Search your PC & the web

Start Button

Pinned Apps

In the middle of the taskbar, you'll see your main icons. The first icon is the Start button, which opens the Start menu. The search button allows you look for apps, files, and search the web. The Task View icon shows currently running apps and virtual desktops. Next to these, you'll see pinned and currently running apps. As you open apps, the icons appear along the taskbar with a line underneath indicating that the app is running. The taskbar also acts as a shortcut bar so you can pin apps you use often and switch between running apps.

Over on the right-hand side you'll see your system clock; click this to open the notifications and calendar sidebar. Next to that, you'll see the Quick Settings icon. Click on this to open Wi-Fi and network settings, Focus Assist, Bluetooth, volume control, and screen brightness. You can quickly toggle these settings on or off, or click the small arrow beside

Corner Icons Overflow

Clock, Calendar, notifications

ENG UK   13:42 7/7/21

Corner System Icons

Keyboard & Display language

Quick Settings

each one for more options. The other icons to the right are called corner system icons. These are usually background apps such as OneDrive, Windows Security, Touch Keyboard, or Pen Menu. The small up arrow to the left is called the corner icons overflow area. These are icons that don't fit in the visible tray.

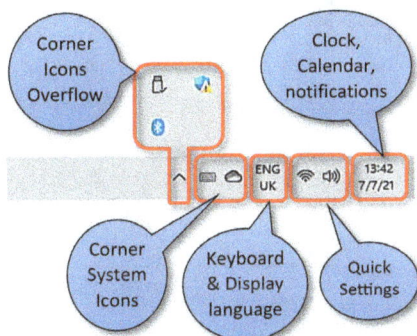

## Jump Lists

Apps that appear on the taskbar have a recent files list called a jump list. To open a jump list, right click on the app's icon on the taskbar.

Here, you'll be able to re-open any of your recently accessed files for that particular app. As well as pin the icon to the taskbar so it doesn't disappear when the app is closed.

## Pin Icons to your Task Bar

For more convenience, you can pin all your favourite apps to your task bar along the bottom of your screen. To do this, open the start menu, then right click on an app. If your app isn't there, click 'all apps' on the top right of the menu. From the menu that appears, select 'pin to taskbar' (select 'more' if it isn't there).

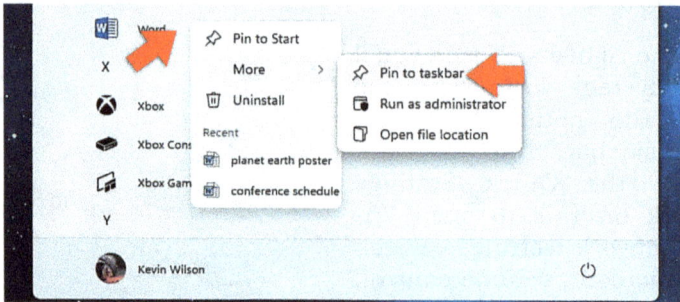

You'll see the icon has been added to your taskbar.

If you want to remove the icon, right click on the icon, select 'unpin from taskbar'.

**184**

# Widgets Panel

The widgets panel opens up on the left hand side of your screen and contains small applets called widgets for web search, weather, stock, news, photos and so on.

## Opening

To open the widgets panel, click on the widgets icon on left of the taskbar, or press **Win W** on your keyboard. You can also swipe inwards from the left hand side, if you're using a touch screen device.

The panel is split into two sections. The left hand side of the panel contains your widgets, such as weather, traffic, reminders and so on. You can select which widgets you want to show in this section

The right hand side of the panel is a live feed of news articles, stories, and other recommended content.

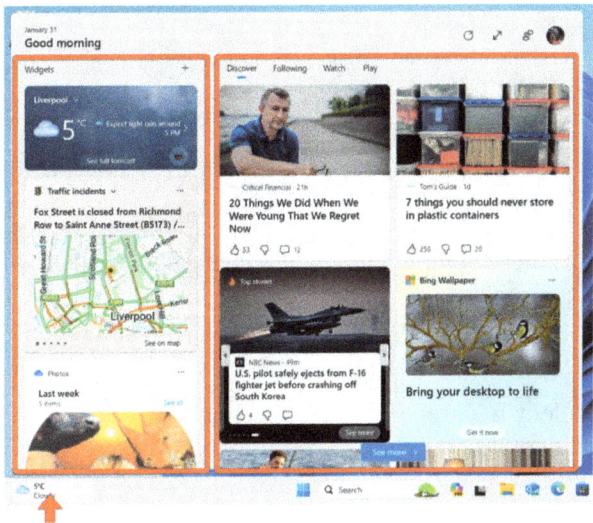

Along the top of the righ hand panel, you'll see four tabs. Let's take a look at what each tab contains.

**Discover** is a section where you can find new content suggestions based on your interests and past activities.

**Following** tab contains content from sources you have chosen to follow such as favorite news outlets, blogs, websites, or topics you've shown interest in.

**Watch** is a curated list of video content such as news video clips, trailers, tutorials, or any other video content tailored to your interests or viewing history.

**Play** tab suggest new games, updates on games you play, streams from popular gamers, or other game-related news and content.

## Add Widget

To add a widget, open the widget panel, then click the '+' icon at the top of the widgets panel.

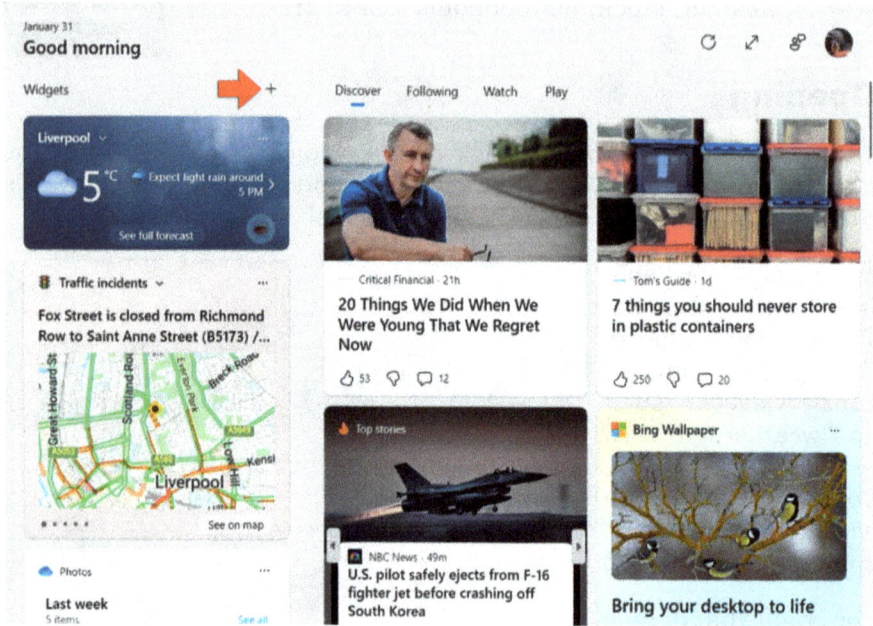

Select a category from the list on the left, then click pin to add the widget to the widgets panel. Click the 'x' on the top right to close the 'widget settings' dialog box.

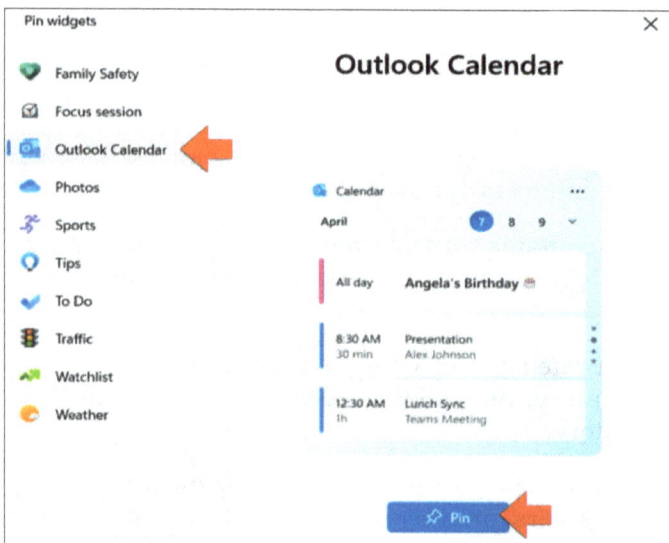

## Customise Widget

Open the widgets side panel, click on the three dots icon next to the widget you want to customise. Here, you can change the size - select small, medium, or large. To customise the settings, click 'customise widget'.

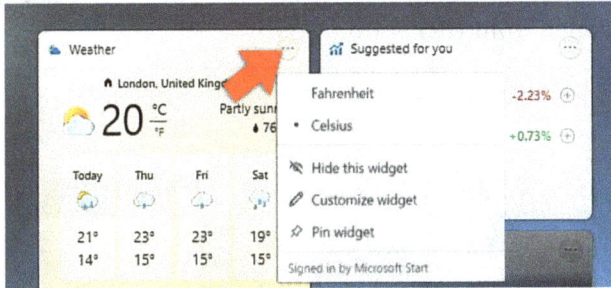

Here, you can customise the widget. The actual settings will depend on the widget you're customising, but in this case, the weather app, I can search for my location.

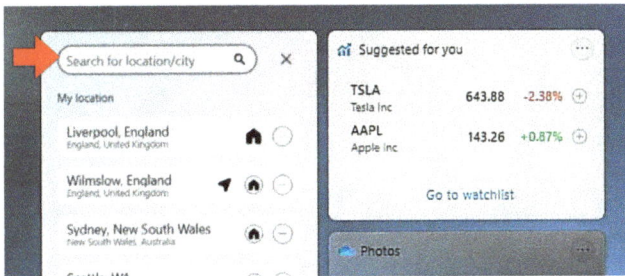

## Remove Widget

To remove a widget, open the widget side panel, click on the three dots icon on the top right of a widget. Select 'hide this widget'.

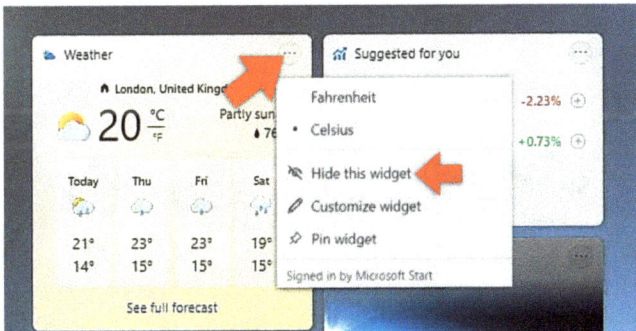

## Customize News Feed

The right hand side of the panel is a live feed of news articles, stories, and other recommended content. On the 'discover' tab, hover your mouse pointer over one of the thumbnail articles in the feed. Click the 'x' to remove the article. Or click the three dots icon, then select 'block...' to stop receiving articles from this source, or click 'follow...' to see more articles from this source.

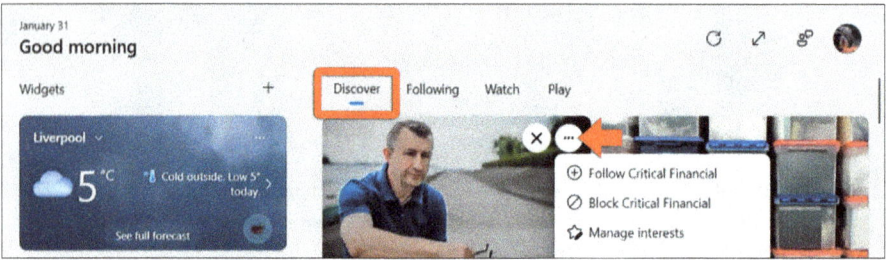

You can select channels and sources whose articles you want to see in your feed. To do this, select the 'following' tab.

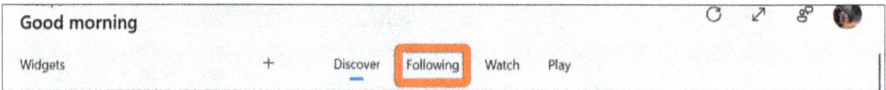

Click 'add channel'.

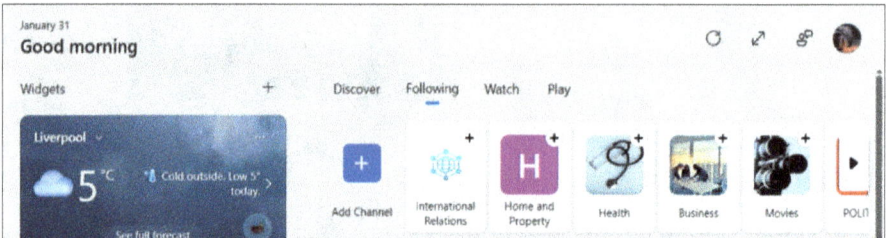

Click on the '+' icons to select a channel to follow. You can also use the search field at the top to search for interests.

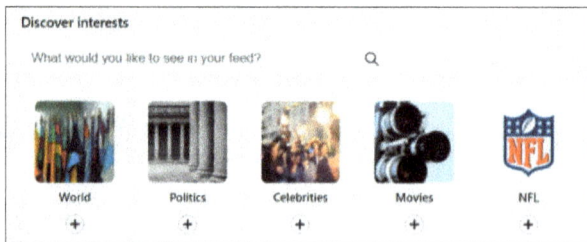

You'll see content from these channels show up in the 'following' tab.

# Windows Search

With Windows search you can search for files, apps, email, music, people, and settings on your PC, as well as a web search.

Scan for Video

You'll find the search field on the taskbar next to the start button. Click in this field to open the search panel.

On the top right, you'll find the search and indexing settings as well as your Microsoft account.

On the left hand side, you'll see a list of all the recent searches. You can click on any of these to revisit. Over on the right, you'll see all the latest trending web searches for the current day. These are called 'search highlights'. You can click on any of these to visit the web link.

# Searching for Files

Click on the search field on your taskbar, then type in your search. This could be the name of an app, a document, email, or website.

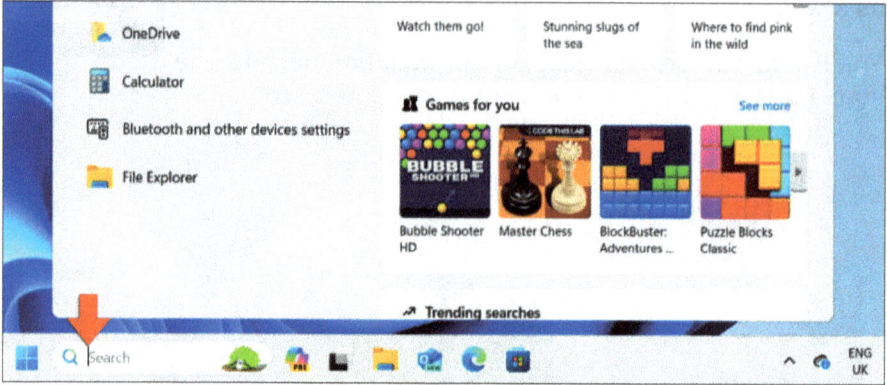

On the left hand side of the search results, you'll see a list of files, apps, and web search suggestions.

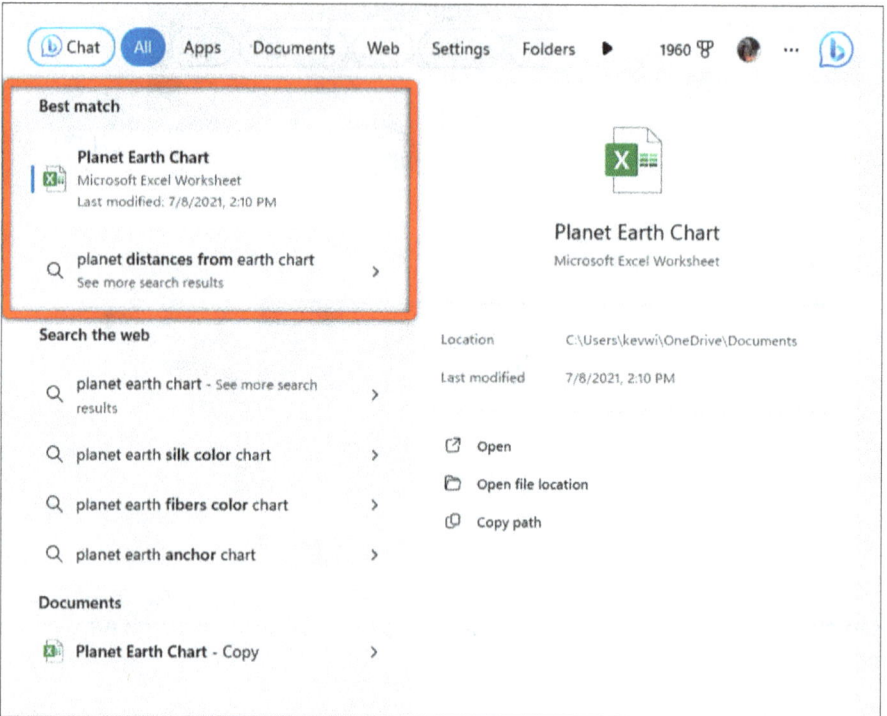

Press the down arrow key on your keyboard to scroll down the list to see some details about the search result.

These details will appear in the right hand half of the window.

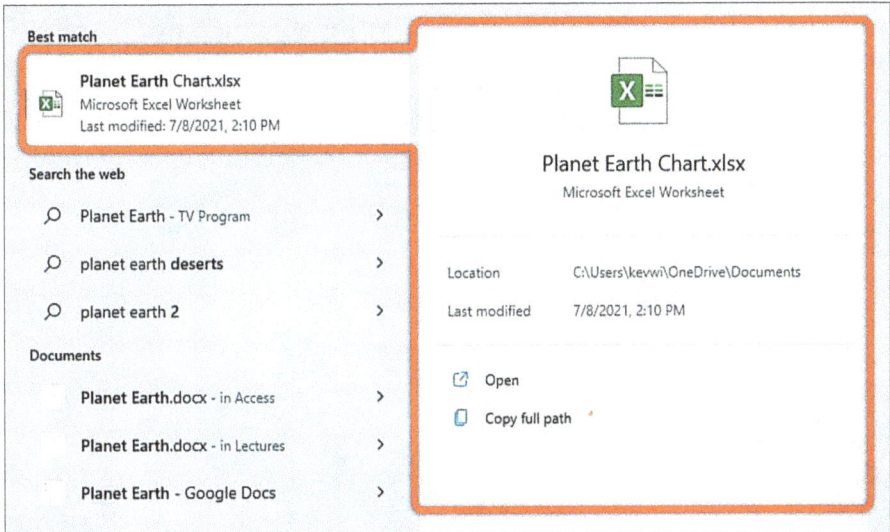

Click on a match from the search results. In this case I was searching for my 'planet earth' chart which happens to be the 'best match' at the top.

## Searching for Apps

You can also search for apps. Click on the search field on the taskbar next to the start button, then type the name of the app into the search field at the top of the search window.

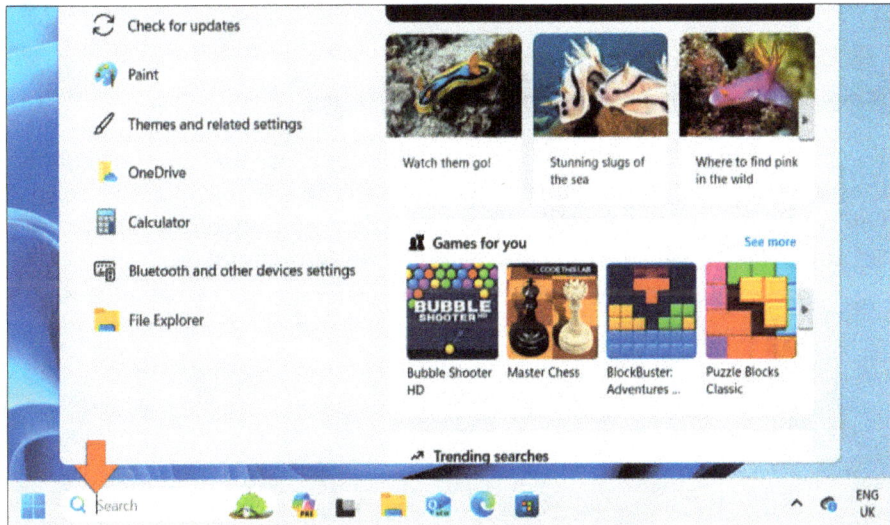

In the search results, you'll see the app name appear under 'best match' on the left. On the right, you'll see some options. Here, you can open the app normally, or run it as an administrator - useful if you need the app to edit system files or change settings. You can pin or unpin it on the start menu or taskbar, and you can edit the app settings - useful if you want to reset the app or repair it. You can also share the app or uninstall it. Most apps, you can just open normally. To do this click on 'open'.

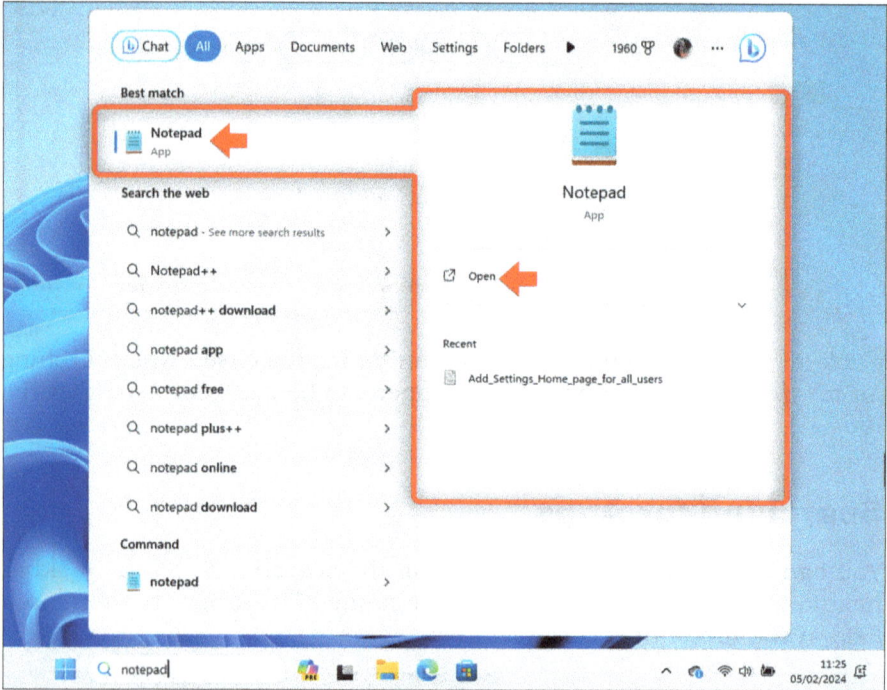

## Searching for Windows Settings

You can search for settings. To do this click on the search icon on the taskbar next to the start button. Type the setting into the search field at the top of the window. For example, you can search for printer settings, Wi-Fi, BlueTooth, display settings and so on.

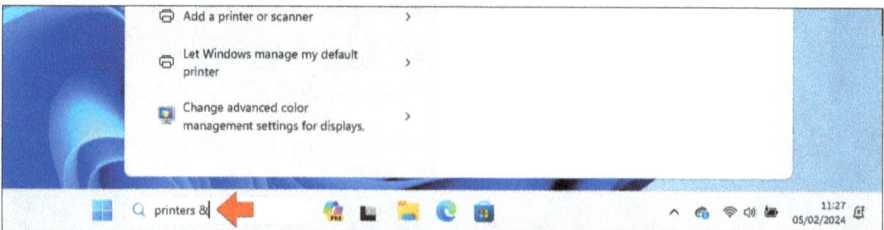

Select the setting from the search results.

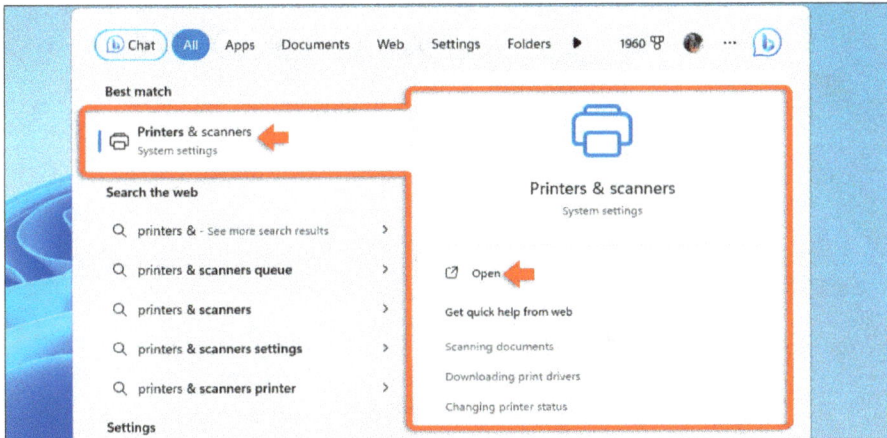

## Narrowing Down the Search

Along the top of the window, you'll see a bar with some options. These allow you to refine your search to apps, documents, email, web, folders, music, people, photos, settings, or videos (click 'more' to see the rest of the options).

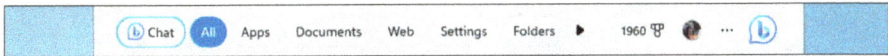

So, if I was searching for my 'planet earth' documents, I'd type 'planet earth' into the search field.

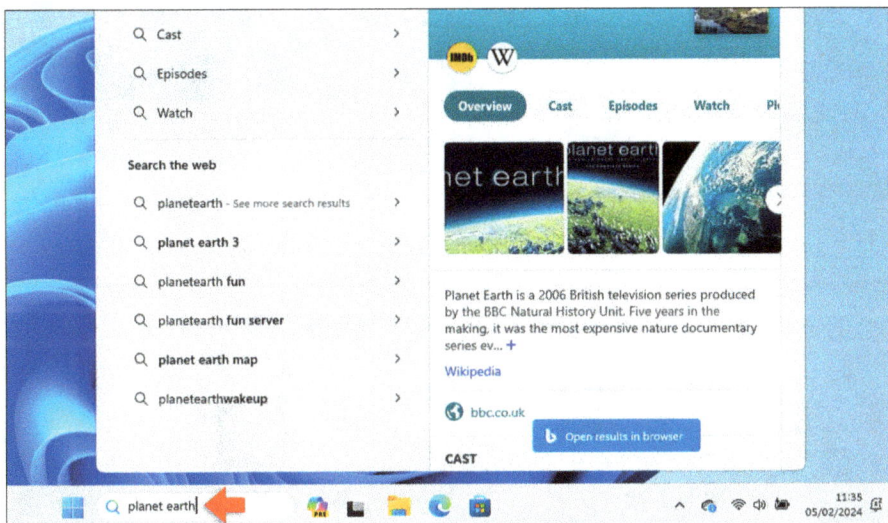

Then from the options, I'd select 'documents'.

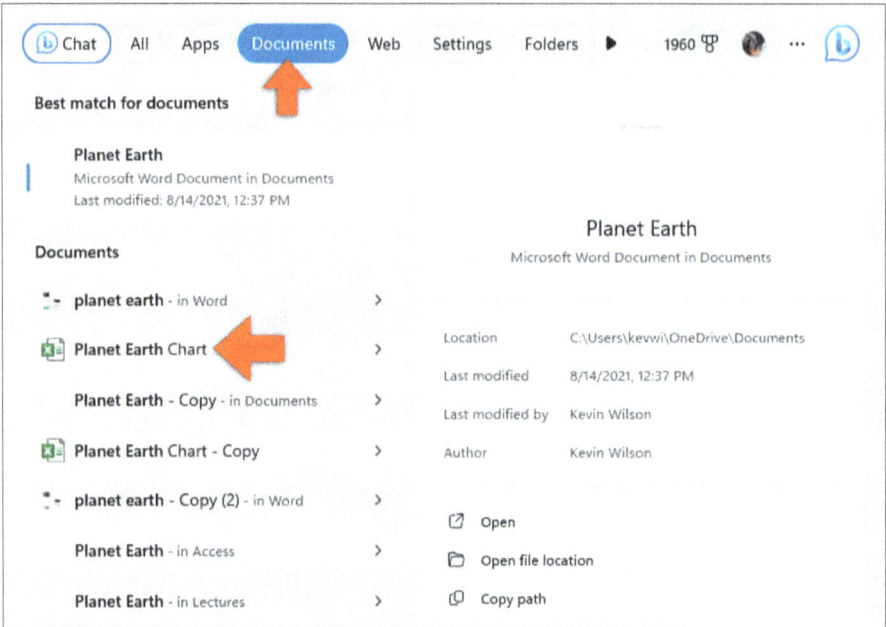

If I just wanted to search the web, I'd select 'web' from the options.

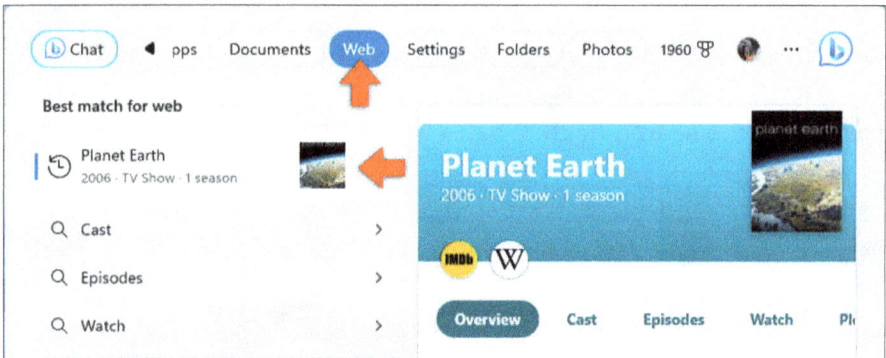

Or if I wanted to search for photos, I'd select 'photos'.

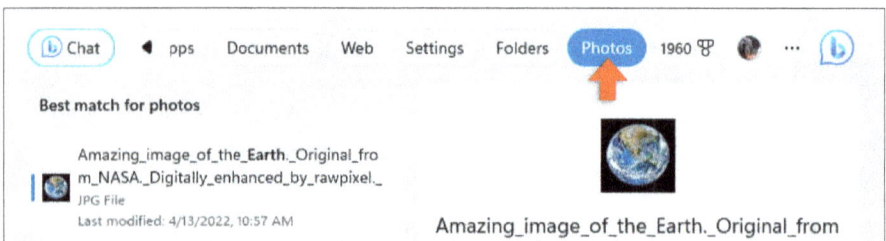

# Virtual Desktops

Using 'Multiple desktops' is almost like having two or more desks in your office, where you can do your work. You could have a desktop for your web browsing and email, another desktop for your word processing, another desktop for your photo editing and sharing and so on. Multiple desktops help to organise your tasks, so you can keep things you are working on together.

## Task View

To access your virtual desktops, click the task view icon on your taskbar, or press Win Tab on your keyboard.

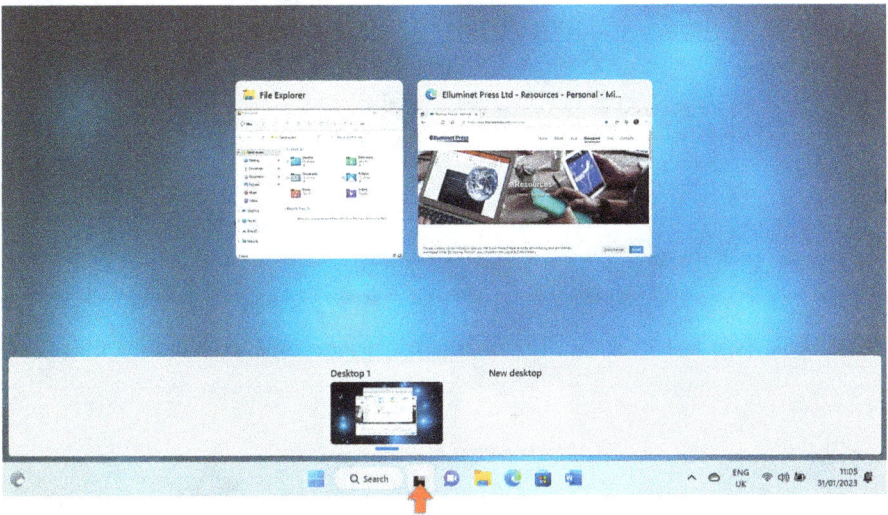

## Creating a New Desktop

To create a new desktop, click the task view icon on your taskbar, then click 'new desktop' from the thumbnails along the bottom of the screen.

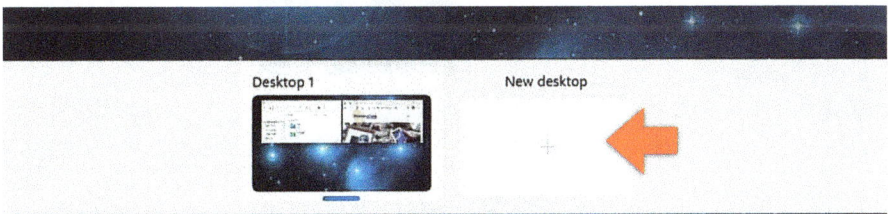

Click on the desktop thumbnail icon to switch to the new desktop.

Now, you can open apps as you would on any desktop.

# Change Background

You can set different backgrounds to help you distinguish between your desktops. To do this, open the taskview, then right click on the thumbnail of the desktop you want to change. Select 'choose background' from the popup menu.

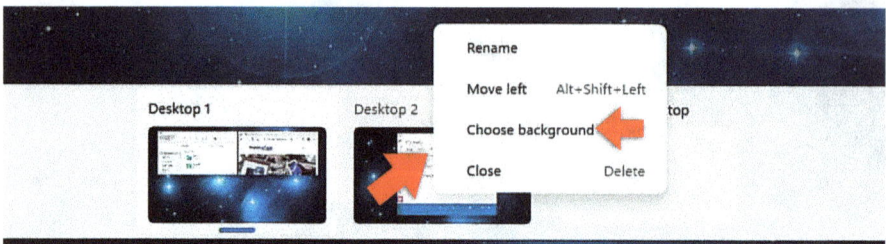

Here, you can select a background, or choose one from your photos.

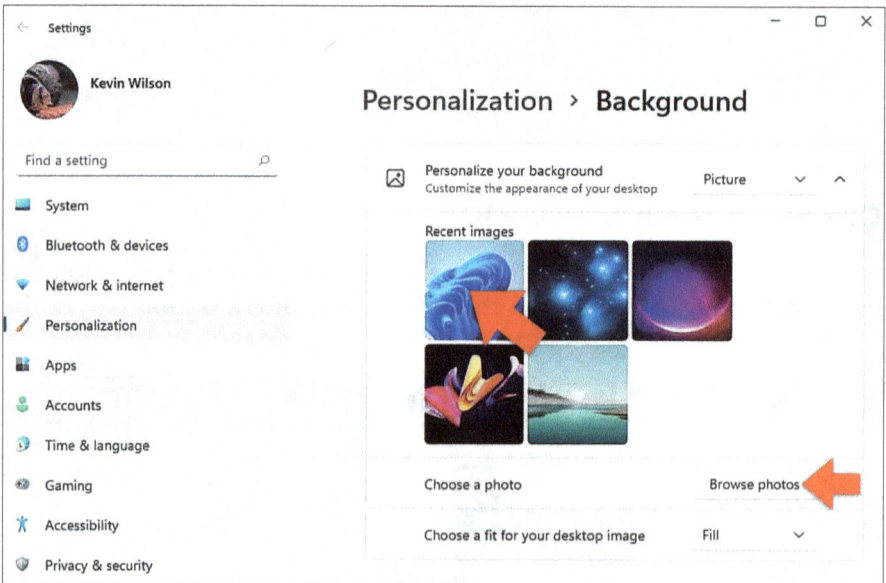

## Renaming

You can name your desktops. To do this, open your taskview, then click on the name of the desktop you want to change.

Type in a meaningful name.

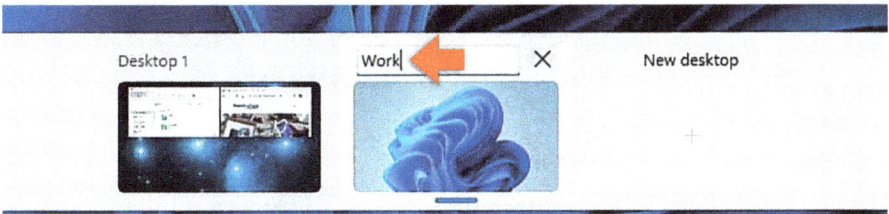

## Reordering

You can reorder your desktops. Just click and drag the thumbnail icon.

## Quick Access

For quick access to your desktops, hover your mouse over the taskview icon on the taskbar.

# Quick Settings

Quick Settings is a compact control panel in Windows 11 that lets you instantly adjust key system functions without opening the full Settings app. Designed for speed and convenience, it provides quick access to essential features like Wi-Fi, Bluetooth, volume, brightness, and more—all in one place with just a single click..

To open quick settings, click the icon on the bottom right of the screen.

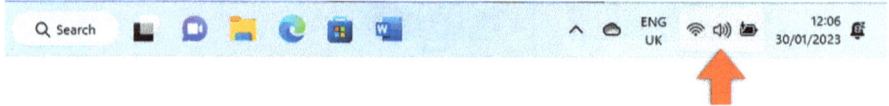

Along the top you'll see media controls if you're are listening to music in spotify or watching a video on YouTube or some other media player. In the panel underneath, you'll see some buttons for Wi-Fi, bluetooth, airplane mode and accessibility settings.

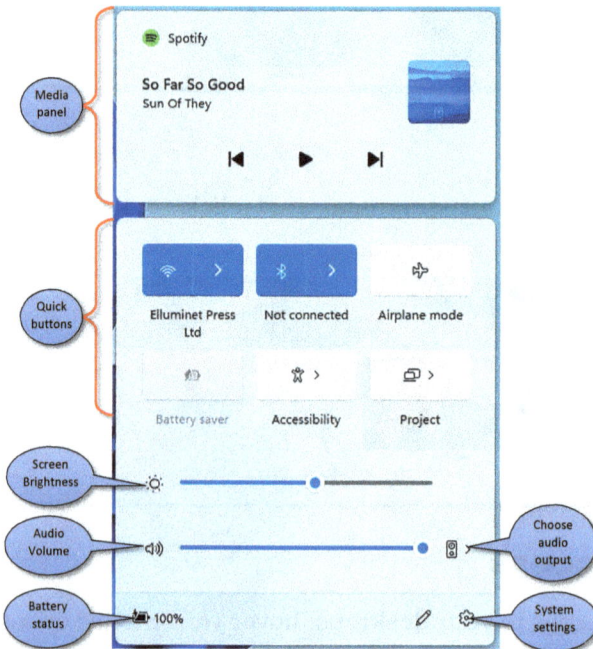

Along the bottom, you'll see a slider to control your audio volume, and if you're using a laptop or tablet, you'll see a screen brightness control.

On the bottom right of the window, you'll see some icons. One allows you to add or remove buttons from the quick settings window, the other opens the settings app.

# Notifications

You'll see notifications and messages. These could be email message that have just arrived, system messages or status alerts from applications. *See page 137 for settings and configuration.*

To open notifications, click on the clock on the bottom right of the taskbar.

Along the top section of the sidebar you'll see all the notifications from apps and system events such as antivirus, etc.

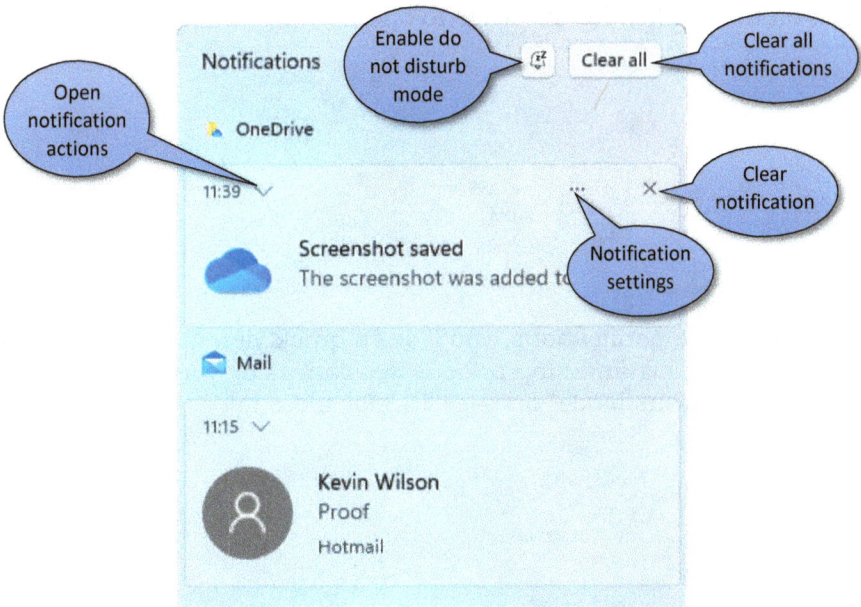

Click the down arrow under the app name to view actions to deal with the notification.

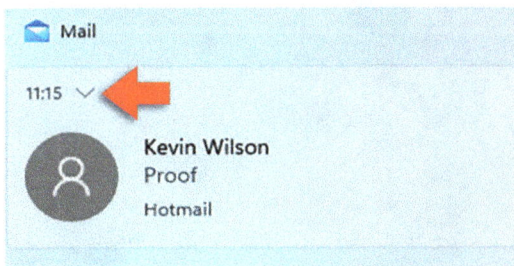

**199**

Here, you'll see a preview of the notification from the app, with some action buttons along the bottom. Depending on the app, you can set a flag, archive, or dismiss the notification

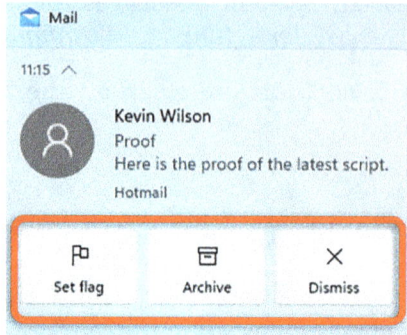

Click on the notification message to open it up.

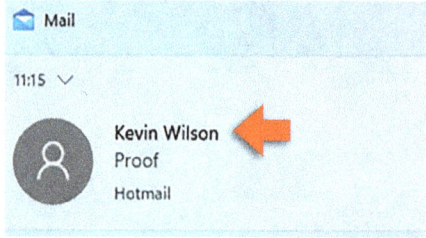

Underneath the notifications, you'll see a quick view of your calendar. You can also start and stop a focus session using the buttons along the bottom. "Focus Mode" on page 132 for more info.

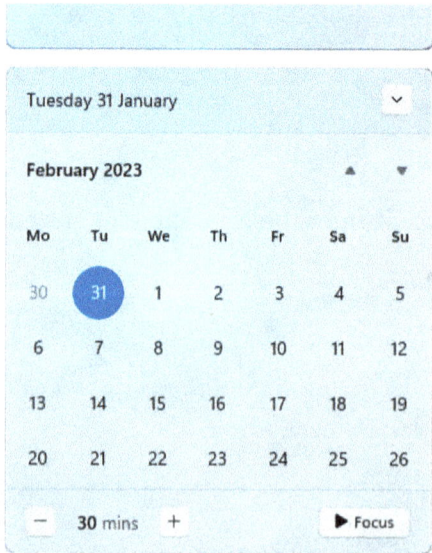

# Windows Ink

Windows Ink is a feature in Windows 11 that contains apps and features that are designed to make use of a touch screen and a pen.

The windows ink icon will appear on the bottom right of your screen when a pen is paired with your device.

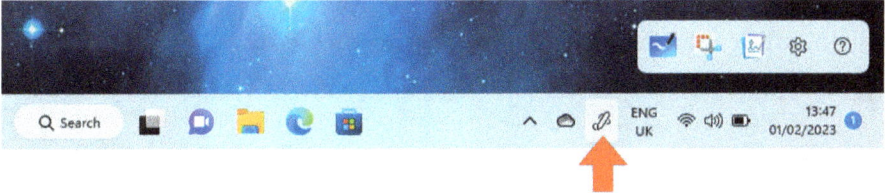

A small popup pen menu will appear. Here, you can open whiteboard, the snipping tool, and journal See page 410 to page 425 for information on how to use these apps. The fourth icon along changes pen settings and allows you to edit the pen menu.

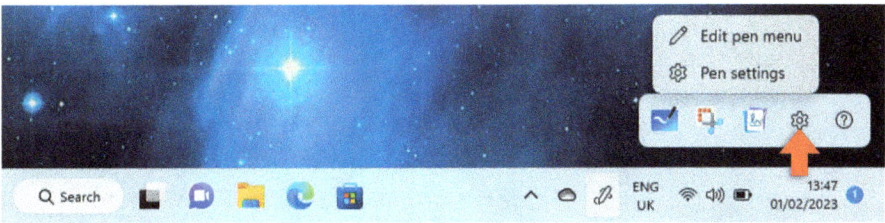

To add/remove icons from the pen menu, click the settings icon, then select 'edit pen menu'. Here you add or remove icons from the menu.

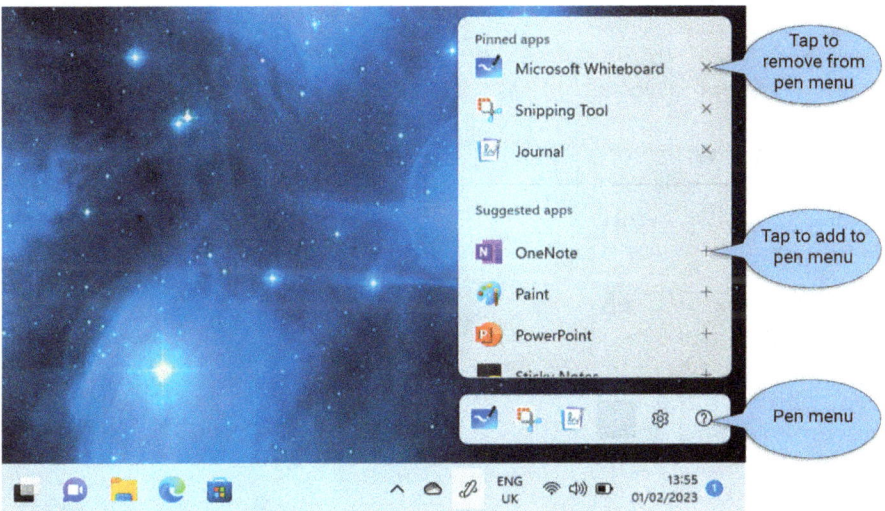

To change your pen settings, click the settings icon, then select 'pen settings'. Here, you can choose which hand you write with: left or right.

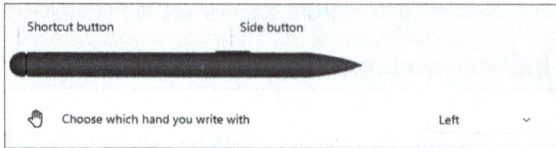

Click on the small side arrows to expand the sections underneath.

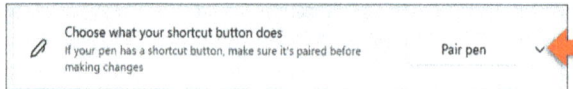

Choose what happens when you press the shortcut button or side button on your pen.

For example, you can set the shortcut button to open the whiteboard app with a single click, or open the journal app with a double click.

Further down the page, you can enable/disable visual effects, or the mouse cursor.

You can enable 'ignore touch input'. This ignores all touch input except your pen, meaning if you rest your hand on the screen it will not interfere with your pen.

At the bottom you can show/hide the pen icon until you use your pen, or show the on-screen keyboard when no physical keyboard is present.

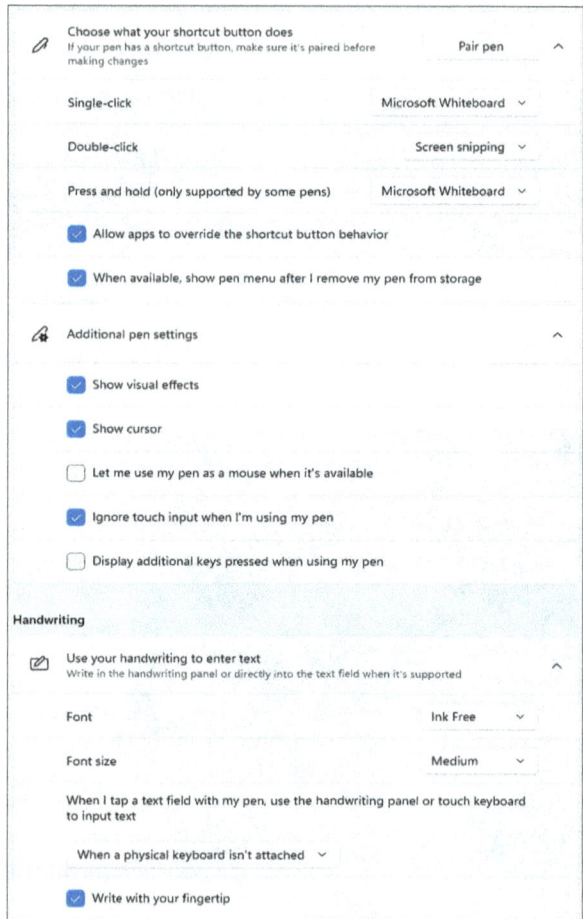

# Arranging Windows on the Desktop

It's useful when working in Windows 11 to arrange the windows on your desktop, especially when you're using more than one application at a time. For example, you could be browsing the web and writing a Word document at the same time - perhaps you're researching something, you could have Word open and your web browser next to it on the screen.

Take a look at the 'resizing and moving windows' demo in the video resources. Open your browser and navigate to the following website:

```
elluminetpress.com/win-11-nav
```

## Moving a Window

Move your mouse pointer to the title bar at the top of the window.

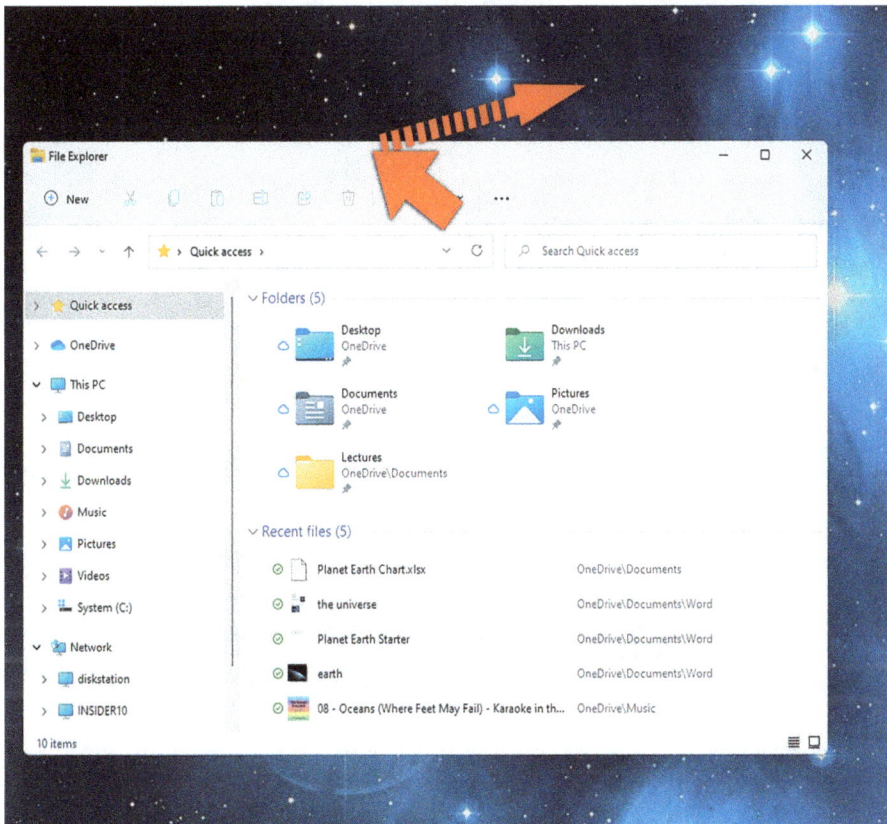

Now click and drag the window to your desired position on the screen.

## Resizing a Window

To resize a window, move your mouse pointer to the bottom right corner of the window - your pointer should turn into a double edged arrow.

The double edged arrow means you can resize the window. Now click and drag the edge of the window until it is the size you want.

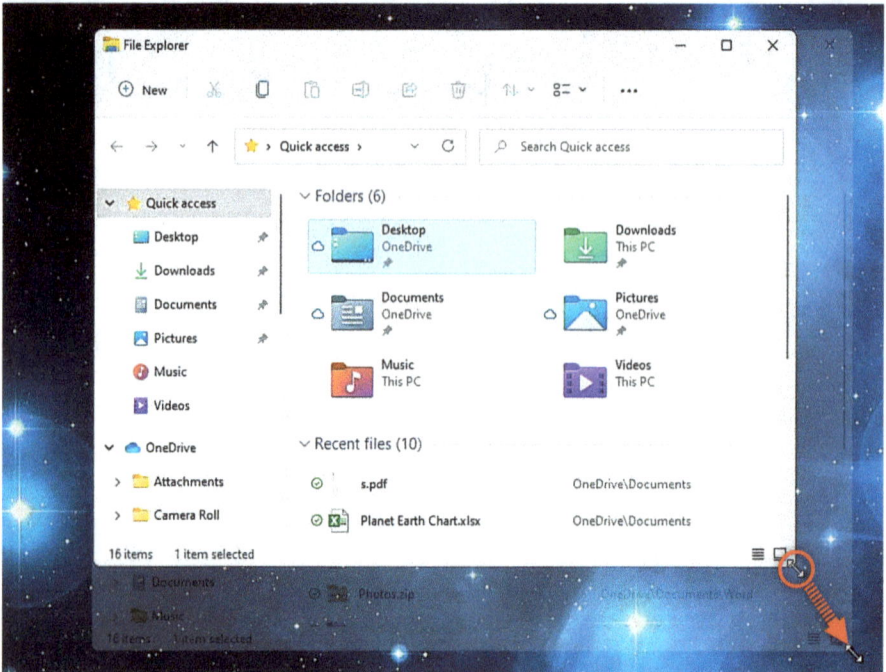

You can drag any edge of the window - left, bottom or right edge, but I find using the corner allows you to freely resize the window much more easily.

If you're on a touch screen, tap and drag the corner of the window.

**204**

## Minimise, Maximise & Close a Window

On the top right hand side of every window, you'll see three icons. You can use these icons to minimise a window, ie reduce it to the taskbar essentially hiding the window from the desktop. With the second icon, you can maximise the window so it fills the entire screen, or if the window is already maximised, using the same icon, restore the window to its original size. The third icon you can use to close a window completely.

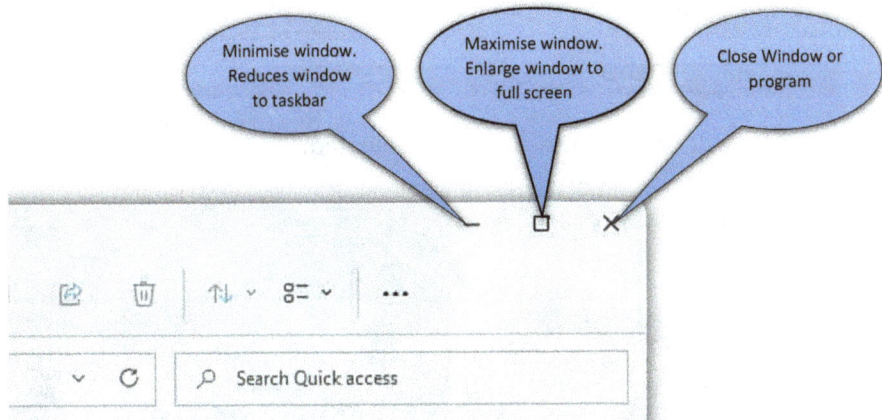

Minimise window. Reduces window to taskbar

Maximise window. Enlarge window to full screen

Close Window or program

Search Quick access

## Snap Layouts

Snap layouts allow you to quickly arrange applications and other windows on your screen according to pre-set template (called a layout) such as the layouts shown below. You can snap two apps side by side, with both the same size, or the left app larger then the right app.

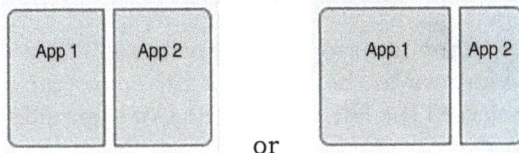

App 1   App 2

App 1   App 2

or

Or you can snap three apps - one large down the left, and two underneath one another on the right. Or you can snap four apps, one in each corner.

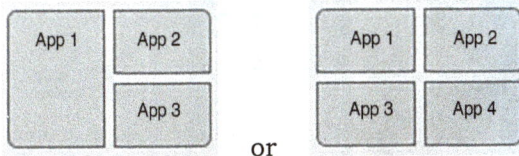

App 1   App 2
        App 3

App 1   App 2
App 3   App 4

or

**Scan for Video**

# Chapter 5: Getting around Windows 11

## Snapping Windows

To snap a window, hover your mouse over a window's maximize button, then select a zone on one of the layouts to snap the window to. Or press **Win Z** on your keyboard.

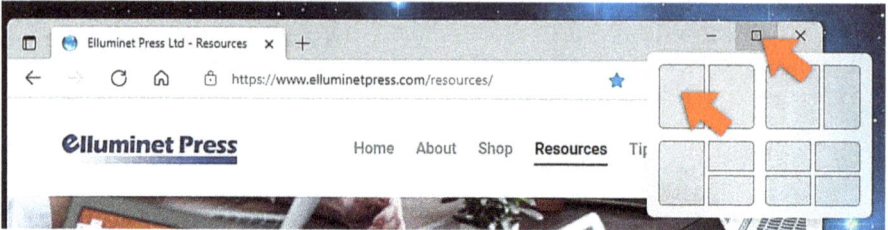

The window will snap to the zone you selected.

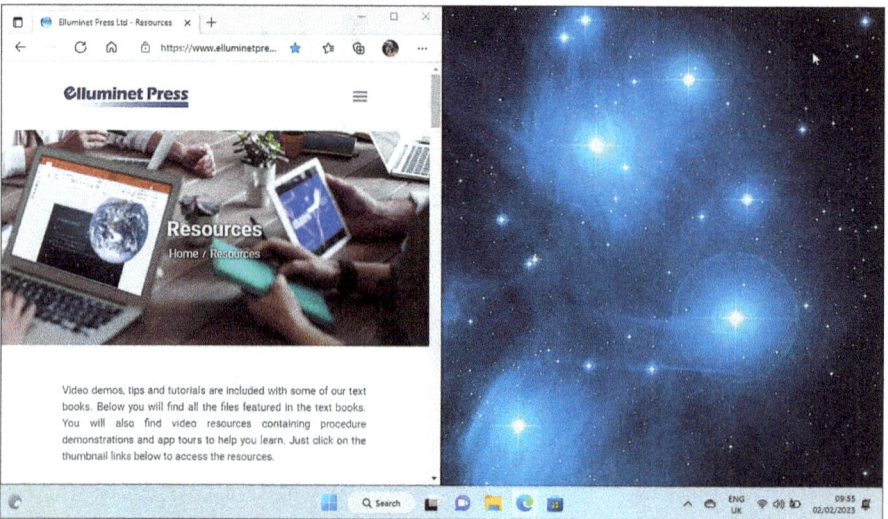

If you have any other apps open, snap assist will ask you to snap the rest of the windows to the layout of the zone you selected earlier. Remember we selected the left zone on the two apps side by side layout.

So, if I had Edge and Word running, the snap assist will ask me to snap Word to the second zone on the layout I selected.

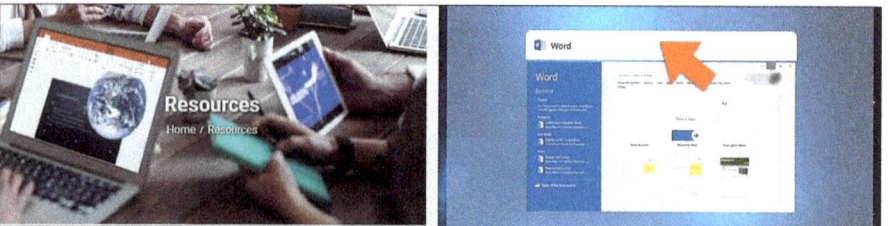

## Dragging Windows

You can also drag windows directly to the snap layout. To do this, click and drag the app window to the top middle of the screen. You'll see a marker appear.

When the layouts appear, drag the window to the area on the layout where you want to put it. For example, here I'm going to drag my browser window to the left hand side of the first layout. This will put the window on the left half of the screen.

## Snap Groups

Snap groups are a way to easily switch back to your snapped windows. Hover over one of the open apps on the taskbar, you'll see a snap group. Click on the group to switch back.

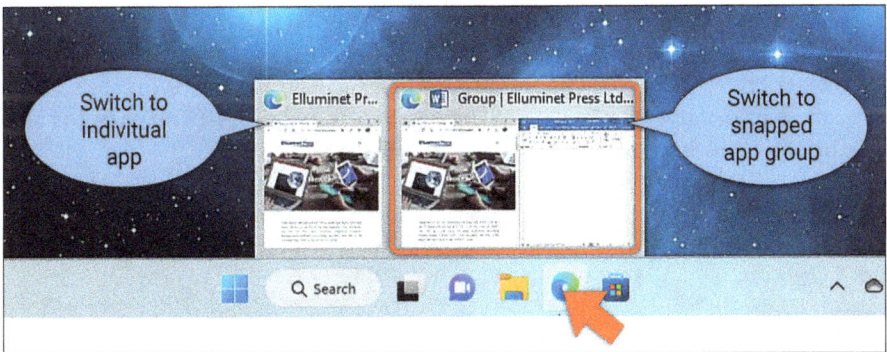

# Multiple Screens

You can plug in more than one screen into most modern computers or tablets if you have the correct adapters.

Scan for Video

To set up multiple monitors, open the Settings app, select System from the list on the left, then click on Display.

At the top of the display settings, you'll see numbered rectangles representing your connected screens. If you don't see both screens, scroll down to the Multiple displays section and set the drop-down to Extend these displays.

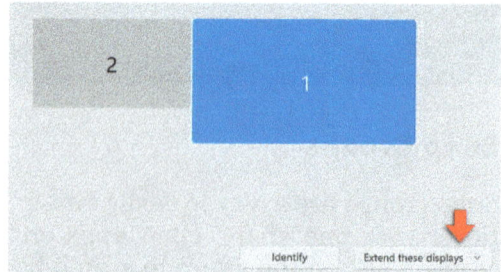

These rectangles represent connected screens. The idea is to arrange the rectangles so they match the physical layout of your desk. In the photo at the top of the page, screen 1 is physically on the left, and screen 2 is on the right. Click Identify to display the numbers on the actual screens so you know which is which.

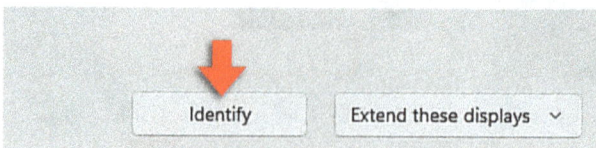

Now, click and drag these rectangles to match the physical positions. Here screen 1 needs to be on the left hand side of screen 2.

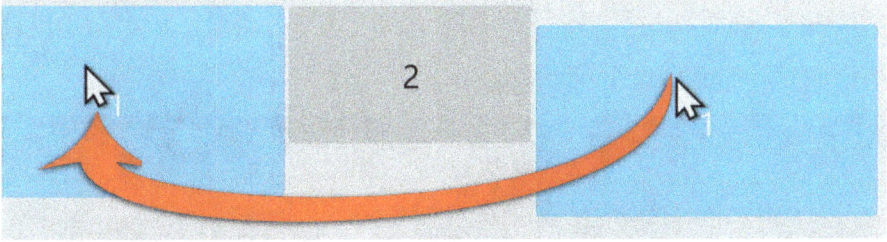

Next set your main display. The main display is the screen where the system tray (clock, network, volume icons), system notifications appear, and apps open by default. It also displays the login and lock screen when the computer is first started or awakened. This display is the central point of interaction in a multi-screen setup. To make a screen your main display, click on its rectangle, open the 'multiple displays' section, then click 'make this my main display'.

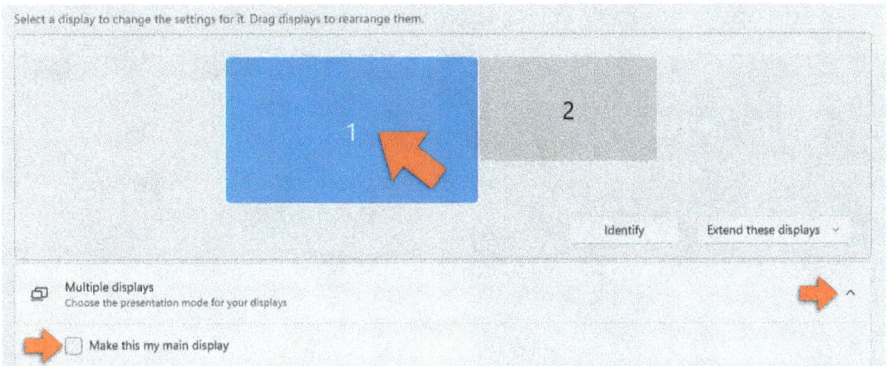

This setup allows you to extend your desktop across multiple screens— whether that's a second monitor, a TV, or a projector. When your displays are set to extend, you can drag windows or apps between screens. In the photo below, Microsoft Edge is being dragged from screen 1 onto screen 2.

## Using Projectors

Much like using multiple screens, you can also use a projector as your second display.

Press **Win P** on your keyboard.

From the options panel, select the display you want.

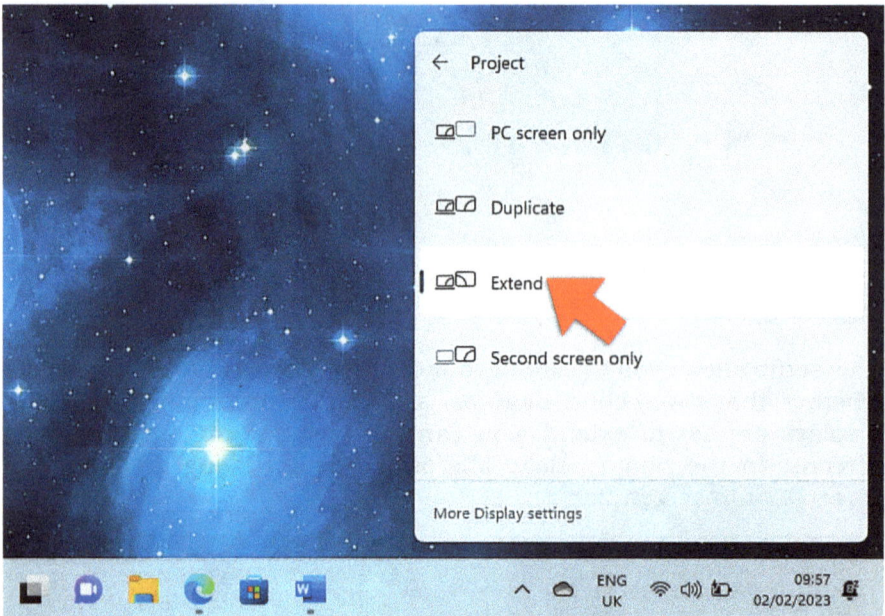

Here, you can project to your PC screen only, you can mirror or duplicate the screens so they both display the same thing, or you can extent the screen making the projector or second screen an extension to your PC screen. Or you can project to the second screen or projector only, leaving your PC screen blank.

**210**

# Duplicate PC screen onto Second Screen

Everything you do on the laptop screen (PC Screen) will be duplicated on the second screen (eg projector). So both screens will show the same image.

## Second Screen Only

This disables your PC's monitor and allows the display to only appear on the second screen.

## PC Screen Only

This disables the projector and allows the information to be seen only on the PC's monitor.

## Extend PC screen onto Second Screen

The second screen (such as a projector) acts as an extension to your laptop screen (PC Screen), rather than just a duplicate. So you can have something on your laptop screen and show different images on the projector as shown below.

This allows you to move windows from the laptop's screen (PC Screen 1) to Screen 2 (eg projector) and vice versa.

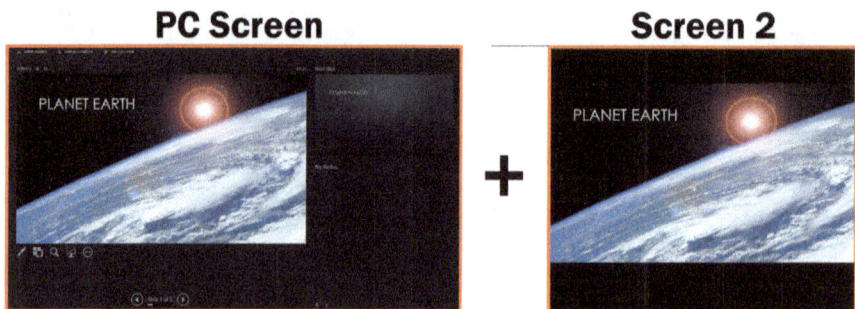

Screen 2 becomes an extension of the PC Screen. Ideal for using presentation software such as Pro Presenter or PowerPoint.

## Docking

If you use a laptop or a windows tablet, sometimes you want to connect it to a larger monitor with an external keyboard and mouse. This could mean you simply plug in an external monitor, keyboard and mouse, or use a docking station. In the image below, you can see my laptop is docked with a docking station. There is a large external monitor connected to the docking station, as well as a keyboard and mouse.

When you un-dock the laptop, the windows on your external monitor will be minimized. Here, below on the laptop's screen, you can see the two apps I had open on my external monitor have been minimised.

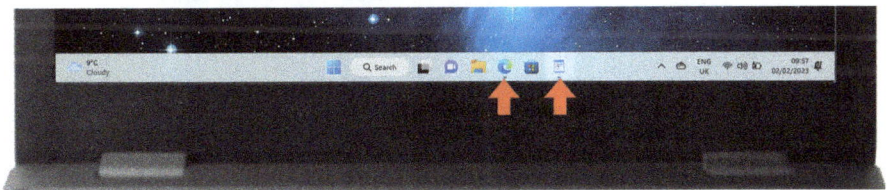

This is indicated with a small dot under the icon. You can click on these icons to open the apps you were working on.

**213**

When you re-dock your laptop, Windows returns the apps you had open on the external monitor, as shown below.

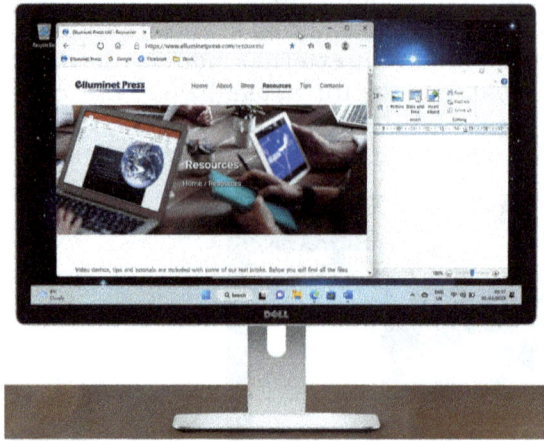

To find the settings of this feature, open your settings app then select 'system' from the list on the left. Click on 'display', then select 'multiple displays'.

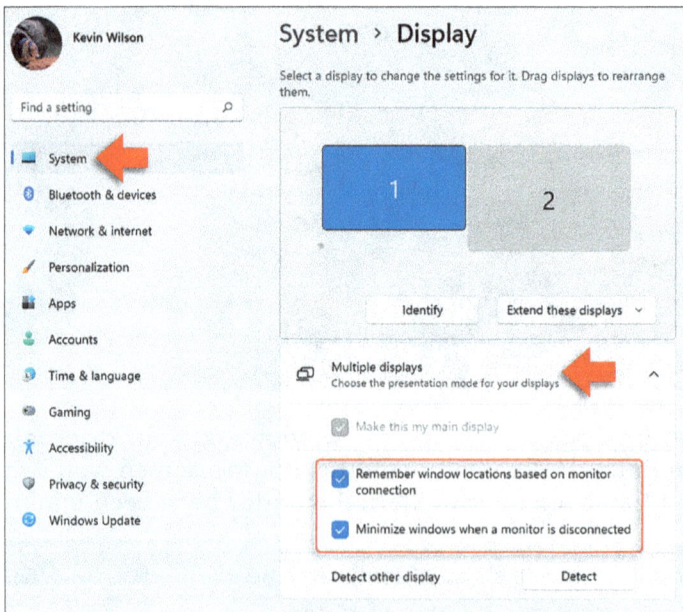

Here, you can enable/disable the 'remember window locations' on your external monitor. You can also enable whether you want the apps to be minimized when you un-dock your laptop, or you can disable 'minimize windows' to have the apps you had on your external monitor, simply transfer to your laptop screen when un-docked.

**214**

# Cloud Clipboard

Cloud clipboard allows you to copy & paste multiple items across all your devices. So for example, you could copy a paragraph off a Word document on your laptop, and paste it into a document on your surface tablet.

To open cloud clipboard, hold the windows key, then tap V.

You'll see a small window appear on the right hand side of the screen. When you do this for the first time on your device, Windows will ask you to turn on clipboard history.

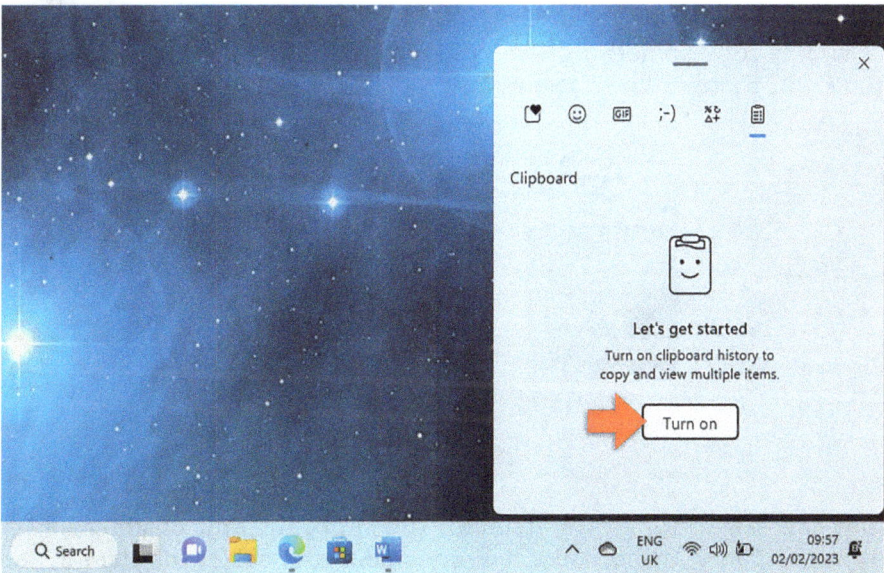

Click 'turn on' to enable clipboard history.

# Copying Multiple Items

If you are doing something that requires you to copy and paste different images or text, you'll find yourself re-copying the same piece of text or image multiple times. Cloud clipboard allows you to copy multiple images or blocks of text, so you can store them on your clipboard, then select and paste in what you need.

You can see below, as we've copied the paragraph, it has been added to the clipboard.

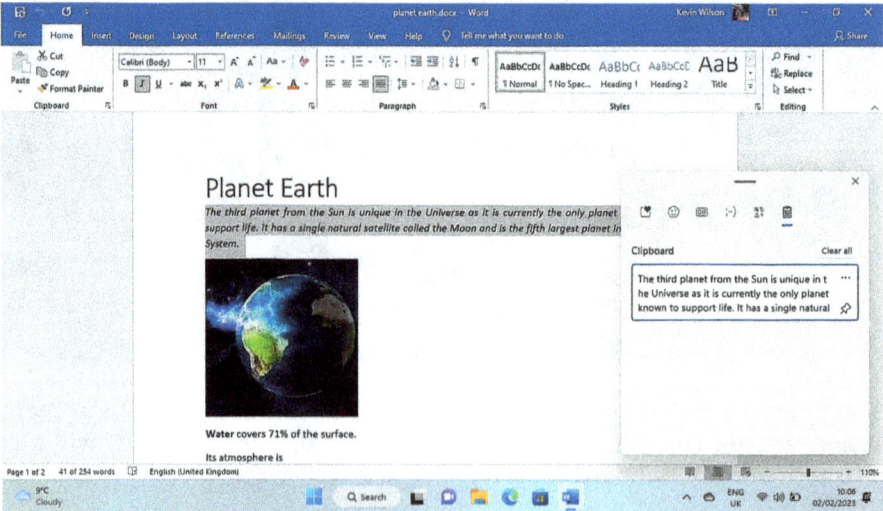

Now, lets copy something else. You can see in the clipboard panel on the right, there are now two items.

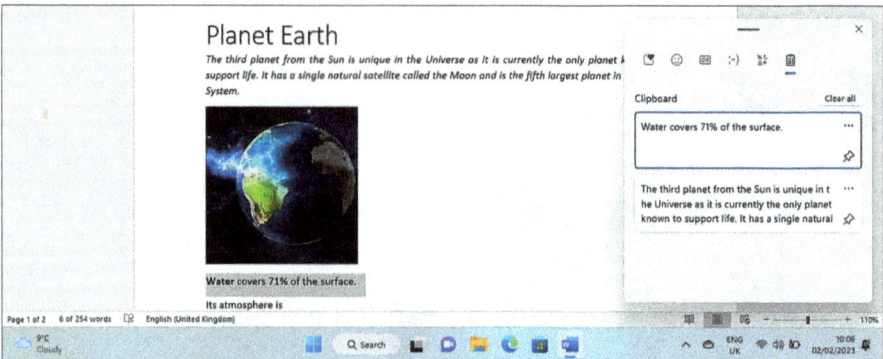

You can select any of the items in the clipboard and paste them in. Just position your cursor in the document and select the item in the clipboard you want to paste. Remember press windows key & V to open the clipboard panel, if it disappears.

# Copying Across Devices

To sync your clipboard across all your devices, first check that this feature is enabled and you are signed into your device using your Microsoft Account. To check, open your settings app, click 'system', then select 'clipboard' from the list on the right hand side.

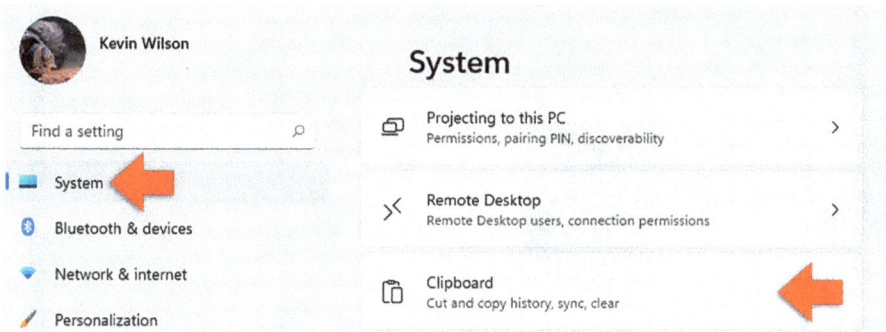

Turn on 'sync across your devices'.

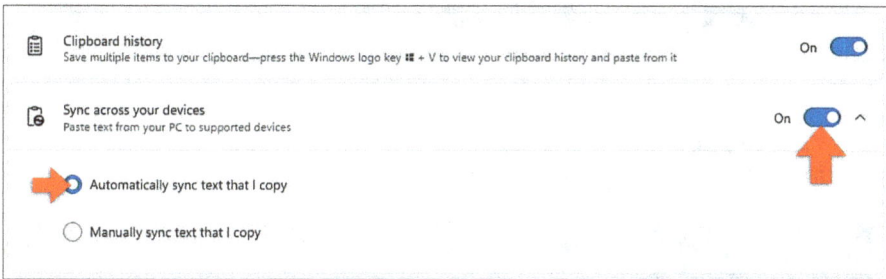

Do this on all your devices. All devices need to be signed in with the same Microsoft Account for this to work.

Now that we have enabled cloud clipboard, in this demo we are going to copy a paragraph from a Word document on the laptop on the left, and paste it into another document on a surface tablet on the right. You can see this setup in the photograph below.

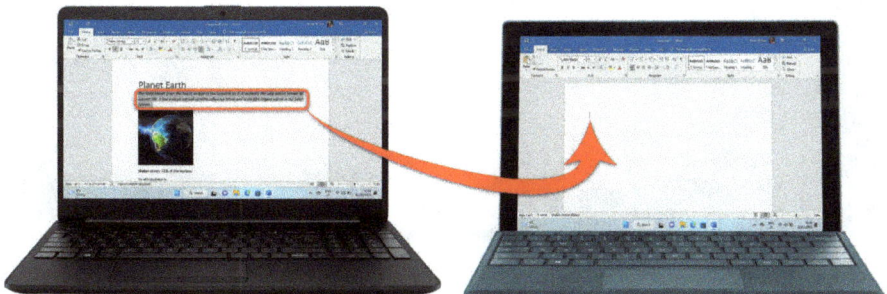

## Chapter 5: Getting around Windows 11

On the laptop, select the text, then click copy, or press Control C.

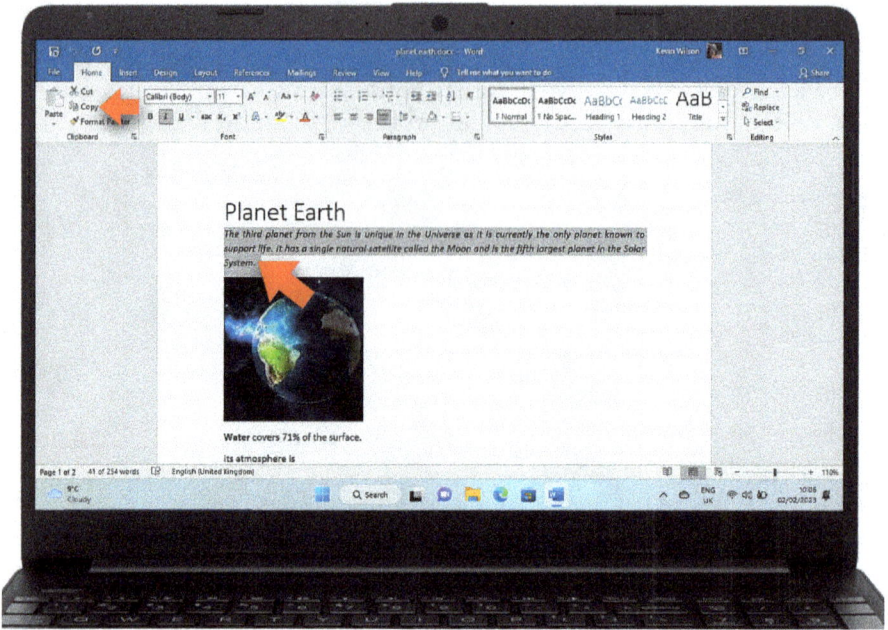

Now go onto the other device - the surface tablet. Open up the app you want to paste the text into. Eg Word. In the document, click on the position where you want to paste the text.

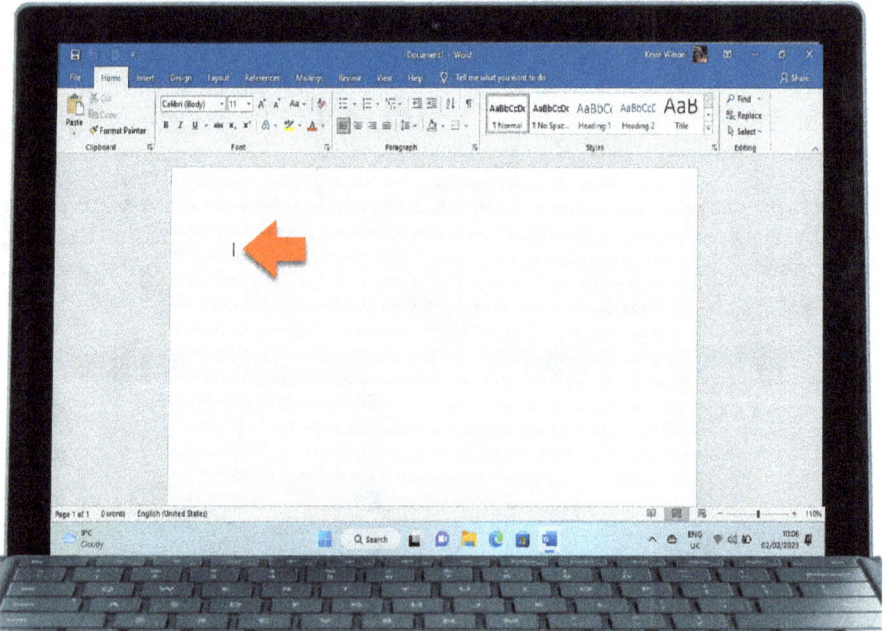

Hold down the windows key, then press V. You'll see the clipboard window open up on the bottom right hand corner of the screen.

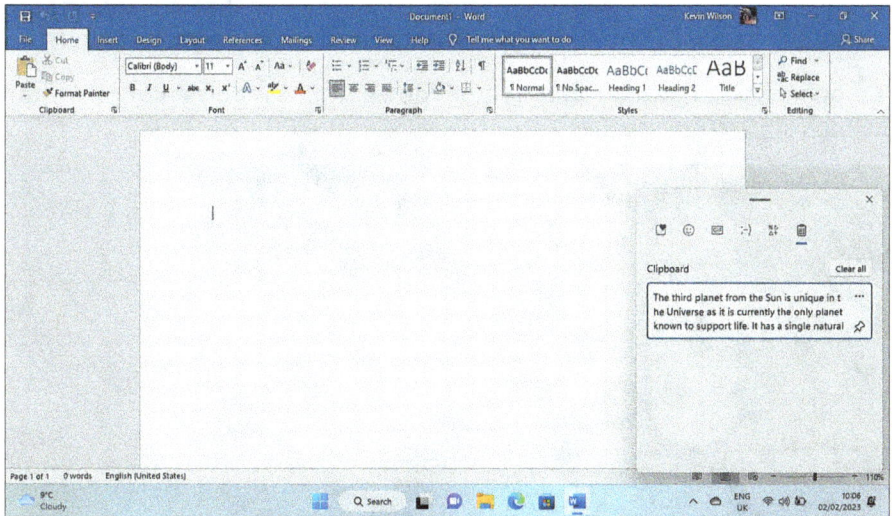

Along the top of the window, you'll see a row of icons. Click on the clipboard icon on the far right, then select the clipping you wan to paste into the word document.

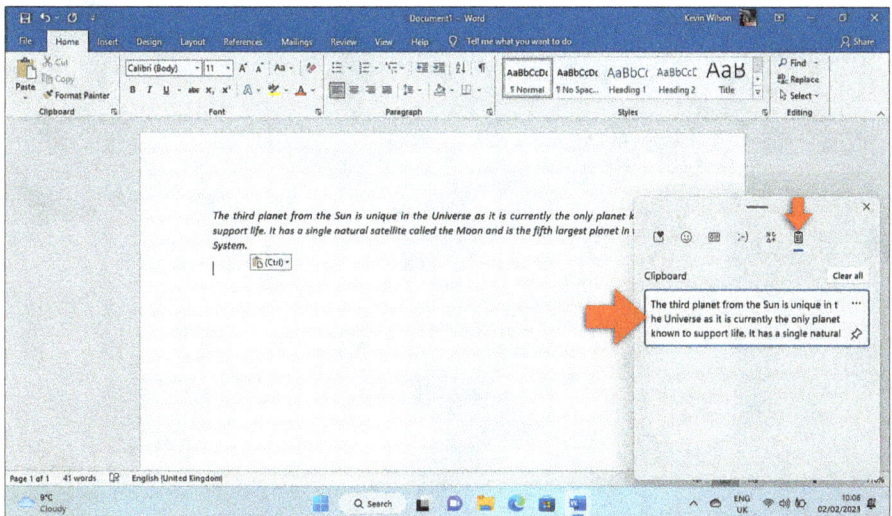

You can do this with text and images. Anything you can copy and paste, you can now paste to any device you've signed into with your Microsoft Account.

*Note that all your devices must be running Windows 11, or the October 2018 Update (1809) of Windows 10 or later for this feature to work.*

# Character Map & Symbols

The character map is useful for inserting symbols that do not appear on your keyboard. These could be mathematical symbols or emojis.

To open the character map, hold down the windows key on your keyboard, then press ;

Along the top of the panel, you'll see six icons.

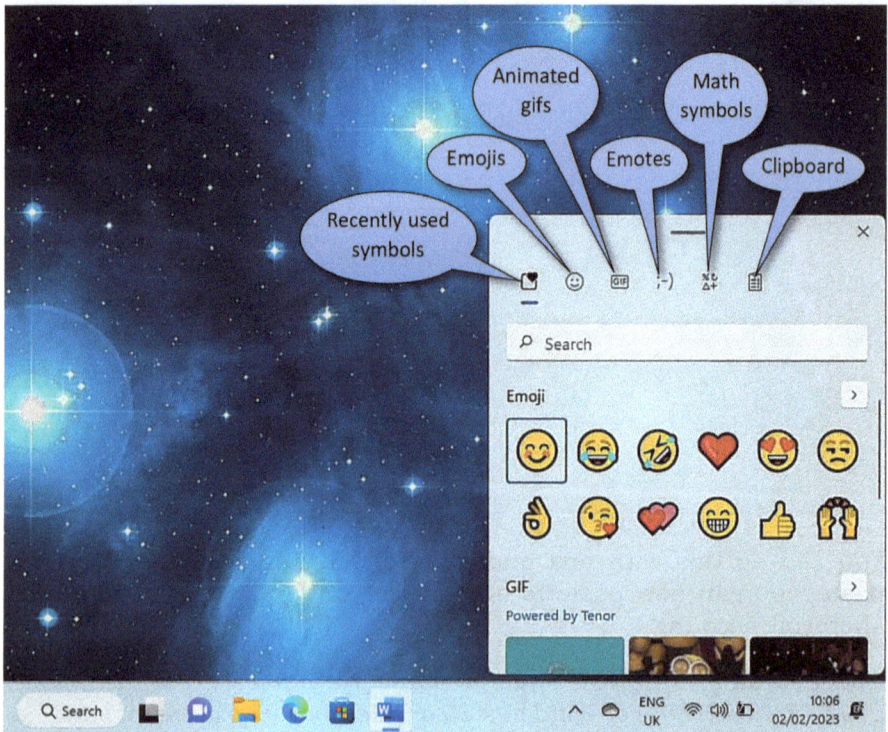

Here, you can add currency, mathematical and language symbols. Select the symbols icon from the top of the panel, then select a symbol group from the list along the top

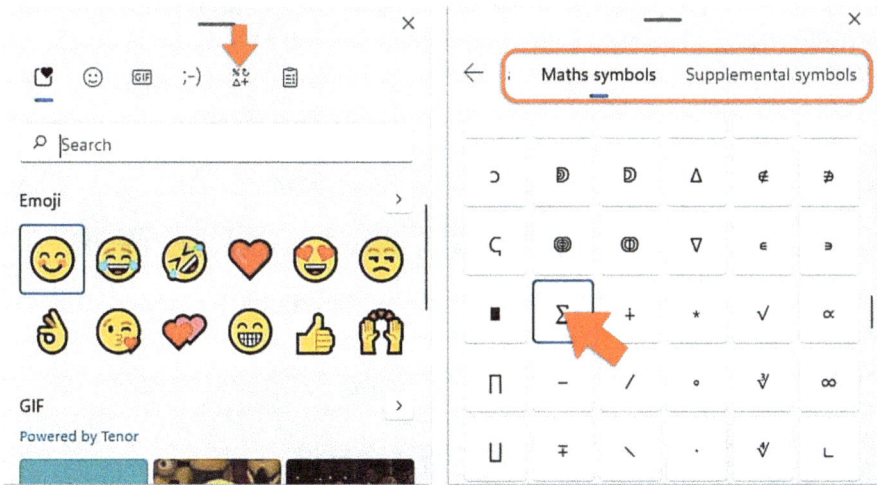

You can also add emojis, select the emoji icon from the icons along the top

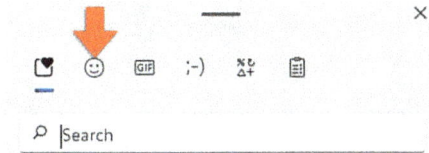

Select an emoji from the icons.

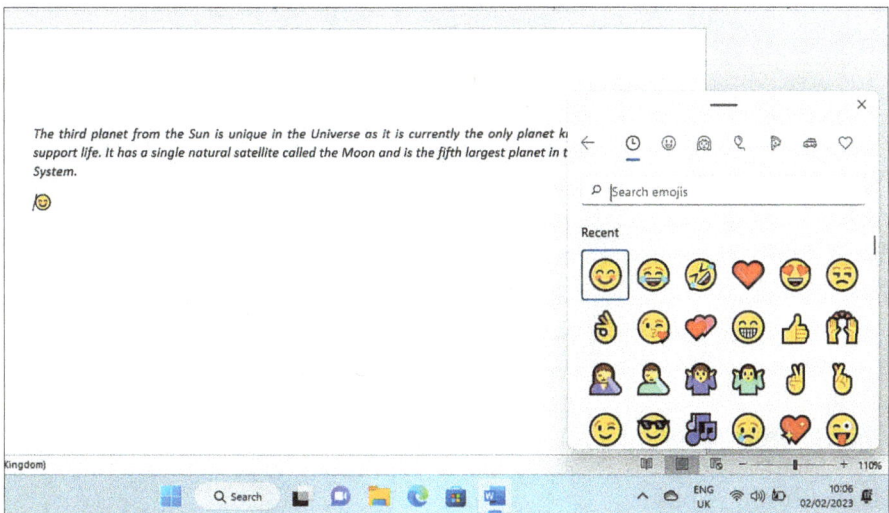

# Taking Screenshots

You can take screenshots using the screen snip feature. Use it to save and share recipes, stories, articles and so on. Screenshots are saved to your clipboard. You can then paste them into an email, message, Word document, or graphics application.

To take a full screen screenshot, press print screen on your keyboard.

To take a screenshot of only part of the screen, hold down the Windows Key and the Shift key, then press S.

Along the top of your screen you'll see a toolbar with some options.

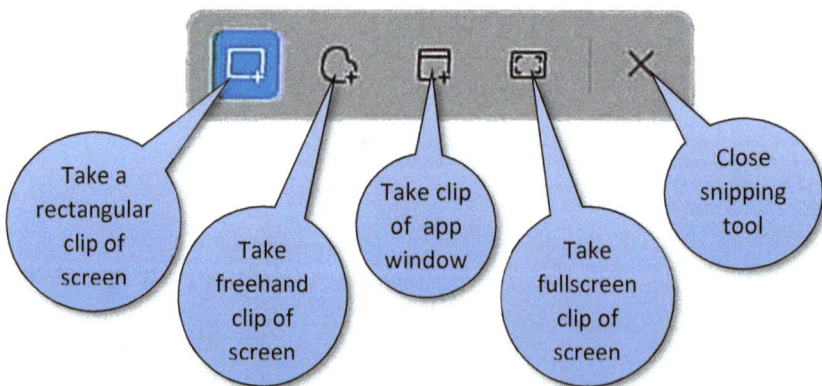

Take a rectangular clip of screen

Take freehand clip of screen

Take clip of app window

Take fullscreen clip of screen

Close snipping tool

Select which type of clip you want to capture. The rectangular or fullscreen clips are the most useful. You can also take a freehand clip or capture a window.

To take a rectangular clip of the screen, click and drag the rectangular box highlight around the area that you want.

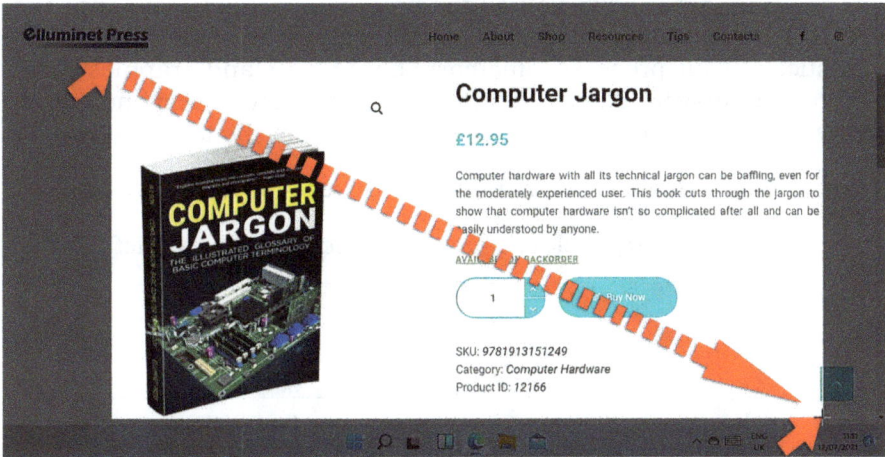

To take a freehand clip of the screen, select the freehand slip icon, then click and draw around the section of the screen you want.

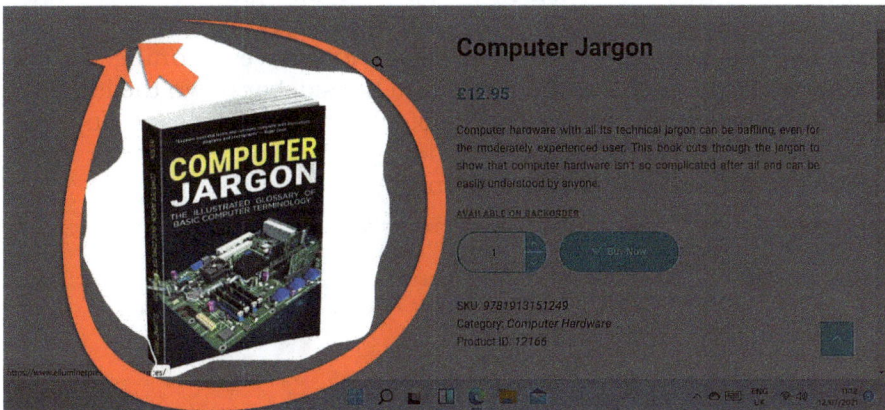

You'll be able to find the clips of the screen on your clipboard. Press Windows V to view your clipboard. Here, you'll be able to paste into a message, document, image editor or email.

**223**

# Task Manager

The task manager shows you all the processes, services and apps that are currently running on your machine, as well as some performance statistics of your processor, memory, hard drives and graphics cards. The task manager is also useful if a program stops responding and freezes up - you can terminate the program from the task manager.

To open task manager, press **control-shift-esc** on your keyboard

To reveal the sidebar, click the hamburger icon on the top left.

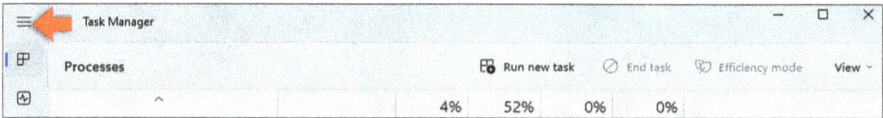

## View Running Apps, Tasks & Processes

Here you will see some tabs down the side of the window. This will show you running processes, apps and tasks. Next, you'll find computer performance charts for memory, WiFi, CPU and graphics card. You'll also find a history of apps you've used, apps that run at start up, apps used by a specific user, details of apps and services running. To view the information, just select the tab from the sidebar down the left hand side. Here below, we can see the list of all running processes, apps and tasks. Over on the right hand section, you'll see the resources each app, task and process are consuming.

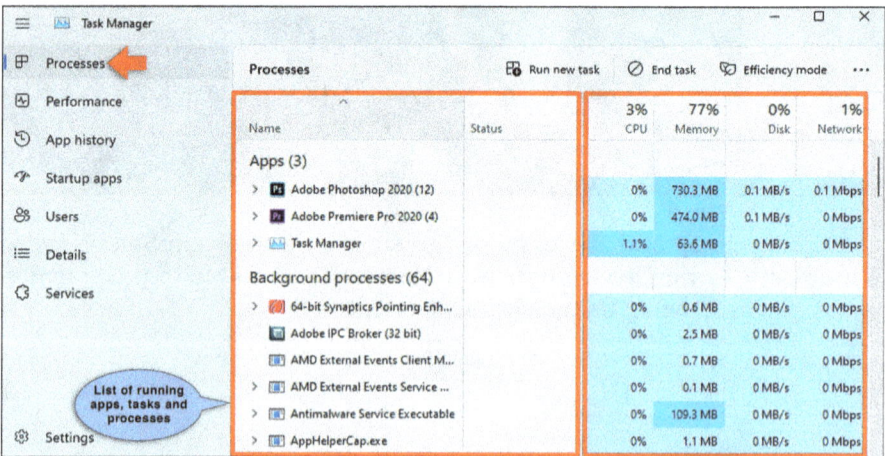

You can also terminate some of these apps - to do this click the service/ app then click 'end task'. You should only do this if the particular app/ service is causing a problem. Don't start terminating services as it can cause your machine to become unstable.

Task manager is useful to terminate apps that have crashed or 'not responding'.

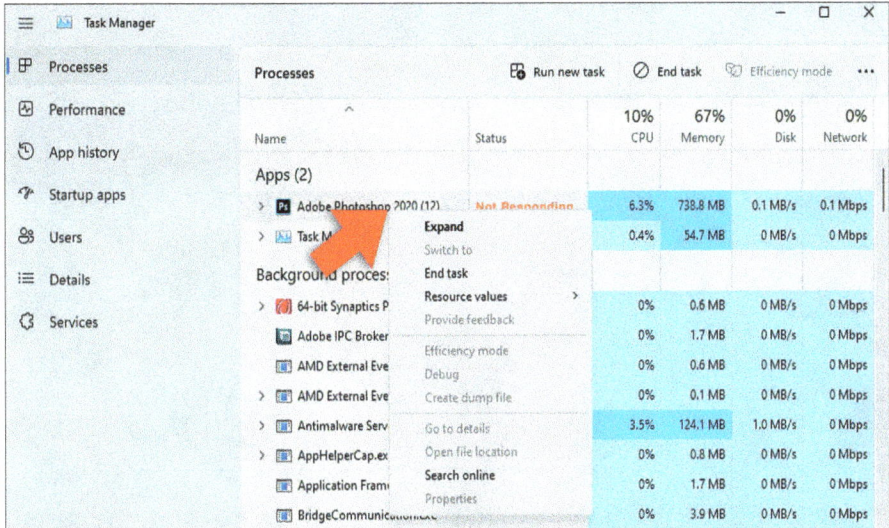

To do this, find the app in the 'processes' tab. The app that has crashed is usually marked with 'not responding'. Right click on the app then from the popup menu, select 'end task'.

## Performance

You can also sort the processes according to the resources they are using. For example, if you want to see what processes are hogging all the CPU resources, click the CPU column. As you can see, the photos app is using a lot of the CPU.

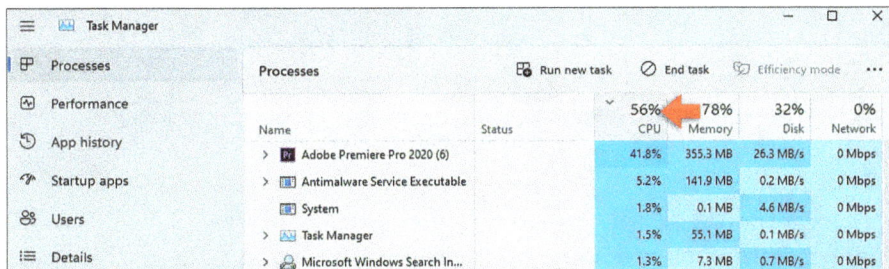

You can do the same for memory, disk, network and GPU.

You can also check the performance of your machine. To do this select the 'performance' tab from the list down the left hand side. In the performance section, you'll see a list of resources: CPU, Memory, Disk Drives, WiFi/Network and GPU (graphics card). Click on any of these to see details. For example, below I've select 'Disk'.

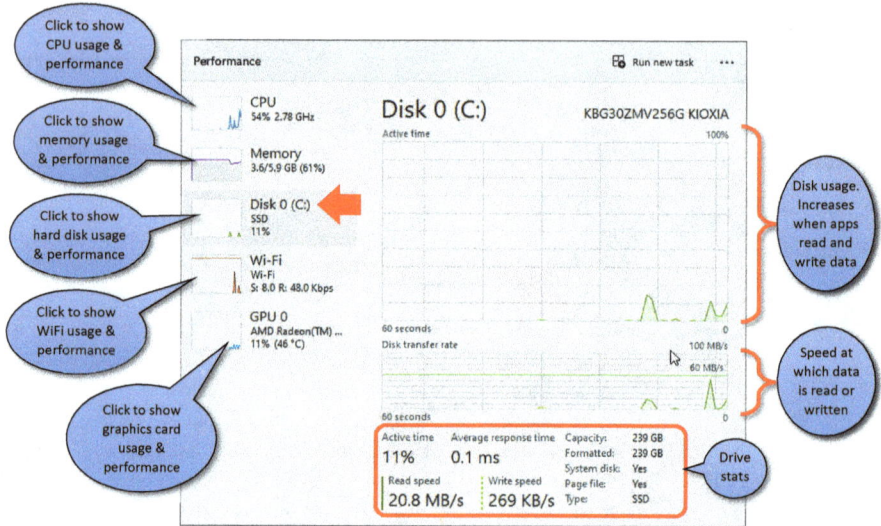

If you select CPU, you'll see the cores of the CPU and the graph indicates the activity - how much each core is being used to execute various tasks.

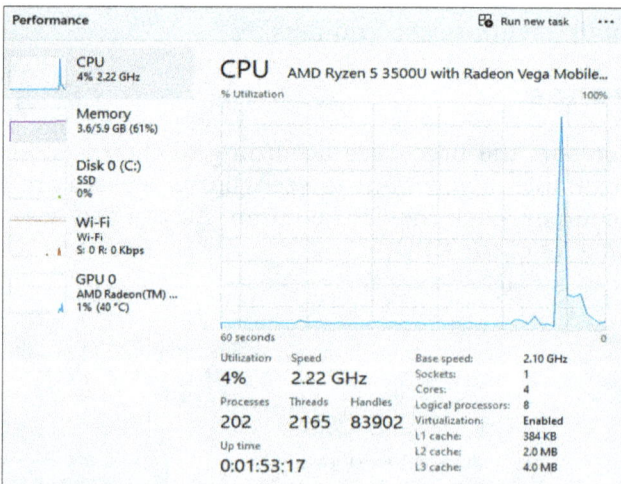

Underneath you'll see some stats for clock speed in GHz, cache sizes, cores and sockets, the up time, as well as the number of processes currently running.

# App History

The app history shows you a list of apps you've used. You can sort the list by the amount of CPU time they've used - ie the most intensive apps, you can also sort the list by the amount of network resources they've used - if an app is downloading large amounts of data

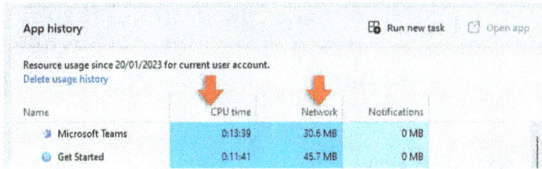

# Startup Apps

Start up apps shows all apps that will load automatically when you log into windows. You can enable and disable the apps here, just right click on the app in the list, then select 'enable' or 'disable' from the menu. If you find your computer is taking a long time to start up, try disabling some of these apps - just don't disable anything to do with antivirus, mouse drivers, OneDrive, etc

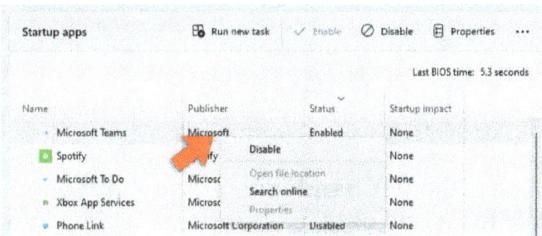

# Users

This section shows other users that are signed in on your computer if you have multiple accounts set up. You can also disconnect a user/log them off, and see apps the user is running.

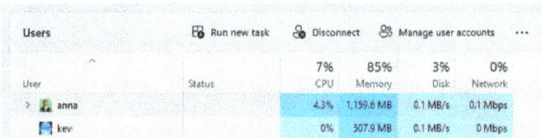

# Details & Services

The details section shows details of all apps and tasks. Services shows details of any installed services. Right click on the task/app/service name to end task, or start/stop/restart a service.

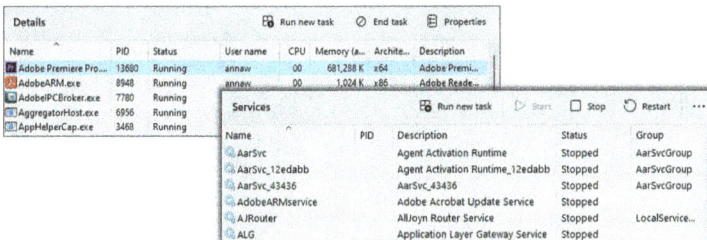

**227**

# File Explorer

File explorer can be used to find your files on your computer, access your OneDrive, network resources, and external hard drives or flash drives.

Scan for Video

## Launching

You'll find file explorer on your taskbar, or on your start menu.

## Anatomy

Down the left hand side of the main window, you will find a list of all file locations on your computer. Home lists the folders and documents you've most recently used. OneDrive contains all your files saved to OneDrive. This PC lists all the local file resources such as local disk drives and folders. Network lists all the other devices and machines on your current network.

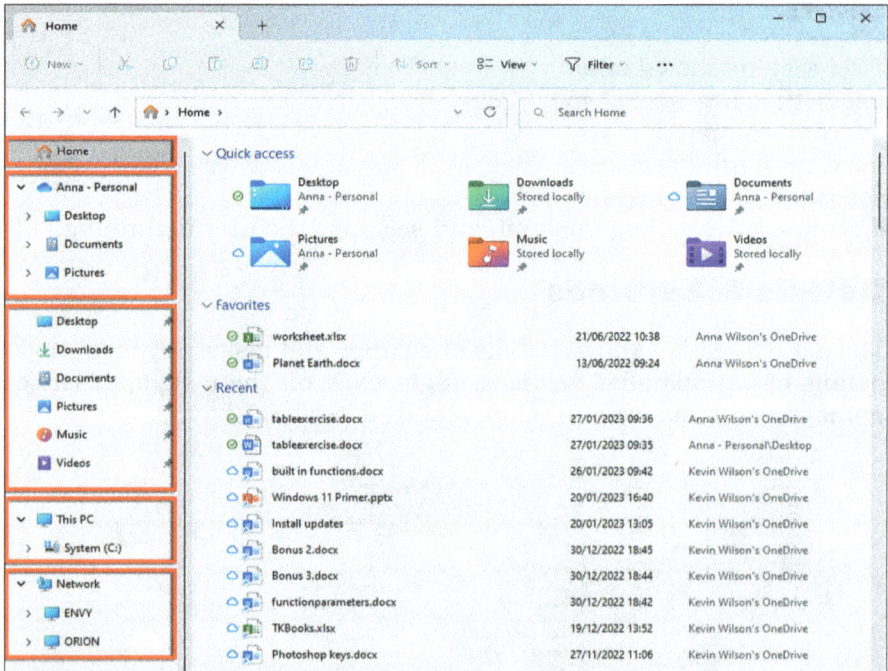

Along the top of the window, you'll see the toolbar. Here, you'll find tools to cut, copy, and paste a selected item (a file or folder). You can also rename, share and delete the item. You'll also see icons to sort your files, and display them as a list or icons. With the three dots icon you can burn the selected items (or files) to a CD/DVD, or you can compress them into a Zip file. The icon on the far right is your OneDrive account and status. You'll see the amount of space used, an option to purchase more space or access your settings.

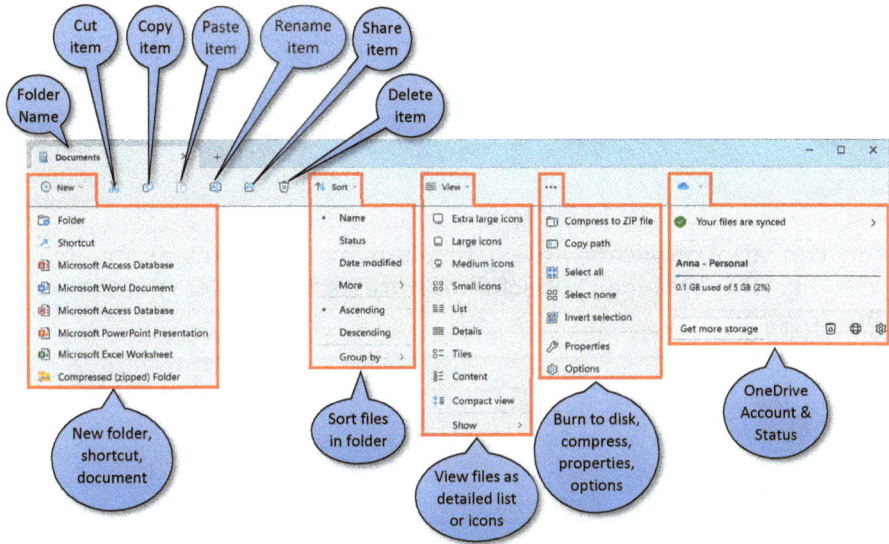

Underneath you'll see an address bar and search field. Here, you can type in a network path to a shared folder, a drive, or folder.

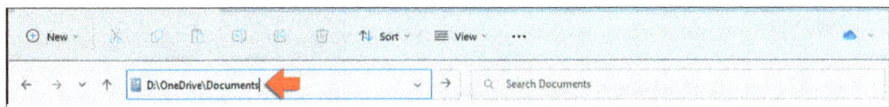

You can also search for files and folders using the search field.

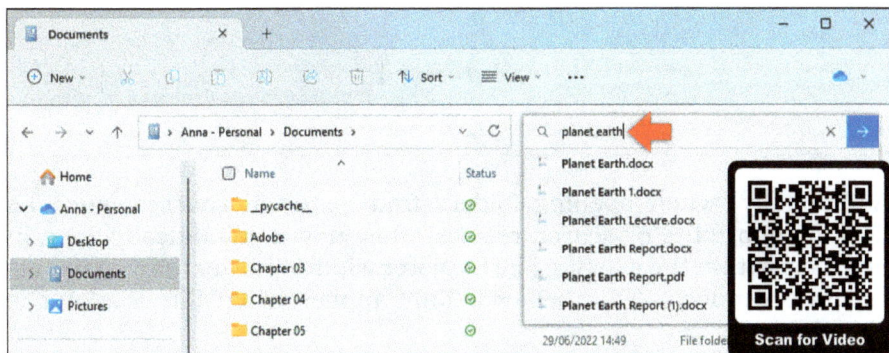

# Chapter 5: Getting around Windows 11

File Explorer tabs have received several improvements. These function much like browser tabs, allowing you to open and manage multiple folders within a single window. This helps reduce clutter when working with files and folders. You'll see any open tabs along the top of the windows.

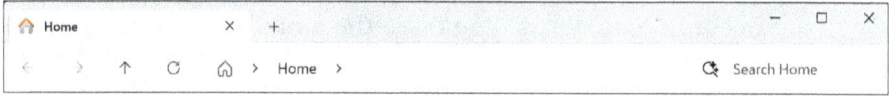

To open a new tab, click the + icon on the right hand side of the tab bar.

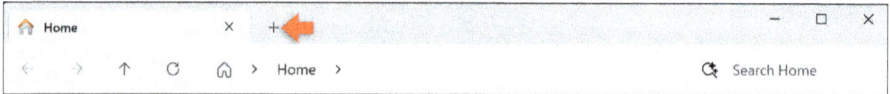

You can also duplicate an existing tab by right-clicking on it and selecting "Duplicate tab"—useful for working in parallel with the same directory.

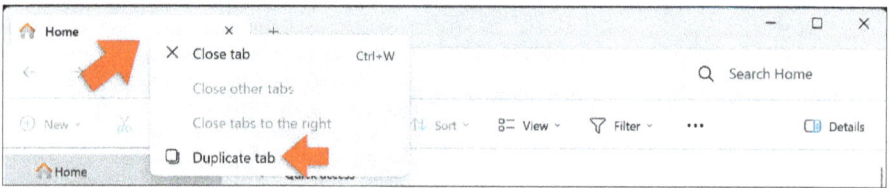

If you want to open a folder in a new tab, right click on the folder you want to open, then select ' open in new tab'.

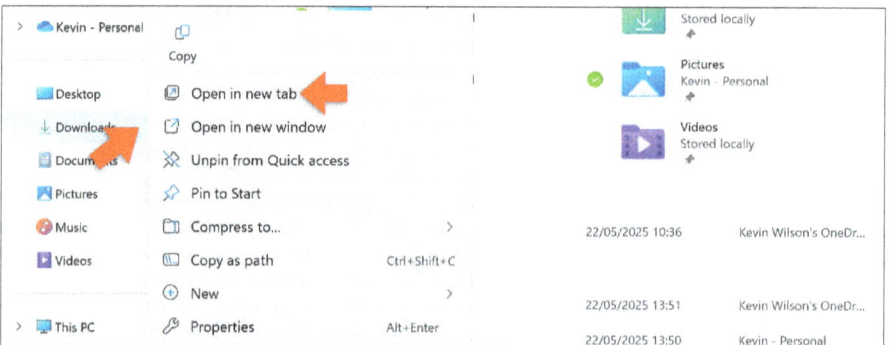

Additionally, when opening folders from external sources (such as desktop shortcuts or search results), they now automatically open in new tabs within the existing File Explorer window rather than spawning separate windows. This behavior only applies when File Explorer is already open.

# Managing your Files

Windows 11 stores data in files and organises the files into folders. Files and folders are saved onto a Drive which is allocated a drive letter such as C, D, E and so on. C is usually reserved for the system drive - ie the drive Windows itself is installed onto.

Scan for Video

## Windows Folder Structure

Windows stores files in folders (sometimes called directories). Here is a typical folder structure on the C drive.

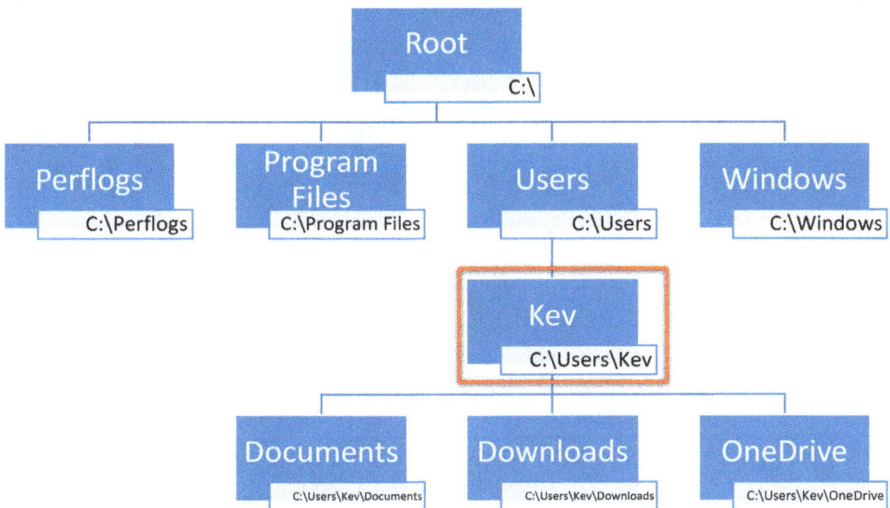

```
                          Root
                          C:\

Perflogs    Program      Users       Windows
            Files
C:\Perflogs  C:\Program Files  C:\Users    C:\Windows

                          Kev
                          C:\Users\Kev

            Documents    Downloads   OneDrive
            C:\Users\Kev\Documents  C:\Users\Kev\Downloads  C:\Users\Kev\OneDrive
```

The top of the drive structure is called the root directory. All other files, folders/directories are created in the root directory.

**Perflogs** contains performance related reports and system logs and is a folder you usually never have to worry about.

**Program Files** contains all the apps and programs you've installed on your device. *On some systems you'll also see another folder called* Program files (x86)*, this is for older 32bit software.*

**Users** folder contains all the personal folders for each user you've created an account for.

**Windows** is a folder that contains all the system files and folders required to run Windows. This is a folder you don't normally have to worry about and should keep clear of unless you know what you're doing.

# Files & Folders

There are many different types of file types; files for photos, videos, documents, spreadsheets, presentations and so on. These files are identified by a file extension.

```
filename.extension
```

So for example...

A photograph is usually saved as a JPEG or JPG. Eg *photo-of-sophie.jpg*. This could be from a graphics package or a camera.

A document is usually saved as a DOC or DOCX. Eg: *production-resume.docx*. This is usually from a word processor such as Microsoft Word.

The 3 or 4 letters after the period is called a file extension and it is what Windows uses to identify the application needed to open the file.

It's best to save all your files into your OneDrive.

Windows stores your files in a hierarchical tree like structure.

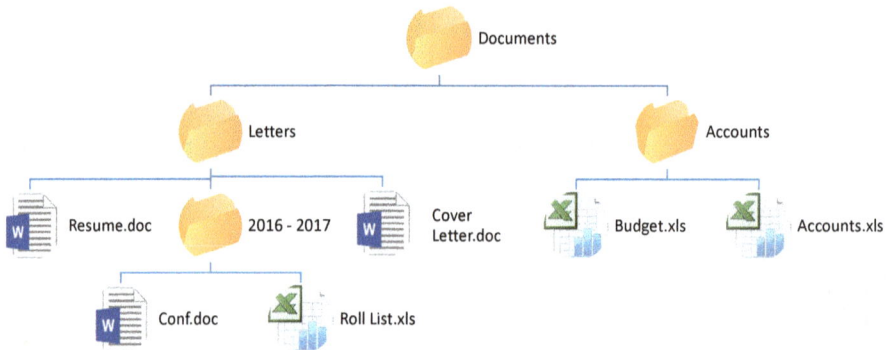

You can create yellow folders to store files of the same type or for the same purpose.

In the example above, letters to various recipients are stored in a 'letters' folder. This can be further divided into year folders, so you have one for each year.

Similarly, all files to do with the accounts are stored in an 'accounts' folder.

Storing files in this fashion keeps them organised and makes them easier to find.

# Creating Folders

It's a good idea to create folders to help organise all your files. You could have a folder for your personal documents, work documents, presentations, vacation/holiday photos, college work and so on. To do this open your File Explorer.

On the left hand side of your screen, navigate to the place you want to create a folder. In this example, I'm going to create a folder in my 'OneDrive' 'Documents' folder.

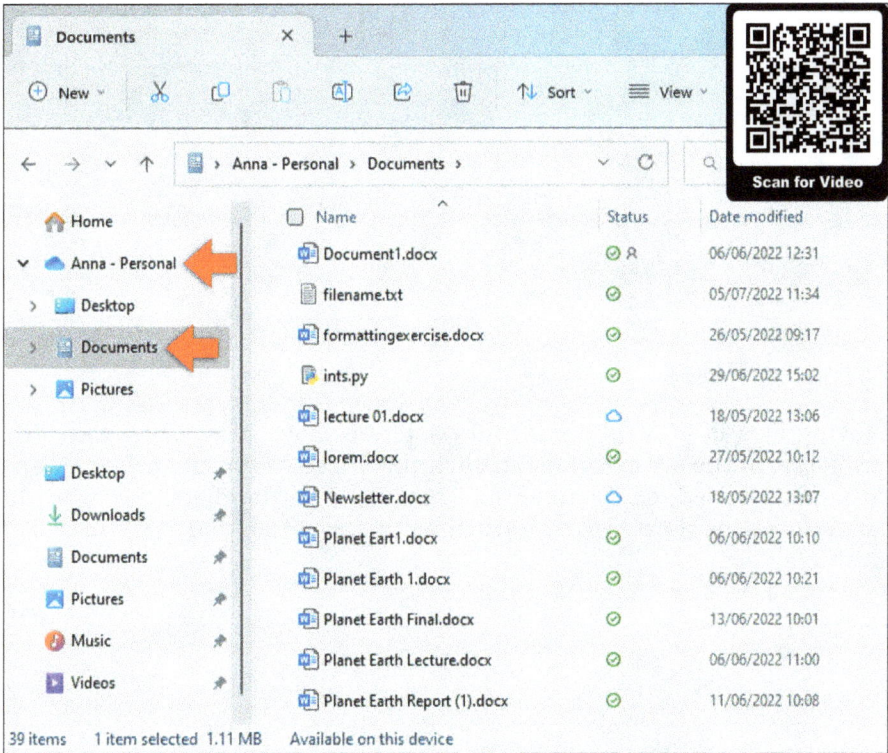

From the toolbar along the top of your screen, click 'new'. Select 'new folder' from the drop down menu.

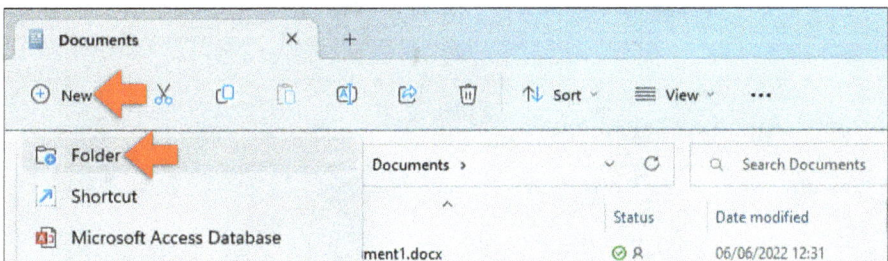

You'll see a new folder appear called 'new folder'. Delete the text 'new folder' and type in a meaningful name - ideally the name of the group of documents you are saving into this folder.

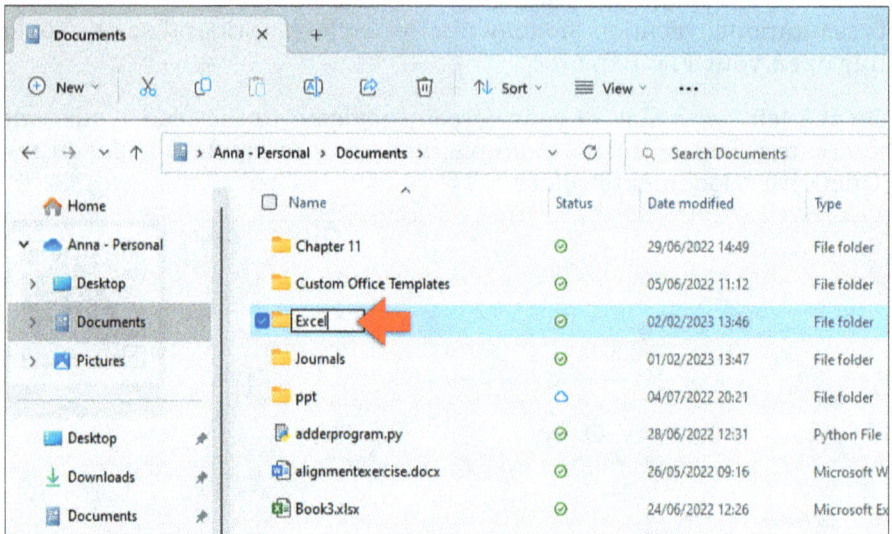

## Moving Files

Moving files is a bit like cut and paste. To move files, open your File Explorer. In the left hand pane, click the folder where the file you want to move is saved, eg documents. Then click on the file(s) you want to move to select them. Hold down the ctrl key while you click to select multiple files.

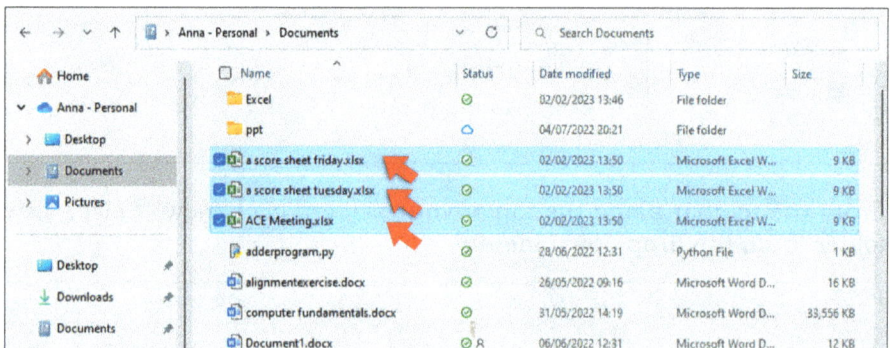

From the toolbar select 'cut'.

Using the left hand pane, navigate to the folder you want to move the file to, eg documents > excel. Click the small side arrows on the left of the folder names to open the folders. Click the folder you want to move the files to.

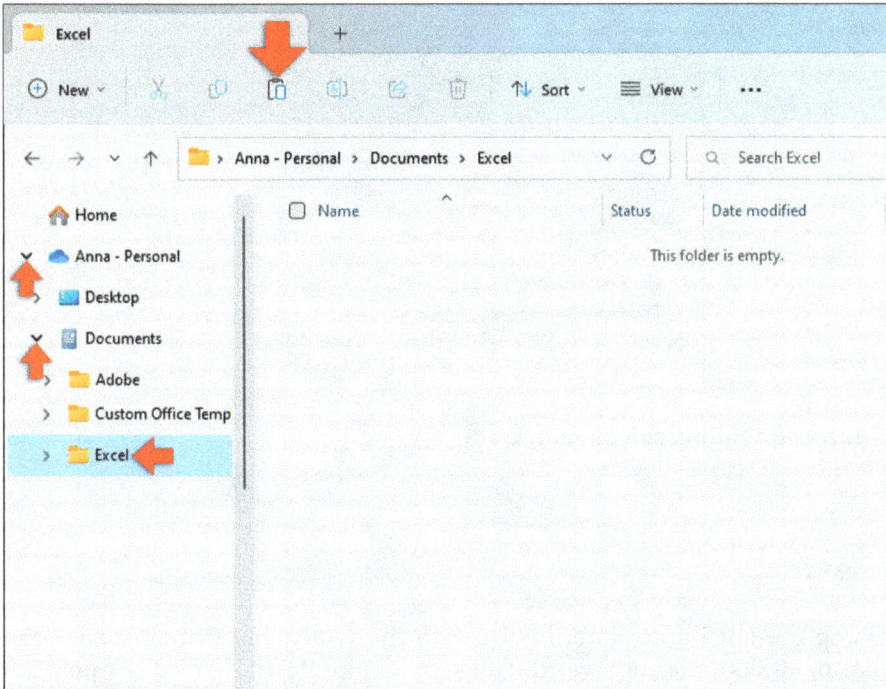

Select 'paste' from the toolbar.

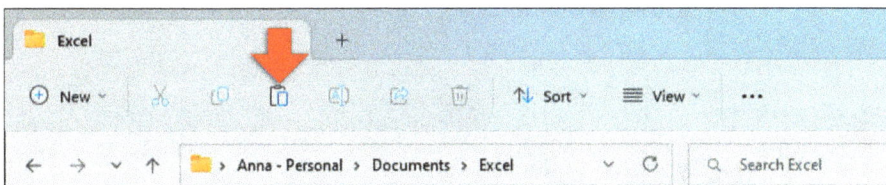

Windows will move the file into the folder.

## Copying Files

Copying files is a bit like copy and paste. To copy files, open your File Explorer.

## Chapter 5: Getting around Windows 11

In the left hand pane, click the folder where the file you want to copy, is saved, eg documents. Then click on the file(s) you want to copy to select them. Hold down the CTRL key while you click to select multiple files.

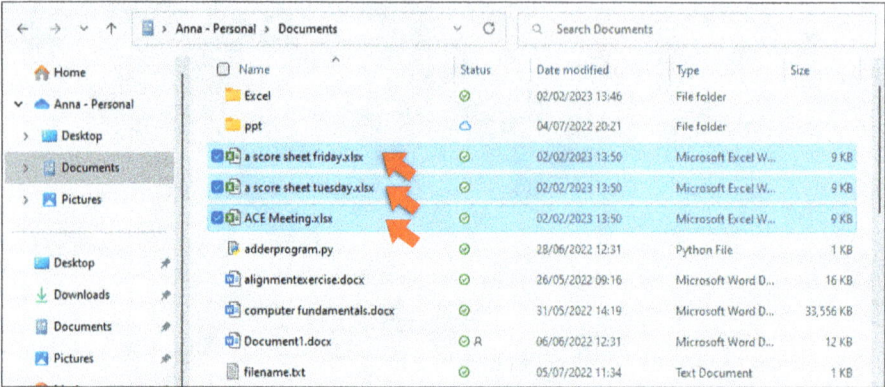

From the toolbar select 'copy'.

Using the left hand pane, navigate to the folder you want to move the file to, eg documents > word. Click the small down arrows to open the folders. Click the folder you want to move the files to.

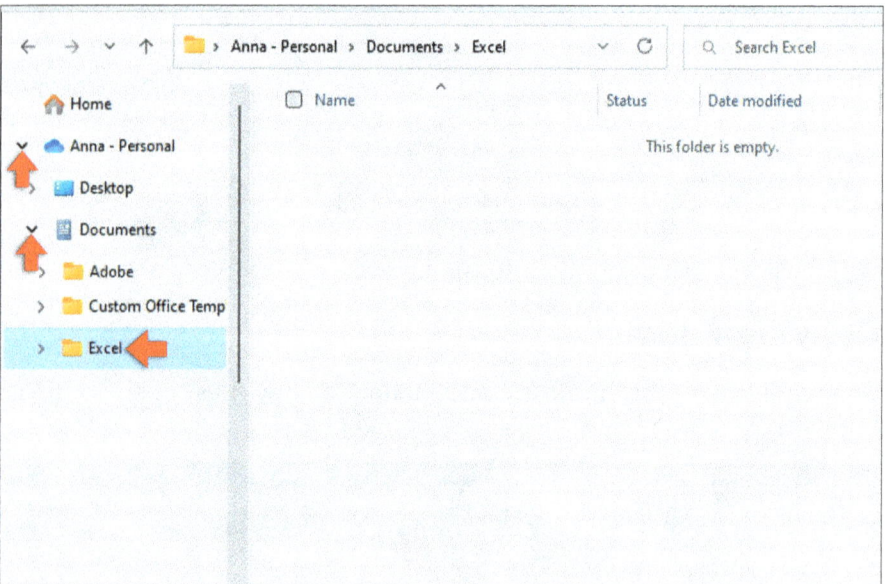

Select 'paste' from the toolbar.

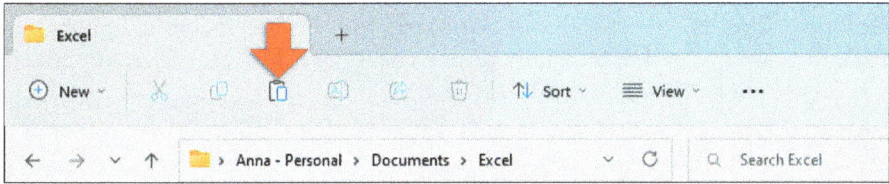

Windows will copy the file into the folder.

# Renaming Files

To rename a file, open up your File Explorer and find the file you want to rename. Navigate to the folder your file is saved in. In this demo it's in the OneDrive > documents folder. Click on the file to select it.

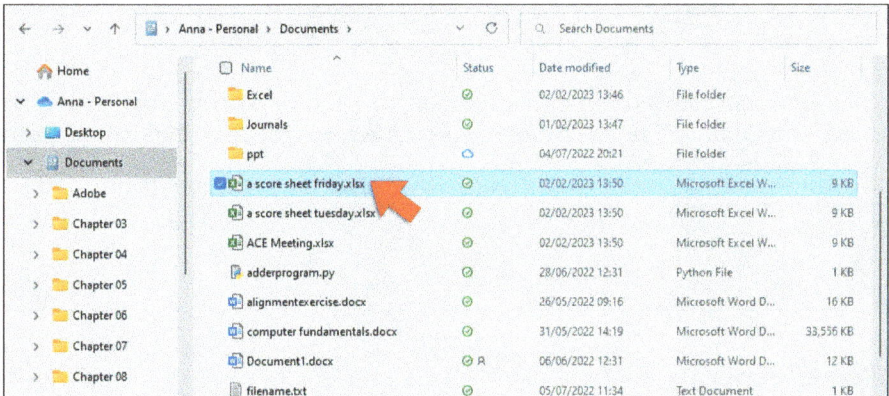

From the toolbar click 'rename'.

You'll see the name of the file highlighted in blue. Now type in a name for the file. Press 'enter' on your keyboard when you're done.

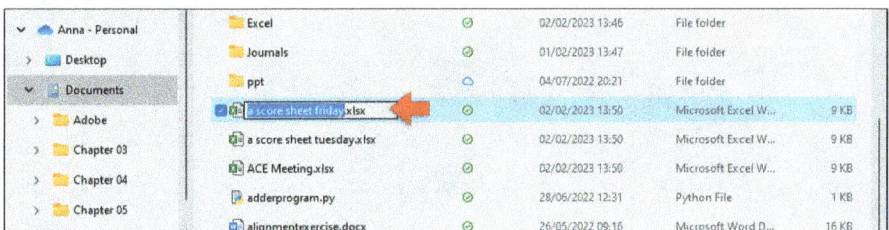

# Deleting Files

Deleting files is fairly straight forward. In File Explorer, click on the files you want to delete. Hold down the CTRL key on your keyboard while you click to select multiple files.

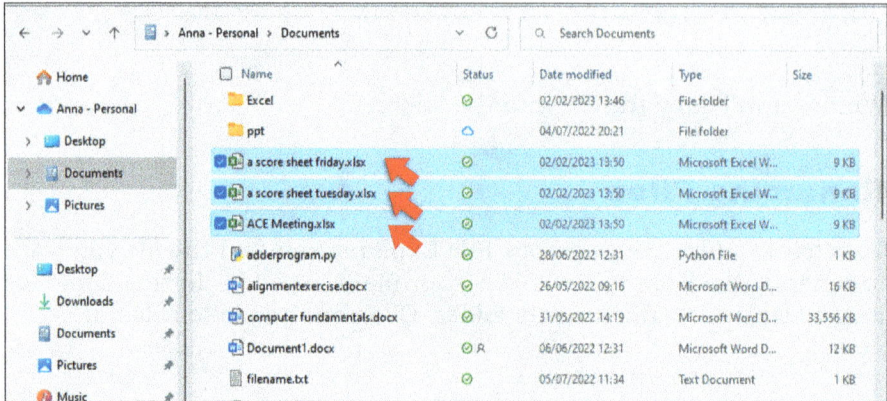

Click the 'delete' icon on the toolbar in File Explorer. You can also press the DEL or DELETE key on your keyboard. Any files you delete will be moved to the recycle bin.

# Restoring Files

When you delete a file, Windows moves the file to the trash (or recycle bin). You'll find the recycle bin icon on your desktop - double click the icon to open it up.

Click 'empty recycle bin' to permanently delete all files in recycle bin. Click 'restore all items' to put all the files back where they were deleted from. Or select a file and click 'restore the selected items' to restore individual files. *If you don't see these icons, click the three dots icon on the far right on the toolbar.*

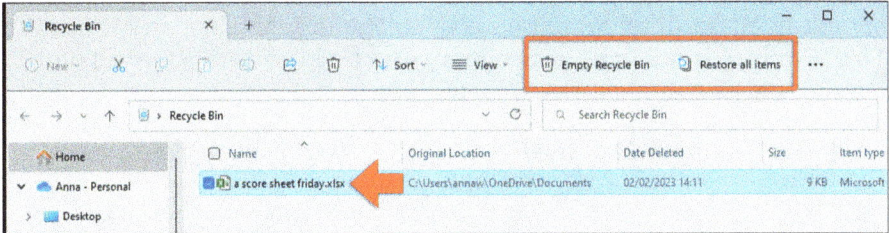

## Compressing Files

You can compress files into a .zip, .7z (7zip), or .tar archive using File Explorer. To do this, select the files you want to compress. Hold down the CTRL key on your keyboard while you click to select multiple files.

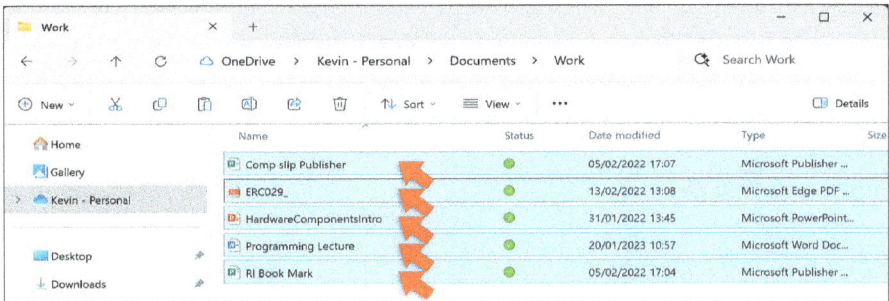

Right click on the selection, go to 'compress to', then select the type of archive you want to create (ZIP, 7z, or TAR). The most common on Windows is a Zip file.

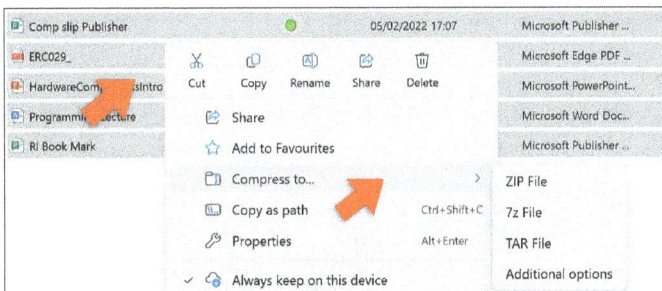

If you want to customize compression, select 'Additional options'.

In the additional options, the "Archive format" dropdown lets you choose the type of archive to create (.7z, ZIP, or TAR). 7z offers high compression, ZIP is widely supported, and TAR is common on Unix systems. The "Compression method" defines how files are compressed. For 7zip, LZMA2 is the default, offering strong compression. For TAR, you can choose methods like BZip2 (slower but compact), Gzip (fast and compatible), xz (high compression), or Zstandard (fast and efficient). The "Compression level" slider lets you choose faster compression or smaller file size (higher compression).

Once the files have been compressed, you'll see the archive appear in the folder. Give the file a meaningful name.

## Sorting Files

Within File Explorer, you can sort files alphabetically by name, or by size and date created. This makes it easier to find files especially when you have a lot of them in one folder. To sort your files, select the folder from the left hand side of File Explorer, eg, 'documents'.

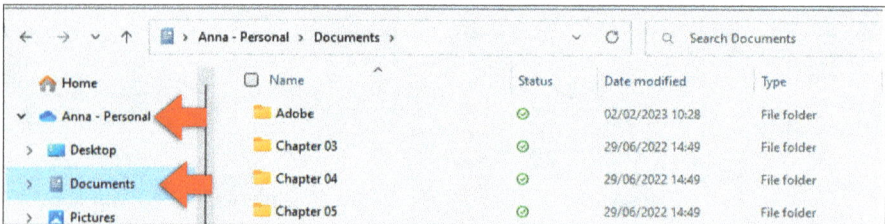

To sort the files, select 'sort by', then select what you want to sort your files by. This could be date modified - so the latest files appear at the top. Or by name - so your files appear in alphabetical order by file name.

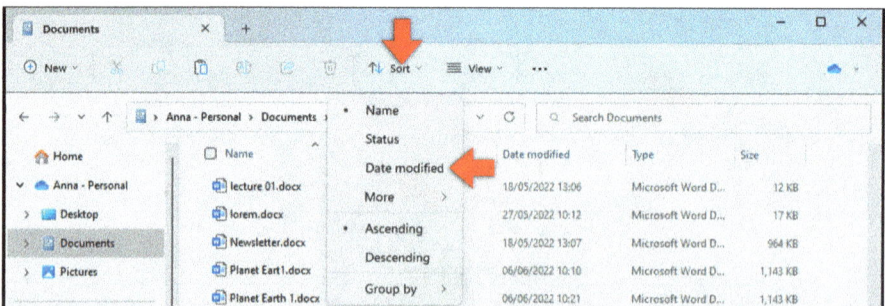

At the bottom of the menu, select ascending or descending order.

**240**

# Searching for Files

You can search for files within File Explorer using the search field on the top right of the window. First, select the location to search from, eg OneDrive, This PC. Then type your search keywords into the search field. You'll see a list of suggestions appear, to select, click on one in the list.

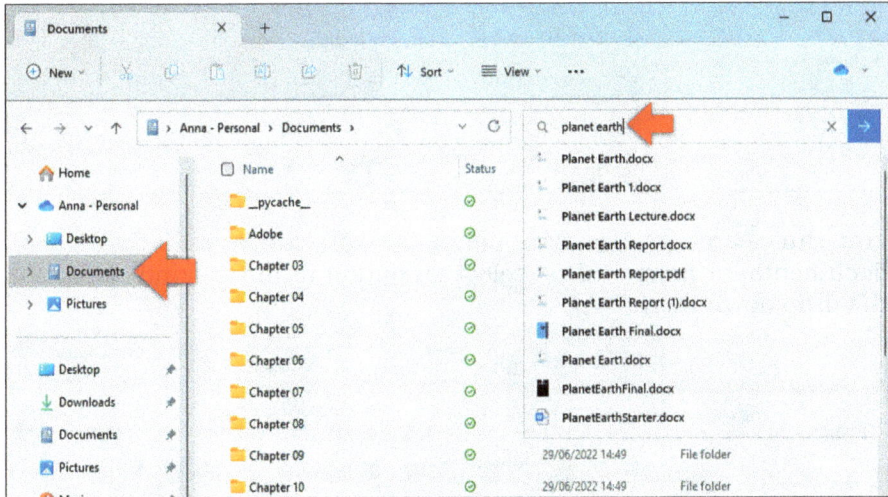

To perform a full search, click the blue arrow icon to the right. A list of matching files will be listed. From here, you can refine your search. - just click 'search options'.

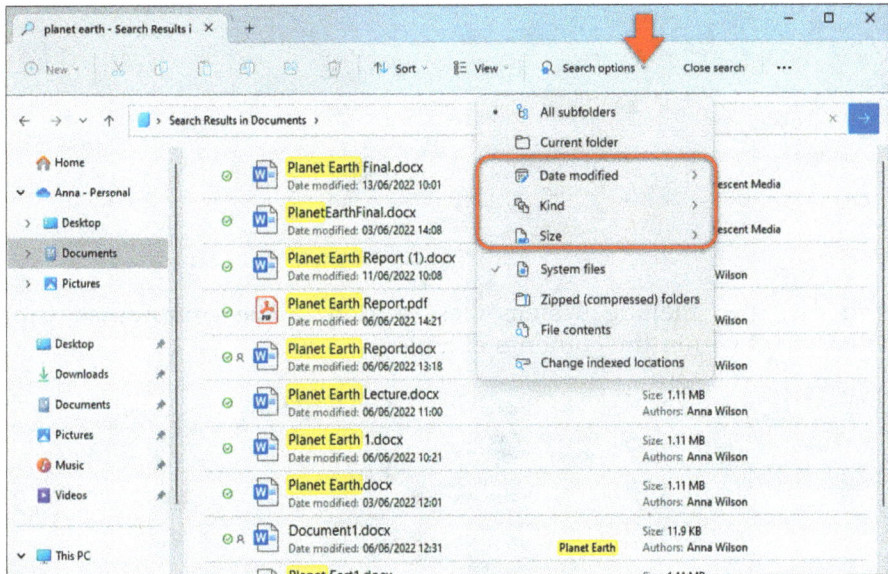

You can search by date modified (eg files you've used today, yesterday, or in the last week. Just select an option from the 'date modified' option on the drop down menu.

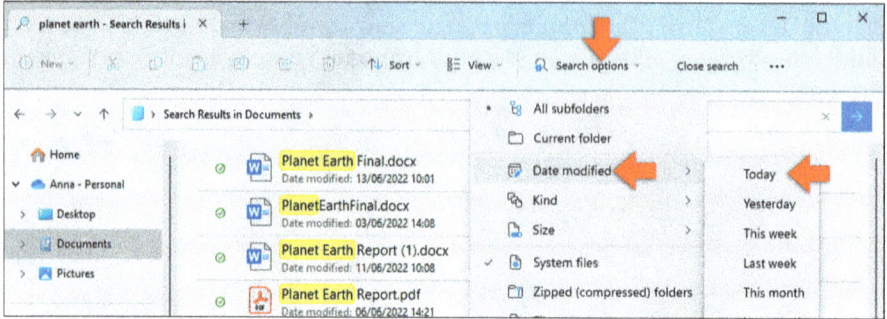

You can search by file type (kind), so you can search through all documents, or images. Just select an option from the 'kind' section of the drop down menu.

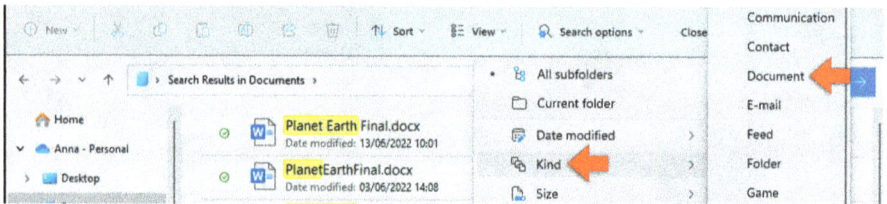

Or files of a particular size

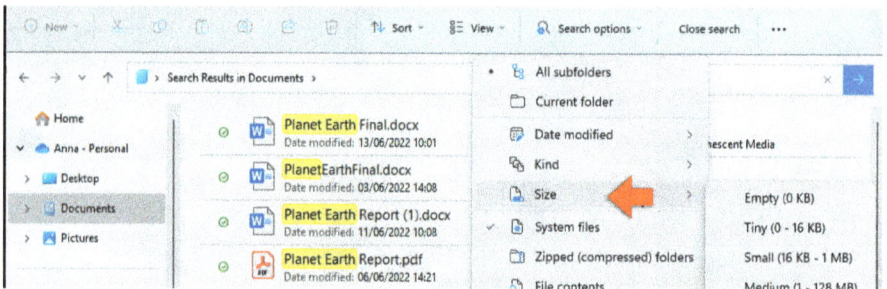

You can also include system files, search inside compressed (zip) folders and within the contents of a file.

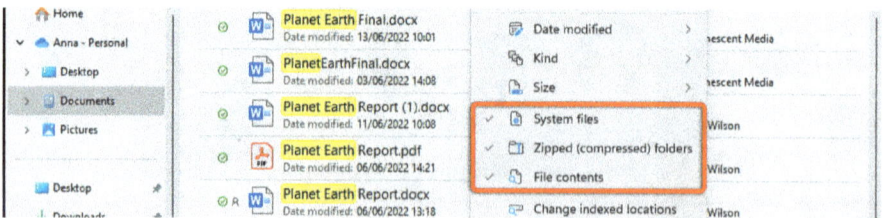

# Address Bar

The Address bar is located at the top of File Explorer and displays the path of the currently selected folder.

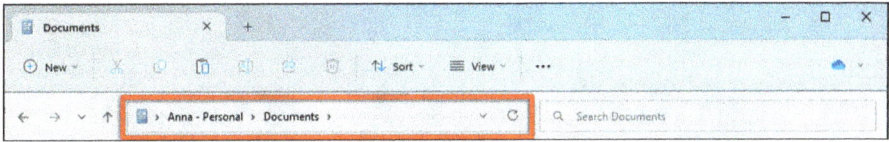

To view the folders at the same level as the current folder (eg in OneDrive), click on the right pointing arrow to the right of that folder in the Address bar. You'll see a drop down menu appear. This lists all the folders at that level.

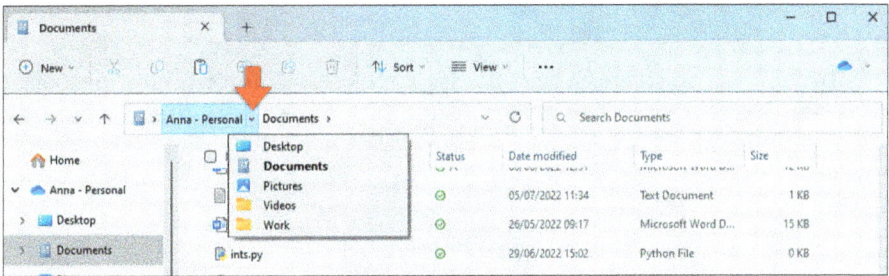

Click in the address field, you'll see the full path to the currently selected folder. In this example, the documents folder on OneDrive.

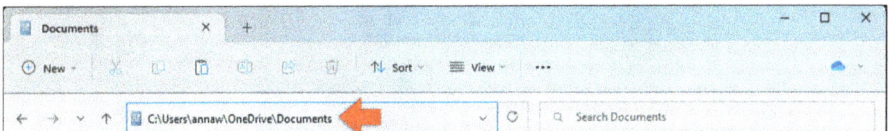

You can type in a folder path, eg if we had a downloads folder on drive E, we'd type `E:\downloads`

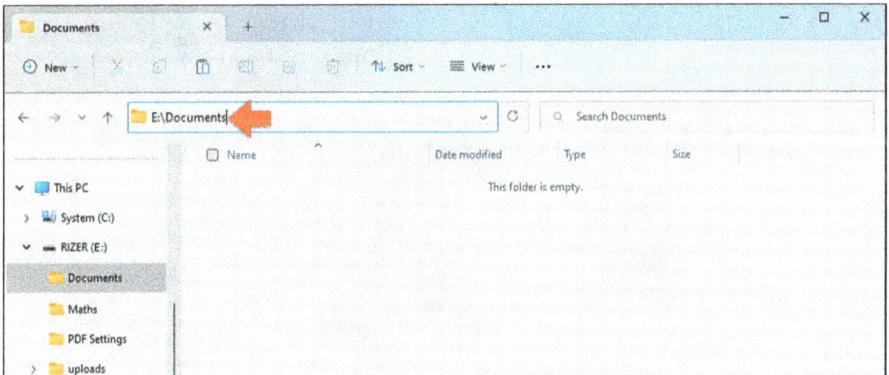

Remember the address bar follows the folder structure of the drive. Here, we can see the downloads folder on drive E.

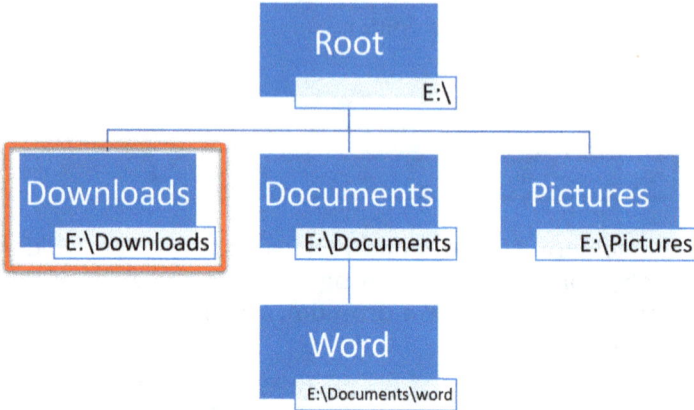

If your folder is on Drive C, the folder structure is different. Your personal files will be stored in the 'users' directory under your username (my username is 'kev'.

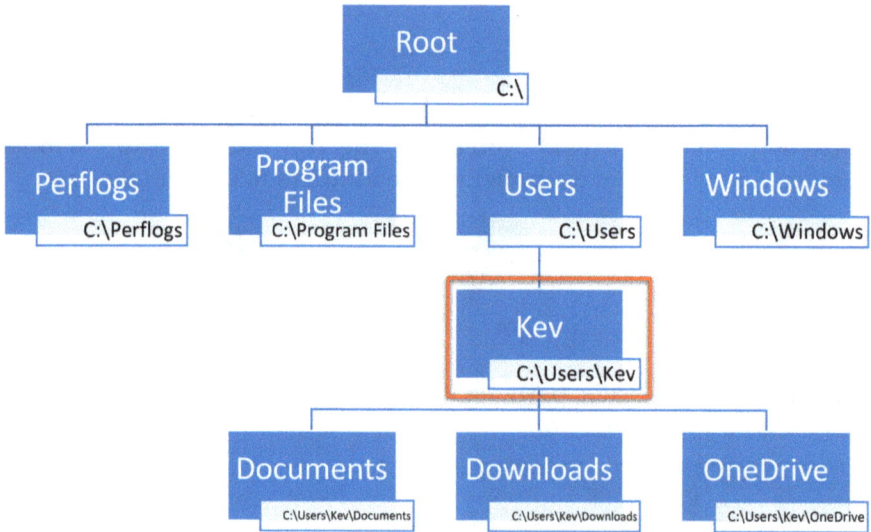

If you click the down arrow to the right of the address bar, you'll see a history of the folders or folder paths you've typed in.

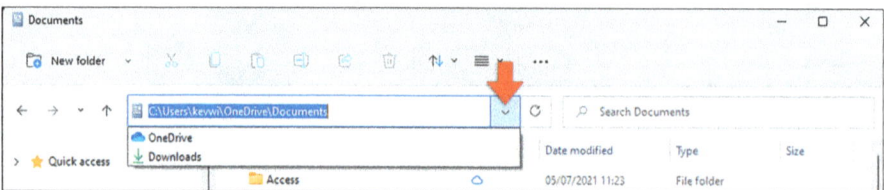

# External Drives

You can attach storage devices such as USB sticks, external hard disk drives and memory cards to your computer.

Scan for Video

## External Hard Disks & USB Sticks

The most common ones are memory sticks - also called usb keys, usb sticks, flash drives or thumb drives. The other type is the portable hard drive.

Memory sticks are usually smaller in capacity ranging from 1GB all the way up to 256GB. Portable hard drives can be larger than 1TB.

To read the drive, plug the device into a USB port on your computer, then select file explorer from the task bar.

The drive will show up in File Explorer, under 'This PC' section.

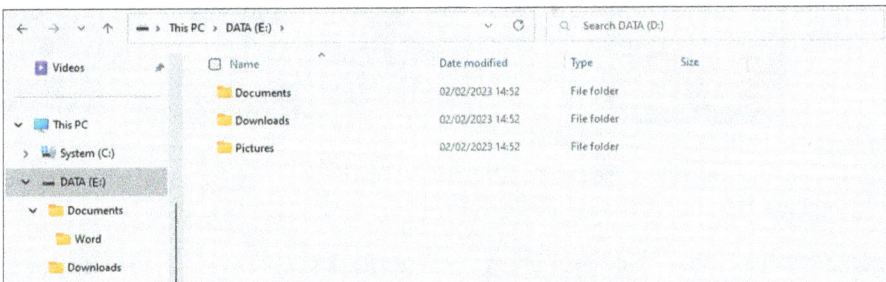

Click on the small arrow to the left of 'this PC'. Then click the drive icon to display the contents of the drive. The external drive will normally be any drive letter after C. In this case it's drive E.

## Memory Cards

Many laptops and tablets now have memory card readers built in. The most common memory card being the SD Card. This can be a full sized SD card or a Micro SD card.

Standard SD     Micro SD     SD Card Adapter

Standard SD cards are commonly used in digital cameras, and many laptops have standard size SD card readers built in. Tablets, phones, and small cameras usually use micro SD cards.

You can get an SD Card adapter if your SD card reader does not read Micro SD cards.

There are various types of SD cards available, each are marked with a speed classification symbol indicating the data transfer speed. If you are merely storing files, the data transfer speed doesn't really matter as much, however, if you are using the card in a dash cam or digital camera, the faster data transfer speeds are necessary. To be safe, the higher the speed the better. You can see a summary in the table below.

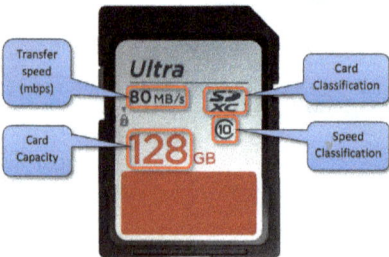

| Speed Classification | Min Speed | Use |
| --- | --- | --- |
| Ⓒ2 | 2MBps (16mbps) | Storing files and documents |
| Ⓒ4 | 4MBps (32mbps) | Storing Photographs and SD video |
| Ⓒ6 | 6MBps (48mbps) | Photographs and SD video |
| Ⓒ10 U1 V10 | 10MBps (80mbps) | Full HD video, Digital cameras |
| U3 | 30MBps (240mbps) | 4K & Full HD video, Digital Cameras |

SDHC stands for "Secure Digital High Capacity", and supports capacities up to 32 GB.

SDXC stands for "Secure Digital eXtended Capacity", and supports capacities up to 2 TB.

SDUC stands for "Secure Digital Ultra Capacity", and supports capacities up to 128 TB.

To read your SD Card, slide it into the card reader on your tablet or laptop. If your laptop or tablet has a built in reader, it is usually on either of the side panels or the front panel.

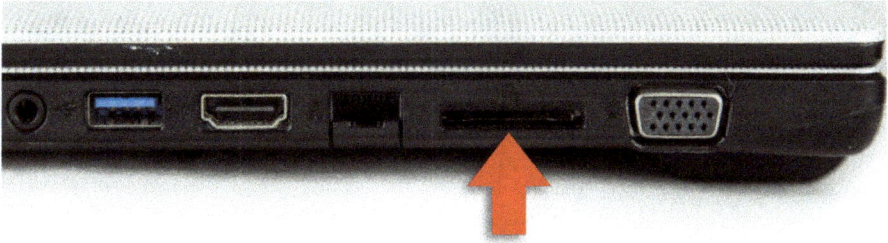

Select file explorer from the task bar.

The card will show up as another drive in file explorer, under 'This PC' section.

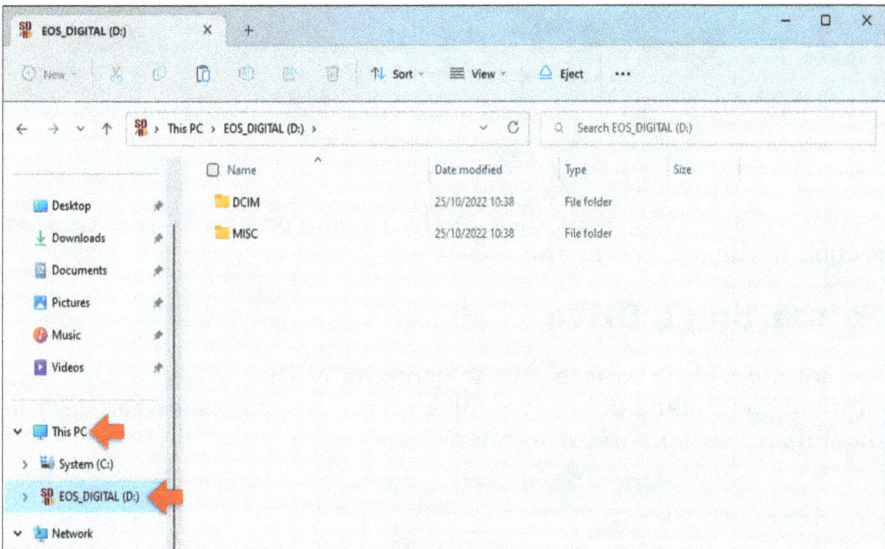

Click on the small arrow to the left of 'this PC'. Then click the drive icon to display the contents of the drive. The external drive will normally be any drive letter after C. In this case it's drive D.

To release the card, press the it inwards and it will pop out. Some other cards will just slide out, depending on your card reader.

## Copying Files to an External Drive

You can copy files to and from the card as you would with a normal disk drive.

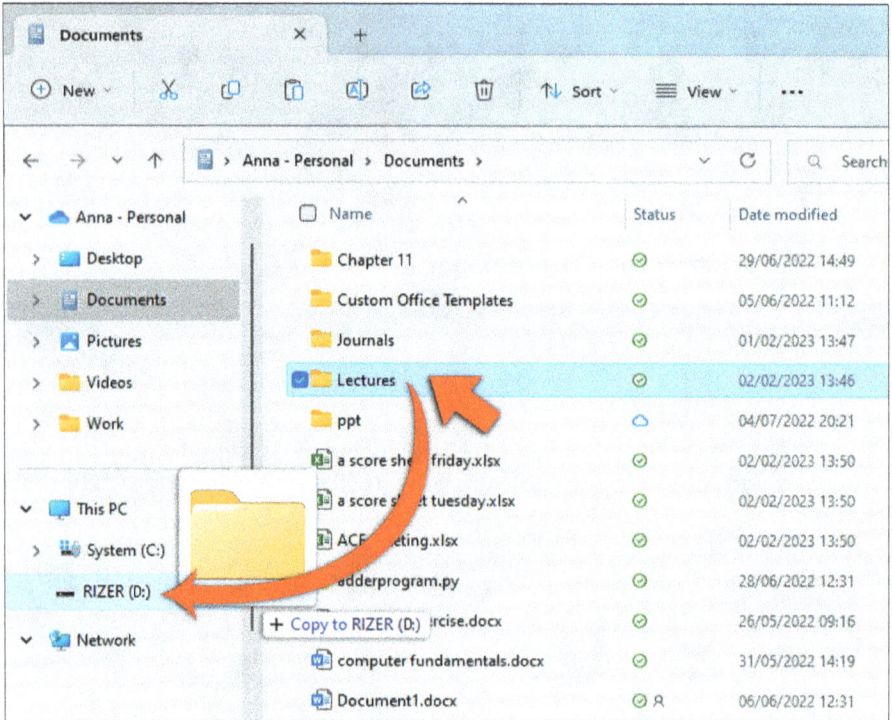

Just click and drag your files to the drive icon under the 'this pc' section in the left hand pane.

## Formatting a Drive

Formatting a drive erases all the contents of that drive, so use with caution. To format a drive, open file explorer, right click on the drive in the 'this pc' section on the left hand side.

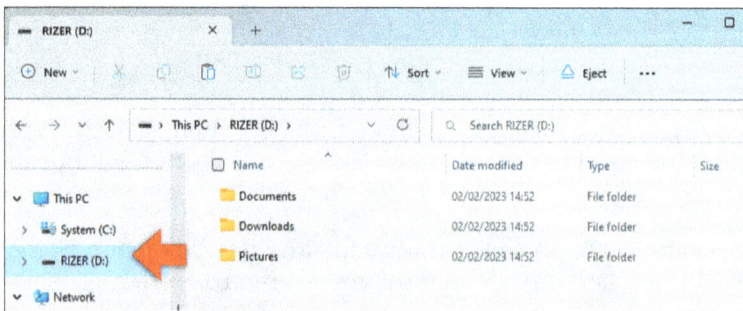

From the popup menu, select 'format'.

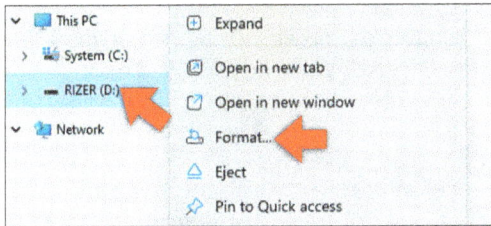

Here, you'll see the capacity of the drive and the file system. Select a file system from the drop down box.

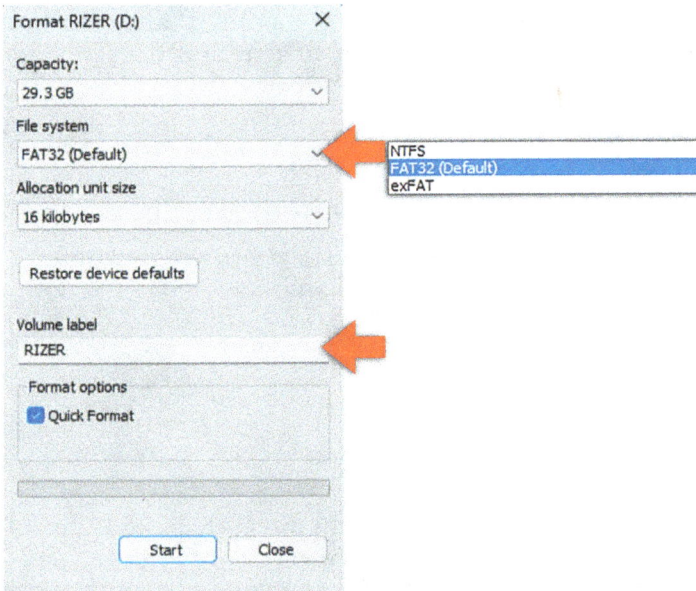

**NTFS** is the native file system for Microsoft Windows and is best suited for your system drive and other internal drives that will only be used with Windows. NTFS has no file-size or partition size limits.

**FAT32** is an old file system that works with all versions of Windows, and Mac, as well as Linux and Game Consoles. This makes it ideal for use on memory sticks and external drives where you need compatibility. This file system has a 4 GB maximum file size limit and Windows will only format drives up to 32GB using the FAT32 file system.

**exFAT** is compatible with Windows and Mac, making it ideal for portability with no file-size or partition-size limits. This is the ideal file system to use for external drives and memory sticks larger than 32GB.

In the 'volume label' field, give your drive a meaningful name. Click 'start' to begin formatting.

**249**

# Copilot

Copilot is an AI assistant powered by advanced language models, including OpenAI's GPT, developed by Microsoft for use in Windows 11 and Microsoft 365. There are three main Copilot offerings available to users.

In Windows 11 version 24H2, Microsoft transitioned Copilot from a built-in feature to a standalone application. While it is installed by default on many new devices, it can also be installed or uninstalled via the Microsoft Store (just search for copilot). This app provides general-purpose assistance—such as adjusting settings, launching applications, summarizing on-screen content, and responding to natural language queries. It is free to use and does not require a Microsoft 365 subscription.

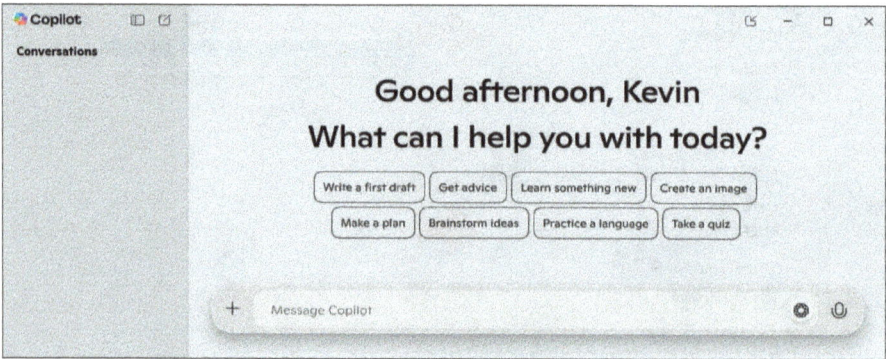

Microsoft 365 Copilot is an AI assistant integrated into Microsoft Office applications such as Word, Excel, PowerPoint, Outlook, and Teams. It can generate documents, analyze spreadsheets, draft emails, and automate workflows. Full access to Microsoft 365 Copilot requires both an eligible Microsoft 365 subscription—such as Microsoft 365 E3, E5, Business Standard, or Business Premium—and a separate Microsoft 365 Copilot add-on license, which is purchased independently at an additional cost per user.

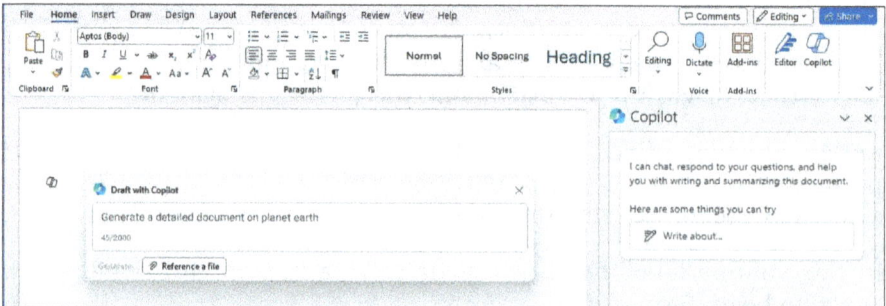

Copilot Pro is a premium add-on subscription targeted at individual users, including those with Microsoft 365 Personal or Family plans. It provides enhanced access to AI features, including priority access to the latest models (e.g., GPT-4 Turbo), faster response times, and early access to new features across Word, Excel, PowerPoint, and Outlook. Copilot Pro requires an active Microsoft 365 Personal or Family subscription, along with the Copilot Pro add-on, which is billed monthly per user.

# Copilot+ PCs and AI Capabilities

Copilot+ PCs are a new class of Windows 11 PC that feature a built-in Neural Processing Unit (NPU)—a specialized chip engineered to accelerate artificial intelligence and machine learning tasks directly on the device, without depending on cloud-based processing. This hardware enables advanced AI functionality that runs locally, improving both performance and privacy.

These AI powered devices introduce a suite of exclusive features designed to take advantage of the NPU's capabilities.

## Recall

Windows Recall is available exclusively on Copilot+ PCs and passively captures snapshots of your screen over time, creating a searchable, visual timeline of your activity. You can retrieve previously viewed content simply by describing it in natural language.

For example, Recall allows you to quickly find and revisit anything you've seen or done on your PC—such as documents you've edited or websites you've visited—even if you didn't save or bookmark it. All captured data is stored locally on your device, and access is protected by Windows Hello to ensure it remains secure.

### Configuration

Recall isn't enabled by default, so if you want to use it, you'll need to enable it. To do this, open the settings app, select 'privacy & security', then click 'recall & snapshots'. Click the toggle switch to turn it on.

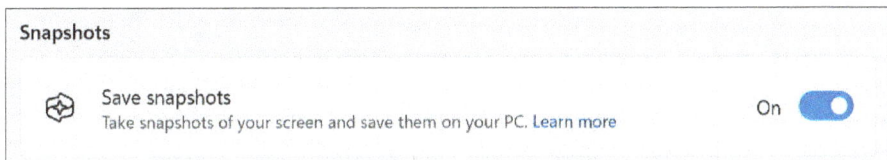

| Snapshots | | |
|---|---|---|
| Save snapshots<br>Take snapshots of your screen and save them on your PC. Learn more | | On ⬤ |

You can configure recall using the settings on this page. The "Storage" section displays the current amount of disk space used by Recall to store snapshots locally on your PC.

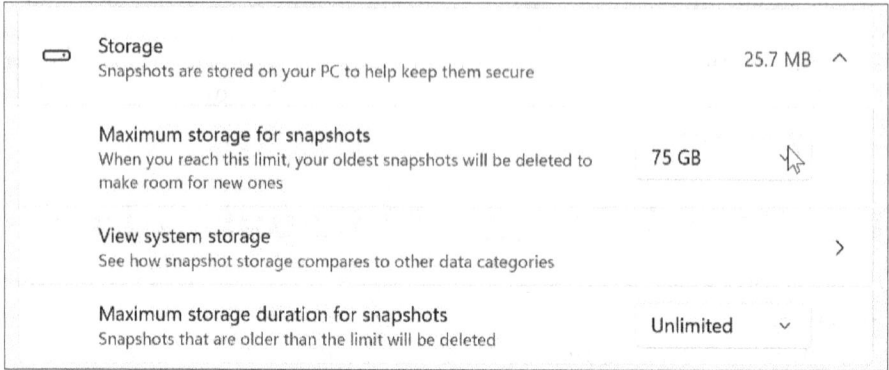

| | Storage | | 25.7 MB ^ |
| --- | --- | --- | --- |
| | Snapshots are stored on your PC to help keep them secure | | |
| | **Maximum storage for snapshots** | | |
| | When you reach this limit, your oldest snapshots will be deleted to make room for new ones | 75 GB | |
| | **View system storage** | | > |
| | See how snapshot storage compares to other data categories | | |
| | **Maximum storage duration for snapshots** | Unlimited ∨ | |
| | Snapshots that are older than the limit will be deleted | | |

The "Maximum storage for snapshots" setting defines the maximum amount of disk space Recall is allowed to use; when this limit is reached, the oldest snapshots are automatically deleted to free up space for new ones.

The "View system storage" option opens a detailed view showing how Recall's storage usage compares to other categories of data on your device.

The "Maximum storage duration for snapshots" setting specifies how long snapshots are kept; any snapshot older than the selected time limit will be deleted automatically.

In the "Delete snapshots" section, you can select a specific time range—such as the past hour—and delete only the snapshots captured during that period.

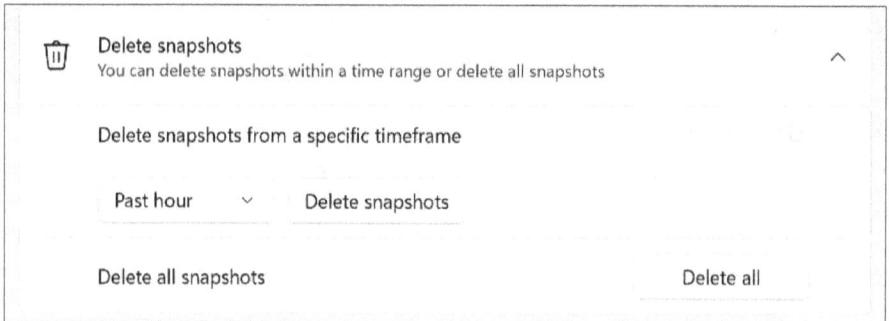

| | Delete snapshots | | ^ |
| --- | --- | --- | --- |
| | You can delete snapshots within a time range or delete all snapshots | | |
| | **Delete snapshots from a specific timeframe** | | |
| | Past hour ∨ | Delete snapshots | |
| | **Delete all snapshots** | Delete all | |

The "Delete all snapshots" button allows you to permanently erase all saved snapshots from the system at once.

Filter sensitive information prevents Recall from saving snapshots when potentially sensitive content—such as passwords, credit card numbers, or other private data—is detected on the screen.

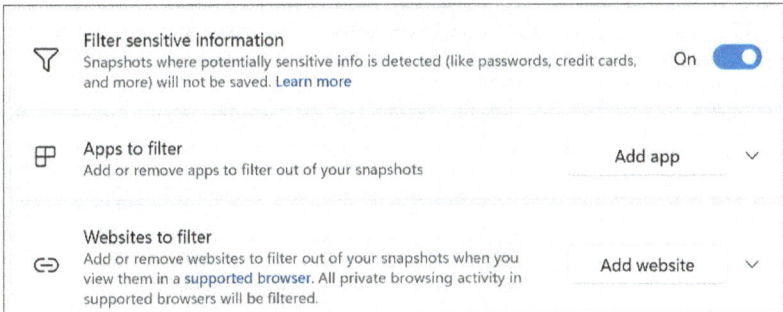

Apps to filter lets you choose specific applications to exclude from snapshot capture, so that any activity in those apps will not be recorded by Recall.

Websites to filter allows you to exclude particular websites from being included in snapshots when you visit them in supported browsers. Private browsing sessions are also automatically excluded.

## Using Recall

Once Recall has been activated, it will start collecting snapshots. You'll also see a new icon in the system tray on the right hand side. Press Windows key + J on your keyboard to open Recall.

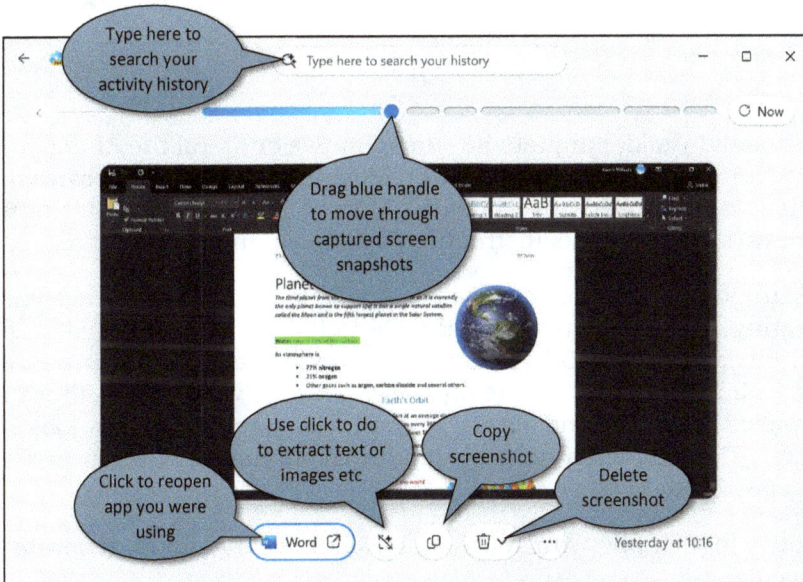

## Cocreator

Cocreator is a real-time AI-assisted drawing tool. As you draw on the canvas, the AI uses your strokes and the provided text prompt to generate enhanced imagery in real time, layered over or around your sketch.

You'll find the Cocreator under the copilot icon on the top right of the toolbar.

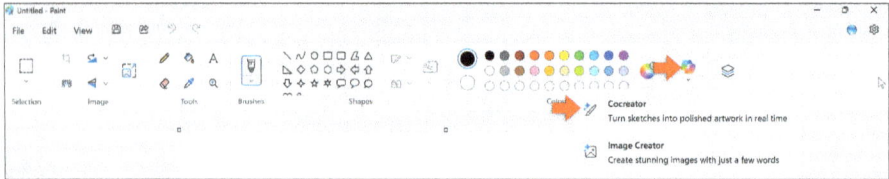

This will open the Cocreator panel on the right hand side. Type in a descriptive text prompt in the field at the top, then begin sketching. Cocreator will generate an image for you. This works best when you have a touch screen device where you can use a pen.

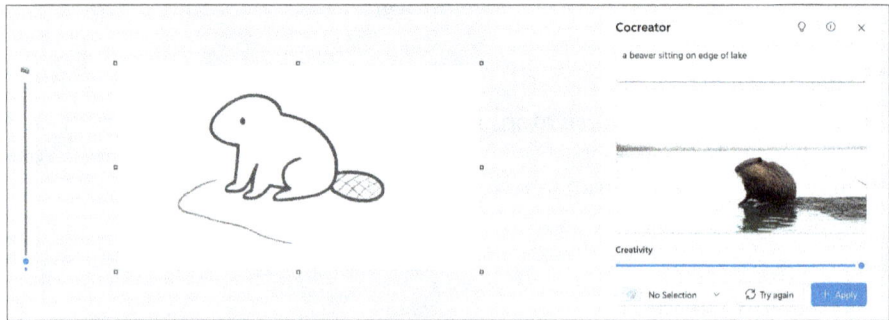

The creativity slider adjusts how imaginative or literal the AI-generated image is in response to your prompt. Moving it to the left generates more realistic and conservative images. Moving it to the right introduces more variation, artistic abstraction, or surreal interpretations.

The dropdown lets you choose an art style for the generated image. Selecting one applies that visual style to the output—Watercolor gives soft, blended colors; Oil Painting adds texture and depth; Ink Sketch creates line drawings; Anime stylizes the image with bold outlines and simplified features; and Pixel Art produces a retro, low-res look. "No Selection" generates a neutral, photorealistic image without applying any specific style.

If you're not happy with the results, click 'try again' to generate the image again.

# Click to Do

Click to Do provides intelligent, context-aware suggestions based on the content currently visible on your screen. For example, while reviewing a document or webpage, you can summarise the text or translate it into another language, with relevant options appearing alongside the content. To use Click to Do, press Windows + Q to activate screen selection. Then, select the text or area you want. Right-click the selection to choose from options such as Summarise, Convert to List, or Rewrite in a different tone or style.

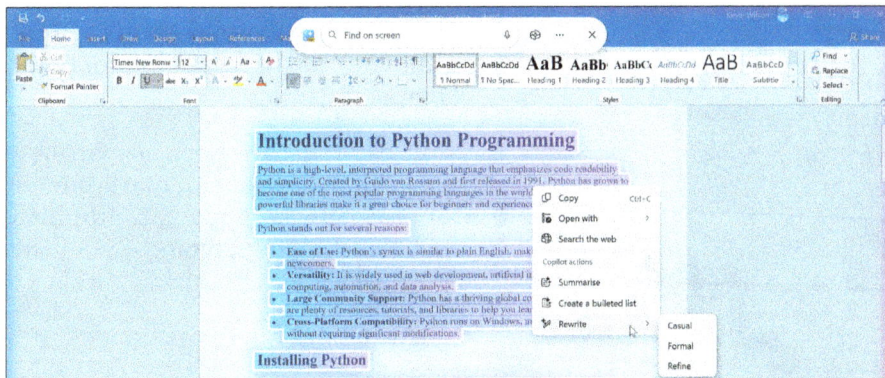

# Live Captions with Translation

Live Captions with Translation extends the real-time captioning system in Windows 11 by adding on-device translation for spoken audio. Supporting over 40 languages, this feature works system-wide across browsers, streaming services, media players, and communication apps—making spoken content accessible even when subtitles are unavailable. Live Captions with Translation is only available on Copilot+ PCs.

To open Live Captions, press Win + Ctrl + L.

# Auto Super Resolution

Auto Super Resolution enhances gaming experiences by using AI to upscale supported games in real time, improving visual sharpness and frame fluidity without significantly increasing GPU load. This delivers a higher-quality gaming experience while maintaining smooth performance. Auto Super Resolution is only available on Copilot+ PCs.

To enable it, open the Settings app, go to System > Display, then click Graphics. Turn on Auto Super Resolution and Optimizations for windowed games.

# 6

# Using Apps

There are thousands of Apps available for download from the Microsoft Store.

You can get an app for virtually anything, from games, entertainment to productivity apps for graphics, writing, drawing, typing and word processing.

In this chapter we'll take a look at

- Searching the Microsoft Store
- Downloading Apps
- Weather App
- News App
- Clock App
- Sound Recorder
- Calculator App
- To Do App
- PowerShell
- Apps from Outside Microsoft Store
- Linux Apps
- Intel, AMD, and ARM

To help you better understand this section, take a look at the video resources. Scan the QR code, or open your web browser and type the following directly into the address bar at the top (don't use a search engine):

elluminetpress.com/win-11-using

# Microsoft Store

Originally known as the Windows Store, Microsoft Store offers apps, games, music, films, and TV series.

You'll find the Microsoft Store on your start menu.

In Windows 11, the store has been redesigned. Along the top of the app, you'll see a search field - here you can search for your favourite apps, TV programmes, movies and games.

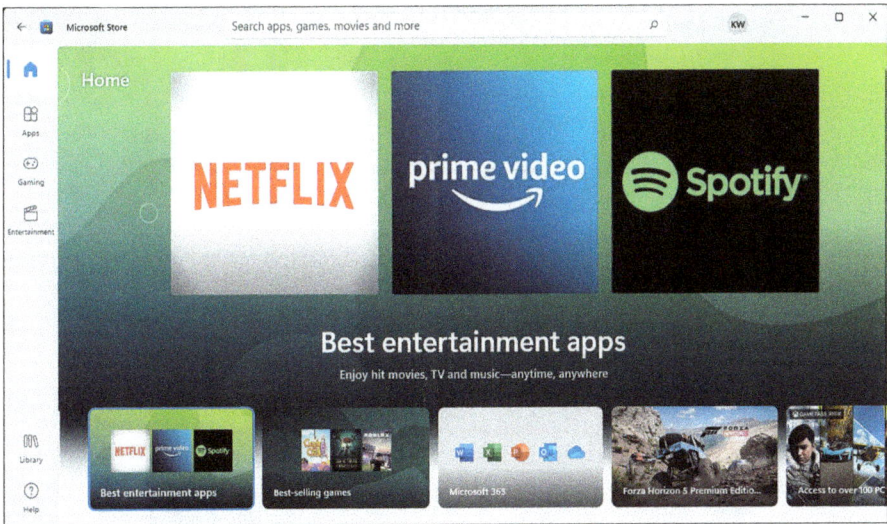

Down the left hand side, you'll see some icons. You'll automatically hand on 'home' where you'll see recommended apps, trending games, TV programmes, movies and so on. Click 'apps' to browse through various different apps from productivity, social media, to photography, as well as tablets and laptops for sale. Click 'gaming' to browse through the latest games, consoles, gaming PCs and accessories. Some apps and games you will need to pay for so you'll need to add payment details, and some are free. Click 'entertainment' to browse through the latest films, TV programmes and music albums.

On the bottom left, you'll see your 'library' and 'help'. The 'library' is where you'll find all the apps and games you've downloaded, as well as any TV Programmes or movies you've purchased.

## Searching the Store & Downloading Apps

You can also search for specific types of apps by using the search field on the top right of the screen. Type what you're looking for into the search field, eg 'theory test'. Press 'enter' on your keyboard.

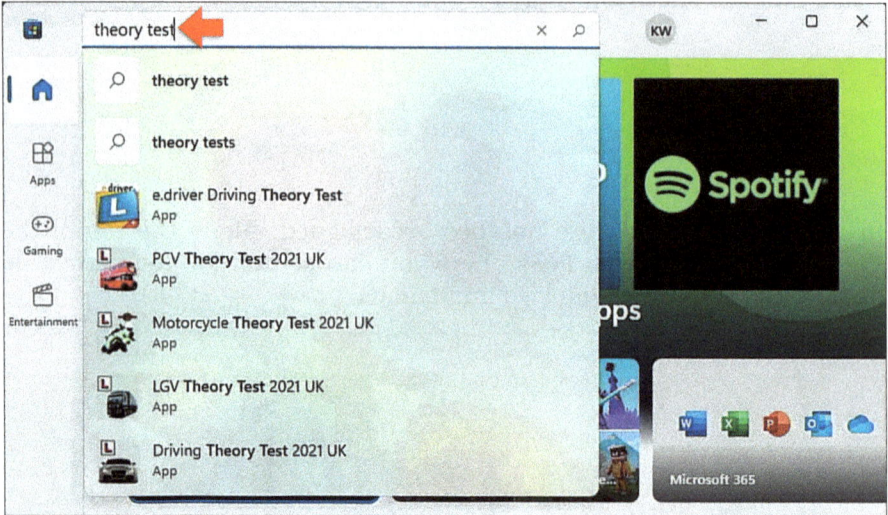

You can further narrow down the search using the options along the top of the window. You can search in all, in apps only, games, movies or tv shows.

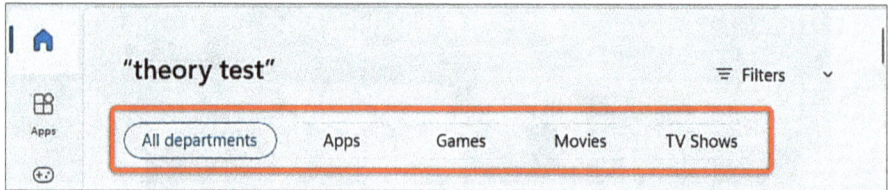

Click on the app's icon to show a summary of what the app is and what it does.

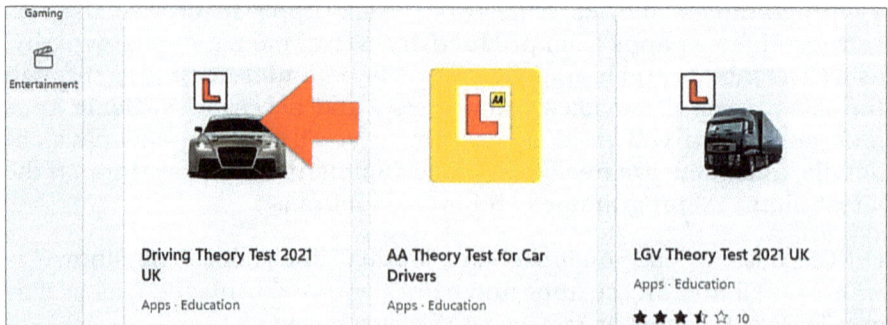

Here, you'll see screenshots of the app, reviews and information. Click the blue price tag or 'free' on the top right to purchase and download the app. You'll need to enter your Microsoft Account email address and password.

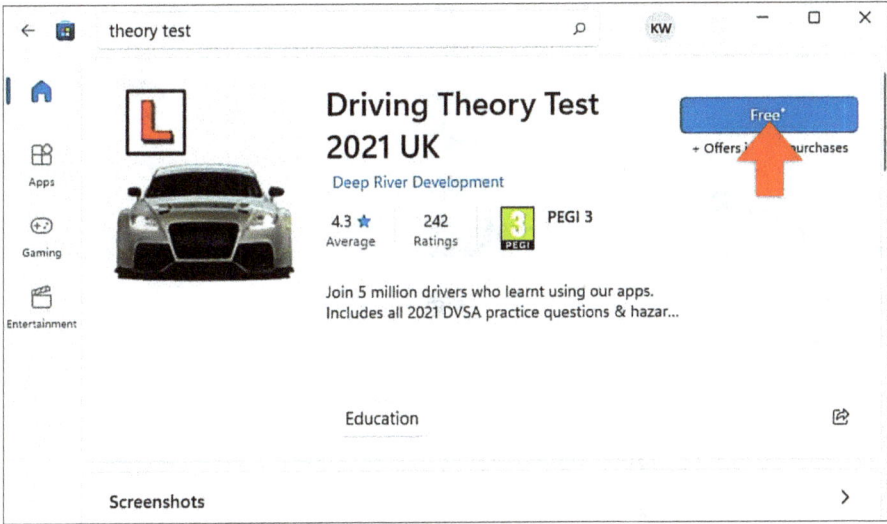

Once the app has downloaded and installed, you will be able to start your app using the start menu. If you downloaded a movie, or TV programme, you'll find it in your 'library' on the bottom left of the screen.

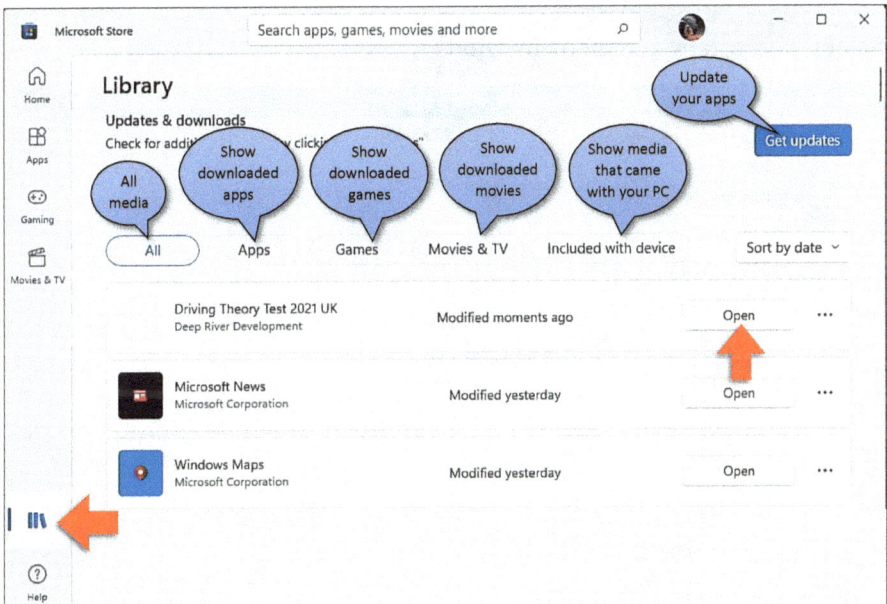

## Payment Options

To enter or check your payment method, click your Microsoft Account icon on the top right of the screen and select 'payment methods'.

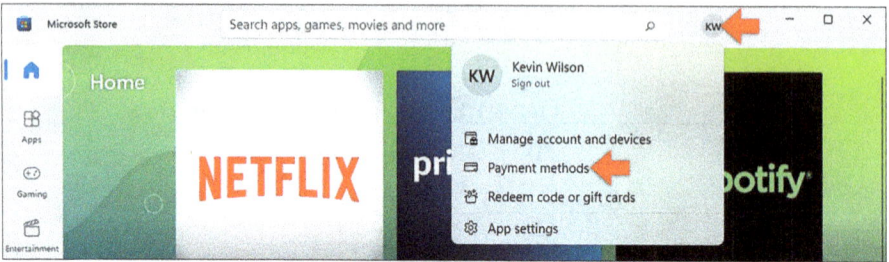

When your web browser opens, sign in with your Microsoft Account username and password.

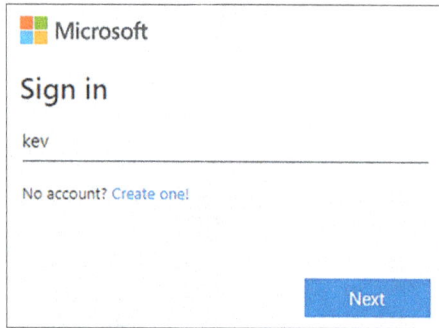

Select 'add a new payment method'.

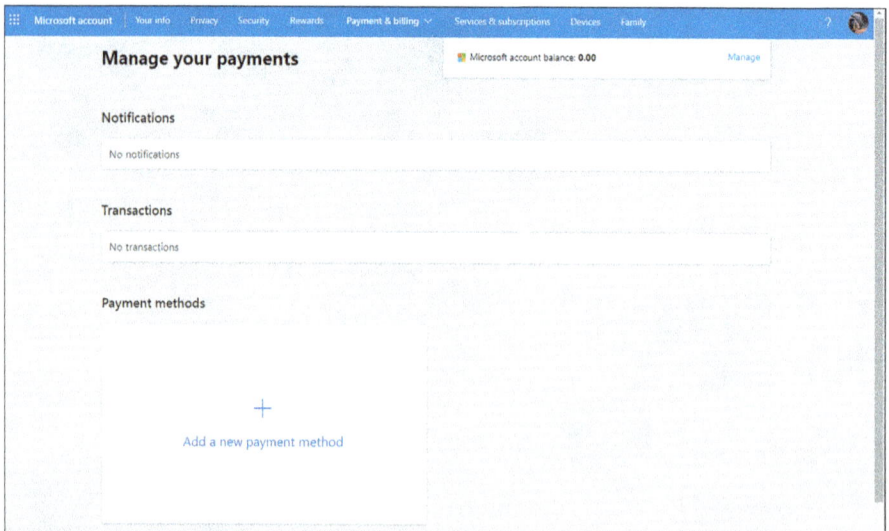

Select your country from the drop down menu at the top, then select the type of payment, eg credit card, mobile billing, or paypal. Scroll down the panel to view other payment methods.

Enter your details in the panel on the right.

Click 'next' or 'save', then follow the instructions on the screen.

# Weather App

The weather app can give you a forecast for your current location or any location you choose to view. Click the weather icon on your start menu. If you don't see it, click 'all apps'.

When you first start weather app it will ask for your location, unless you have location services enabled, then it will automatically find your location. If not, type it into the field in the middle of the screen.

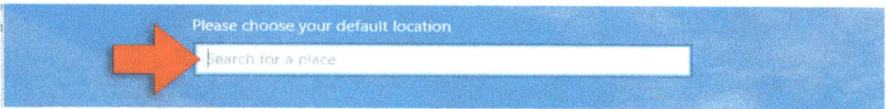

Please choose your default location

Search for a place

Once you have entered your location the weather app will show you a summary of the local weather conditions.

You can tap on each day to see more details, you may need to scroll down the page to see them.

Down the left hand side you have your navigation icons where you can see local weather, animated radar weather maps, historical weather and view your favourite locations list.

You can also find weather forecasts for other places. If for example you are going on holiday/vacation, you can enter the location's name into the search field and get a weather forecast.

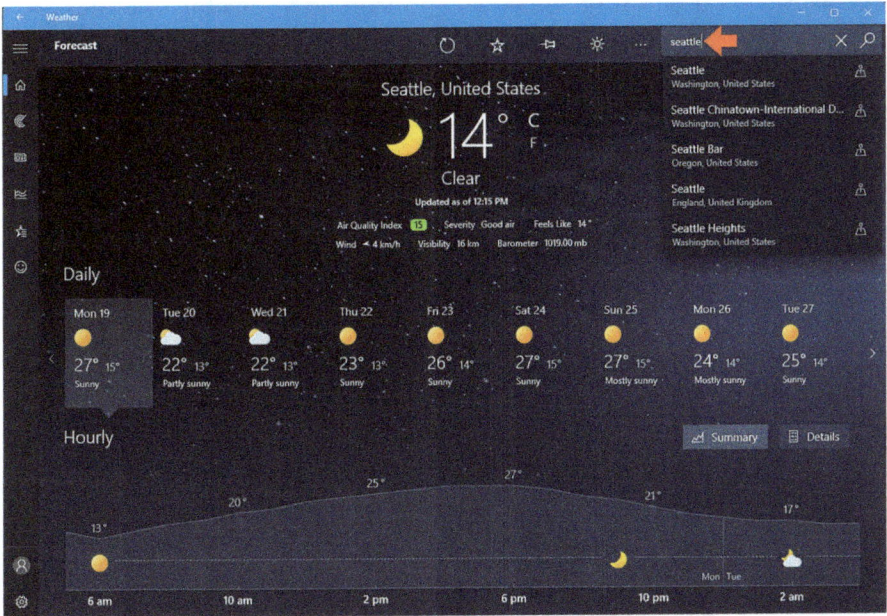

You can also add forecasts for locations to your favourites list so you don't have to keep searching for them.

To do this, just tap the 'add forecast location to favourites' icon along the top of your screen.

# News App

The news app brings you local news headlines and stories from around the world. You can find the news app icon on your start menu.

Along the top of the window, you can pin articles to your taskbar, open the articles in a web browser or share the article with someone else. Down the left hand side you have your navigation icons where you can browse different news sources such as news or sports channels.

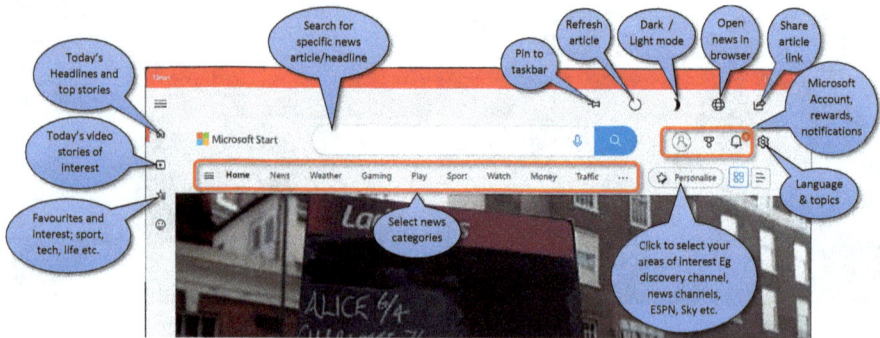

In the main window, you can read the headlines, or local news, just click on the article for more information . You can also watch video articles and reports - select the 'video stories' hub icon from the bar on the left hand side.

To personalise the articles that appear, click 'personalise' on the top right, then select a category from the list on the left. Click the '+' on any area of interest you like.

To search, type in an area of interest using the search field. Click the '+' icon next to the area of interest to add.

**264**

# Clock App

With the clock app, you can set alarms to alert you, or set timers, world clocks and timers. You'll find the app on your start menu.

| Alarms & Clock | Notepad | Paint | File Explorer | Movies & TV | Tips |

## Timers

Along the left hand side, you can set a timer to time something.

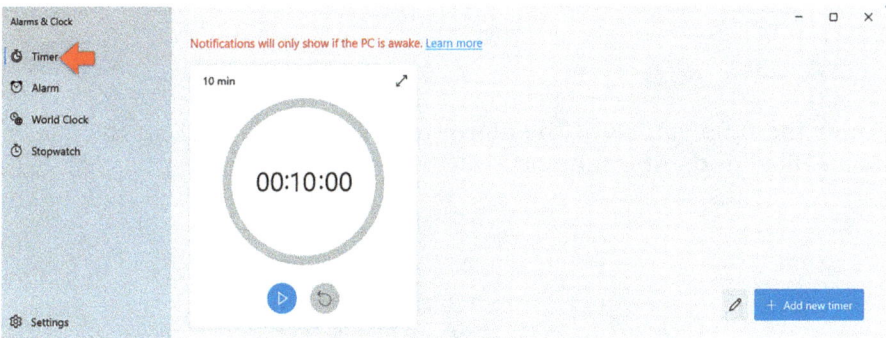

Click 'add new timer' on the bottom right, then set the time duration. Give the timer a name. Click 'save'

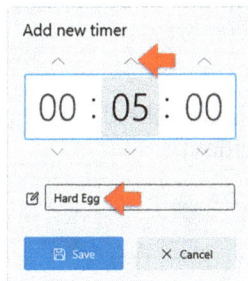

To run the timer, click the play button on the timer screen.

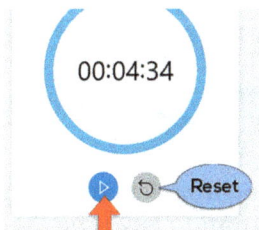

# Chapter 6: Using Apps

## Alarms

To set an alarm to sound at a particular time. For example, setting a time to get up in the morning. Select 'alarm' from the list on the left, then click 'add an alarm' on the bottom right.

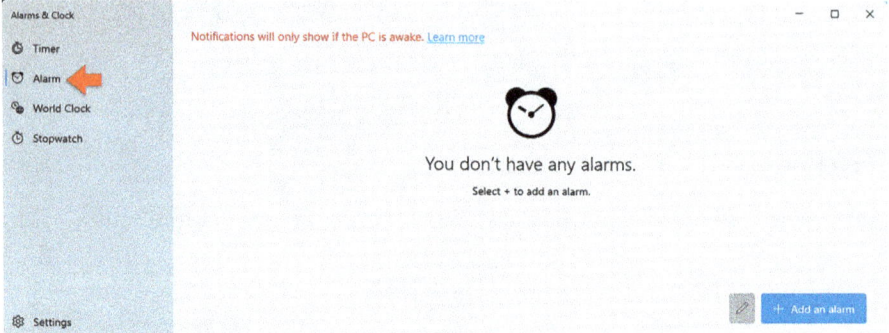

Enter the time you want the alarm to sound. Then click in the 'alarm name' field and enter a name.

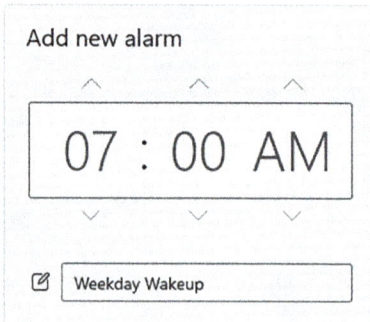

Click in the 'repeats' field, select the days you want the alarm to sound, eg week days (monday - friday).

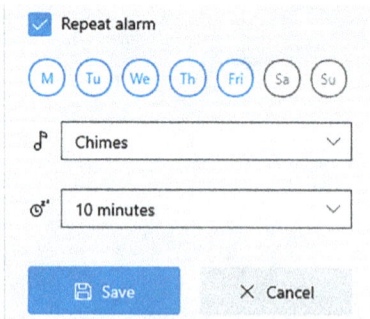

Choose a chime sound, and a how many minutes you want to 'snooze'. Click the 'save' on the bottom to save the alarm.

**266**

To set your alarm, click the switch on the top right of the alarm in the 'alarms' page.

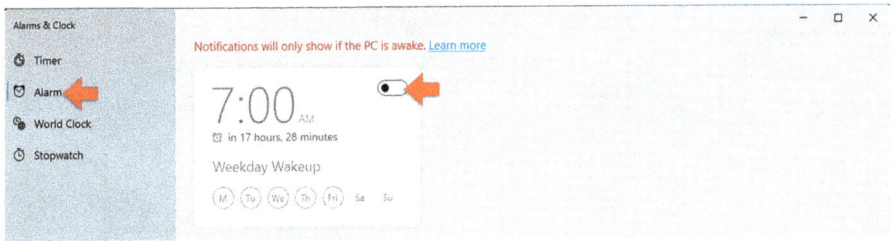

# World Clock

This can be useful if you have colleagues or family in other countries, or just want to know what time it is there so when you skype them you aren't disturbing them in the middle of the night. To add a clock for another city in the world, click 'world clock', then click 'add new city' on the bottom right.

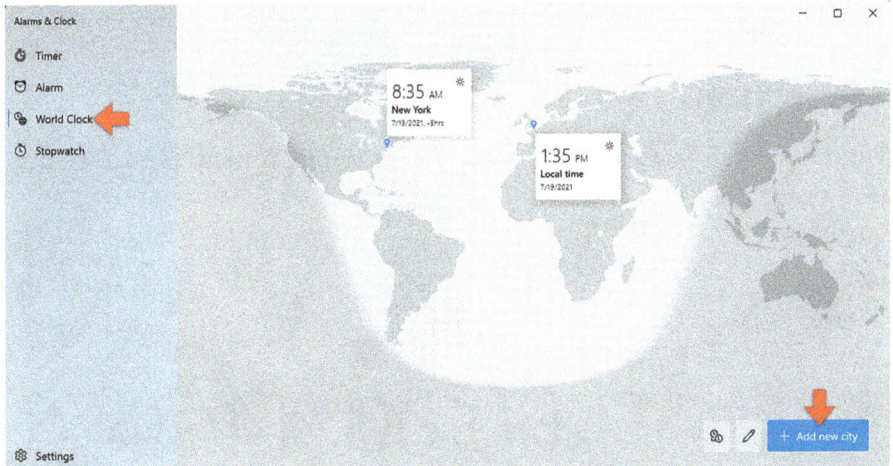

Enter the city/country name in the search field. Click the match in the search results.

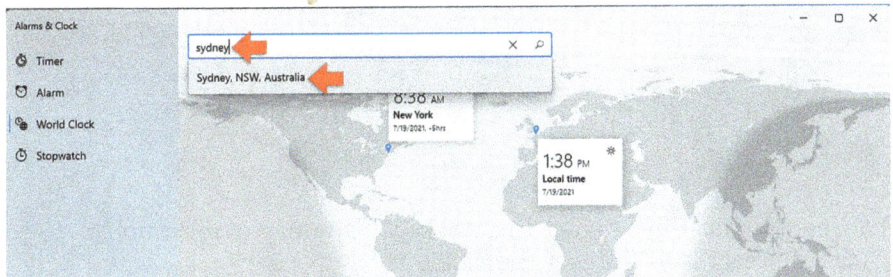

You'll see the city appear on the map

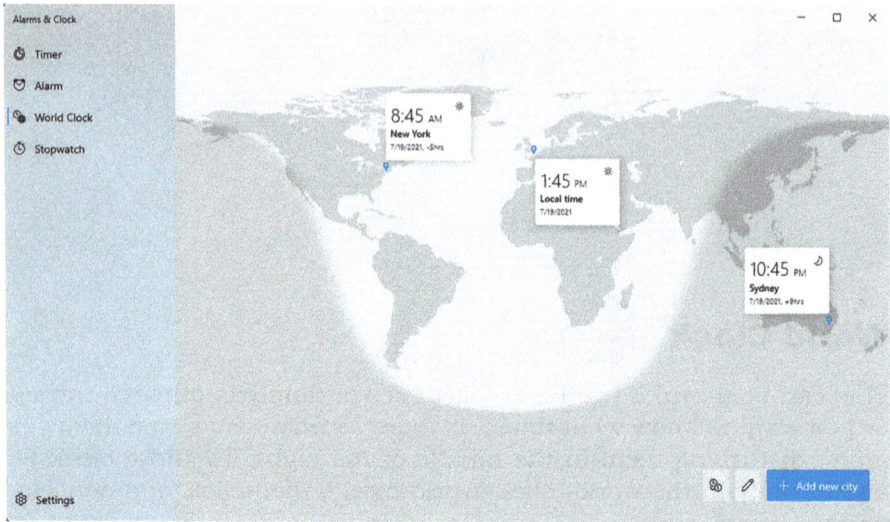

To remove a city, right click on the city, select 'delete'.

## Stopwatch

Tap stopwatch to time something, for example, a race, lap times and so on.

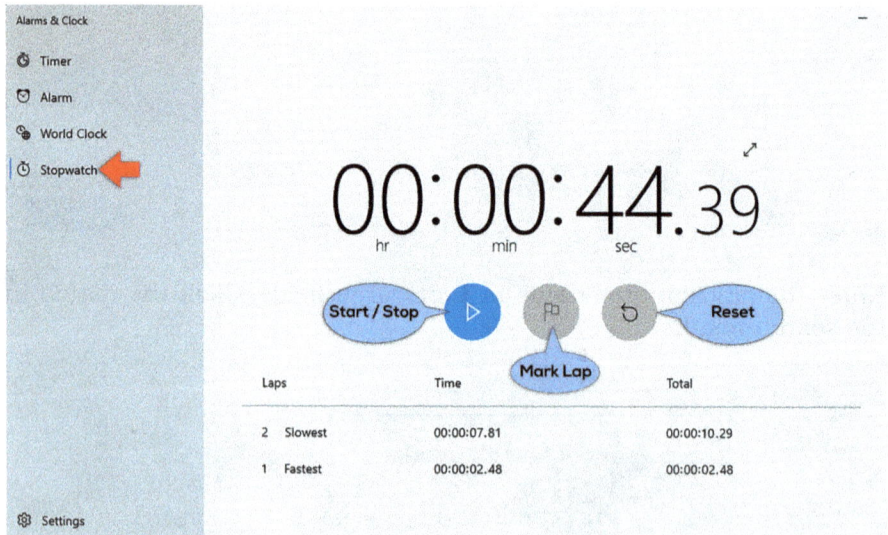

Hit the play button to start the clock. Hit the flag icon to mark a lap. Click the reset icon to reset the clock.

# Sound Recorder

Sound Recorder (formally Voice recorder), is your on-board dictation machine. You can make voice notes, record lectures, interviews and so on. To start recording just hit the microphone icon on the screen.

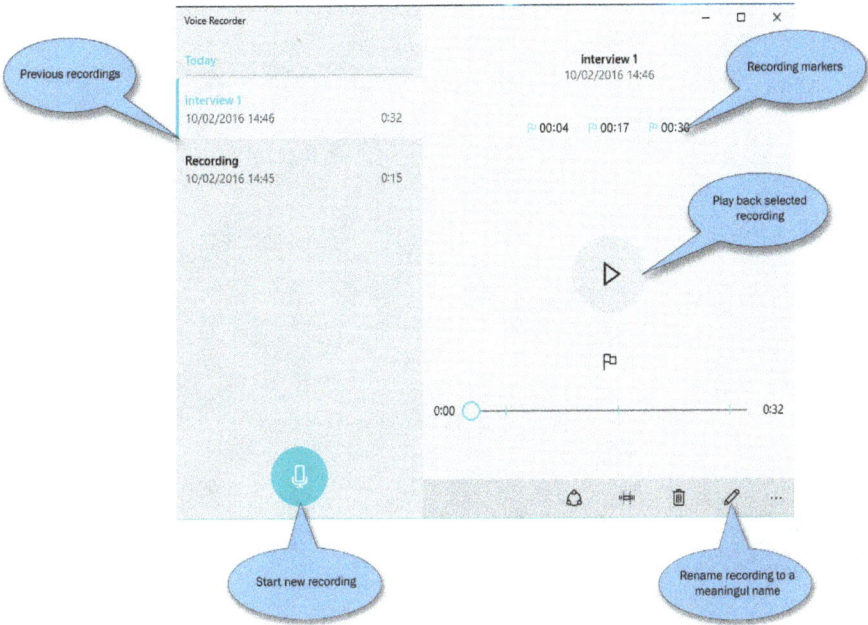

You can even add markers at important points during a recording.

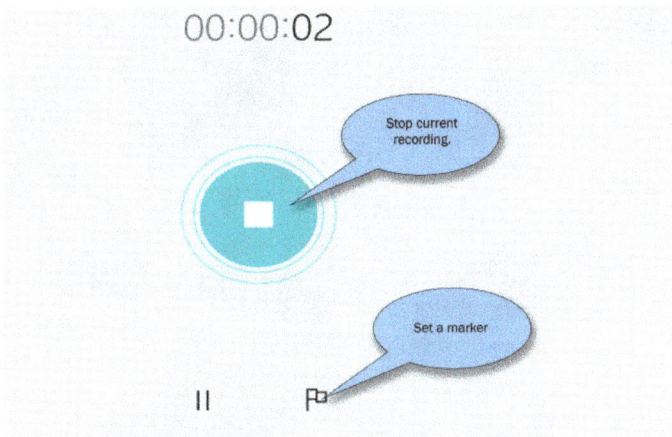

This way when you play back the recordings, you can go directly to the important points by clicking on these recording markers, illustrated in the top diagram.

# Calculator App

The calculator app works like any calculator. You can choose the type of calculator you want; just a standard calculator for adding a few numbers together or a full scientific calculator for working out more complex equations.

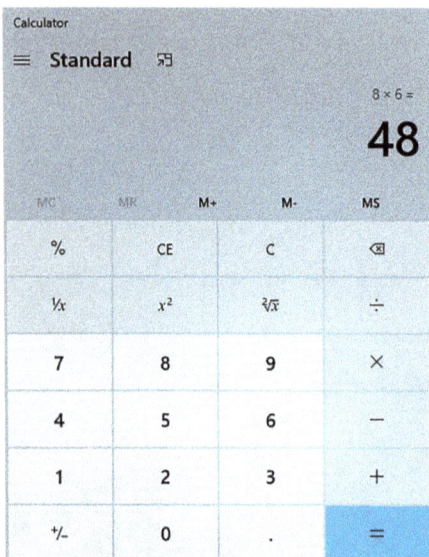

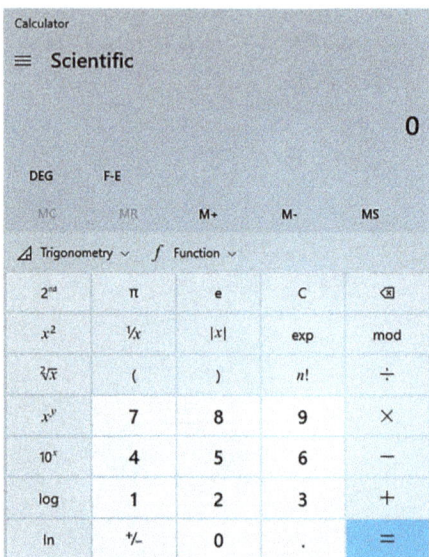

| Calculator | | | | |
|---|---|---|---|---|
| ≡ Standard ⊞ | | | | |
| | | | | $8 \times 6 =$ |
| | | | | **48** |
| MC | MR | M+ | M- | MS |
| % | CE | C | ⌫ | |
| $1/x$ | $x^2$ | $\sqrt[3]{x}$ | ÷ | |
| 7 | 8 | 9 | × | |
| 4 | 5 | 6 | − | |
| 1 | 2 | 3 | + | |
| +/- | 0 | . | = | |

| Calculator | | | | |
|---|---|---|---|---|
| ≡ Scientific | | | | |
| | | | | **0** |
| DEG | F-E | | | |
| MC | MR | M+ | M- | MS |
| ◁ Trigonometry ∨ | $f$ Function ∨ | | | |
| $2^{nd}$ | π | e | C | ⌫ |
| $x^2$ | $1/x$ | $|x|$ | exp | mod |
| $\sqrt[3]{x}$ | ( | ) | $n!$ | ÷ |
| $x^y$ | 7 | 8 | 9 | × |
| $10^x$ | 4 | 5 | 6 | − |
| log | 1 | 2 | 3 | + |
| ln | +/- | 0 | . | = |

To change the calculator click the icon on the top left of your screen, and select 'scientific'.

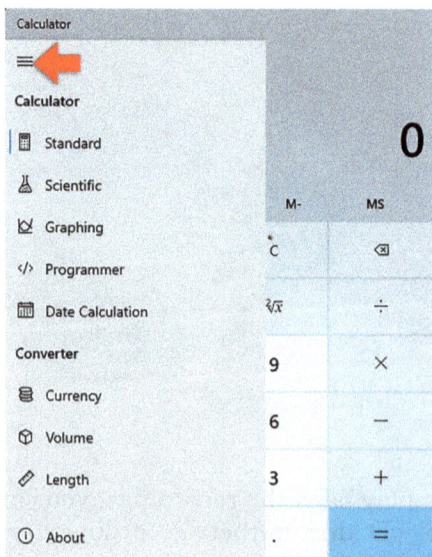

| Calculator | | |
|---|---|---|
| ≡ ⬅ | | |
| **Calculator** | | |
| 🔲 Standard | | **0** |
| ⚗ Scientific | | |
| | M- | MS |
| 🗠 Graphing | ⋮ | |
| | C | ⌫ |
| </> Programmer | | |
| 📅 Date Calculation | $\sqrt[3]{x}$ | ÷ |
| **Converter** | | |
| 🖥 Currency | 9 | × |
| ⊕ Volume | | |
| | 6 | − |
| ✏ Length | 3 | + |
| ⓘ About | . | = |

# Unit Converter

You can also convert different units. You can convert between different currencies, weight, length, temperature, energy and so on. To open the converter, click the icon on the top left of your screen, shown below. Scroll down the list to the converters and select one, eg 'length'.

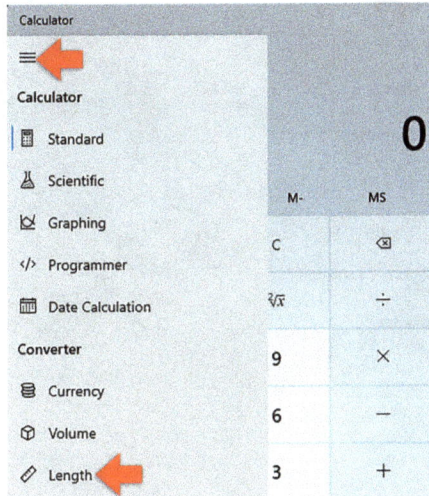

Useful if you want to convert metric measurements to ones you're familiar with. Eg: To convert from millimeters to inches, change the first one to millimeters and the second one to inches - indicated by the red arrows below.

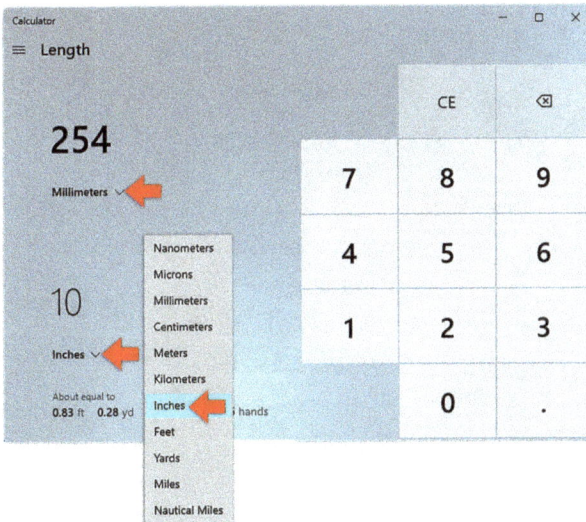

Click on the top number - it will turn to bold text. Now type in a value.

# Currency Converter

Click the icon on the top left of your screen and select 'currency' from the drop down menu.

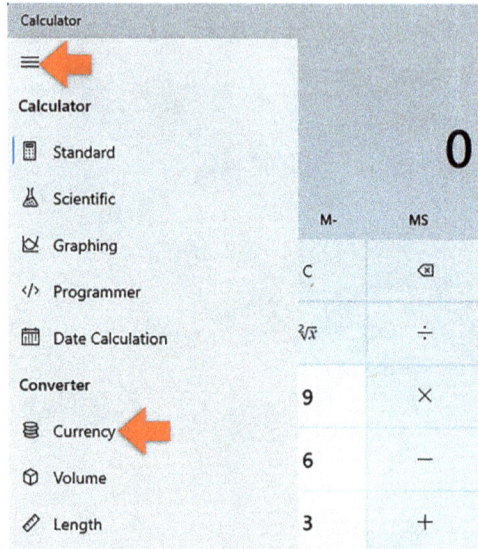

To change the currencies, click the currency name under the value, shown below. From the popup menu, select the currency you want.

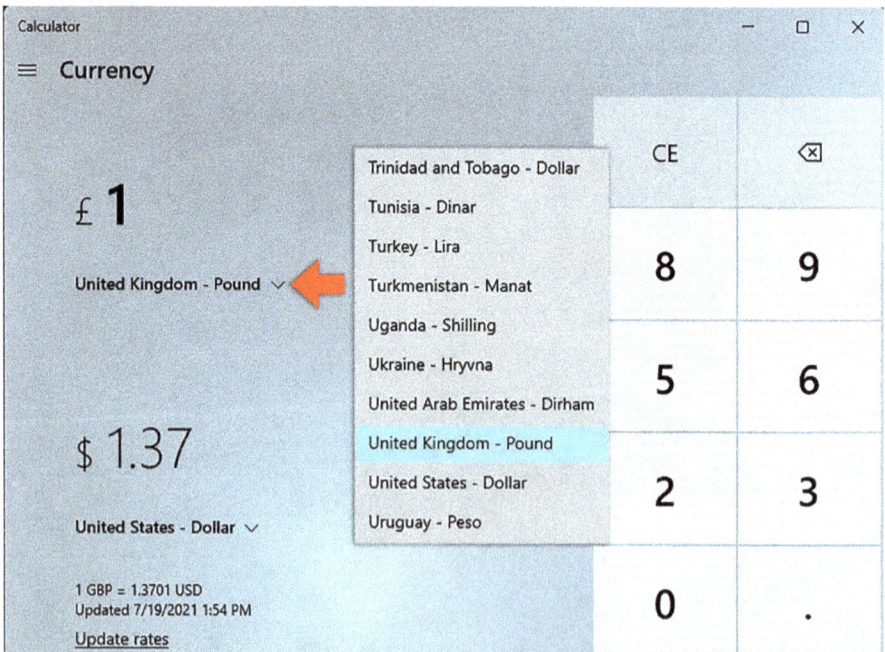

Click on the currency numbers and enter a value using the on screen keypad, as shown below. In the example below, I'm converting from British Pounds to US Dollars.

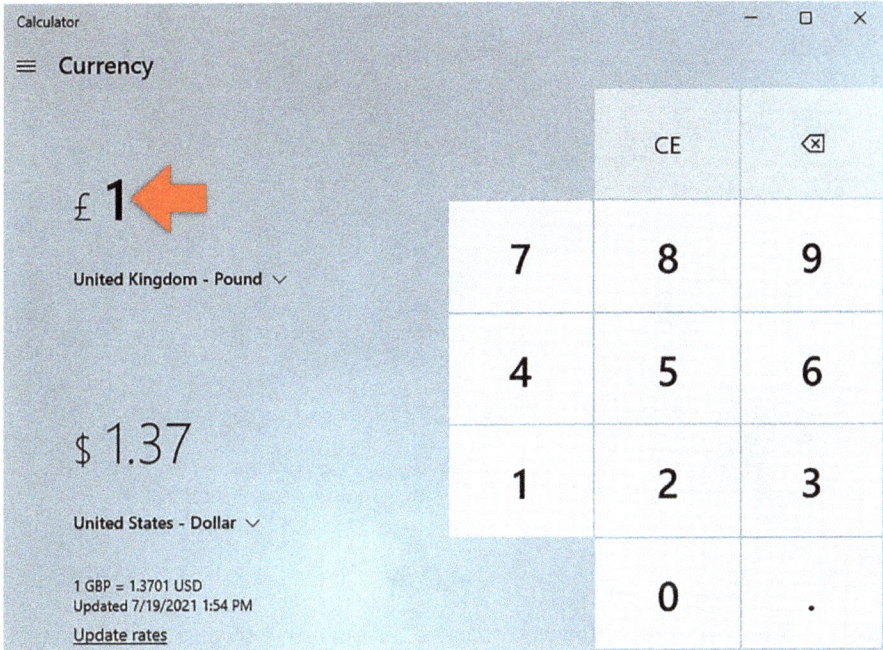

## Graphing

With the graphing feature, you can plot various equations on the graph. To use the feature, click the icon on the top left of the screen and select 'graphing' from the menu.

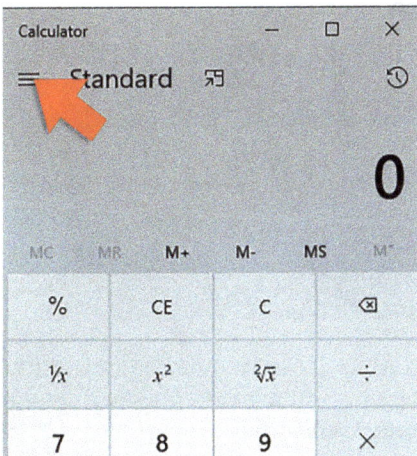

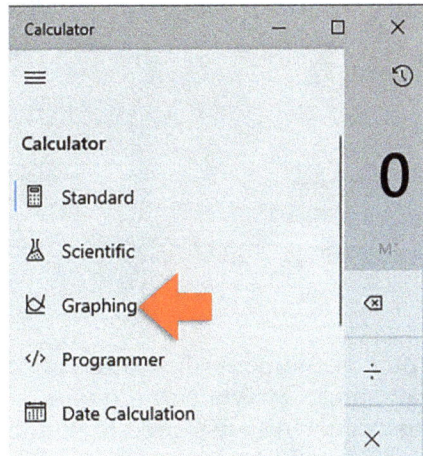

Make the window bigger, or go into full screen. As you do this, you'll see the graphing functions appear on the right.

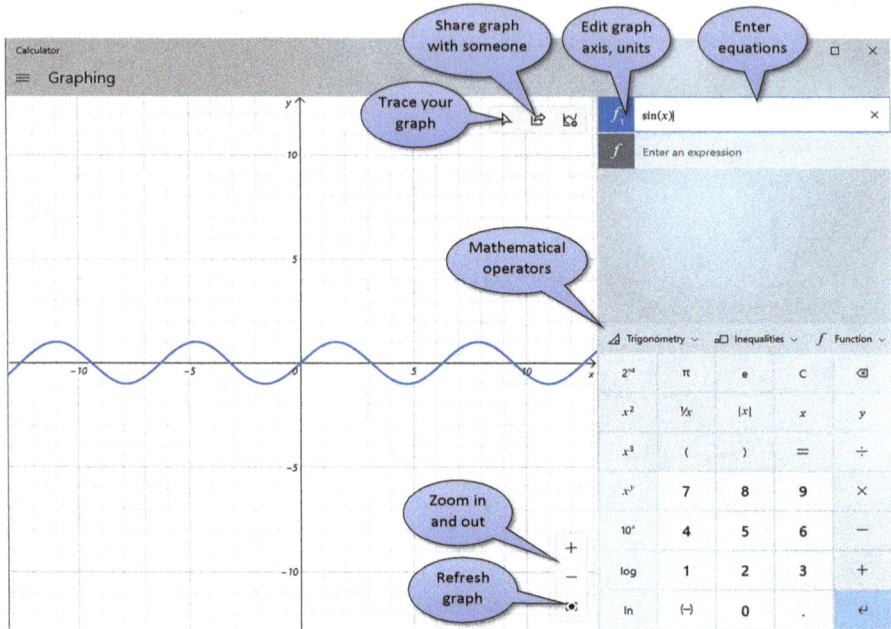

On the top right, enter your equations. Press enter to plot on the graph.

# To Do App

The To Do App is a cloud based task management utility that allows you to set tasks and make to do lists. You'll find the icon on your start menu.

Once the app opens, you'll land on the main screen.

You'll see a menu down the left hand side. Here, you'll see options to view tasks for your day, tasks marked as important, planned tasks, tasks currently assigned to you, all tasks, and task lists.

To create a new list, click 'new list' on the left hand side. Give the list a name.

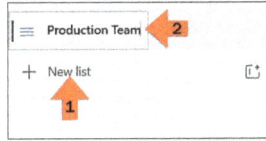

Click the share icon on the top right to invite other people in the team to join the task list. Select 'invite via email'. Enter the person's email address in the email app, then click send.

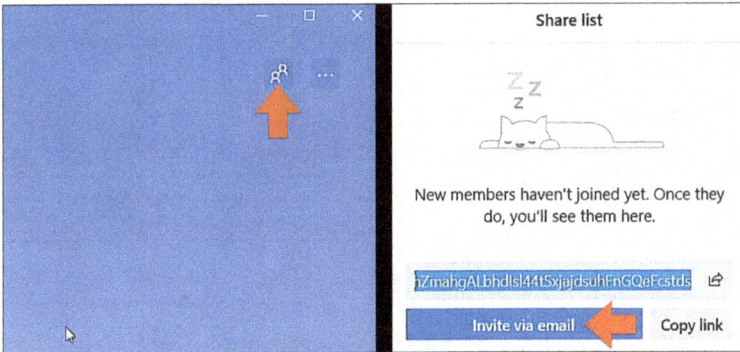

To add a task, type the activity into the 'add a task' field. Type @ then select the name to assign the task to someone.

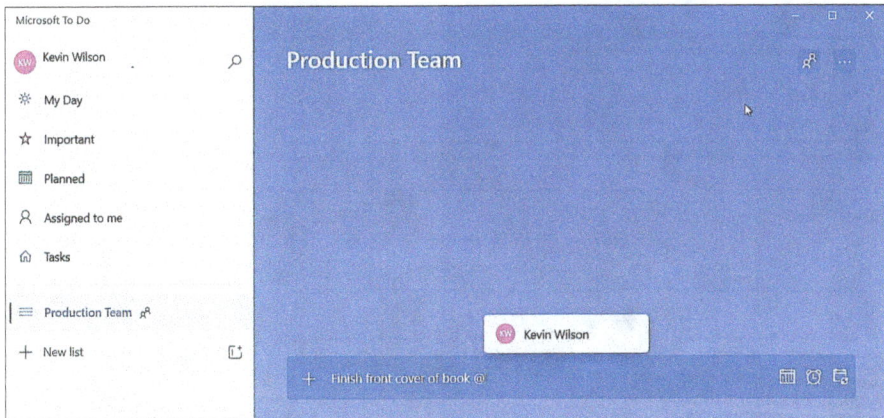

Click the calendar icon then select a due date. Click the alarm clock icon to add a reminder. Click the repeat icon to create a repeating task (daily, weekly, monthly etc).

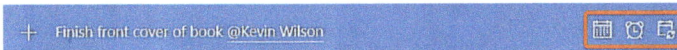

# PowerShell

The powershell is a command-line interface that allows you to execute commands by typing them in. Command line interfaces were the standard for computers in the early 1980s before the introduction of graphic user interfaces as seen in Windows or Mac.

To open the powershell, right click on the start button, select 'windows terminal' from the options. 'Windows Terminal' opens powershell as a standard user, 'Windows Terminal (admin)' opens the powershell as an administrator and is the option you choose if you want to run system utilities.

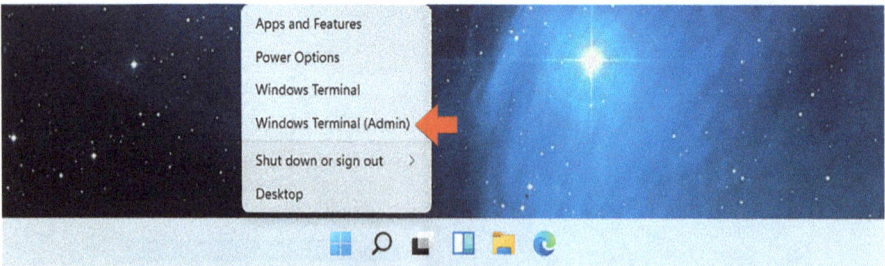

You'll see a window pop up, with a command prompt similar to the following.

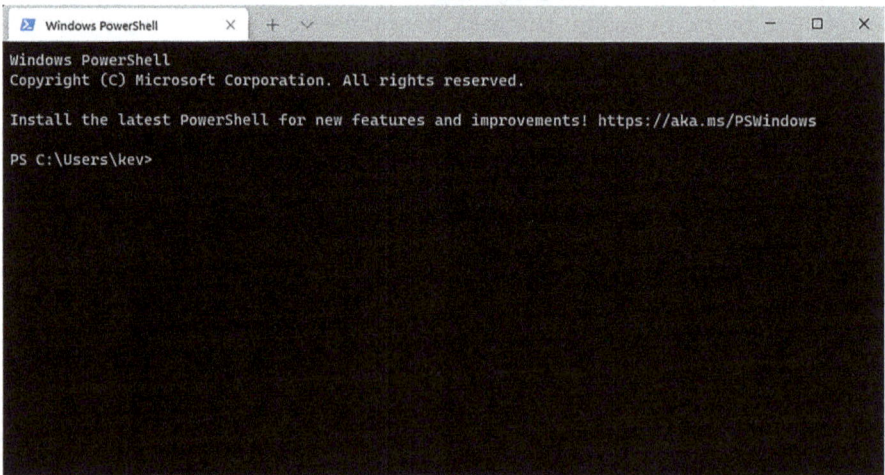

Here, the command prompt is made up of the letters 'PS' - meaning you're using PowerShell, followed by a drive letter, and the folder you're currently in with a greater than sign at the end.

This is where you type in your commands. For example, to list all files in the current directory (downloads), type `dir` then press enter.

```
PS C:\Users\kev> dir


    Directory: C:\Users\kev


Mode                 LastWriteTime         Length Name
----                 -------------         ------ ----
d-r---        05/07/2021     11:20                Contacts
d-----        05/07/2021     11:23                Documents
d-r---        11/07/2021     10:57                Downloads
d-r---        05/07/2021     11:20                Favorites
d-r---        05/07/2021     11:20                Links
d-r---        05/07/2021     11:20                Music
dar--l        19/07/2021     13:06                OneDrive
d-r---        05/07/2021     11:20                Saved Games
d-r---        05/07/2021     11:30                Searches
d-r---        05/07/2021     12:00                Videos


PS C:\Users\kev>
```

The powershell will return a list of files in the directory.

You can use sl or cd to move between folders. For example, from the folder listing we got in the previous step, if I wanted to move down to the OneDrive folder...

```
PS C:\Users\kevwi> dir


    Directory: C:\Users\kev


Mode                 LastWriteTime         Length Name
----                 -------------         ------ ----
d-r---        05/07/2021     11:20                Contacts
d-----        05/07/2021     11:23                Documents
d-r---        11/07/2021     10:57                Downloads
d-r---        05/07/2021     11:20                Favorites
d-r---        05/07/2021     11:20                Links
d-r---        05/07/2021     11:20                Music
dar--l        19/07/2021     13:06                OneDrive
d-r---        05/07/2021     11:20                Saved Games
d-r---        05/07/2021     11:30                Searches
```

Use the sl or cd command followed by the folder name. So in this case to get to the OneDrive folder type `sl OneDrive`

```
PS C:\Users\kev> sl OneDrive
```

To create a new folder in the current folder use `mkdir` followed by the folder name.

```
PS C:\Users\kev\OneDrive> mkdir Work
```

**277**

To copy a file use the copy. To copy a file from the documents folder to my new work folder. First we need to go into the documents directory so we type `sl documents`.

```
PS C:\Users\kevwi\OneDrive> sl Documents
```

To copy a file use the `copy` command. The folder 'work' isn't in the documents folder so we need to tell the copy command where the folder is. Remember the folder tree. We need to go back a folder, then into the work folder

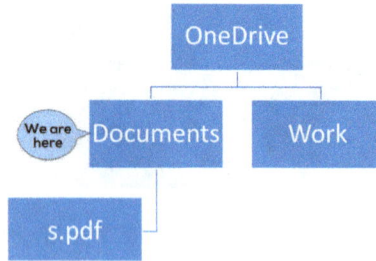

To do this use the double dot. So we type:

```
copy s.pdf ../work
```

The '..' means go back a folder. So the copy command will go back to OneDrive folder, then into the 'work' folder.

If we look in the 'work' folder, you'll see the file we copied.

```
PS C:\Users\kev\OneDrive\work> dir

    Directory: C:\Users\kev\OneDrive\work


Mode                 LastWriteTime         Length Name
----                 -------------         ------ ----
-a---l         25/01/2021     14:59         131077 s.pdf
```

You can open new powershell tabs, open the old command prompt, or an azure cloud shell. Click the arrow to the right of the tabs.

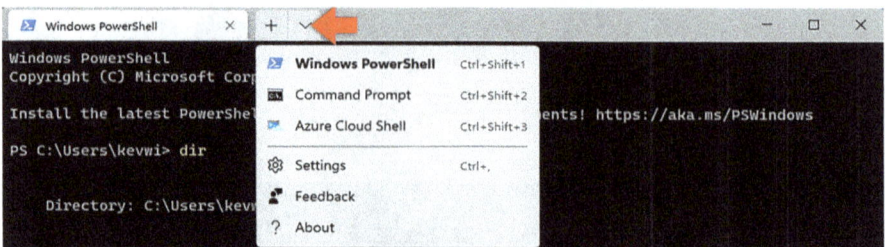

# Apps from Outside Microsoft Store

While the Microsoft Store provides a convenient and secure way to download a wide range of applications, many of the most powerful, specialized, or widely used Windows applications are distributed outside the Store. These applications are typically available as .exe (executable) or .msi (Microsoft Installer) files and can be downloaded directly from the software vendor's website such as the following.

- Google Chrome – `google.com/chrome`
- Mozilla Firefox – `mozilla.org/firefox`
- VLC Media Player – `videolan.org`
- Steam (for games) – `store.steampowered.com`
- OBS Studio, Notepad++, Visual Studio Code, Python, and many others.

**Remember, only download applications from official websites or well-known, trusted sources. Avoid third-party download sites, which may bundle software with adware or malware. Never download apps from links in unsolicited emails, pop-up ads, or unknown messages, as these are common vectors for malicious software and cyber attacks.**

For example to install Mozilla Firefox, first download the installer from the website if you haven't already done so.

Open File explorer, then navigate to the 'downloads' folder in file explorer. Double-click it to launch the installer. Follow the on-screen instructions to complete the installation.

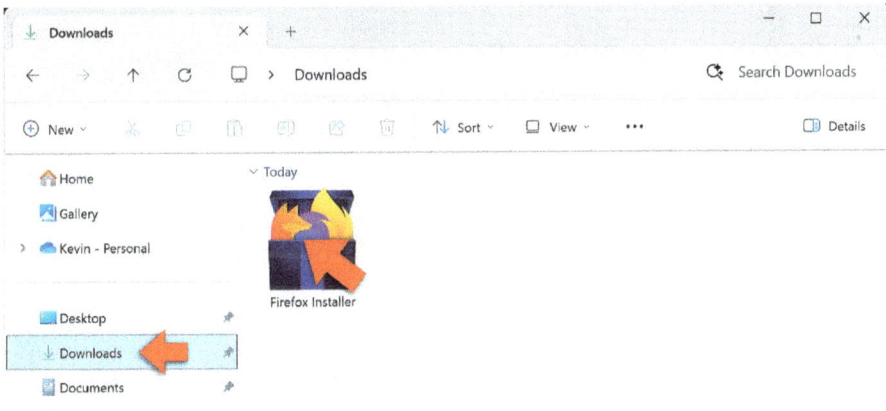

If the installer is stored on an external drive or a different folder, browse to that location using File Explorer.

**279**

If you encounter an error stating that Windows has blocked the installation, it may be due to a system setting that restricts app installations to the Microsoft Store.

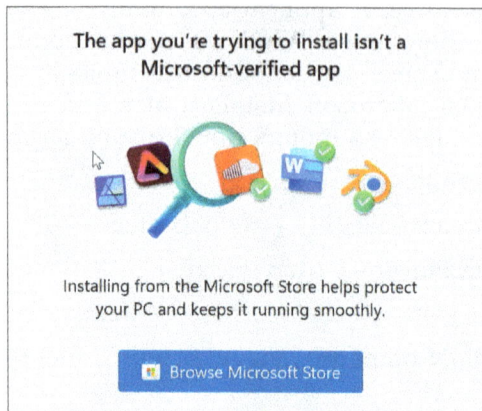

If this is the case, open the settings app, navigate to Apps > Advanced App Settings. Change 'choose where to get apps' to 'anywhere'.

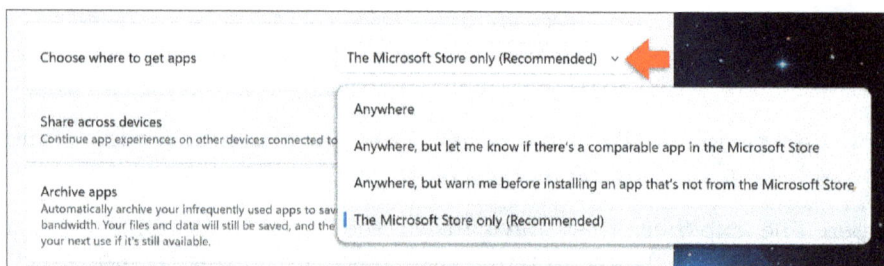

Once the application has been successfully installed, remember to change this setting back to "The Microsoft Store only". This reduces the risk of inadvertently installing unsafe software in the future.

# Linux Apps

As of Windows 11 version 24H2, Microsoft continues to support running Linux applications through Windows Subsystem for Linux (WSL), a powerful compatibility layer that enables native-like Linux development on Windows machines.

See "Windows Subsystem for Linux" on page 153 for information on how to enable this.

Once installed and setup, open your Linux distribution from the start menu. Eg 'Ubuntu'.

At the command prompt type the following

```
sudo apt update
```

```
sudo apt upgrade -y
```

To install the app (Gimp in this example), type the following command.

```
sudo apt install gimp -y
```

Allow the installer to download and install the app.

To run the installed app type the following

```
gimp
```

Once you enter the command, the app will open.

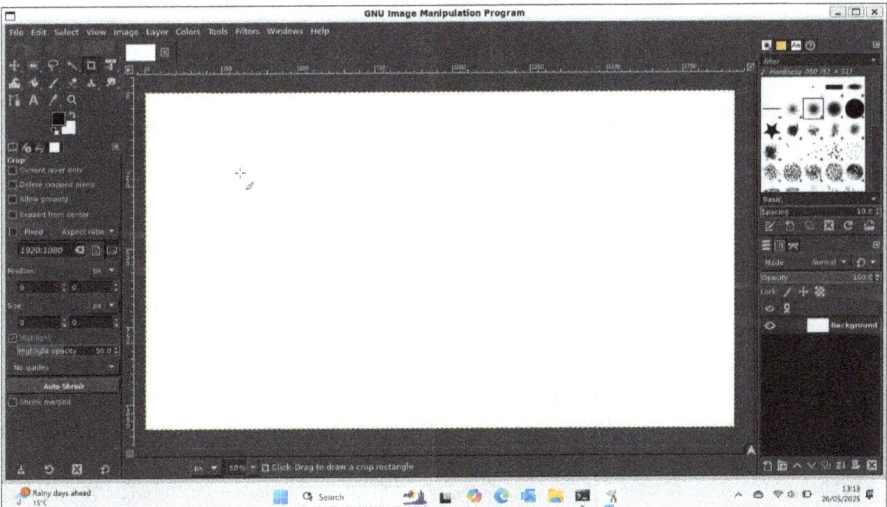

You can view and copy files created by Linux apps from Windows using this path in File Explorer. Change your-linux-username for the username you setup when you installed the Linux Distribution.

`\\wsl$\Ubuntu\home\`**`your-linux-username`**

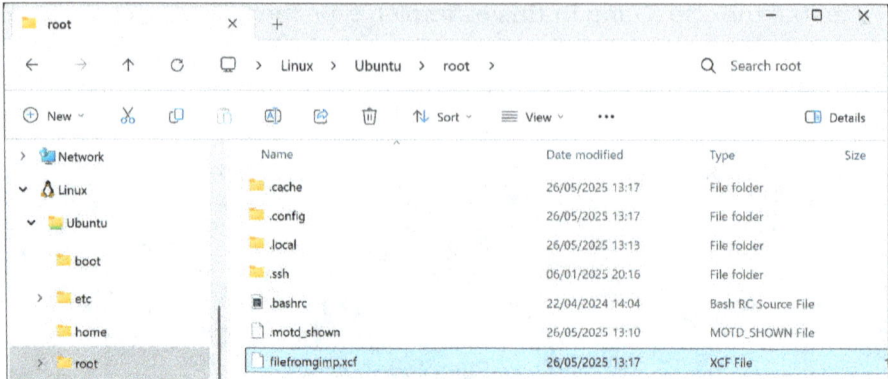

Some other commonly used Linux apps

| App | Description | Install Command |
|---|---|---|
| gimp | Advanced image editor (like Photoshop) | `sudo apt install gimp` |
| inkscape | Vector graphics editor | `sudo apt install inkscape` |
| firefox | Web browser | `sudo apt install firefox` |
| libreoffice | Full-featured office suite | `sudo apt install libreoffice` |
| vlc | Media player for audio/video | `sudo apt install vlc` |

# Intel, AMD, and ARM

Windows 11 is designed to run across a range of hardware platforms—including traditional Intel and AMD processors using the x64 architecture, as well as newer ARM-based systems powered by Qualcomm Snapdragon chips, such as those found in Copilot+ PCs.

Architecture refers to the fundamental design of the processor—specifically, how it processes instructions, manages data, and interacts with memory and hardware.

It defines the instruction set the processor understands (such as x64 or ARM64), which is the low-level language used by software to communicate with the CPU. In other words, architecture determines what kind of software can run on a processor and how efficiently it will run. Two processors with different architectures—like x64 and ARM64—require software to be built or adapted specifically for them, because the instructions each one understands are different.

Traditional Windows PCs are built on the x64 architecture and run natively on Intel or AMD processors. ARM-based Windows devices, including those with Snapdragon processors, use the ARM64 (also known as AArch64) architecture and are becoming increasingly common in the ultraportable laptop segment and among energy-efficient, AI-enhanced devices such as Copilot+ PCs.

If you're using an ARM-based PC, you can install and run the majority of Windows applications just as you would on a traditional Intel or AMD system. Applications do not need to come from the Microsoft Store; standalone installers such as .exe and .msi files downloaded from websites can be installed and executed normally.

The best performance is achieved on ARM based PCs when applications are compiled specifically for the ARM64 architecture. Many widely used Windows applications already offer native ARM versions, including Microsoft 365 apps (Word, Excel, PowerPoint, Outlook), Microsoft Edge, Zoom, Visual Studio Code, Creative Cloud, and many others.

For applications that have not yet been recompiled for ARM, Windows 11 includes built-in support for x64 emulation. With Windows 11 version 24H2, Microsoft introduced a next-generation emulation engine called Prism, which significantly improves the performance, compatibility, and energy efficiency of emulated apps compared to earlier versions. Prism replaces the previous x64 emulation layer and makes it possible to run most traditional desktop software—including productivity, communication, and media applications—on ARM-based systems with minimal user intervention.

From the user's perspective, the experience is virtually identical: installations, file handling, updates, and shortcuts behave just as they do on x64 systems.

Although the emulation layer is highly capable, there may be slight performance or power efficiency penalties when running demanding applications or those that depend heavily on plug-ins, low-level drivers, or legacy APIs. For optimal performance—especially on AI-capable Copilot+ PCs—users are encouraged to install ARM-native applications whenever available. These apps are optimized to take full advantage of the underlying hardware architecture and the Neural Processing Unit (NPU), which in Copilot+ PCs can deliver over 40 TOPS (trillion operations per second) to accelerate on-device AI workloads such as real-time image editing, background removal, and live transcription.

# 7

# Internet and Comms

In this chapter, we'll take a look at the browser Microsoft Edge. We'll also take a brief look at Google Chrome as it is a good alternative to Microsoft Edge.

We'll also take a look at

- Edge Browser
- Outlook App
- Calendar
- People & Contacts
- Microsoft Teams
- Remote Desktop
- FTP
- SSH with PuTTY
- SSH from Windows Terminal
- Folder Sharing on a LAN
- Access a Shared Folder on a LAN
- Mobile Hotspot
- Phone Link

We'll also take a look at how to get started using Microsoft Teams for making calls and collaboration.

To help you better understand this section, take a look at the video resources. Scan the QR code, or open your web browser and type the following directly into the address bar at the top (don't use a search engine):

elluminetpress.com/win-comms

# Microsoft Edge Browser

You'll find Edge on your start menu or taskbar. Click the icon to start the app.

Mail    Microsoft Edge    Calendar    Microsoft Store    Alarms & Clock    Settings

## Main Screen

When Edge starts, you'll see the main screen. The icons along the top of the window represent various functionalities and tools available. Lets take a look at what they do.

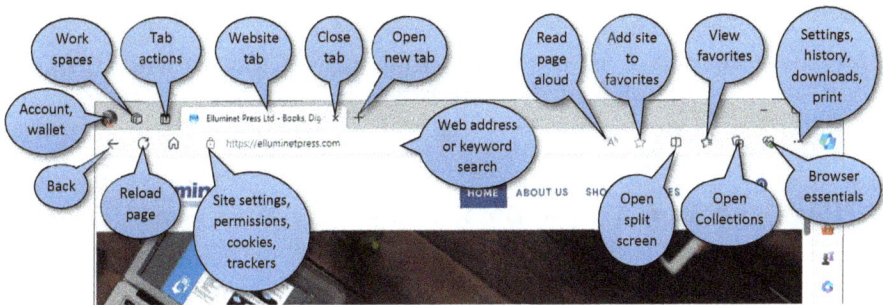

**Account Icon** indicates the user profile that is currently active in the browser. Clicking on it will allow you to manage profiles, sync settings, or log in/out.

**Workspaces** allows users to organize tabs into different workspaces. It's like having multiple desks, each with its own set of related tabs open. This can be helpful for separating different projects or topics you're working on.

**Tab Actions** encompasses a variety of options you can take with your tabs such as pinning tabs. This keeps a tab in a fixed position, usually to the left of the tab bar. Tab Groups allows you to group related tabs together.

**Back and Forward Arrows** allow you to navigate to previously visited pages.

**Refresh Icon** reloads or refreshes the current webpage.

**Home Icon** this takes you to the homepage set in the browser's settings.

Scan for Video

**285**

**Address Bar/Search Bar** is where you can type in URLs or Bing search queries. You'll also see a lock icon indicating a secure connection to the site.

**Favorites (Star Icon)** provides access to saved web pages. Also called bookmarks.

**The Collections icon** opens a sidebar you can use it to keep track of websites, images, text snippets, and other information as you browse. This feature is particularly useful for projects where you're gathering information on a topic, as it allows you to save all relevant information in one place, which can then sync across your devices if you are signed in to your Microsoft account.

**Split Screen Icon** allows you to work on multiple websites side-by-side within a single browser tab. This enhances productivity by facilitating multitasking.

**Browser Essentials** is a feature that provides you with insights into the performance and security of your browser in a single, easy-to-understand view. It offers helpful suggestions for optimizing performance and enhancing browser protection.

**Settings and More (Three Dots)** opens a menu with more browser options such as settings, history, downloads, etc.

## The Sidebar

Down the right hand side of the browser window, you'll see a sidebar.

**Copilot:** An AI assistant that helps you navigate and perform tasks in the browser efficiently.

**Search:** Allows you to perform web searches without leaving your current page.

**Shopping:** A feature designed to assist with finding deals, price comparisons, and managing coupons as you shop online.

**Tools:** A suite of utilities such as calculators, converters, or other small apps to facilitate quick tasks.

**Games:** Provides quick access to games directly within the browser without needing to visit a separate website.

**Microsoft 365:** Provides a direct link to Microsoft Office applications and documents for editing and collaboration.

**Outlook Email:** Enables you to check your Outlook email without having to navigate away from your current tab.

**Image Creator:** A creative tool for editing or generating images directly within the browser.

**Drop:** A feature that simplifies the process of sending files and notes across your devices.

You can customize the sidebar by adding or removing features. To add a feature, click the '+' icon on the bottom of the sidebar, then select a feature. To remove an icon from the sidebar, right click on the icon, then select 'quit app'.

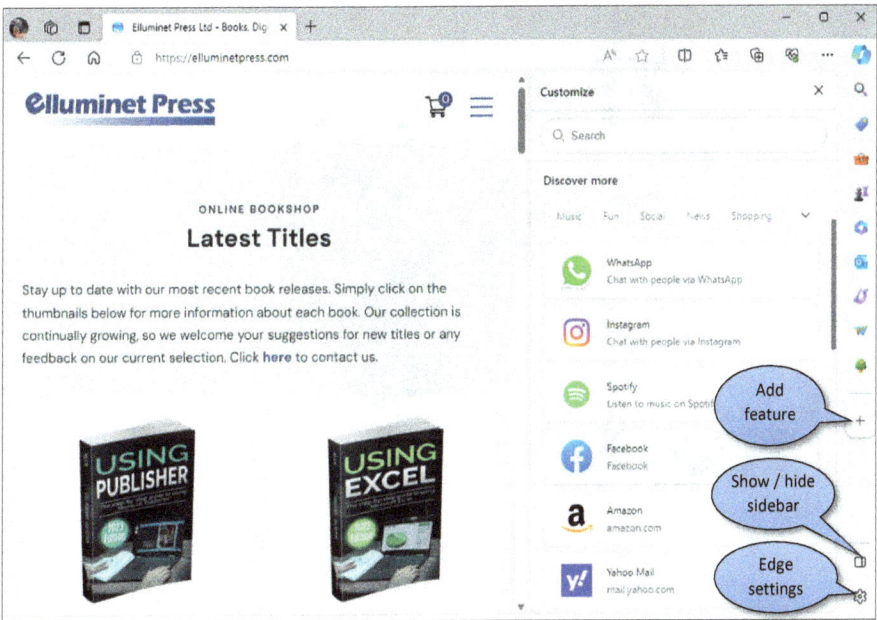

The sidebar can also be hidden or shown. To do this, click the 'show/hide' toggle icon located just above the gear icon at the bottom of the sidebar.

The gear icon at the bottom opens Sidebar settings, where you can customize which tools appear, rearrange icon order, and set whether the sidebar opens automatically on startup.

The sidebar is designed to help you multitask more efficiently without switching tabs or losing focus on your current work. It integrates productivity tools—like calculators, file sharing, quick notes, and even full apps like Word or Outlook—into a single panel that stays accessible as you browse.

## Set your Home Page

Setting a home page allows you to set a page to show when you first start Edge or when you click the home icon on the toolbar. Ideally you should set the home page to a website you use most often such as Google search.

To set your home page, click the 'three dots icon' on the top right of the screen, then from the menu select 'settings'.

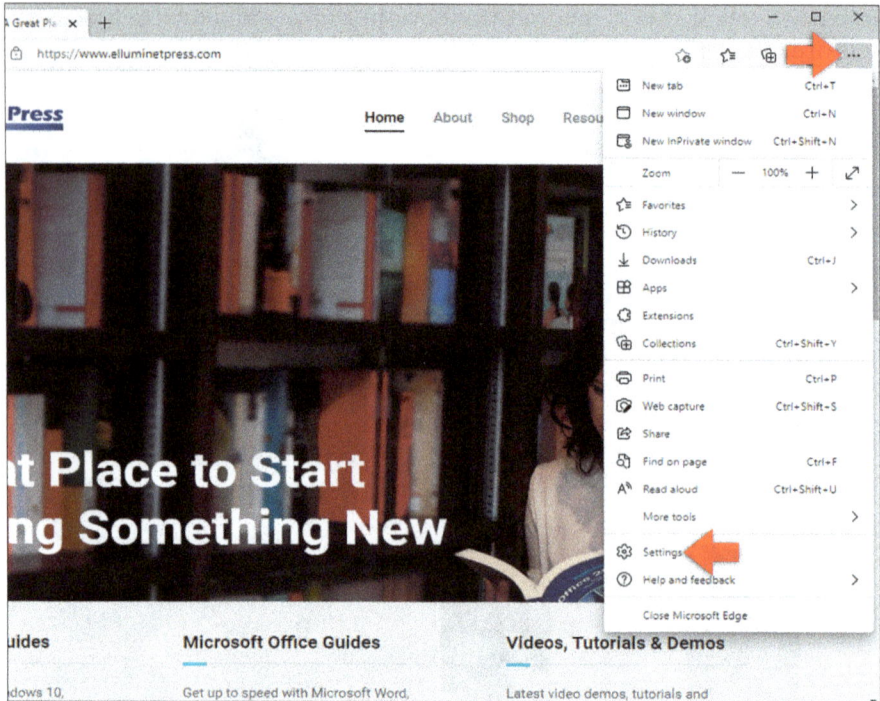

On the left hand panel click 'start, home and new tabs'.

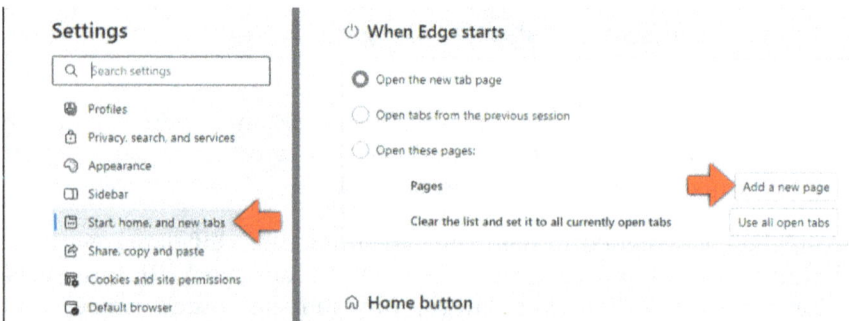

Select 'open a specific page or pages', then click 'add new page'

Enter the website address (URL) into the field (eg www.google.com).

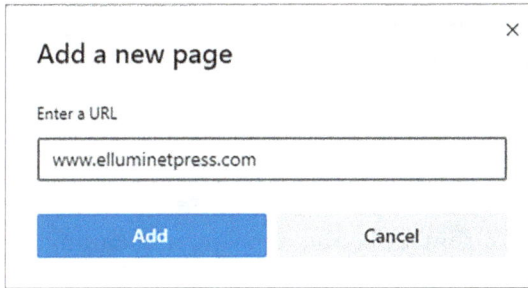

Click 'add'.

## Favorites Bar

The favorites bar is where you can save websites. The bar shows up just below the address bar at the top of the screen. I'd advise you to only pin the websites you use most often to this bar, otherwise it can get a bit cluttered.

To enable the favorites bar, click the 'favorites' icon on the top right of the screen.

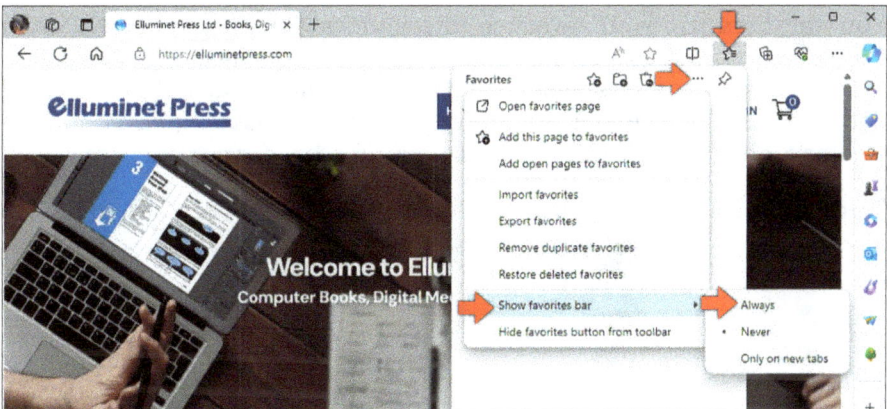

From the drop down menu, click on the 'three dots' icon on the top right.

From the popup menu, go down to 'show favorites bar'. Select 'aways' from the slideout menu.

## Add Website to Favorites Bar

To add a website, first navigate to the page you want to add, then click the star icon on the top right of the address bar.

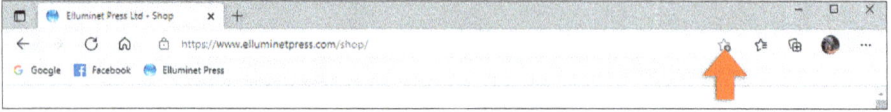

In the dialog box that appears, type in a meaningful name for the website.

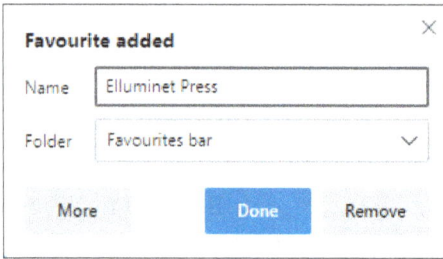

Click on the drop down box next to 'folder'. Select 'favorites bar' to add the website to the favorites bar, or select the folder you want to save the website into.

Click 'done' at the bottom of the dialog box.

## Organising the Favorites Bar

You can organise your favorites into folders. This helps keep sites of the same genre together. For example, you could have a folder called 'work' for all your business sites, a folder called 'social' for all your social media, or a folder for any interests you have eg gardening or photography. Create these on your favorites bar for easy access.

To create a folder, right click on the favorites bar, select 'add folder'.

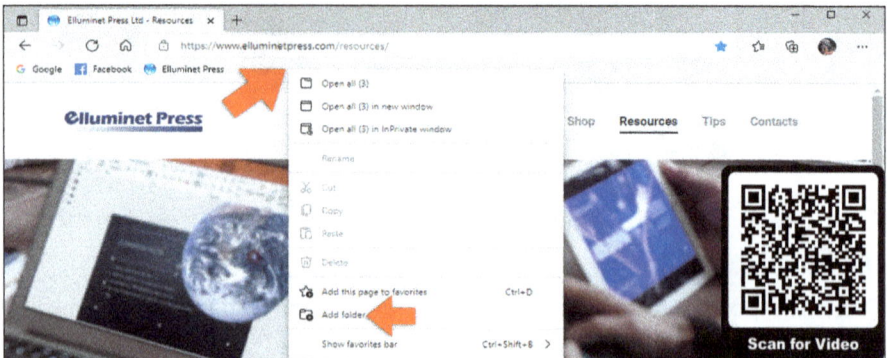

Make sure you've selected 'favorites bar', then type in a meaningful name for the folder, eg: 'work'.

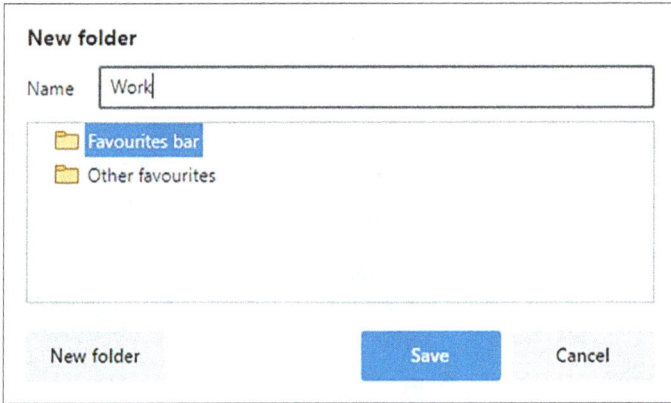

**New folder**

Name | Work

📁 **Favourites bar**
📁 Other favourites

New folder          Save          Cancel

You'll see your folder appear on the favorites bar.

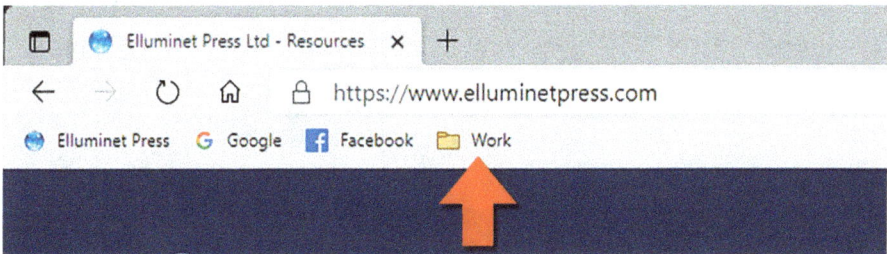

You can click & drag any favorite into the folder.

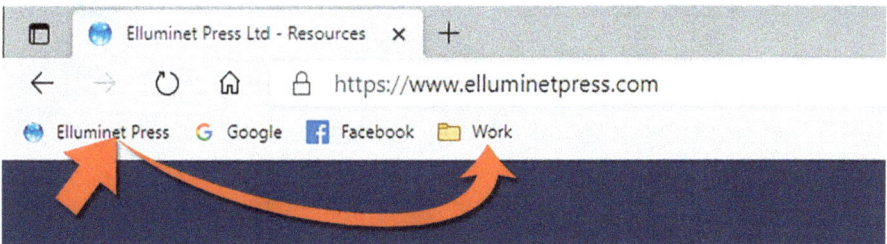

Click on the folder name to open it up

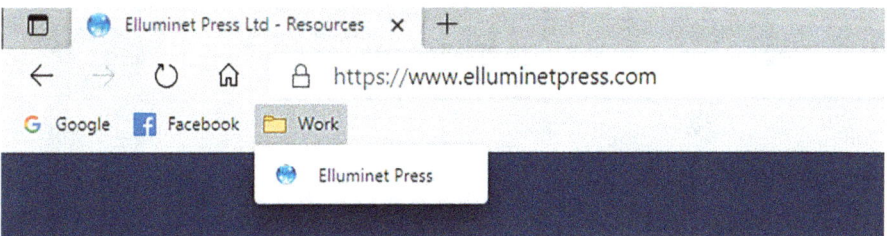

## Revisit a Website on Favorites

To revisit your favorite sites just select them from the favorites bar.

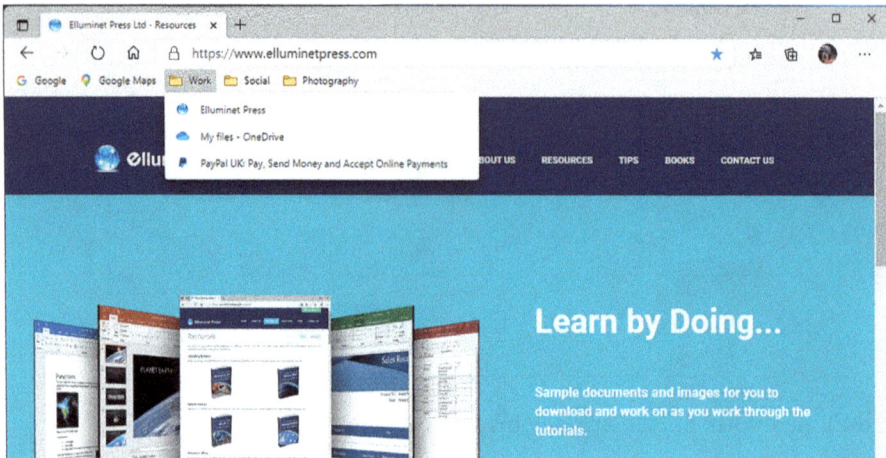

You'll also find your favorites using the 'favorites' icon on the top right of the screen.

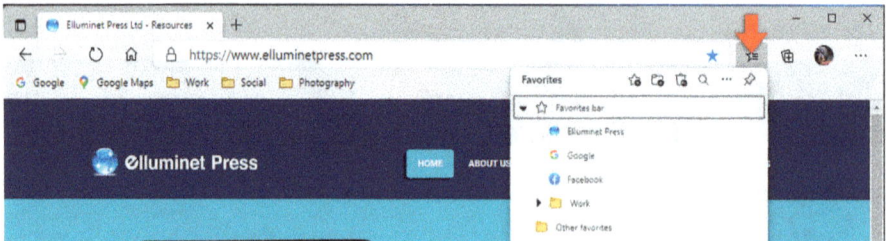

## Managing Favorites

Click the 'favorites' icon on the top right of the screen. Select 'open favorites page'.

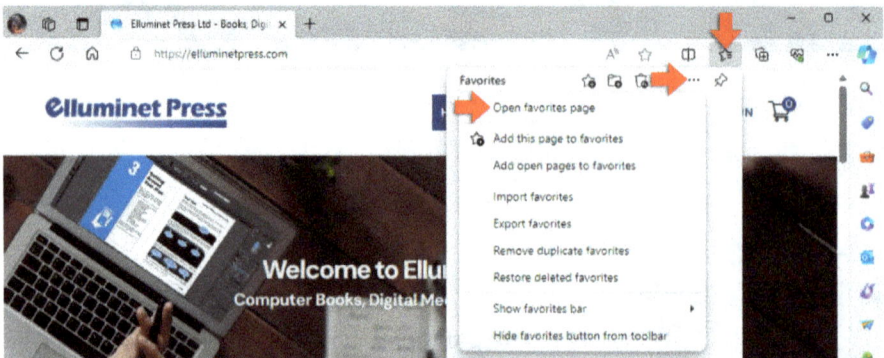

From here, you can drag sites into folders, change the order, create new folders, as well as delete favorited sites.

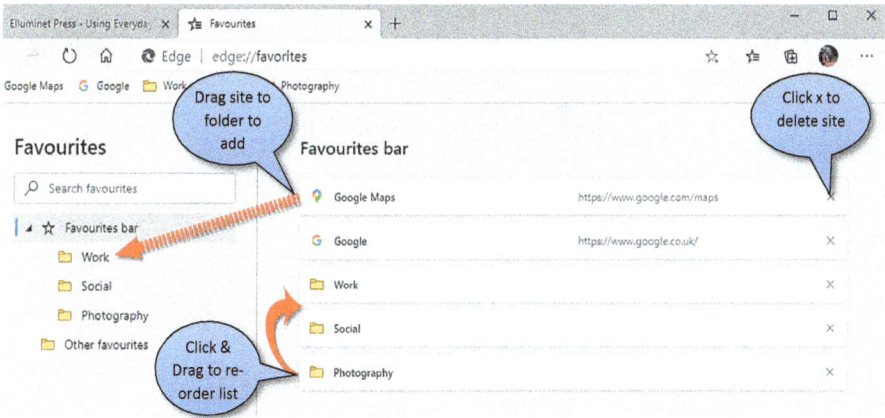

# Collections

Collections allow you to organize content you browse on the web. You can gather text, images from the web and then place them inside a note page and share organized sets and export them to Office apps.

## Create a Collection

To create a collection, click the collections icon on the top right of the toolbar. This will open the collections panel.

Then click 'start new collection'.

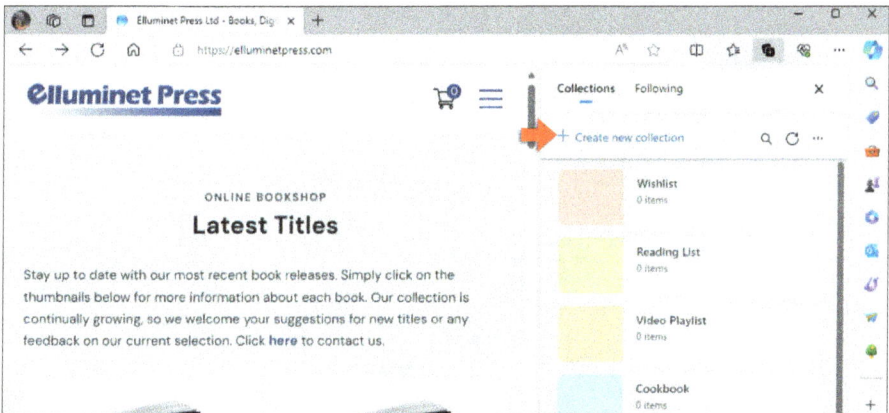

Give it a meaningful name, then click 'save'.

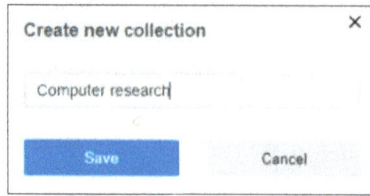

You'll see your new collection appear on the collections panel on the right hand side of the screen.

## Add Content

If you want to add a paragraph or some text from a website, click and highlight the text with your mouse.

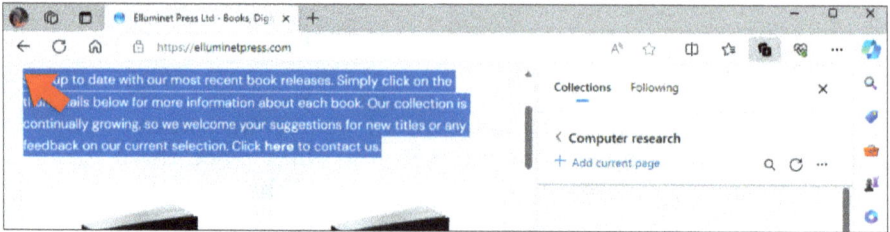

Right click on the selection, select 'add to collections'. From the slideout menu, select the collection you want to add the selection to.

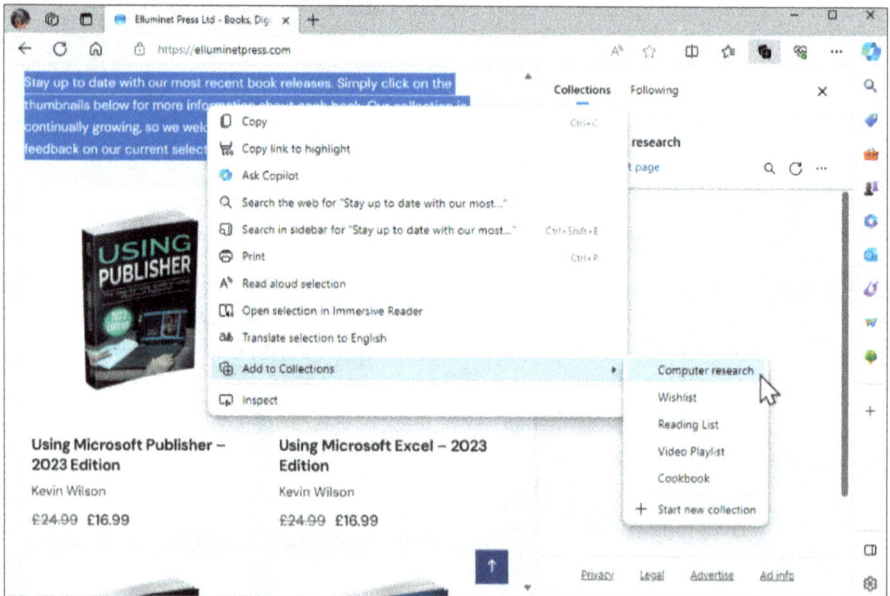

## Add a Page

You can add a whole page to your collections. To do this, open the collections panel if you haven't already done so, then select the collection you want to add the page to (eg 'computer research').

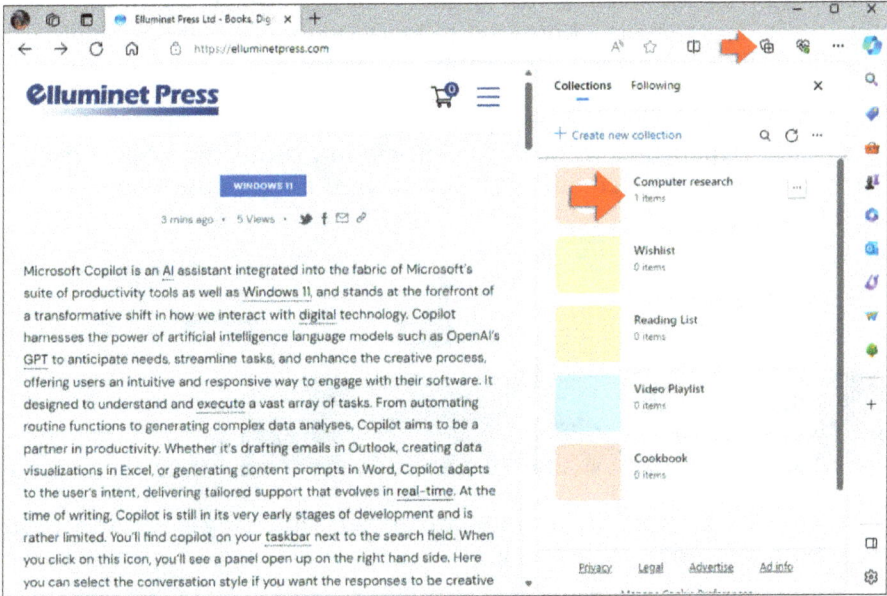

From the collections panel, click 'add current page'.

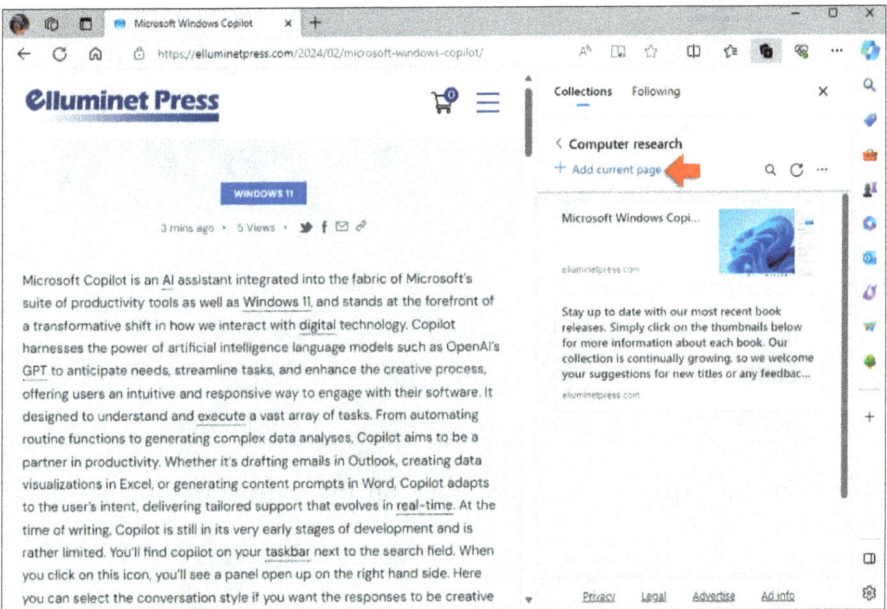

## Split Screen

The split screen feature allows you to view and interact with two websites simultaneously in a single tab. For instance, you could have a document open on one side of the screen while researching information on the web on the other. This feature can be particularly useful for comparison shopping, referencing while writing, or simply multitasking more effectively within the browser.

To open a link in a split screen, right-click on a link within a webpage and select 'Open link in split screen window' from the popup menu. For example, in the screenshot below, I want to open the 'courses' link in split screen mode.

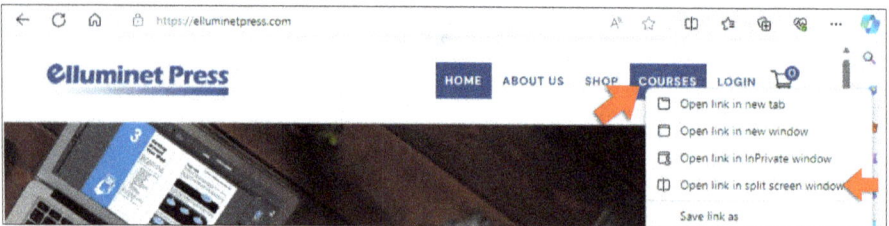

The screen will then divide into two panels, allowing you to interact with both sites simultaneously.

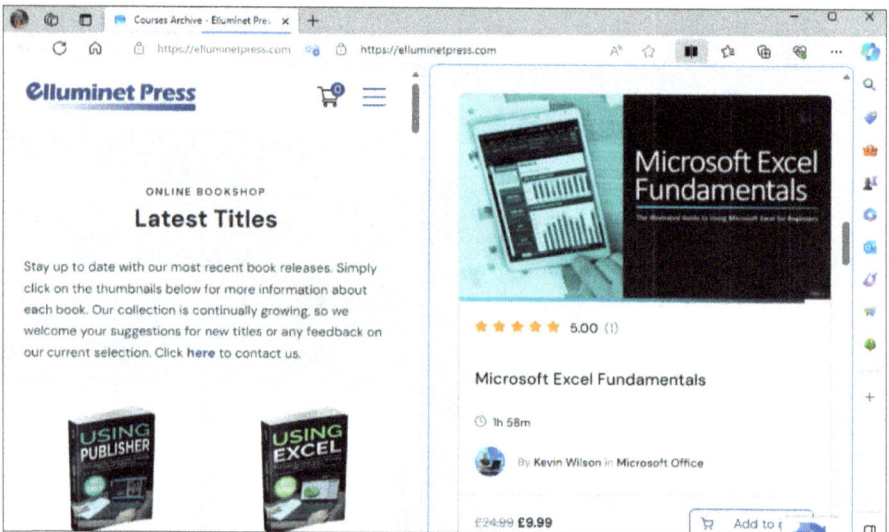

To remove the split screen, just click on the split screen icon on the toolbar.

# Visual Search

Visual Search is a feature powered by Microsoft Bing that allows you to search the web using images instead of words. This technology uses advanced computer vision to identify objects within images and find related information or similar items online.

Visual Search is particularly useful for shopping. If you see a product you like, such as furniture or clothing, you can use Visual Search to find where to buy it or explore similar products across different retailers.

To perform a visual search, navigate to any webpage and find an image you're interested in. Hover your mouse pointer over the top right of the image, you'll see a 'visual search' icon appear. Click on the icon

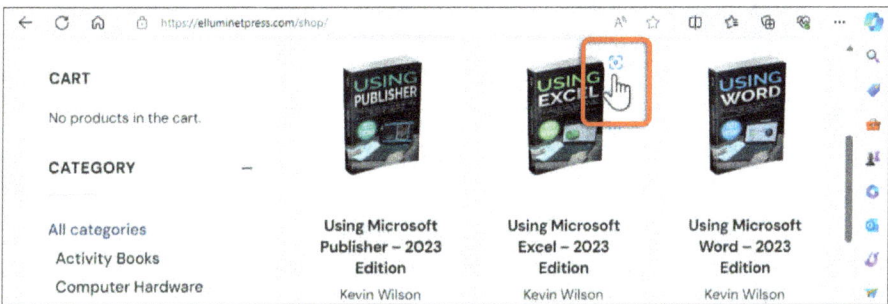

Microsoft Edge will then use Bing to perform a visual search, displaying results in a sidebar. These results can include similar images, product listings, and more, depending on the image content. Using the tabs you can filter the search results to show only pages that contain the image, pages with related products, and related content.

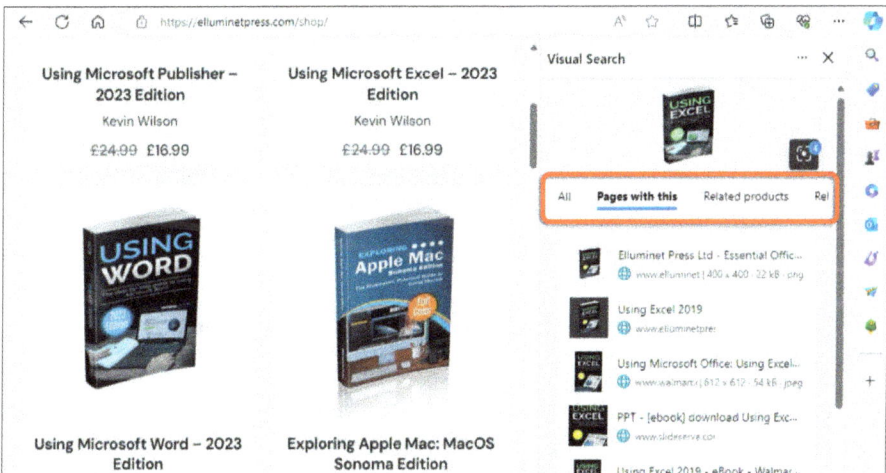

## Finding Files you've Downloaded

Whenever you download files from a website, you'll find the files in your downloads folder.

To open your downloads folder, click the 'three dots icon' on the top right of the screen, and select 'downloads'

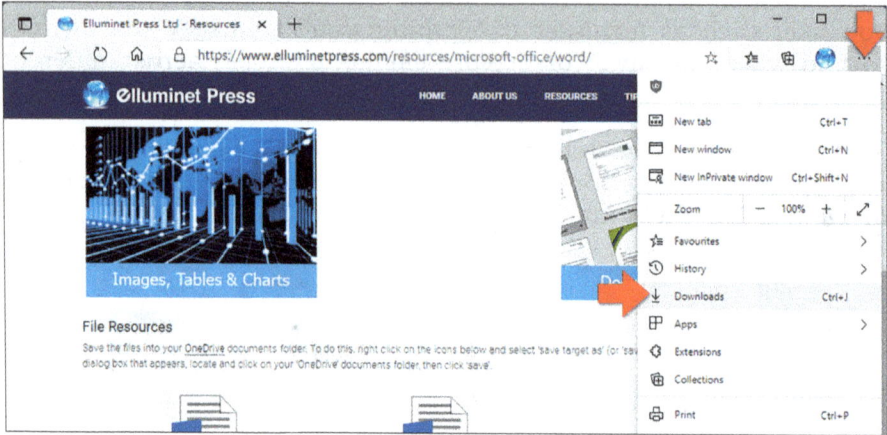

Here, you'll see a history list of all the files you've downloaded. Down the left hand side, you can search for downloads, or you can use the categories in the list to find a specific type of tile such as an app, image or video.

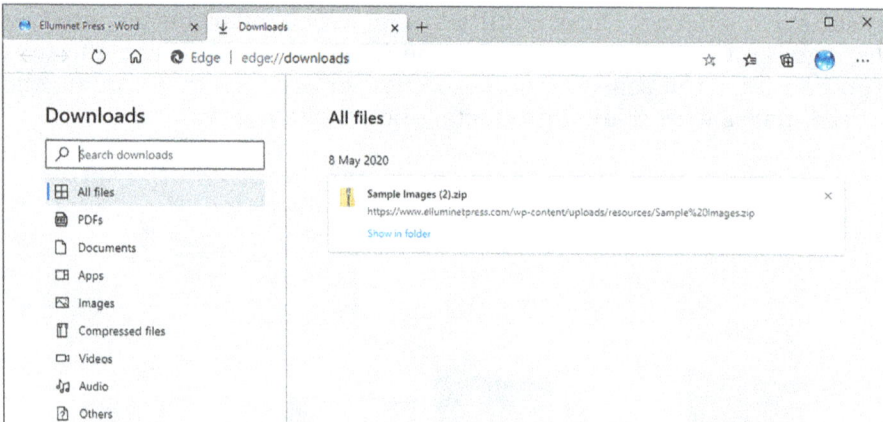

To open or run any of these downloads, double click on the link in the list.

To open your downloads folder in File Explorer, click 'show in folder'. From File Explorer, you can double click on the file to open it or run it.

# Browsing History

Edge keeps a list of every website you visit. To find your browsing history, click the three dots icon on the top right. Select 'history'.

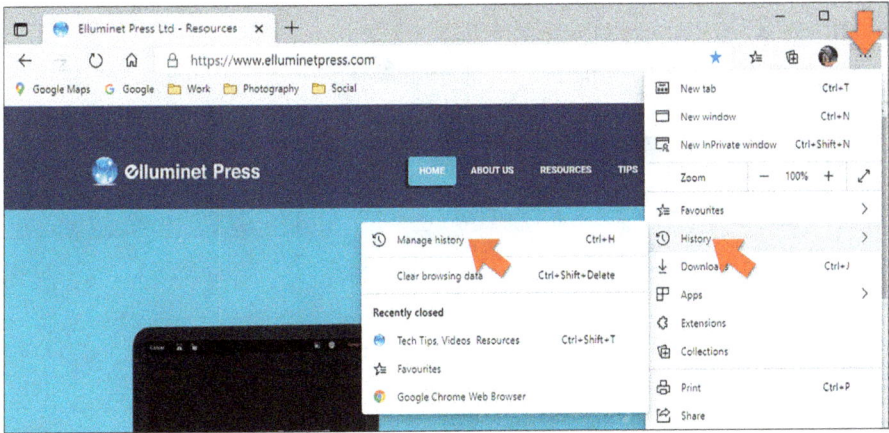

You'll see a list of the sites you've visited. Click on a site to revisit. To clear the history click 'clear browsing history on bottom left.

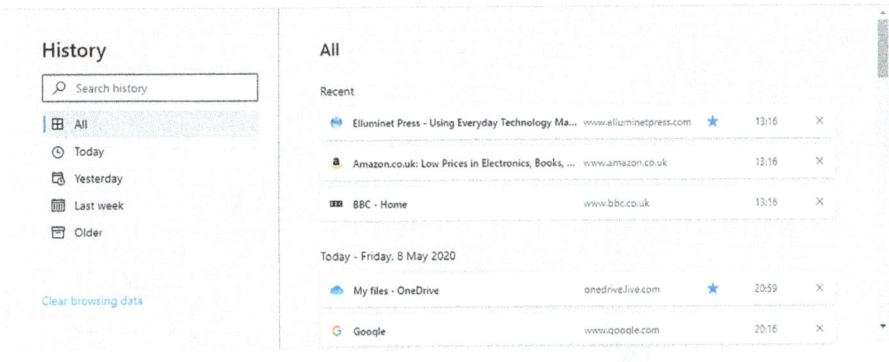

You can also see a list of sites you've visited while you've been browsing if you click and hold your mouse pointer on the back icon.

Click any of the links to return to the website.

## Reading Mode

Some websites, especially those with a lot of text can be difficult to print or read on screen. You can use the immersive reader feature. To use this feature, click the reader icon to the right of the address bar. Or press F9.

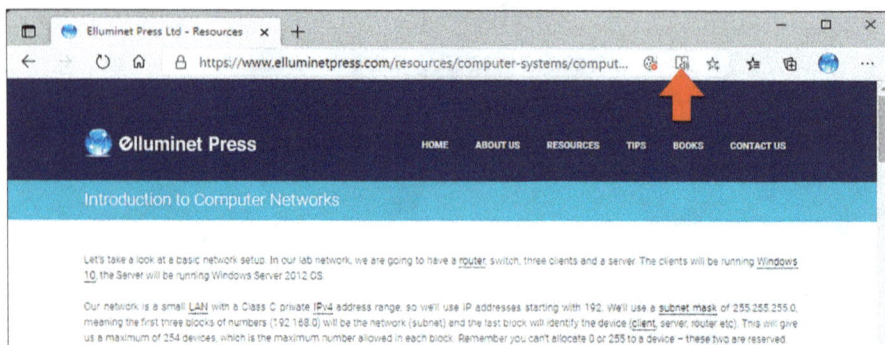

From here, you can read the main text without adverts or any other distracting parts of a website.

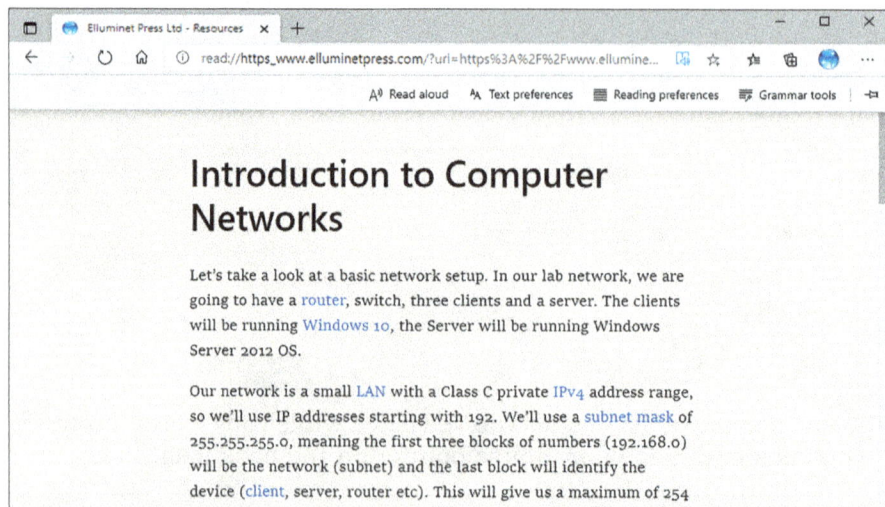

You can get Edge to read the document aloud - click 'read aloud'. You can change the size of the text or the background color - click 'text preferences'. You can enable 'line focus' that allows you to concentrate on each line as you read - click 'reading preferences'. You can also highlight syllables, verbs, nouns and adjectives in the text using the grammar tools. Give it a try.

To exit reader mode, click the reader icon again or press F9

# Page Translator

You can translate any page into another language. To do this, right click your mouse on the web page, then select 'translate to...'

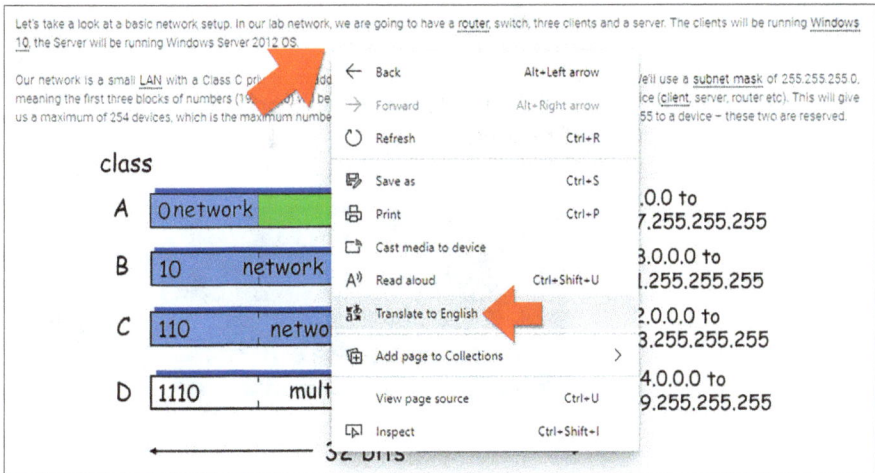

In the drop down box, select the language you want to translate the page into. Lets try Portuguese... Click 'translate', or 'try again'.

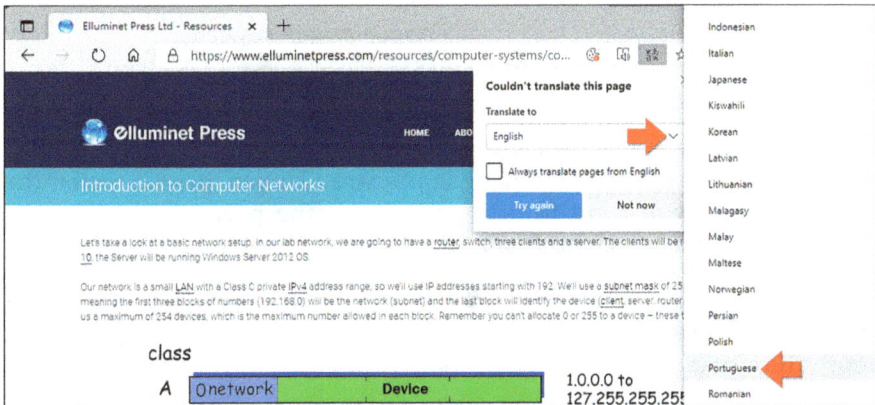

Here you can see Edge has attempted a translation. Translations aren't 100% accurate but will give you the general idea.

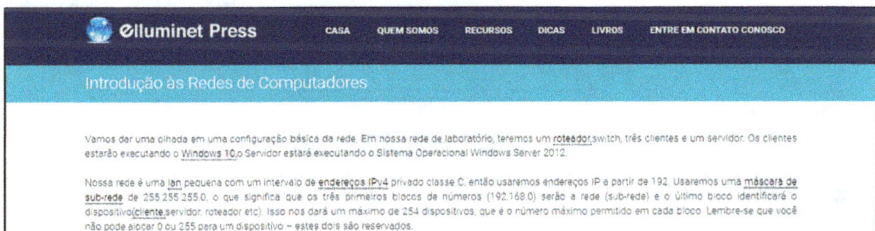

## Print a Page

To print a web page, click the three dots icon on the top right of the screen, then select 'print' from the drop down menu.

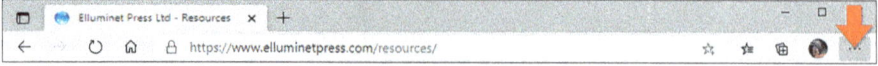

From the panel on the left hand side, select the printer. Under 'copies', enter number of copies if needed.

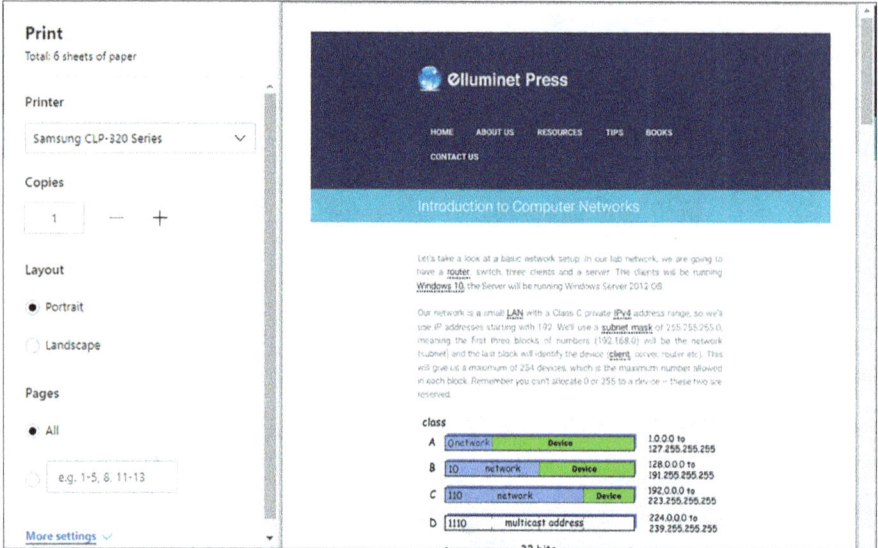

Under 'layout', select portrait or landscape. Under 'pages', enter the page numbers you want to print. You'll see the page numbers in the print preview on the right if you scroll down the page.

Click 'more settings' on the bottom left. From here you can print background graphics, add or remove headers and footers, or print more than one page to a sheet of paper, and change the paper size.

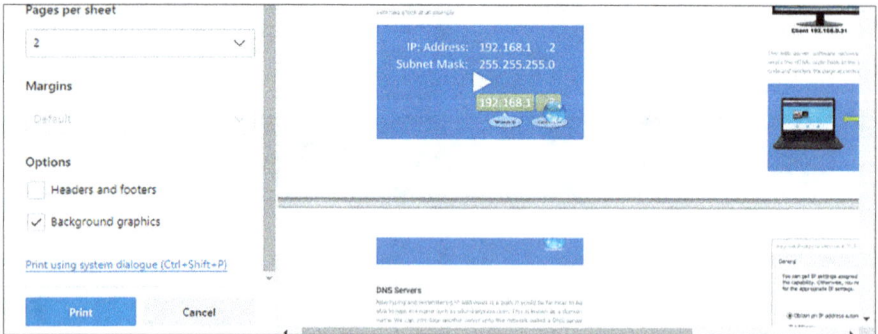

# Share a Page

You can share a web page with anyone on your contact list using email, chat, teams, messages and so on.

To share a page, click the three dots icon on the top right of the screen. From the drop down menu, select 'share'.

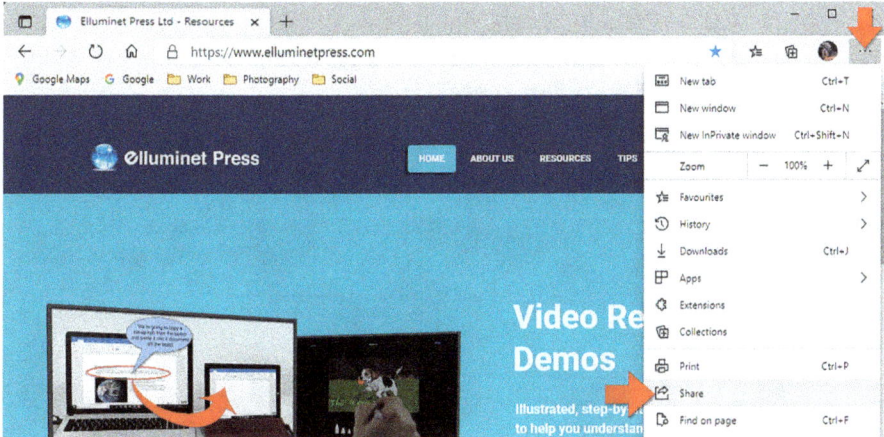

From the dialog box, select the person you want to share the page with, or select an app to share the page. Eg, email. Click 'find more people' or 'find more apps', if you can't see the person or app.

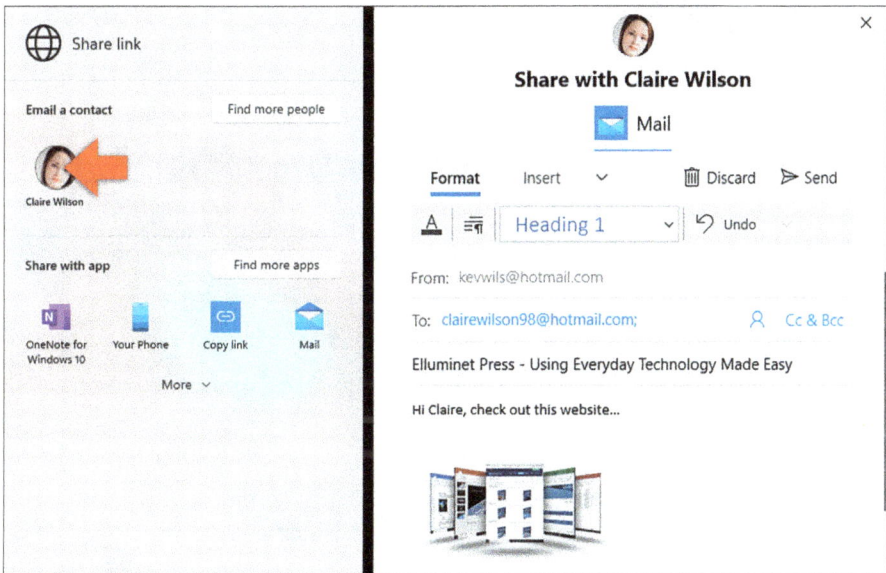

Type in a message, click 'send'.

# Pin Website to TaskBar

A useful feature of Microsoft Edge is the ability to pin a website shortcut onto your taskbar. You should only really use this feature for websites you visit very often, as you can quite easily fill up your taskbar with clutter. Perhaps if you use a web based email or facebook - create a taskbar short cut.

To do this, open the website you want to pin in Microsoft Edge. Click the three dots icon on the top right, go down to 'more tools', select 'pin to taskbar' from the slide out menu.

Give the site a name, then click 'pin'.

You'll see the website link appear on your task bar. The icon depends on the website's own icon.

## Tabbed Browsing

Tabbed browsing allows you to have multiple websites open at the same time. Websites open up as tabs along the top of the browser window, this is known as horizontal tabbing. Here below, you can see there are three tabs open.

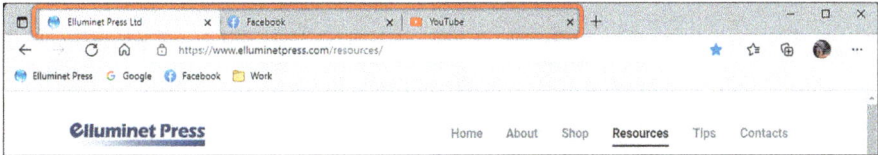

This makes it easier to switch between different websites you have open.

### New Tabs

To open a new tab, click the 'plus' icon to the right of the browser tab.

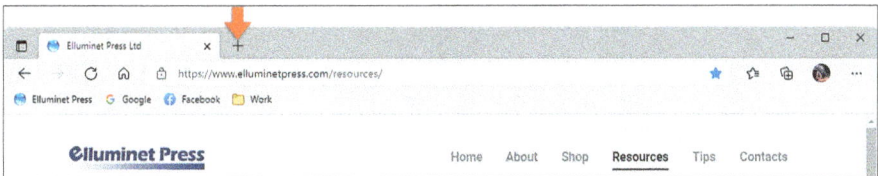

A new tab will open up. You can navigate to any website from here. Use the address field at the top of the screen to do a web search or type in a website address.

### Switching Tabs

You can switch between tabs using the tab bar at the top of the screen. Just click on the tab you want to return to. You can also press Ctrl Tab on your keyboard.

### Duplicate Tab

To duplicate a tab means to open a tab with the same website. To do this, right click on the tab, select 'duplicate tab' from the popup menu.

# Chapter 7: Internet and Communication

## Pin Tab

You can pin tabs to your tab bar. This is useful for websites you visit frequently. Right click on the tab you want to pin. Select 'pin tab' from the popup menu.

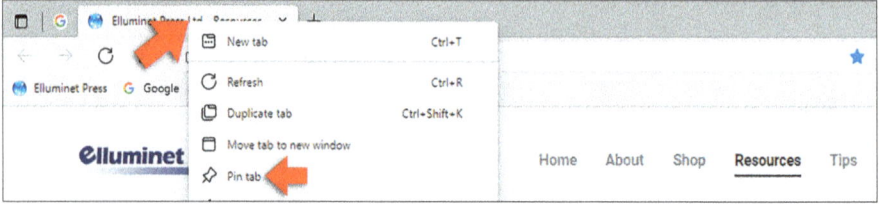

Pinned tabs appear on the top left.

## Vertical Tabs

Vertical tabs are similar to the horizontal tabs we looked at in the previous section. The difference is, the tabbed websites are listed down the left hand side of the screen. To turn on vertical tabs, click the icon on the top left, then select

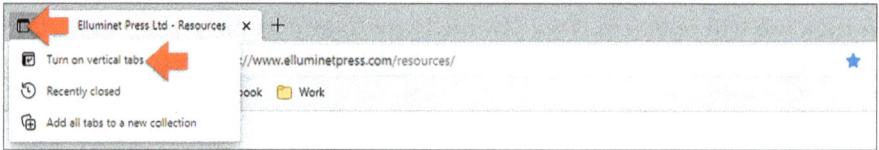

You'll see a sidebar open up on the left. Here, you can switch to other tabs in a similar fashion as before.

To go back to horizontal tabs, click the icon on the top left of the vertical tabs sidebar, select 'turn off vertical tabs'.

# Edge Extensions

Extensions add functionality to the Edge Browser. To add extensions to Edge, click the three dots icon on the top right of your screen and select 'extensions'.

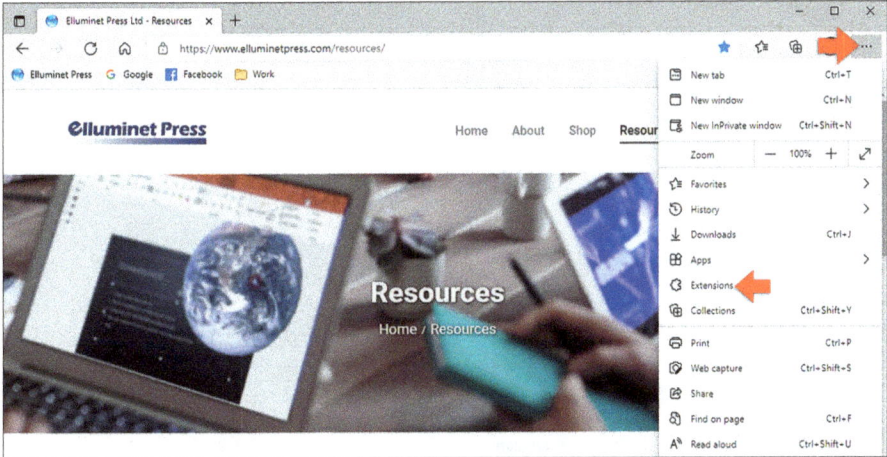

You'll see a list of any extensions that have been installed on the right. To install a new extension, click 'get extensions for Edge'.

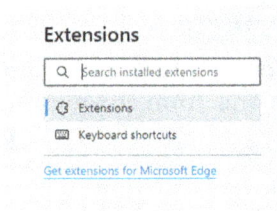

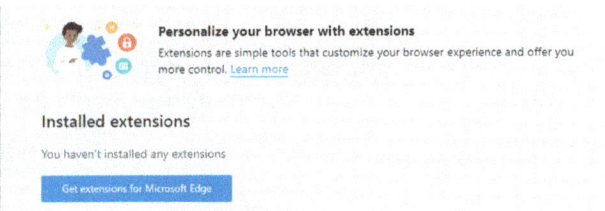

The Microsoft Store will open up showing the newest extensions available. In this example, I'm going to add the uBlock extension. So click 'uBlock Origin'.

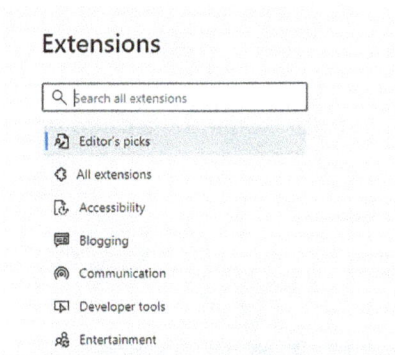

# Chapter 7: Internet and Communication

From the extension details page, click 'get'.

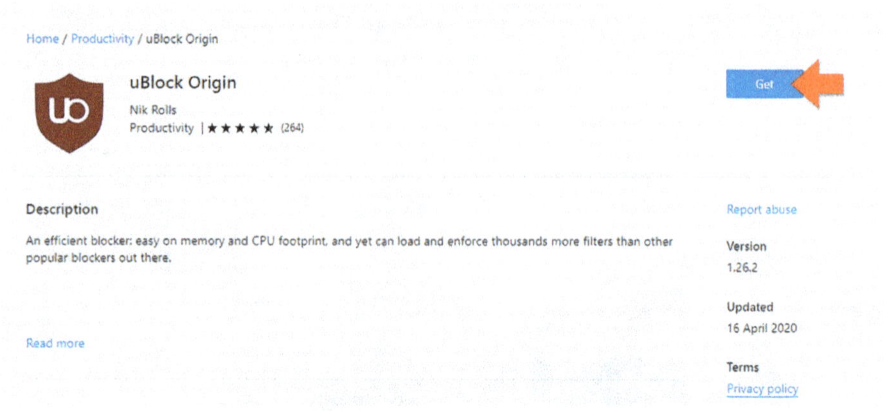

Click 'add extension' on the confirmation dialog box.

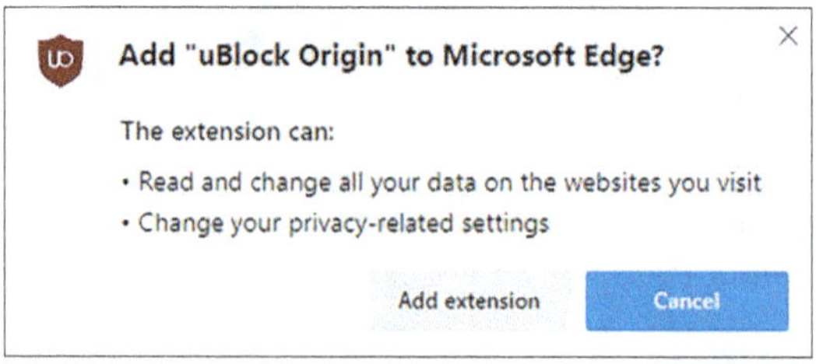

You can access your extensions anytime, just click the three dots icon on the top right of your screen and select 'extensions' from the menu.

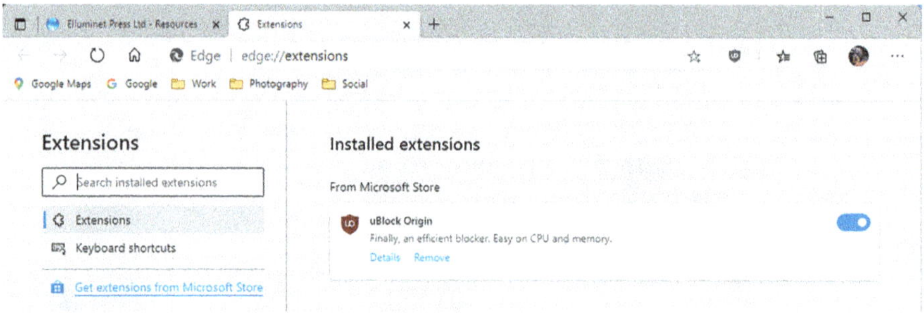

Any installed extensions will appear on the right. Click the icon to open the extensions settings.

You'll also see an icon appear on the toolbar.

# Install Chrome Extensions in Edge

With the new Edge browser, you can install chrome extensions from the chrome web store. To do this, you first need to enable extensions from other stores.

Click the three dots icon on the top right, select 'extensions' from the drop down menu.

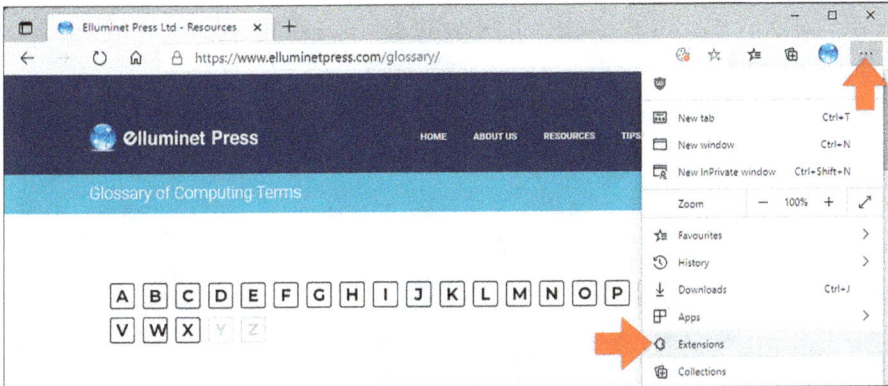

Enable 'allow extensions from other stores', on the bottom left.

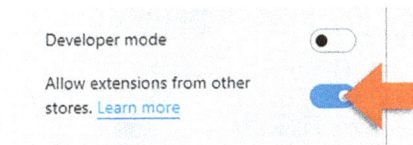

Type `chrome.google.com/webstore` into the search bar in Edge.

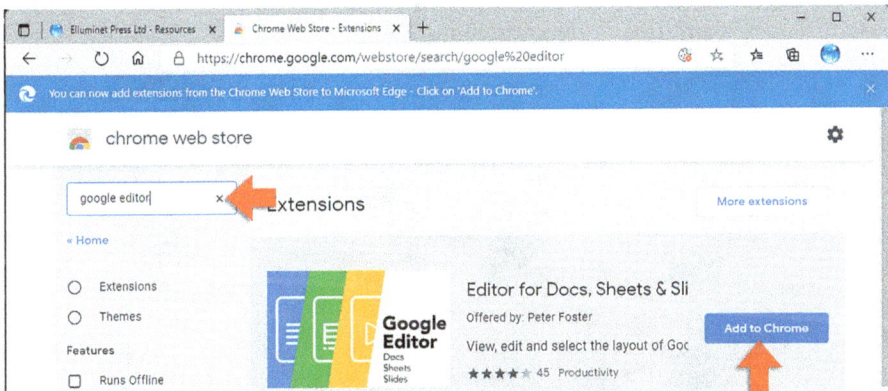

Use the search bar on the left hand side in the chrome web store to search for apps.

Click 'add to chrome' to install any app.

## Import Browser Data

Importing data into Microsoft Edge from another browser is typically done for convenience and to maintain continuity in your browsing experience when switching to Edge.

Edge allows you to import favorites, passwords, search engines, browsing history, and other data from browsers such as Internet Explorer, Google Chrome, and Mozilla Firefox. This allows you to keep your bookmarks and favorites, retain saved passwords, and preserves your browsing history.

To import data from another browse, click on the three-dot menu at the top right of the Edge window. Select 'settings' from the menu.

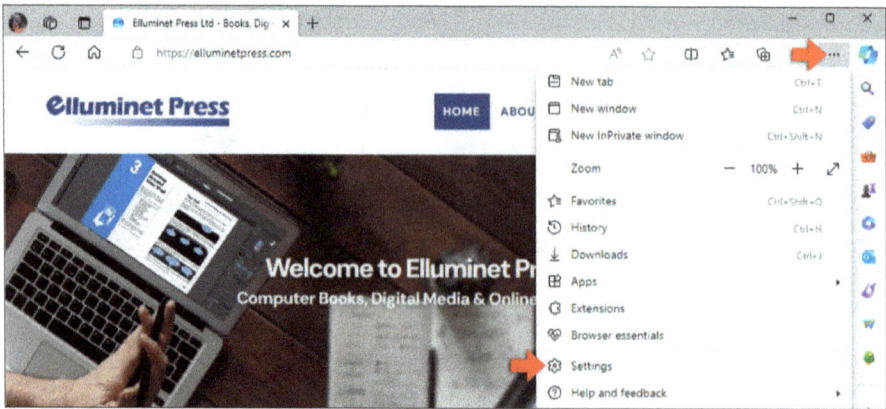

Click on 'profiles' from the list on the left. You may need to sign in with your Microsoft Account email address and password. In the 'profiles section', click on 'Import browser data'.

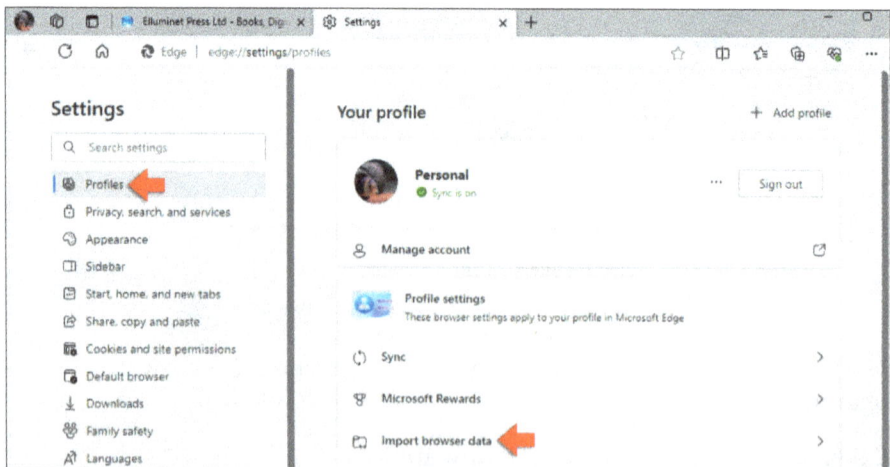

Under 'Import from other browsers', click on 'choose what to import'.

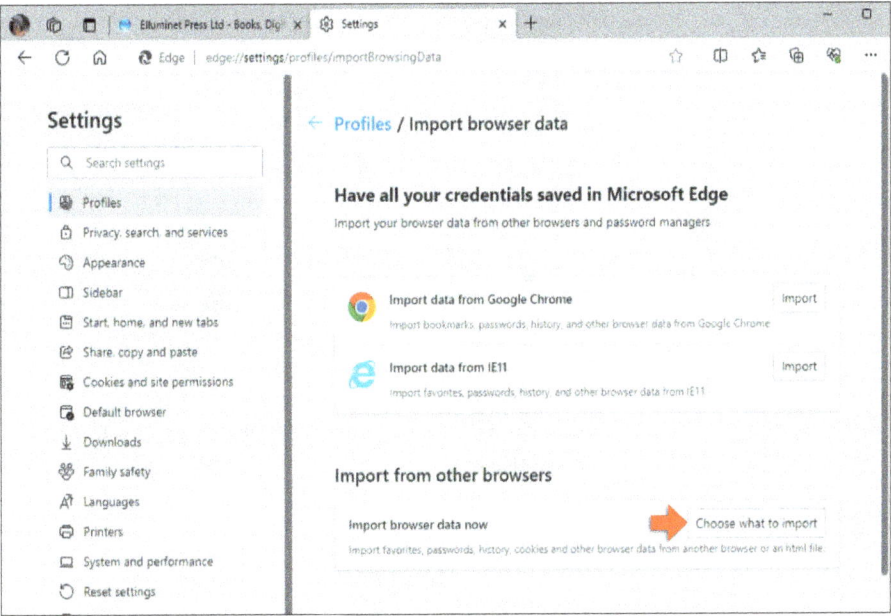

Select the browser you want to import from (eg Google Chrome). Select your profile if you have more than one.

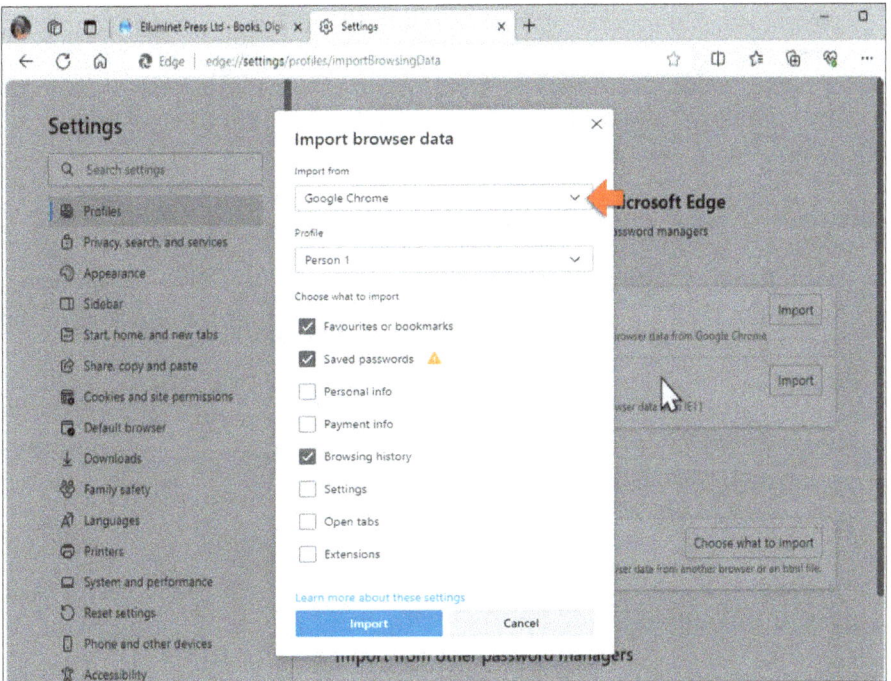

Choose what to import. Here, you have a list of items you can import.

**Favourites or bookmarks** will import your bookmarks from your other browser.

**Saved passwords** will import passwords saved in your other browser.

**Personal info** will import personal data such as addresses and phone numbers you've saved in forms on web pages.

**Payment info** will import credit card information and other payment details for quicker transactions online.

**Browsing history** will import the history of websites you've visited in in your other browser.

**Settings** will import the browser configuration settings such as the start page, search engine preferences, and privacy settings.

**Open tabs** will import any currently open tabs from your other browser into Edge.

Click 'import' when you're done.

## Edge Security

Microsoft Edge is designed with security in mind, offering a suite of features aimed at safeguarding online activities. With the integration of Microsoft Defender SmartScreen, Edge provides real-time protection against phishing attacks, malicious software, and fraudulent websites, ensuring users navigate the web safely.

### Microsoft Defender SmartScreen

Protects against malicious websites, downloads, and phishing scams.

To access SmartScreen settings in Microsoft Edge:

1. Open Edge and click the three dots in the top-right corner to access the menu.

2. Select Settings, then navigate to Privacy, search, and services.

3. Scroll down to the Security section.

Here, you'll find the toggle for Microsoft Defender SmartScreen to enable or disable it.

## Password Monitor

Alerts you about any saved passwords that have been exposed in data breaches.

To view alerts:

1. Go to Settings in Microsoft Edge.

2. Choose Profiles and then Passwords.

3. If any breaches are detected, you'll see notifications here with advice on changing compromised passwords.

Here, you can view an assessment of your saved passwords' strength and any recommended actions.

## Website Typo Protection

Prevents navigation to potentially malicious sites due to URL typos. If Edge detects a typo that could lead to a malicious site, it will alert you with a warning and suggest the correct site.

To access Website Typo Protection settings in Microsoft Edge:

1. Open Edge and click the three dots in the top-right corner to access the menu.

2. Select Settings, then navigate to Privacy, search, and services.

3. Scroll down to Security.

4. Enable/disable Website Typo Protection.

## Enhanced Security Mode

Offers extra protection by applying tighter security settings on unfamiliar sites. This help prevent users from landing on potentially harmful sites.

To enable Enhanced Security Mode:

1. Open Settings in Microsoft Edge.

2. Click on Privacy, search, and services.

3. Under Security, find Enhanced Security Mode and select your preferred level of protection.

# Chapter 7: Internet and Communication

## Browser Essentials

Browser Essentials shows your browser's performance and security status and aims to enhance your browsing experience by providing intuitive suggestions for optimization and protection.

To view browser essentials, click on the 'heart pulse' icon on the top right of the Edge window.

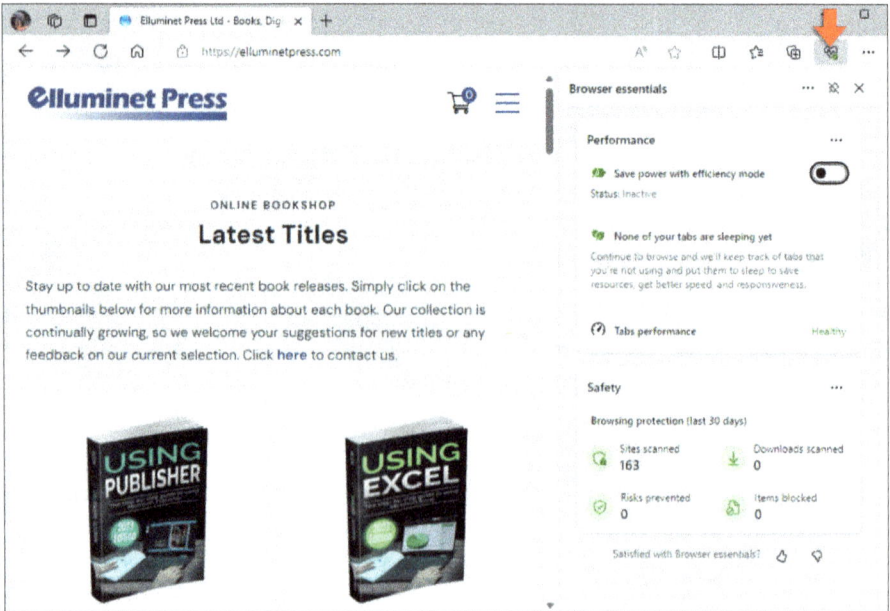

The Browser Essentials panel will display insights into your browser's performance, such performance. It also shows security scans powered by SmartScreen on the 'safety' card.

## Passkeys

Passkeys provide a more secure sign-in method than traditional passwords by using unique, biometrically verified codes. They eliminate the risk of security breaches associated with traditional passwords by utilizing device-specific biometrics such as facial recognition or fingerprint scanning for authentication. These one-time use codes are linked to your device and Microsoft account meaning they can't be used elsewhere.

Creating a passkey involves opening a supported website or app, selecting the 'create passkey' option. Not all websites and apps support passkeys, but they will eventually adopt the new technology.

**314**

When you click sign in on a website that supports passkeys, you'll be prompted to create a passkey. For example, here I'm signing into my Ebay account. Once I click 'sign in' for the first time, I'm prompted to create a passkey. Click 'add a passkey' and run through the steps.

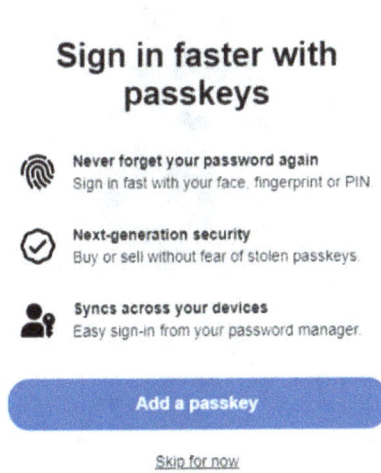

**Sign in faster with passkeys**

**Never forget your password again**
Sign in fast with your face, fingerprint or PIN.

**Next-generation security**
Buy or sell without fear of stolen passkeys.

**Syncs across your devices**
Easy sign-in from your password manager.

**Add a passkey**

Skip for now

Authenticate the passkey with your PIN, Facial Recognition or Fingerprint if you have them installed.

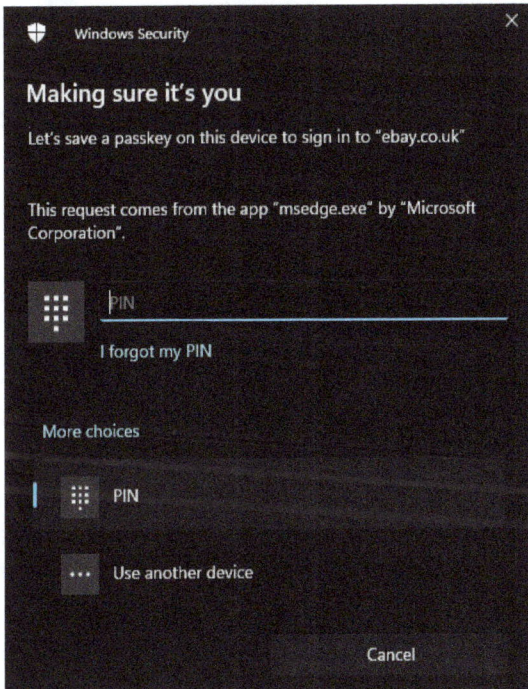

Windows Security

**Making sure it's you**

Let's save a passkey on this device to sign in to "ebay.co.uk"

This request comes from the app "msedge.exe" by "Microsoft Corporation".

PIN

I forgot my PIN

More choices

PIN

Use another device

Cancel

Once the passkey has been saved, you'll see a prompt. Click ok.

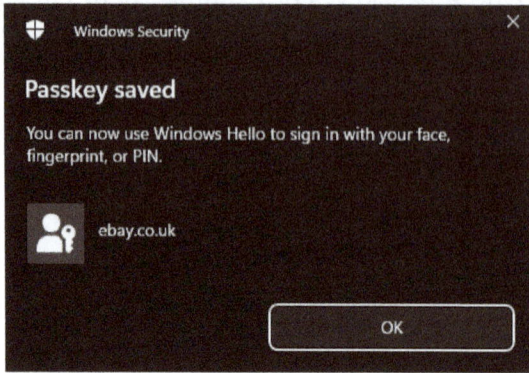

Now when you need to sign into the website, you can sign in with the passkey instead of a password.

## Password Generator

The Password Generator automatically generates and saves strong passwords when you're creating a new account or changing a password. Edge suggests a strong password, which you can accept and will be saved automatically.

The password generator generates passwords that consist of uppercase letters, lowercase letters, numbers, and special characters. The passwords generated by password generator are stored securely within the browser's password manager.

They are typically encrypted and protected by your Microsoft account credentials or your device's biometric authentication if you've set it up.

To generate a password, right click in the password field on the sign up, or change password form on the website. Select 'suggest strong password'.

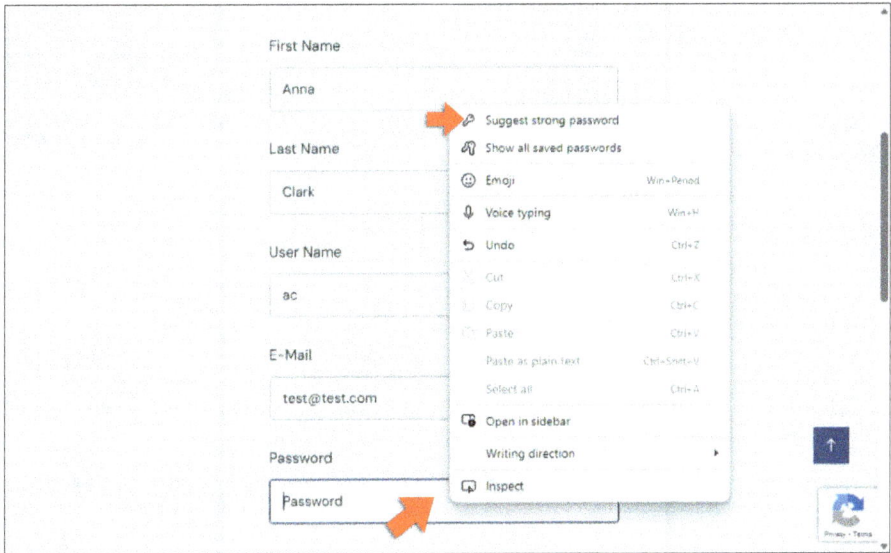

Select the password that has been suggested. After generating a password, Microsoft Edge will prompt you to save it to the browser's password manager. This feature ensures that you don't forget the password and can easily access it when needed.

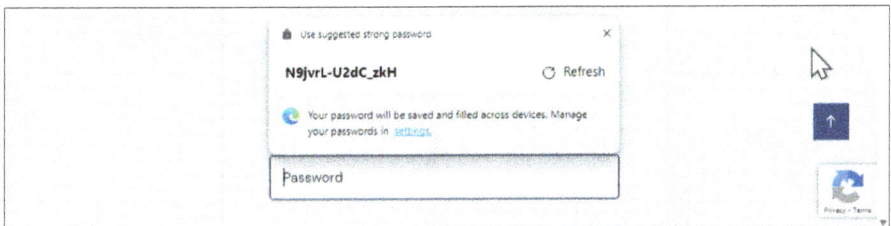

Whenever you need to sign back into the website, you just select the saved username/email address and password from the saved accounts.

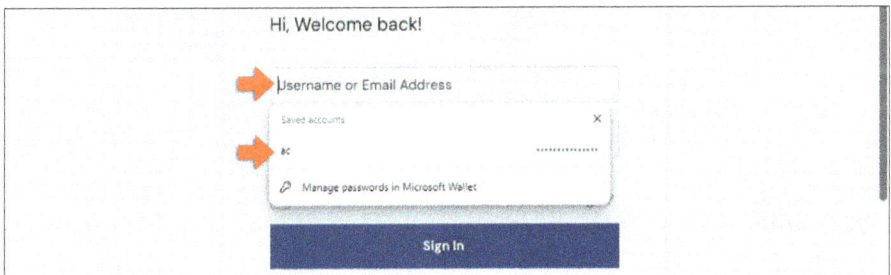

# Outlook for Windows

Outlook for Windows is a new email app intended to replace the old mail app, and is designed to help improve personal productivity and email organization.

With this app, you can check your Microsoft Account email, as well as other email accounts from Yahoo or Google you might have.

**Scan for Video**

## Main Screen

When you start the app, you'll land on the home screen. Along the top, you'll see the ribbon (home, view, etc).

Underneath, the screen is divided into three sections. The section on the left is called the sidebar. This is where you'll find your email accounts, inbox, sent items, drafts and deleted items.

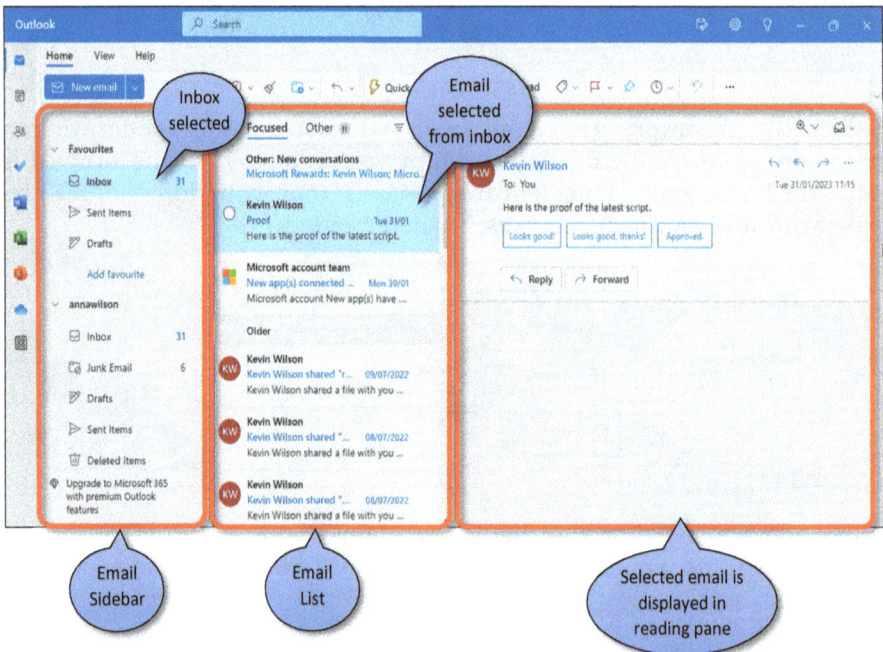

The middle section displays all the messages in the folder you selected from the sidebar. For example, in the image above, I've selected the inbox.

The middle section lists all the messages contained in the inbox. Any unread messages are displayed in bold.

The section on the right will display the contents of the message you've selected from the middle section. This is called the reading pane.

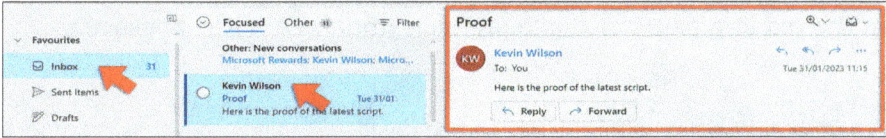

At the top of your inbox, you'll see two options: 'focussed' and 'other'. This separates your inbox into two tabs. Your most important email messages are on the 'focused tab' while the less important emails stay out of the way in the 'other tab'. Just click on a tab to select.

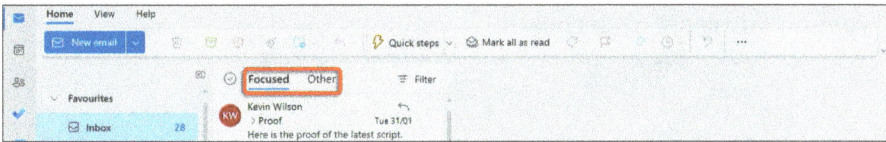

# Compose New Message

To send a new email message to someone, click 'new email' on the top left of the 'home' ribbon tab.

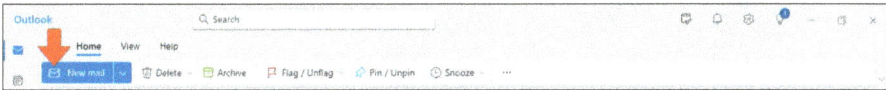

On the right hand side of your screen, you'll see a new blank message appear. Add the recipient's email address in the 'to' field.

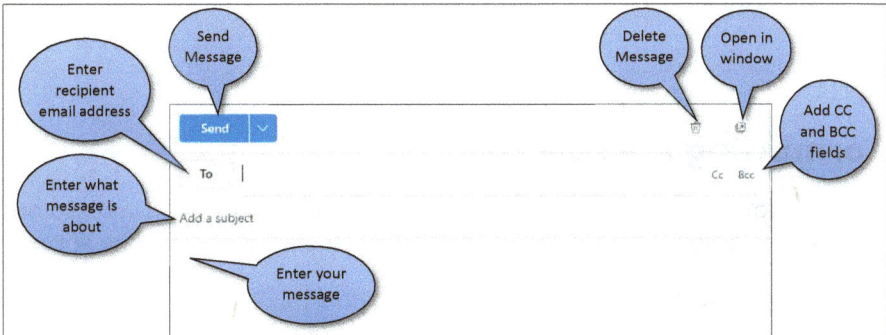

You can also add CC and BCC fields if you want to send someone else a copy. Enter a subject in the 'subject' field, then type in your message. See page 320 for information on formatting your message. See page 321 for information on adding an attachment. See page 323, and page 324 for information on how to insert pictures, tables and emojis. Click 'send' when you're done.

**319**

## Replying to Messages

To reply to a message, click the reply icon on the top right of the message in the reading pane, or the 'reply' icon underneath the message.

Type in your reply underneath.

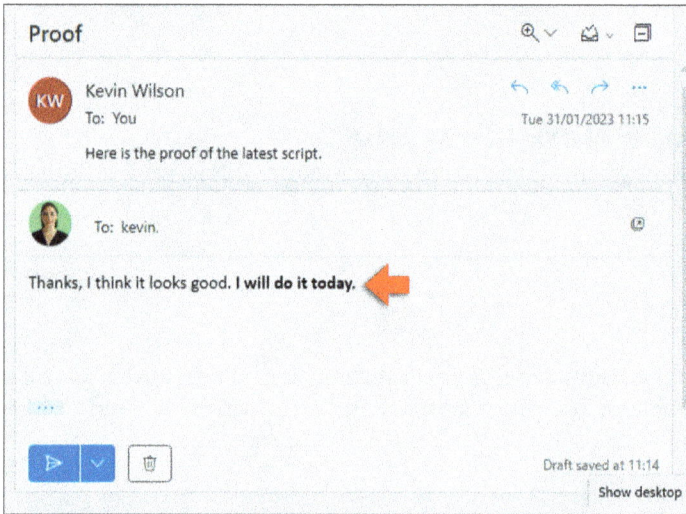

## Formatting a Message

You can format your message, change font sizes, align text and so on. You can do this using the 'message' ribbon along the top of the screen.

To do this, select the text you want to format.

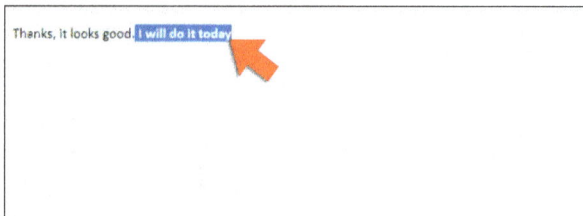

Then from the 'message' ribbon tab, select your formatting. Here, you can change the font size, typeface, make the text bold, italic or underlined. You can change the font color, as well as add emojis.

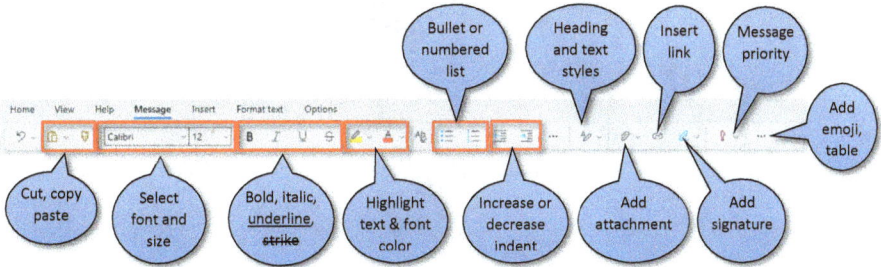

If you click on the 'three dots' icons, you'll see some more options such as indents, text alignments, pictures, emojis and tables.

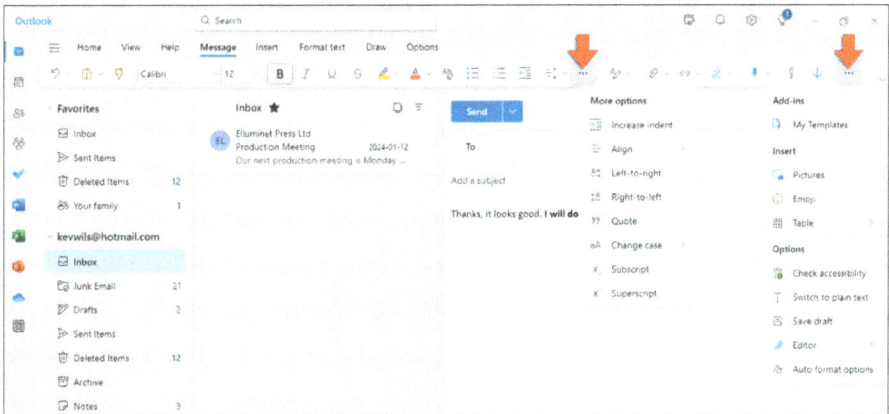

## Adding an Attachment

If you want to add an attachment such as a photograph or file, click on the paperclip icon on the toolbar. From the drop down menu, select where the file is saved. In this example, I'm going to attach a PowerPoint presentation that is saved on my computer, so I'd select 'browse this computer'.

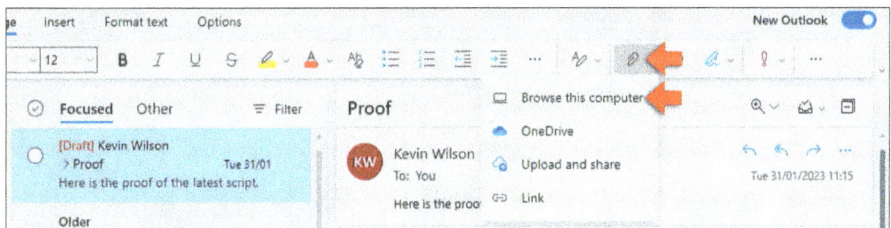

# Chapter 7: Internet and Communication

Locate and select the file from the dialog box, then click 'open'.

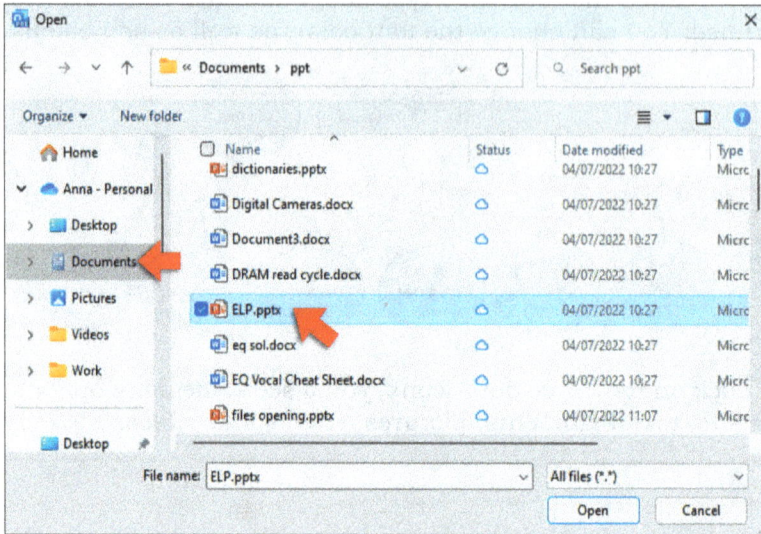

You'll see the attachment appear at the top of your reply.

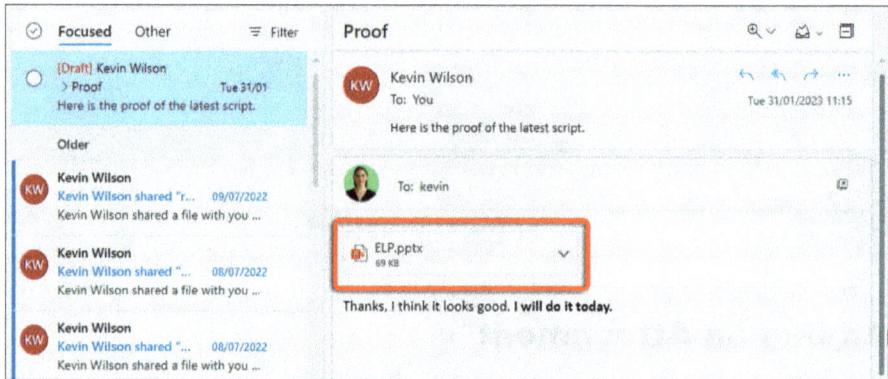

Once you're done, click the 'send' icon at the bottom of the message.

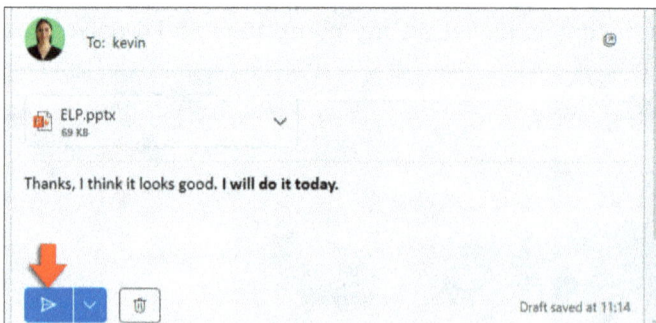

Your reply will be added to the email conversation.

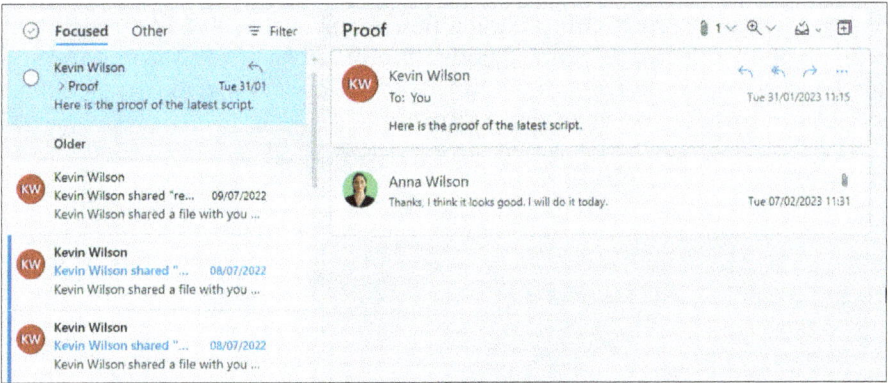

# Insert Picture

Start by creating a new email message. Then go to the 'Insert' ribbon tab at the top of the window.

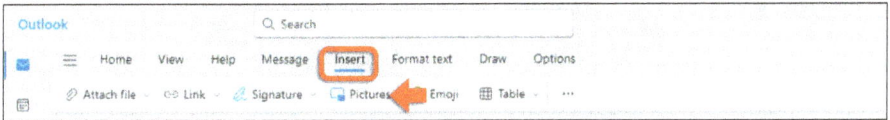

Click on the 'Pictures' icon. Browse your computer and select an image you want to insert.

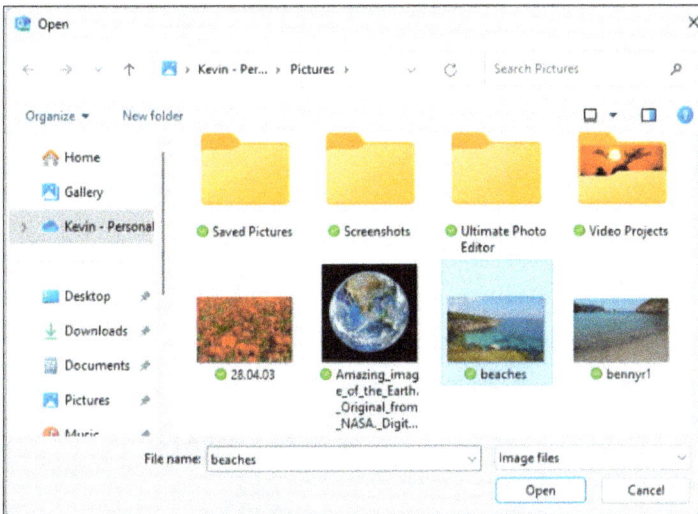

Click 'Open' when you're done.

## Insert Table

To insert a table, start composing a new email. From the 'Insert' ribbon tab, click on the 'Table' icon. Choose the number of rows and columns for your table. To do this, hover your mouse over the grid, then click to select the number of rows and columns.

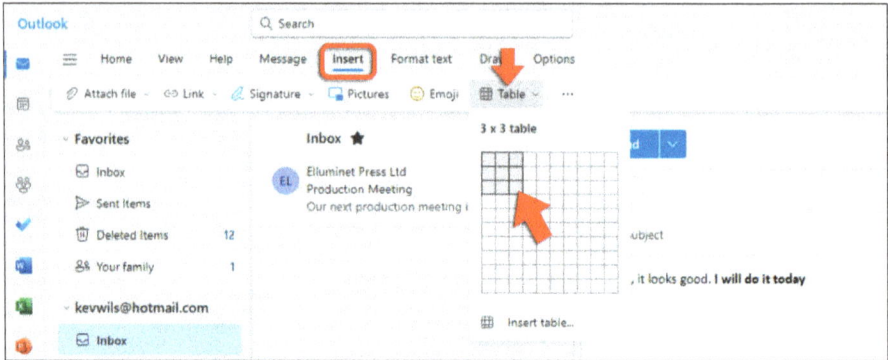

## Insert Emoji

To insert an emoji, start composing a new email. From the 'Insert' ribbon tab, click on the 'Emoji' icon.

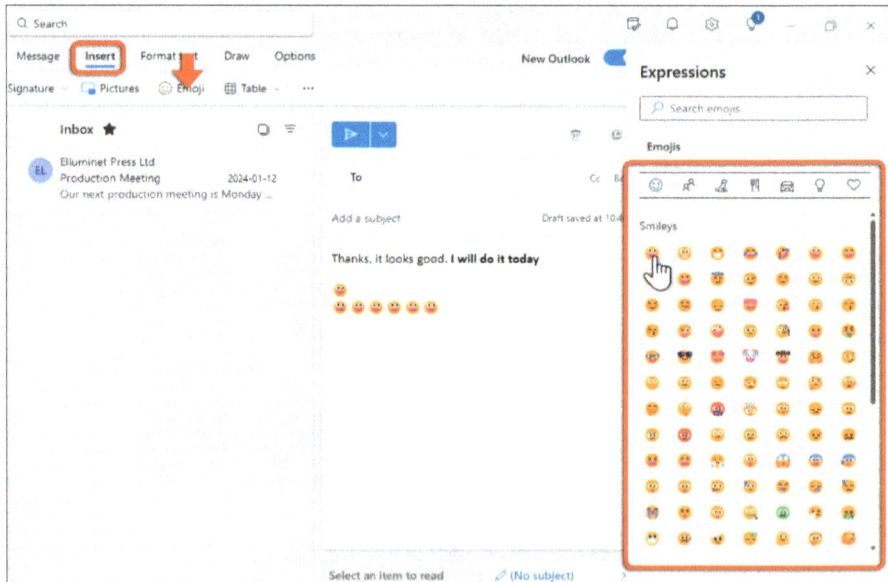

Browse through the emojis in the panel on the right. Click on the one you wish to insert into your email.

# Calendar

The new Outlook app integrates several features such as calendar, people and email management. This version focuses on a modern and simplified design, aiming to streamline the workflow for both personal and professional communication.

## Getting Started

To find your calendar, open the new outlook app, then select the 'calendar' icon from the toolbar down the left hand side of the screen.

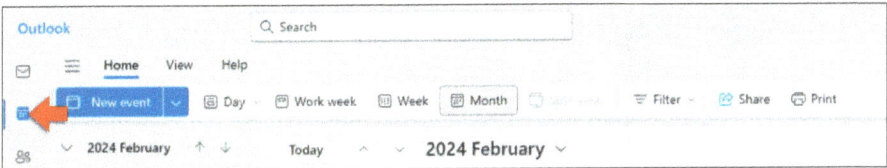

The top ribbon menu currently shows the home tab, and offers options for creating a 'New event', different viewing formats ('Day', 'Work week', 'Week', 'Month', 'Split view'), and other actions like 'Filter', 'Share', and 'Print'.

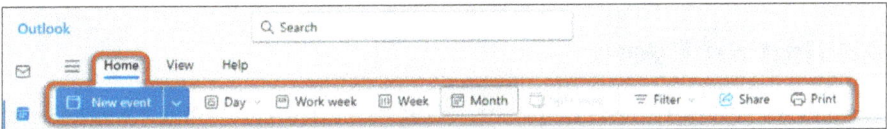

Here in the screenshot below, app is currently displaying in a monthly view, with the month and year shown at the top. Each date block contains events or appointments that have been scheduled. The highlighted box shows the current day.

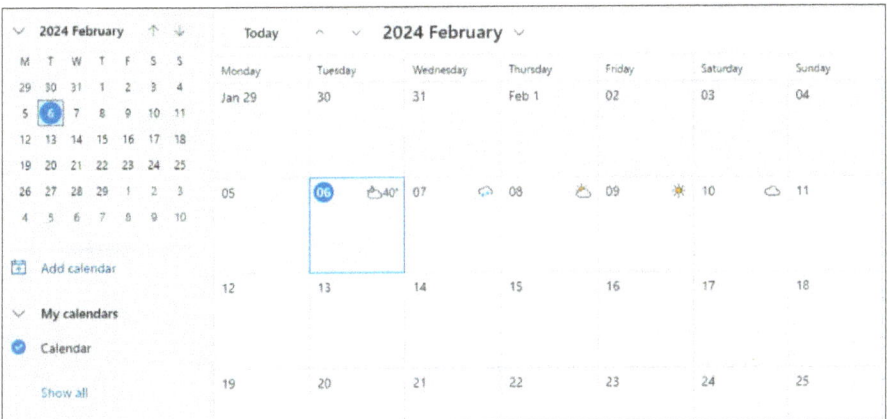

On the left hand navigation pane you'll see your primary calendar which shows the full month. The 'Add Calendar' button allows you to add additional calendars, perhaps for different accounts and purposes.

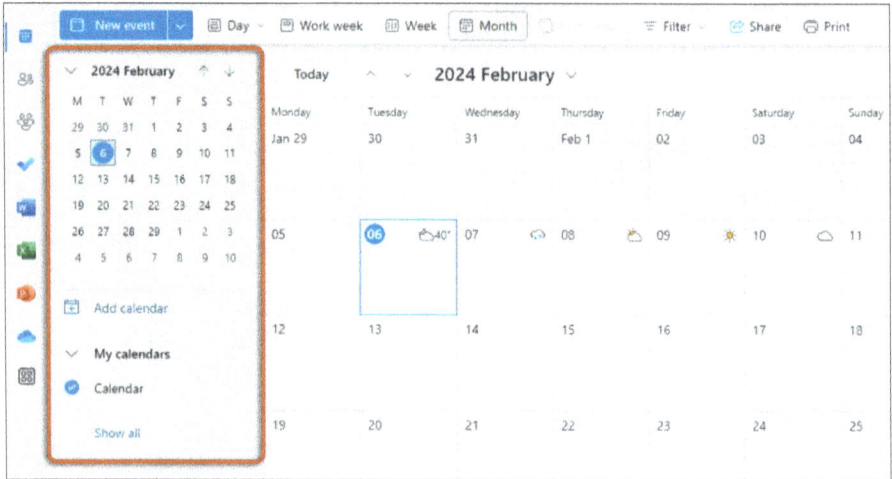

The 'My Calendars' section allows you to view and manage your personal calendars and any other calendars you've added such as holidays and sporting events.

## Adding an Event

To add an appointment or event, click the button labeled "New event" on the left hand side of the home ribbon tab.

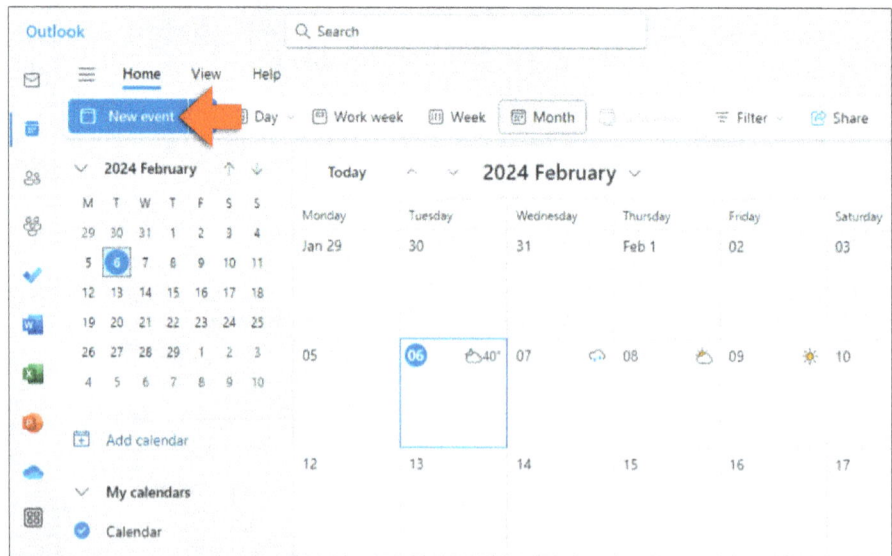

In the event creation window, you can enter details such as the event's title, location, start and end times, and any notes or descriptions. You may also have the option to add attendees, set a reminder, categorize the event, or set it as a recurring event.

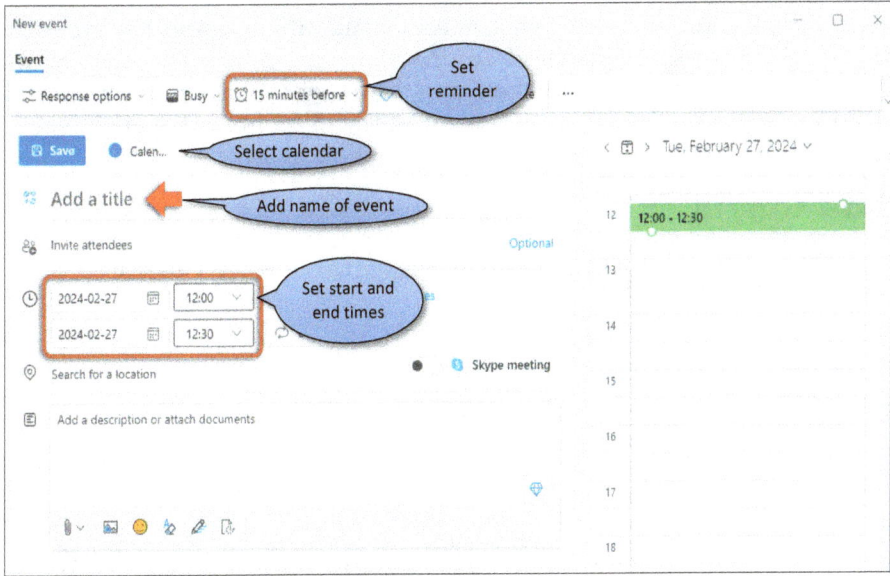

After you've entered all the necessary information, click "Save", on the top left hand side of the window.

Your appointment or event will appear on the calendar under the date you entered. If you want to edit the event, or delete it, right click on the event, then select the option from the popup menu.

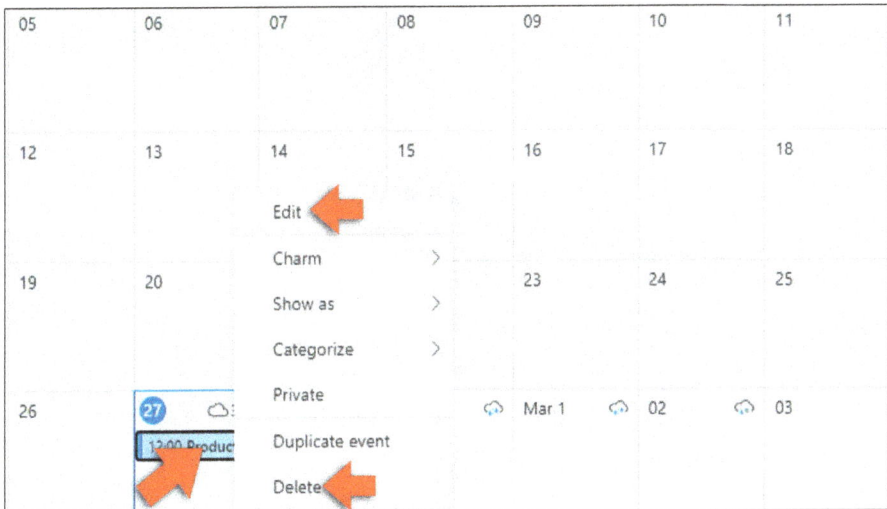

# Calendars

Managing time efficiently has become a necessity in both personal and professional life. You might want to keep your work, personal, family, or hobby-related events separate. For instance, you could have one calendar for your professional appointments and another for your personal or family events and so on. Some calendars are specifically for holidays, sports schedules, school terms, or other recurring events. Adding these can help you plan around these events more effectively.

# Add Calendar

Switch to calendar view, then on the left, below the calendar grid, select 'Add Calendar'.

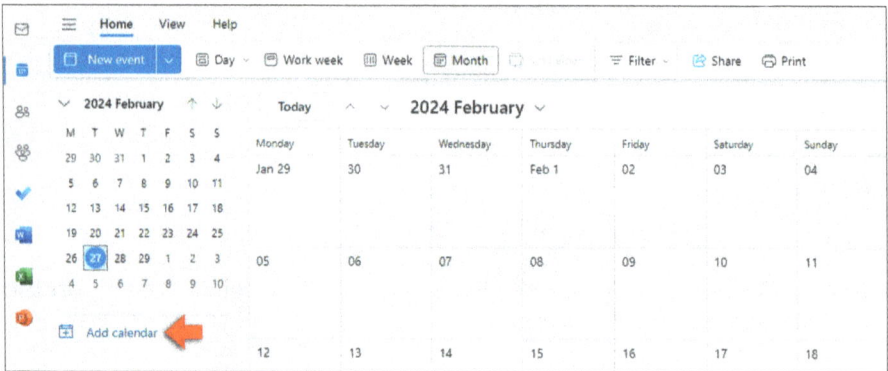

You'll see a window appear with some options.

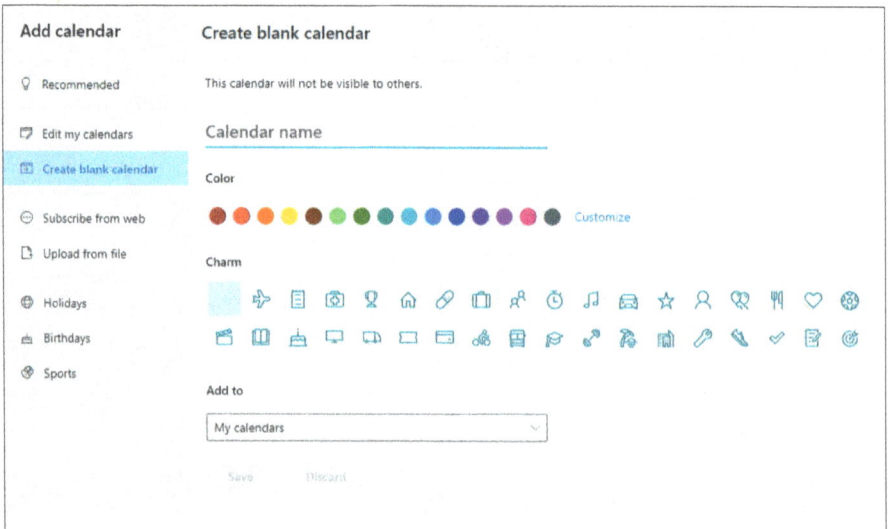

# Chapter 7: Internet and Communication

Down the left hand side of the 'add calendar' window, you have some options as to what calendar to add.

Edit my calendars allows you to manage your existing calendars. You can rename them, change their color or charm, merge them, or adjust their settings.

**Edit my calendars**

Select a calendar below to rename or customize your calendars

Select a calendar

Create blank calendar will start the process of creating a new calendar from scratch. You would give it a name, choose a color, and select a charm to represent it.

**Create blank calendar**

This calendar will not be visible to others.

Calendar name

Color

Customize

Charm

Subscribe from web allows you to subscribe to a calendar that is hosted on the internet. This could be a public calendar or a shared calendar from a specific organization or group.

**Subscribe from web**

Paste the url for the calendar you would like to subscribe to below. Any edits that the author of the calendar makes will be updated

Example: webcal://www.contoso.com/calendar.ics

Import

329

# Chapter 7: Internet and Communication

Upload from file allows you to add a calendar file (commonly in .ics format).

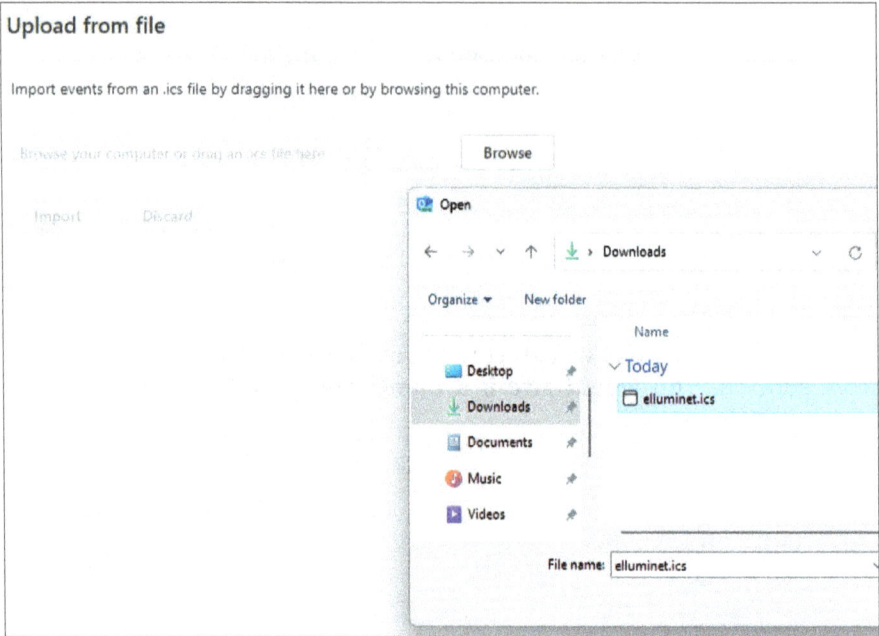

Upload from file

Import events from an .ics file by dragging it here or by browsing this computer.

Browse your computer or drag an .ics file here

Browse

Import          Discard

Open

←  →  ∨  ↑    ↓  › Downloads                    ∨   ↻

Organize ▾    New folder

                                              Name

Desktop        📌        ∨ Today

Downloads      📌          ☐ elluminet.ics

Documents      📌

Music          📌

Videos         📌

File name:  elluminet.ics

Holidays automatically add a calendar with national or religious holidays based on your location or preferences.

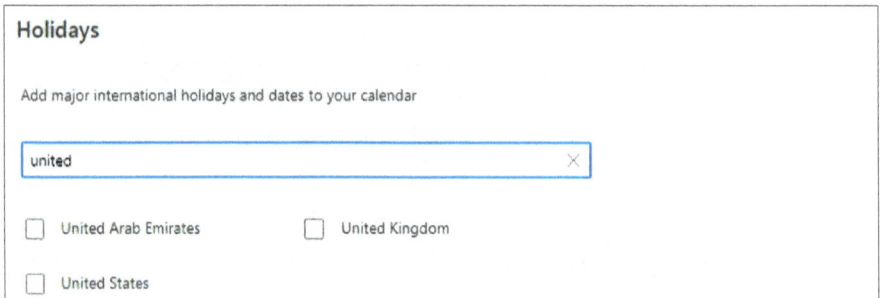

Holidays

Add major international holidays and dates to your calendar

united                                                    ✕

☐  United Arab Emirates        ☐  United Kingdom

☐  United States

Birthdays will automatically create or integrate a calendar that keeps track of all the birthdays in your contact list.

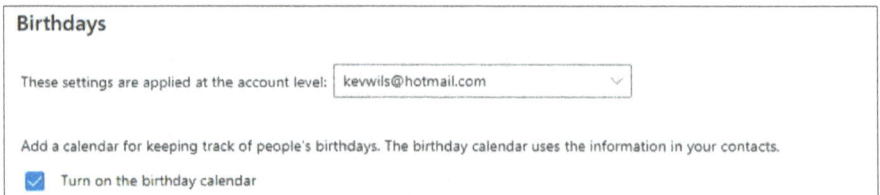

Birthdays

These settings are applied at the account level:  kevwils@hotmail.com        ∨

Add a calendar for keeping track of people's birthdays. The birthday calendar uses the information in your contacts.

☑  Turn on the birthday calendar

Sports allows you to add a calendar related to sports events, like the game dates for your favorite team.

Once you've added a calendar, for example, here I've added US holidays. You'll see the calendar appear under the 'my calendars' section on the left hand side. You'll also see the holiday events appear on the main calendar.

# Address Book (Contacts)

The new Outlook app integrates several features such as calendar, people and email management. This version focuses on a modern and simplified design, aiming to streamline the workflow for both personal and professional communication.

## Getting Started

To find your address book, open the new outlook app, then select the 'people' icon from the toolbar down the left hand side of the screen.

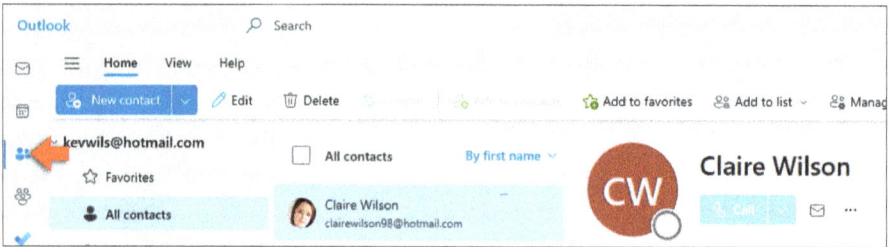

Along the top of the screen, you'll see the familiar ribbon menu. The screen underneath is split into three sections.

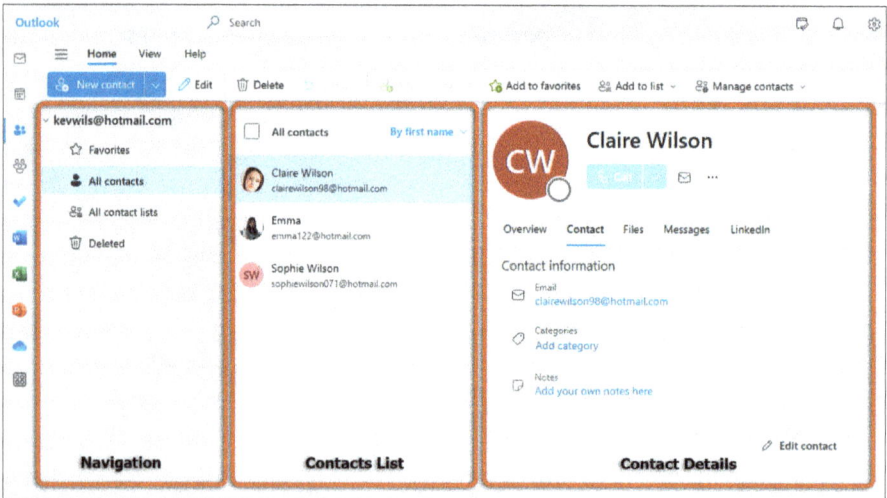

**Navigation** Pane is where you can navigate between different email accounts that have been added to outlook. Each account contains categories such as 'Favorites', 'All contacts', 'All contact lists', and 'Deleted'. Contacts can be sorted into these. In the screenshot, 'All contacts' is highlighted, meaning that it is the currently active view.

**Contacts List** Pane shows the list of individual contacts from the category selected in the navigation pane. In the example the selected category in the navigation pane is 'all contacts'. There are three contacts are shown.

**Contact Details** Pane displays detailed information for the contact selected in the contacts list, which in this case is Claire Wilson. It provides an overview of the contact's information, including email address and other fields like 'Categories' and 'Notes' which have not been filled in. There are also tabs for additional details such as 'Contact', 'Files', 'Messages', and 'LinkedIn', as well as a 'Call' button and email icon.

# Add Contact

From the home ribbon tab, select 'new contact'.

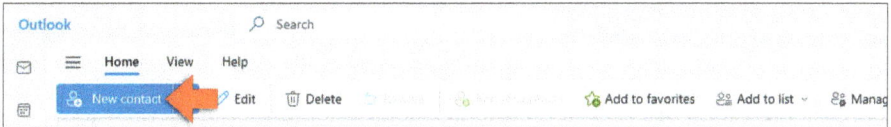

Fill in the contact's details. Click the camera icon at the top if you want to add a picture or profile photograph. Go through the rest of the fields and add the contact's name and contact details such as email address and phone number.

**First Name & Last Name:** Enter the contact's first and last names.

**Add Email:** Click "Add email" to enter the contact's email address.

**Add Chat:** If applicable, you can add chat contact details, such as a Skype or Teams.

**Add Phone:** Click "Add phone" to include the contact's mobile phone number.

**Add Address:** You can enter the contact's physical address here.

**Company:** If relevant, include the name of the contact's employer.

Click 'save' when you're done.

# Edit Contact

To edit a contact's details, first select 'all contacts' from the navigation pane, then from the contacts list in the middle, select the contact you want to edit. In the contact details on the right hand side, you'll see an 'edit contact' button on the bottom right. Click on this to edit the details.

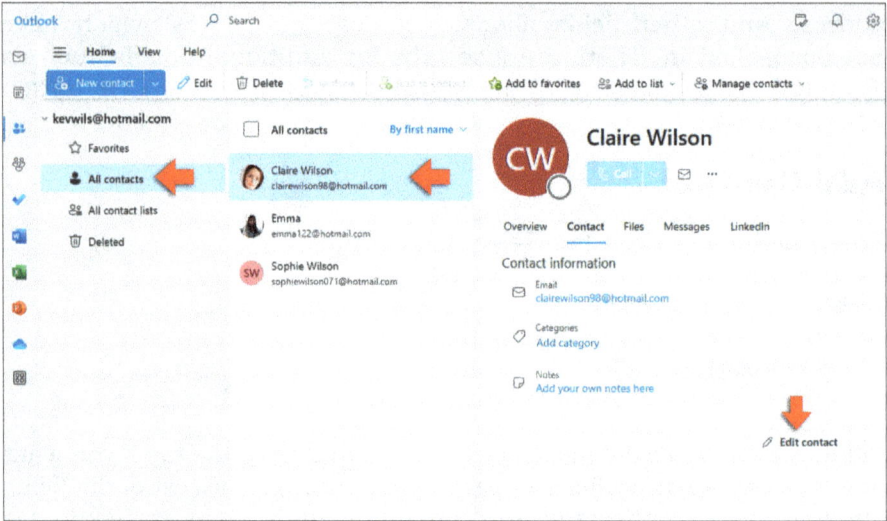

Make edits to the contact details as required. Click 'save' on the bottom of the window when you're done.

# Contact Lists

A contact list is a collection of email addresses that you can use to send an email to a group of people simultaneously. Instead of entering each email address individually, you can create a contact list (sometimes referred to as a distribution list) and send an email to the list, which then distributes the email to all the addresses within that list. This is particularly useful for sending newsletters, announcements, or updates to a group of people, such as family members, colleagues, or club members.

To create a contact list, select the 'people' icon from the toolbar down the left hand side of the screen.

On the home ribbon tab, click the dropdown arrow next to 'New contact'. Then select 'New contact list'.

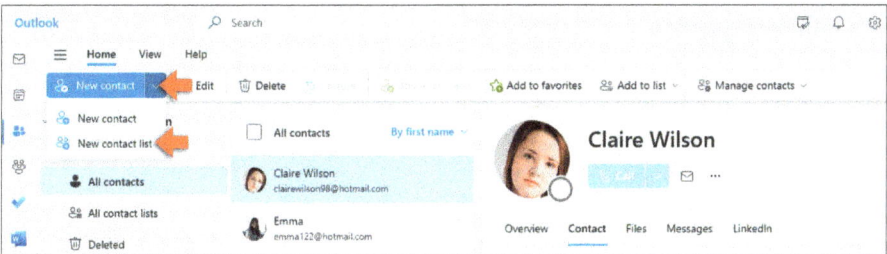

Name your list and add contacts by typing their names or email addresses.

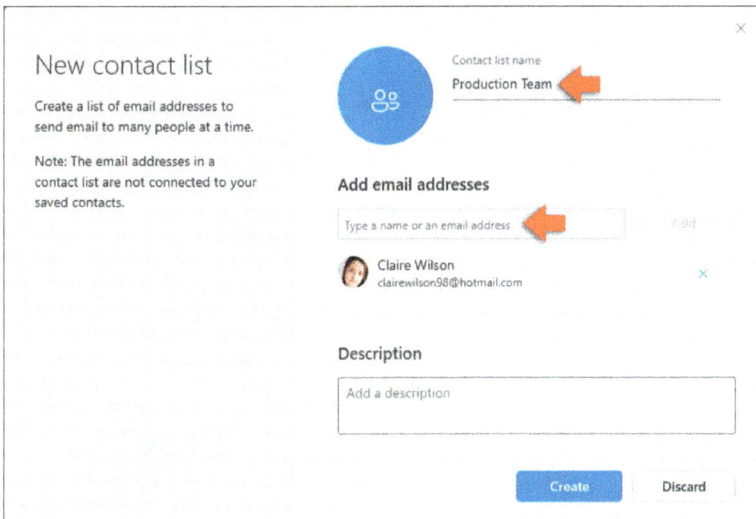

When finished, click "Create".

## Send Message to Contact List

First switch to emails, select the 'mail' icon from the toolbar down the left hand side of the screen.

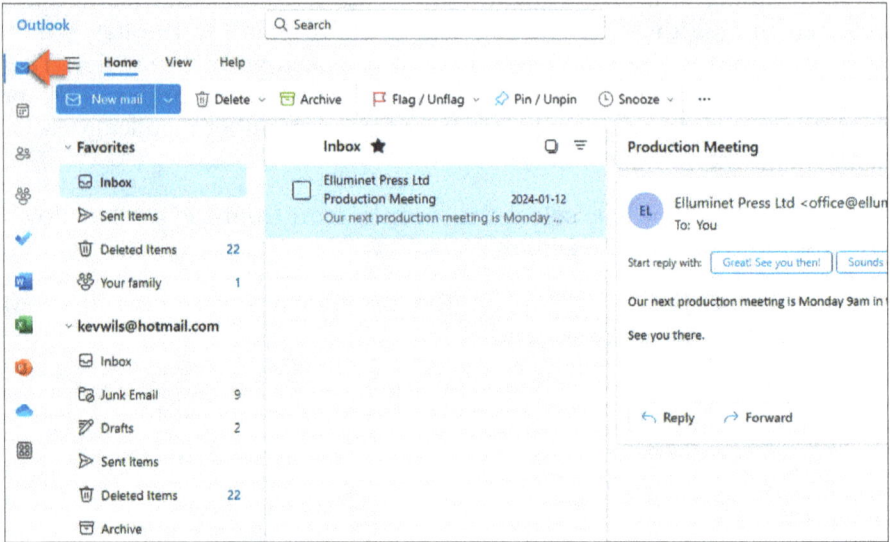

When you want to send an email to the contacts list, create a new email message, then type the name of the contacts list in the 'to' field.

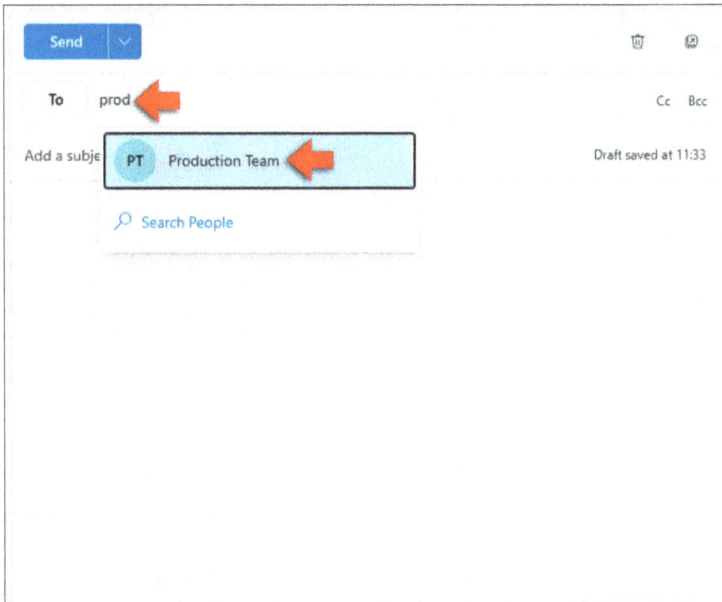

Enter your message as normal, then click 'send' when you're done.

# Add Contact from Email Message

To add a contact from an email message, select the message, then right click on the email address at the top. From the popup window, select the three dots icon on the top right, then select 'add to contacts' from the drop down menu.

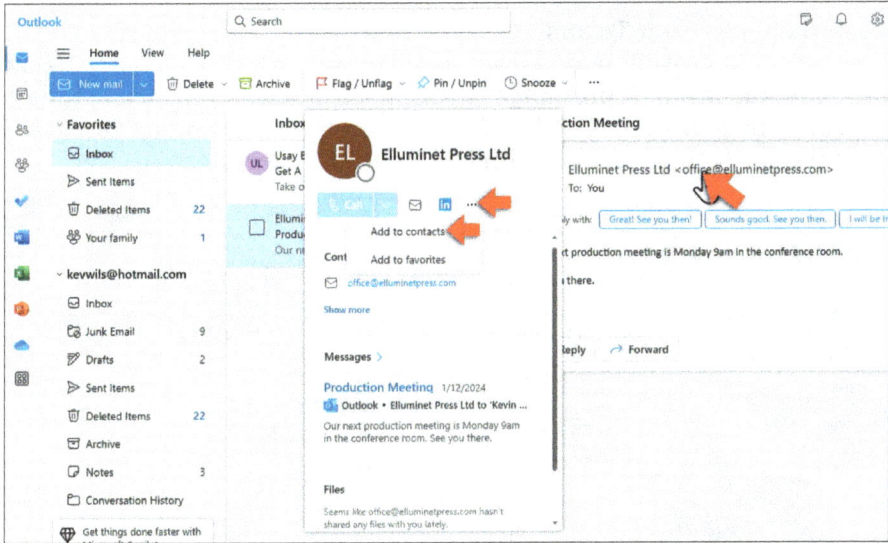

Fill in any additional information you want to add, then click 'save' at the bottom of the contacts details.

# Chat with Friends & Family

Microsoft Teams (free) lets you connect with friends, family, or colleagues through video calls, messaging, screen and file sharing. You can launch it from the Start Menu, or install it via the Microsoft Store if it's not already on your computer.

To launch Microsoft Teams, open the Start Menu and go to "All Apps", then select Microsoft Teams from the list. Sign in using your Microsoft account credentials if prompted. Upon first launch, Teams may request permissions to access your Microphone and Camera. Ensure you grant permission as these are essential for calls and meetings.

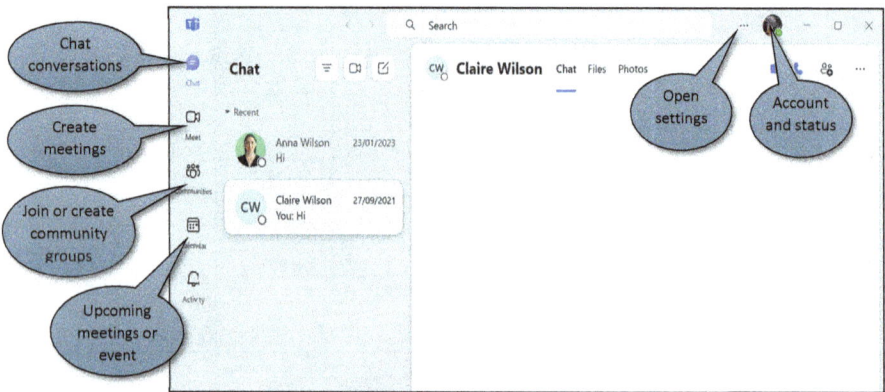

## Start a New Video Chat

To start a video chat, select 'chat' from the left hand panel, then click the 'meet now' icon.

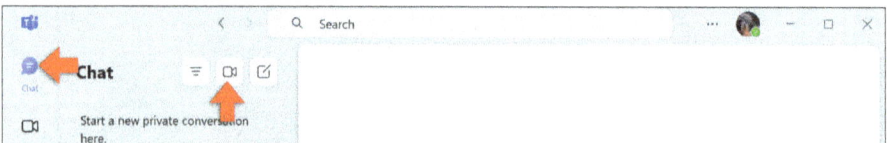

Enter the person's name or email address, then select the match that appears below.

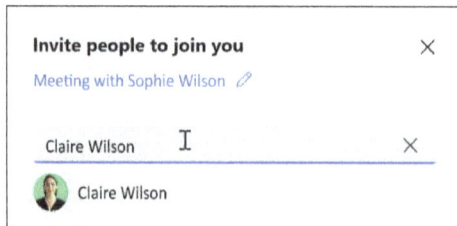

Wait for the other person to join the meeting. Once they do, you'll both appear in the call window where you can use video, audio, screen sharing, and chat tools. You can also enable your camera and mic.

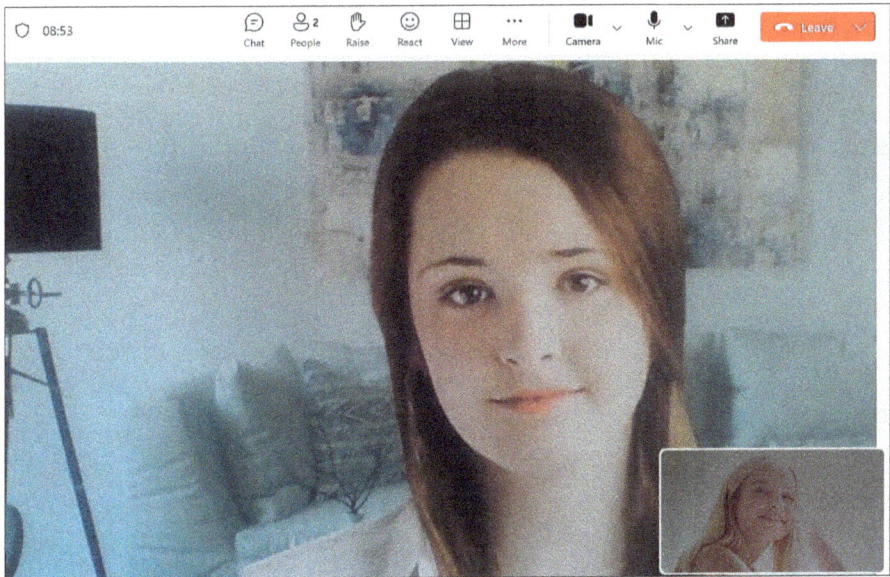

The large video feed shows the other participant in the call. The smaller video feed in the lower-right corner is a preview of your own webcam. This helps you monitor how you appear to others.

On the toolbar along the top of the window, the timer on the top left indicates how long the meeting has been ongoing.

- The chat icon opens the in-call text chat sidebar.
- The people icon opens the participant list.
- The raise icon lets you raise your virtual hand to signal that you want to speak.
- The react icon opens emoji reactions (e.g. thumbs-up, heart, clap).
- The view icon lets you change how participant video feeds are arranged.
- The three dots 'more' icon opens additional options, such as device settings, background effects, or meeting settings.
- The camera icon toggles your webcam on/off, and the mic icon toggles your microphone on/off.
- The share icon shares your screen or app window with the other participant(s).
- The leave icon ends your participation in the meeting.

# Screen Sharing

While in call, you can share your screen. To do this click the 'share' icon on the toolbar at the top of the screen. From the drop down menu, you'll see two options.

If you share your screen, everyone on the call will be able to see what is on your desktop, so make sure its clear with no sensitive information showing. To do this, select 'share' from the icons along the top of the window.

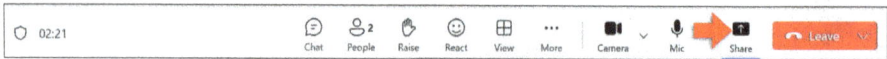

From here, you can choose what type of content you want to share—your entire screen, a specific app window, or a browser tab. This panel is central to delivering presentations, demonstrations, or collaborative reviews.

The **include sound** toggle lets you share your computer's audio along with the visual content. This is especially useful when showing videos or playing audio clips during a presentation. By default, the switch is off, meaning participants will only see what you share, but won't hear system sounds or media playback unless you enable this option.

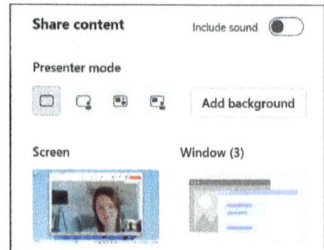

The **Presenter mode** section allows you to control how your camera feed is displayed alongside shared content. The four available modes are:

- **Content only** shares your screen or window without showing your webcam.
- **Standout overlays** your webcam video on top of your shared content, useful for keeping yourself visually present while presenting.
- **Side-by-side** places your camera view beside the content in a split layout.
- **Reporter** places your webcam feed in a styled layout, mimicking a news anchor next to graphics.

In this example I'm going to select side by side.

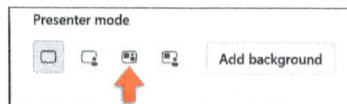

The **Add background** button lets you apply a virtual background behind your video feed while using presenter mode. This can help reduce distractions or maintain privacy by obscuring your physical surroundings. It is especially useful in professional or educational settings.

At the bottom, selecting the screen option will broadcast everything on your screen to the participants—including your taskbar, open windows, and notifications. It's ideal when switching between multiple apps or showing workflows that span the desktop. The window option displays a list of individual application windows currently open on your PC. You can select one to share just that app, without revealing the rest of your desktop. This is the best option for focused presentations where you want to keep your content controlled and avoid exposing unrelated material.

In this example, I'm going to select window, as I only want to share the browser app I have open. If you selected 'window' select from the list of open apps that appear. Once you select this, you'll see a preview of your camera on the bottom right. The app that you're sharing will have a red border around it.

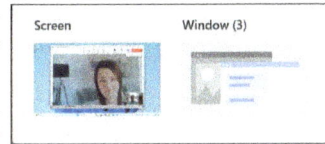

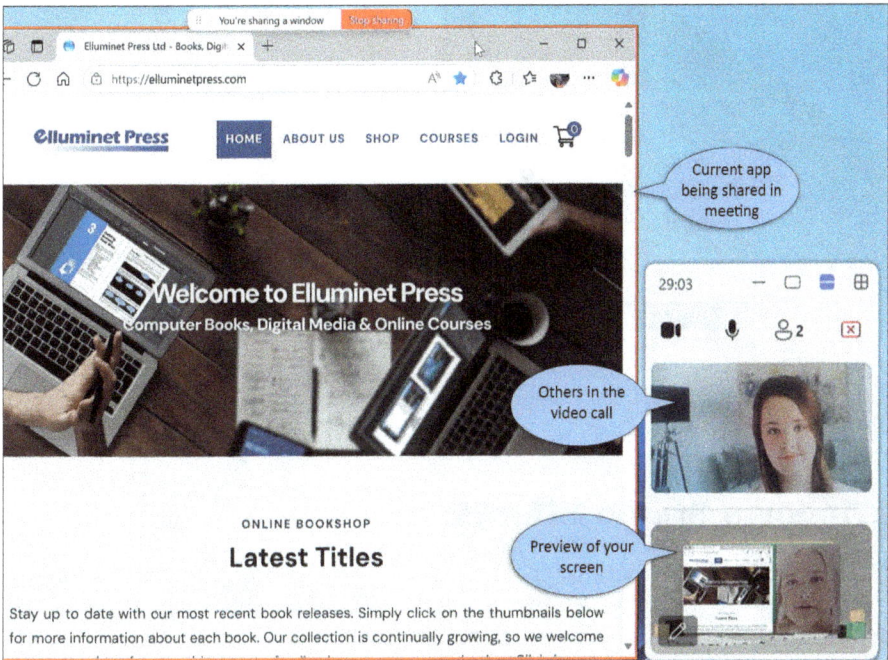

To stop sharing click 'stop sharing' on the top middle of the screen.

## Background Effects

You can apply various background effects to your camera. For example, you can blur the background, or you can add a virtual background to your cam. To do this, during a call, click on the 'more' icon on the toolbar along the top of the screen. From the drop down menu, select 'video effects and settings'.

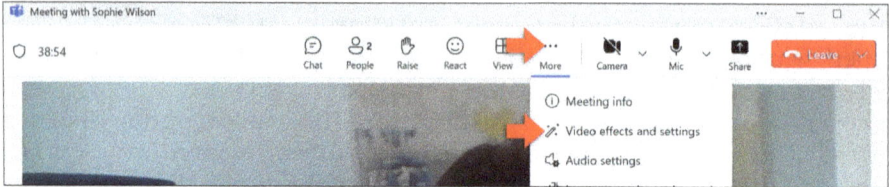

On the right hand side, you'll see a list of effects. Click on one to try it out. Click 'preview' to see what it looks like, or click 'apply and turn on video', then 'apply'.

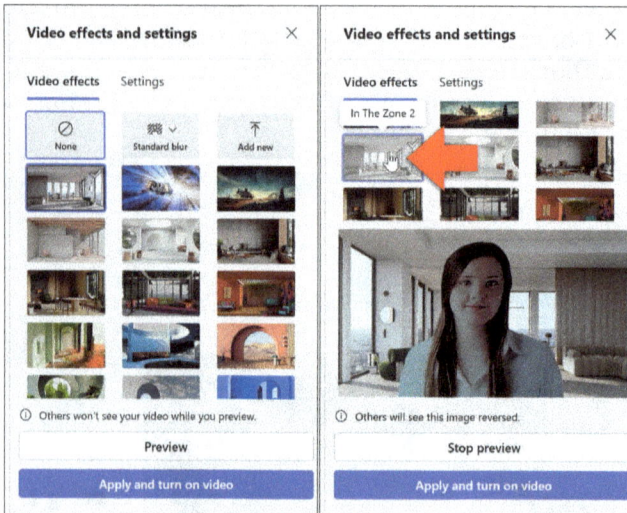

To turn the effect off, go back up to the 'more' icon, select 'video effects and settings', then click 'none', then 'apply'.

## Windows Studio Effects

Windows Studio Effects uses AI to elevate the quality of video calls and recordings. It includes features such as background blur, automatic framing, eye contact correction, and voice focus. These enhancements work in real time and are supported across major conferencing platforms like Microsoft Teams and Zoom.

**342**

All of these capabilities are designed to operate entirely on the Copilot+ PC using the on board NPU. Microsoft has emphasized that these are not simply software upgrades—they require dedicated AI hardware and architectural support that only Copilot+ PCs provide.

To apply these effects, click on the quick settings icon on the bottom right of the taskbar. From the settings menu, select 'studio effects'.

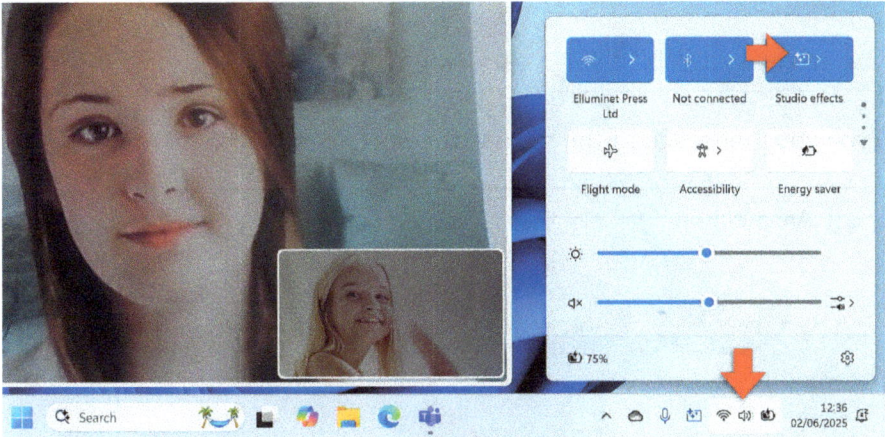

Now you can apply various studio effects to your camera. Just select the ones you want from the options. **Portrait Light** enhances lighting on your face to create a more flattering and well-lit appearance.

**Background Blur** softens the background to reduce distractions and focus attention on you.

**Creative Filter Illustrated** applies a hand-drawn cartoon-style effect to your video feed. **Creative Filter Animated** adds stylized, motion-based visual effects for a dynamic appearance. **Creative Filter Watercolor** gives your video the look of a soft, painted watercolor portrait.

**Eye Contact Standard** adjusts your gaze slightly to simulate natural eye contact with the camera. **Eye Contact Teleprompter** shifts your gaze more directly toward the camera for a presenter-style look.

**Automatic Framing** automatically zooms and pans to keep you centered in the camera view.

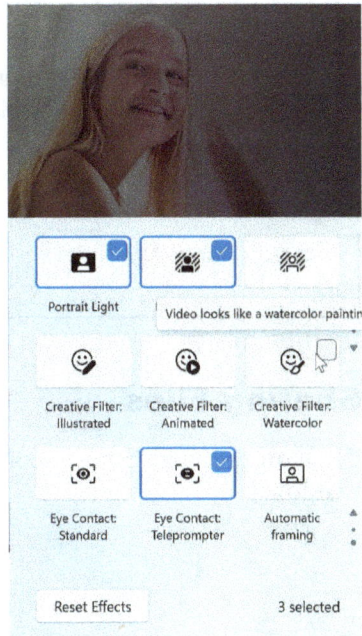

## Text Chat

To start a text chat with a new person, on the main window click 'new chat'. Or if you've chatted to the person before, you'll find their name in the 'recent' list on the main screen.

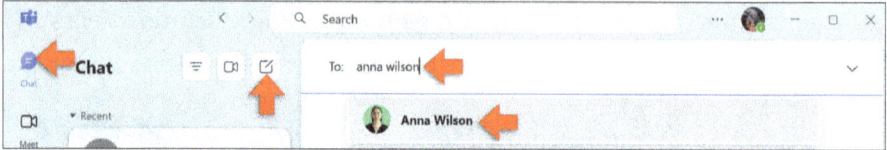

Type your message in the field at the bottom of the chat window.

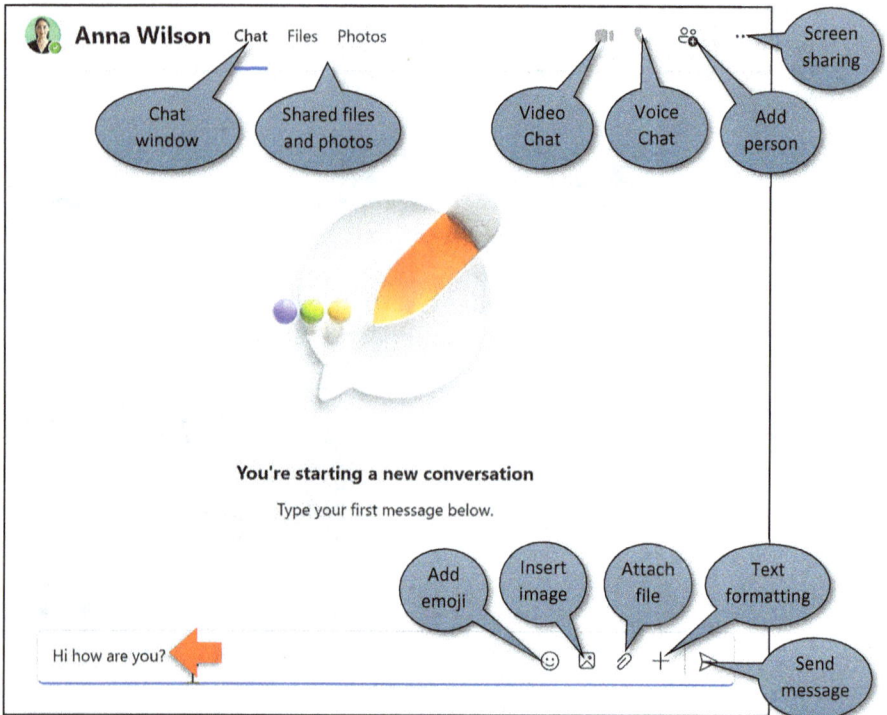

## Sharing Files

Click on the attachment icon on the bottom right hand side of the chat window.

Click 'upload from this device'. Select the file you want to send.

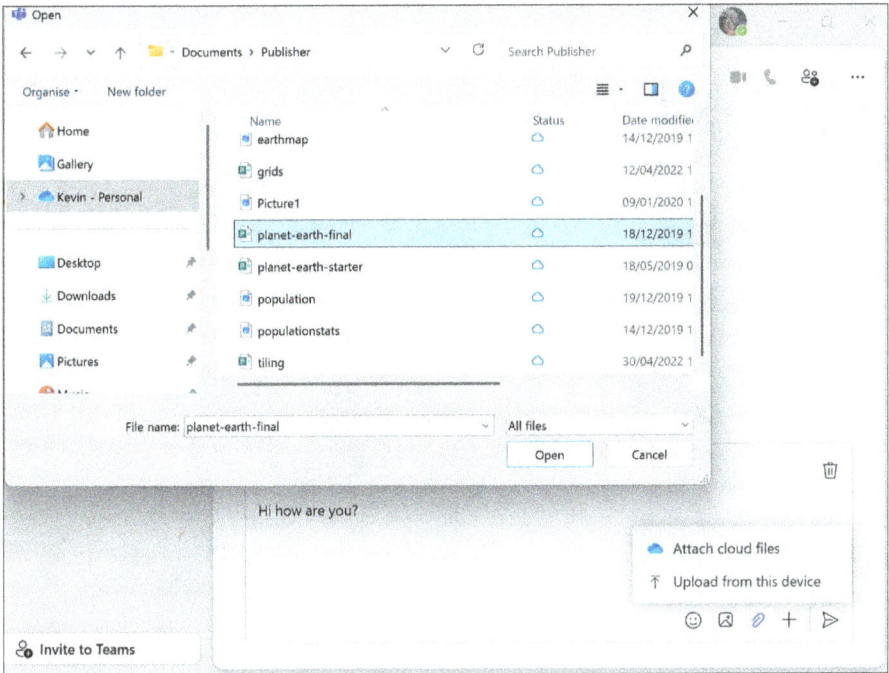

Once the file has been added to your message. Click on the send icon.

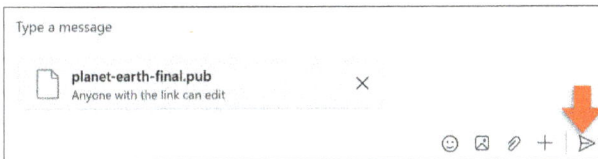

# Schedule a Meeting

From the sidebar on the left, click 'calendar', then click on a date and time on the calendar.

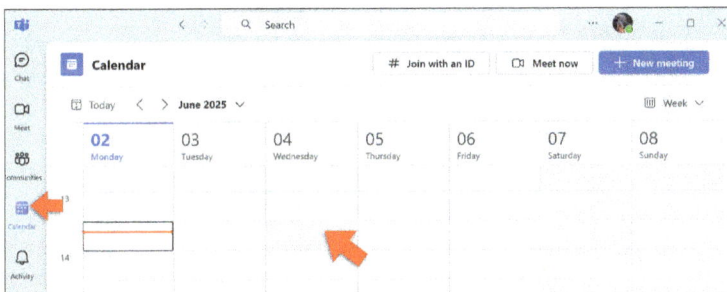

# Chapter 7: Internet and Communication

A scheduling window will appear where you can fill in the meeting details. Give your meeting a title, then add the email addresses of the people you want to invite. You can also add a short description or agenda in the message box, and adjust the start and end time or choose whether the meeting repeats (e.g. daily, weekly). Click 'send'. Everyone who was invited to the meeting will find an invite on their chat window or email.

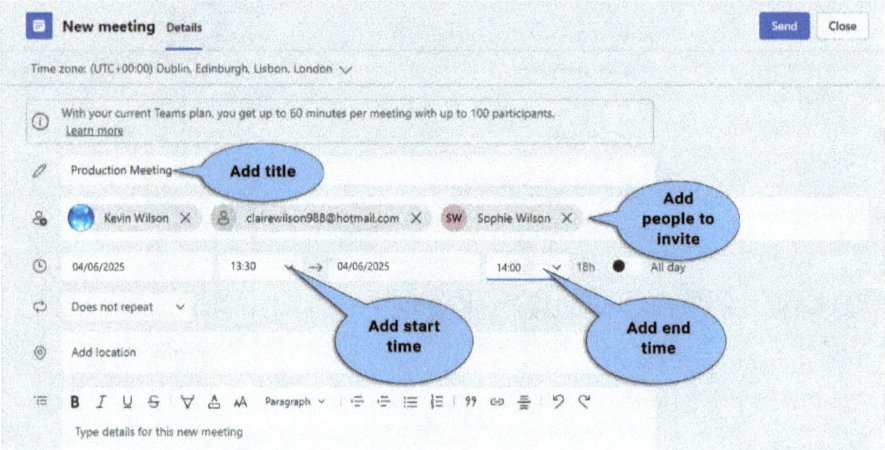

Everyone you've invited will receive a calendar invite by email, and the meeting will appear on their Teams calendar (if they use Teams) and their email calendar (if supported by their email provider). You'll also see the event appear in your own calendar within Teams as shown in the screen below.

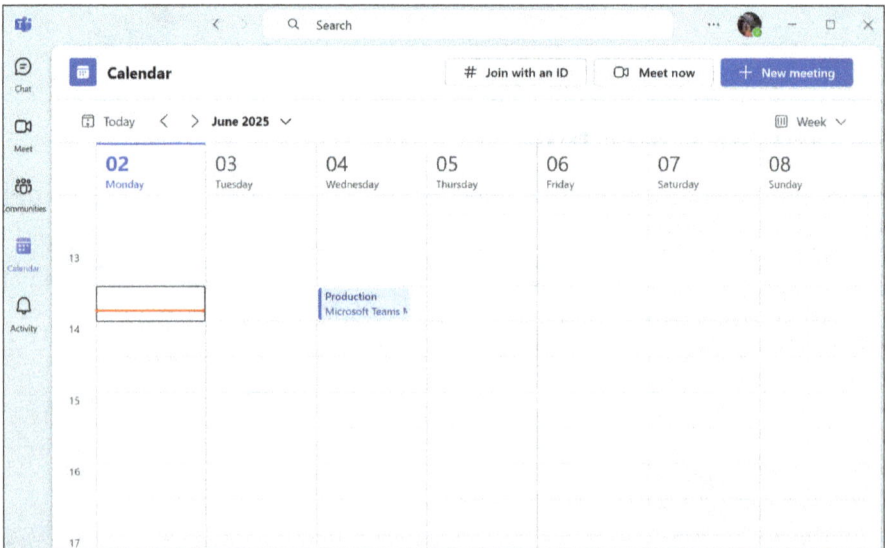

## Accepting a Call

When someone calls you in Teams, a pop-up incoming call window appears on your screen, even if you're not actively using the app. This window includes the caller's name and options to respond. Click 'accept' to accept the call or 'decline' to decline the call.

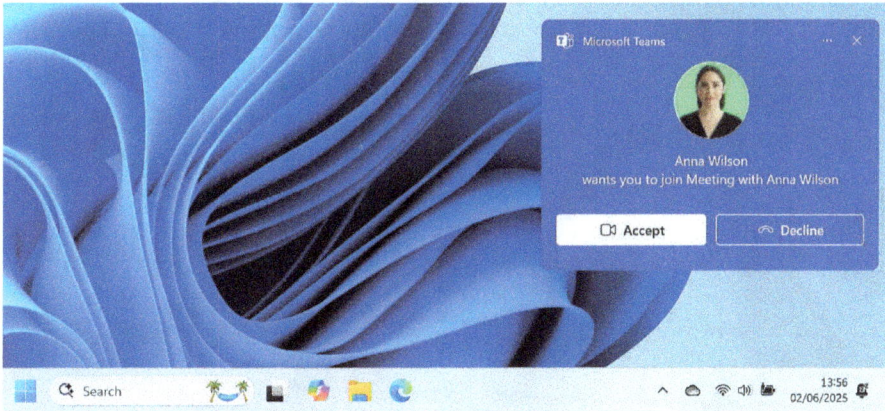

If it's a video call, you may be prompted to turn your camera on or off before connecting. Similarly you can activate/deactivate your microphone. Turn both of these on.

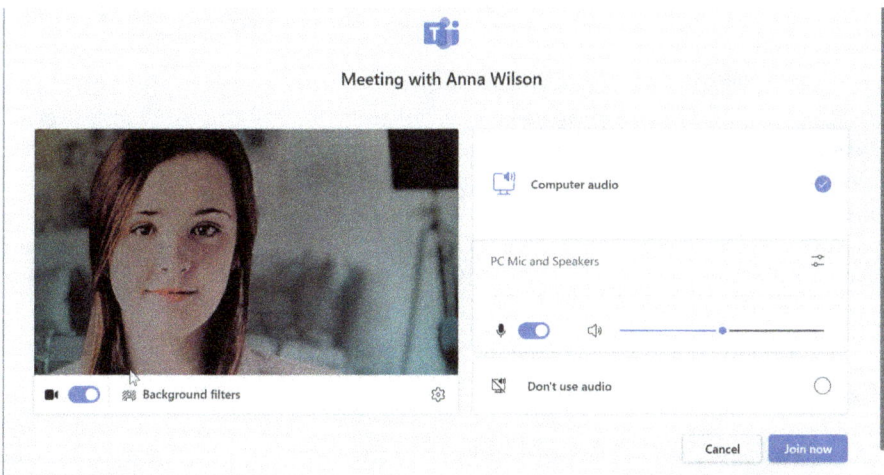

You see a live preview so you can check your appearance before joining. Below the preview, there's a button labeled Background filters, which allows you to apply a blurred or virtual background. A small gear icon beside it opens additional camera settings. On the right, you can adjust your microphone level and access further audio settings to select your preferred input and output devices.

**347**

## Headsets & External Mics

Using a headset, earbuds, or external microphone with Microsoft Teams can significantly improve your audio experience during calls and meetings. When you connect a wired or Bluetooth headset, Teams will often detect it automatically and switch your input and output devices accordingly. This ensures your microphone captures your voice more clearly and that you hear others with better sound isolation, especially in noisy environments.

You can manually select your audio devices from the pre-join screen by clicking the sliders icon or gear symbol next to "PC mic and speakers." This opens the audio settings, where you can choose your microphone, speakers, or headset from the available device list. If your headset has a built-in mic, it will usually appear as a combined device (e.g. "Headset (Hands-Free AG Audio)")—make sure you select the correct one, as Teams sometimes defaults to the wrong mode, especially for Bluetooth devices.

## Adjusting Settings

To access settings, click your profile picture in the top-right corner of the Teams window and select Settings from the dropdown menu.

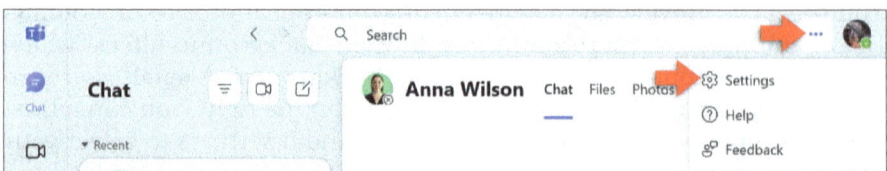

The settings panel opens in a new window with several categories down the left-hand side.

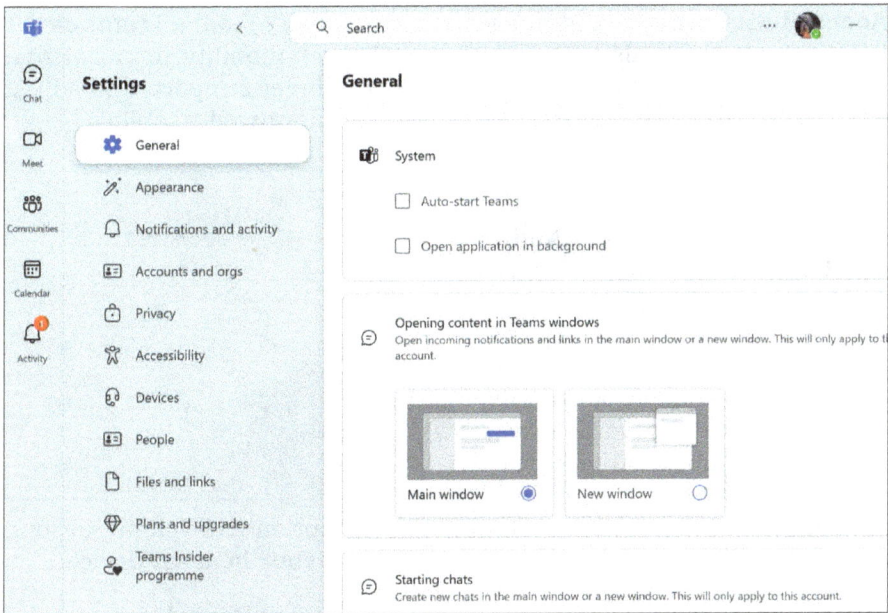

**General** includes basic app behavior and layout preferences. Here, you can choose your language, select how Teams launches and behaves on startup, and enable or disable features such as hardware acceleration. It's where you define the default experience for how Teams functions on your device.

In **Appearance**, you can select the visual theme for Teams—choosing between Light, Dark, and High Contrast modes, or allowing it to follow your system settings. This section is useful if you want to reduce eye strain or match Teams to your desktop environment.

**Notifications and Activity** lets you manage how Teams notifies you about messages, mentions, calls, and other events. You can configure banner alerts, sound notifications, and notification frequency, allowing you to stay informed without being overwhelmed.

**Accounts and Orgs** shows which Microsoft account you're signed into and any organizations you're connected to. Here you can switch between personal and work/school accounts or sign out of the app. This is also where you manage linked tenants if you belong to multiple Teams environments.

**Privacy settings** allow you to control who can contact you, enable or disable read receipts, and manage your blocked contacts list.

It's especially useful for limiting unwanted communication or managing your availability in personal Teams chats.

**Accessibility** section contains features designed to make Teams easier to use for individuals with visual, hearing, or mobility impairments. You can enable keyboard shortcuts, screen reader support, and adjust animations and other interface elements for improved usability.

**Devices** panel lets you select and test audio and video hardware. In the **Audio section**, you can select which microphone and speakers to use such as built-in hardware, a headset, or earbuds. You can enable automatic mic sensitivity to help balance your voice levels, and turn on noise suppression to reduce background sounds. If your headset has built-in buttons, the sync option lets Teams respond to controls like mute or volume directly from your headset device.

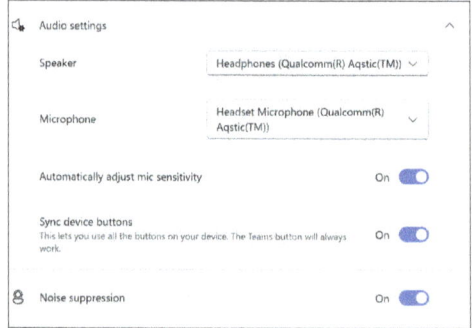

The **Video section** allows you to choose your preferred camera and adjust basic video settings. You can preview your camera feed to check framing and lighting before calls, and make adjustments to brightness or contrast. Teams will use this camera by default for video meetings, screen sharing with camera overlay, or when using background effects.

**People** section helps manage your Teams contacts. You can view your saved contacts, block or unblock users, and manage suggested contacts based on previous interactions. It's useful for keeping your communication organized.

**Files and Links** section provides access to file sharing preferences and saved links. It gives you a centralized view of the files and resources you've shared or received through chats and meetings.

# Remote Desktop

Remote Desktop, also known as terminal services allows you to connect to another machine remotely over a network connection. The user interface is displayed from remote machine onto the local machine and input from the local machine is transmitted to the remote machine – where software execution takes place. Only Windows 10 or 11 Professional allows remote access and isn't available in the home edition. To enable remote connections, open the settings app, select 'system' from the list on the left. Scroll down the list on the right, select 'remote desktop'.

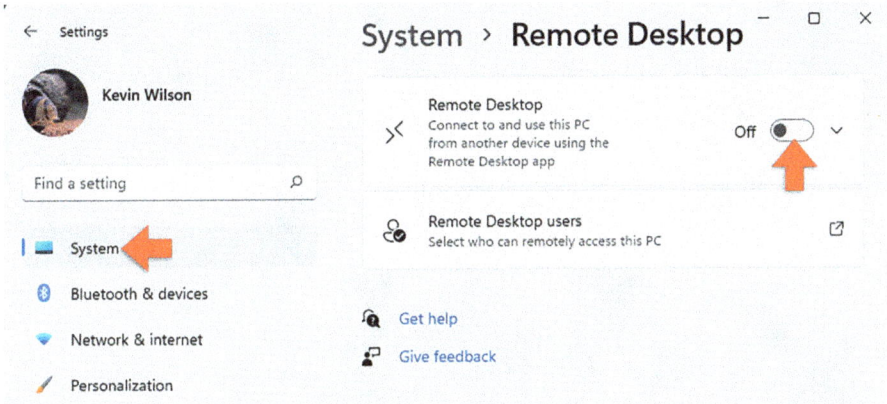

Set the 'enable remote desktop' switch to on. This allows other machines to connect to this PC. Click 'confirm' on the blue dialog box.

Now you need to find out the IP address of the machine. To do this open the Windows terminal. Right click on the start button, select 'windows terminal' or 'windows powershell'.

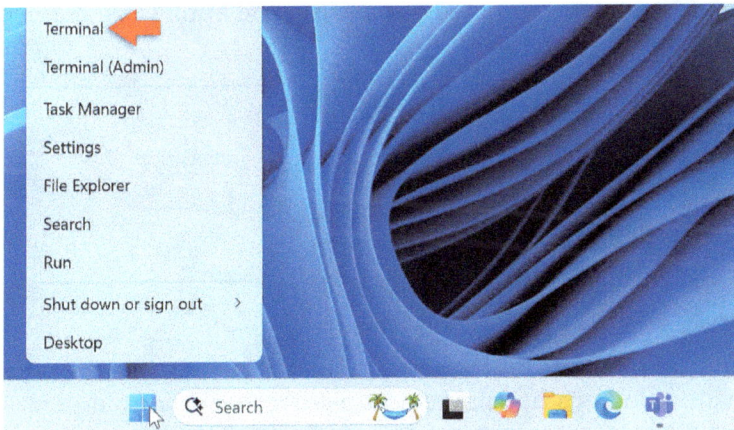

**351**

Now, type ipconfig and find the IPv4 address. In this case 192.168.1.13. Note down this IP address, you'll need it later.

```
Connection-specific DNS Suffix  . : lan
IPv6 Address. . . . . . . . . . . : fdaa:bbcc:ddee:0:a508
Temporary IPv6 Address. . . . . . : fdaa:bbcc:ddee:0:4557
Temporary IPv6 Address. . . . . . : fdaa:bbcc:ddee:0:a149
Link-local IPv6 Address . . . . . : fe80::a508:a9b3:78e1
IPv4 Address. . . . . . . . . . . : 192.168.1.13
Subnet Mask . . . . . . . . . . . : 255.255.255.0
Default Gateway . . . . . . . . . : 192.168.1.1
```

Now you can connect from another machine on the LAN. To do this, on another machine, open the remote desktop connection app. Type 'remote desktop connection' into the search field on the bottom left.

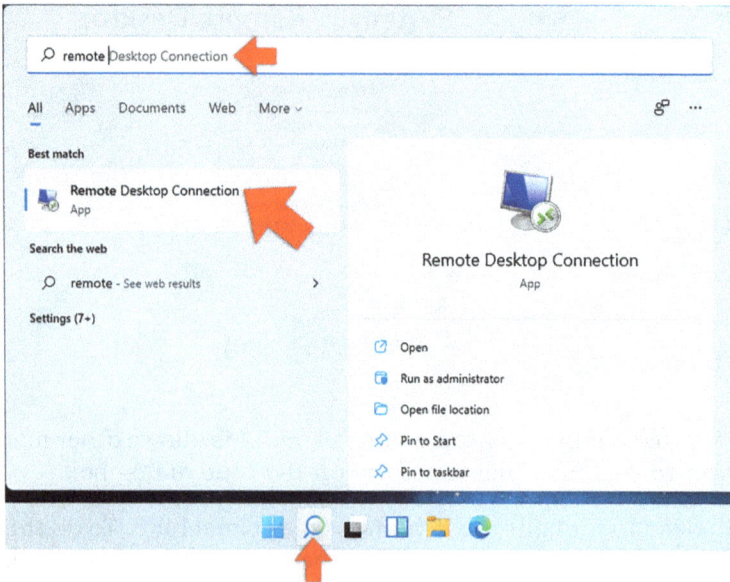

Type the IP address you noted earlier into the app. Click 'connect'.

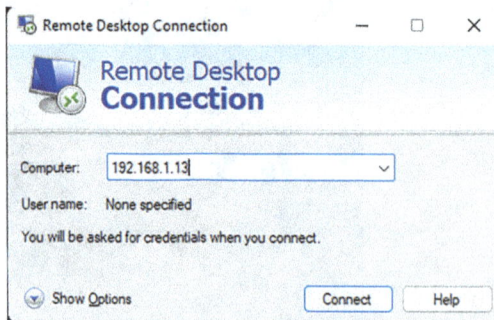

Enter your windows username and password when prompted. You'll see your desktop appear in the remote desktop window.

# FTP

FTP (File Transfer Protocol) is a protocol for transferring files to and from a remote machine. You can connect using a program called FileZilla.

```
filezilla-project.org
```

First you need to download and install the program. You can download FileZilla here. Double click on `FileZilla_..._win64-setup.exe` to begin the setup. Follow the instructions on screen to install.

To connect to an FTP server click the 'site manager' icon on the top left.

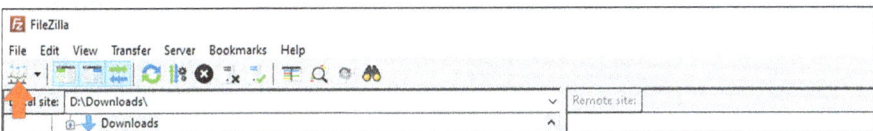

Click 'new site' on the bottom left, in the 'general' tab on the right, select a protocol from the 'protocol' drop down list - usually SFTP or FTP.

In the 'host' field, enter the server name or IP address of the server you're connecting to.

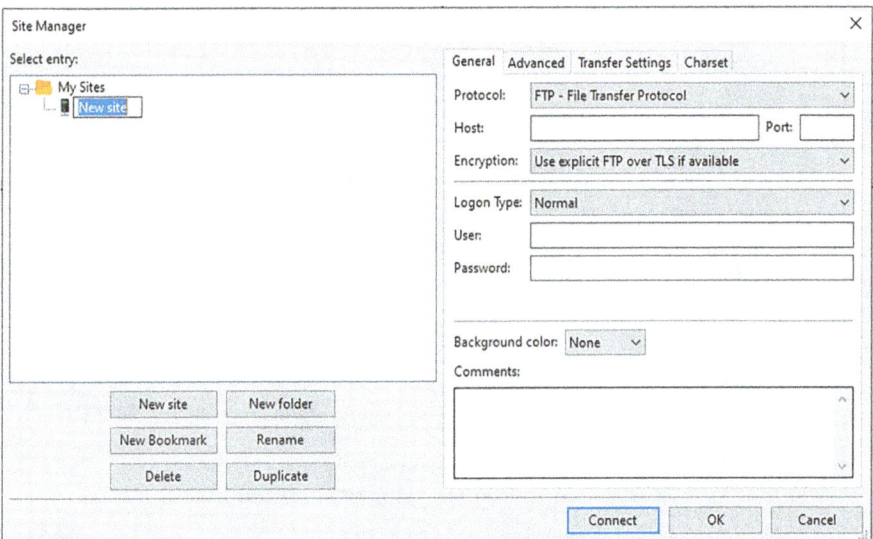

In the 'user' and 'password' field, enter the username and password for the server you're connecting to. Click 'connect' when you're done.

Now you can transfer files.

# SSH with PuTTY

SSH (or Secure Shell) is a protocol for secure remote login to another machine. This provides a command prompt where you can issue commands to execute programs or perform tasks on the remote machine. You can connect using a program called PuTTY or using the command prompt.

First you need to download and install the program.

    www.putty.org

Go to your downloads folder then double click `putty-64bit-...-installer.msi` to install PuTTY. Follow the instructions on screen.

Once installed, launch the app from your start menu, then in the configuration window, enter the IP address or hostname of the machine you're connecting to.

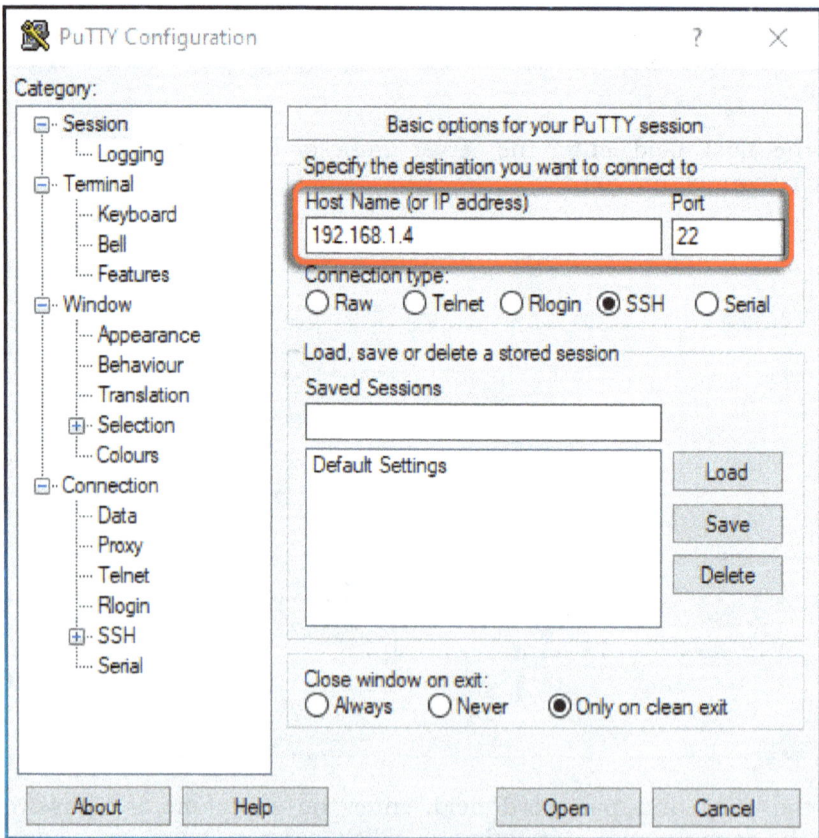

Enter the port number – usually 22. Click 'open'.

When a connection is established, enter your username and password for the machine you're connecting to.

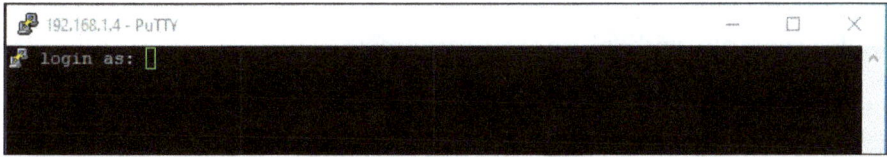

Once authenticated you can issue various commands from the command prompt.

# SSH from Windows Terminal

First, open windows terminal. Right click on the start button, select 'windows powershell' or 'terminal' from the popup menu.

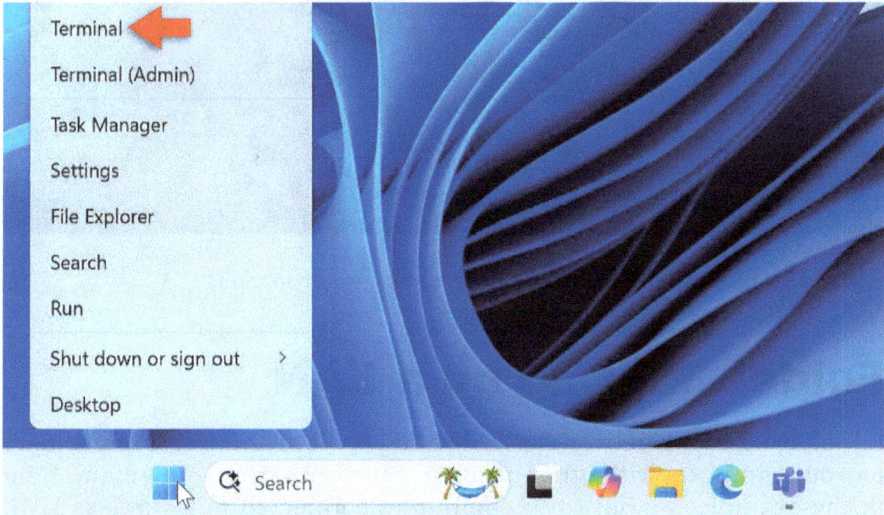

You'll land on the PowerShell windows terminal.

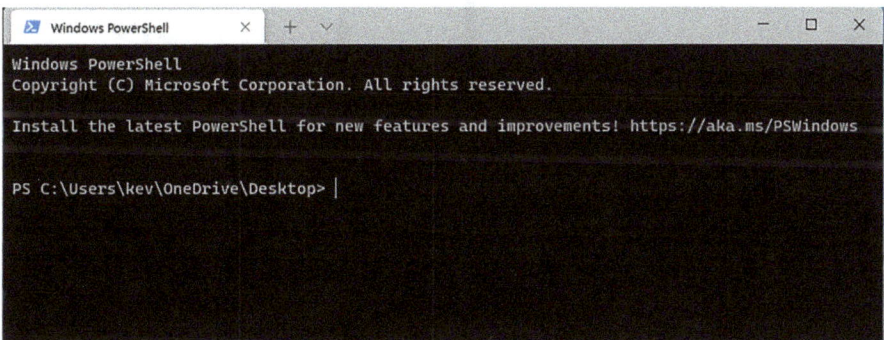

To connect to the server type:

```
ssh username@hostname
```

So for example, with 'pi' as the username:

```
ssh pi@192.168.1.3
```

Enter the password for the username when prompted.

# Folder Sharing on a LAN

File sharing over a network (or LAN) allows you to share files and folders on your computer with other users in your workgroup or domain. Here in the example, we have two computers connected to a wireless LAN. Were are going to share a folder on PC 1, then connect to it from PC 2.

PC 1

PC 2

Device Name: **Gigabyte**
Shared folder: **Documents**

First, on the PC you're sharing the folder from (PC 1), you need to create usernames for the people you want to share the folder with.

To do this, see page 108 for information on creating local user accounts on your machine.

## Sharing a Folder

Now on PC 1 ie the PC you're sharing the folder from, open file explorer then navigate to the folder you want to share. To share a folder, right click on it, then select "properties" from the popup menu.

Select the "sharing" tab, then click "advanced sharing".

Click "share this folder", then select "permissions".

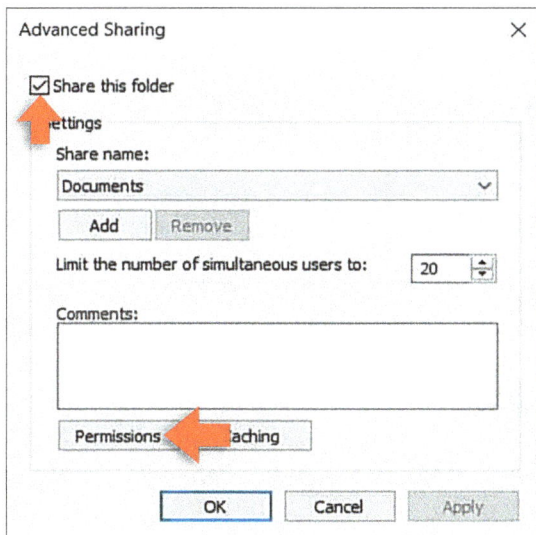

Set the permissions for this folder. In other words choose the people you want to have access to this folder. Note that you will need the account you created earlier. To add a user, click "add".

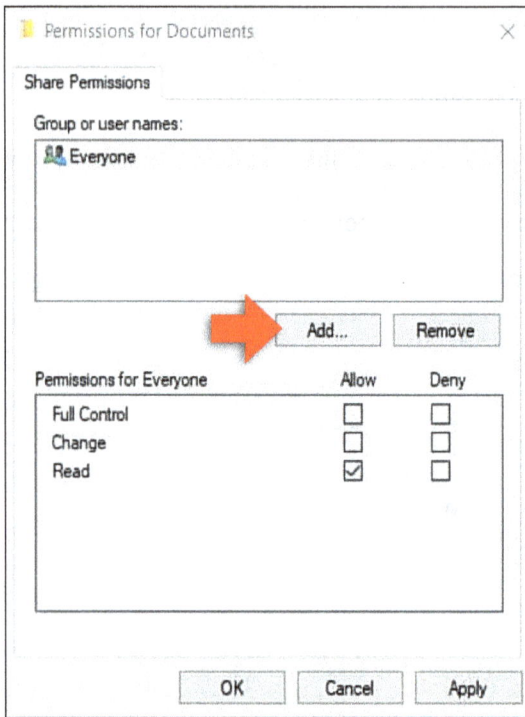

Type the person's username in the field below, then click "check names". Click "ok".

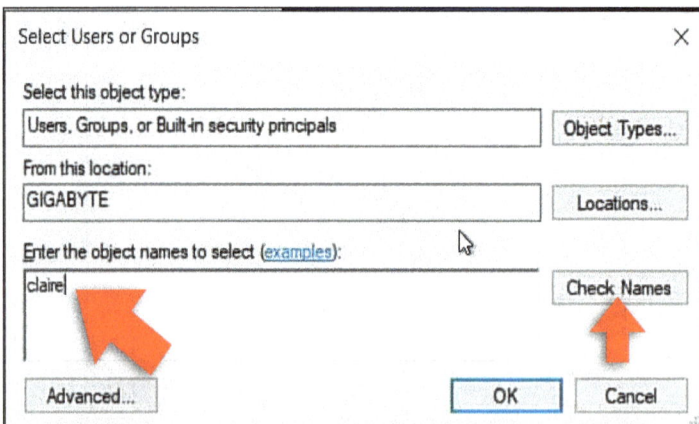

*If it doesn't work, click 'advanced', then click 'find now'. Select the username from the list.*

Now set the permissions. If you select "everyone", this means anyone connecting to your PC can view the folder. This might be ok on a small private network, but on larger networks, you should only allow the people you want to grant access to.

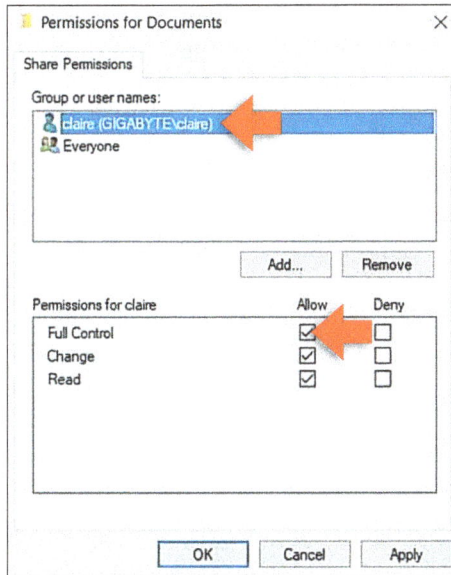

To grant access, in the top panel of the dialog box, click on the user you just added. In the panel underneath, click "full control" to allow the user to add files, as well as read and write to existing files. If you just want them to view files, select read only. Click 'ok'.

# Access a Shared Folder on a LAN

If we wanted to connect to the shared folder we created in the previous section (the folder on PC 1), we need to know the PC's name and the name of the shared folder.

On the PC sharing the folder (ie PC 1), you can find the PC's name in the settings app. Click on "system". Select "about" from the list on the right.

You'll see the PC's name under "device name".

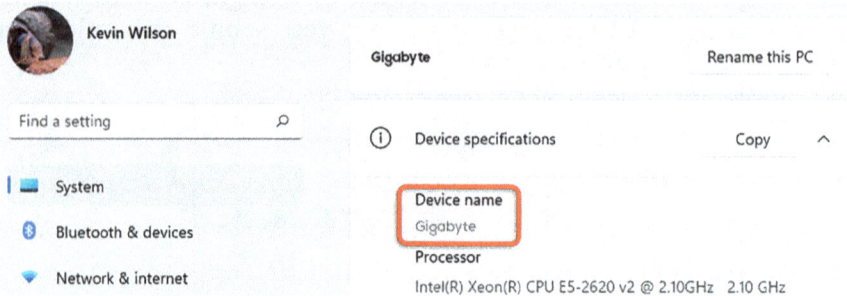

*If it's too difficult to remember, click "rename this PC" then enter a name". Click "next".*

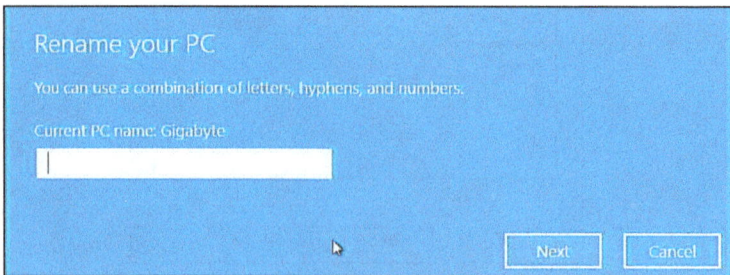

*Restart your PC for the change to take effect.*

To connect to a shared folder, you'll need to enter the UNC path to that folder. The UNC path is the name of the PC sharing the folder, followed by the folder name.

```
\\PC-Name\Shared-Folder-Name
```

On another machine on the network (PC 2 in our example), open File Explorer.

PC 1

PC 2

Device Name: **Gigabyte**

Shared folder: **Documents**

Type the UNC path to the shared folder into the address bar along the top of the window. In this case:

```
\\gigabyte\documents
```

Press enter when you're done.

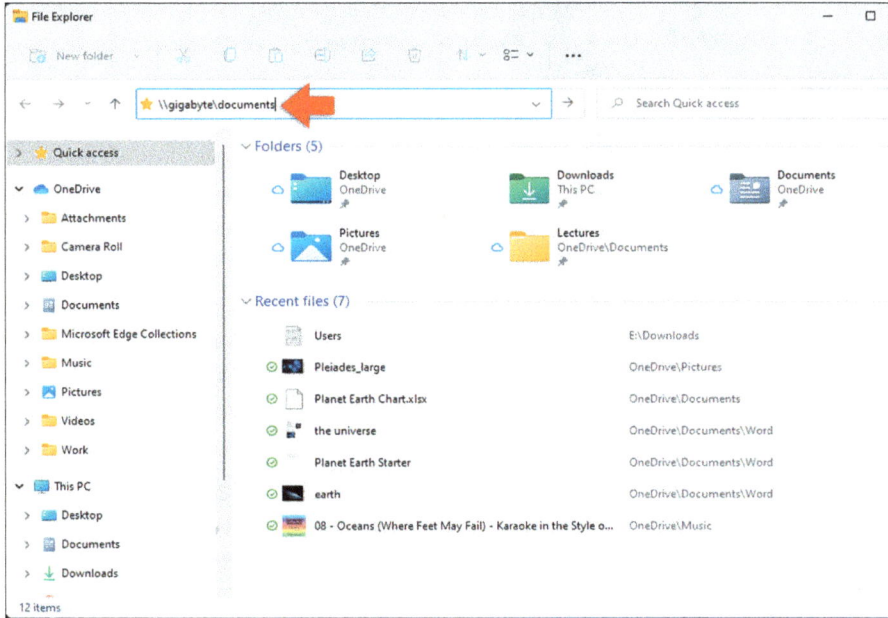

Enter the username and password you created for this user (the username and password you created on page 357)

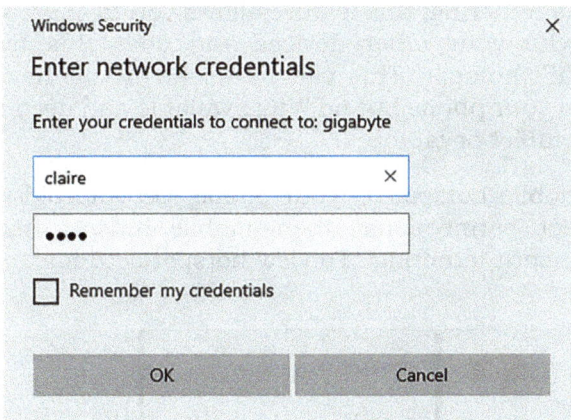

If you connect to this folder often, click 'remember my credentials'.

Click 'ok' when you're done.

Your PC will connect to the shared folder. Here, you can see we're now connected to the documents folder on PC 1.

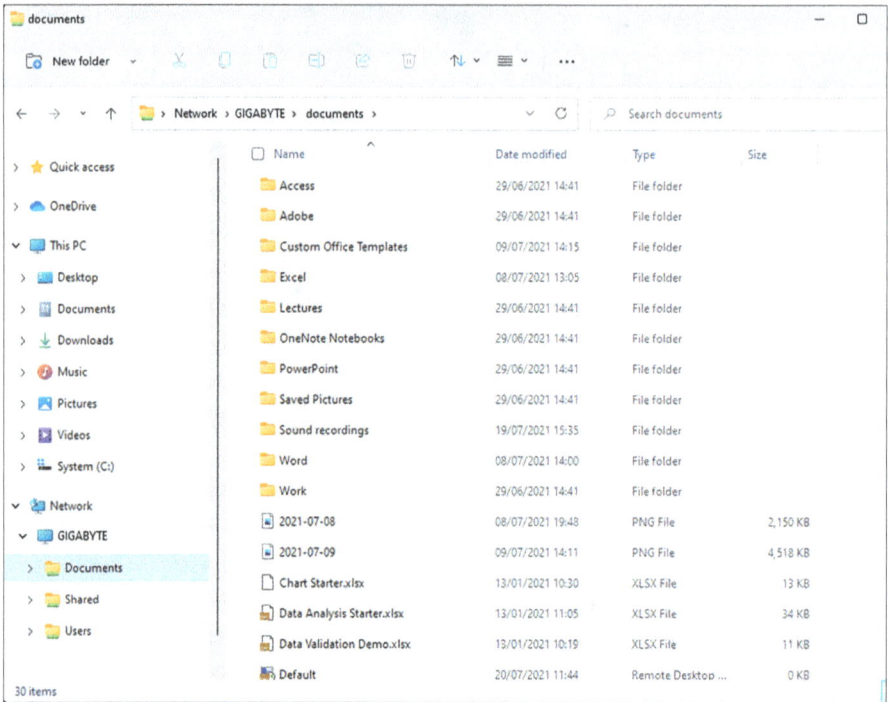

# Mobile Hotspot

Also known as tethering, this feature allows you to share your internet connection with your other devices and does this by creating a temporary WiFi hotspot. This can be useful if you have a 4G data connection on your phone but no WiFi available and need to access the internet on a tablet or laptop.

Enable the mobile hotspot on your phone. On Android phones go to settings, select 'connections', then 'mobile hotspot and tethering'. Turn on 'bluetooth tethering'. To view hotspot settings, tap on 'mobile hotspot'.

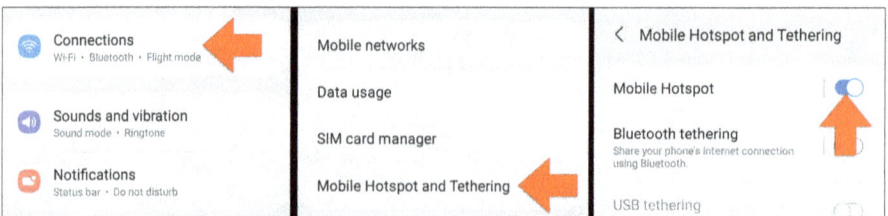

On your laptop or tablet, tap on the WiFi icon on the right hand side of your taskbar to reveal the available networks.

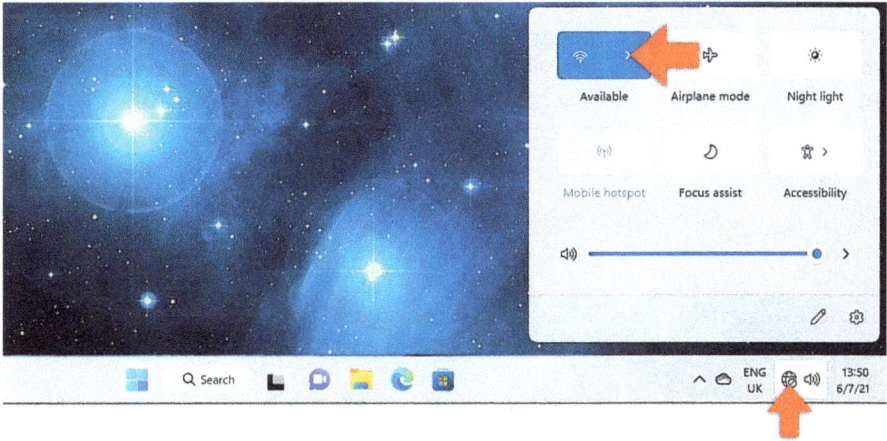

The network name is usually the name of your phone. Look at the mobile hotspot settings. You'll find the network name and password.

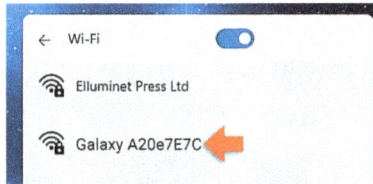

On your laptop or tablet, select the network name from the list and enter the password. Click 'next'.

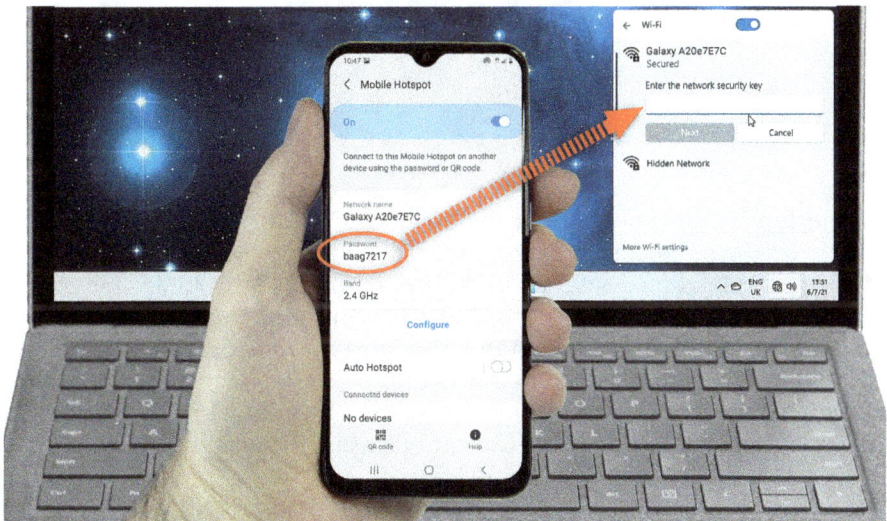

# Phone Link

Phone Link (formerly "Your Phone") is pre-installed on most Windows 11 PCs, and is a feature that allows you connect your smartphone to your PC. Once linked, your PC can display your phone's notifications, let you send and receive text messages, browse your photos, and even make or take phone calls—depending on the phone and features supported.

Phone Link communicates with a companion app installed on your phone. On Android, the app is called Link to Windows, and it's available in the Google Play Store. On iPhone, Phone Link uses a Bluetooth-based integration, available from Windows 11 version 22H2 onwards—but with limited functionality compared to Android.

See page 125 for information on how to set up phone link.

Open the Phone Link app, you'll find it on your start menu.

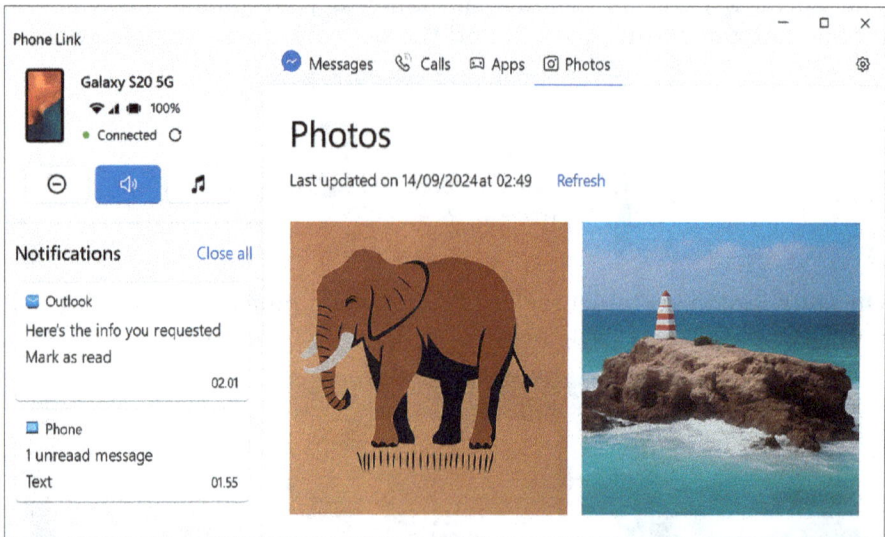

At the top of the Phone Link window, you'll find the navigation bar, which lets you access key features of your connected phone. The Messages tab allows you to view and send SMS or MMS messages directly from your PC. Selecting Calls lets you make and receive phone calls using your PC's microphone and speakers, while routing the call through your phone's cellular connection. The Apps tab—available on supported Android devices such as Samsung Galaxy and Surface Duo models—lets you launch and use mobile apps in resizable windows, as if they were native desktop applications.

The Photos tab displays a gallery of the most recent images stored on your phone, allowing you to view, copy, or drag them into other apps or folders. On the top right, the Settings (gear icon) opens the configuration panel, where you can manage permissions, device preferences, and notification behavior.

On the top left, you'll see device-specific information. The Device Name field displays the name of the connected phone—in this example, "Galaxy S20 5G" Underneath this, a series of status icons show the phone's battery level, Wi-Fi signal strength, and whether it's currently connected. The Connection Indicator, which shows a green "Connected" label, confirms that the phone is actively linked to the PC. Below these indicators, volume and audio controls allow you to quickly toggle between sound modes on the phone: silent, vibrate, or ring. These controls can be especially useful when managing calls or notifications from your desktop.

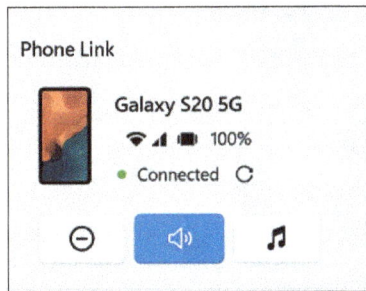

Phone Link

Galaxy S20 5G

📶 ▄ 🔋 100%

● Connected ↻

Below the device specific information, you'll see the notifications panel. This mirrors your phone's notifications in real time. Here, you can see messages, missed calls, app alerts, and calendar reminders as they arrive. You can dismiss notifications, reply to messages from supported apps, or take quick actions such as calling back missed calls—all without needing to pick up your phone. This panel helps streamline multitasking by keeping all your alerts visible on your PC while you work.

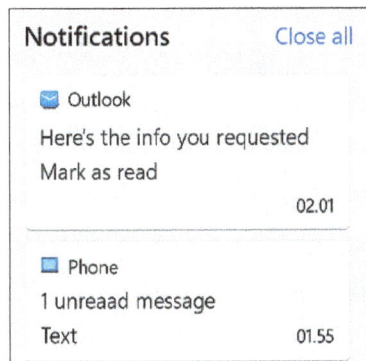

Notifications                    Close all

✉ Outlook

Here's the info you requested

Mark as read

                                        02.01

⬜ Phone

1 unreaad message

Text                                    01.55

# 8

# Multimedia Apps

Windows 11 has several multimedia applications available. There is an app to organise and enhance your digital photos whether it be from your phone or digital camera. There is also an app to take photographs using a windows tablet.

We'll also take a look at

- New Photos App
- New ClipChamp Editor
- Movies & TV App
- Media Player
- Playing DVDs & Blu-Rays
- Spotify
- Microsoft Paint

Windows 11 doesn't come with the ability to play DVDs but you can download some software that will allow you to still enjoy your DVD collection.

Let's begin by taking a look at the Photos app.

To help you better understand this section, take a look at the video resources. Scan the QR code, or open your web browser and type the following directly into the address bar at the top (don't use a search engine):

elluminetpress.com/win-mm

# Photos App

The Photos app has undergone significant enhancements, offering users a more intuitive and enriched photo viewing and editing experience. Microsoft has revamped the user interface, making it sleeker and more user-friendly, ensuring that navigation and photo organization are seamless. Additionally, the app now integrates advanced editing tools, allowing users to make professional-grade adjustments to their images without needing third-party software. With AI-driven features, the Photos app can automatically enhance images, recognize faces, and even suggest edits.

Once you start the photos app, you'll land on the main screen. Let's take a look around.

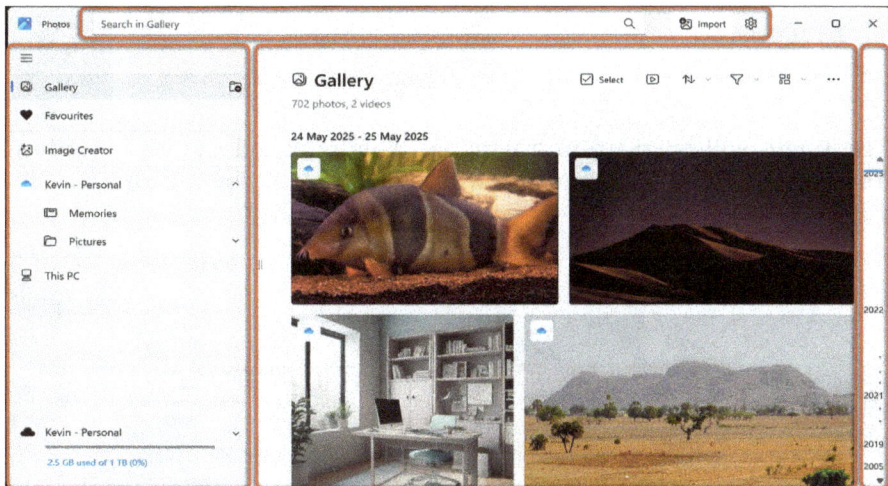

**Top Menu Bar** includes options to search through your collection, import new photos, and access the app settings.

**Navigation Pane** on the Left area allows you to select different views of your photo library, such as "All Photos", "Favorites", "Folders", and any albums you've created. At the bottom of the navigation pane you'll see your OneDrive storage. As well as a new "Image Creator" section.

**Timeline** on the right allows you to quickly navigate through years to find photos from specific periods. This timeline only appears once you move your mouse pointer over to the right edge of the screen.

**Photo Collection Area** in the Center displays thumbnails of your photos and videos. It is showing a range of dates at the top, suggesting that the photos are organized chronologically.

# View a Photo

To view a photo, double click on the thumbnail in the photo gallery section.

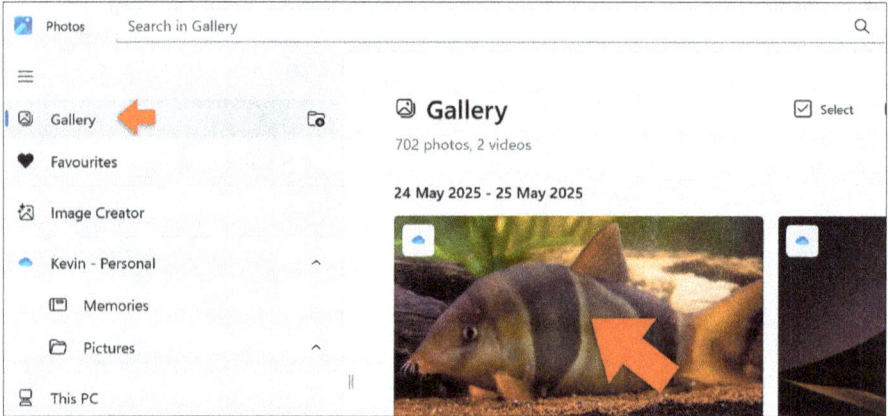

The photo will open up in a window. This is called the view window. You'll see the photo in the main window and along the top and bottom, you'll see some icons.

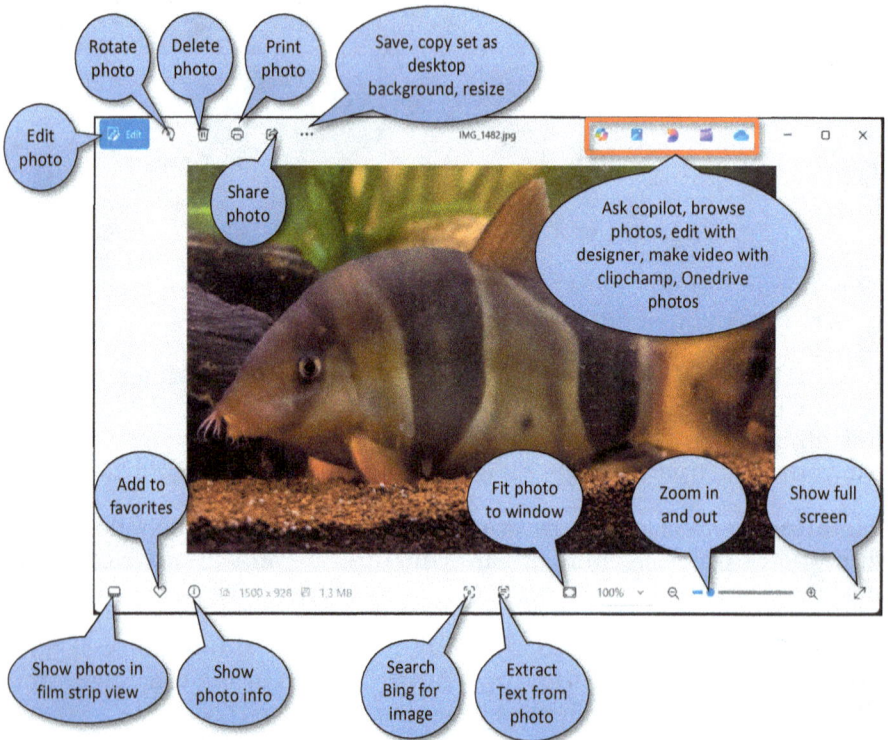

# Adjust a Photo

To adjust a photo, you'll need to open it in view mode as shown in the previous section on page 368.

Once you've opened the photo, select the 'edit' icon from the toolbar along the top of the 'view window'.

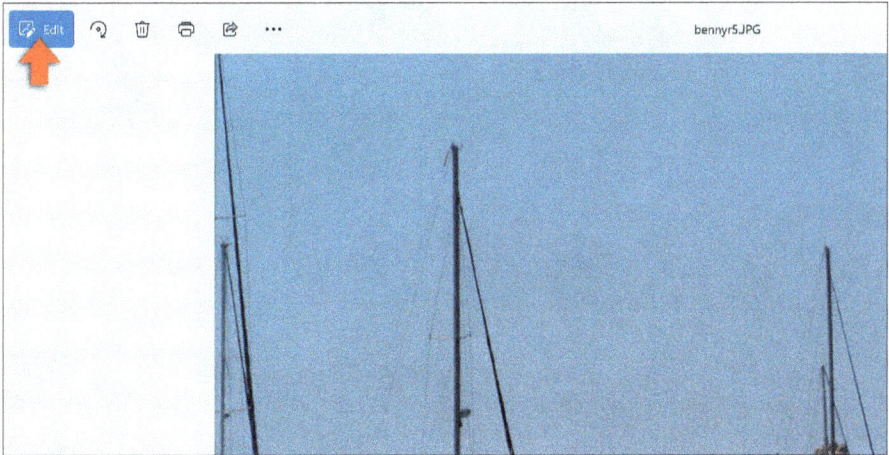

This will open the 'edit window'.

## Crop & Rotate

In the 'edit window', select the 'crop' icon from the toolbar along the top. Click and drag the blank markers around the part of the image you want to keep.

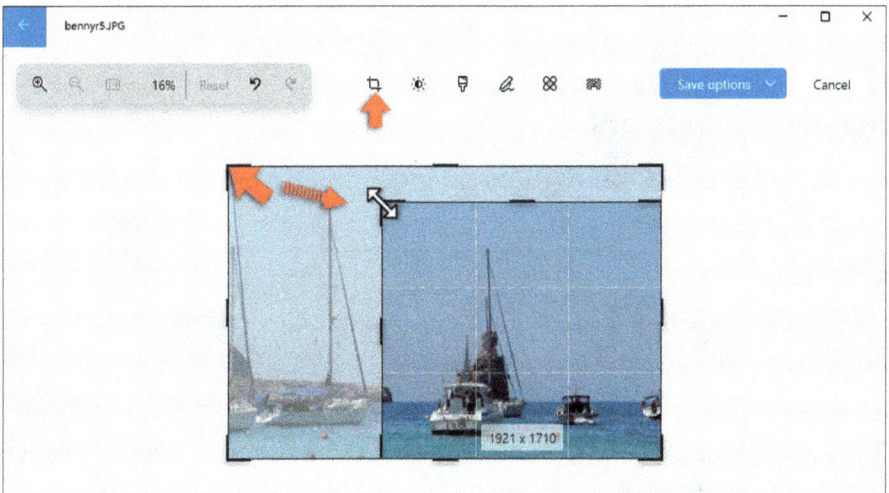

To rotate the image, use the rotate bar at the bottom of the window. Click and drag the black marker in the middle left or right to rotate the image.

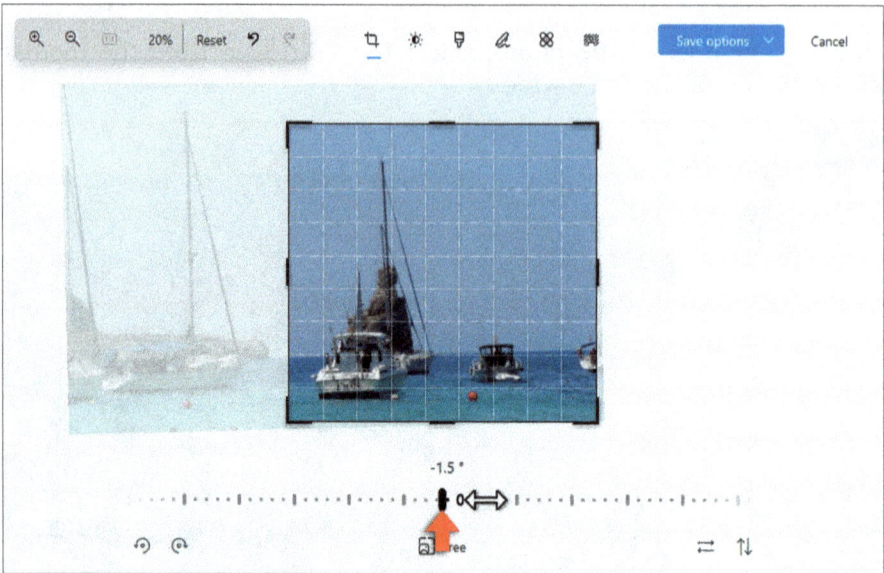

You can also rotate the image using the two controls on the bottom left. You can crop to a predefined size such as square, 4:3 or 16:9 using the 'free' icon on the bottom middle. You can also flip the image horizontally or vertically using the controls on the bottom right.

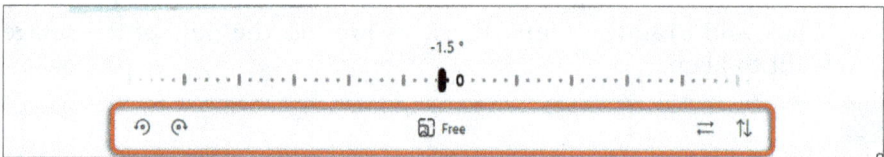

## Making Adjustments

In the 'edit window', select the 'adjustment' icon from the toolbar along the top.

You'll see a panel of sliders down the right hand side. Drag the slider left or right to make the adjustments.

**Brightness** adjusts the overall lightness or darkness of the image.

**Exposure** alters the image as if it were exposed to more or less light during shooting. Increasing exposure brightens the image, while decreasing it darkens the image.

**Contrast** changes the difference between the dark and light areas of the image. Increasing contrast makes the darks darker and the lights lighter, while decreasing it makes the image look more flat.

Light

| | |
|---|---|
| ☀ Brightness | 0 |
| ◕ Exposure | 0 |
| ◑ Contrast | 0 |
| ○ Highlights | 0 |
| ● Shadows | 0 |
| ▢ Vignette | 0 |

**Highlights** affects only the brightest parts of the image such as the sky. Moving the slider up makes the highlights brighter, and moving it down makes them less intense.

**Shadows** adjusts the darkness of the shadows in the image without affecting the brighter areas. Moving the slider up lightens the shadows, while moving it down darkens them.

**Vignette** adds or removes a darkening around the corners and edges of the photo. This can be used to draw attention to the center of the image or to give a photo a more dramatic or old-fashioned look.

By adjusting these sliders, you can correct lighting issues in a photo or create a particular mood or effect.

If you scroll down the list, you'll see another section called 'color'. These sliders allow you to adjust the color cast of the image.

**Saturation** controls the intensity of the colors in the image. Moving the slider to the right increases saturation, making colors more vivid and pronounced. Moving it to the left decreases saturation, which can lead to a more muted or even black-and-white image.

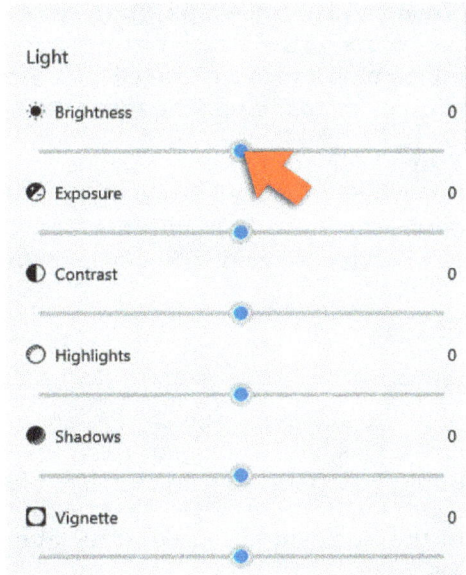

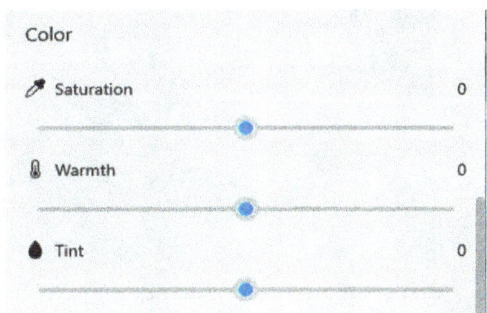

Color

| | |
|---|---|
| ✐ Saturation | 0 |
| 🌡 Warmth | 0 |
| ◗ Tint | 0 |

**Warmth** also known as white balance, adjusting this slider can make the colors in the image warmer (more yellow or orange tones) or cooler (more blue tones). It's used to correct color casts from different light sources or to change the mood of the photo.

**Tint** slider adjusts the balance between green and magenta tones in the image. Moving it one way will add a green tint, while moving it the other way will add a magenta tint. This can be used for creative effect or to correct specific color balance issues in the photo.

## Filters

Filters are pre-set adjustments that change the color and tone of a photo to achieve a specific look or effect. Filters can simulate different film styles, add vintage or retro effects, alter mood with color changes, or apply artistic conversions like black and white or sepia tones.

In the 'edit window', select the 'filters' icon from the toolbar along the top.

Select a filter from the options on the right hand panel.

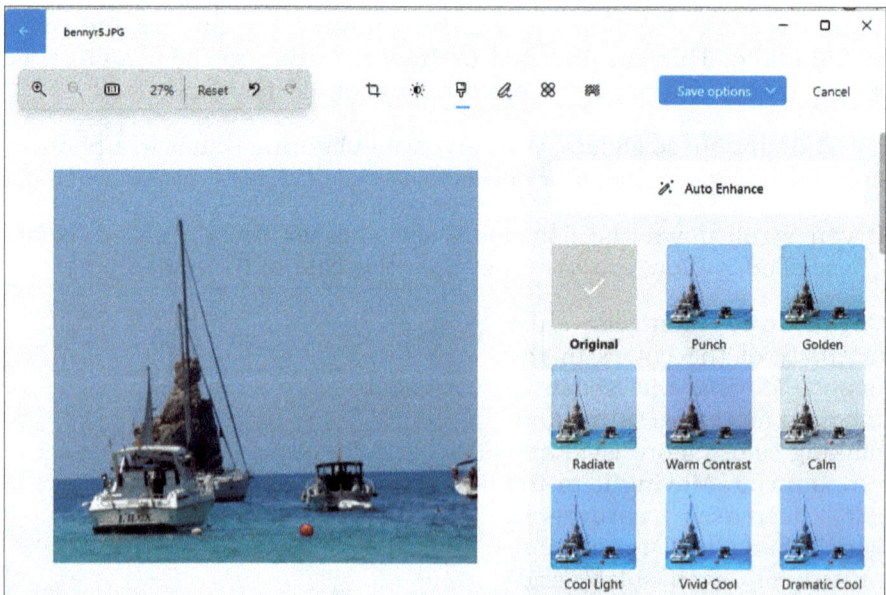

## Markup

This allows you to draw on the photograph using a pen. In the 'edit window', select the 'markup' icon from the toolbar along the top.

Use the tools along the bottom of the window to select your pen or marker to draw directly on the image.

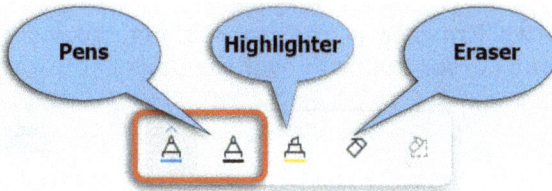

Select a pen, color and size.

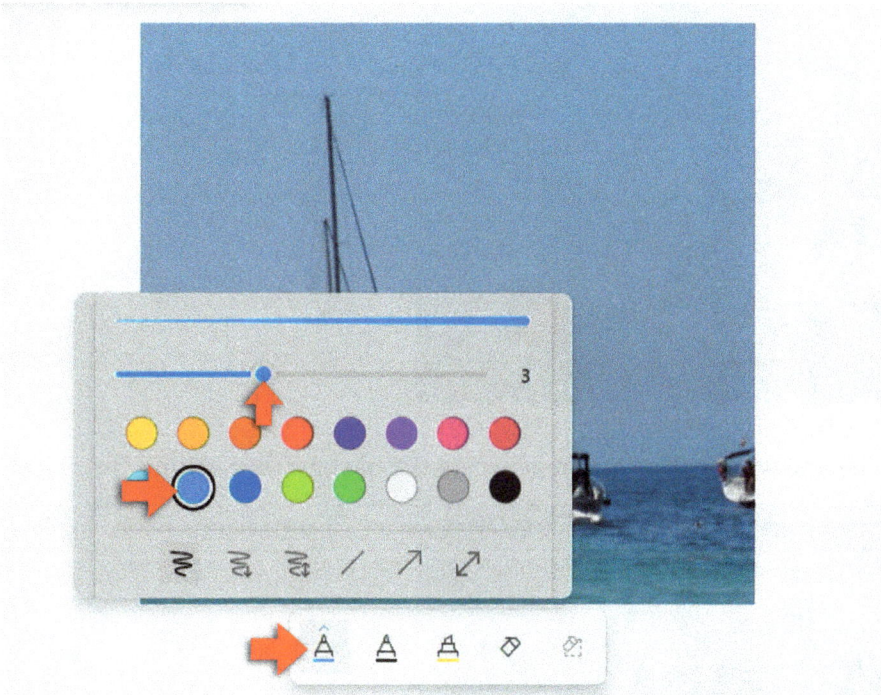

Then add your markups.

## Generative Erase

Allows you to remove unwanted elements from a photo. The app fills in the erased area using AI-generated content that blends naturally with the surrounding pixels. Only available on Copilot+ PCs with on-device NPU processing.

Double click on the photo from the photo gallery, then click 'edit' on the top left.

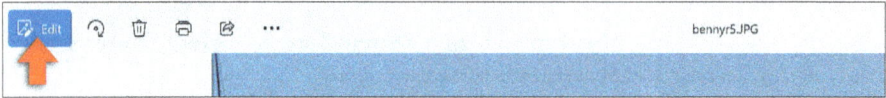

Select Generative Erase from the icons along the top middle of the screen. Use your cursor to brush over the object you want to remove.

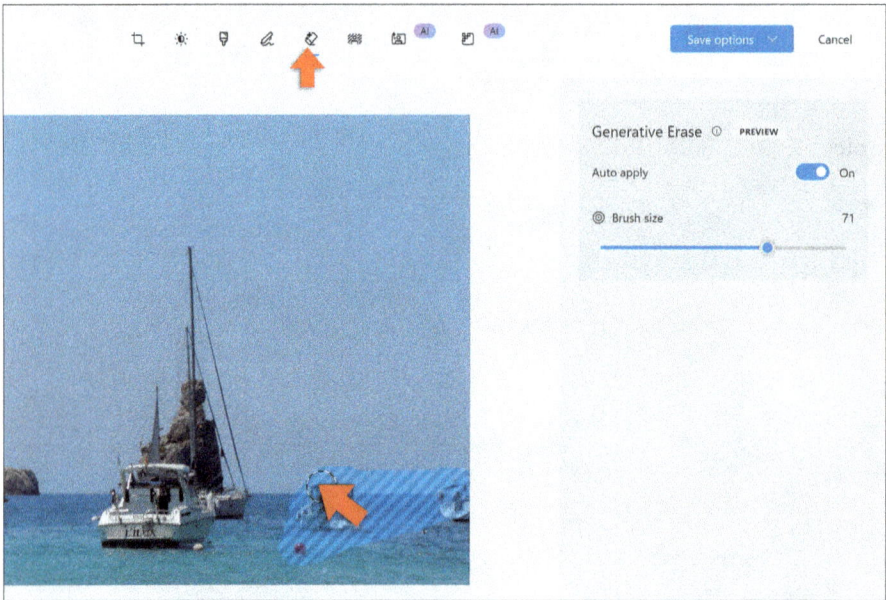

The app will analyze and regenerate the background behind the object.

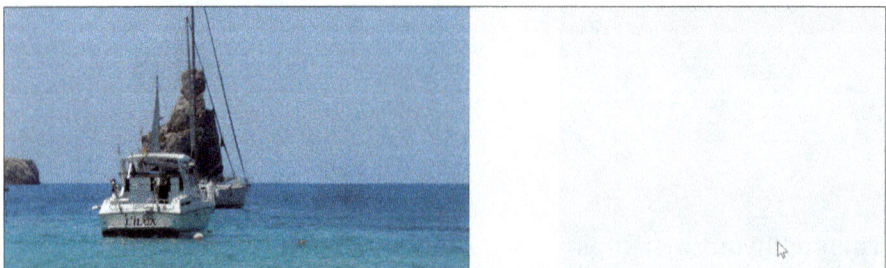

# Background Blur and Replacement

Applies an artificial blur to the background or replaces it with a different scene, similar to portrait effects on phones.

Double click on the photo from the photo gallery, then click 'edit' on the top left.

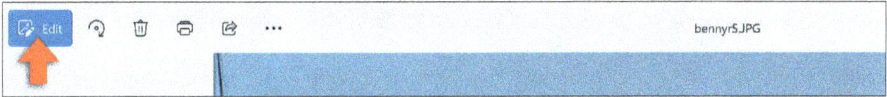

Select Background from the icons along the top middle of the screen.

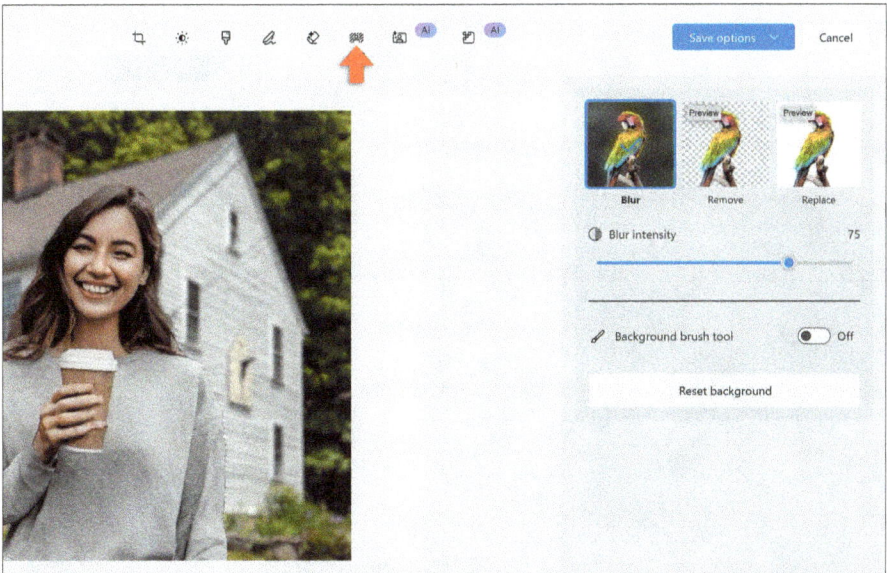

**Blur** softens the background using AI while keeping the subject in focus to create a portrait-style effect.

**Remove** deletes the background entirely, isolating the subject on a transparent layer.

**Replace** swaps the original background with a different color or image using AI-based segmentation.

**Blur Intensity Slider** adjusts how strongly the background is blurred, from minimal softening to a heavy blur effect.

**Background Brush Tool** allows you to manually refine which areas are treated as background by brushing over parts of the image to include or exclude them from the effect.

**375**

## Restyle Image

Applies artistic or themed filters to your photo using AI (e.g., turning a photo into a sketch, painting, or a specific visual style). Exclusive to Copilot+ PCs.

Double click on the photo from the photo gallery, then click 'edit' on the top left.

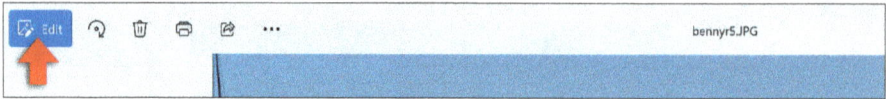

Select restyle from the icons along the top middle of the screen.

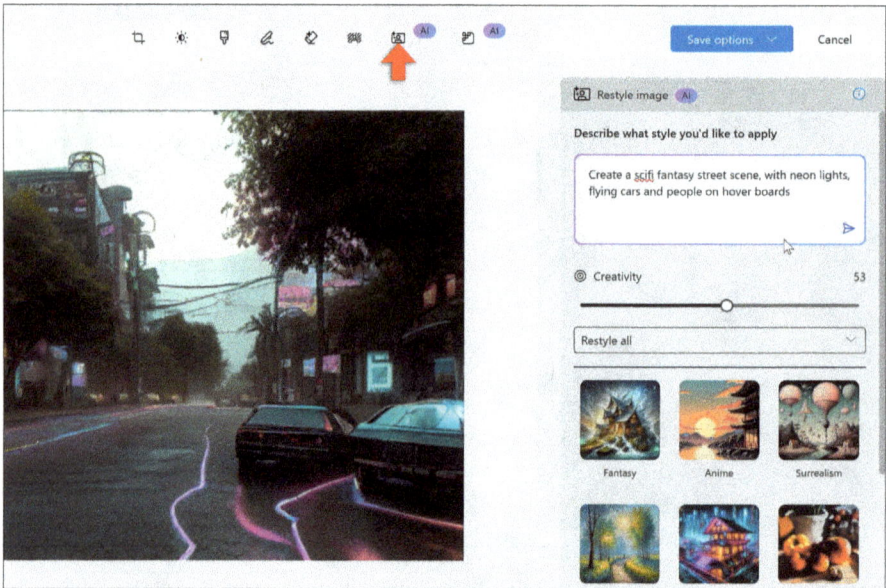

In the editing sidebar, choose from a range of AI-generated styles—these might include options like Sketch, Watercolor, Cartoon, Vintage, or other creative looks. Alternatively, you can type your own specifications or style prompts into the text field at the top to generate a custom visual transformation based on your input.

The Creativity Slider allows you to control how dramatically the AI transforms your image. At lower values, the result stays close to the original photo. As you increase the slider to medium levels, the AI introduces more noticeable changes in tone, detail, and atmosphere. At higher settings, the transformation becomes bold and imaginative, with the AI potentially altering the background, reshaping elements, or fully reinterpreting the scene to match your style prompt.

# ClipChamp Video Editor

ClipChamp is a video editor that allows you create videos using titles, filters, and other visual effects.

To start ClipChamp, open your start menu, select 'all apps' on the top right. Scroll down and select ClipChamp. If you don't see the app, open the Microsoft Store, search for ClipChamp then click 'get'.

Once the app opens, you'll need to sign up for a new account. Enter your date of birth and country/region. Click 'continue'.

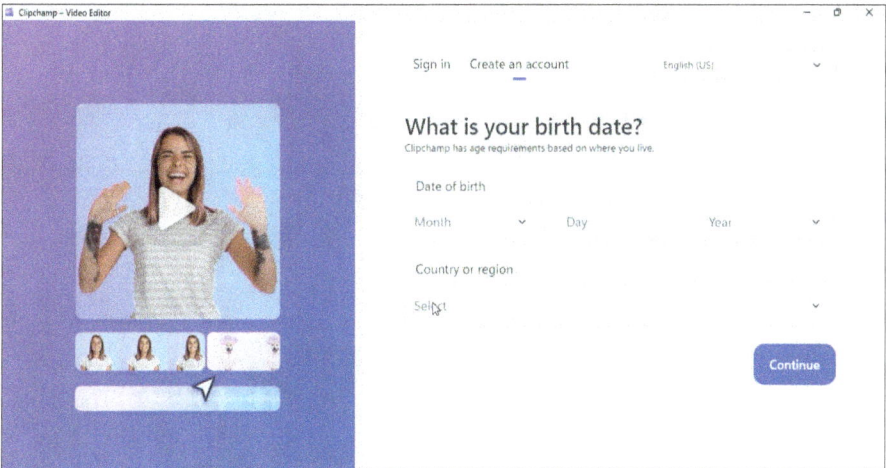

Once you've done that, you'll land on the home screen.

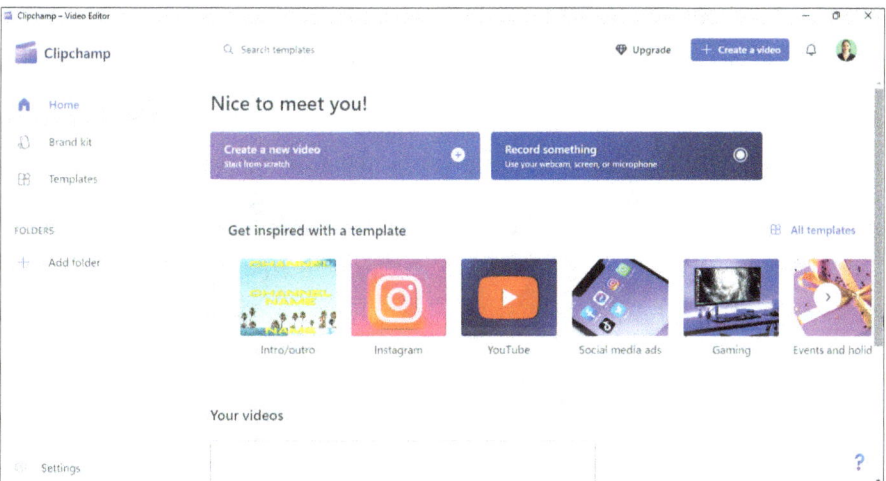

To create a new video, click 'create video' on the top right of the screen.

## Edit Screen

You'll land on the edit screen. Along the left hand side, you'll see some icons. Here you can import videos and photos stored on your OneDrive or device, you can record from your screen or webcam, you can choose from a list of ready made templates complete with graphics and text. Further down you can add music and sound effects, you can find a list of ready to use stock videos and photos, as well as shapes and stickers you can use to spice up your videos. Keep in mind that some of the stock photos and videos aren't free - the ones marked 'premium' will need to be paid for.

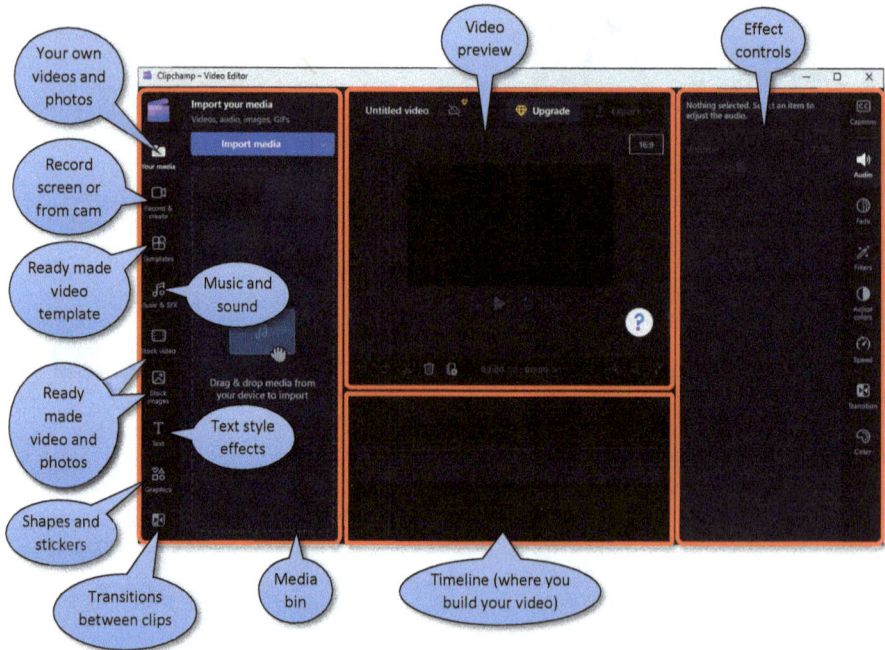

In the middle of the screen, you'll see a preview window. This is where you'll be able to watch the video you're creating. Underneath the preview window, you'll see the timeline. This is where you place all your video clips, photos and graphics to build up your video.

Over on the right hand side you'll see all the effect controls. This allows you to edit the sound, change brightness, add filters and so on.

## Adding your own Videos & Photos

The first thing you might want to do is add some of your video. To do this, select 'your media' from the toolbar on the left. Then click 'import media'

**378**

From the dialog box, browse to and select the video or photo you want to add

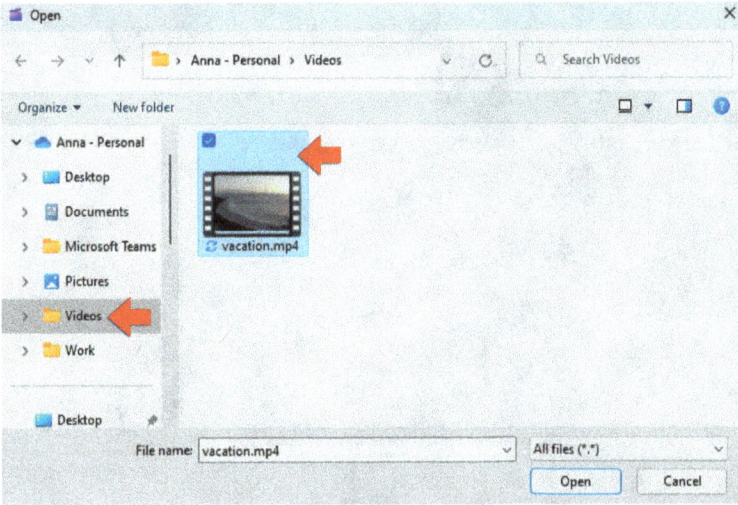

Your file will appear in the media bin. To add the file to the timeline, click and drag the file to the area on the bottom center of the screen.

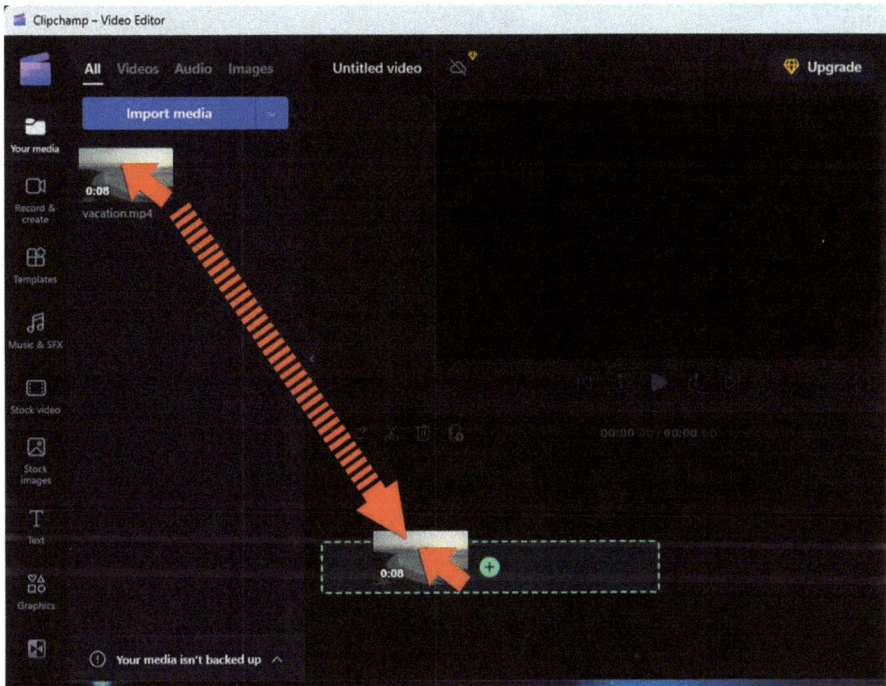

Do the same with all other media you want to add

# Chapter 8: Multimedia Apps

You'll see a preview appear at the top of the screen and your clip will appear on the timeline.

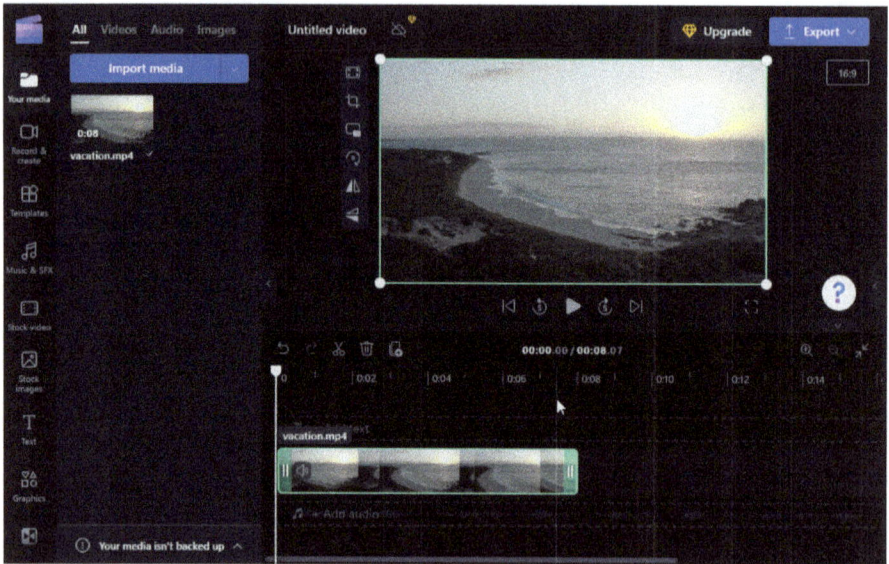

Use the markers on either side of the clip on the timeline to trim the clip.

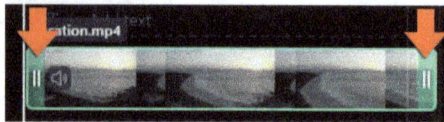

Try adding some stock videos, photos and music using the options on the toolbar on the left hand side.

To export the clip, click 'export', then choose the quality: 720p or 1080p.

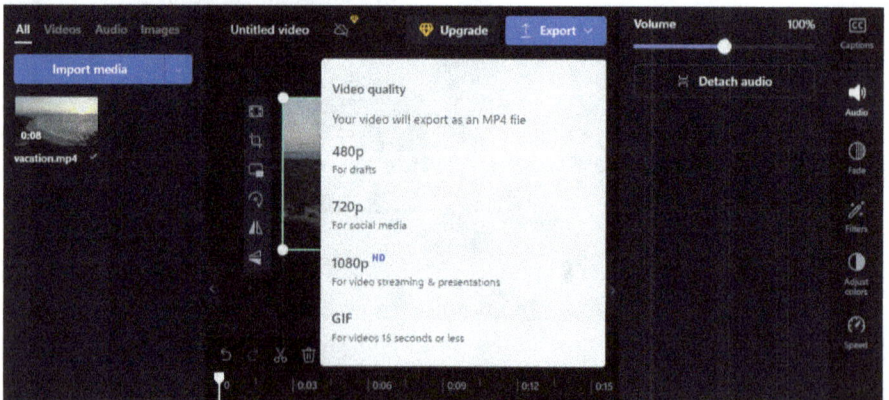

# Camera App

The camera app makes use of the on board camera on your windows tablet to take photographs. To start the camera app, open the start menu, select 'all apps' on the top right, click on 'camera'.

Camera

Your tablet usually has two cameras: a front facing camera, and a rear camera. The rear camera is usually higher quality and for taking photos/videos of things, while the front facing camera is usually for video calls and selfies.

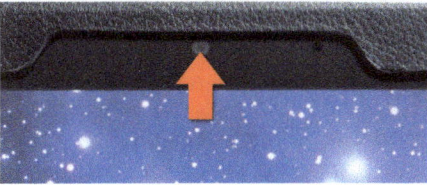

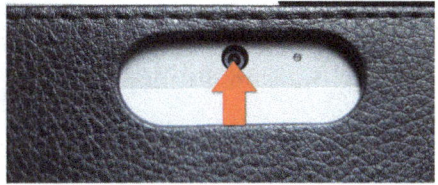

When you start up the camera app, you'll see an image from your camera on screen.

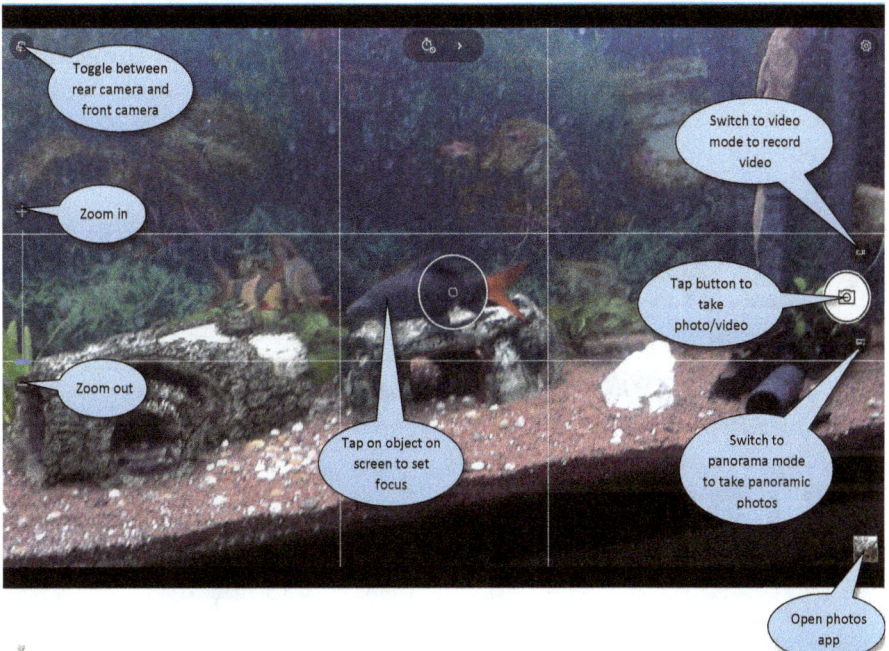

Tap on the small camera icon to take a photo.

Once you have taken your photo, you can view them by tapping/ clicking the icon on the bottom right to view in photo app.

You can also take movies by tapping on the 'switch to video' icon, on the right hand side. This works just like a video camcorder.

You can also take panoramic photos. To do this, tap the panoramic photo icon, on the right hand side. You'll see a square box appear along the centre of the screen. Point the camera at the position in the scene you want the panoramic photo to start. Tap the large white button, on the right hand side of your screen. Now, pan the camera to your right, rotating around your hips/shoulders, until you have covered the scene. You'll see the box in the centre of the screen start to build your image.

Tap the large white button again, to finish.

You can also adjust your exposure settings such as ISO, White Balance, Shutter Speed and Brightness on your camera, as well as set a timer delay. To access these settings, tap the 'pro' icon on the top of your screen.

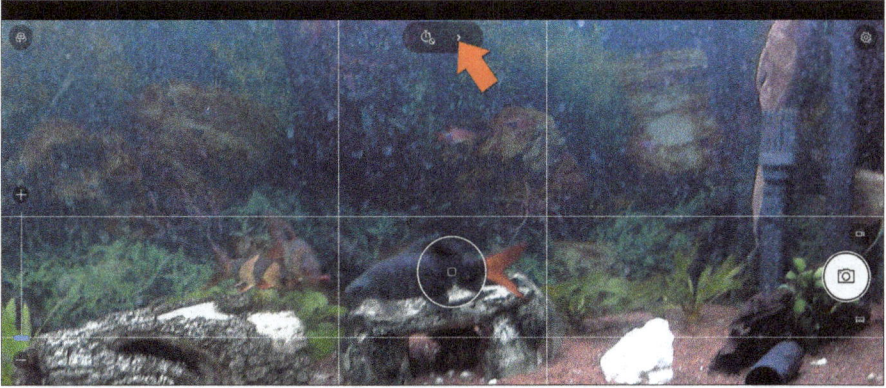

This will reveal the exposure settings.

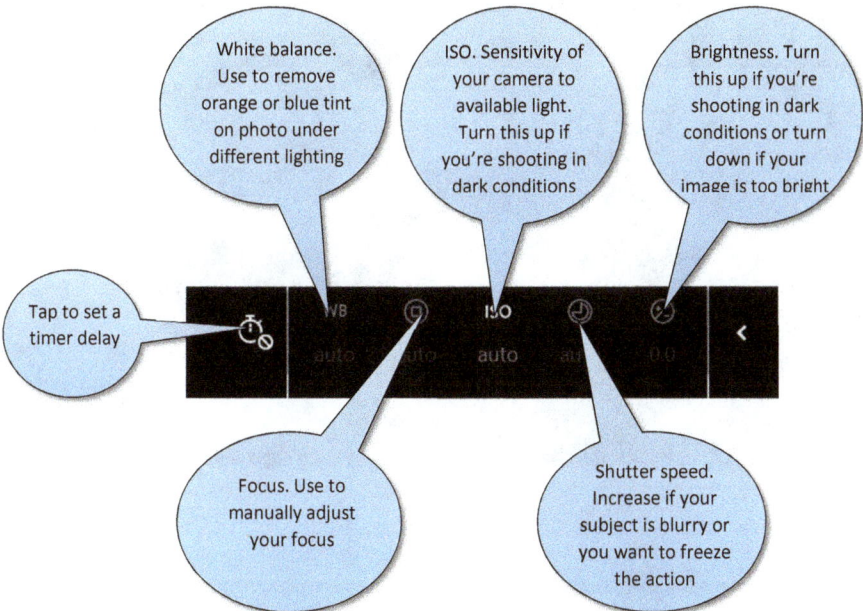

To adjust the settings, tap on one of the icons.

In this example, I am going to adjust the ISO. So tap on the ISO icon.

When you do this, you'll notice a semi-circle control appear around the 'take photo' icon, on the right hand side of your screen.

**383**

To make the adjustment, tap on 'ISO', on the right of the screen, then drag this upwards to increase the ISO, drag it downwards to decrease the ISO, as illustrated below.

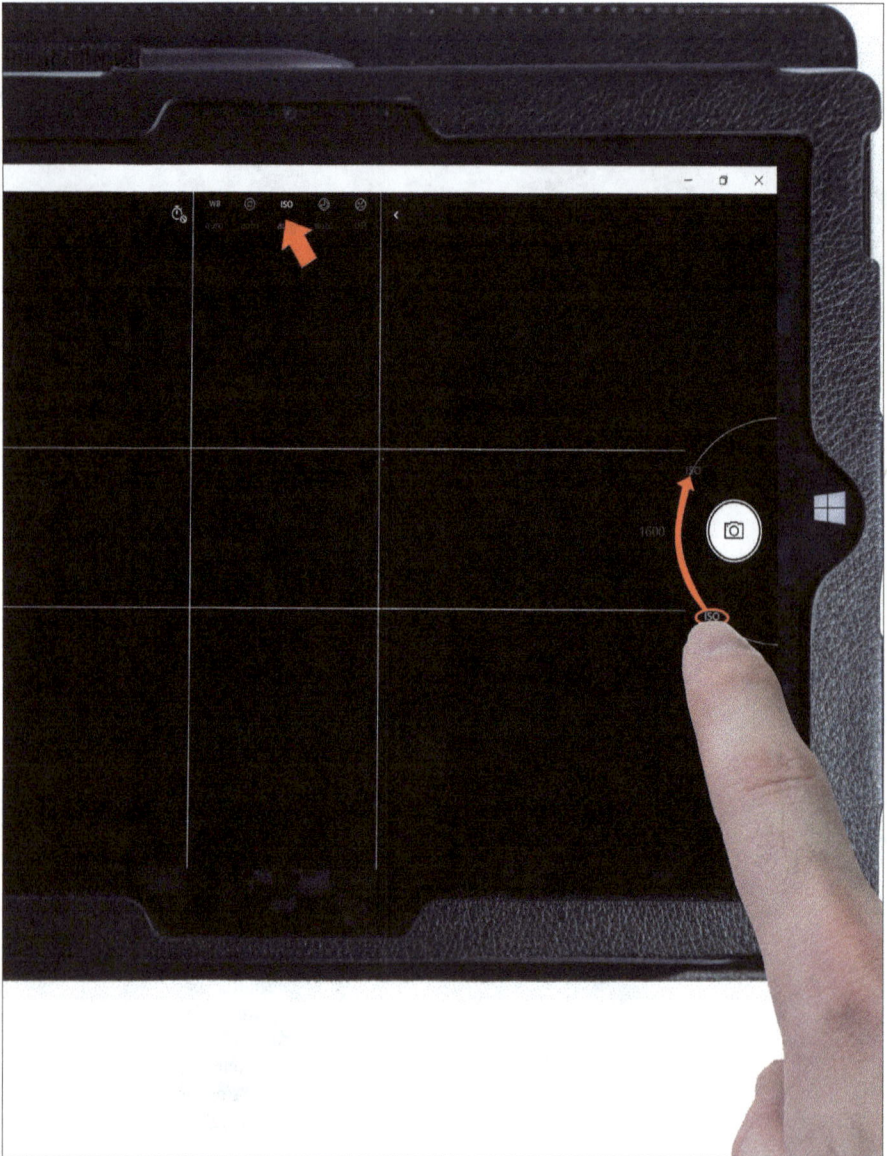

You'll see the value in the centre increase or decrease as you make your adjustment. In this example, I've set the ISO to 1600.

You can use this technique for the other settings too (white balance, focus, shutter speed and brightness).

# Movies & TV App

With the Movies & TV app (Films & TV in some regions) you can watch the latest TV shows and movies, as well as your own video content you've taken with your phone or a digital camera. This app is no longer pre-installed, however you can download it from the Microsoft Store.

Once you've downloaded it, you will find the Movies & TV app on your start menu.

Movies & TV

Along the top of your screen you'll see three categories: Explore, Purchased and Personal.

Browse latest films and tv shows

View TV shows and films you've purchased

View your own video content from phone or digital camera

Search for shows, films, actors etc

Browse films & TV shows in Microsoft Store

Adjust settings

Explore film and TV trailers for the latest content

Explore 360 videos where you can 'look' around a 3D video

Explore the latest film releases in your region

Explore the latest TV Show releases in your region

Click thumbnail to view movie or TV show details

In the 'explore' category you'll be able to browse through the latest TV shows and movies that have been released in your region/country. You can scroll down the page and select the ones you're interested in.

In the 'purchased' category, you'll see a list of all the movies and TV shows you have purchased. This is where you can select them to watch.

The 'personal' category will show you video content you have taken with your camera

## Purchasing Content

Once you have found the movie or TV show you want to watch, select the thumbnail cover to view the show's details.

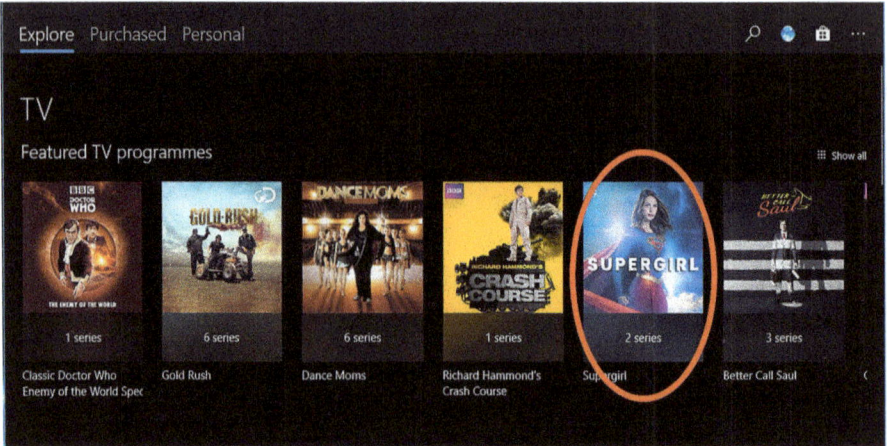

You'll be redirected to the Microsoft Store. On the store page you'll see some details about the series or movie. To buy the movie, or buy a whole season if it's a TV show, click the 'starts at' or 'buy' button.

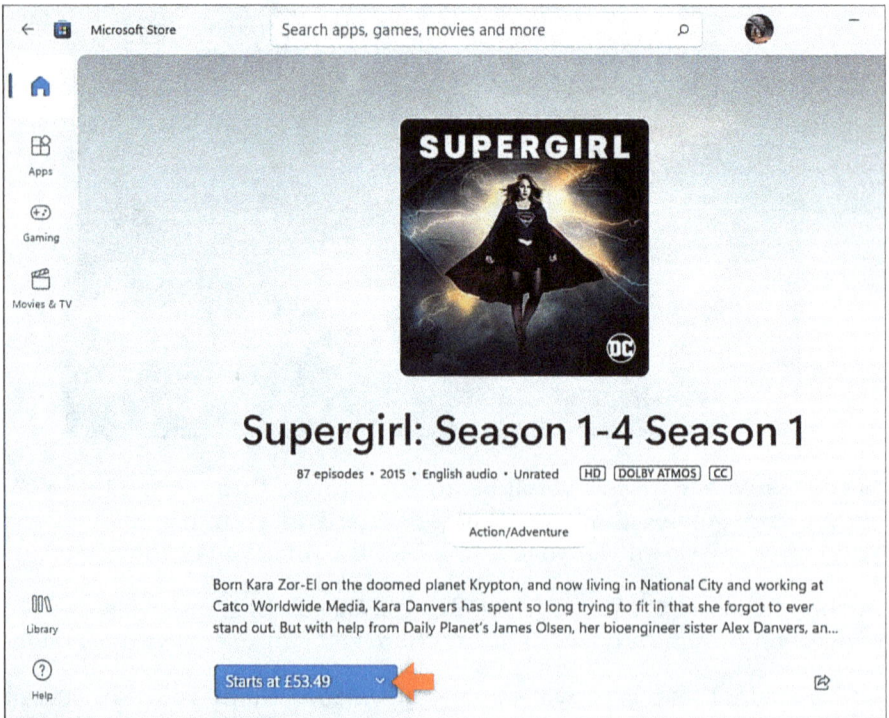

Scroll down further and you'll see a list of each episode. Here you can purchase individual episodes. To do this just click the price button next to the episode you want

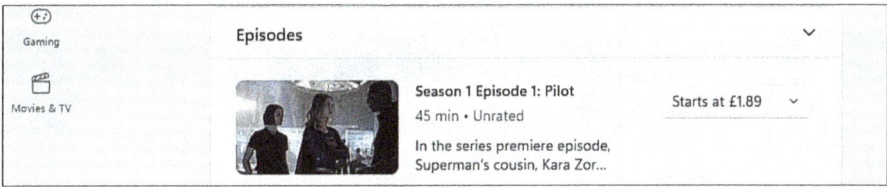

Select 'High Definition' if prompted, then enter your microsoft account email and password, along with payment details. Follow the instructions on screen.

## Viewing Purchased Content

You'll find all the movies and TV shows you have purchased in the 'purchased' section on the main screen.

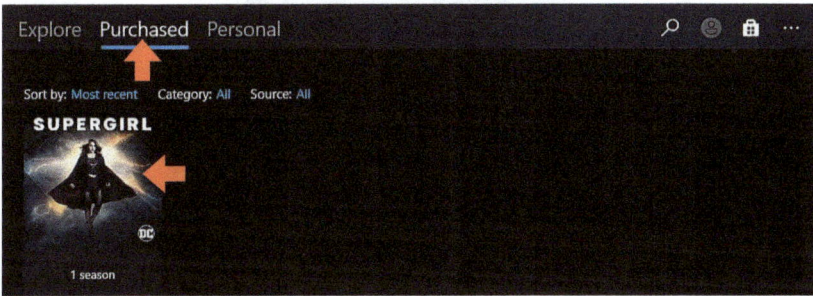

Click thumbnail to play, then select an episode if you're watching a TV show.

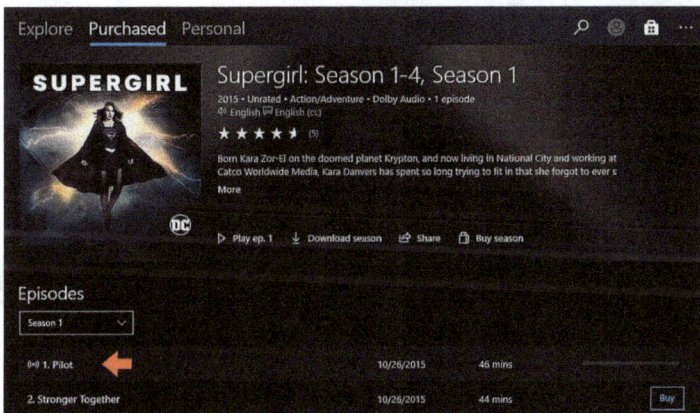

Make sure you click the little play button next to the episode title.

## Search for New Content

To search for TV shows and movies, click the magnifying glass icon on the top right of your screen.

In the search field, type in the show's name or the film's title. Press enter

By default, the search algorithm searches your purchased collection. To search for new content, you'll need to select 'search in microsoft store'

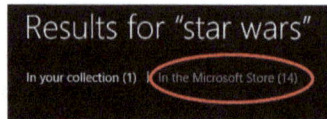

Here you'll be able to click on the thumbnails to view details and purchase the content.

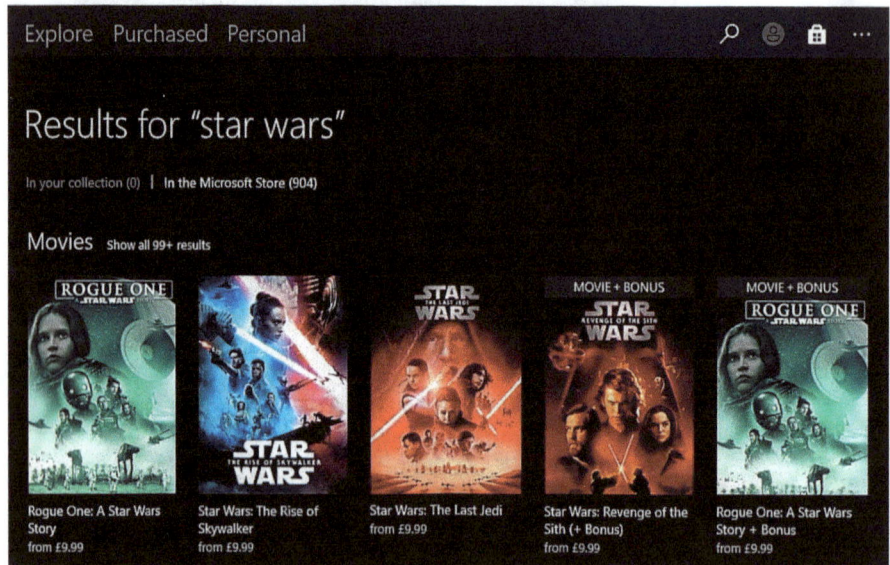

Just click on the cover of the movie you want to watch.

You'll find all the movies and TV shows you have purchased in the 'purchased' section on the main screen.

## Personal Content

This is where you can see the video content you have taken with your camera. Select the 'personal' category from the top of the main screen.

Along the top of the personal content window you'll see: 'video folders', 'removable storage' and 'media servers'.

Select 'video folders' to see video clips stored on your device or PC. You can also add other folders - to do this click 'add folder'.

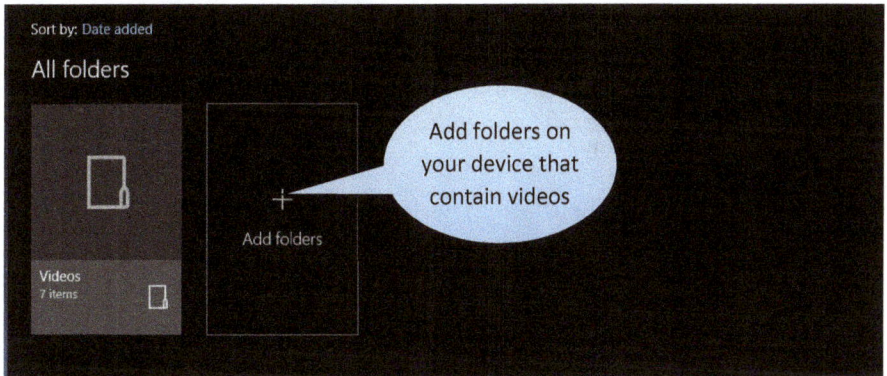

Scroll down a bit further to see all the clips in the folder.

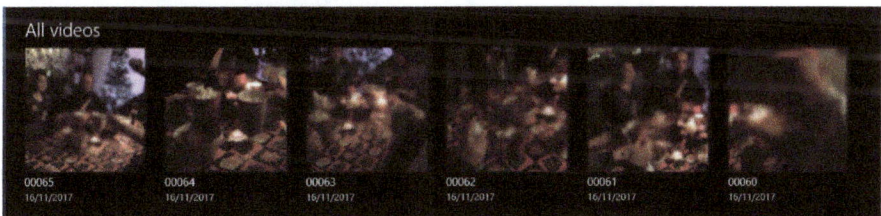

Click on one of the clips to view.

**389**

# Media Player

With the release of Windows 11 version 24H2, Microsoft has introduced a significantly enhanced Media Player, designed to unify and modernize the Windows media playback experience. The updated Media Player integrates functionalities from the legacy Groove Music and Movies & TV applications, providing a consolidated platform for both audio and video playback. Media Player scans default folders (such as Music, Videos) automatically, but you may need to add media manually if stored elsewhere.

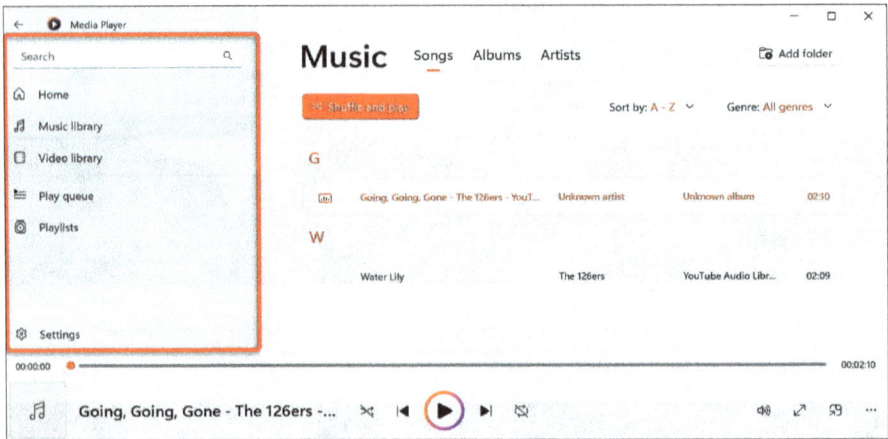

On the navigation bar on the left hand side, the **Search** bar at the top lets you quickly find specific songs, albums, artists, or videos by typing a keyword.

**Home** returns you to the main overview screen, where you can access recent content or continue listening to recently played media.

**Music library** shows all the audio content found in the folders you've added, organized by songs, albums, and artists.

**Video library** displays the video files from your added video folders, allowing you to browse and play movies or clips.

**Play queue** shows the list of tracks currently lined up for playback, including upcoming songs and the current one playing.

**Playlists** lets you access, create, edit, and play your saved custom playlists.

**Settings** at the bottom of the pane opens the app's configuration options, where you can manage library folders, playback behavior, storage, and privacy settings.

At the bottom of the window is the playback bar. This displays the currently playing track, including the title and artist. A timeline at the top shows playback progress from start to finish. Playback controls in the center include options to shuffle tracks, skip to the previous track, play or pause, skip to the next track, and repeat the current track or playlist. Over on the right, additional controls let you adjust the volume, and toggle between full screen and mini-player modes. The three dots icon on the right opens settings to cast to another device, playback speed, and the graphic equalizer.

You can create playlists of your favorite music. In the left sidebar, click on Music library, then select Songs, Albums, or Artists to browse your collection.

Find a song you want to add to a playlist. Right click on the song title. Select Add to > New playlist.

A small box will appear—type a name for your playlist (e.g., "Road Trip") and press Enter. To add additional songs, right click on another song, select Add to, then choose the name of the playlist you previously created. The song will be added to that playlist immediately. You can repeat this process to add as many songs as you like.

You'll find the playlist on the playlists section on the left hand side.

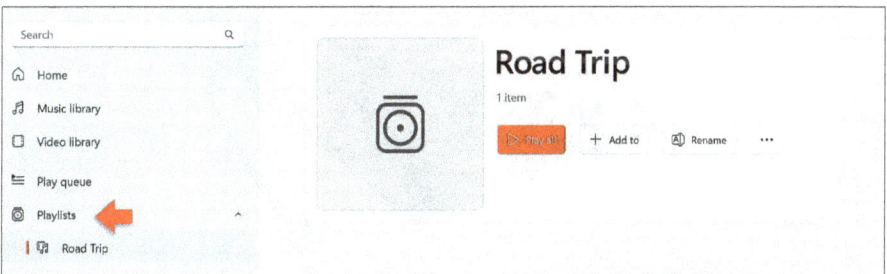

# Playing DVDs & Blu-Rays

If you like watching DVDs or Blu-rays on your PC, Windows 11 can't play them out of the box, nor do the latest devices have DVD drives, so you'll need an external DVD drive and a free media player.

The best one I found is VLC Media Player, which can play DVDs, Blu-ray, CDs and a range of other file types.

Just go to the following website and download the software.

```
www.videolan.org
```

Click the 'Download VLC' on the homepage.

Click 'Run' when prompted by your browser and follow the instructions on screen.

DVDs & Blu-rays are becoming obsolete, thanks to high speed internet services available to most homes, video/film streaming services that allow you to access on demand films, and television programs you can access from the comfort of your favourite arm chair.

Many computers, particularly laptops and mobile devices no longer include a Blu-ray/DVD drive. You can still buy external USB DVD / Blu-ray drives if you need them.

Once you've installed VLC player, you'll find it on your start menu. Click 'all apps', then scroll down to 'VideoLAN', then click 'VLC Media Player'

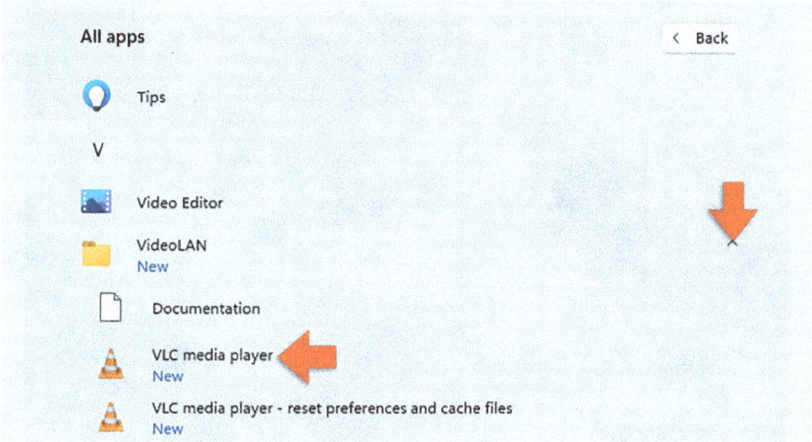

Insert the disc into the DVD/Blu-ray drive either on your computer or an external USB drive.

Click the play button on the bottom left of the VLC Media Player window.

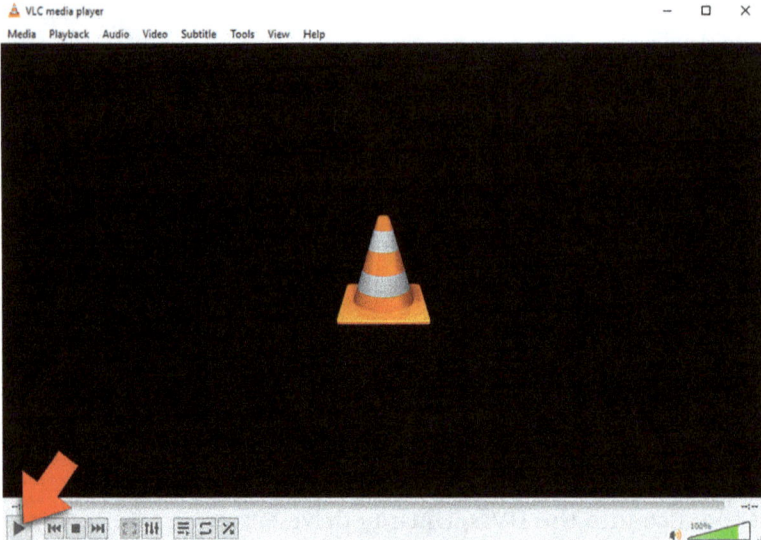

From the pop up dialog box, select the 'disc' tab along the top.

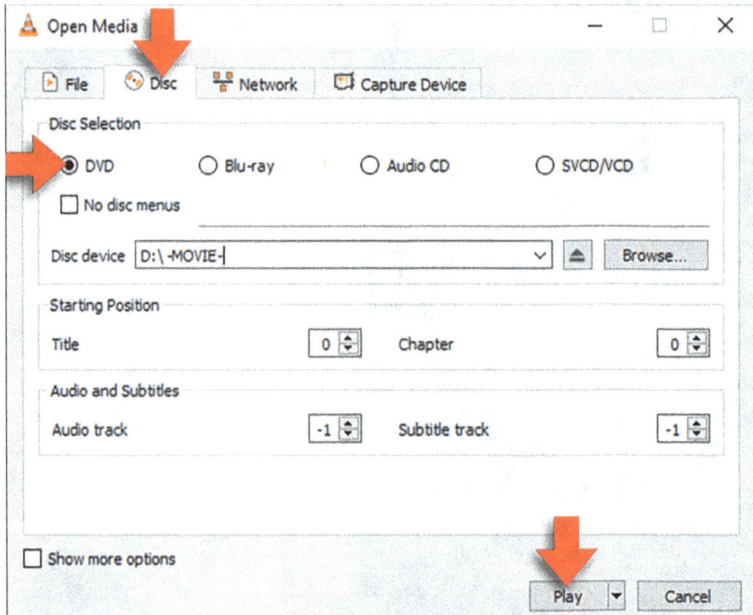

Make sure 'DVD' is selected from the 'disc selection' options for DVD movies, and 'blu-ray' for blu-ray movies. Click 'play' to start playing the movie.

**394**

# Spotify

Spotify is a music streaming app where you can stream all your favourite music for free. The free service is supported by adverts, although you can subscribe to the service for £9.99 a month ad free.

You'll find the Spotify music app on your start menu.

*If you don't see it, go to the Microsoft store, then search for and download Spotify.*

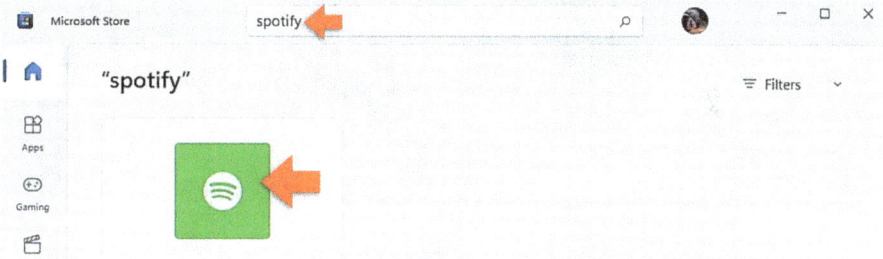

Once downloaded and installed, you can start the Spotify app from your start menu. You'll need to sign up for a free account. Click 'sign up for free' and fill in your details. If you already use Spotify, click 'log in'.

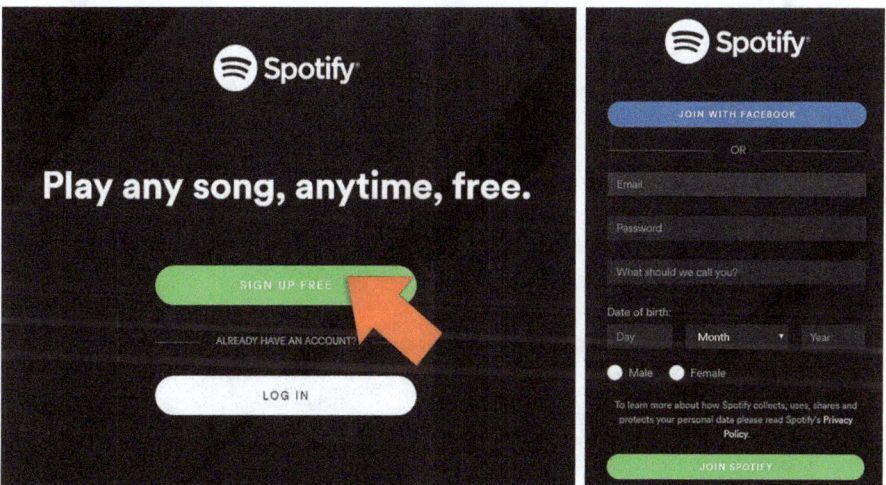

Click 'join Spotify' when you're finished.

## Chapter 8: Multimedia Apps

With Spotify, you can search for any song, album or artist you like. Just type it into the search field at the top of the screen.

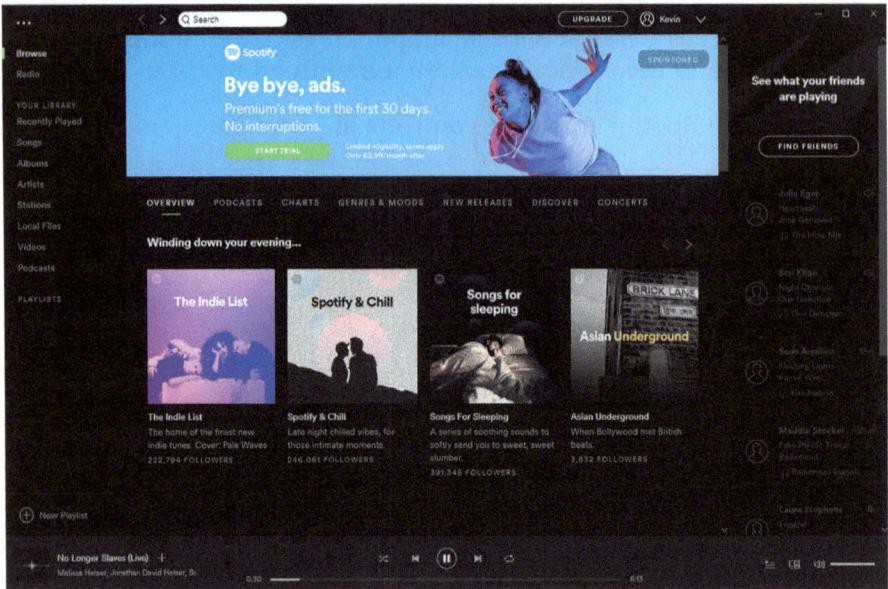

You can scroll down the main page and browse through the genres. Once you've found a song, either by searching or browsing through your favourite genres, you can add them to your library. To do this, click the '+' sign to the left of the track name.

You'll find the tracks in your library on the top left of the main screen

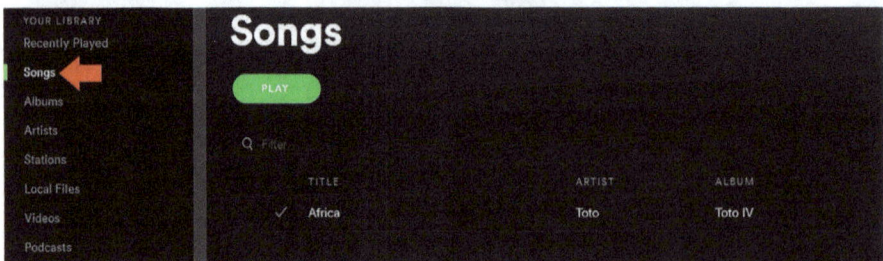

Click on the track to play.

# Microsoft Paint

Paint is a simplified graphics editor able to edit Windows bitmap, JPEG, GIF, PNG, WEBP, HEIC, ICO and single-page TIFF formats.

You'll find the paint icon on your start menu.

Paint

## Drawing

Once paint opens, you'll land on the main screen. Along the top of the window you'll find your tools. Select a brush, a size, then a color.

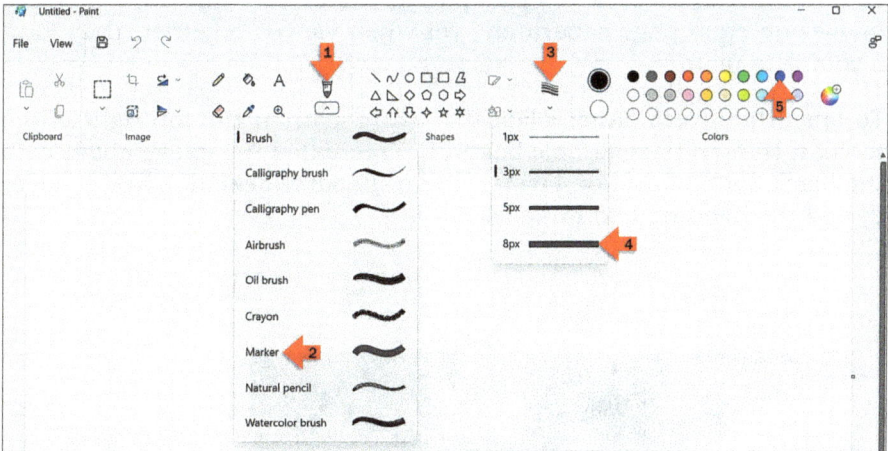

Now you can draw on the canvas.

# Chapter 8: Multimedia Apps

## Layers

A highly requested feature, layers give users more control over their creations. This allows for the editing, managing, and composing of images with more depth and detail, without affecting other parts of the work.

Layers in image editing are akin to transparent sheets stacked on top of each other where each layer can contain different parts of an image or effect. This concept allows artists and designers to work on individual elements of a graphic without altering the parts on other layers. Think of it as organizing your work into a stack of clear pages, where you can draw or place images on each page separately, yet when viewed together, they form a complete picture.

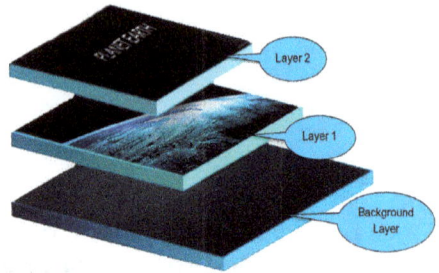

To open the layers panel, click the layers icon on the top right of the toolbar. Here in the example below, I've recreated the image above with the black background on layer 1, the transparent earth image on layer 2, and the heading text on layer 3.

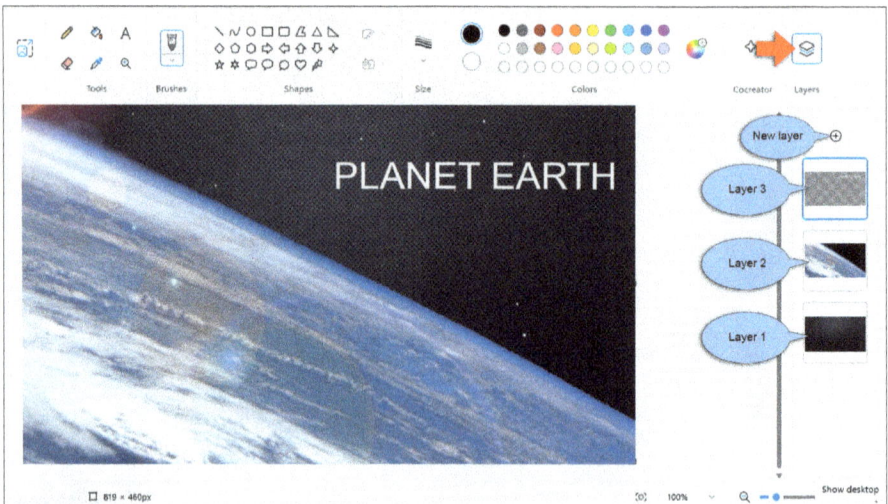

Layers are a cornerstone of digital imaging, allowing for non-destructive editing and complex composition. They enable designers to work on individual elements of an image separately, without affecting other parts. This modular approach allows adjustments, and refinements with ease without having to redo any work.

**398**

# Copilot Features

The Copilot features in Microsoft Paint introduce AI-assisted tools designed to extend the app's image editing capabilities. You'll find basic copilot tools under the copilot menu. If you have a Copilot+ PC.

**Image Creator** generates images from text prompts using AI, allows you to type a short description (e.g., "a mountain landscape at sunset"), and Paint creates an image matching your prompt using a cloud-based AI model (currently based on OpenAI's DALL·E). This feature requires a Microsoft account and a Microsoft 365 subscription (or Copilot Pro) to access AI credits.

To use the feature, select Image Creator from the Copilot menu.

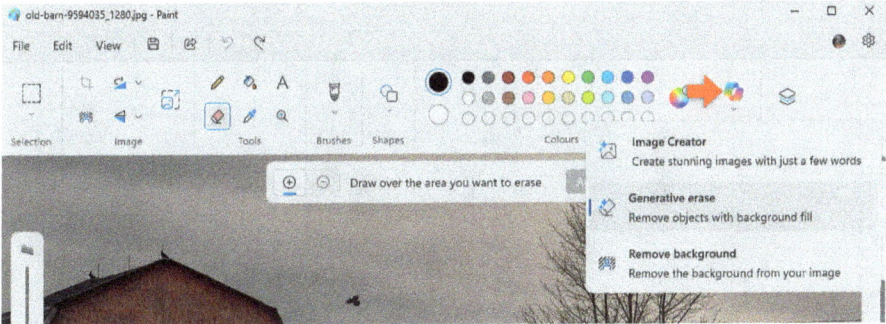

Type your prompt in the textbox at the top, then click 'create' to generate the image. Select a style using the selection box, then click on one of the variants below to add the image to your canvas.

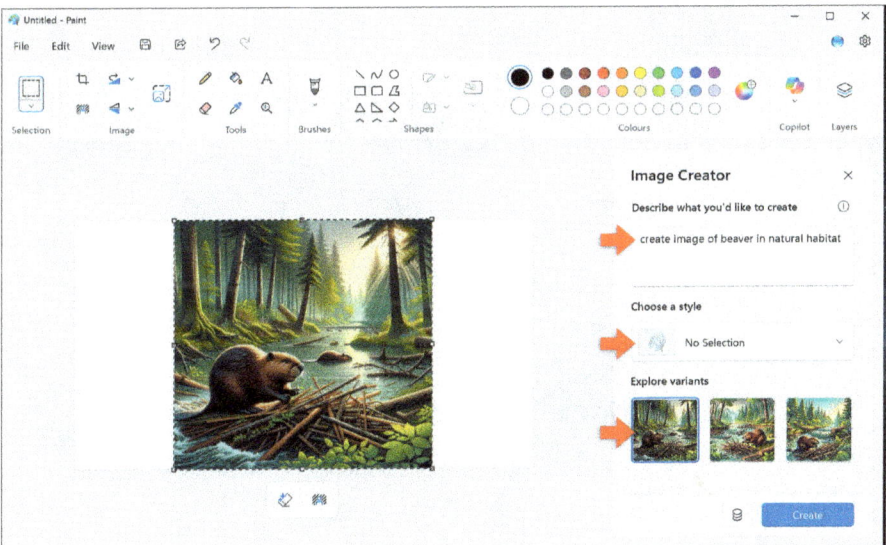

## Chapter 8: Multimedia Apps

**Generative Erase** removes unwanted parts of an image and fills in the background automatically using AI. You select the area you want to erase, and Paint intelligently reconstructs the missing background so it blends seamlessly. This is useful for cleaning up photos by removing objects like power lines, people, or text.

To use the feature, select Generative Erase from the Copilot menu.

Select the brush size using the slider on the left. Drag the brush over the object you want to remove. Click 'apply' when you're done.

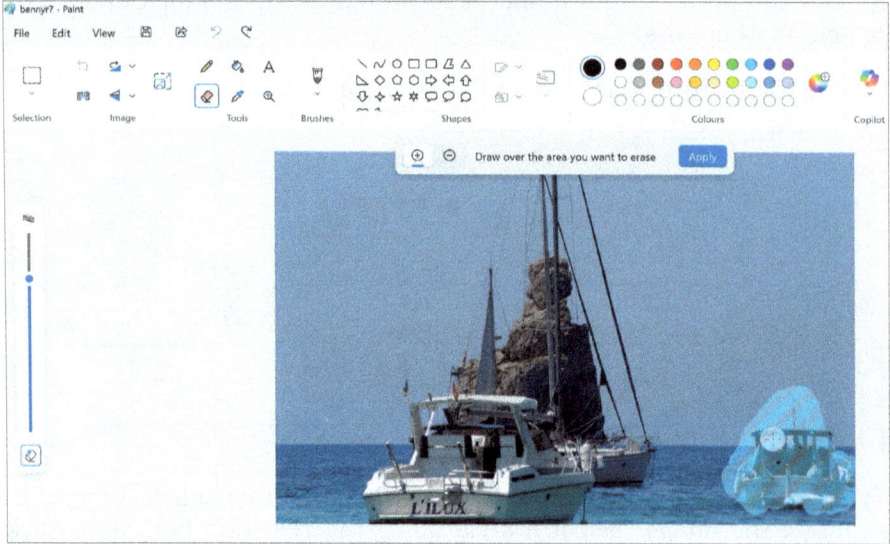

Copilot will remove the object from the photo.

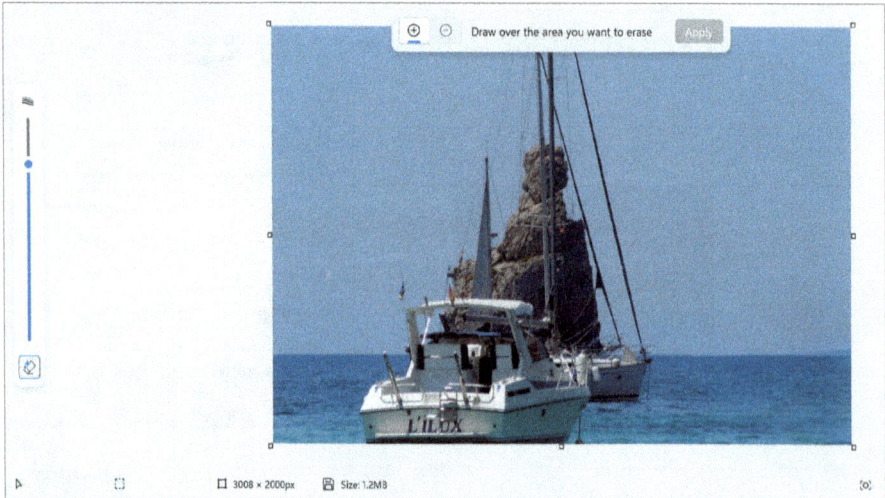

**Remove Background** automatically removes the background from an image, isolating the main subject.

To use the feature, click Remove Background in the Copilot menu.

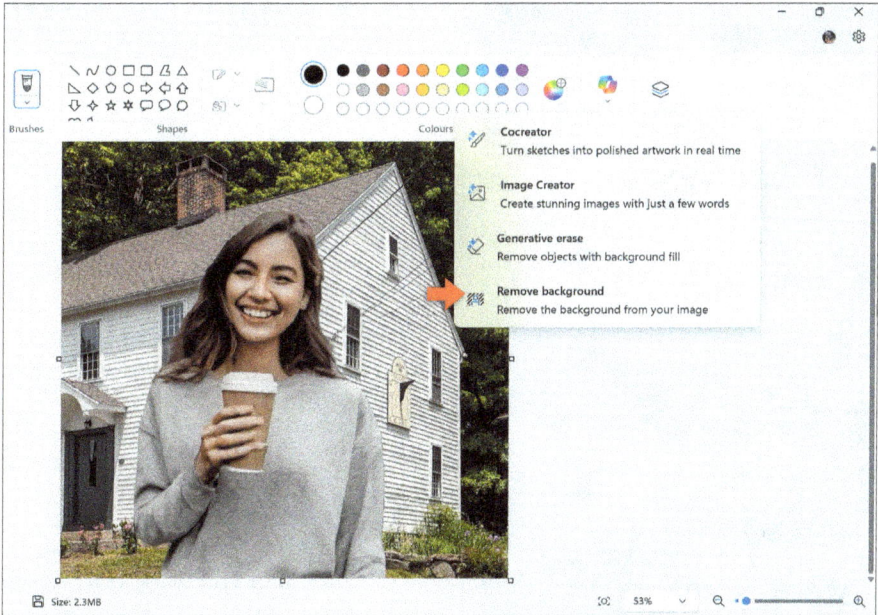

Paint will process and isolate the subject automatically.

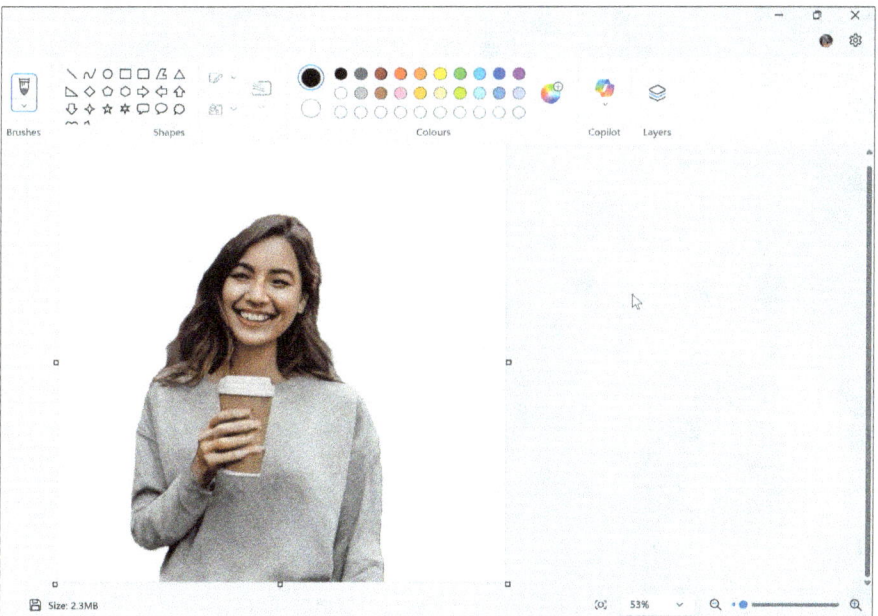

# 9

# Tablets & Touchscreens

Windows 11 is designed to run on a tablets and touchscreen devices. There is no more tablet mode like there was in Windows 10. In Windows 11, you get a much more consistent experience across devices.

In this chapter, we'll take a look at

- Touchscreens
- Touchscreen gestures
- How to Tap, Drag, and Zoom In & Out
- The Widgets Panel
- The Notifications Panel
- On-screen Keyboard
- Changing Keyboards
- Snipping Tool
- Sticky Notes
- Microsoft Whiteboard
- Microsoft Journal
- Using Pens
- Cases
- External Keyboards
- Hybrid Devices

To help you better understand this section, take a look at the video resources. Scan the QR code, or open your web browser and type the following directly into the address bar at the top (don't use a search engine):

elluminetpress.com/win-11-nav

# Touchscreens

Windows 11 supports touch screens. Here in the image below is Windows 11 running with a keyboard attached. You'll notice the interface is geared towards point and click navigation using a mouse pointer.

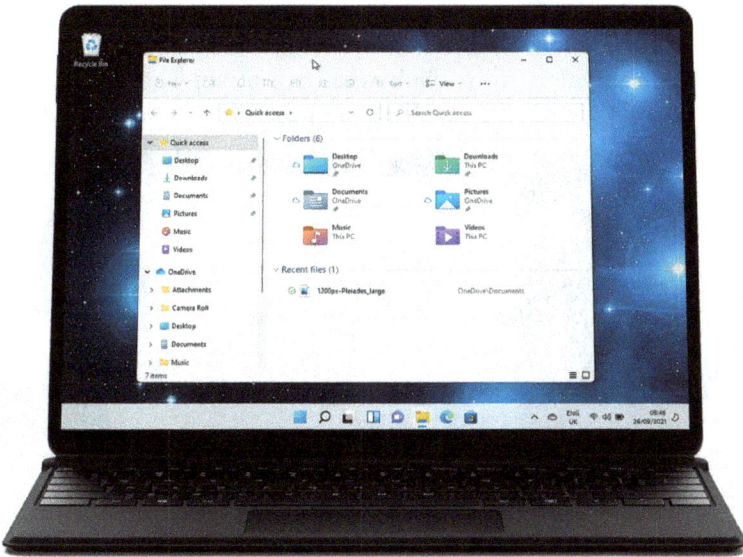

When you remove a keyboard from a device, such as a Surface Tablet, the icons on the taskbar appear more spaced out, making it easier for you to tap on the icon with your finger. Scroll bars and window edges are also a bit bigger making them easier to drag or resize. Here in the image below is Windows 11 running without a keyboard. Windows 11 automatically adjusts to touch oriented navigation.

# Touchscreen Gestures

On your tablet's touch screen, you can use various gestures using your forefinger and thumb.

## Tap (Left Click)

Tap with one finger to select icons, links, files, or open apps on the start menu- equivalent to a click with a mouse. Tap twice with your finger to 'double click' - eg use this to open a file in file explorer.

## Two Finger Tap (Right Click)

Tap two fingers on your screen. This is equivalent to the right click on a mouse, and is used to invoke a context menu.

# Drag

Use this to move objects such as windows and icons around the screen. Tap on an object, then without lifting your finger, slide your finger across the screen. This is the same as click and drag with the mouse.

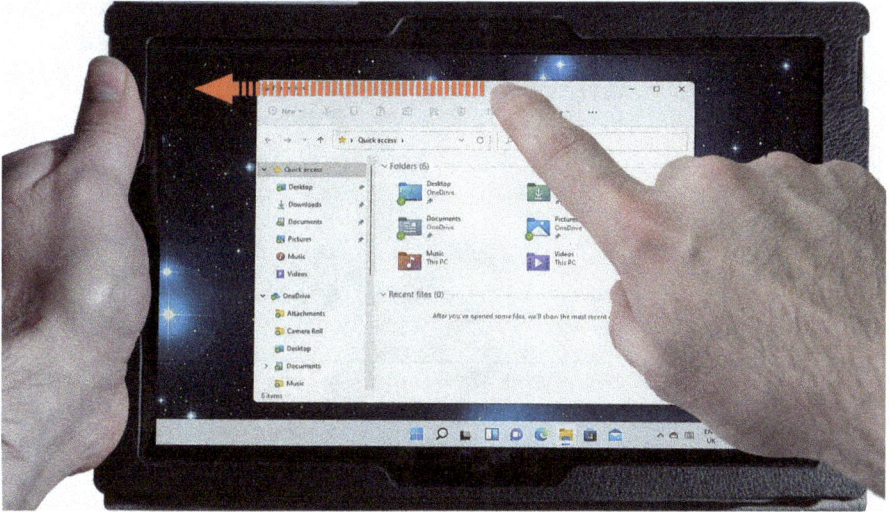

# Zoom In & Out

Use your forefinger and thumb to zoom in and out. Spread your finger and thumb apart to zoom in, pinch your thumb and finger closer together to zoom out. Use this gesture on maps or when viewing photos.

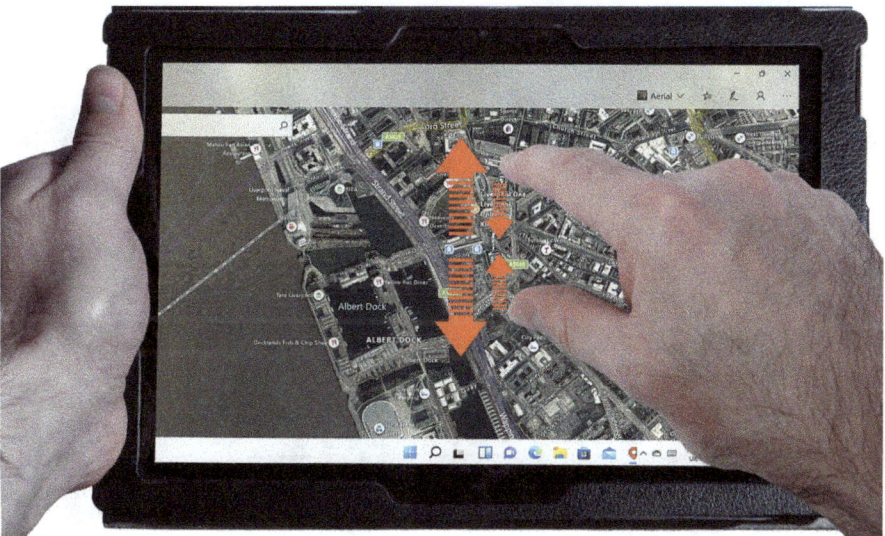

# Open Widgets Panel

Swipe from the left edge of the screen opens the widgets panel on the left hand side.

# Open Notifications Panel

Swipe from the right edge of the screen opens your notifications.

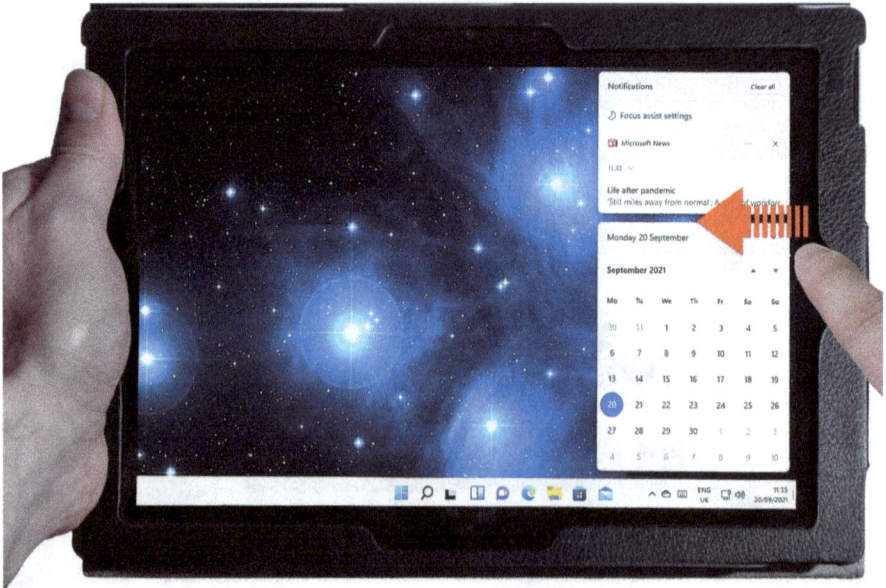

# On-screen Keyboard

Your on-screen keyboard will appear whenever you tap inside a text field. To bring up the keyboard at any other time, tap the icon on the right hand side of the task bar. Note this icon wont appear if you have a keyboard plugged into your tablet.

Your keyboard will open up on the bottom third of the screen.

You can type normally using the keys. To quickly type in a number, use the keys on the top row, you'll notice a small number in the top left hand side of the key. To do this, tap and hold your finger on the key with the number you want to type, eg press and hold 'r' for the number 4. Tap the number in the popup.

If you're typing in more than one number, tap the '&123' icon on the bottom left of the screen and use the keypad. Tap 'abc" to get back to the standard keyboard.

## Changing Keyboards

You can also select different keyboards: default which is a standard keyboard, small - which is a small floating keyboard, split keyboard is one where the keyboard is split in half - one half on each side of the screen, and a traditional keyboard which is similar to a hardware keyboard.

To change the keyboard, tap the settings icon on the top left of the keyboard. Tap 'keyboard layout', then select a keyboard from the list.

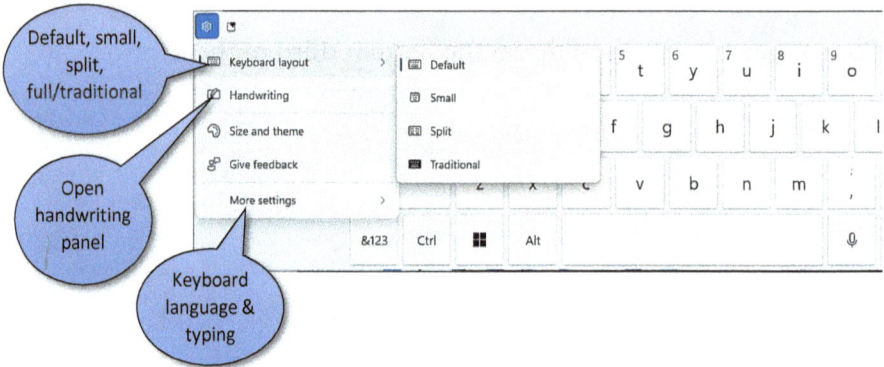

On a split keyboard, half appears on the left and the other half appears on the right. This can be more comfortable to type.

A small floating keyboard is useful if the default keyboard gets in the way.

You can drag a floating keyboard anywhere on the screen.

The on-screen keyboard also has a hand writing recognition feature that instead of typing, you can actually write words and sentences using your pen or finger.

To do this, tap the settings icon on the top left of the keyboard, then select handwriting from the drop down menu.

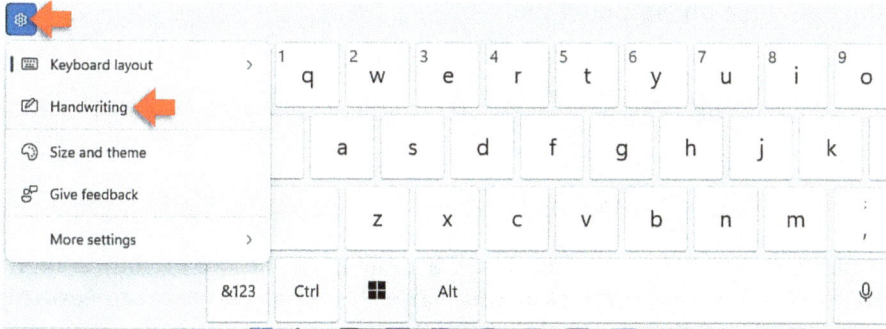

You'll see a panel open up. Tap in the field you want to enter text into. Write the text you want to 'type' in on the line. For example, when saving a file, you can write the file name instead of typing it, and the text appears in the text field.

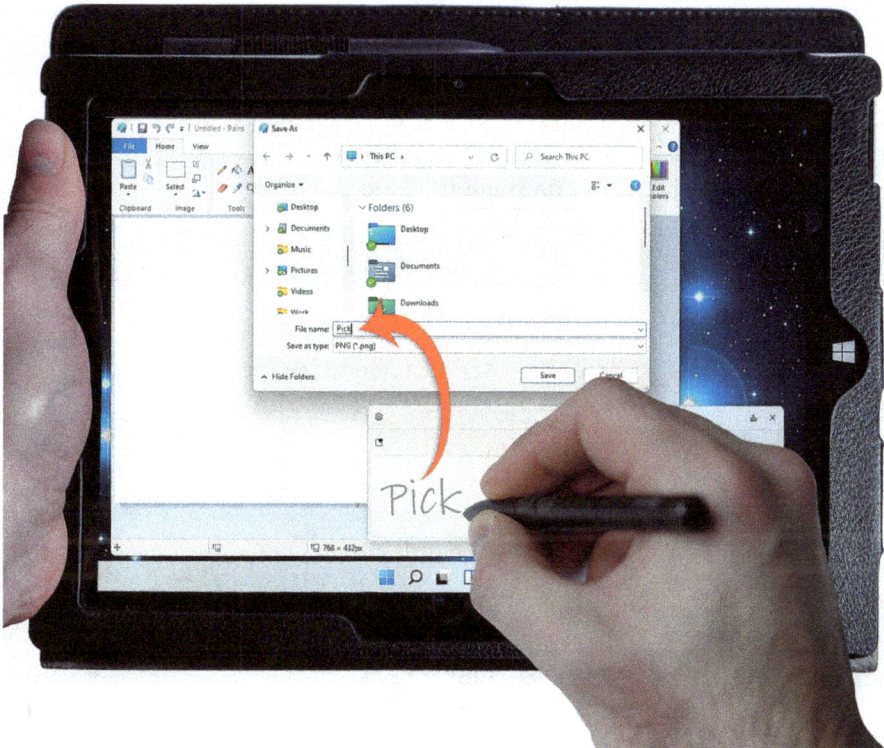

**409**

# Snipping Tool

With the snipping tool, you can take a screenshot of whatever app you have open and handwrite annotations onto it with your pen. You can 'snip' the whole screen or just a section of it. To open the snipping tool, click on the start button, select 'all apps' on the top right, scroll down the list, click on 'snipping tool'.

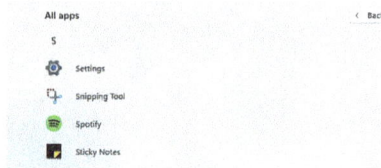

When you start the app, you'll see a toolbar at the top of your screen. Here, you can create a new screen snip, set what you want to capture - rectangle, a window, whole screen or draw a shape.

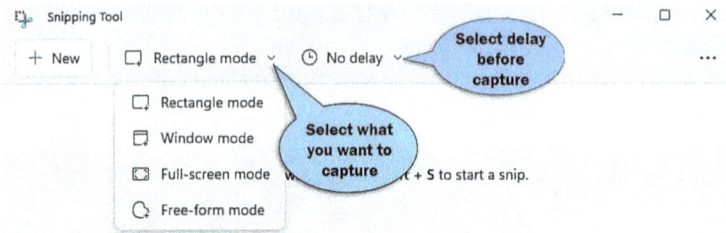

Open up the app you want to capture. In this case, I'm taking a rectangular screen ship of a page in Edge.

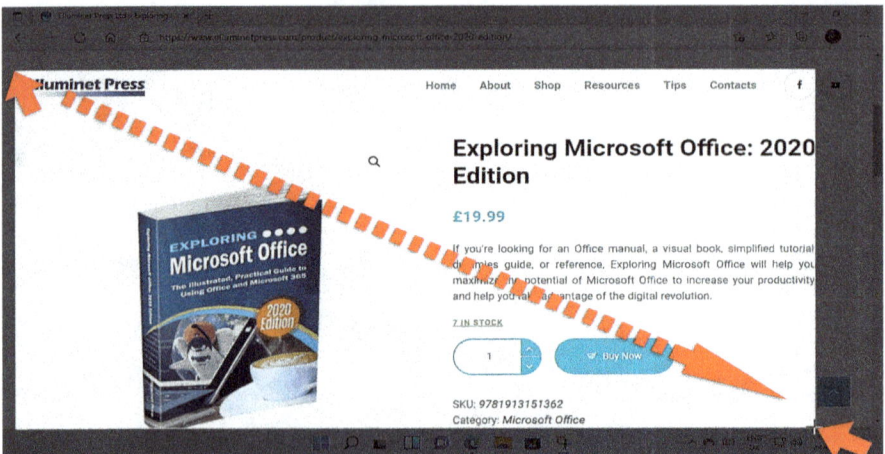

Click and drag the marker around the part of the page you want.

This is where you'll find pens and highlighters for you to annotate the screenshot.

If you want to choose the pen, tap on its icon, on the tool bar. To change the color and size, tap and hold your pen on the pen icon until a drop down menu appears. Tap on the color and sizes you want.

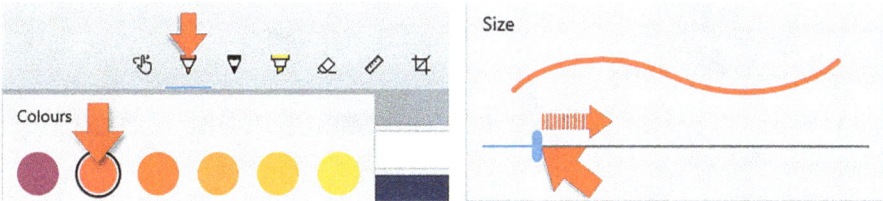

Draw directly onto the screen with your pen. If you want to change color or size, select the pen icon again then choose a color. You can also use a highlighter, to do this click the highlighter icon on the toolbar, select a color and size from the drop down.

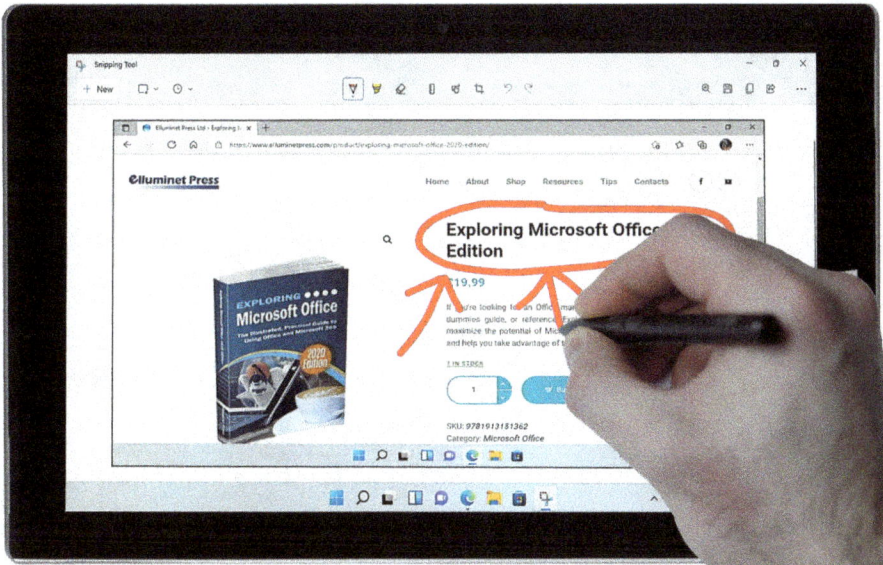

You can **save** your annotation as an image. To save, tap the 'save' icon on the top right of the screen. Enter a filename, then tap 'save'.

# Chapter 9: Tablets & Touchscreens

To **share**, tap the 'share' icon on the top right of the screen.

Tap the app you want to use to share, eg mail.

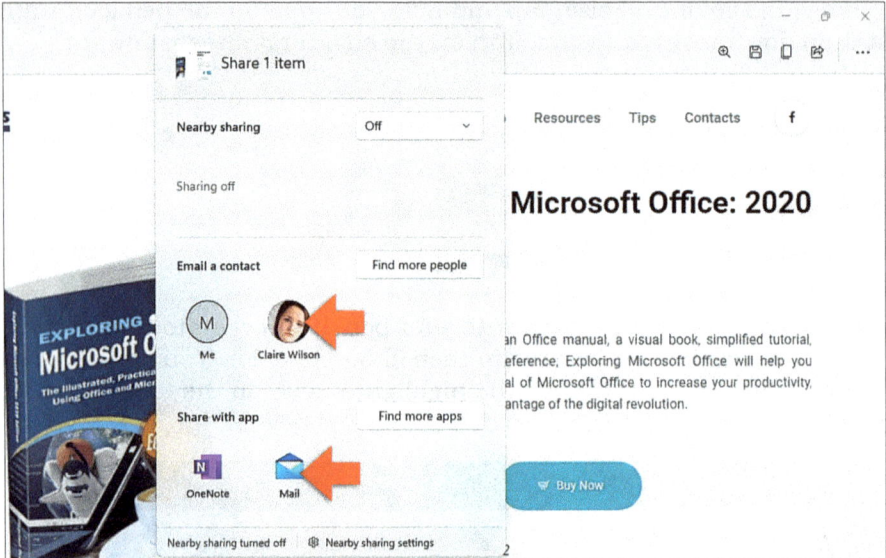

Fill in the email address and write a message, then tap the send icon.

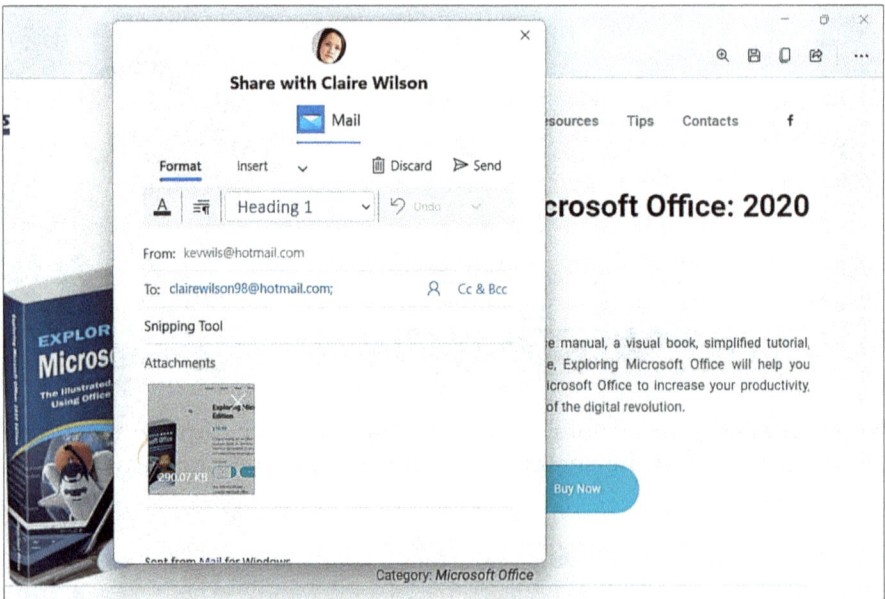

# Sticky Notes

Sticky Notes allow you to hand write or type notes that you can pin to your desktop. You'll find sticky notes on your start menu, select 'all apps', scroll down, click on 'sticky notes'.

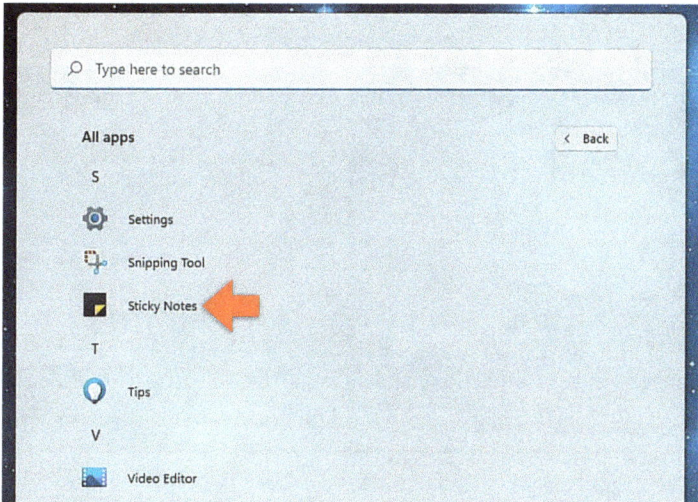

You can write notes, delete notes, and add new notes using the icons indicated below.

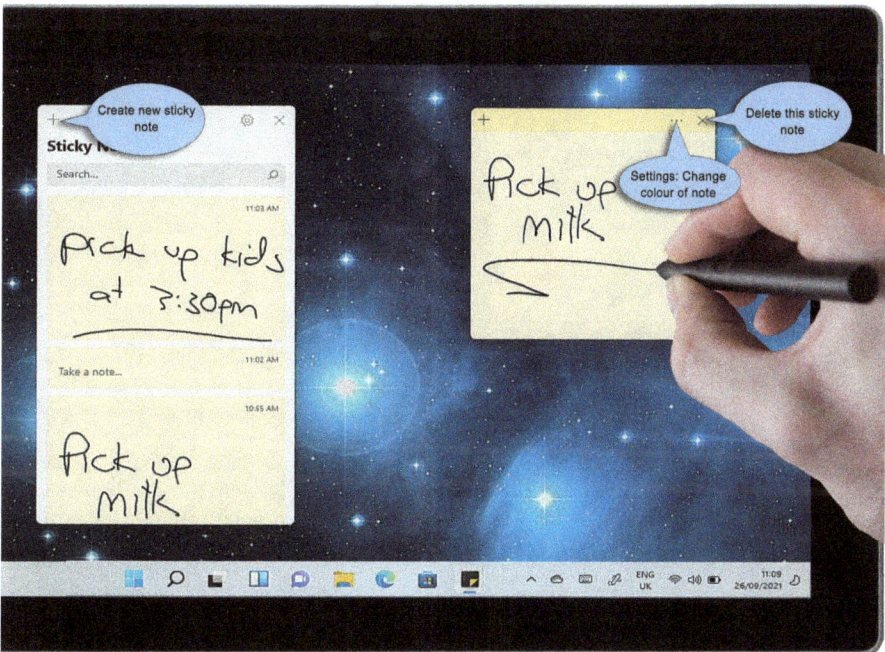

# Microsoft Whiteboard

Microsoft Whiteboard is useful when giving presentations, teaching, online collaboration, or drawing. You can also save and share your illustrations created while using Whiteboard. You'll find the whiteboard app on your start menu, or on the Windows Ink pen menu on the bottom right of your screen.

On the start screen, you'll see a thumbnail list of all the whiteboards you have created. Click on one to revisit. To create a new whiteboard, click 'create new whiteboard'.

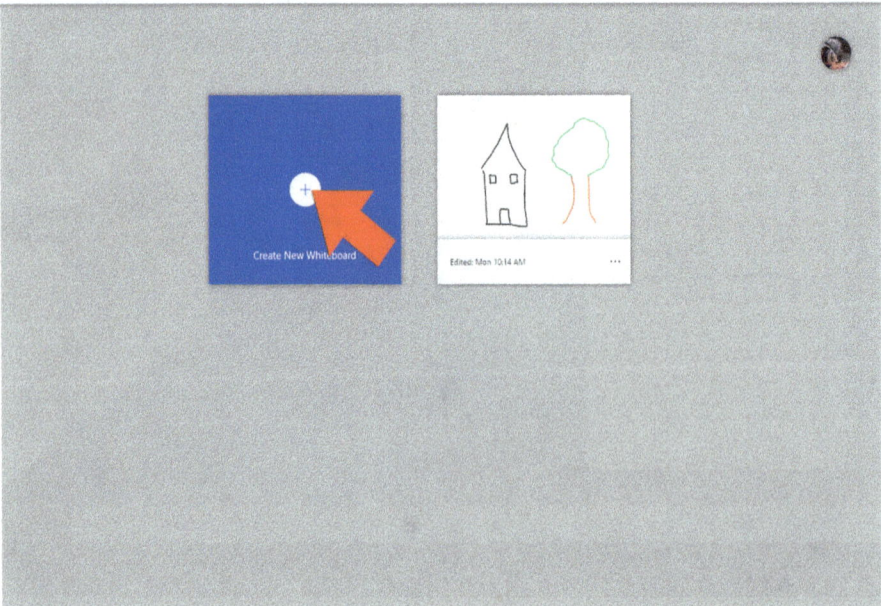

# Getting Started

Select a template from the panel on the left hand side, or tap on the blank screen to start from scratch.

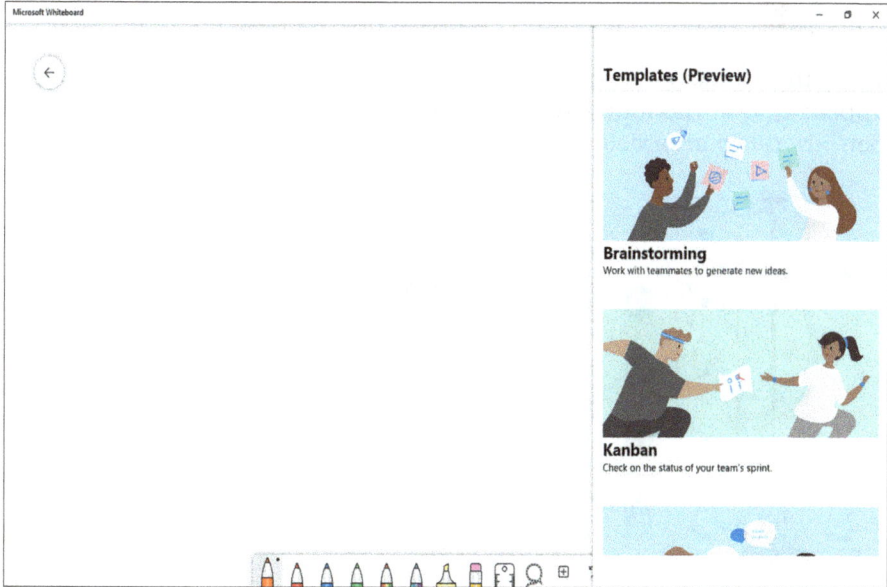

In the screen that opens, you'll see a tool bar appear along the bottom of your screen. Here, you'll find your pencils, pens, and highlighters you can use to draw onto the screen. Let's take a look:

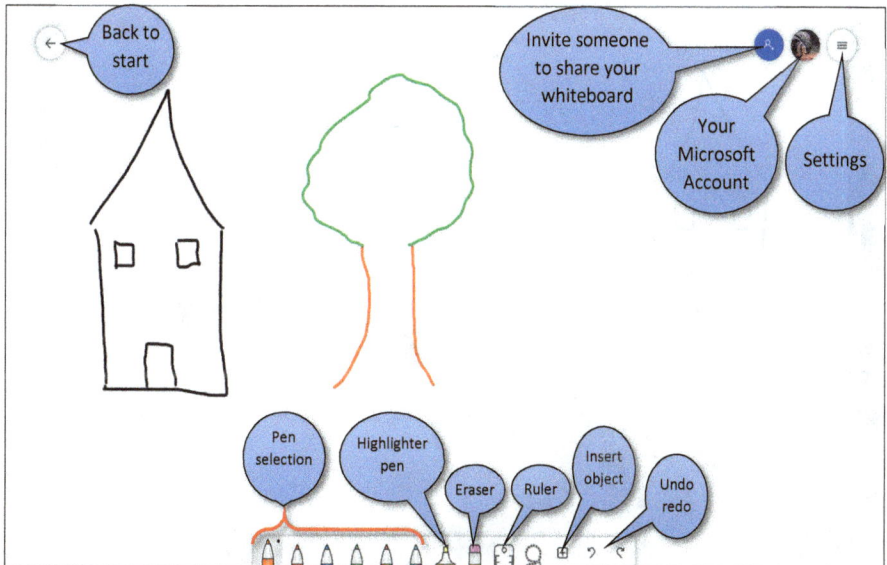

If you want to choose the pen, tap on its icon, on the tool bar.

To change the color and size, tap on the pen icon until the popup menu appears. Use the four circles on the left to select the thickness of the pen, then tap on a color.

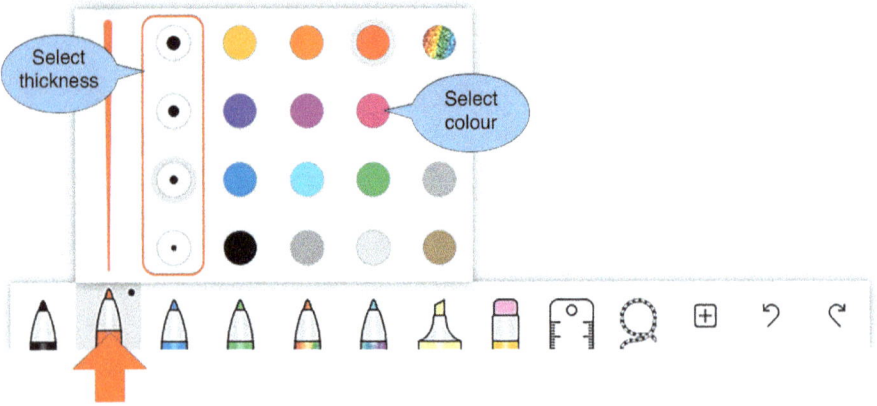

Now you can draw directly onto the screen with your pen.

# Inserting Objects

You can insert objects such as photographs, diagrams, tables, notes, as well as insert office documents and PDFs. To do this, tap the insert icon on the toolbar along the bottom of your screen. Select the object type you want to insert (eg an image)

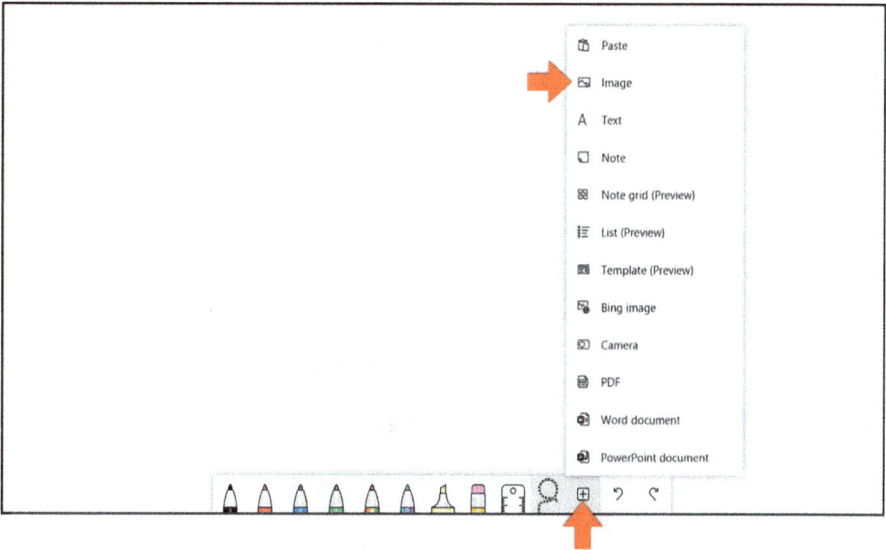

From the dialog box, select the image you want to insert.

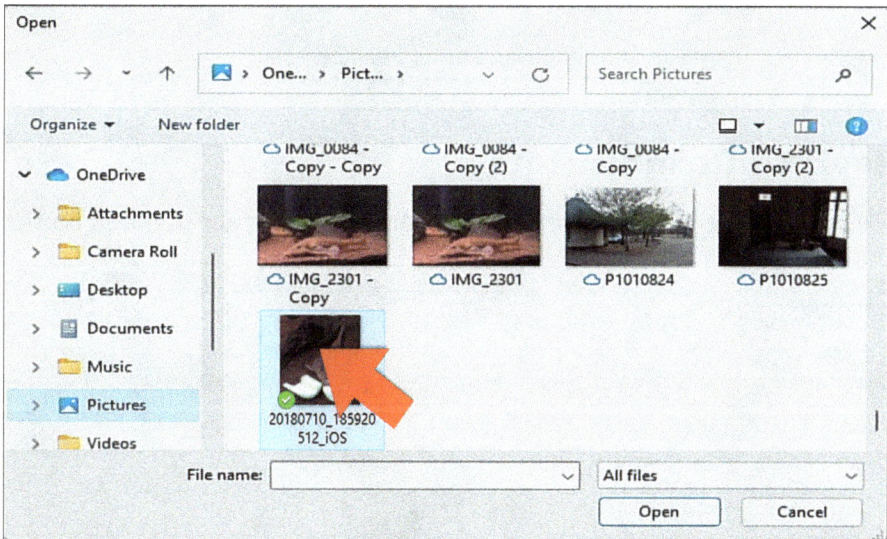

Click 'open'

Place the image on your whiteboard. Click and drag the image into position. You'll see a toolbar appear above the image.

## Inviting Collaborators

To invite other people to your whiteboard, click the sharing link on the top right of the screen.

Turn on 'web sharing link'. Whiteboard will generate a link you can send to other people.

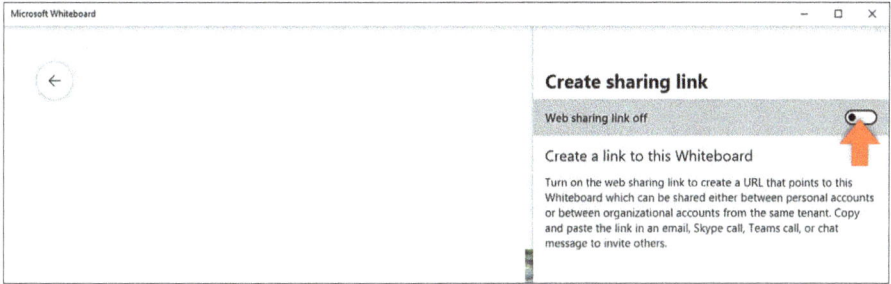

Now, once the link has been generated, click 'copy link' and paste it into an email or message to send to other people.

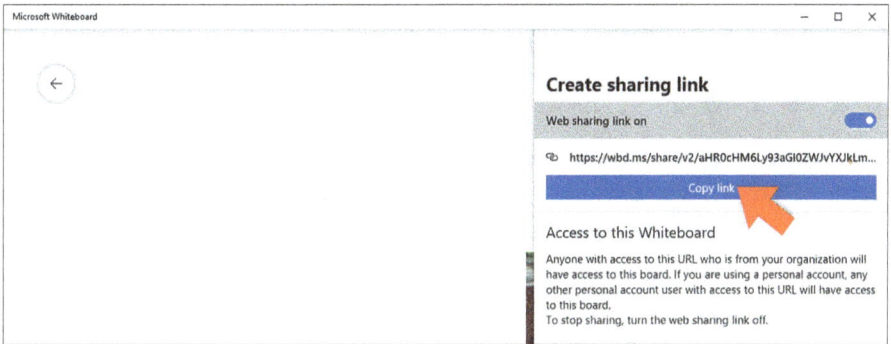

Once other people join, you'll see their contributions marked with their badge.

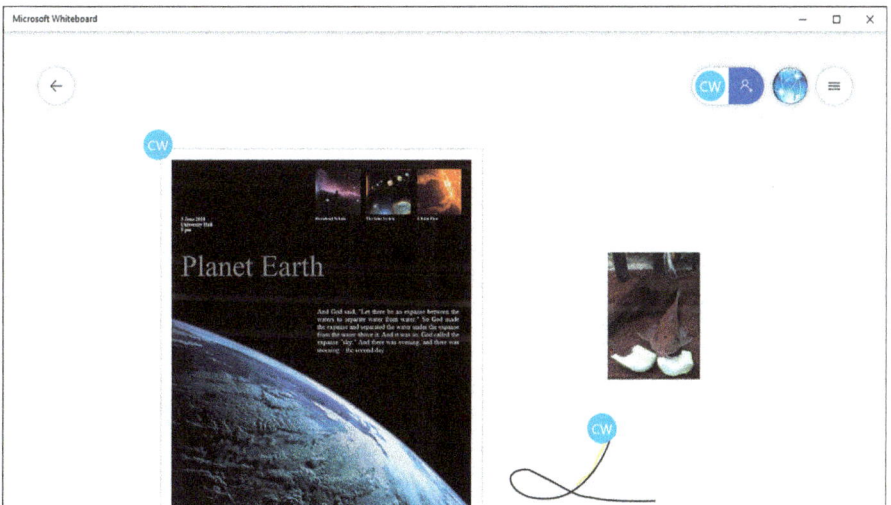

# Ink to Shape

This feature creates clean geometric shapes from your drawings, such as squares, circles, etc. To enable ink to shape, click the hamburger icon on the top right.

Select 'ink to shape'.

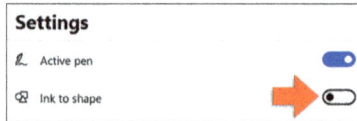

Draw your shape on the canvas.

# Ink to Table

This feature allows you to create clean tables by drawing them on your screen. To enable ink to table, click the hamburger icon on the top right.

Select 'ink to table'.

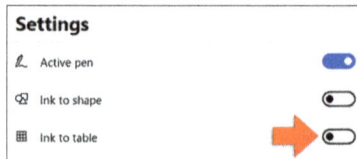

To draw your table, first draw a square. Then divide the square in half.

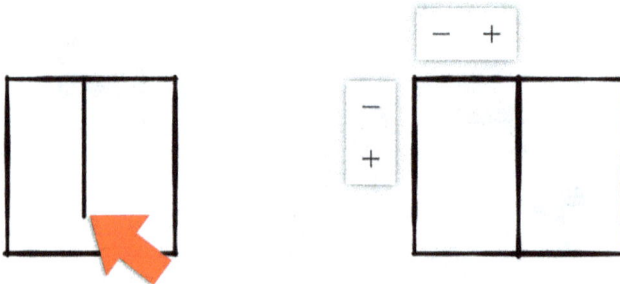

# Microsoft Journal

Microsoft Journal is an app that allows you to create drawings, annotations, notes, sketches and other ideas using a pen. It's designed for people who thrive when writing out their ideas, notes, and sketches.

You'll find Journal on your start menu. If not, then open the Microsoft Store, search for Microsoft Journal and install the app.

Once Journal starts, you'll land on the home screen. Here, you'll see a list of all the journals you've created. To create a new blank journal, click 'new journal' on the top left of the screen.

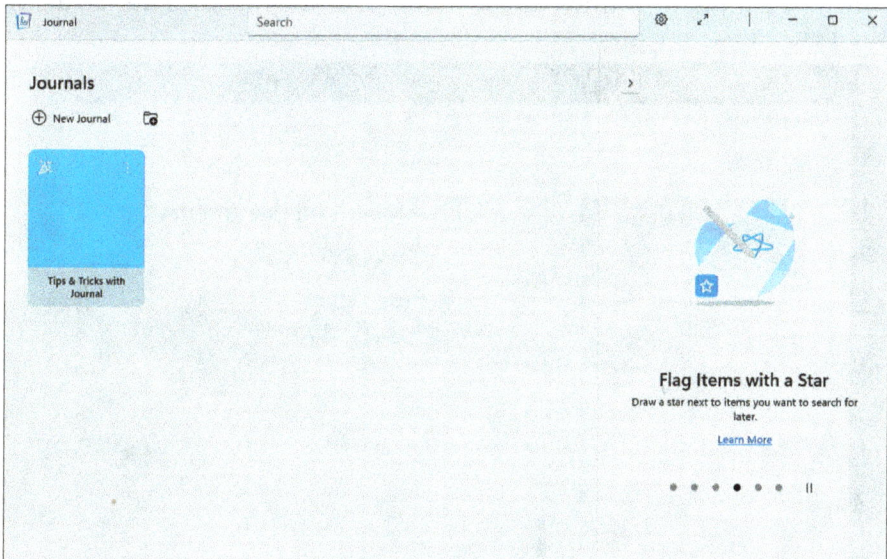

Give your journal a meaningful name, select an identifying color and icon if you want to. Click 'ok' when you're done.

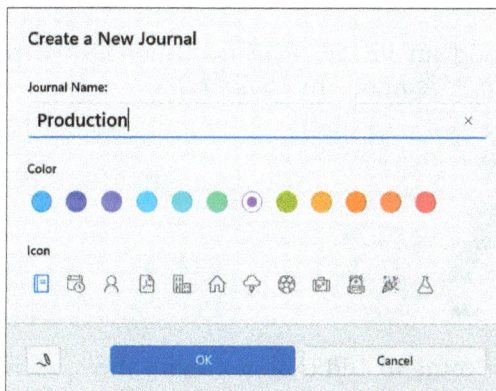

Next, you'll see your journal. Select a pen, size and color from the toolbar along the bottom of the screen.

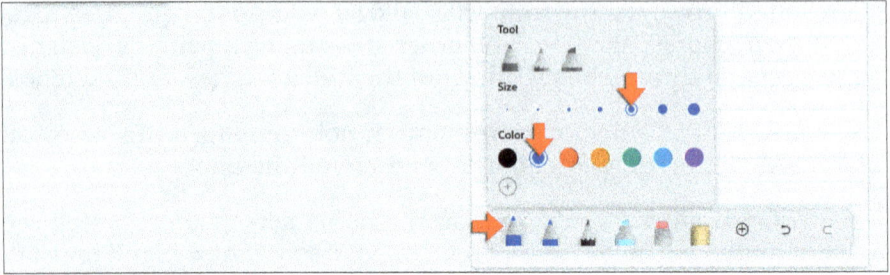

Now you can write or draw directly onto your touchscreen device using the pen.

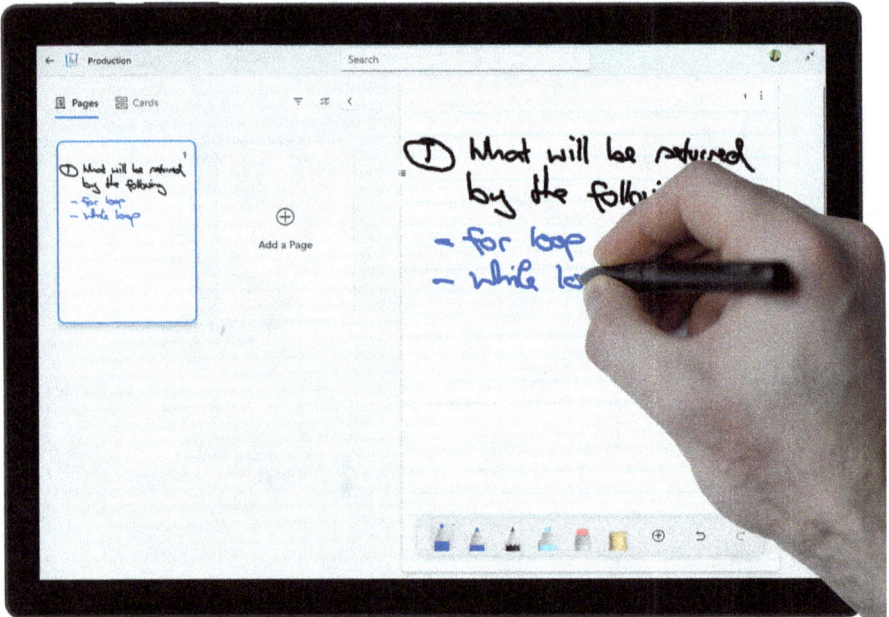

If you want to add an image, PDF document, or a photo from your camera, click the '+' icon on the toolbar.

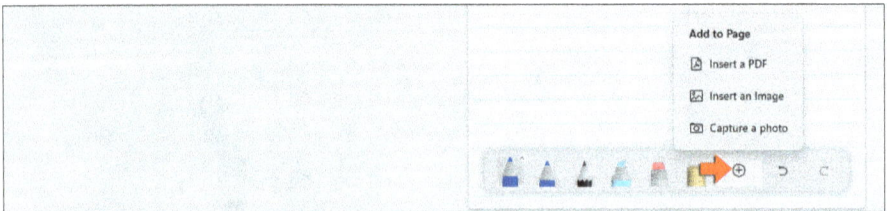

For example, I'm going to add a photo using the camera on my surface tablet. So I'm going to select 'capture a photo'.

Take the photo using the camera. Tap the photo icon on the right hand side of the window

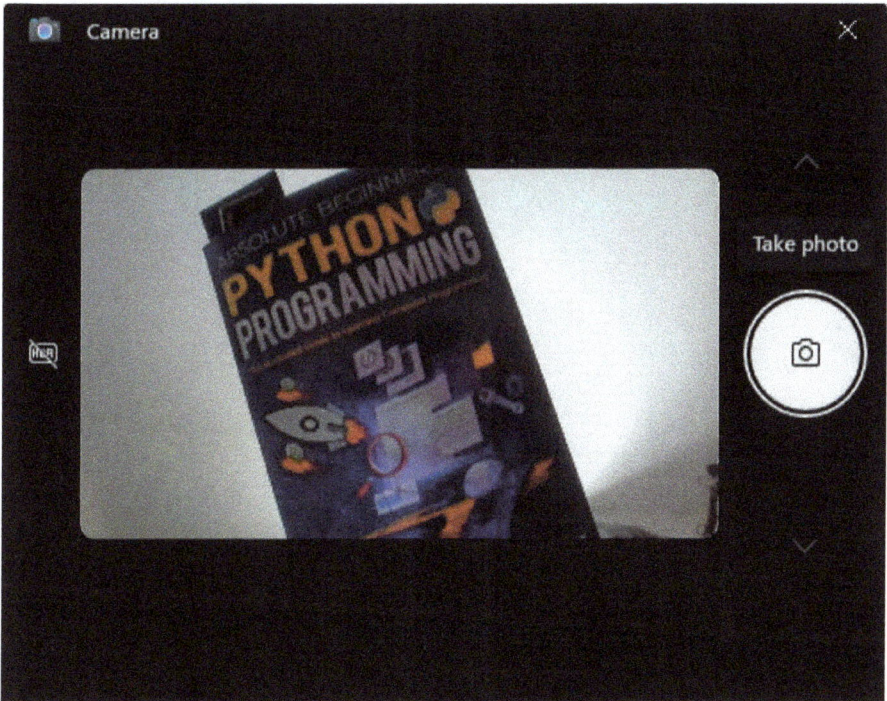

Click 'done' if you're happy with the photo

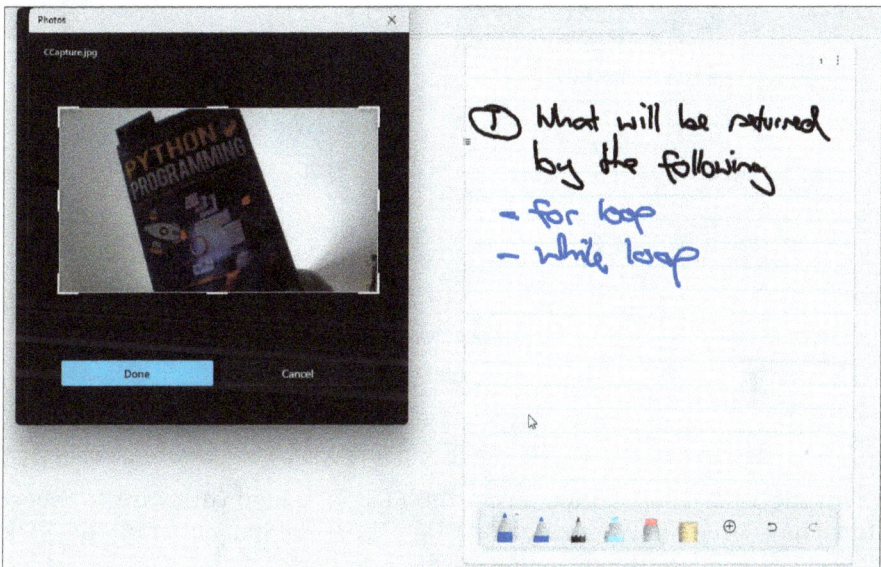

The photo will drop onto your journal page. Drag the photo into position

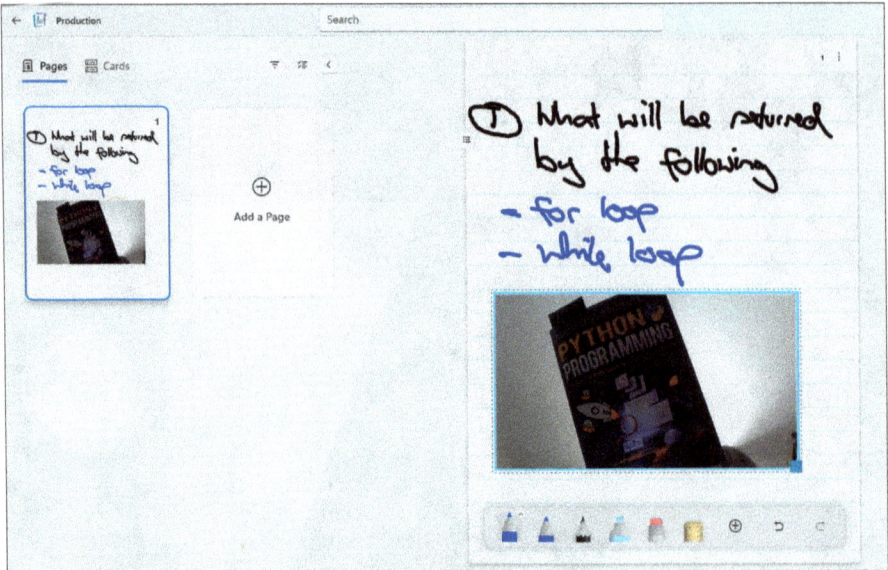

If you want to insert a PDF or image, click the '+' icon on the toolbar along the bottom of the screen, then select the option from the menu.

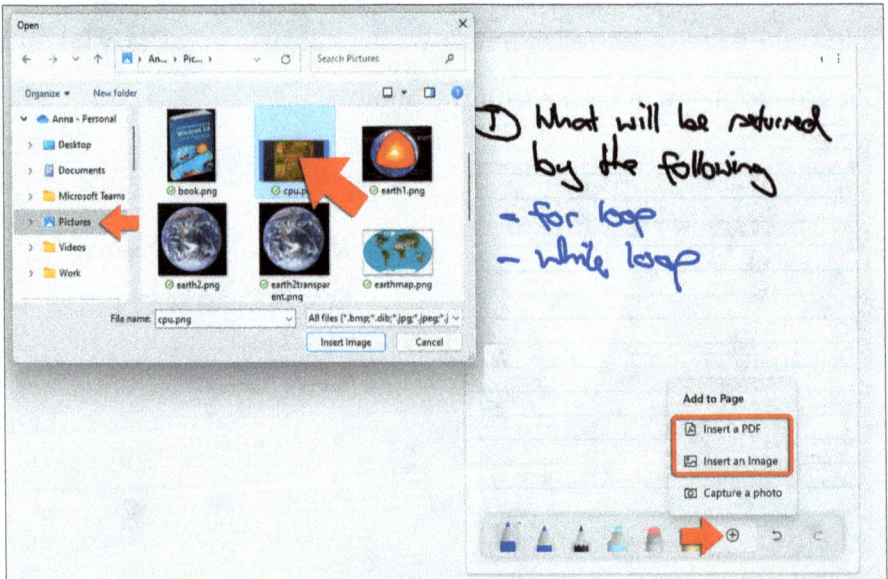

From the 'open' dialog box, select the PDF or image you want to insert into your journal. If you add a PDF, then the pages from the PDF document will be added to your journal.

# Pens

You can buy pens and styluses to use with your tablet. These come in useful for Windows Ink & OneNote, as well as any art apps out there that you can find in the Microsoft Store.

Here is the Microsoft Surface Pen that is used with many surface tablets and laptops.

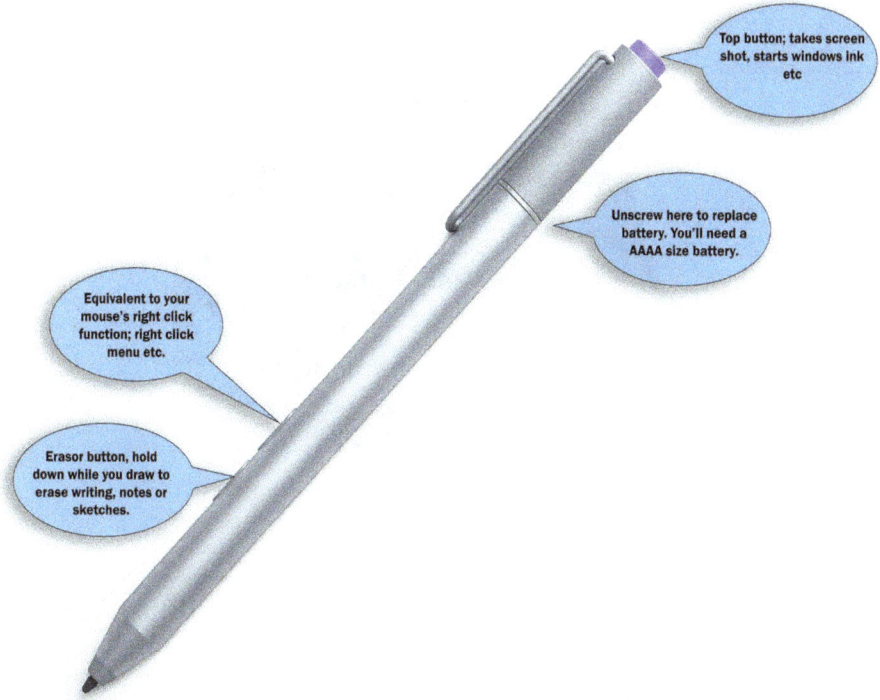

These come in various types but the ones that work best have bluetooth capability, meaning you can pair the pen with your tablet giving you extra features such as shortcut buttons, mouse button equivalents and so on.

Third party pens also work well. You can pick these up quite cheaply in any electronics store.

# Cases

A case is a must for any tablet. A case helps to protect your tablet from scratches. Some cases double as a stand to allow you to prop your tablet up which is useful if you want to watch a movie. Some also come with pockets and a place to keep your pen.

# External Keyboards

Some cases come with built in keyboards. Most of these types connect to your tablet using bluetooth. You can pair them in the usual way - see pairing bluetooth devices on page 89.

# Hybrid Devices

Hybrid devices are a combination of a tablet and a laptop. They often have detachable keyboards such as the surface tablet...

...or keyboards that flip back behind the screen such as the lenovo yoga.

When you attach your keyboard, the display is optimised for point and click desktop use. When you detach the keyboard, the icons become larger and further apart making it easier to use on a touch screen.

# 10

# System Maintenance

Computer maintenance keeps your computer in a good working order.

In this chapter, we'll take a look at

- Backing Up your Files
- PIN Recovery
- Password Recovery
- Changing Passwords
- Windows Update
- Activating Windows
- System File Check
- Managing Drives
- Add/Remove Windows Features
- Maintaining Apps
- System Recovery
- Windows Security
- Windows Firewall
- Anti Virus Software

Let's begin by taking a look at some backup strategies.

To help you better understand this section, take a look at the video resources. Scan the QR code, or open your web browser and type the following directly into the address bar at the top (don't use a search engine):

elluminetpress.com/win-sys

# Backing Up your Files

If you have ever lost data because of a computer glitch or crash you know how frustrating it can be. So we all need a good backup strategy. I'm going to go through the strategy I have found that has worked well over the years.

Windows 11 has a built in backup utility called File History that allows you to select files and back them up to an external hard drive.

## Creating a Backup

First of all go buy yourself a good external hard disk - go for at least 1TB. This is a small device that plugs into a USB port on your computer.

Plug in your external drive into a free USB port.

# Chapter 10: System Maintenance

To open File History, click the search icon on your taskbar, type

```
File History
```

Click on 'File History' in the search results.

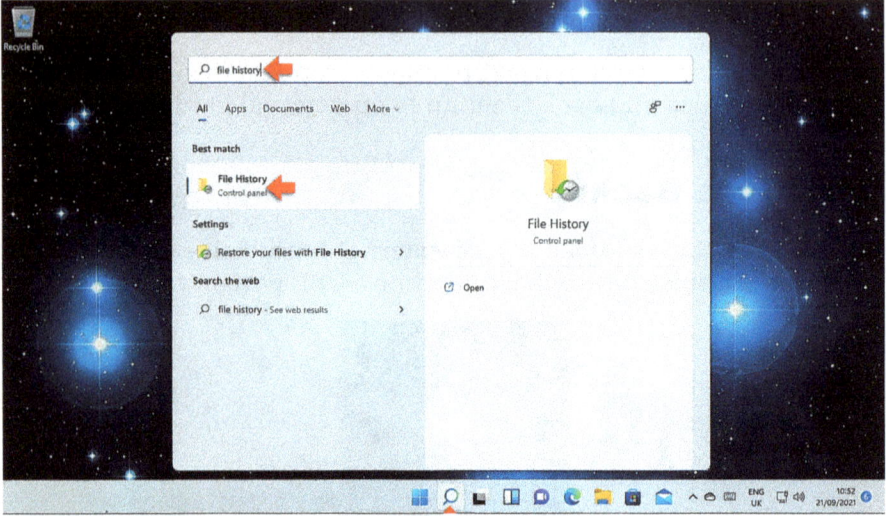

On the screen that appears, click 'Turn On' to enable File History.

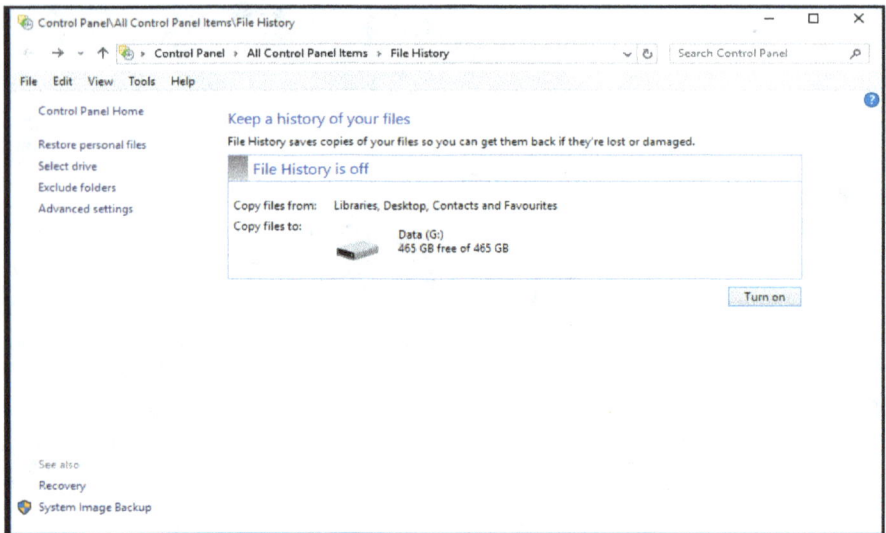

Once you have turned on File History, it will start to copy files from your libraries (documents, pictures, music etc) onto your external hard drive.

## Adding Folders

If you want to add folders to your backup, just add them to your libraries. Remember your desktop, documents, photos, music & videos folders and their contents are already included.

For example, if I wanted to include my downloads folder which is on another hard drive, open file explorer, right click on the folder you want to backup, then go down to 'show more options'.

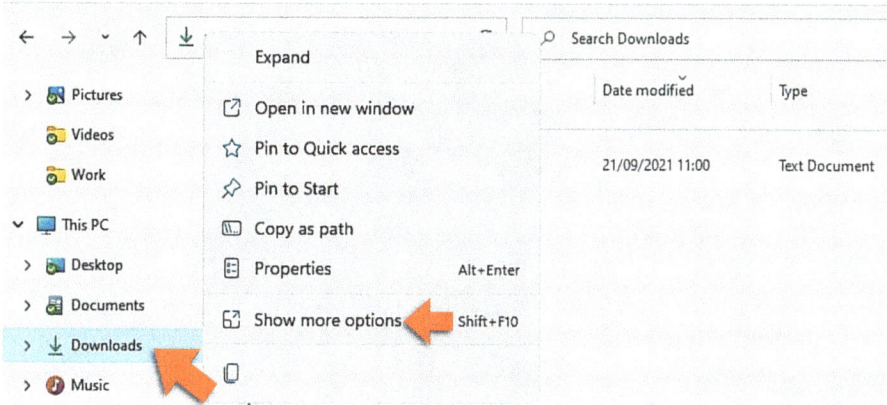

Then from the legacy menu, click 'include in library'. From the slide-out menu, select 'create new library'.

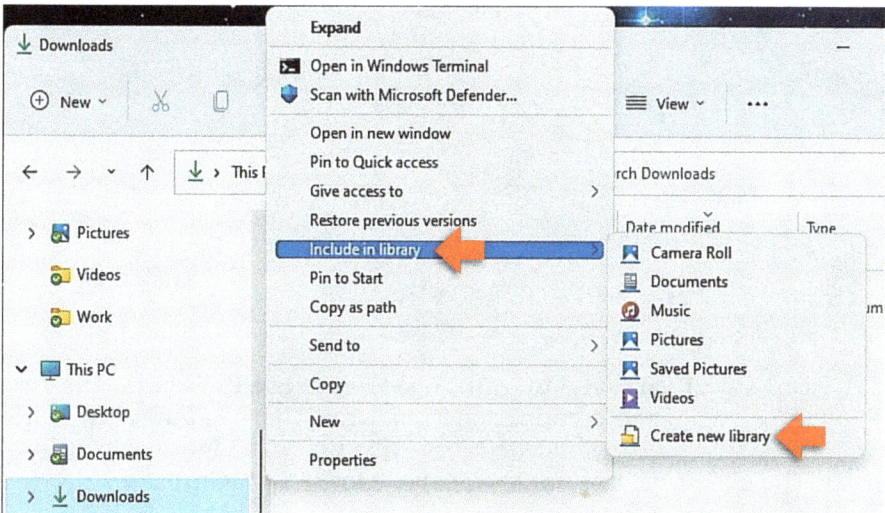

This folder will now be backed up with the rest of your libraries.

## Setting Backup Schedules

By default, File History saves files every hour, but you can change this by clicking on "Advanced Settings" listed down the left hand side of the screen.

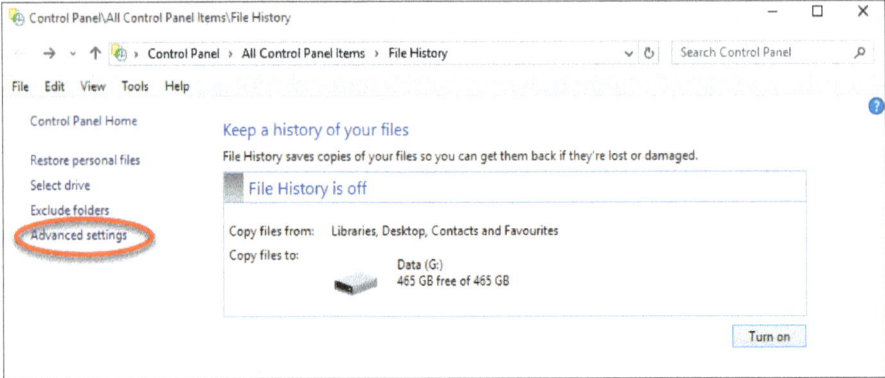

A good guide is to set how often File History saves files to "Daily". This will tell File History to save copies of your files once a day. For most users this is sufficient.

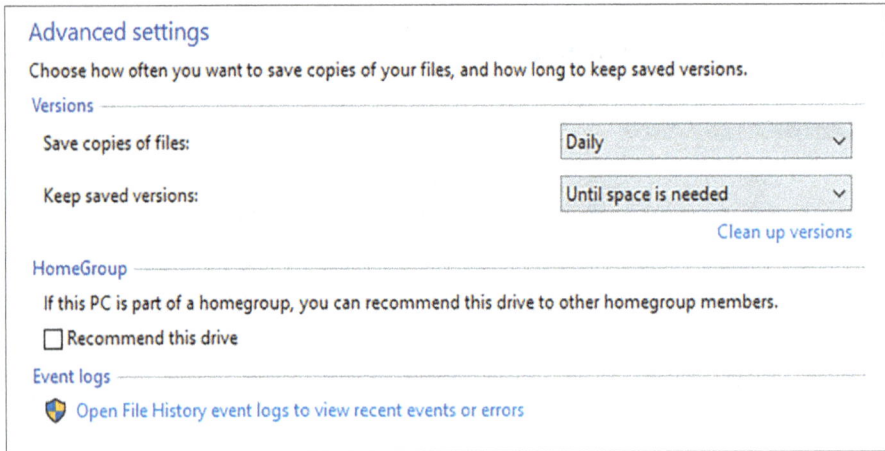

Set 'keep saved versions' to 'until space is needed'. This means that File History will keep creating backups while there is sufficient space on the hard drive, then once the drive fills up, File History will start to delete the oldest backups to make space for new backups.

Good practice would be to plug in your external drive at the end of each day to back up what you have done throughout the day.

Backups can take a while depending on how much you have done.

**432**

# Restoring Files

Plug in your external Hard drive. Open up File History and click 'Restore Personal Files'

Use the left and right arrows at the bottom to navigate to the date backed up when you know your file still existed or was working.

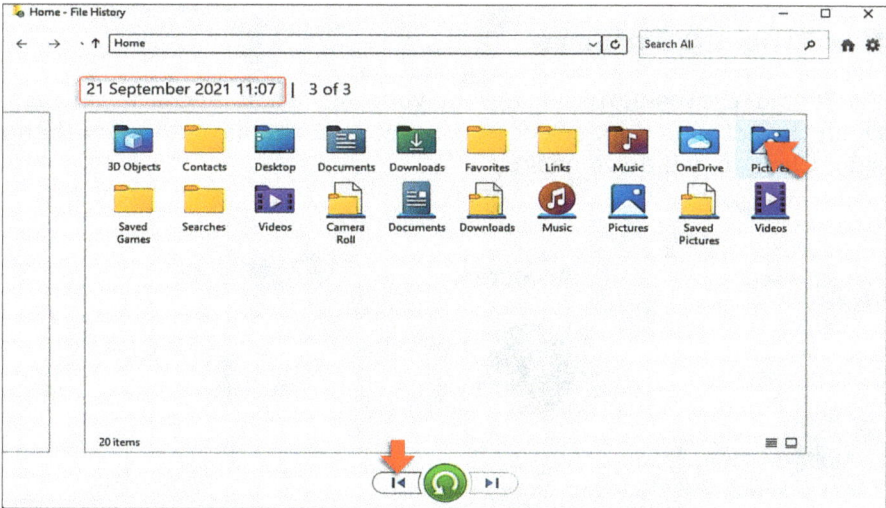

Then in the library section double click in the folder the file was in eg pictures if you lost a photo.

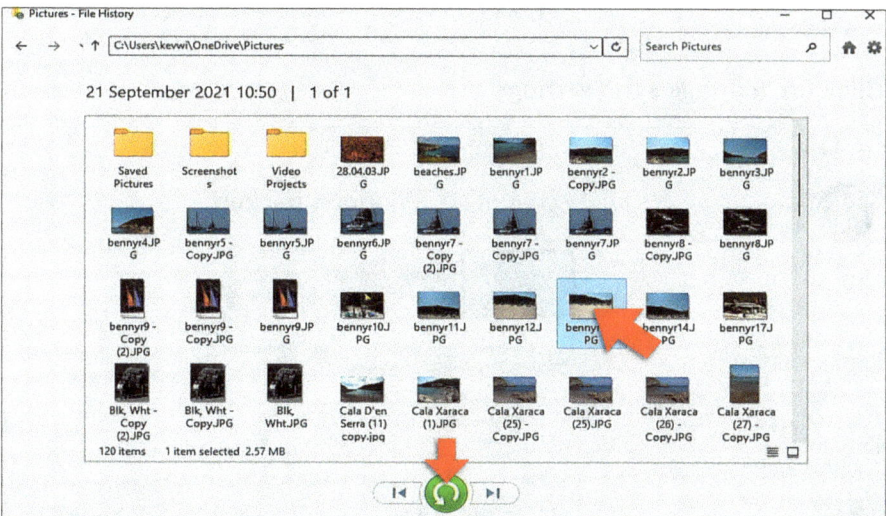

Select the photo and to restore it click the green button at the bottom of the window.

# Windows Backup App

The Windows Backup app in Windows 11 allows you to back up folders, apps, settings, and credentials to OneDrive. It simplifies backing up personal files and settings but cannot create full system backups or save data locally.

## Backing up Folders

You'll find the backup settings in your Microsoft Account settings. Open the settings app, select 'accounts' from the list on the left hand side. Click on 'windows backup'.

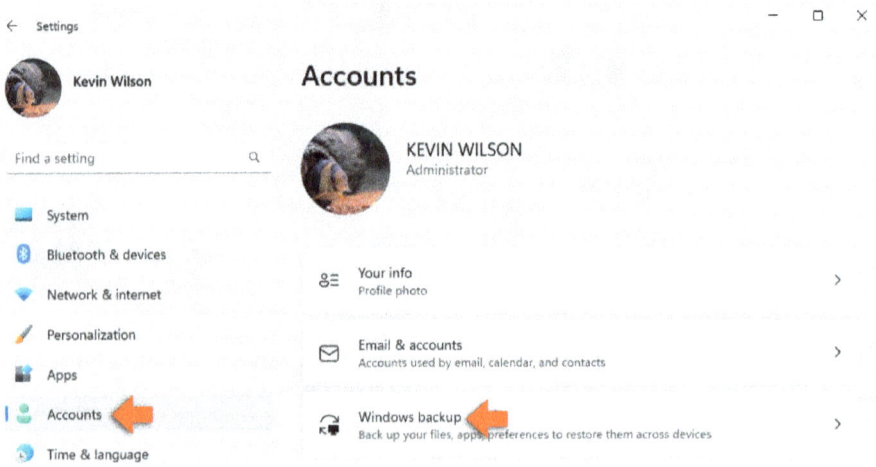

Click on 'manage sync settings'

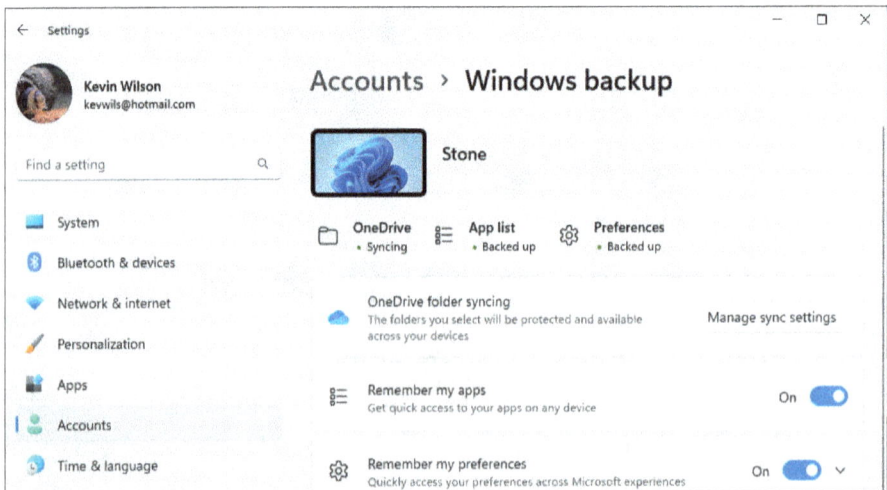

Turn on the switches next to the folders you want to back up. Click 'save changes' when you're done

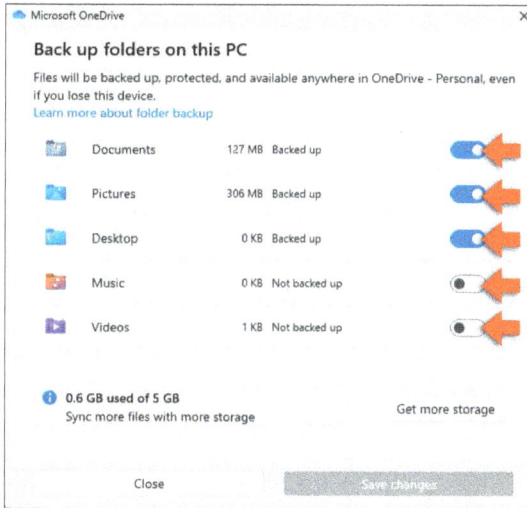

Note that you only get 5GB of storage space with a free Microsoft Account. If you need more you'll have to pay a subscription. To do this click 'get more storage' and follow the prompts. If you have a Microsoft 365 subscription, you'll already have 1TB of space.

## Backing up Settings, Apps & Credentials

Open the settings app, select 'accounts' from the list on the left hand side. Click on 'windows backup'.

Scroll down turn on 'remember my apps, and 'remember my preferences'

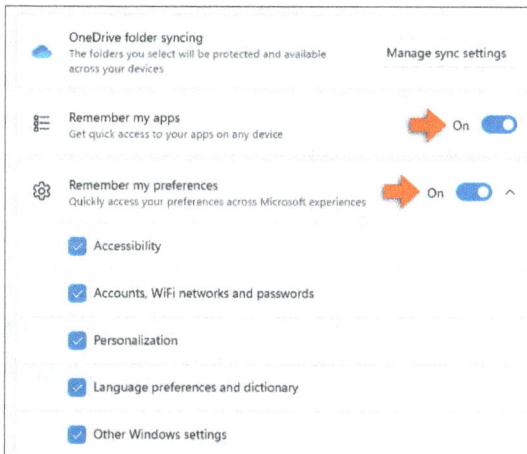

**Remember my apps:** saves the apps you use and install on your device, and you will have the option to sync these apps across other devices that you sign into with the same Microsoft account. This can be useful if you want a consistent app experience across multiple devices.

**Remember my preferences** will allow Microsoft to remember various user preferences and apply them across different Microsoft services and devices. Within this category, there are several sub-settings:

**Accessibility** will save screen reader preferences or magnification settings, will be remembered and applied across devices.

**Accounts, WiFi networks and passwords** will save information about your accounts as well as known WiFi networks and passwords will be synchronized across devices, making it easier to connect to networks you've previously used.

**Personalization** will save settings related to the appearance and behavior of Windows, such as your wallpaper, theme, and other personalization settings.

## Restoring

When you get a new PC or if you have to reinstall Windows for whatever reason, you'll get an option to restore the latest backup when you log in with the same Microsoft account that you used to make the backup.

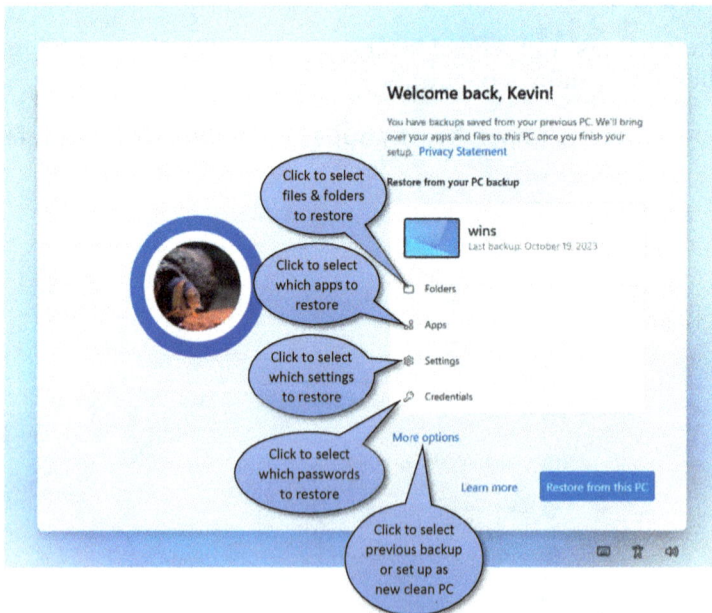

If you only want to restore specific settings, click 'settings' and select what you want to restore. Do the same for apps, folders and credentials.

Restore from your PC backup

**wins**
Last backup: October 19, 2023

📁 Folders

o8 Apps

⚙ Settings

🔑 Credentials

If you have more than one device backed up, select 'more options' and select the backup you want to restore.

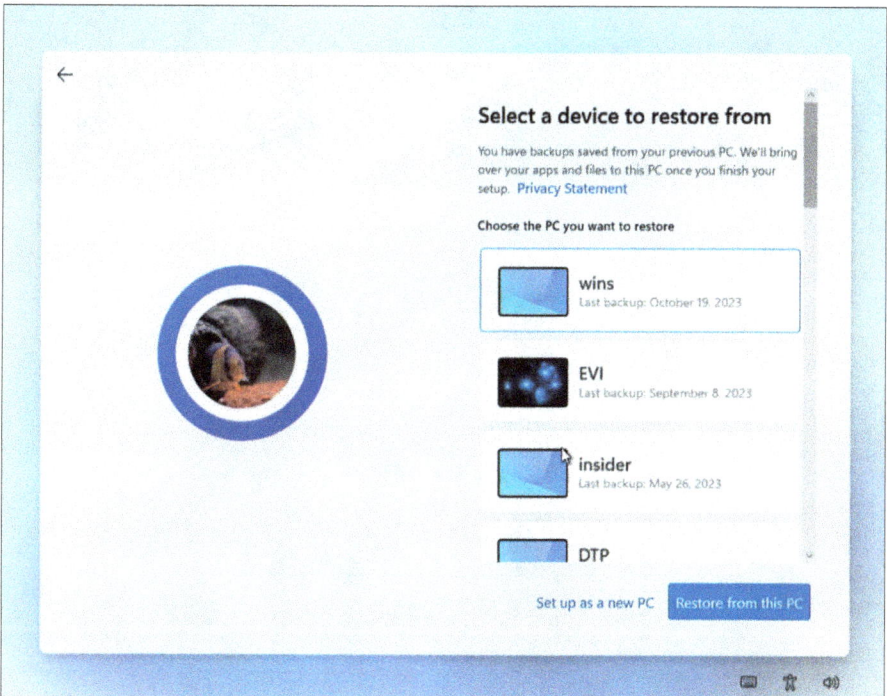

**Select a device to restore from**

You have backups saved from your previous PC. We'll bring over your apps and files to this PC once you finish your setup. Privacy Statement

Choose the PC you want to restore

**wins**
Last backup: October 19, 2023

**EVI**
Last backup: September 8, 2023

**insider**
Last backup: May 26, 2023

**DTP**

Set up as a new PC    Restore from this PC

All your personal files will have been synced to OneDrive and will be available when you sign back in using your Microsoft Account.

Click 'restore from this PC' when you're done.

# PIN Recovery

You can recover a forgotten Microsoft Account password from the login screen. Click 'I forgot my PIN' underneath the password field. If you don't see this field, it usually appears after you've entered an incorrect PIN.

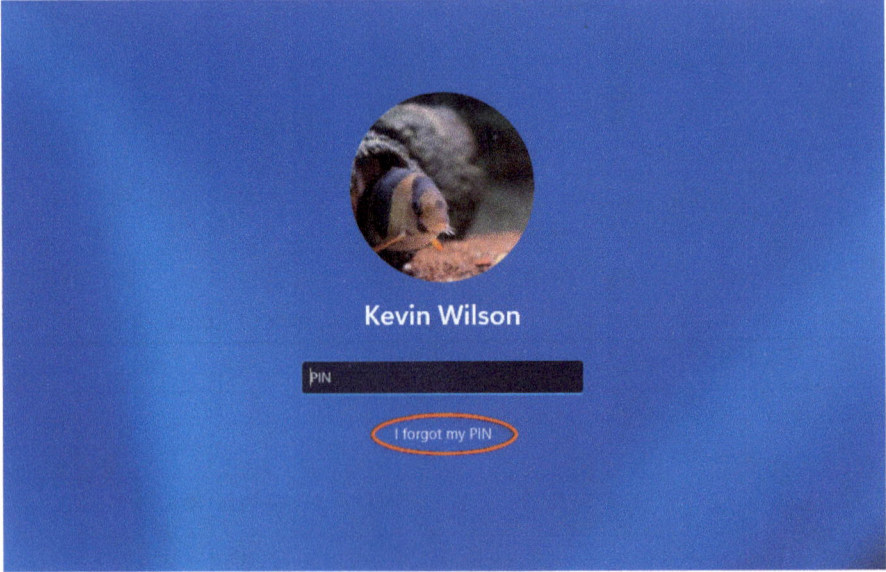

Enter your Microsoft Account Password.

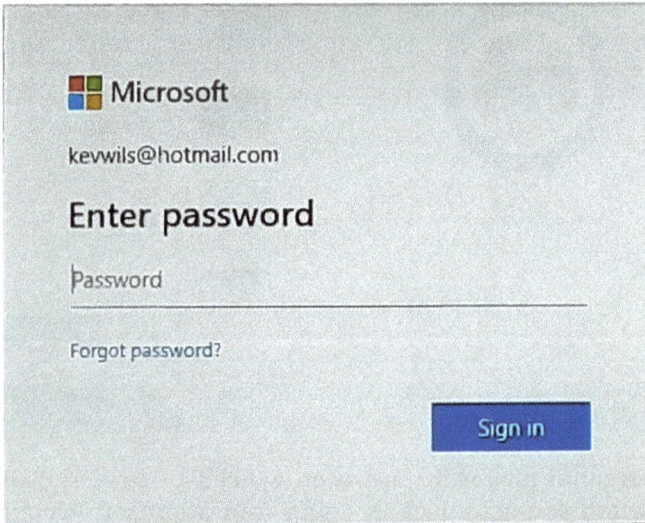

Click 'sign in'.

Select your recovery email address. This is the email address you entered when you signed up for a Microsoft Account. Select the email address, then type in your email address to confirm. Click 'send code'.

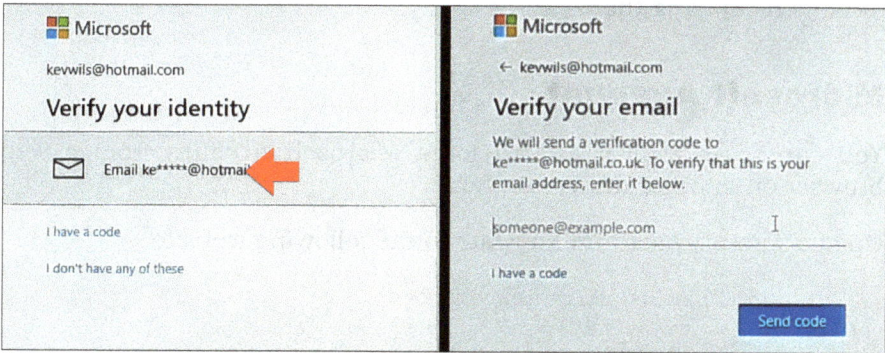

Now, go and check that email address - the account for the email address you just entered above. You'll see an email from 'microsoft account team' with a code. Enter the code in the field below and click 'verify'.

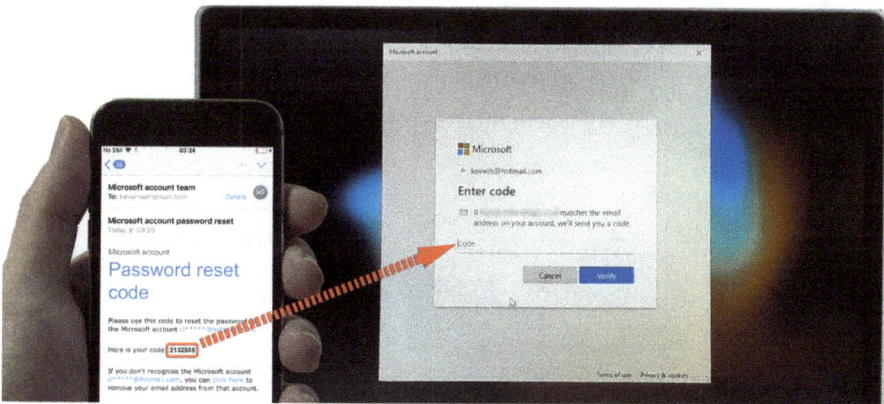

Click 'verify'. Click 'continue' on the 'are you sure' confirmation screen.

Now enter your new PIN, then click 'ok'.

# Password Recovery

You should make every effort to remember passwords and keep them safe, as recovering them can be tricky.

## Microsoft Account

You can reset your password for a Microsoft Account from a web browser on another device or phone.

Open a web browser and navigate to the following website.

```
account.live.com/password/reset
```

or

```
account.live.com/acsr
```

Follow the instructions on the screen.

## Local Account

Select the Reset password link on the sign-in screen. The reset link only appears after you enter an incorrect password.

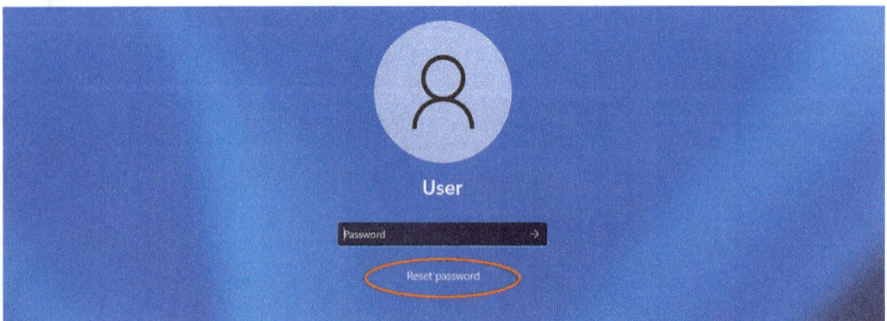

Answer the security questions you setup when you created the account.

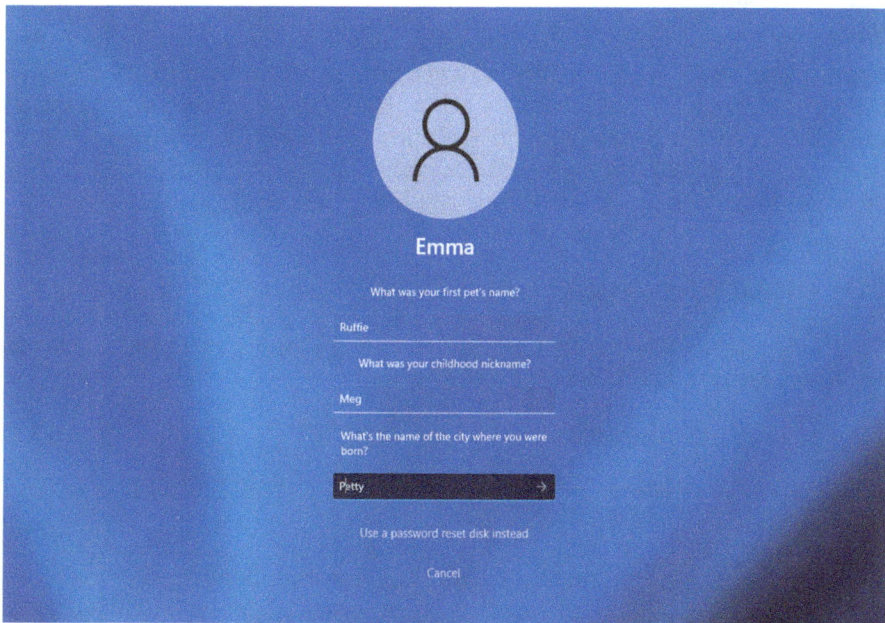

Enter a new password, then click the small arrow to the right.

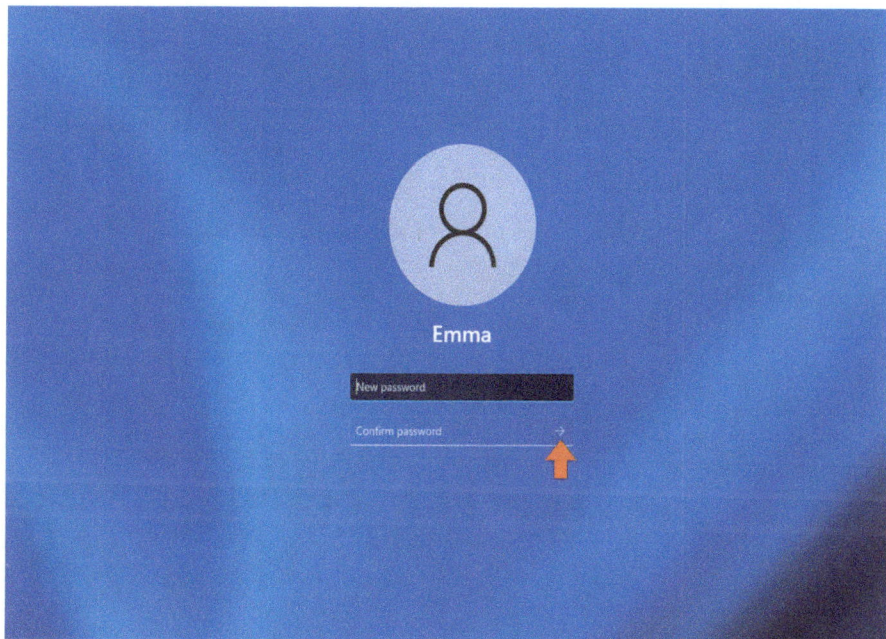

Sign in as usual with the new password.

# Changing Passwords

Windows 11 encourages the use of Windows Hello — which includes sign-in methods such as PIN, fingerprint, or facial recognition — for faster and more secure authentication. However, traditional password-based sign-in is still supported for both Microsoft accounts and local user accounts. If Windows Hello is not available or configured, users can continue to sign in with their regular password.

## Microsoft Account

To change your Microsoft Account password, open your web browser then navigate to the following website

```
account.microsoft.com
```

*Sign in with your Microsoft Account Email address and current password if prompted.*

At the top of the page, on the right, click 'change password'.

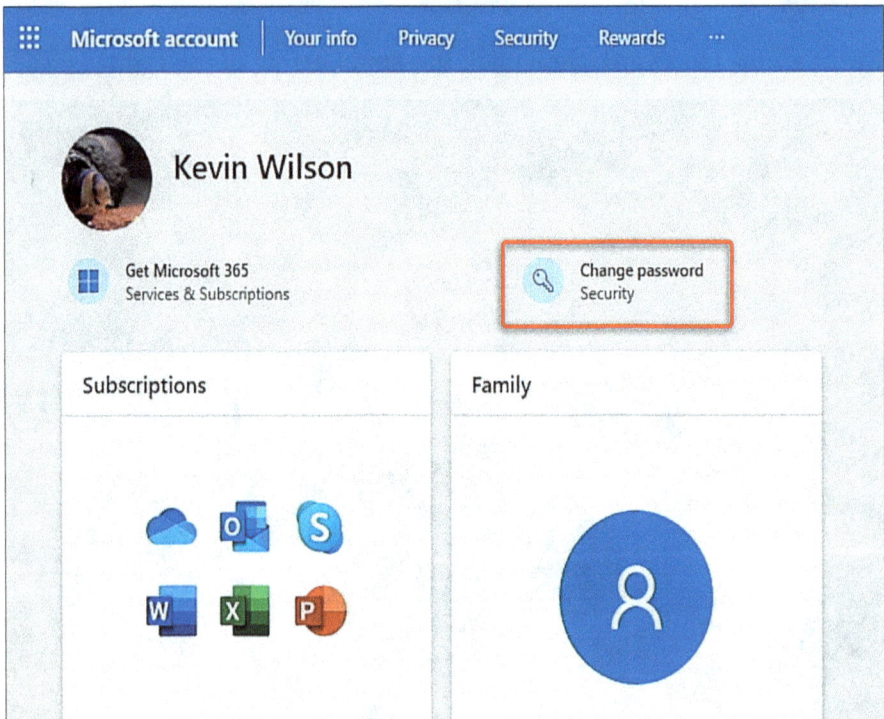

Follow the instructions on screen to change your password.

# Windows Update

Windows update usually automatically downloads and installs all updates available for Windows.

Scan for Video

## Settings

You can find Windows Update in the Settings App on the start menu. Select 'windows update'.

You'll land on the Windows Update page. At the top, you'll see available updates. Click 'check for updates' to check, click 'download now' to download updates.

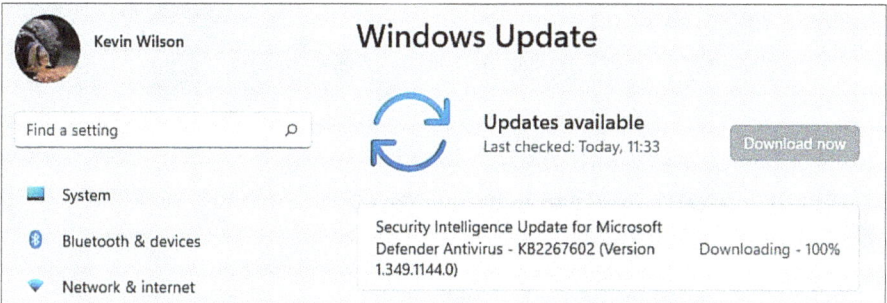

At the bottom you'll see some options. Here, you can pause updates for a set amount of time - this prevents updates from being installed during this period. You can also see a list of updates in update history

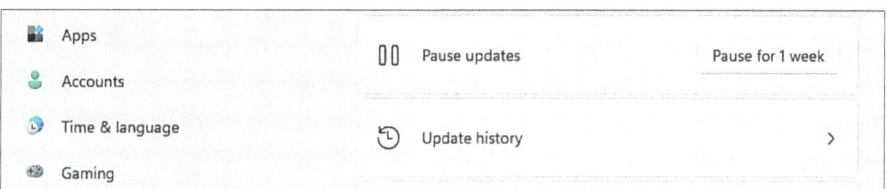

# Chapter 10: System Maintenance

At the bottom, you'll see advanced options.

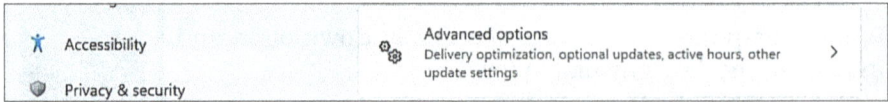

| | | |
|---|---|---|
| 🏃 Accessibility | ⚙️ | Advanced options |
| | | Delivery optimization, optional updates, active hours, other update settings  > |
| 🛡️ Privacy & security | | |

Let's take a look at the advanced options.

### ··· > Advanced options

Turn this on if you have Office, or other Microsoft apps installed

↻ Receive updates for other Microsoft products
Get Microsoft Office and other updates together with Windows updates — **On** ⬤

This one is usually best left off for most situations to minimise interruptions

⏩ Get me up to date
Restart as soon as possible (even during active hours) to finish updating, and notify me 15 minutes before restarting so I can make sure this device is on and plugged in — **Off** ⬤

Best left off to save your cellular/mobile data. Use WiFi to update windows

⊘ Download updates over metered connections
Data charges may apply — **Off** ⬤

🔔 Notify me when a restart is required to finish updating
Show notification when your device requires a restart to finish updating — **Off** ⬤

Set the times you use your device. This will prevent windows update interrupting you

🕘 Active hours
We won't restart your device during these hours — Currently 08:00 to 17:00 ⌄

To change active hours, click 'active hours', select 'manual', then choose a start time and an end time.

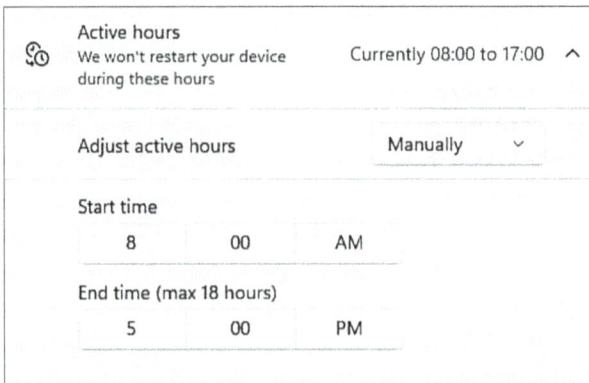

| | | |
|---|---|---|
| 🕘 Active hours<br>We won't restart your device during these hours | Currently 08:00 to 17:00 ⌃ | |
| Adjust active hours | Manually ⌄ | |
| Start time | | |
| 8 | 00 | AM |
| End time (max 18 hours) | | |
| 5 | 00 | PM |

At the bottom of the page, you'll see optional updates. These are usually optional windows features, or device drivers. Click on 'optional updates' to view the options.

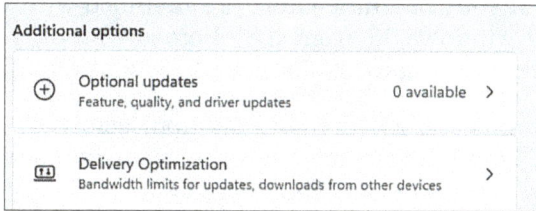

Additional options

| | | |
|---|---|---|
| ⊕ | **Optional updates**<br>Feature, quality, and driver updates | 0 available > |
| 🔲 | **Delivery Optimization**<br>Bandwidth limits for updates, downloads from other devices | > |

Underneath you'll see delivery optimization. If you have multiple windows 11 devices on your home or office network you can use Delivery Optimization to reduce internet bandwidth consumption by sharing the downloaded updates among the multiple devices on your network. This means that the update packages are downloaded from the internet to a device on the network, the update packages are then shared from this device and made available to other devices on the network, so they can update without having to download the package again from the internet.

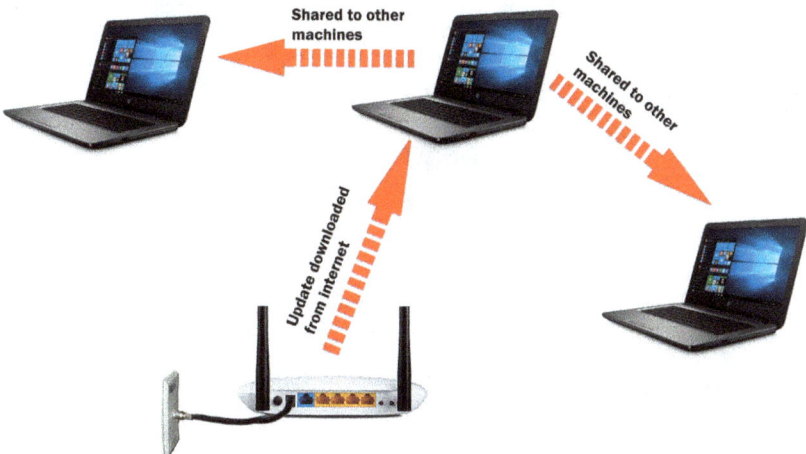

To enable delivery optimisation, click 'delivery optimization'. Click the slider switch to turn it on and select 'PCs on my local network'.

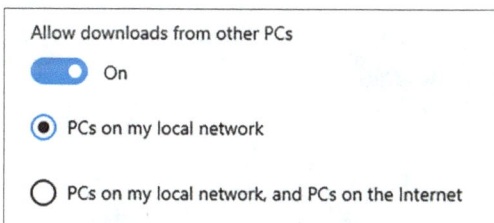

Allow downloads from other PCs

🔵 On

🔘 PCs on my local network

⚪ PCs on my local network, and PCs on the Internet

# Activating Windows

To activate windows, you'll need a license with a product key or a digital license. If your machine came pre-installed with windows 11 or you purchased windows 11 from the Microsoft Store, you most likely have a digital licence meaning Windows 11 will automatically activate.

To activate Windows, open the settings app, select 'system' from the list on the left. Scroll down the list on the right then select 'activation'

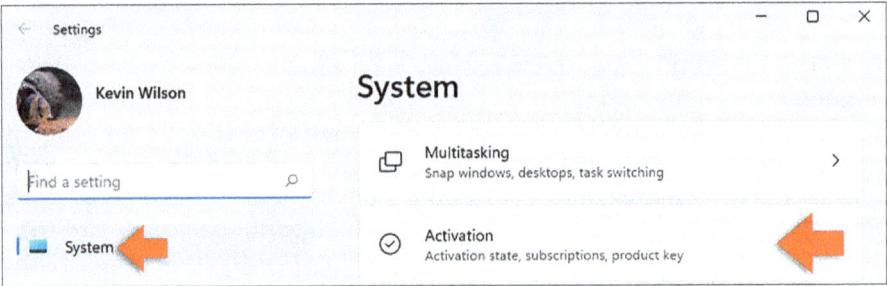

Click 'change product key'.

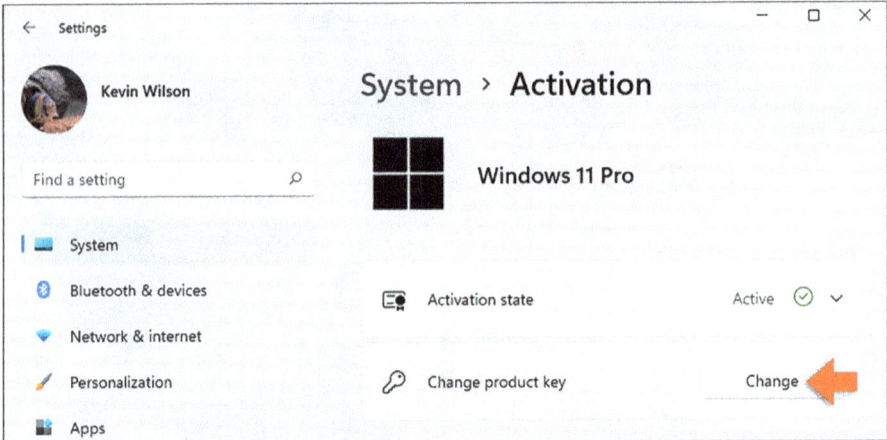

Enter your product key into pop-up box. Click 'next'.

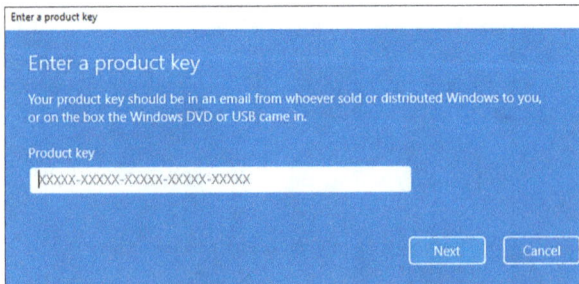

# System File Check

System File Check or SFC, is a command line tool that allows you to scan for and restore corrupted windows system files. Useful when troubleshooting certain windows problems.

Open the windows terminal as an administrator - right click on the start button, then select 'windows terminal (admin)' from the popup menu.

Type the following command

```
sfc /scannow
```

SFC will scan your system files and replace any it finds to be corrupt.

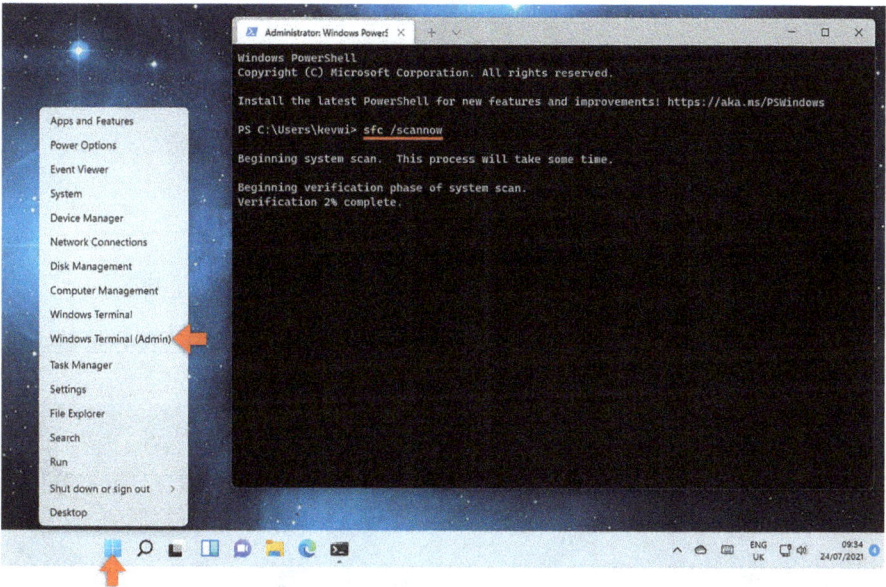

To check the log file, type:

```
notepad $Env:WinDir\Logs\CBS\CBS.log
```

This will open the log file in notepad.

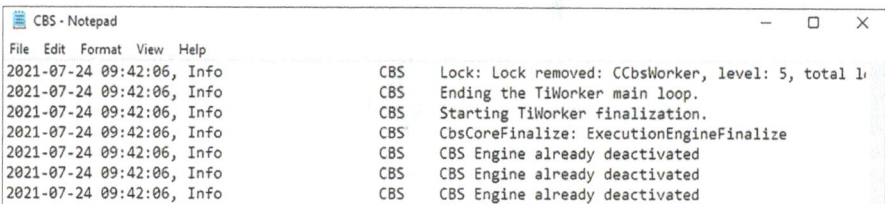

# DISM

DISM stands for Deployment Image Servicing and Management and is a command-line tool on all Windows computers used to modify, and repair windows images. A Windows image contains a list of all of the components (the windows component store), settings, and packages that are available for install. The Windows Component Store is used for customizing and updating Windows such as enabling or disabling features, and system recovery.

You can check the Windows Component Store for errors. To do this, open the windows terminal as an administrator - right click on the start button, then select 'windows terminal (admin)' from the popup menu. Type the following command

```
DISM /Online /Cleanup-Image /RestoreHealth
```

The **Online** option means DISM will be service the Operating System you're running the command on. In other words DISM will work on files for your operating system instead of an offline image.

The **RestoreHealth** option automatically scans and repairs common issues.

The **Cleanup-Image** option performs an extensive error check.

Once you execute the command, the DISM tool will start to repair the Windows Component Store if it finds any errors.

```
Windows PowerShell
Copyright (C) Microsoft Corporation. All rights reserved.

Install the latest PowerShell for new features and improvements!
s

PS C:\Users\kevwi> DISM /Online /Cleanup-Image /RestoreHealth

Deployment Image Servicing and Management tool
Version: 10.0.25252.1000

Image Version: 10.0.25252.1010

[==                        4.2%                           ]
```

This might take a while. DISM will report any errors it finds.

**448**

# Managing Drives

You can defragment and optimize your drives, as well as clean up temporary files.

## Disk De-fragmentation

Data is saved in blocks on the surface of the disk called clusters. When a computer saves your file, it writes the data to the next empty cluster on the disk, even if the clusters are not adjacent. This allows faster performance, and usually, the disk is spinning fast enough that this has little effect on the time it takes to open the file.

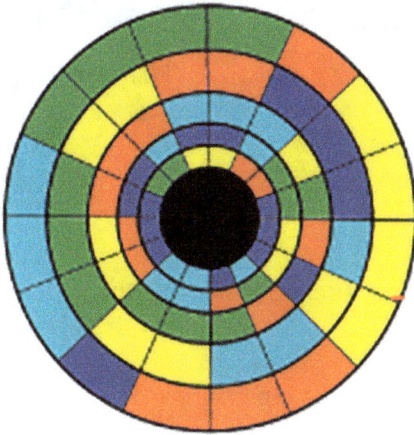

**Fragmented Files**                    **De-Fragmented Files**

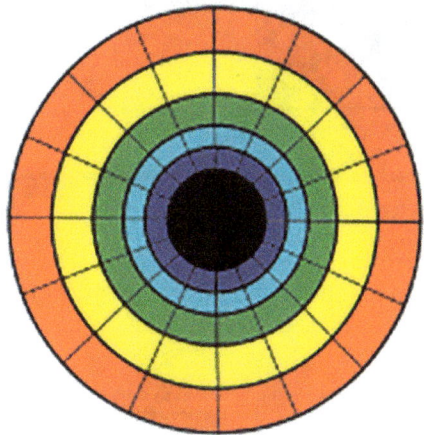

However, as more and more files are created, saved, deleted or changed, the data becomes fragmented across the surface of a disk, and it takes longer to access. This can cause problems when launching software (because it will often load many different files as it launches). So bad fragmentation just makes every operation on the computer take longer but eventually fragmentation can cause applications to crash, hang, or even corrupt the data.

It's a good rule of thumb to do this roughly once a month, to keep things running smoothly.

Disk defragmentation only applies to hard drives with mechanical spinning disks (HDD). If you have a solid state drive or SSD, then you don't need to worry about defragmentation. Windows 11 will automatically maintain the SSD using the TRIM command, not defragmentation. TRIM helps the SSD manage deleted data efficiently and prolongs its lifespan

# Chapter 10: System Maintenance

To defragment the disk in Windows 11, click the search icon on the taskbar, then type 'defragment'. Click 'Defragment and optimise your drives'.

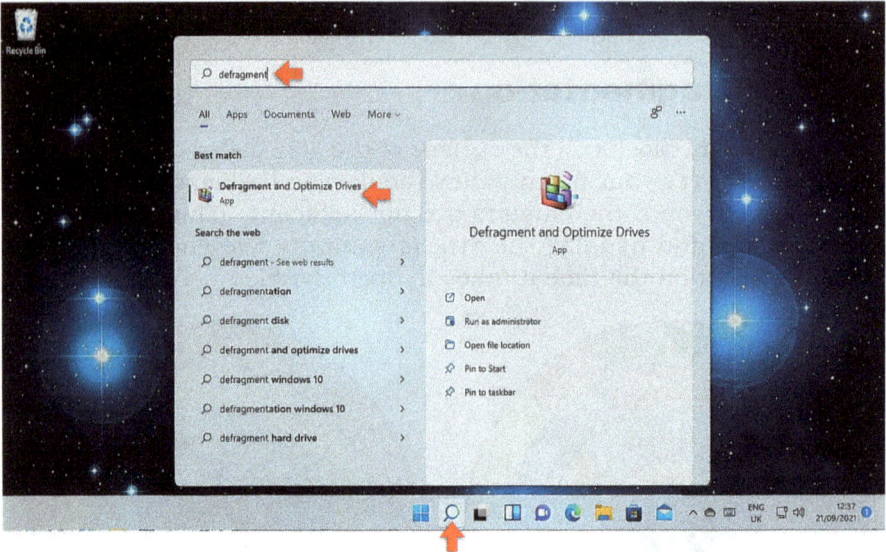

Select the drive you want to defrag. Click the 'optimize' button.

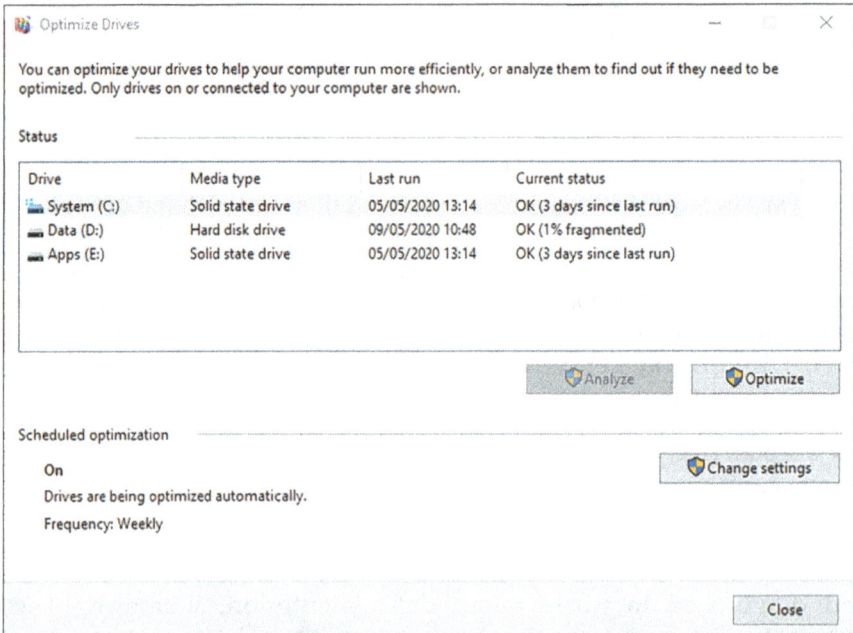

This will start de-fragmenting your disk. This process can take a while.

# Disk Clean-Up

Over time, windows gets clogged up with temporary files from browsing the internet, installing and un-installing software and general every day usage. Doing this once a month will help keep things running smoothly.

Click the search icon on the taskbar then type 'disk cleanup'.

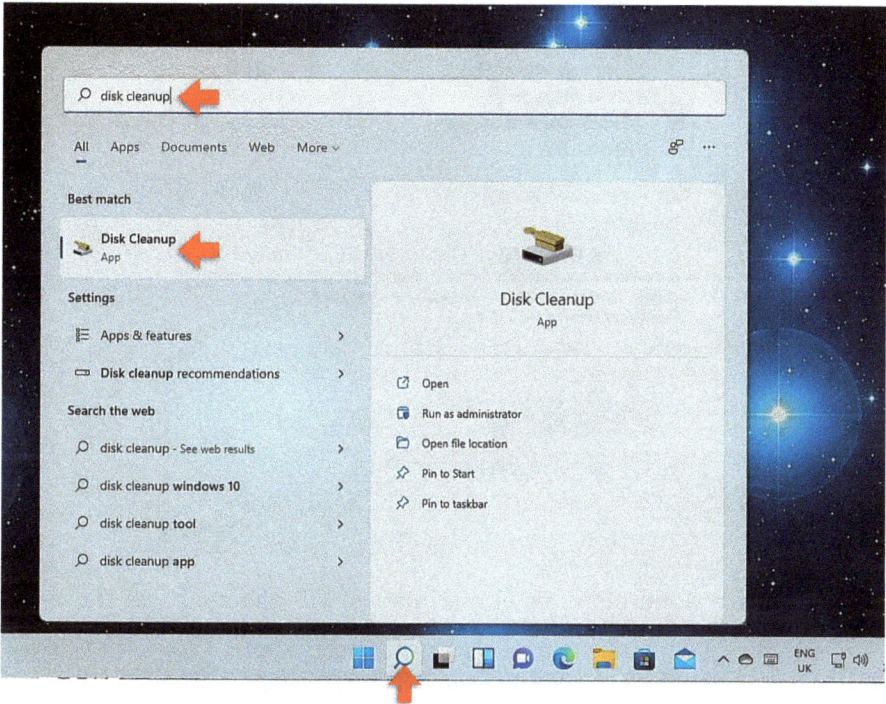

Click 'clear disk space by deleting unnecessary files'

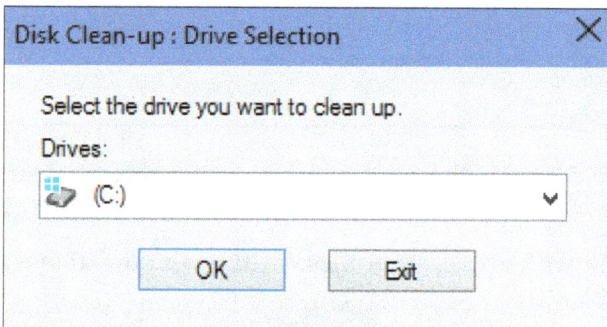

Select drive C, click 'ok'.

# Chapter 10: System Maintenance

In the window that appears you can see a list of all the different files and caches. It is safe to select all these for clearing.

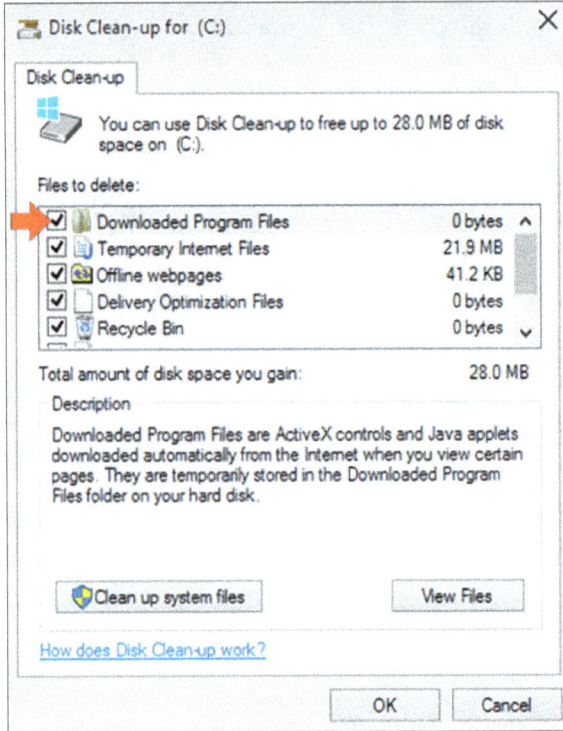

Once you are done click ok and windows will clear out all those old files.

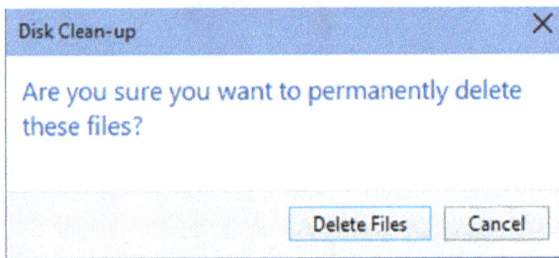

Click 'delete files' on the confirmation dialog box to clear out all the old files

Do the same with the system files. In the window above, click 'clean up system files'.

This helps to keep your system running smoothly. A good rule of thumb is to do this about once a month.

# Disk Manager

This utility allows you to view and manage disk drives, partitions and volumes. You can also manage external drives such as USB drives (flash drives), and external hard drives. **Use this utility with caution as you can wipe drives, volumes and partitions, which means the data on those drives and partitions will be lost.**

To open disk manager, right click on the start button, select 'disk management' from the menu.

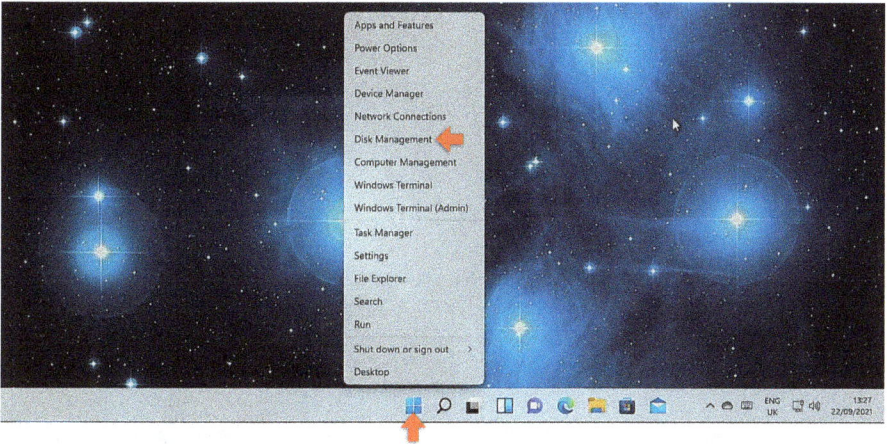

Let's take a look at the main screen.

# Chapter 10: System Maintenance

## Drive Volumes

Find the drive you want to create a volume on. Disk 1 on this PC is an external hard drive I plugged into a USB port. In this demo, I'm going to create a new volume on this drive.

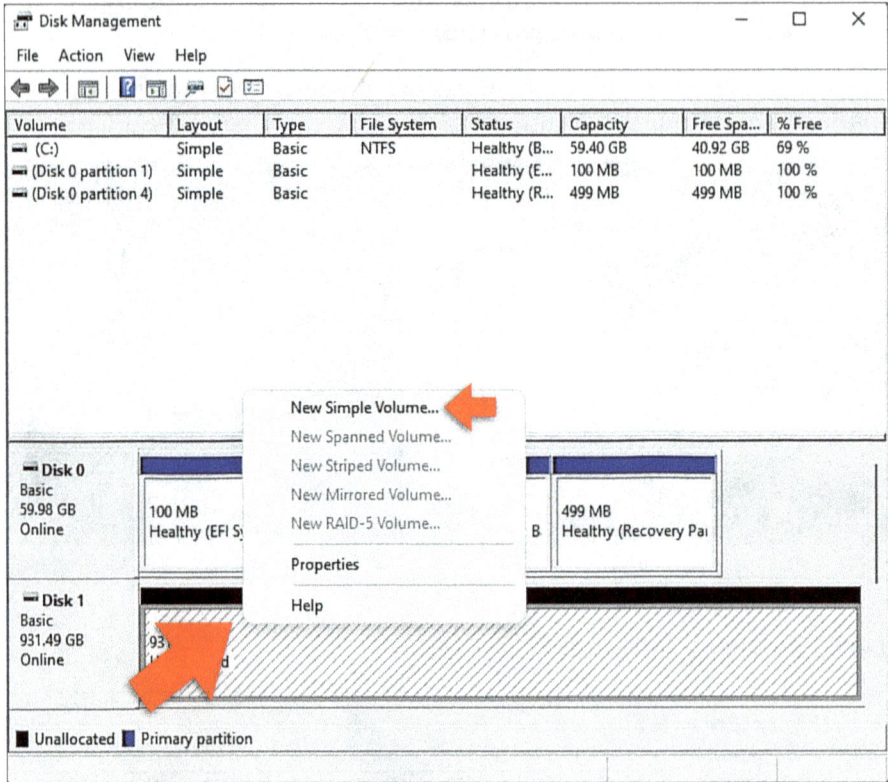

In the lower half of the screen, right click on the unallocated part of the disk, select 'new simple volume' from the popup menu. Click 'next'.

Enter the size of the volume in MB, or leave it as the default if you want to use the whole drive. In this example, I'm creating a volume that is 4GB (4096MB) in size. Click 'next'.

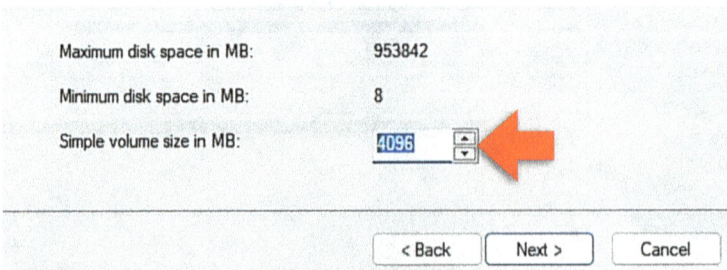

Assign a drive letter, eg Drive D: Click 'next'.

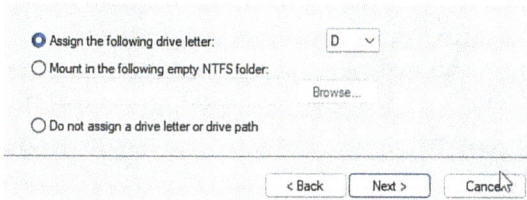

Under 'file system' select a file system. Select NTFS if you use the drive on Windows only. Select exFAT or FAT32 if you use the drive on a Mac, Linux and Windows.

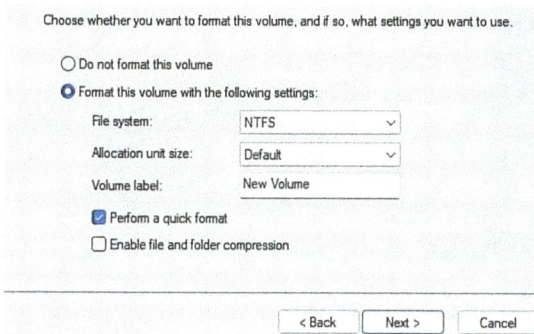

Under 'volume label' give the drive a meaningful name. Click 'next', then 'finish'.

You'll see the partition appear in the bottom half of the screen.

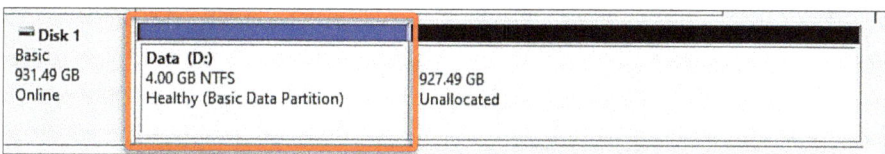

To delete a volume, right click on the volume then select 'delete volume' from the menu. **Use with caution as doing this will wipe the data off the volume.**

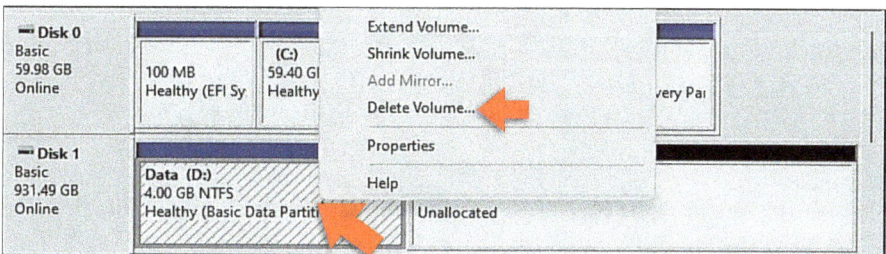

# Add/Remove Windows Features

You can turn on/off various features in Windows 11. To do this click the search icon on the taskbar, then type 'turn windows features on or off'. Click 'turn windows features on or off' in the search results.

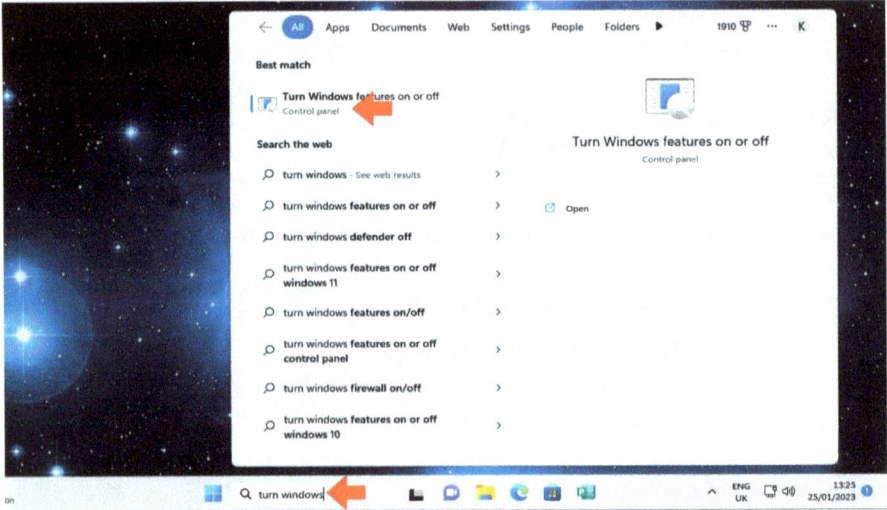

Scroll down the list, select the options you want to install, and deselect the ones you want to remove.

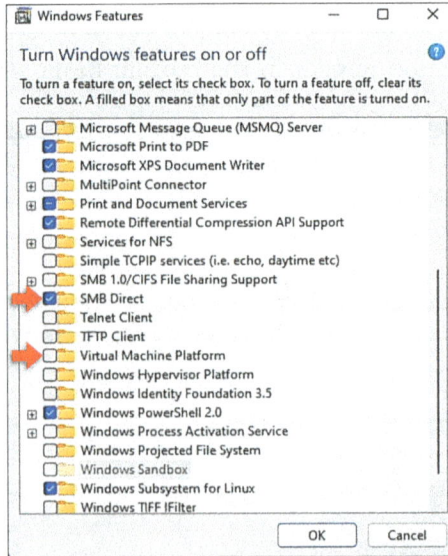

Click 'ok', when you're done. Windows will restart and add/remove your selections.

# Maintaining Apps

In Windows 11, you can remove apps you don't use, you can reset apps if they're not working correctly, and you can change which apps run at windows startup.

## Removing Apps

To remove apps and programs from your computer, right click on the start button, select 'apps and features' from the menu.

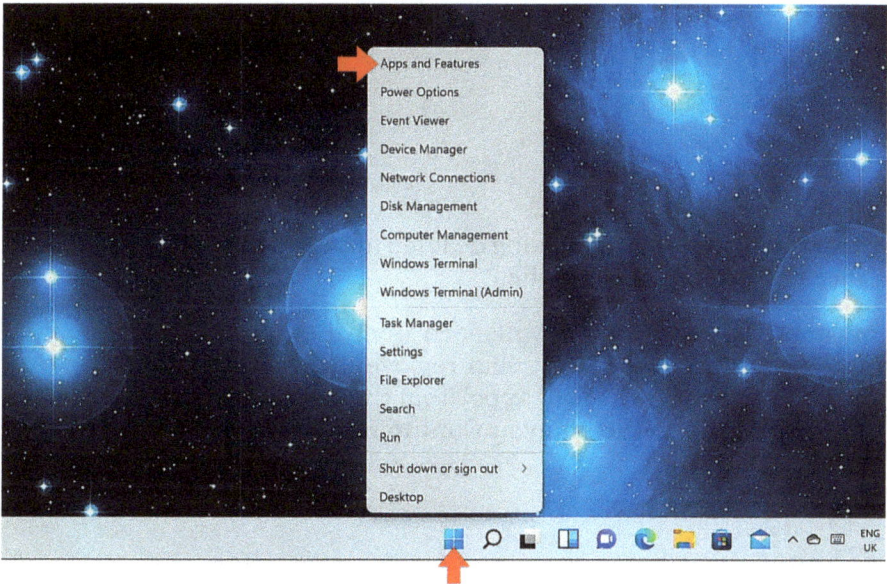

Scroll down to the app you want to remove, then click the three dots icon. Select 'uninstall' from the menu.

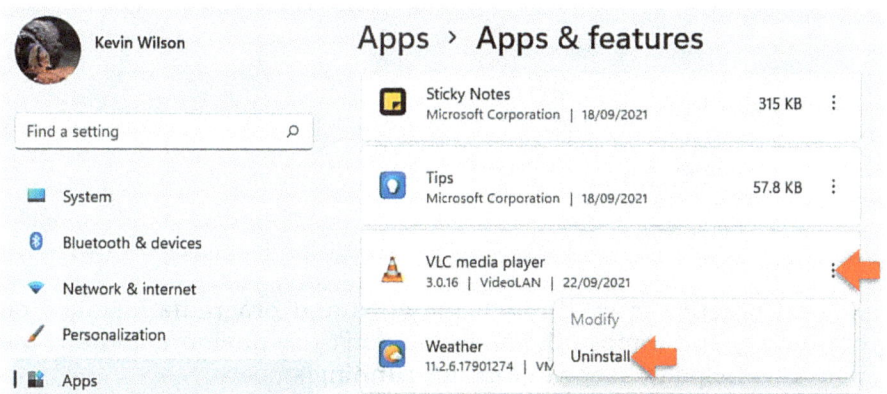

# Chapter 10: System Maintenance

Now, depending on what program you are trying to remove, you might get a screen asking you what you want to do. Click 'next', and run through the wizard.

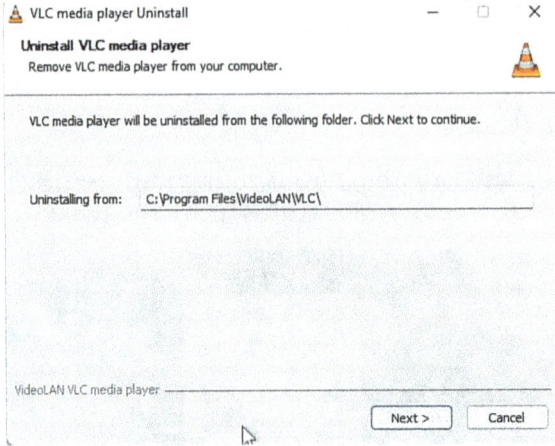

This is the process for removing desktop applications such as Microsoft Office or Adobe Creative Suite.

For apps that you have downloaded from the App Store or ones that come with Windows 11, you can remove them directly from the start menu. To do this, select 'all apps' from the top right of the start menu, then right click on the app you want to remove, select 'uninstall' from the menu.

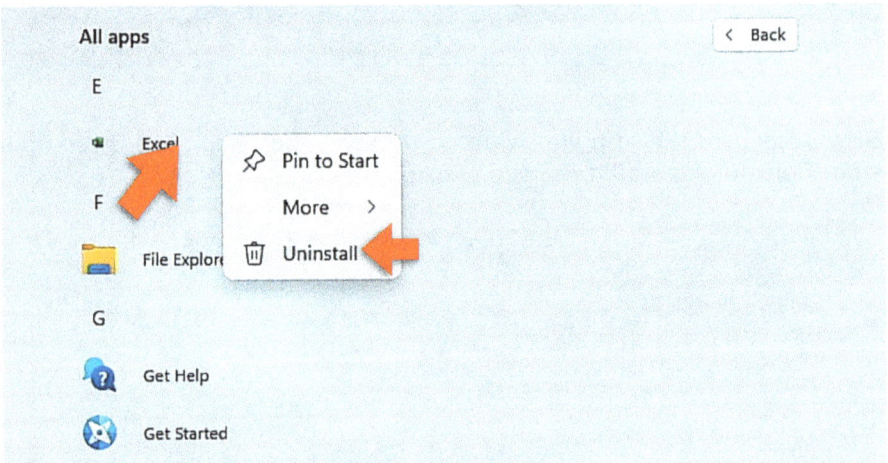

It's good practice to go through the apps and programs installed on your device, and remove the ones you don't use anymore and any old apps. This helps to keep your device running smoothly.

## Resetting & Repairing Apps

Sometimes apps can become slow and unresponsive, so in Windows 11, you have the option to reset or repair the app. This will clear all the App's data, history lists, caches, settings and so on. This doesn't clear any of your personal files etc.

To do this, right click on the start menu, select 'apps and features'.

Click the three dots icon next to the app you want to reset, select 'advanced options'.

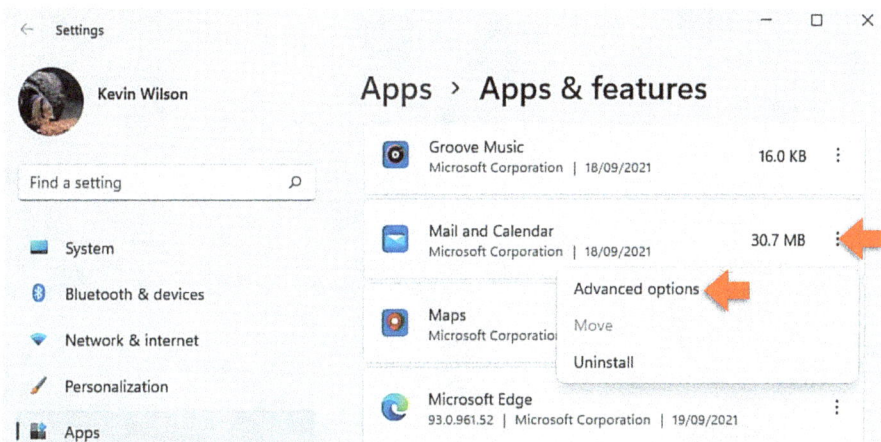

From the advanced options, scroll down the screen, click 'reset' to reset the app, or repair to repair the app.

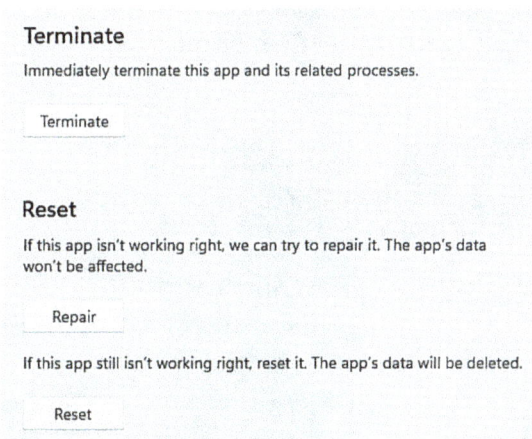

Click 'terminate' to close the app down. You can start it up again from the start menu.

# Startup Programs

Start up programs automatically start when you start up Windows - this can cause Windows to become very sluggish during start up. These are usually 'helper' apps that are installed with certain pieces of software and most can be disabled without any problem.

To find your startup programs, open your settings app, then select 'apps' from the list on the left hand side. Scroll down, then click 'startup'.

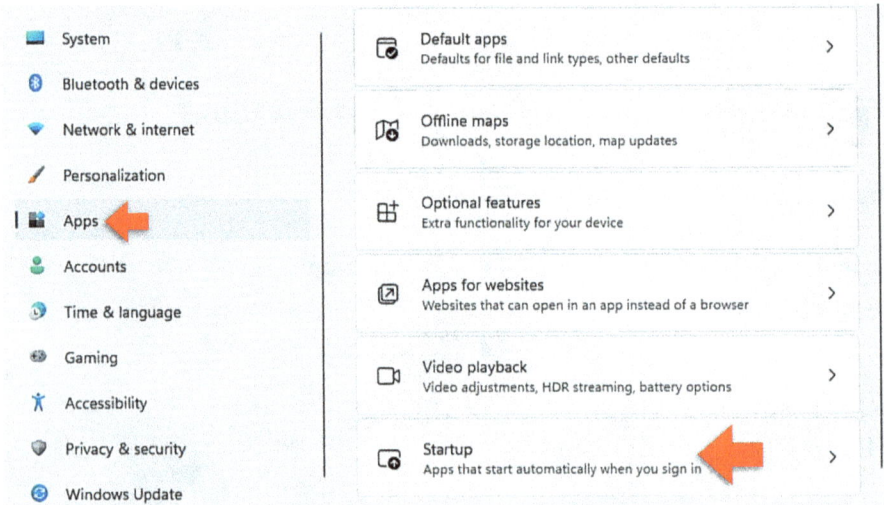

On this screen you'll see a list of apps that are configured to start when Windows starts. Click the sliders next to each app to either enable or disable them - you can turn then on or off.

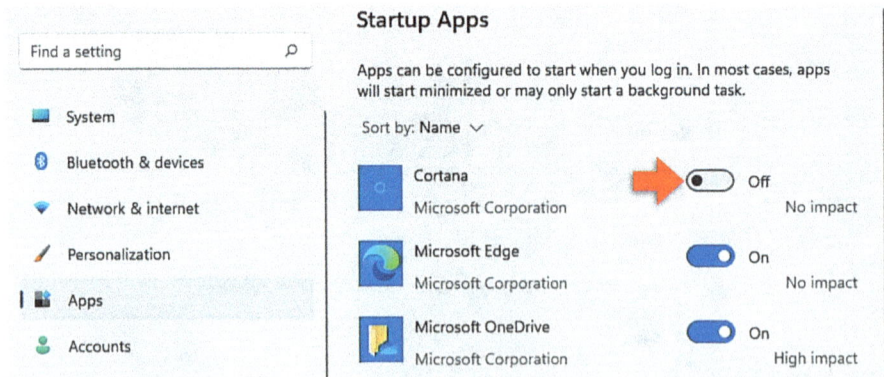

You can turn off most of these, except anti-virus, onedrive, and anything to do with your graphics or sound cards.

# System Recovery

If you are having problems, Windows 11 has a section to recover your computer. You can boot to the recovery environment from the settings app. Windows 11 will also startup into the recovery environment after two failed attempts to restart.

To find the recovery options in Windows, open the settings app, select 'system' from the list on the left. Scroll down, click 'recovery'.

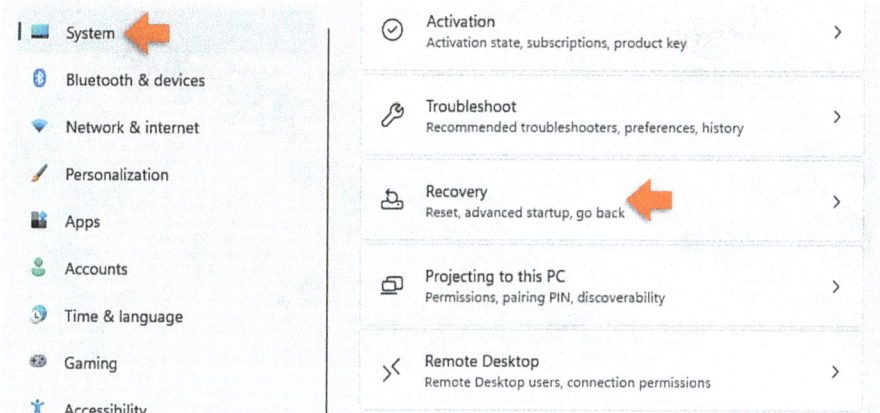

| | |
|---|---|
| **System** | ✓ Activation — Activation state, subscriptions, product key › |
| ⓘ Bluetooth & devices | 🔧 Troubleshoot — Recommended troubleshooters, preferences, history › |
| ▼ Network & internet | |
| ✏ Personalization | 🔄 Recovery — Reset, advanced startup, go back › |
| 🗐 Apps | |
| 👤 Accounts | 🖥 Projecting to this PC — Permissions, pairing PIN, discoverability › |
| 🕘 Time & language | |
| 🎮 Gaming | ✕ Remote Desktop — Remote Desktop users, connection permissions › |
| ✦ Accessibility | |

In the first section, under 'recovery options' you can reset your PC - this re-installs Windows 11 leaving all your personal files intact. To do this click 'Reset PC'.

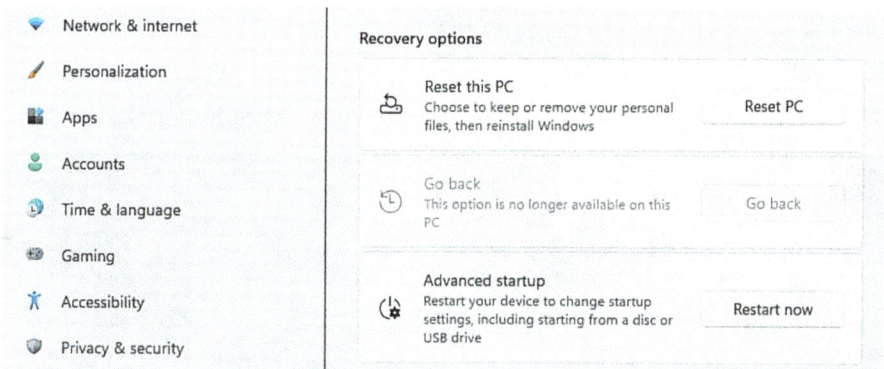

| | Recovery options | |
|---|---|---|
| ▼ Network & internet | | |
| ✏ Personalization | **Reset this PC** — Choose to keep or remove your personal files, then reinstall Windows | **Reset PC** |
| 🗐 Apps | | |
| 👤 Accounts | Go back — This option is no longer available on this PC | Go back |
| 🕘 Time & language | | |
| 🎮 Gaming | **Advanced startup** — Restart your device to change startup settings, including starting from a disc or USB drive | **Restart now** |
| ✦ Accessibility | | |
| 🛡 Privacy & security | | |

Scroll down to the next section. Here, you can go back to a previous version of Windows 11 - useful if you've installed an update but are having problems. To do this click 'Go back'.

In the section at the bottom, you can boot to the recovery environment under the 'advanced startup' section. To do this click 'restart now'.

# Force Windows into the Recovery Environment

If you're having trouble starting Windows, you can force windows 11 to boot into the recovery environment.

To do this, start your machine, then when you see the start up logo screen, hold down the power button until your screen goes blank. *If you don't see the logo you'll need to boot from the installation media - see 'boot from external drive' on page 465 for details.*

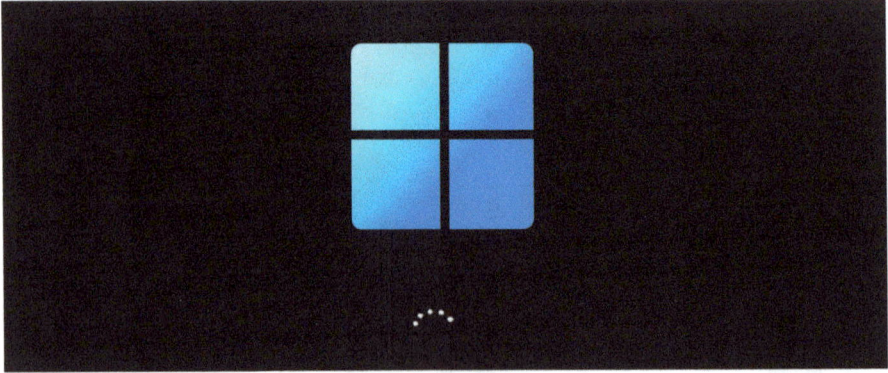

Wait a few seconds, then press the power button again to start your machine.

When you see the start up logo screen, hold down the power button again until your screen goes blank.

Wait a few seconds, then press the power button again to start your machine.

This time, allow your device to fully restart. You should see this screen.

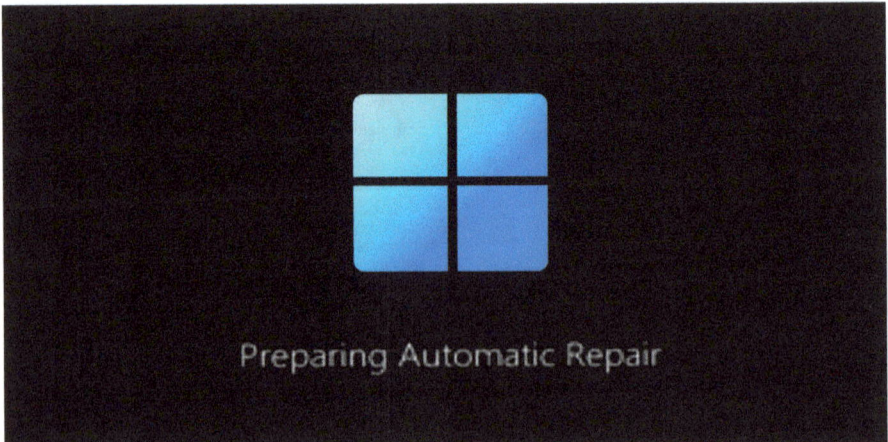

Once the WinRE environment starts, you'll see the 'automatic repair screen'.

## Automatic Repair

Automatic Repair couldn't repair your PC

Press "Advanced options" to try other options to repair your PC or "Shut down" to turn off your PC.
Log file: C:\Windows\System32\Logfiles\Srt\SrtTrail.txt

Shut down     Advanced options

Click 'advanced options' to begin.

## Reset your PC

Boot into the recovery environment as shown in the previous section.

To reinstall Windows 11 for your PC, click 'troubleshoot'.

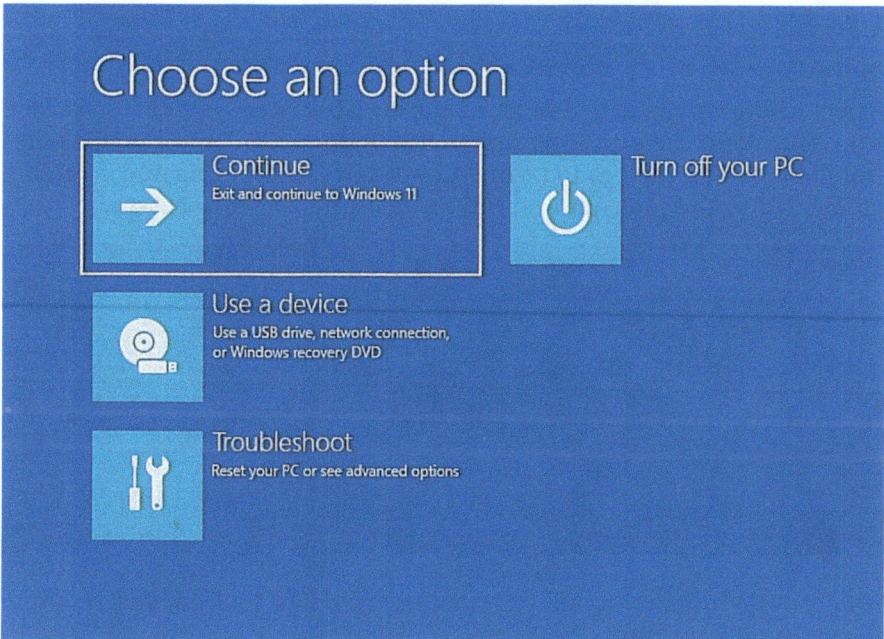

## Choose an option

→   Continue
    Exit and continue to Windows 11

⏻   Turn off your PC

💿   Use a device
    Use a USB drive, network connection,
    or Windows recovery DVD

🛠   Troubleshoot
    Reset your PC or see advanced options

From the 'troubleshoot' screen, click 'reset this PC'.

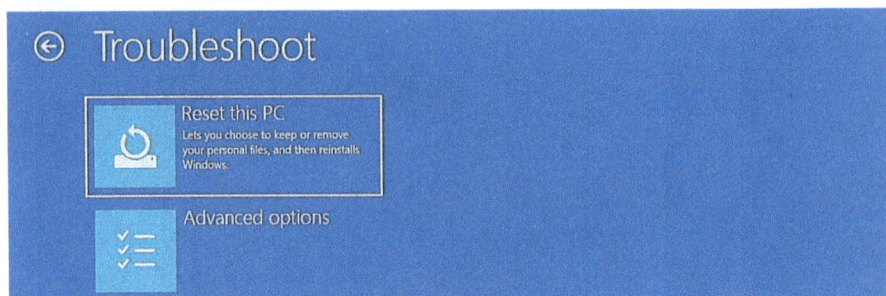

⊙ Troubleshoot

Reset this PC
Lets you choose to keep or remove your personal files, and then reinstalls Windows.

Advanced options

From here you can do a complete re-install by clicking on 'remove everything'. This will remove all your files and applications and reset Windows 11 back to its factory default. Click 'keep my files' to refresh Windows 11. This will delete all your installed applications and settings. Your personal files and data will remain intact.

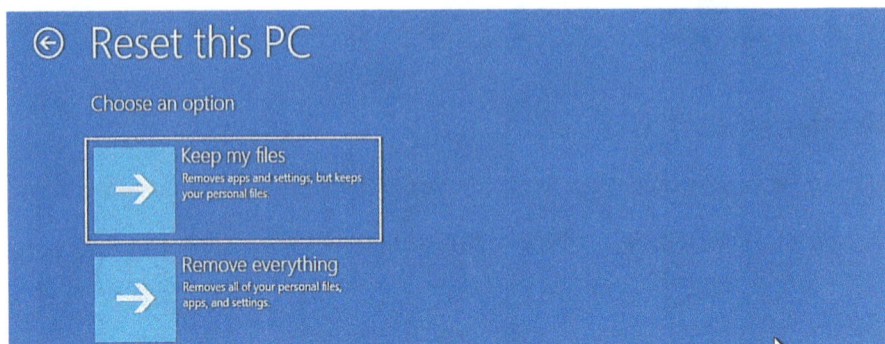

⊙ Reset this PC

Choose an option

Keep my files
Removes apps and settings, but keeps your personal files

Remove everything
Removes all of your personal files, apps, and settings

Select where you want to download the installer from. You can download from the cloud meaning the installer will download` the installer files from Microsoft's servers to re-install windows. Select this one if you are connected to the internet and have a fast internet connection.

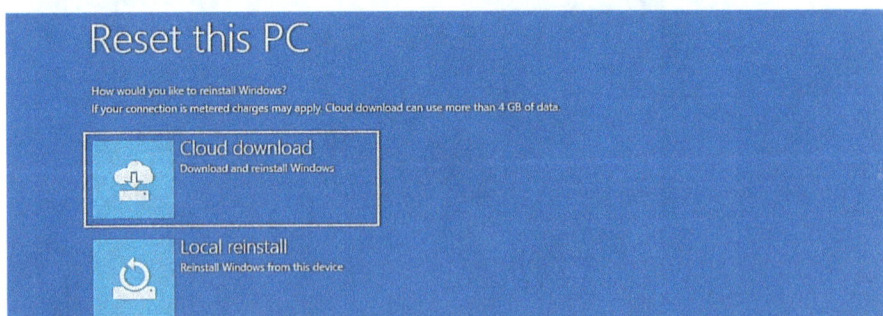

Reset this PC

How would you like to reinstall Windows?
If your connection is metered charges may apply. Cloud download can use more than 4 GB of data.

Cloud download
Download and reinstall Windows

Local reinstall
Reinstall Windows from this device

If not, click 'local reinstall' to reinstall Windows 11 from the recovery partition on your hard drive.

**464**

# Boot from External Drive (USB)

First, insert the USB drive into a USB port on your PC, then power on or restart the machine.

As it boots, watch for the startup screen that briefly displays the hotkey for accessing the boot menu. This key varies by manufacturer but is commonly Esc, F8, F10, F11, or F12. You'll need to press the key quickly—usually just after the power button is pressed—as the startup screen appears only for a brief moment.

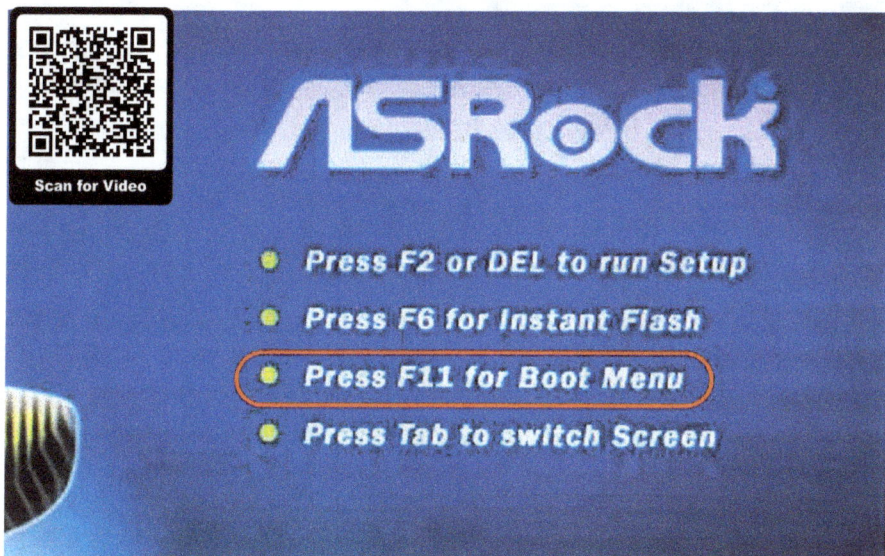

On this particular machine it's F11. *If you're using a surface tablet, press and hold the volume-down button, then press and release the power button.*

Once you find the boot menu select the UEFI USB drive, press 'enter' on your keyboard.

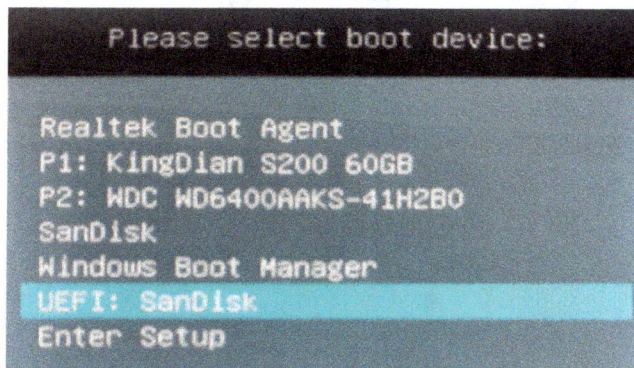

## Re-install Windows from USB Drive

Boot your PC from the USB drive. See page 465 for details. Once you boot from the drive, Windows setup will begin.

Select language, time format and your keyboard layout. Click 'next'.

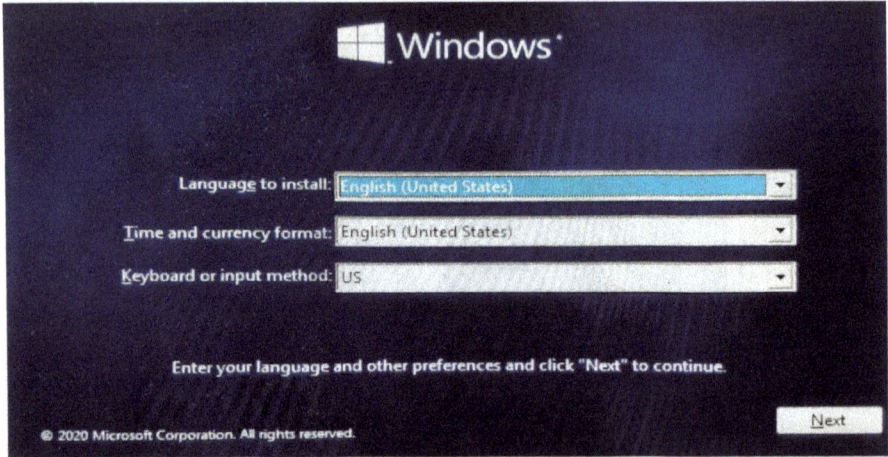

Click 'install now' to re-install windows 11.

On the 'activate windows' screen. Enter your product key - this is usually printed on a label on your PC. If you don't have one, click 'I don't have a product key' on the bottom right, you can activate later.

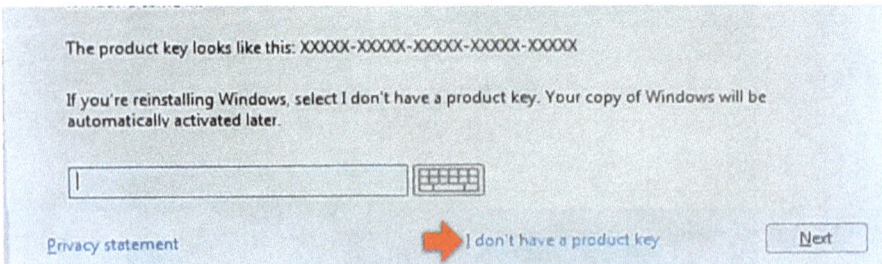

Select the version of Windows 11 you want to install. Eg 'Windows 11 Home', or 'windows 11 pro'. Click 'next'.

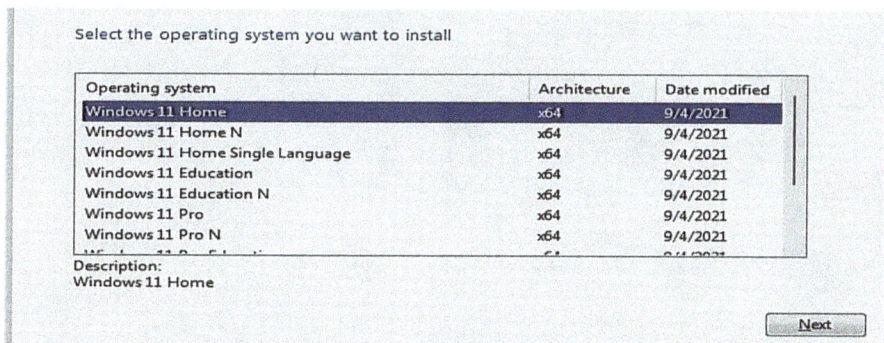

Select the operating system you want to install

| Operating system | Architecture | Date modified |
|---|---|---|
| Windows 11 Home | x64 | 9/4/2021 |
| Windows 11 Home N | x64 | 9/4/2021 |
| Windows 11 Home Single Language | x64 | 9/4/2021 |
| Windows 11 Education | x64 | 9/4/2021 |
| Windows 11 Education N | x64 | 9/4/2021 |
| Windows 11 Pro | x64 | 9/4/2021 |
| Windows 11 Pro N | x64 | 9/4/2021 |

Description:
Windows 11 Home

Next

Accept the license agreement on the following screen.

Click 'next'.

Click 'custom: install windows only'.

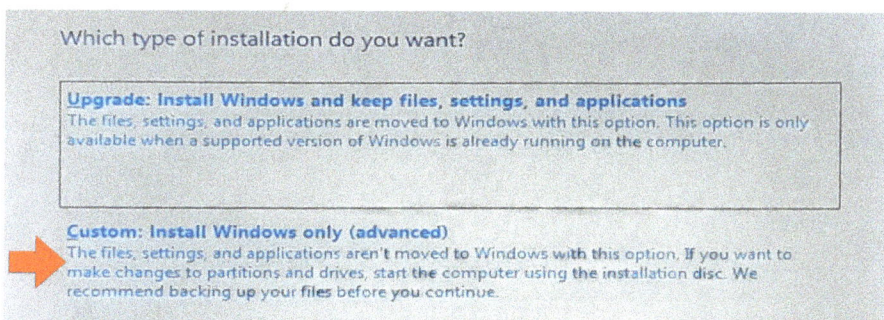

Which type of installation do you want?

**Upgrade: Install Windows and keep files, settings, and applications**
The files, settings, and applications are moved to Windows with this option. This option is only available when a supported version of Windows is already running on the computer.

**Custom: Install Windows only (advanced)**
The files, settings, and applications aren't moved to Windows with this option. If you want to make changes to partitions and drives, start the computer using the installation disc. We recommend backing up your files before you continue.

If you see 'partition 1', 'partition 2', and so on, click on each of these then select 'delete'. *Note that this will delete all the information on these partitions - so use with caution. Make sure all this data is backed up if you want to keep it.* This ensures you have a clean drive.

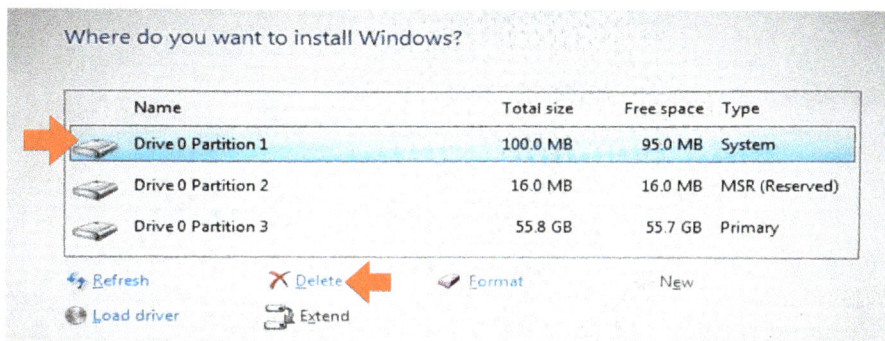

Where do you want to install Windows?

| Name | Total size | Free space | Type |
|---|---|---|---|
| Drive 0 Partition 1 | 100.0 MB | 95.0 MB | System |
| Drive 0 Partition 2 | 16.0 MB | 16.0 MB | MSR (Reserved) |
| Drive 0 Partition 3 | 55.8 GB | 55.7 GB | Primary |

Refresh    ✕ Delete    ✔ Format    New
Load driver    Extend

**467**

Once all partitions have been deleted, select the drive you want to install windows onto. You should see 'unallocated space' next to the drive.

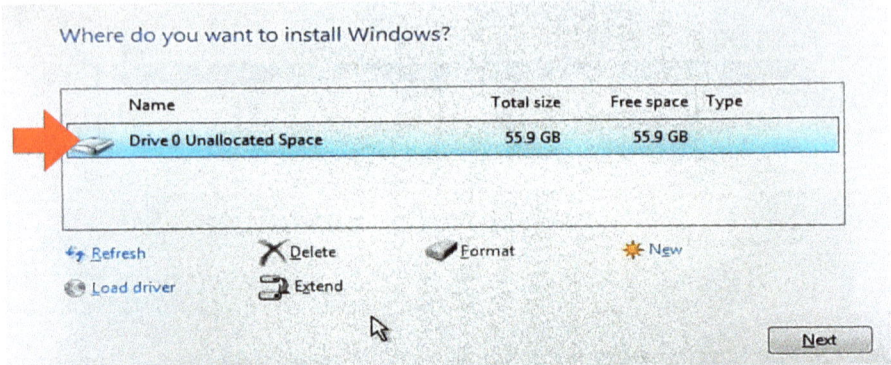

Where do you want to install Windows?

| Name | Total size | Free space | Type |
|---|---|---|---|
| Drive 0 Unallocated Space | 55.9 GB | 55.9 GB | |

Refresh       ✗ Delete       ✓ Format       ✳ New

Load driver       Extend

Next

Click 'next' to begin.

Allow Windows to install.

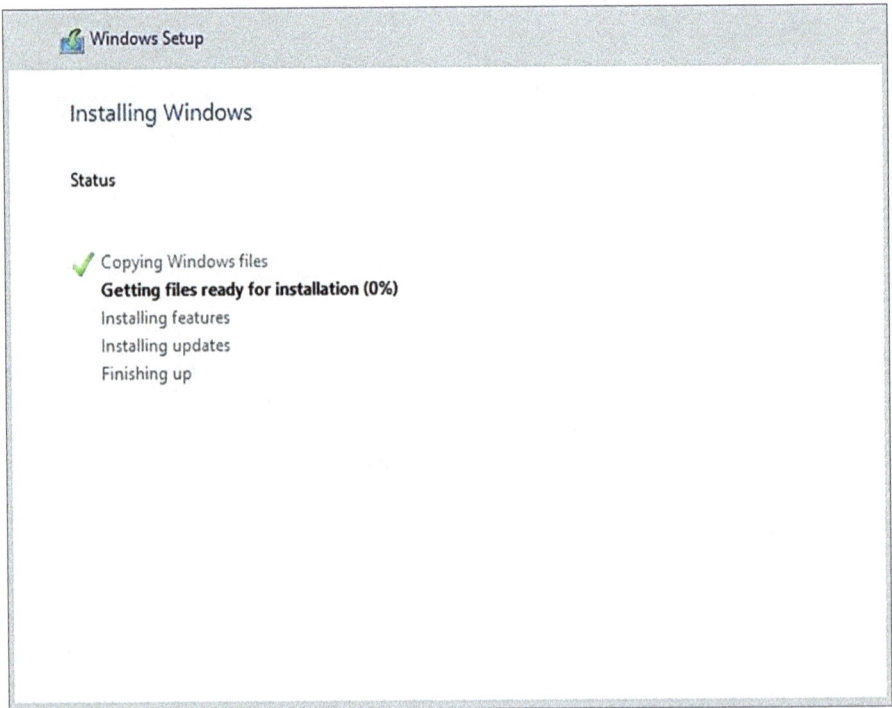

Windows Setup

Installing Windows

Status

✓ Copying Windows files

**Getting files ready for installation (0%)**

Installing features

Installing updates

Finishing up

Windows will reboot and continue the setup. This will take a while. When complete, you'll need to run through the initial setup again. See "Running Windows 11 the First Time" on page 35

# Enter UEFI BIOS

Open the settings app, select 'system', then scroll down, select 'recovery'. Under 'recovery options' click 'restart now'.

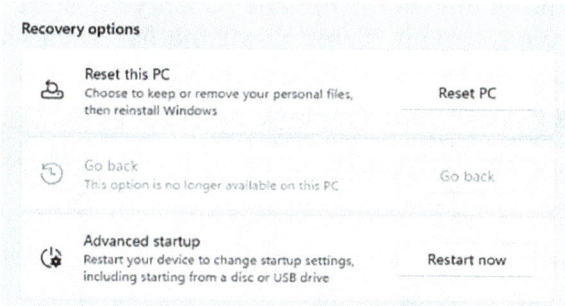

From the recovery screen, choose Troubleshoot, then Advanced options.

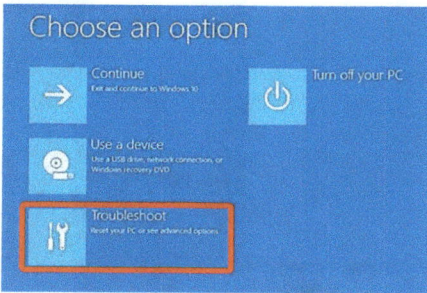

Select UEFI Firmware Settings. Click 'restart'. Allow your machine will reboot to the UEFI screen.

As an alternative method, you can enter the UEFI by pressing a specific hotkey during startup. As soon as the computer powers on, repeatedly press the appropriate key for your device's UEFI or boot menu. This key varies depending on the manufacturer, but it is typically one of the following: Esc, F1, F2, F10, F11, F12, or Del. Because the startup screen is only visible for a brief moment, it's important to press the key quickly—ideally as soon as the device begins to boot.

# Windows Security

Windows Security is the hub for all security features including virus protection, device health, networking, firewalls, internet security, app control and family safety options. Open your start menu, select 'all apps' on the top right. Scroll down the list, then click 'windows security'.

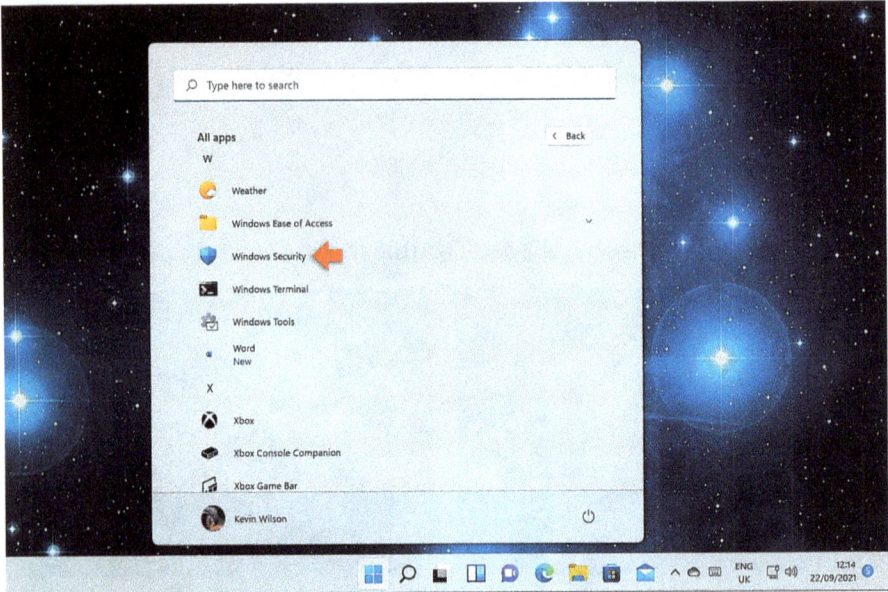

Down the left hand panel and on the 'home' page, you have some options:

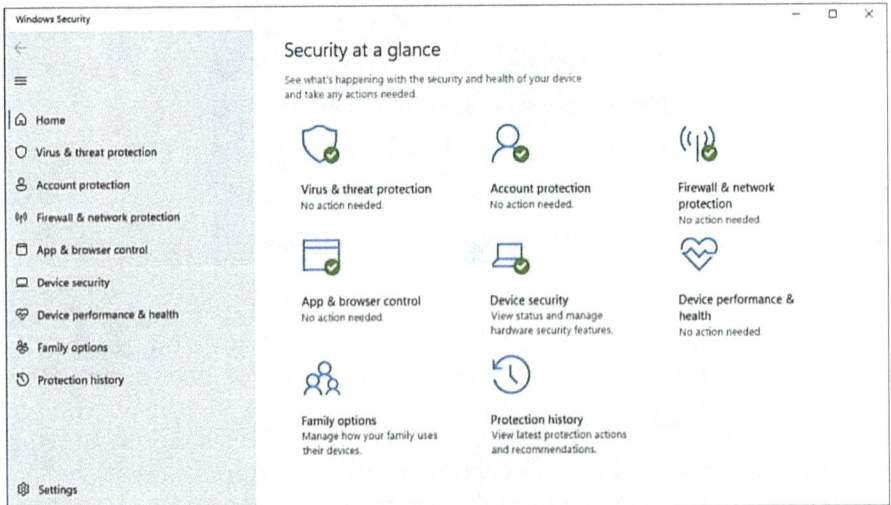

**Virus & Threat Protection.** From here you can scan for threats with a full system scan which scans system files, apps, as well as your files. You can also perform an 'offline scan', where your system will restart into a 'secure mode' to scan for threats. This scan is useful for removing malware that isn't removed with a full or quick scan. Most detected threats are automatically quarantined.

**Account Protection.** Security settings for your Microsoft Account, manage sync settings between devices, adjust windows hello sign in options, enable/disable dynamic lock.

**Firewall & network Protection.** Here you can troubleshoot network issues with WiFi or internet connectivity and adjust your firewall settings. You can also access firewall settings.

**App & Browser Control.** Here you can adjust your browser and application security settings such as SmartScreen filter that helps protect you against malicious websites, apps and downloads.

**Device Security.** Enable/disable core isolation and memory integrity preventing and attack injecting malicious code into processes.

**Device Performance & Health.** Here you can see any issues arising with drivers, updates, battery life and disk storage space. You also have the option to refresh Windows 11, meaning you can re-install Windows if it is not running smoothly while keeping your personal files safe.

**Family Options.** This section links you to your family options using your web browser and allows you to monitor your kids' online activity.

**Protection History.** This shows actions taken on various potential threats, as well as any recommended actions.

# Running a Virus Scan

You can run a quick scan that checks your folders, or a full scan that scans every file on your PC. To start, select 'virus & threat protection' from the panel on the left hand side

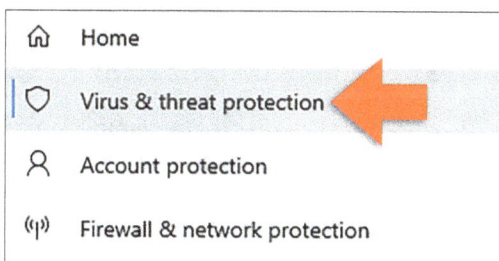

From the 'scan screen' click 'scan options'.

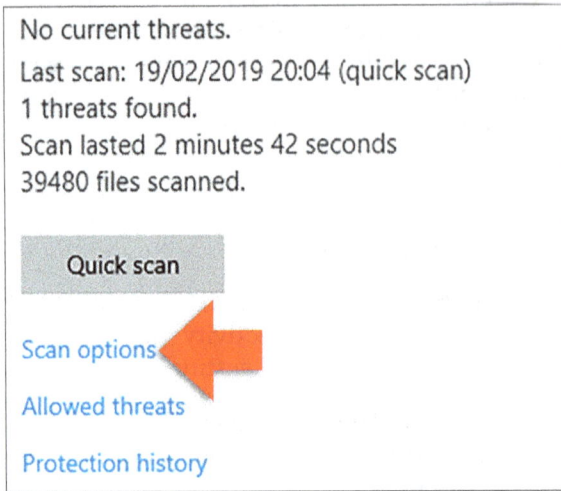

No current threats.

Last scan: 19/02/2019 20:04 (quick scan)
1 threats found.
Scan lasted 2 minutes 42 seconds
39480 files scanned.

Quick scan

Scan options

Allowed threats

Protection history

Select either 'quick scan' to scan system files as well as your personal files. Click 'full scan' to scan every file on your PC.

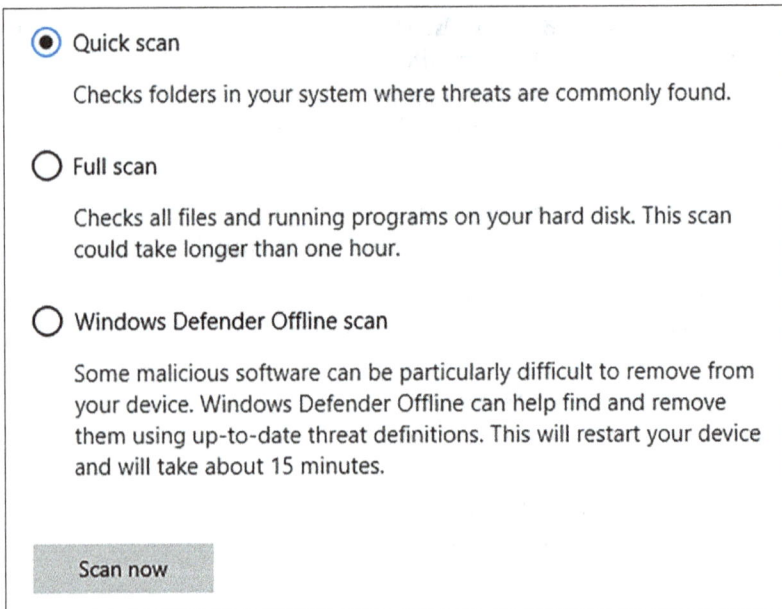

◉ Quick scan

Checks folders in your system where threats are commonly found.

◯ Full scan

Checks all files and running programs on your hard disk. This scan could take longer than one hour.

◯ Windows Defender Offline scan

Some malicious software can be particularly difficult to remove from your device. Windows Defender Offline can help find and remove them using up-to-date threat definitions. This will restart your device and will take about 15 minutes.

Scan now

If you are trying to remove malware or a virus and the quick or full scan doesn't remove it, use 'windows defender offline scan' to restart your PC in a secure environment.

Click 'scan now'.

If you selected the 'windows defender offline scan', windows will reboot into a secure environment and scan your system

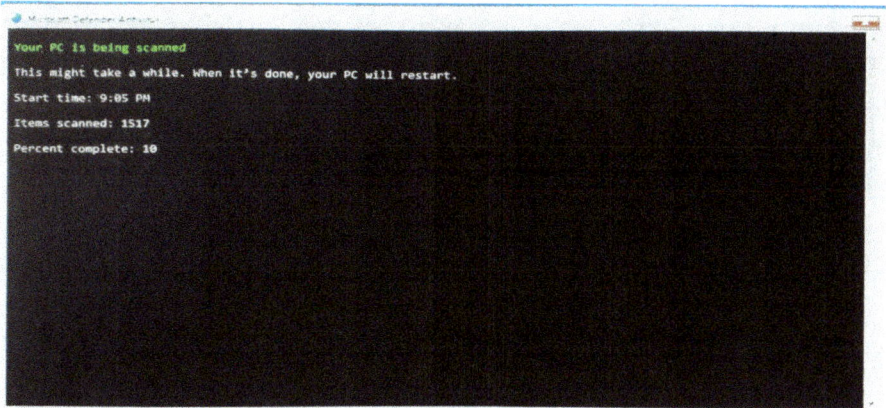

Any malware or viruses that are found will be removed or quarantined. You'll find the results in 'virus & threat protection' under 'protection history'.

## Scan a Specified File or Folder

To scan a particular file or folder, open up File Explorer and navigate to the file or folder you want to scan.

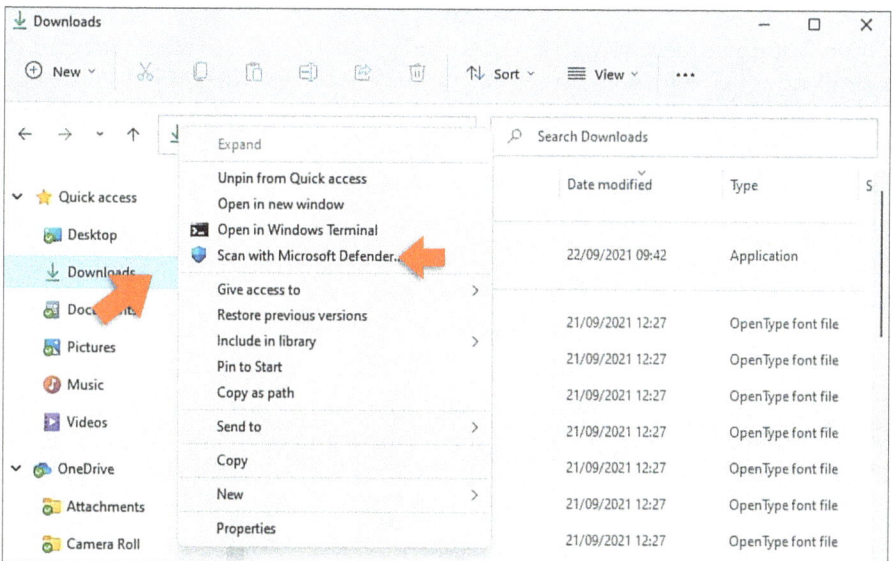

Right click on the folder, select 'show more options', then click 'scan with Microsoft Defender'.

## Dealing with Threats

If any of the virus scans detect a threat, they'll appear on the 'scan options' screen. Click on the threat to view details. Select an action, eg 'remove'.

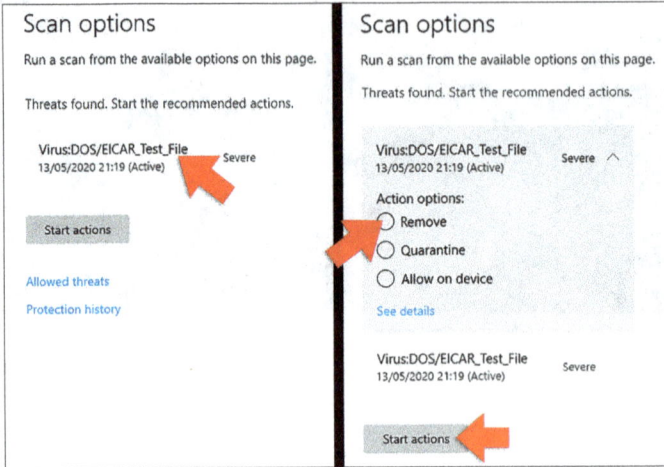

Click 'start actions' to clean.

## Threat Protection Settings

Open windows security app, then select 'Virus & Threat Protection'. Scroll down to 'virus & threat protection settings', then click 'manage settings'.

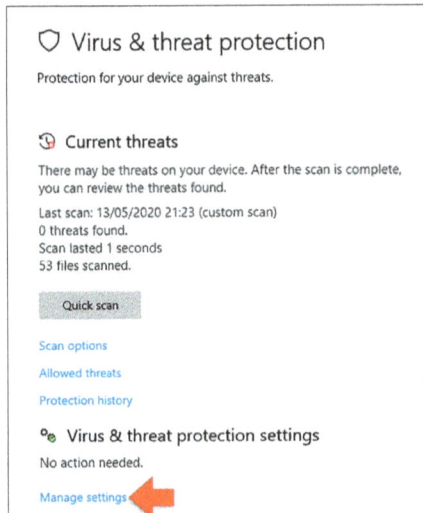

Here, you can enable/disable 'real time protection', 'cloud delivered protection', 'automatic sample submission', 'tamper protection', 'file exclusions', and 'notifications'.

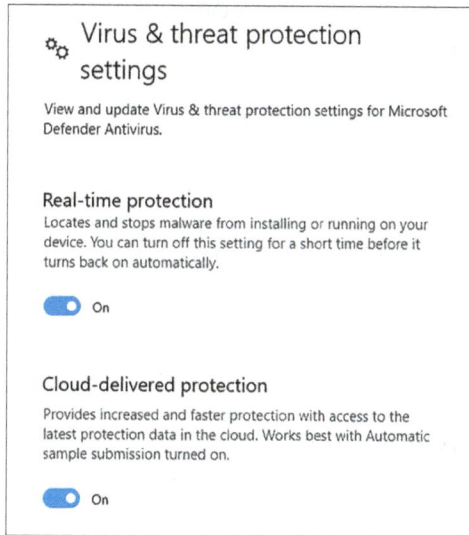

## Controlling Folder Access

This feature allows you to protect files & folders from modification by unapproved applications and malware. If any of these applications try to modify files, you'll get a notification allowing you to block the action.

To enable this feature, open Windows Security, Click 'virus & threat protection', scroll down the page, then select 'Manage Ransomware Protection'. Set the 'controlled folder access' switch to 'On'.

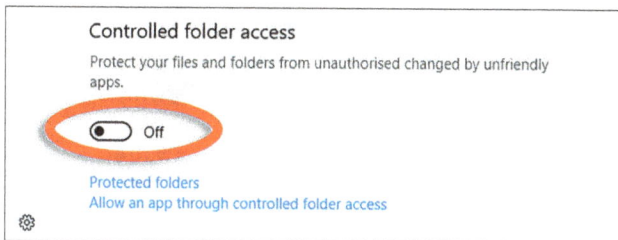

Windows Security will normally allow most known applications to access and change data in the folders on your machine. If Windows Security detects an app it doesn't recognise, you'll receive a notification that it has been blocked. Some of the time this will be a legitimate application, so you might need to add the application to the safe list.

To add other applications to the 'safe list', click 'allow an app trough controlled folder access'. Then click 'add an allowed app'.

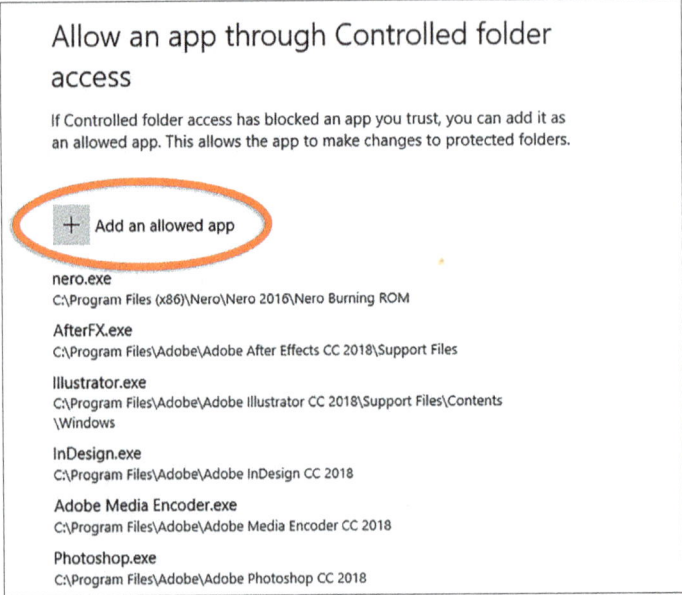

Now in the dialog box that appears, navigate to the folder where the application is installed. This will usually be "C:\Program Files". In this example, I'm going to add 'Adobe After Effects'. So navigate to the folder in 'program files'. Make sure you select the file with the EXE extension, as shown below.

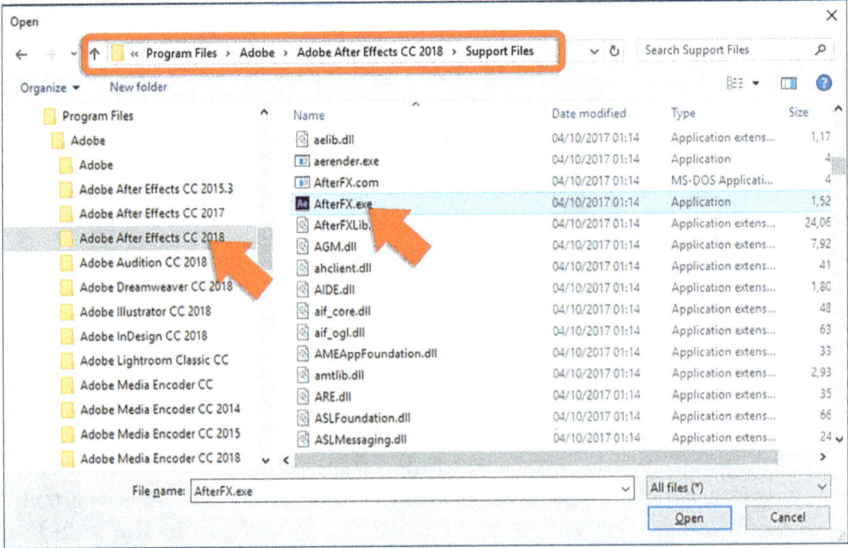

Windows Security will automatically add your system folders and most of your personal folders. You can add any others if you need to. To do this, click 'protected folders' on the 'virus & threat protection' screen.

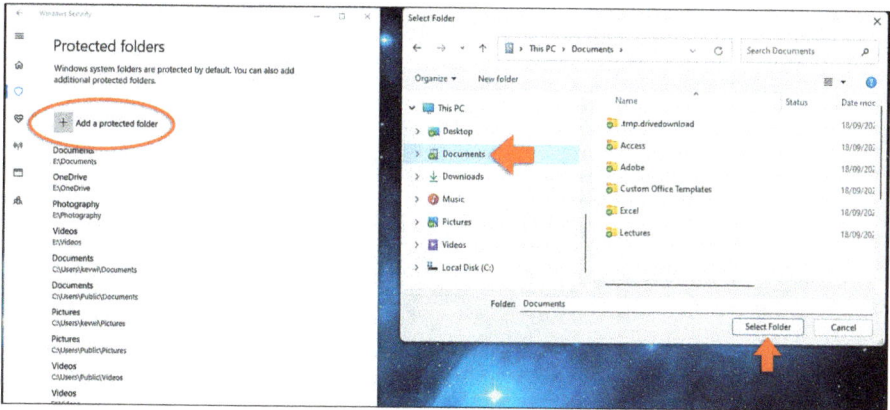

Click 'add a protected folder', then from the dialog box that appears, navigate to the folder you want to protect, click on it, then click 'select folder'.

# Exploit Protection

This feature is designed to protect your PC from various types of exploits out of the box and shouldn't need any configuration.

To find this feature, open Windows Security, click 'App & browser control' then select 'Exploit protection' at the bottom of the page.

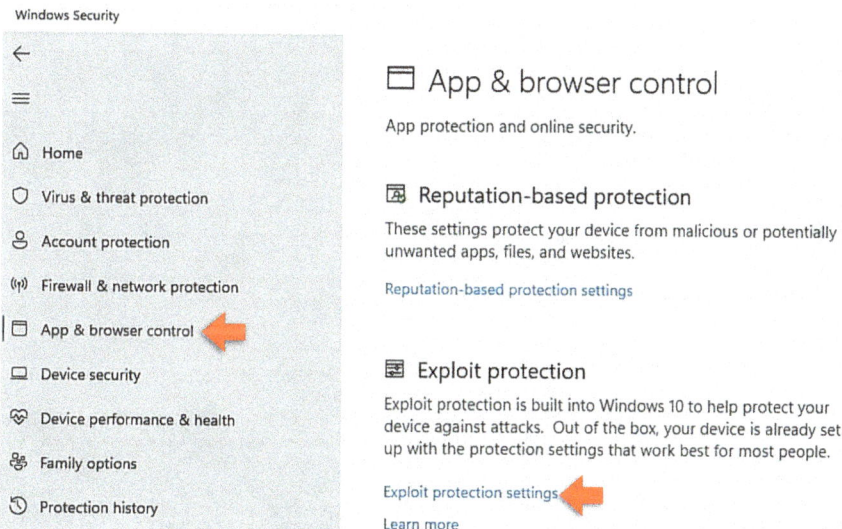

## Chapter 10: System Maintenance

The exploit protection settings are divided into two categories: system settings and program settings.

System settings allows you to set the exploit protection globally - for all the programs.

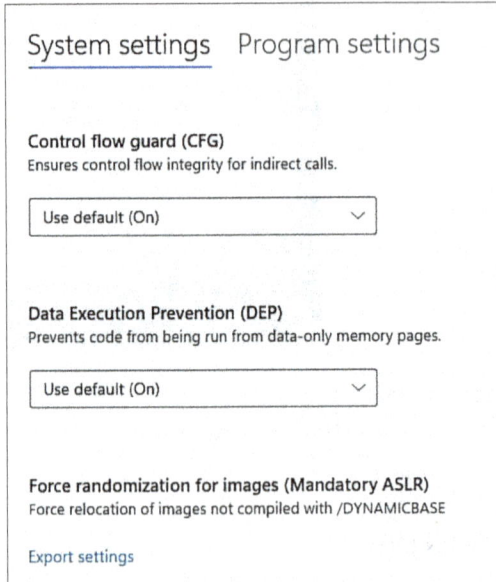

System settings   Program settings

**Control flow guard (CFG)**
Ensures control flow integrity for indirect calls.

Use default (On)                          ∨

**Data Execution Prevention (DEP)**
Prevents code from being run from data-only memory pages.

Use default (On)                          ∨

**Force randomization for images (Mandatory ASLR)**
Force relocation of images not compiled with /DYNAMICBASE

Export settings

The program settings allows you to override the global system settings for an individual program.

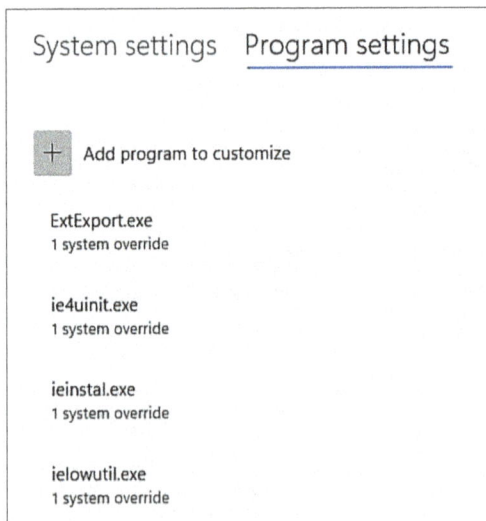

System settings   Program settings

+   Add program to customize

ExtExport.exe
1 system override

ie4uinit.exe
1 system override

ieinstal.exe
1 system override

ielowutil.exe
1 system override

Most of these settings can be left on the default.

# Windows Firewall

Windows Firewall is a security feature built into Windows 11. It is designed to filter network traffic to and from your computer and block any malicious attempts to connect to your machine or potentially harmful programs attempting to transmit data.

To open the firewall settings, start windows security - you'll find the icon on your start menu. Select 'firewall & network protection'

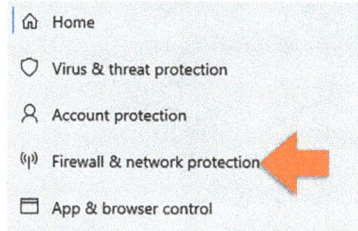

## Enable or Disable

Select the network profile. The one your PC is using with have 'active' written next to it. Home networks use the 'private' profile.

**Private.** Networks where computers at home or office connected to a private, internal network usually a small workgroup.

**Domain.** Networks where computers are part of an Active Directory domain usually found on large networks in schools, colleges and businesses.

**Guest or Public.** Networks that are not secure such as wifi hotspots you'd find in a coffee shop, library or any public place.

It's best practice to enable the firewall on all three profiles.

To enable/disable, click on the network profile. Eg 'private network'.

Set the slider to 'on' to enable, 'off' to disable.

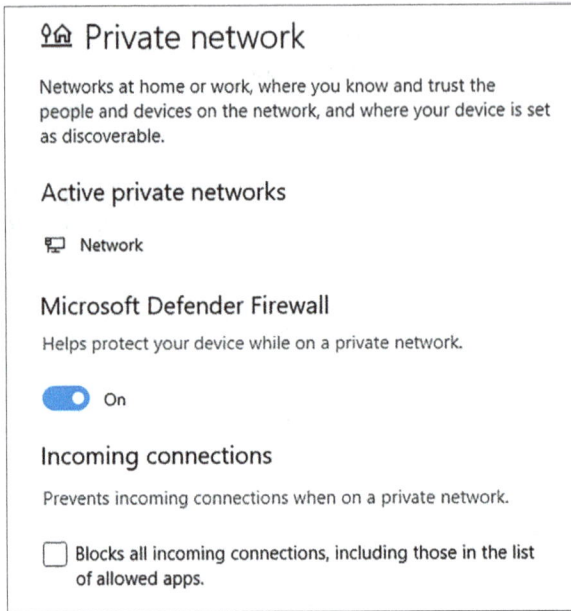

If you're on a public wifi network, enable 'block all incoming connections' on the active network profile.

## Allow or Block an App

Select 'firewall & network protection' in Windows Security, then click 'allow an app through firewall'.

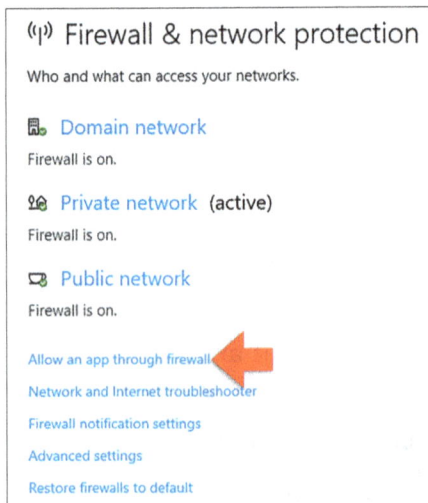

Click 'change settings', enter your administrator password if prompted.

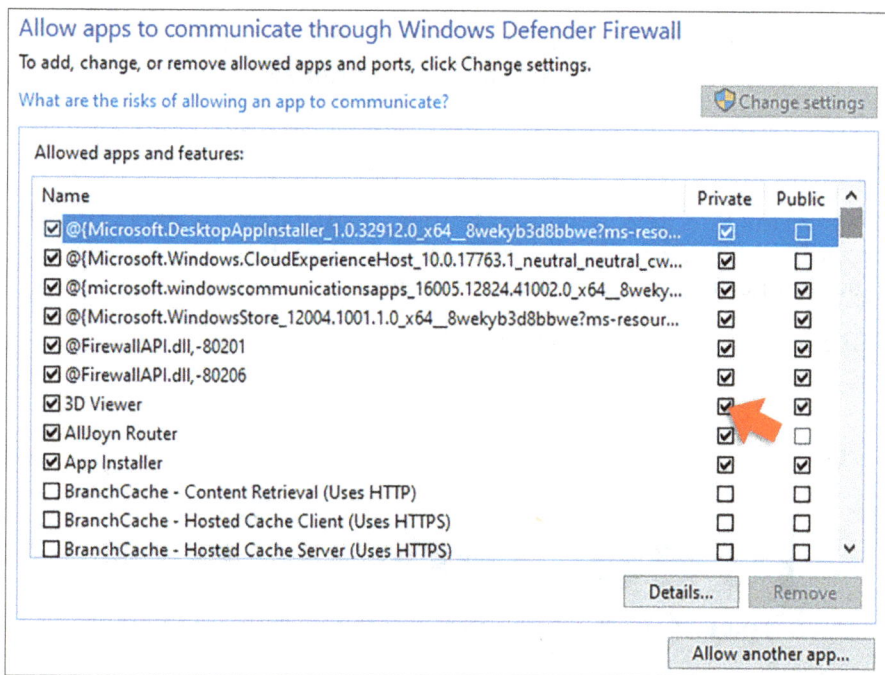

Scroll down the list, click the box next to the app name. Add the tick to allow the app on private and public networks. Remove the tick to block the app.

If you app isn't in the list, click 'allow another app'.

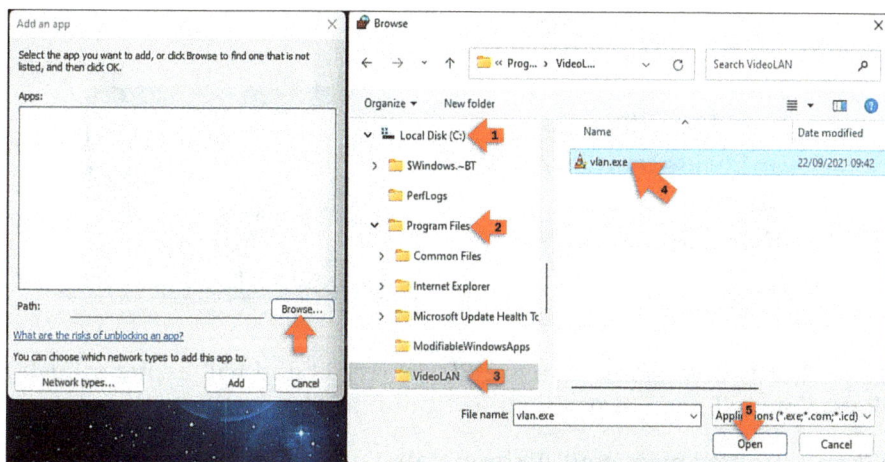

Navigate to the app. This is usually in the 'program files' on the C drive. Click 'open', then back on the 'add an app' screen click 'add'.

# Anti Virus Software

Windows security does a reasonable job at keeping you safe, however there are some free third party anti virus utilities worth noting.

## Avast

Avast scans and detects vulnerabilities in your home network, checks for program updates, scans files as you open them, emails as they come in and fixes PC performance issues.

You can download it from their website.

```
www.avast.com
```

Scroll down the page until you find 'free download'.

The other two versions here are 30 day trials and will expire after 30 days. You will need to pay a subscription to continue.

When prompted hit 'install'. If the installation doesn't run automatically, go to your downloads folder and run 'avast_free_antivirus_setup.exe', follow the on screen wizard.

## AVG

AVG blocks viruses, spyware, & other malware, scans web, twitter, & facebook links and warns you of malicious attachments.

You can download it from their website.

```
www.avg.com
```

Scroll down and click 'free download'.

The other versions here are 30 day trials and will expire after 30 days. You will need to pay a subscription to continue.

The free version is good enough for home users.

## Avira

Avira scans and detects vulnerabilities in your home network, checks for program updates, scans files as you open them, emails as they come in and fixes PC performance issues.

You can download it from their website.

```
www.avira.com
```

Scroll down the page until you find 'download for free'.

## Avira Free Antivirus for Windows

—

Award-winning protection, and free forever

✓ **Top antivirus:** blocks spyware, adware, ransomware, etc.
✓ **Real-time** protection & updates
✓ **Light and fast:** doesn't slow down your PC

[Download for free]

The other versions here are 30 day trials and will expire after 30 days. You will need to pay a subscription to continue.

The free version is good enough for home users.

## MalwareBytes

Malwarebytes offers a free antivirus solution that is useful for removing malware threats from your Windows PC. You can download it here

```
www.malwarebytes.com
```

Click on 'free download'

**Malwarebytes**     Personal  Business  Pricing  Partners  Resources  Support     FREE DOWNLOAD

## FIX TODAY. PROTECT FOREVER.

Secure your devices with the #1 malware removal and protection software*

**Protect your device**
Scan your device today and see why millions trust Malwarebytes to keep them protected.
[Free Download]

**Protect your business**
Enterprise-grade protection. Built for resource-constrained IT teams.
[Learn More]

Follow the on screen prompts to install the software.

# Bitlocker & Drive Encryption

BitLocker is a full-disk encryption feature built into Windows 11 Pro, Enterprise, and Education editions. It helps protect your data by encrypting your entire drive so that unauthorized users cannot access your files — even if the device is lost or stolen. When BitLocker is enabled, all data on the drive is encrypted using advanced encryption algorithms (typically AES). Without the correct key — either stored securely in a Trusted Platform Module (TPM) chip or entered manually — the drive cannot be accessed.

BitLocker is available in Windows 11 Pro, Enterprise, and Education editions. To enable BitLocker in Windows 11 Pro, type `Control Panel` into the search field. Go to System and Security, and then click on BitLocker Drive Encryption.

You will be prompted to back up your recovery key. You can choose to save the key to your Microsoft account, save it to a local file, or print a physical copy. It is recommended that you save the recovery key to your Microsoft account if available, and keep an additional copy stored securely in a separate location.

Choose how much of the drive you want to encrypt. For best security, it is recommended to select Encrypt entire drive. This ensures that all data, including residual or deleted files, is encrypted.

Select the encryption mode. For internal system drives, it is recommended to use the new encryption mode.

Before encryption begins, you will see an option to run a BitLocker system check. This test verifies that the recovery and encryption keys are accessible and functioning properly. When you're ready, click Start encrypting. BitLocker will begin the encryption process..

Devices running Windows 11 Home do not include the full BitLocker feature set, but some newer models support a streamlined version known as Device Encryption. This feature uses the same underlying encryption technology as BitLocker but with fewer configuration options and less user control.

To enable Device Encryption on Windows 11 Home, open the Settings app, select Privacy & security, then click on Device encryption. If your hardware supports it, you can toggle the switch to turn encryption on or off. This is a simplified version of BitLocker with no advanced configuration options.

# Video Resources

To help you understand the procedures and concepts explored in this book, we have developed some video resources and app demos for you to use, as you work through the book.

As well as the video resources, you'll also find some downloadable files and samples for exercises that appear in the book.

To find the resources, scan the QR code, or open your web browser and type the following directly into the address bar at the top (don't use a search engine):

`elluminetpress.com/win-11/`

Do not use a search engine, type the website into the address field at the top of the browser window.

At the beginning of each chapter, you'll find a website that contains the resources for that chapter.

# Using the Videos

Type the website URL into the address bar at the top of your browser.

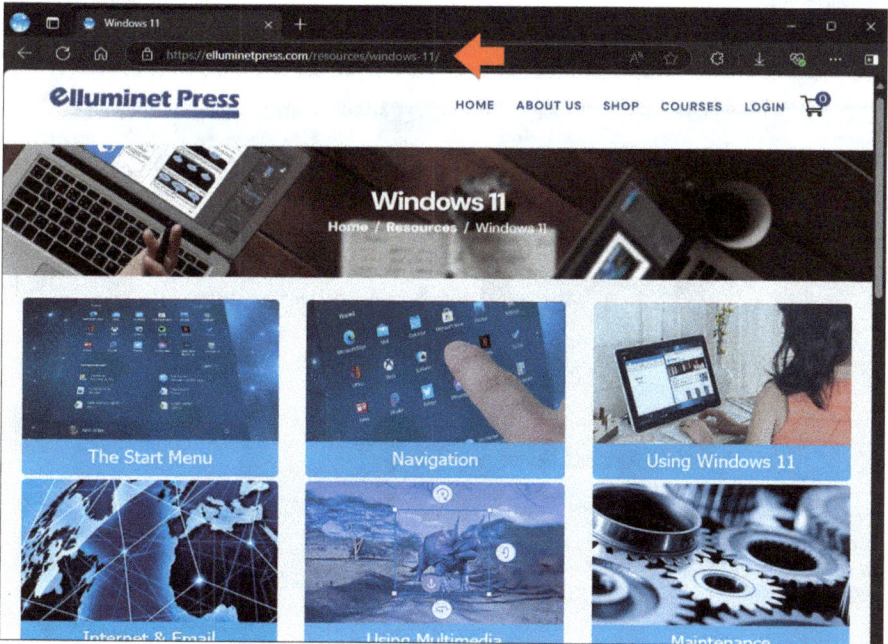

You'll see different categories. Click on these to access the videos.

When you open the link to the video resources, you'll see a thumbnail list at the bottom.

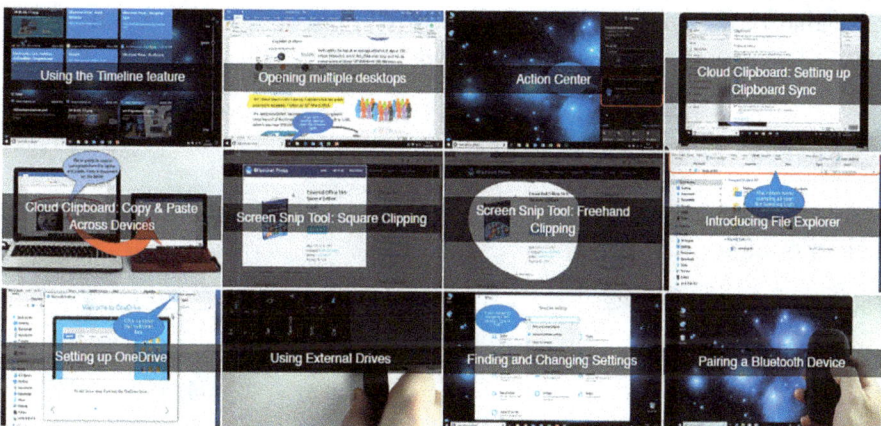

Click on the thumbnail for the particular video you want to watch. Most videos are between 40 and 90 seconds outlining the procedure, others are a bit longer.

## Video Resources

When the video is playing, hover your mouse over the video and you'll see some controls...

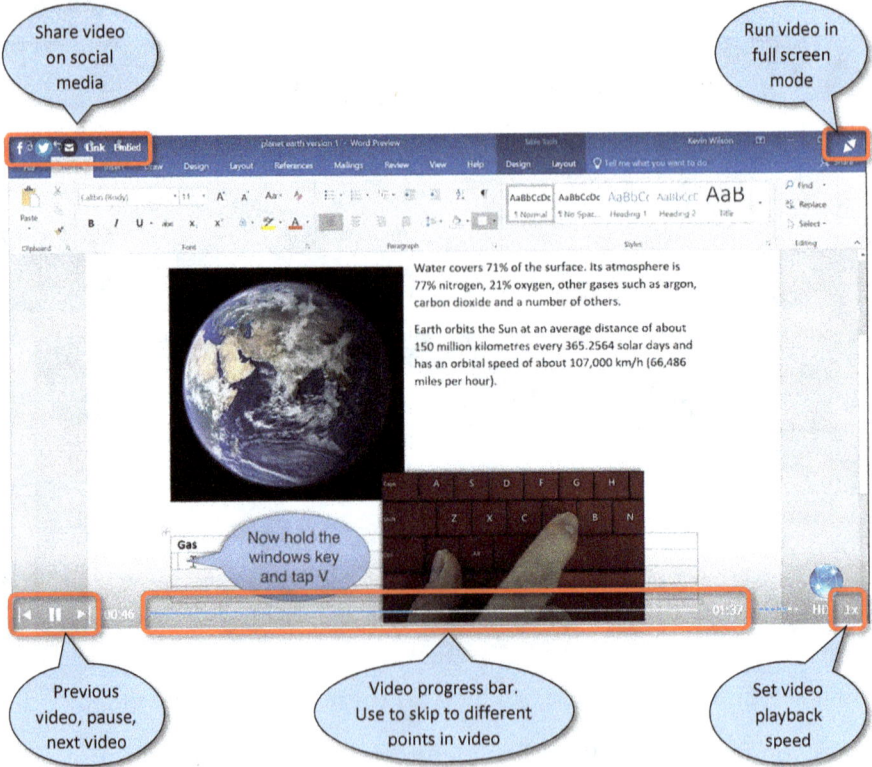

Share video on social media

Run video in full screen mode

Now hold the windows key and tap V

Previous video, pause, next video

Video progress bar. Use to skip to different points in video

Set video playback speed

Here, you can share the video on social media, make it full screen. You can also play/pause the video, jump to a particular part of the video using the progress bar and set the playback speed.

# Other Resources

You'll also find cheat sheets, short-cuts, updates, tips and frequently asked questions.

Bonuses

Click on the icons below to download the files onto your computer.

Keyboard Shortcuts Cheat Sheet

Common Windows 11 Questions & Answers

Legacy Photos App

Legacy Mail App

Windows 11 Tips

Computer Glossary

Windows Cheat Sheet

Windows FAQ

Printers Cheat Sheet

You'll also find a tips section. Here, we'll keep you up to date with the latest tips and tricks to help you get the most out of Windows 11.

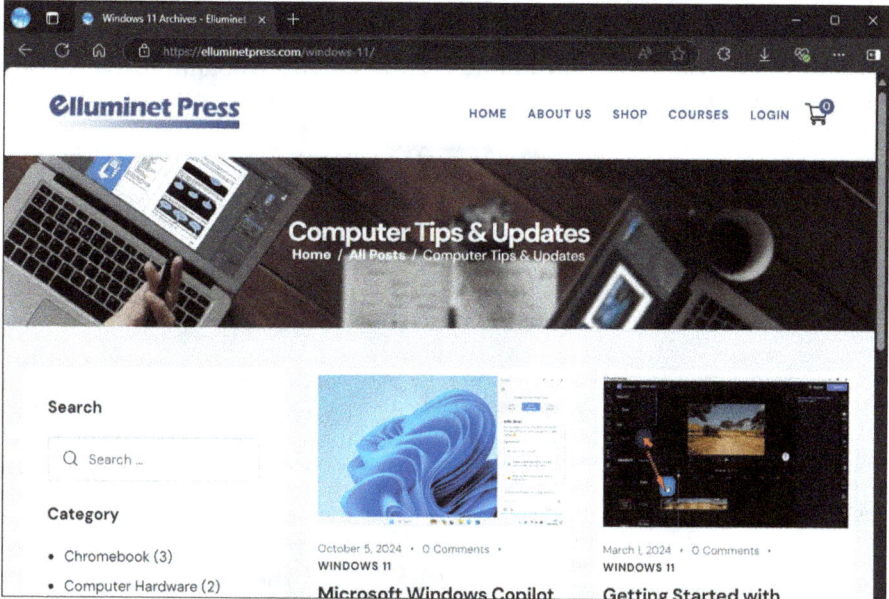

Finally, you'll find a glossary of computing terms.

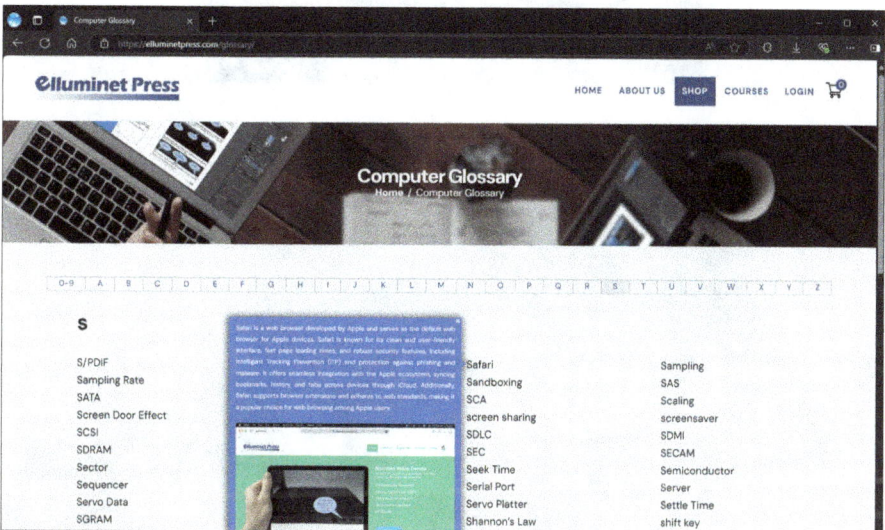

You can find the index here:

`www.elluminetpress.com/glossary`

This is integrated into the resources section.

# Scanning the QR Codes

QR codes are placed at the beginning of each chapter and alongside key procedures within the chapter. You can scan these codes with your phone to access additional resources, downloadable files, and video demonstrations..

## iPhone

To scan the code with your iPhone/iPad, open the camera app.

Frame the QR code in the center of the screen. A banner will appear at the top or bottom—tap on it to open the webpage in Safari.

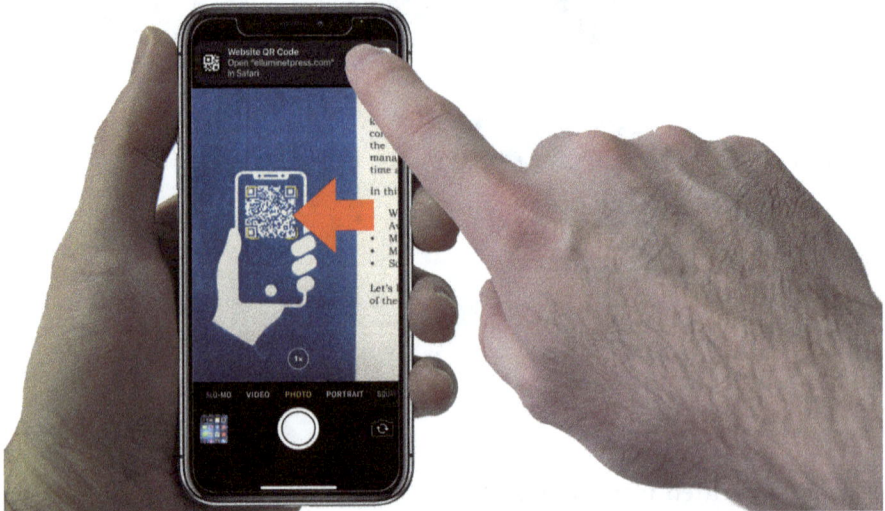

# Android

To scan the code with your phone or tablet, open the camera app. You can also use Google Lens to scan QR codes. Lens is available in the Camera app on many devices, or as a standalone feature in the Google app.

Frame the code in the middle of the screen. Tap on the website popup at the top.

If it doesn't scan, turn on 'Scan QR codes'. To do this, tap the settings icon on the top left. Turn on 'scan QR codes'.

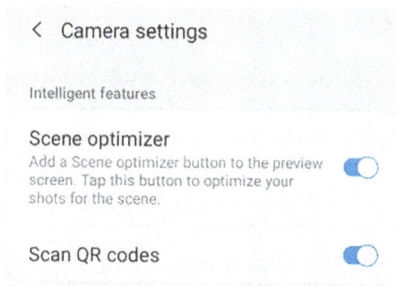

If the setting isn't there, you'll need to download a QR Code scanner. Open the Google Play Store, then search for "QR Code Scanner".

# Index

# Index

## E

# Index

# Index

**N**

# Index

**500**

**Q**

## Index

### R

### S

# Index

## T

# Index

# X

# Y

# Z

# SOMETHING
# NOT COVERED?

**We want to create the best possible resources to help you learn and get things done, so if we've missed anything out, then please get in touch using the links below and let us know. Thanks.**

**office@elluminetpress.com**

**elluminetpress.com/feedback**

SCAN ME